Advanced PUBLIC SPEAKING

Advanced

PUBLIC

SPEAKING

Edward Rogge

James C. Ching

both of Tulane University

HOLT, RINEHART AND WINSTON, INC.

New York · Chicago · San Francisco · Toronto

ACKNOWLEDGMENTS

The American Association for the Advancement of Science, for permission to reprint *The Moral Un-Neutrality of Science*, by C. P. Snow. Copyright © 1961 by the American Association for the Advancement of Science.

American Psychological Association, publishers of *Journal of Abnormal Social Psychology*, for adaptation of table from Donald Fiske's article, "The Consistency of Factorial Structures of Personality Ratings from Different Sources."

America, The National Catholic Weekly Review, New York, for excerpt from Thomas M. Garrett's article, "TV: Who's to Blame?" Reprinted with permission.

Appleton-Century-Crofts, for excerpts from *Classified Speech Models of Eighteen Forms of Public Address*, by William Norwood Brigance (Copyright 1928). Excerpts from: *Fundamentals of Public Speaking*, 3rd Ed., by Donald C. Bryant and Karl R. Wallace. Copyright © 1953, 1960, Appleton-Century-Crofts, Inc. Reprinted by permission of Appleton-Century-Crofts, Division of Meredith Publishing Company. Excerpts from *The Psychology of Communication* by Jon Eisenson, J. Jeffery Auer, and John V. Irwin. Copyright © 1963 Meredith Publishing Company. Reprinted by permission of Appleton-Century-Crofts, Division of Meredith Publishing Company.

The Atlantic Monthly, for permission to reprint excerpts from "The Act of Faith," by Archibald MacLeish. Copyright © 1950, by The Atlantic Monthly Company, Boston 16, Massachusetts.

The Bobbs-Merrill Company, Inc., for excerpt from *Famous Speeches in American History*, by Glenn R. Capp (Copyright © 1963), by The Bobbs-Merrill Company, Inc., reprinted by permission of the publishers.

Bennett Cerf, President, Random House, Inc., for permission to quote excerpts from his book, *An Encyclopedia of Modern American Humor* (New York: Doubleday & Company, Inc., Copyright © 1954).

City News Publishing Co., publishers of *Vital Speeches of the Day*, for numerous excerpts and complete speeches.

The Clarendon Press, for permission to reprint excerpts from the Oxford Translation of Aristotle's *Rhetorica*, by permission of the Clarendon Press, Oxford.

The Colorado Quarterly, Winter 1961 (Vol. 9, No. 3), The University of Colorado, Boulder, Colorado, for excerpt from "The Conquest of Space," by Willy Ley.

CBS News, A Division of Columbia Broadcasting System, Inc., for excerpt from radio broadcast by Edward R. Murrow. Printed by permission of Columbia Broadcasting System, Inc.

Crosscurrents Press, Inc., for excerpts from *Khrushchev in America*, by Nikita S. Khrushchev (Copyright © 1960); *Khrushchev in New York: A documentary record of Nikita S. Khrushchev's trip to New York, September 19 to October 13, 1960, including all his speeches and proposals to the United Nations and major addresses and news conferences* (Copyright 1960); and *Mikoyan in Cuba: Full texts of the speeches made by Anastas I. Mikoyan First Vice Chairman of the USSR on his tour of Cuba February 4–13, 1960* (Copyright © 1960).

Crowell Collier and Macmillan, Inc., for excerpt from *Practical Public Speaking: A Guide to Effective Communication*, by Eugene E. White and Clair R. Henderlider (Copyright 1954).

E. P. Dutton & Co., Inc., for speech in *For Victory in Peaceful Competition with Capitalism*, by Nikita S. Khrushchev (Copyright © 1960).

Donald W. Fiske, Department of Psychology, University of Chicago, for permission to adapt a table from the *Journal of Abnormal Psychology*, 1949, Vol. 44.

Samuel B. Gould, President, State University of New York, Albany, for permission to quote from his speech, "A Flavor for our Daily Bread."

Harcourt, Brace & World, Inc., for excerpts from *Introduction to Psychology*, 2d ed., by Ernest R. Hilgard, Copyright 1953, © 1957, by Harcourt, Brace & World, Inc. and reproduced with their permission. From *Human Behavior: An Inventory of Scientific Findings* by Bernard Berelson and Gary A. Steiner © 1964, by Harcourt, Brace & World, Inc. and reprinted with their permission. For permission to quote from *The Misanthrope* by Molière, translated by Richard Wilbur (Copyright 1954 © 1955, by Richard Wilbur). Reprinted by permission of Harcourt, Brace & World, Inc.

iv

Harper & Row, Publishers, for excerpts from *American Forum: Speeches on Historic Issues, 1788–1900,* by Ernest J. Wrage and Barnet Baskerville (Copyright © 1960); *Mark Twain's Speeches* (Copyright 1910); *The Public Papers and Addresses of Franklin D. Roosevelt,* Vol. 10: *The Call to Battle Stations,* and Vol. 12: *Victory and the Threshold of Peace,* Samuel I. Rosenman, comp. (Copyright 1950); and *The Public Papers of Woodrow Wilson,* Vol. 2: *War and Peace: Presidential Messages, Addresses, and Public Papers (1917–1924),* by Ray Stannard Baker and William E. Dodd, eds. (Copyright 1927).

James W. Harris, Public Relations Staff, Ford Motor Company, Dearborn, Michigan, for supplying visual aids.

Holt, Rinehart and Winston, Inc., for permission to adapt from *The Logic and Rhetoric of Exposition,* Rev. Ed., by Harold C. Martin and Richard M. Ohmann (Copyright © 1963) by Holt, Rinehart and Winston, Inc.

Joe B. Humphreys, Vice-President, Westminster College, Fulton, Missouri, for permission to quote from *Westminster College Bulletin.*

Jenkin Lloyd Jones, Editor, *The Tulsa Tribune,* for permission to quote excerpt from his speech, "Who Is Tampering With the Soul of America?"

Manuel I. Kuhr, Chairman, Department of Speech, Slippery Rock State College, Slippery Rock, Pennsylvania, for copy from [Chicago] *Herald,* September 17, 1897.

B. H. Lim, Government Printer, State of Singapore, for permission to quote speech from *Legislative Assembly Debates: State of Singapore Official Report.*

Louisiana State University Press, Baton Rouge, for excerpts from *Pitchfork Ben Tillman: South Carolinian,* by Francis B. Simkins (Copyright 1944).

McGraw-Hill, Inc., for modification of table from *Introduction to Psychology,* 2nd Ed., by Clifford T. Morgan (Copyright © 1961), McGraw-Hill Book Company. Excerpts from *Social Psychology,* 3d ed., by Richard F. La Piere and Paul R. Farnsworth (Copyright 1949) and William Norwood Brigance, *A History and Criticism of American Public Addresses,* Vol. 2 (Copyright 1943). Used by permission of McGraw-Hill Book Company.

Archibald MacLeish, for permission to use excerpts from speeches.

Miloard Mijović, Chief and Managing Editor, Federation of Yugoslav Journalists, *Medunarodna Politika,* Belgrade, Yugoslavia, for material from "Belgrade Conference."

Arjay Miller, President, Ford Motor Company, Dearborn, Michigan, for permission to quote his report to stockholders, 1964.

Richard T. Mittauer, Public Affairs Officer for Space Science & Applications, National Aeronautics and Space Administration, Washington, D.C., for permission to quote "Mariner IV Briefing for the President of the United States," and for supplying visual aids.

National Education Association of the United States, for excerpts from *Addresses and Proceedings of the Ninety-ninth Annual Meeting Held at Atlantic City, New Jersey June 25–June 30: 1961* (Washington, D.C.; Vol. 99, p. 19, 20) Copyright © 1961, *and Addresses and Proceedings of the One-Hundredth Annual Meeting at Denver, Colorado July 1–July 6: 1962* (Washington, D.C.; Vol. 100, p. 100) Copyright © 1962.

New York *Herald Tribune* for excerpt from speech delivered by John Crosby, reprinted from New York *Herald Tribune,* Section 9, October 28, 1951.

The New York *Times* for numerous excerpts and entire speeches. © 1942, 1944, 1945, 1948, 1956, 1961 by The New York Times Company. Reprinted by permission.

Phi Delta Kappa, for excerpt from *Dissemination and Implementation: Third Annual Phi Delta Kappa Symposium on Educational Research,* Keith Goldhammer and Stanley Elam, eds. Copyright © 1962).

G. P. Putnam's Sons & Coward-McCann, Inc., New York, and McClelland and Stewart, Ontario, Canada, for excerpts from *Blood, Sweat, and Tears,* by Winston Churchill (Copyright 1941).

Loren Reid, Department of Speech, University of Missouri, for valuable criticism in the preparation of this book.

Frederick C. Schwarz, President, Christian Anti-Communism Crusade, Long Beach, California, for permission to quote from his book, *You Can Trust The Communists (. . . to do exactly as they say!)* (Englewood Cliffs, New Jersey: Prentice-Hall, Inc., 1961).

Charles Scribner's Sons, Publishers, for excerpt from *The Works of Theodore Roosevelt,* Vol. 16: *American Problems* (Copyright 1926).

The Secretary General, Office of the Ministry of Information and Tourism, Democratic Republic of the Congo, Léopoldville, for permission to quote Justin Bomboko's speech, "Allocution radiodiffusée de M. Justin Bomboko, Ministre des Affaires Etrangères."

Robert Sargent Shriver, Jr., Director, Peace Corps, Washington, D.C., for permission to quote his speech, "The Job Was Tough: Our Success Has Been Your Success."

Rabbi Charles E. Shulman, Riverdale Temple, New York, for permission to quote from his speech before Ad-Sell League, Omaha, Nebraska.

Simon and Schuster, Inc., for excerpts from *A Treasury of the World's Great Speeches,* Houston Peterson, ed. (Copyright 1954).

Robert W. Smith, Assistant Professor of Speech, Alma College, Alma, Michigan, for permission to reprint his transcribed version of Edward VIII's abdication address as it appeared in "Rhetoric in Crisis: The Abdication Address of Edward VIII," Vol. 30, *Speech Monographs* (November 1963).

C. P. Snow, for permission to print his speech "The Moral Un-Neutrality of Science."

Edna Lamprey Stantial, Secretary, Alice Stone Blackwell Memorial Committee, Pond Acre, Chilmark, Massachusetts, for permission to quote excerpts from speeches in *Lucy Stone: Pioneer Woman Suffragist* (Norwood, Massachusetts: The Plimpton Press, 1930).

Theatre Arts Books, New York, and Heinemann Educational Books, Ltd., Tadworth, Surrey, England, for speech copyrighted by Michel Saint-Denis in *Theatre: The Rediscovery of Style.* Copyright © 1960.

The *Times-Picayune,* New Orleans, Louisiana, for excerpt, reprinted from The *Times-Picayune.*

United Press International, New York, for dispatch.

University of North Carolina Press, Chapel Hill, for excerpt from *Henry George: Citizen of the World,* by Anna George de Mille (Copyright 1950).

H. W. Wilson, Co., for selections from *I Am Happy to Present: A Book of Introductions* (Copyright 1953).

William Work, Executive Secretary, Speech Association of America, for permission to quote from Robert W. Smith's article.

Yale University Press, for excerpts from *Communication and Persuasion,* by Carl I. Hovland, Irving L. Janis, and Harold H. Kelley.

Young Socialist Forum, New York, for excerpt from *Castro Speaks on Unemployment* (Copyright © 1961).

PREFACE

This is a book about public speaking and about methods that we believe should be used in the marketplace of ideas. This is not a book that teaches students to use all effective methods in securing acceptance of ideas; nor is it a book that treats only what we wish would be effective methods of gaining acceptance. Although we share Aristotle's idealistic conclusion that "we ought in fairness fight our case with nothing but the bare facts," we also share his belief that a speaker must recognize that he deals with people; and there is some question how much people base decisions on bare facts. Bertrand Russell argues that "desires, emotions, passions (you can choose whichever word you will), are the only possible causes of action. Reason is not a cause of action but only a regulator."[1]

As speech teachers we interest ourselves in improving the decision-making process in a democratic society. However (and we hope this marks us as good teachers rather than as cynics), we agree with F. L. Lucas: "It is futile to preach changes of heart; the human heart does change—but in the slow course of generations, not overnight."[2] Although we think it futile to *preach* changes in heart, we believe it possible to *teach* modest changes and to encourage speakers to use those methods that best serve them and their society. Furthermore, we believe that speakers should provide maximal opportunity for hearers to make rational choices. This does not mean we renounce our stated belief that human beings are sometimes irrational; nor does it mean we have forgotten that issues must be decided. Rather, it means we combined—in what seems the most reasonable portions—the ideal and the practical, cognizant that while all speakers may be considered self-serving, our democracy is based on the belief that ideas need a hearing to determine their validity. We can never hold that certain ideas, even unpopular and repugnant ones, should be proscribed.

Our hope is that ideas will be advanced and advocated by methods that

[1] *Human Society in Ethics and Politics* (New York: Simon and Schuster, Inc., 1955). p. vii.

[2] *Literature and Psychology* (Ann Arbor, Michigan: University of Michigan Press, First American Edition Revised, 1957), p. 21.

permit hearers to determine their acceptability. A desire to aid in implementing that objective led us to discuss certain methods of gaining acceptance for ideas and to exclude others from consideration. For instance, in keeping with our belief that auditors should be aware, as far as possible, of the reasons why they accept or reject an idea, we did not develop techniques for the use of *suggestion* (the uncritical acceptance of an idea), even though such a technique provides a powerful source of persuasion. If it be objected that as members of a democracy we have not the right to exclude a persuasive means, we answer that all authors of speech texts exercise the function of teachers in a democracy, and therefore exclude some things. For surely there are techniques of lying; yet we know of no modern text amplifying Quintilian's suggestions on how to commit perjury and 'get away with it.'

If this book were limited to a description of speech techniques, we would have included a summary of all methods used. Our purpose, however, is to describe *and* exhort.

Although this book may be used in first courses in public speaking, we wrote primarily for the advanced public speaking student. We excluded comprehensive consideration of certain principles covered adequately in an earlier course. We have no chapters on delivery, selecting a topic, gathering material, or voice improvement. Although we comment on some of those areas as they apply to particular speeches, we believe that the fundamental principles were covered earlier in any beginning public speaking course using any of the standard texts. Should the book be used in a beginning course, those areas might need covering by supplementary readings or lectures.

The exclusion of certain principles gave us room to treat the heart of rhetoric, or the management of ideas, more comprehensively. Consequently, we devote more space than usual to the reasoning process and to language. We also had room to describe the various situations in which students might expect to speak. And, more importantly, we had room to reprint and analyze speeches.

As Donald Lemen Clark said, "Modern teachers would make their teaching more effective if they made fuller use of the exercises of imitation." Imitating models, said Clark, "is one technic of holding fast that which is good." Precept "tells the learner what to do. Imitation shows him how others have done it."[3]

We also reprint the speeches of others to help students realize that rarely are important events in history disassociated from public address, that public speaking has been a force in history, and that it has called forth the best efforts of our best men. As Benjamin Franklin explained:

> *history* will show the wonderful Effects of ORATORY, in governing, turning and leading great Bodies of Mankind, Armies, Cities, Nations. When the Minds

[3] *Rhetoric in Greco-Roman Education* (New York: Columbia University Press, 1957), pp. 175 and 144.

of Youth are struck with Admiration at this, then is the Time to give them the Principles of that Art, which they will study with Taste and Application.[4]

Although we use the traditional term *speech models,* we do not intend that the speeches reprinted here should be regarded as archetypes. Rather, we intend that they be regarded as examples for study. Some of the features are worthy of emulation; others are not. We expect that students will at times disagree with our evaluations. That is as it should be, for, as an art, speech making recognizes no individual's evaluation as final or beyond question. Even when there is agreement that a certain speech fulfilled the objectives at the time of delivery, there is little likelihood that the same situation will again occur. Furthermore, tastes in art change. What was praised a century ago will seem too grandiloquent now. We applaud Abraham Lincoln's Gettysburg Address; but Lincoln's contemporaries applauded Edward Everett's Gettysburg Address.

We admit leaning heavily on classical rhetoricians, particularly Aristotle. Since rhetoric, however, has no subject matter exclusively its own, we also borrowed freely from the logician, psychologist, sociologist, historian, and linguist.

We hope that *Advanced Public Speaking* contradicts a minimum of what was taught in a first course. There are, however, ways and *ways* of building a speech. We think our approach will supplement basic principles and, hopefully, give new perspective to students. Our aim is not to undo what students learned; rather it is to draw them into deeper consideration of public speaking principles and perhaps to open new directions for them.

Because we believe there are various ways of building a speech and that public speaking is an art, we found occasional disparities—even inconsistencies—between what one of us had written and what the other believed. Although the inconsistencies were resolved, differences in emphasis remain. While we both stand by what follows in this book, the principal responsibility for the various chapters is as follows: Rogge, chapters 1, 2, 4, 5, 9, 10, 15, and 16; Ching, chapters 3, 6, 7, 8, 11, 12, 13, 14, 17, and 18.

E. R.
J. C. C.

New Orleans, Louisiana
January 1966

[4] *Proposals Relating to the Education of Youth in Pennsylvania* (Philadelphia: University of Pennsylvania Press, Facsimile Reprint, 1931), p. 21.

CONTENTS

Advanced PUBLIC SPEAKING

PART ONE

1   Point of View

As a student begins the study of this book, he should understand that its development, both as to what principles are discussed and the way they are organized into chapters, is influenced by the authors' views concerning, first, the nature of the public-speaking situation and, second, the elements essential to success in speaking.

As a student begins to apply the principles and to seek the success his authors wish for him, he should know, first, how much help he can expect from an understanding of principles and, second, how much he must help himself.

Those four points are developed here.

THE PUBLIC SPEAKING SITUATION

Public speaking is usually defined from the standpoint of a speaker's purpose and media. Such definitions, while useful, do not include the significant aspect of how a listener regards the situation. Success of any communication act depends in part on the listener's expectations. If we expect to be a listener to a public speech, we are disappointed (or pleased) when we learn we do not have to assume the role. Conversely, if we join a group in which we expect to hear discussants, we may be distressed (or pleased) if we discover that we are to be part of an audience for a speech. Hence, it may be useful to define a public speaking *situation* and look at speech from the viewpoints of both speaker and listener.

For the speaker a public speaking situation exists if the communication, principally through speech and gesture, attempts to influence hearer action in a significant way.

For the listener a public speech situation exists if the communication, again through speech and gesture, is of sufficient length, formality, and one-sidedness for him to regard it as a speech situation.

We do not suggest that a public speech must fail if a listener regards the communication act as something other than a speech event. Most of us have participated in occasions where the principal communicant enjoyed considerable success without seeming to make a public speech, and the absence of any appearance of a speech contributed to that success. Conversely, we have been in situations when the speaker did such a superficial or unsatisfactory job of communicating that we designated the attempt as mere babble, regardless of what he considered it. Perhaps the most auspicious occasion is one where both speaker and audience expect a public speech, and after the event both feel a fulfillment of that expectation.

Two aspects of our definition of a public speaking situation from the speaker's viewpoint need clarification: that the communication seeks to influence action, and that the action influenced must be significant.

A public speech is designed to make people act in a different way than they probably would have acted had they not heard it. For example, a speaker seeks to change or strengthen an attitude of listeners or to impel them to react differently to the object of that attitude whenever they deal with it. Or he attempts to add to his listeners' knowledge because he hopes that the knowledge will enable them to react differently in any situation where it is applicable. This does not mean that hearers seek knowledge only when information has immediate or obvious applicability; rather it means that few people regard the acquisition of knowledge as an end in itself.[1]

Students will recognize that we included both expository and persuasive speeches in our discussion of influencing conduct. Even the entertaining speech—which sometimes is not considered a species of public address[2]—seeks a response ranging from mirth to interest. This is not, of course, a new concept. William Norwood Brigance wrote: "What possible purposes may a speaker have? Fundamentally, he has just *one*. He wants the audience to *respond* to his speech, to *do something*[3] about what he says."[4] In other words, public speeches of all kinds have at their base the action-response purpose, which speakers seek in a variety of ways. Therefore, to regard the

[1] We make this statement even though we recognize that some knowledge is acquired or imparted for the training in method it provides. We also recognize that there are what psychologist Donald Johnson calls intrinsic motives. Certain activities have "motivation value *for their own sakes*." (*The Psychology of Thought and Judgment,* New York: Harper & Row, Publishers, 1955, p. 59.) For certain people the learning of a new language or understanding of an electronic mechanism has no anticipated value beyond the value in achieving the task itself.

[2] See, for example, Donald C. Bryant and Karl R. Wallace, *Fundamentals of Public Speaking.* New York: Appleton-Century-Crofts, Third ed., 1960.

[3] Brigance made it clear to one of the authors that "to do something" meant active or passive response, and for this reason he did not consider the speech to *actuate* as a true species of speech.

[4] *Speech: Its Techniques and Disciplines in a Free Society* (New York: Appleton-Century-Crofts, Second ed., 1955), p. 188.

methods of exposition as inapplicable to a speech of persuasion, or the reverse, is to allow that speeches occur in "pure" form. We are not suggesting that techniques of making something clear are the same as methods of making something seem desirable. Rather, we contend that rarely does a speech use one set of techniques to the exclusion of others, and consequently a speaker who suffers from a myopic view of speech purpose may well miss his mark for this failing.

Speaking is public speaking only if its purpose is to influence action in a *significant* way. The ritualistic "Good morning," or "How are you?" are frequently intended to do no more than convey a general impression of good will and to elicit no response more comprehensive than the equally ritualistic "Good morning," or "Well, thank you."

Although all public speaking shares in the objective of influencing conduct in a significant way, the action sought can be considered from several points of view: whether it is specific or nonspecific, immediate (including short-lived) or delayed (including sustained), major or minor, and simple or complex. The full significance of the differences in the type of action sought will become apparent in later chapters. Here we but illustrate how the speaker's task differs as the response differs.

When the influence sought is *specific,* a speaker's task is to emphasize the act itself so that listeners will remember it even though they forget the arguments that establish the efficacy of the act. Thus the speaker who seeks support for a specific political candidate will be content if his listeners vote for the right person even though they fail to remember the precise reasons why they decided to support him. If, however, action sought is *nonspecific,* emphasis should be on a body of ideas, for success depends on the audience's acceptance and retention of those ideas so that specific applications of them can be made as appropriate. The speaker who hopes to instill in his listeners standards for the evaluation of public officials must do more than leave his hearers convinced that evaluations should be made, although that is a first step toward his objective. He must also inform them of the standards in such a way that the criteria will be remembered.

Immediate or short-lived action is generally thought of as more easily obtained than is *delayed* or sustained action. Auditors who must delay or sustain their action are subject to subsequent influence of other persuaders, of their own meditations, and of time's eroding influence on recall of specifics.

While inertia is a factor in all attempts at influencing conduct, most people are more willing to accept a speaker's ideas if only *minor* changes in action or reaction are required of them than they would be if *major* changes were required. Without much thought, for instance, you would contribute $.50 towards the purchase of a gift for a friend leaving for Europe. You would likely, however, give thought and require considerable persuasion before you donated $50 to the same purpose.

Finally, listeners can more easily remember how to perform a relatively *simple* action, such as how to use a voting machine, than a *complex* action, such as how to complete an income tax return.

ESSENTIALS OF A SUCCESSFUL SPEECH

Having decided on the action he seeks, the speaker asks, "How may I proceed?" Many ways have been suggested by various authors,[5] particularly as the purpose of the speech changes. We think, however, a sound approach is founded on the assumption that a speech is successful only insofar as it is interesting,[6] clear, and impelling.

Unless the speaker is successful in gaining and holding attention he cannot expect success, because without attention he has not, in a sense, been heard. Indeed, if William James is correct, the speaker's first and only task in persuasion is equivalent to gaining full and favorable attention. In this book we call sustained attention (or, since attention is a fluctuating process, the frequent regaining of attention) *interest*. Because it is no more than theoretically possible to sustain attention throughout an activity as long as a public speech, the speaker must give active concern to gaining and regaining attention (that is, he must maintain interest) if he is to be either informative or persuasive.

Even if a speaker succeeds in keeping his audience interested, his speech must be clear. First, he must have clearly in mind what he wishes to accomplish. Second, what he wants to accomplish and the reasons why certain ideas should be accepted or certain acts performed need to be made clear to his audience. Although the injunction to clarity is stated categorically, we recognize that there may be times when clarity of purpose or thought is not at a premium; but we feel that these instances are so specialized that the injunction is not inappropriately stated.[7]

Finally, even though interest has been maintained and the presentation has been clear, the speaker will achieve his goal only if the listeners also find the speech impelling. In other words, you may listen closely to what the President says, understand him precisely, and still refuse to accept his explanation or his recommendation.

One might argue that making a speech impelling is all that should concern a speaker, for if the speech is impelling then it was of necessity both interesting and clear as well. That may be true. Our point, however, is that

[5] Some of the more recent ways are Alan H. Monroe's "Motivated Sequence," and Brigance's "Seven Lamps."

[6] It is important to realize that we are using interest in a somewhat broader sense than that often used by psychologists.

[7] For an interesting discussion of the usefulness of deliberate ambiguity see "Speech: The Life of a Diplomat," by Ben C. Limb, former Ambassador from the Republic of Korea to the United Nations, in *Quarterly Journal of Speech*, Vol. 43 (February 1957), pp. 55–61.

interest and clarity generally precede, or at least accompany, impulsion, and that interest precedes clarity.

Not only is there a sequence in time of the three factors but they tend to relate to the general purposes of speeches. As Alan H. Monroe points out, the speech to entertain, which has no more ambitious purpose than providing diversion and distraction from a listener's usual concerns and problems, can be regarded as successful if attention is sustained.[8] One may insist, however, that even in the light after-dinner speech, humor should be clear and impellingly funny. The speech purporting to explain an idea, concept, or object must place special emphasis on clarity. Additionally, however, interest must be held and explanation must be impelling (convincing). The speech urging specific action must, of course, be impelling. People frequently do things without knowing why, and often the best-trained analyst fails to offer a clear explanation of motivations. Nevertheless, people like to believe they are rational; they prefer to know that there are cogent reasons for whatever they believe or do.

Our concern in the chapters that follow will center on means whereby a speech can be made interesting, clear, and impelling. The chapters in Part One deal with application of principles to nearly all speeches, regardless of specific purpose or occasion. Part Two will suggest specific applications to speeches of particular purpose and occasions.

PUBLIC SPEAKING AS AN ART

As the reader turns to the next chapters, he should remember Aristotle's contention that public speaking is an art. It is an art, he said, because "it is possible to inquire the reason why some speakers succeed through practice and others succeed spontaneously; and every one will at once agree that such an inquiry is the function of an art."[9] This book rests on the assumption that the old Greek was pedagogically correct, and, consequently, that speech methods, to a degree, can be both analyzed and taught.

Of course, rhetoric is an art in a more common sense: it is a creative process by which the vast resources for oral communication are brought together in a unique, tasteful, and effective way. Can that creative process be analyzed, systematized, and capsulized so that all may use it with equal facility? Probably not. It seems too elusive, too variable, too individual. Even if the process could be capsulized, to know the rules would not ensure that they could be applied. Sense and sensitivity, more than knowledge and respect for rules, determine the speech product. That is why the finest speeches have been and always will be composed by imaginative practitioners who recognize that principles of art (in our case, the body *rhetoric*) are but

[8] *Principles and Types of Speech* (Chicago: Scott, Foresman and Co., Fifth ed., 1962), pp. 280–302.
[9] *Rhetoric*, W. Rhys Roberts, Tr. (New York: Modern Library, Inc., 1954), p. 1354a.

suggestions of what is thought by critics (in our case, *rhetoricians*) as the best practice. We repeat with insistence, therefore, the caution expressed nearly 2000 years ago by Quintilian: "Let no one . . . demand from me a rigid code of rules . . . or ask me to impose on students of rhetoric a system of laws [as] immutable as fate. . . . Rules are helpful all the same so long as they indicate the direct road and do not restrict us absolutely to the ruts made by others."[10]

PUBLIC SPEAKING AS HARD WORK

Though speech composition is an art, it still requires hard work. Novice speakers often underestimate the amount of time and energy devoted to speech preparation by even experienced speakers with exceptional talents. Here is a description of the procedures Lincoln used in building his "First Inaugural," a short speech even by modern standards:

> Lincoln began the actual composition of the address during the anxious days of January, 1861, in Springfield, when the pulse of the Republic trembled with disunion. [Recall that a President was then inaugurated on March 4 rather than January 20.] . . .
>
> One day Lincoln broke loose from the grip of hangers-on and climbed the three flights of stairs leading to a room in a brick office building standing across from the rugged old State House, the scene of many of Lincoln's political speeches. On the shiny surface top of a hardwood table he wrote out the original draft of the address. But he had first compared his own sentiments with what other men, in positions similar to that in which he now found himself, had said. He had reviewed the Republican platform and the much-discussed speech Alexander H. Stephens had recently made. He had arranged with Herndon [his law partner] to furnish him copies of Henry Clay's "Speech of 1850," Andrew Jackson's "Proclamation against Nullification," the "Constitution," and, later, Daniel Webster's "Reply to Hayne." (He regarded this latter argument as a model of American eloquence and had been much influenced by it in composing his speech of June 16, 1858.) Guided by these strong minds, he revised his own version of the address before putting it in the hands of W. H. Bailhache, to be set up and printed on the press of the *Illinois State Journal*. Friends advised him on matters of syntax in the copy.
>
> Lincoln showed a copy of the proposed address to Judge David Davis, who approved every word in it. Senator-elect O. H. Browning recommended that the tone of one passage in it be softened. Francis P. Blair approved of it in its entirety, but William H. Seward suggested no fewer than thirty-six items of revision. Stephen A. Douglas probably proposed one point of revision in it. . . .
>
> Seward aside, Lincoln made nine alterations of the original draft independently, although unnamed persons may have influenced him in this. . . .

[10] *The Institutio Oratoria*, H. E. Butler, Tr. (Cambridge, Mass.: Harvard University Press, 1953), Vol. 2, Sec. 13, pp. 1, 16.

The original text underwent a grand total of at least forty-five modifications. . . .[11]

Granted, that was an inaugural address, important and worthy of greatest care. However, the Gettysburg Address, delivered at an occasion when Edward Everett was to be the main speaker (Everett had already worked five weeks on his speech before Lincoln was even asked to speak), and at which the President was asked to make a "few appropriate remarks," could not be so regarded. The myth that Lincoln wrote his few remarks on the train to Gettysburg belies the care that this consummate artist, engrossed in the problems of leading a nation in the time of its severest trial, devoted to this minor occasion. Three days before the event a reporter asked him if the speech, which Lincoln characterized as "short, short, short," was written. "Well, not exactly written," Lincoln answered, "not finished anyway." The day before he left for Gettysburg, Lincoln read the draft to a friend. On the train he excused himself from a gathering of friends by saying: "Gentlemen, this is all very pleasant, but the people will expect me to say something to them tomorrow, and I must give the matter some thought." He probably did no actual writing on the train. That night at Gettysburg he began at 9 o'clock to rework his speech. From time to time he asked his valet for reactions to what he had written; he asked the chairman of the event to describe what was expected of him the next day; at 11 o'clock he spent ½ hour with Seward; and a little after midnight he retired. The next morning he worked an additional hour on the address.[12] All that for 270 words, just 2 minutes worth.

Even that description of Lincoln's creative process is incomplete. Earl Wiley wrote: "Revision and yet more revision characterized Lincoln's composition method. The few score words he spoke at Gettysburg were months in the making. In a sense, the composing of that address had no beginning that we can identify, for the concepts that stimulated those words had long been in Lincoln's heart."[13]

Or the method of Robert M. La Follette:

What was his own method of preparation for speaking? For important messages and political speeches the first step was to call on authoritative sources for accurate information. Often special research was done by someone, usually a young university-trained man, designated for the task. The next step was for him and Mrs. La Follette—for on such occasions they often worked together— to surround themselves with endless stacks of source material and bury themselves in personal research away from interruptions. For ideas to be included he also welcomed and solicited suggestions from trusted friends and advisers. . . .

[11] Earl W. Wiley, "Abraham Lincoln: His Emergence as the Voice of the People," *A History and Criticism of American Public Address*, William Norwood Brigance, Ed. (New York: McGraw-Hill, Inc., 1943), Vol. 2, pp. 866–868.

[12] Dorothy Meserve Kunhardt, "Lincoln's Gettysburg 'Failure'," *Life* Vol. 55 (November 15, 1963), pp. 116ff.

[13] *A History and Criticism of American Public Address*, Vol. 2, p. 871.

Not only did La Follette solicit suggestions on the ideas and wording of a speech; at least in the early days he sought criticism of his actual speaking. . . .[14]

The experienced and successful speakers, those known for their abilities, realize that abilities become apparent only with careful grooming. Only inexperienced speakers or those content with mediocrity regard the task as minor or wait for what Shelley called the "fading coal" of creativity to come alive from "some invisible influence, like an inconstant wind." In other words, *even great speakers do not rely on inspiration to do their work for them.* The poet-speakers, such as Lincoln, Churchill, and Stevenson, probably have their inspired moments. But even for them inspiration is not a substitute for effort. Edgar Allan Poe described well the creative process:

Most writers—poets in especial—prefer having it understood that they compose by a species of fine frenzy—an ecstatic intuition—and would positively shudder at letting the public take a peep behind the scenes, at the elaborate and vacillating crudities of thought—at the true purposes seized only at the last moment—at the innumerable glimpses of idea that arrived not at the maturity of full view—at the fully matured fancies discarded in despair as unmanageable—at the cautious selections and rejections—at the painful erasures and interpolations—in a word, at the wheels and pinions—the tackle for scene-shifting—the stepladders and demon-traps, the cock's feathers, the red paint and the black patches, which in ninety-nine cases out of the hundred, constitute the properties of the literary *histrio* . . .[15]

And Henry James told Hugh Walpole: "Don't let anyone persuade you—there are plenty of ignorant and fatuous duffers to try to do it—that strenuous selection and comparison are not the very essence of art. . . ."[16]

14 Carroll P. Lahman, "Robert M. La Follette," *A History and Criticism of American Public Address,* Vol. 2, p. 952.
15 *Writers on Writing,* Walter Allen, Ed. (New York: E. P. Dutton & Co., Inc., 1949), p. 65.
16 *Writers on Writing,* p. 147.

Making the Speech Interesting

2

As stated earlier, one of a speaker's prime objectives is to hold his listeners' interest, for interest precedes understanding and conviction. Although interest is emphasized, it is but one segment of the learning process, which starts with *reception* of stimuli and proceeds to giving *attention* to certain of them, maintaining *interest* in those selected for attention, arriving at a *perception* or interpretation of the things toward which attention or interest is shown, *learning* from what is perceived, and, finally, *forgetting* much of what is learned.

RECEPTION OF STIMULI

Whatever we may be, we live in a buzzing, bustling world, particularly when we are in a situation that calls for public speaking. Order comes from the confusion only if there is meaningful reception of some of the stimuli emanating from myriad sources.

Meaningful reception of stimuli requires certain conditions. First, the stimulus must be within our receptor's range of sensitivity. The sound that is insufficiently loud or too highly pitched cannot be received in any meaningful sense. Though a light source may be of sufficient brightness to be detected with sensitive instruments, it may be below the threshold of vision for the unassisted eye. Second, meaningful reception of a stimulus can take place only if the stimulus contrasts with competing stimuli. Sensation, the immediate apprehension of simple stimuli, requires that we be able to separate one stimulus from the galaxy of stimuli competing for reception by sensory apparatus. Thus, any one voice mixed with a multitude of voices that we hear as a roar yields no separate sensation. Our ears may literally ring with sound, but the contrast of the one voice to the many is insufficient for us to receive it specifically, regardless of how urgent a message it may carry.

Surfeit of stimuli is not the only cause of inability to make meaningful

11

reception of a stimulus. Stimuli may lack sufficient differentiation for our receptor and interpretative apparatus to distinguish between them. Whether we lack training in interpretation or our physical mechanism is incapable of reporting fine distinctions, we may receive two musical notes as substantially the same, or regard the shades of green on a visual aid as one color rather than two.

Perhaps every speaker would acknowledge that stimuli must have sufficient strength and contrast for meaningful reception to occur. Nevertheless, many speakers seem insufficiently aware of the extent to which distance between source and receptor modifies the stimulus as received. A sound heard at a certain loudness at 10 feet will have to be increased in intensity four times if it is to be heard with the same loudness at 20 feet. A visual aid that can be seen clearly at 10 feet may become a conglomeration of indistinguishable colors and print at the back of even a small meeting room.

The first problem in maintaining interest, then, is to ensure that stimuli can be received.

ATTENTION AND INTEREST

Of the barrage of stimuli that impinge on our sense organs, only a few of even those we are able to receive meaningfully actually reach our awareness. The rim of your glasses, the sounds from the hall, the feel of the pen in your hand, the too-high temperature of the room remain outside your awareness until your attention is directed to them.

Attention is the process of "focusing on certain aspects of current experience and neglecting others," according to psychologist Clifford T. Morgan. "Attention has a focus in which events are clearly perceived and a margin in which they are less clearly perceived."[1] Attention, then, is a selecting process. We do not react equally to all the stimuli impinging upon us; instead we focus upon a few.

J. Jeffery Auer reminds us that attention is fleeting, that we do not long keep a specific stimulus in focus.

> A listener cannot give continuous attention; even when he tries very hard to attend, he does not hear everything. Attention comes in spurts, like an irregular succession of waves breaking on a beach. While early experimenters estimated that the length of an attention unit is from five to eight seconds, psychologists now conclude simply that the duration of attention is brief, and that it is impossible to specify an absolute time value since that depends upon the intensity of the stimulus.[2]

Whatever the appropriate figure, the problem for the speaker is to gain, regain, and again regain attention. The speaker will be assisted in this

[1] *Introduction to Psychology* (New York: McGraw-Hill, Inc., Second ed., 1961), p. 665.
[2] Jon Eisenson, J. Jeffery Auer, John V. Irwin, *The Psychology of Communication* (New York: Appleton-Century-Crofts, 1963), pp. 237–238.

effort if he knows what determines whether a stimulus will be selected for attention.

Bernard Berelson and Gary A. Steiner believe there are three determinants of major importance:

> . . . the nature of the stimuli involved; previous experience or learning as it affects the observer's expectations (what he is prepared or "set" to see); and the motives in play at the time, by which we mean his needs, desires, wishes, interests, and so on—in short, what the observer wants or needs to see and not to see. Each of these factors can act to heighten or to decrease the probability of perceiving, and each can act on both exposure and awareness.[3]

The first determinant (discussed below in the sections on natural factors of attention and interest) depends on the characteristics of stimuli; the other two (discussed below as individualized attention factors) depend on the individual receiving them.

Natural Factors of Attention

Certain characteristics will enhance a stimulus's attention value regardless of the situation in which it occurs or the particular individual receiving it. Those characteristics are often called *natural* or *primary factors* of attention, and they are unlearned. A speaker must remember that they pertain to the entire context of a public speech. They relate not only to the speaker's voice but also to competing sounds, and not only to the speaker's gesture and movement but also to competing visual stimuli, such as visual aids or ornate head-table centerpieces. Further, although there is some question whether the extrapolation is justified, the attention factors operative with relatively simple and isolated visual and auditory stimuli are often assumed to operate in the involved thought process of the speech itself. That is, the quality that draws attention to an isolated stimulus is assumed to draw attention to a speech if it is present in the overall movement or development of the speech. Because stimuli occur in a complex of competing stimuli rather than independently, there is value in stating these factors in terms of the competition, as the rhetoricians Donald C. Bryant and Karl R. Wallace do and whose terminology we use.[4]

1. "Among competing stimuli, the moving one is preferred to the one at rest." The mobile speaker is more likely to hold attention than is the immobile speaker. We are not advocating that movement or gesture be motivated by a desire to attract attention. Rather, we are pointing out that movement to convey meaning has the additional value of attracting attention. Similarly, a flexible voice used to convey shades of meaning and

---

[3] *Human Behavior: An Inventory of Scientific Findings* (New York: Harcourt, Brace & World, Inc., 1964), p. 100.

[4] *Fundamentals of Public Speaking* (New York: Appleton-Century-Crofts, Inc., 1960), pp. 34–38. We use their terminology through the first four points in this section. We continue to use their format for points five and beyond.

emphasis will additionally assist in gaining and holding attention. Extending the principle to the speech as a whole suggests that the speaker who provides some light touches in an otherwise serious speech, who moves from specific to general statements and back to specifics helps his listeners attend to what he is saying as well as understand the points being made.

2. "Among competing stimuli, the stronger, the more intense stimulus is preferred to the weaker." The loudest sound, the quickest motion, the brightest color are likely to attract our attention.

3. "Among stimuli which vary in size [or duration] the larger [or longer lasting] is preferred." As Bryant and Wallace point out.

> . . . a speaker's full vocal and bodily response creates a stronger stimulus than a small, inhibited response. The well-developed gesture, the full movement, hold attention better than the small, restricted gesture. The facial expression, like the smile or the frown, which is broad enough for all to see is better than the facial expression which is dim, uncertain, and fleeting.

Perhaps this factor can be extended, as Bryant and Wallace extend it, to include the entire process of speech amplification, for amplification is the process of making an idea large.

4. "Among two or more collections of stimuli, the group which is organized has preference over the group which is disorganized; a unified whole is preferred to its separate parts." We tend, in other words, to arrange stimuli into patterns, to make a unit of them if possible. Most people see Figure 2.1 as a circle and a square, rather than as an arc and two lines.

If what is true for visual stimuli applies with equal force to as complex a process as a speech, this principle has important implications for the organization of a speech. Bryant and Wallace point out three factors that determine whether a group of stimuli can be formed into a pattern.

A. "The items in a stimulus-field must be near enough to each other to be taken in as a whole." In Figure 2.2 the lines on the left may appear as isolated lines, while those on the right may form a square.

A speech, lasting many minutes, presents obvious difficulties in making it possible for a listener to see a pattern as the elements appear in relative isolation. Indeed, the very space between the elements may make it probable that unless he is given assistance in remembering, the listener will even forget the earlier segments of the pattern. Ralph Waldo Emerson's "The American Scholar," delivered to the Harvard Phi Beta Kappa Society in 1837 and called by Oliver Wendell Holmes "our intellectual Declaration of Independence," is a long address with a number of ideas. However, through careful use of transition and the language of structure, the parts are brought clearly enough to the forefront and are often enough repeated so that a listener, without deliberate effort on his part, can perceive the pattern. After an introduction and a statement of his topic, Emerson said,

> Let us see him [the American scholar] in his school and consider him in reference to the main influences he receives.
> I. The first in time and first in importance of the influences upon the mind is that of nature. . . .
> II. The next great influence into the spirit of the scholar is the mind of the Past. . . . Books are the best type of the influence of the past. . . .
> III. . . . Action is with the scholar subordinate, but it is essential.
> I have now spoken of the education of the scholar by nature, by books, and by action. It remains to say somewhat of his duties.[5]

Perhaps Emerson thought principally of making himself clear; but the attempt at clarity also assisted in holding attention.

B. "Similar items in a stimulus-field are preferred to dissimilar items." You are more likely to see a pattern in the figures at the left of Figure 2.3 than you are in the figures at the right.

And Bryant and Wallace point out that the words in block B are more likely to seem to constitute a pattern than do those in block A.

A		B	
book	pipe	green	violet
auto	window	blue	color
idea	theater	red	yellow
speech	agriculture	spectrum	orange

[5] Printed in *American Philosophic Addresses: 1700–1900*, Joseph L. Blau, Ed. (New York: Columbia University Press, 1946).

Parallel wording or parallel handling of subpoints and ideas in a speech tend to hold attention.

The pattern of a speech must be artistically revealed. We tend to become incensed when a speaker's overconcern for ensuring that we see his pattern of development makes him seem condescending or patronizing. The problem is to provide enough signposts, but not too many; to show the direction, but not lead an audience by the hand. The golden mean, which permeates Aristotle's rhetoric, is applicable.

C. "Orderly items in a stimulus-field are preferred to items without order." You probably feel more comfortable with the first list of numbers below than with the second, even though the order is contrary to the usual order in which numbers appear. You feel most comfortable of all with the third sequence.

$$9, 7, 5, 3, 1$$
$$1, 2, 6, 8, 5$$
$$2, 4, 6, 8, 10$$

A speaker must remember that audiences have expectations of how items will appear, either from previous handling of the material or from the apparent pattern that the speaker is developing. If a speaker were to say "on the one hand," audiences would be convinced that he had forgotten something if he did not draw a contrast. The speaker who begins by citing several examples of something will be assumed to be working toward a generalization based on those examples. If a speaker spends time developing a problem, people will tend to think that he is moving to a proposed solution, even though his purpose may be only to convince them that a problem exists.

Kenneth Burke believes that a pattern not only facilitates understanding, but has probative value as well:

> We know that many purely formal patterns can readily awaken an attitude of collaborative expectancy in us. . . . Once you grasp the trend of the form, it invites participation regardless of the subject matter. Formally, you will find yourself swinging along with the succession of antitheses, even though you may not agree with the proposition that is being presented in this form. . . . Of course, the more violent your original resistance to the proposition, the weaker will be your degree of "surrender" by "collaborating" with the form. But in cases where a decision is still to be reached, a yielding to the form prepares for assent to the matter identified with it. Thus, you are drawn to the form, not in your capacity as a partisan, but because of some "universal" appeal in it. And this attitude of assent may then be transferred to the matter which happens to be associated with the form.[6]

5. Among competing stimuli, the one that is repeated, will be preferred to the one that is not. This results from what is described as the

[6] *A Rhetoric of Motives* (New York: George Braziller, Inc., 1955), p. 58.

"summation of stimuli." Mothers have learned that they are more likely to elicit a response from a child if his name is repeated several times when he is called. Nearly every student speaker has been criticized for omitting something from a speech when he knows it was included. If a speaker wishes to ensure that his point is heard, he should repeat it. Not everything should be repeated, of course, for repetition is a mode of gaining emphasis as well as attention. Further, artless repetition can lead to monotony. As Auer states, monotony can be avoided

> and even greater potency often achieved if the repeated stimulus is varied slightly in form while retaining the central theme. This application of repetition is a hallmark of good design and composition, whether in music, architecture, stage scenery, or public relations campaigns.[7]

In the speech cited above, Emerson talked at first of the "influences" on the American scholar. When he summarized the "influences," he referred to the "education" of the scholar. This variation introduced variety, probably made his meaning clearer, and by substantial repetition avoided monotony while still achieving the result of repetition.

Natural Factors of Interest

So far we have considered those factors of attention that have to do principally with the nature of visual or aural stimuli, and suggested implications of those factors for a speech. In addition to the attention factors operative in relatively simple and static patterns, factors of attention can be found in certain patterns of activity. They are dependent on a continuing and developing situation. Hence, they are often called *interest factors*. Whereas the implications for speechmaking of the factors already discussed can be gained only by extension, interest factors relate primarily to thought processes rather than perception of relatively isolated stimuli. Hence, their significance for public speaking is apparent.

The point where attention becomes interest is difficult to discover. Auer states,

> In considering functional psychological factors in communicative behavior it is logical to move from attention to interest for they are not only associated but nearly inseparable. As William James . . . put it: "What-we-attend-to and what-interests-us are synonymous terms." The distinction between them, a thin one, is that attention is concerned with the initial organization of our sensory receptors toward a given stimulus and that interest is what maintains subsequent orientation.[8]

Whether the qualities of a developing situation that serve to hold our attention are listed separately as interest factors or as attention factors is a nearly arbitrary decision. We choose to list them separately.

[7] *The Psychology of Communication*, p. 240.
[8] *The Psychology of Communication*, p. 241.

1. *Of competing situations, one which is suspenseful will tend to hold interest better than one which is not.* Imagine how frequently the inanity of a television show, a poor movie, or the unimaginative writing of a mystery story is overcome and attention held through suspense. Frances Taylor Patterson believes that "suspense . . . constitutes the difference between the masterpieces in the Metropolitan Museum of Art and the pictures at the Rivoli or the Rialto Theatres." It is because of this difference, she believes, that "people straggle into the Metropolitan by twos and threes and struggle into the Rialto and Rivoli by hundreds."[9] Oftentimes the suspense is sham; we know how the story will end. Marshal Dillon will capture the bank robber, but he will never marry Kitty. Nevertheless, listen.

Perhaps as important as suspense in holding interest in a developing situation is our concern for completeness. We dislike things that are incomplete. Most of us would feel more comfortable if the lines and arc in Figure 2.1 were completed to form a circle and rectangle.

Suspense in public speaking can be utilized in the total development of the speech, such as when an inductive development leads from the specific points to the generalization or conclusion of the speech. C. P. Snow's famous address "The Moral Un-Neutrality of Science" has some aspects of a jigsaw puzzle as piece by piece is placed in the development and it moves toward the inexorable conclusion. At times the pieces seem not related, but if the conclusion had been revealed prematurely, Snow's audience would have been ill-prepared for his almost audacious conclusion.[10] Although Snow is an accomplished novelist, considerations of making his theme amenable probably had more to do with his pattern of organization than did concern for suspense; but suspense served as the willing handmaiden of the persuasive arguments.

Suspense can be used with great effectiveness in smaller segments of the speech as well. Note these two examples from a speech by Archibald MacLeish (Pulitzer Prize poet, speechwriter to President Roosevelt, Librarian of Congress, Harvard Professor of Rhetoric and Oratory) delivered in 1950 at the inauguration of a president of Wellesley College. The first is the suspense of the periodic sentence.

> Here is a great and distinctly American college making the most emphatic affirmation of belief in the national future of which men are capable. And here, in the same country, and in the same hour, and from one end of the American republic to the other, is something as different from that affirmation, as opposite to it, as contradictory, as the human mind would well conceive: a fear for the future . . .

The next is the suspenseful development of a point:

9 Cited in Walter Lippmann's *Public Opinion* (New York: Crowell Collier and Macmillan, Inc. Paperback Ed., 1961), pp. 164–165.
10 This speech is reprinted in full and analyzed in detail in Chapter 16.

These two things, the act of confidence in the future here, the terror of the future everywhere and here as well, can simply not be reconciled. They cannot live together. And yet they do. They do, within this room. How do they?

Is it because people like us, people of our kind, live our lives in separate compartments?—because we don't permit ourselves to know, as officers and teachers and students and friends of this college, what we know only too well, what we lie awake at night knowing, as men and women?—because we go on with our lives and our occupations out of habit and out of sheer inertia, repeating, now that they are meaningless, the forms and motions that once had meaning when the future was alive?

Is it because we deceive ourselves with hopes which we know only too well are deceptions—the hope that something will turn up now, that something will happen, that Stalin will die or the Communists will change their minds or the Tito-ists will overthrow the Kremlin and everything will be different; the hope that the cold war can be won as a cold war, in spite of the fact that a cold war, by hypothesis, is a war that can never be won because it is waged, not to accomplish something, but to prevent something from happening, and is therefore only effective as long as it goes on preventing?

Is it because we delude ourselves into thinking that somehow, in some way, by some miracle, we will be spared in this holocaust—our lives will be spared, or our days, or our college or this particular new beginning we inaugurate this morning? Is it because we think, like the Princess in Li Po's poem, that the howling of the yellow dogs is not for us?

I, for myself, do not think so. I do not think it is for any of these reasons we are able to do what we are doing here today. I do not think we are deluding ourselves, or hiding our fears from our hopes, or carrying on out of habit, or pretending not to know what in fact we do know.

I think the truth is the opposite. I think the truth is that we do *not* know what we pretend to know—what we pretend to know because we hear ourselves saying it over and over like parrots, or because we read it over and over in the speech the hypnotized politicians are constantly making—the same speech over and over with nothing but the speaker changing.

I think we *do not know*—we here in this room and millions of others in millions of other rooms across this country—I think we *do not* know that our time is a time of ineluctable war, of inescapable struggle for survival, which weapons and warfare must decide because only weapons and warfare can decide it.[11]

Suspense occurs in places where we may not expect it. Irony or sarcasm or satire may have suspense in it, at least until the irony is clear and the speaker reveals whether he can hew to the narrow line separating finesse from boorishness.

John Crosby, radio and television critic for the *New York Herald Tribune,* in 1951 talked about "How To Get Along in a Free World without Being Subpoenaed."

[11] Printed in the *Atlantic Monthly,* Vol. 155 (June 1950).

Well—to get back to the subject—how does one get along with these people who want to shoot everyone? How does one avoid being subpoenaed? How do you hang on to your job, your reputation, your diplomatic career? There are methods. In 1938, let's say, you gave two dollars to some organization to buy an ambulance to pick up the wounded in the Spanish Civil War. This was a fashionable thing to do at the time. It isn't any more. You have since discovered that the organization you gave the two dollars to has grown enormously unfashionable and you are still linked to it.

What to do? Well—give another two dollars. This time you give it to an organization to investigate what happened to that first two dollars.[12]

2. *Of competing situations, one with conflict will hold interest better than will one without.* Kenneth Burke regards rhetoric as a form of conflict. Public debate of issues implies disagreement and therefore at least moderate conflict, he believes. The degree to which conflict can or should be revealed in a speech is, however, a matter of taste. For a variety of reasons, General Douglas MacArthur's address to Congress in April, 1951, held attention of the American public and a good portion of the world; but one reason was an awareness of the conflict out of which the speech grew— President Truman's removal of the General as the Commander in Chief of American forces in the Far East. The conflict was so great that MacArthur sought to minimize it in his speech:

I do not stand here as an advocate for any partisan cause, for the issues are fundamental and reach quite beyond the realm of partisan consideration. They must be resolved on the highest plane of national interest if our course is to prove sound and our future protected.[13]

Political speakers often seek to heighten a sense of conflict to maximize interest in a campaign. Though Truman, too, in 1951 sought to minimize the feeling of conflict between himself and MacArthur, in 1948 he attempted to heighten the conflict between himself and Governor Dewey so that the voters would become concerned about the outcome of the election. Clark Clifford, Truman's principal speechwriter and strategist, likened the campaign to a "razzle-dazzle" football game. Although the "razzle-dazzle" distressed some voters, post-election surveys revealed that many voters admired Truman's spunk, enjoyed his enthusiasm as he began an election "fight" against odds considered by nearly all professional pollsters as insuperable, and became convinced that it did matter who won the election.

3. *Of competing situations, one having a judicious mixture of the familiar and the novel will be preferred to one made up of either entirely familiar or unknown elements.* Although, as Bryant and Wallace state, "among two stimuli, one familiar and the other strange, the familiar one is preferred," we wish to avoid monotony. And yet we dislike too much

12 Printed in *Representative American Speeches: 1951–1952*, A. Craig Baird, Ed.; Vol. 24, No. 3 of "The Reference Shelf" (New York: The H. W. Wilson Co., 1952).
13 Printed in *Representative American Speeches: 1951–1952*.

strangeness. Thus, we are delighted with a visit to a new city; but we are almost equally delighted when we unexpectedly meet an acquaintance there. We greet him warmly, even if we saw him at home but a few days earlier and there exchanged only the perfunctory salutations required by convention.

Only through the process of combining the familiar and the unfamiliar can understanding occur. If one has never seen a mountain, a description of it might include a concept he does know—a hill or knoll. While *understanding* should be the prime justification for combining the known and unknown, the combination also aids in holding interest. Notice how the effectiveness of this paragraph from another speech by Archibald MacLeish is heightened by the use of the ordinary in striking ways:[14]

> It is no longer feared, it is now assumed, that the country is headed back to normalcy, that Harding is just around the corner, that the Twenties will repeat themselves in a blaze of chromium sinks, cabinet radios, glass-topped automobiles and four-color unemployment—and that the peace upon which the hope of the world depends will not be made.[15]

As Auer wrote, "perhaps the most effective presentation combines familiarity and novelty: 'Old wine in new bottles.' In terms of communication this might mean familiar ideas and sentiments applied to new situations and in novel language."[16]

Analogy, metaphor, and comparison all use a combination of the familiar and the novel. Striking statements often achieve their memorable and quotable quality in part because of an unusual use of the familiar. In his address on the American scholar, Emerson stated that it becomes the scholar to "feel all confidence in himself and to defer never to the popular cry. . . . Let him not quit his belief that a popgun is a popgun, though the ancient and honorable of the earth affirm it to be the crack of doom."

4. *Of competing messages, one that is concrete will hold interest better than one that is abstract.* A speaker cannot always be concrete or specific. Often his purpose is to build general concepts that inherently must be abstract. However, the specific can heighten interest. Compare the paragraph from MacLeish's speech cited above with this rewriting.

> It is no longer feared, it is now assumed, that the country will experience the same concern with physical things that it experienced in the Twenties, and that while it tries to develop more impressive material things, it will also experience extensive unemployment and disillusionment over the failure to gain world peace.

[14] Note, too, the emphasis given the failure of the hope for world peace. By talking lightly, almost gaily, about the material things, he achieved a sharp and striking contrast by moving to the no-nonsense last statement.
[15] Printed in *Representative American Speeches: 1943–1944*, A. Craig Baird, Ed.; Vol. 17, No. 4 of "The Reference Shelf."
[16] *The Psychology of Communication*, p. 242.

5. *Of two situations, one that is humorous will hold interest better than one that is not.* Few speakers fail to appreciate the value of humor; rather, they expect too much from it. Humor does heighten interest; and, if the response solicited is laughter and applause, it does assist in making a unit of the audience. But humor alone will not salvage a poor speech. Oftentimes the most effective humor is not the type that brings guffaws from the audience. Adlai Stevenson, one of the most effective speakers in modern times, used humor with considerable skill.[17] In an address at the World Brotherhood Dinner of the National Conference of Christians and Jews, he began:

> I have here, if I may play just a little on a word, what I consider the perfect address for a meeting in behalf of World Brotherhood. It is the address on a letter that figured in Thornton Wilder's play *Our Town*. This is the address: "Jane Crofeet, the Crofeet Farm, Grover's Corners, Sutton County, New Hampshire, United States of America, Continent of North America, the Earth, the Solar System, the Universe, the Mind of God."

The relevancy of the reference became even more apparent as Stevenson made the presentation:

> Ladies and Gentlemen, acting for you, I confer the World Brotherhood Award Citation upon Albert M. Greenfield, Sugar Loaf, Chestnut Hill, Philadelphia, Pennsylvania, United States of America, Continent of North America, the Earth, the Solar System, the Universe, the Mind of God.[18]

Individualized Attention Factors

Thus far we have considered the first of the three determinants of whether a stimulus will be selected for attention and interest: the nature of the stimulus. We turn now to what have been called "acquired determiners of attention," "individualized attention values," or "internal factors." As Berelson and Steiner state, these individualized factors are of two types: what listeners are set to attend to, and the motives operative at any particular time.

1. *Among competing stimuli, we will give attention to those we are set to perceive.* The importance of set in attention is stated by Morgan.

> Of the various factors that determine attention and thus perception, expectancy is probably the most important, for our sets and expectancies largely direct and order the successions of our perceptual experiences. Without them, our perceiving would be largely at the mercy of random fluctuations in the environmental stimuli.[19]

[17] That a little humor can be a dangerous thing came to the forefront clearly in the 1952 presidential campaign. Stevenson received criticism for using what his critics regarded as too much humor in his unsuccessful campaign. Some people thought the office of the President is no joking matter. Four years later Stevenson used less humor in his campaign.

[18] Printed in *Representative American Speeches: 1957–1958*, A. Craig Baird, Ed.; Vol. 30, No. 4 of "The Reference Shelf."

[19] *Introduction to Psychology*, p. 309.

As Morgan suggests, no one can attend to all stimuli. Therefore, a person assumes a set to attend to those that seem important to him in a particular context. Fortunately for the speaker, people who come to hear a speech are likely to assume a set that will enable them to hear the speech and will minimize attention given to competing noises or sights. While a set ordinarily operates powerfully in a speaker's favor, the natural attention factors of distracting stimuli may be sufficient to overcome the set. Indeed, the difficulty in overcoming natural attention factors leads the serious listener to chastise the talking couple sitting next to him in a lecture hall.

2. *Of competing stimuli, those related to a vital interest will be preferred over those that are not.* Andrew Weaver and Ordean Ness relate the story of the physician who sat playing cards with three friends.

> Word was brought to him that a child had suddenly become seriously ill and needed immediate help. As he rose to go, one of his friends remonstrated, "Don't rush off; the child's mother is probably unduly alarmed over the situation. Stay and finish the game."
>
> "That's what you think I ought to do?" queried the doctor.
>
> "Yes," answered his friend, "fussy, nervous people have no right to call a physician after office hours, anyway."
>
> "Very well," said the doctor, "I'll take your advice; it is your child who is ill."[20]

Not all subjects are vital to all audiences. Only when the father realized that his child was ill could the physician assume that the man appreciated the significance of the telephone call. And, as did the physician, a speaker often must point out to the audience that what he speaks of is important to them.

Arthur Vandenberg, Senator from Michigan who was long known to be suspicious of international commitments beyond a war period, announced a reversal of his ideas before the Senate. He stated why he believed clear thinking to be of utmost importance:

> Mr. President, there are critical moments in the life of every nation which call for the straightest, the plainest, and the most courageous thinking of which we are capable. We confront such a moment now. It is not only desperately important to America. It is important to the world. It is important not only to this generation which lives in blood. It is important to future generations if they shall live in peace.[21]

3. *Of competing stimuli, those to which our attention has been directed will tend to gain that attention.* Although he may lack subtlety, the lecturer who tells you, "This is the most important point, I want you to get it," will probably be successful in gaining your attention to his point. However,

[20] *An Introduction to Public Speaking* (New York: The Odyssey Press, Inc., 1961), p. 185.

[21] Printed in *Representative American Speeches: 1944–1945*, A. Craig Baird, Ed.; Vol. 18, No. 3 of "The Reference Shelf."

attention can be directed as well through subtle suggestion. The speaker who wishes to direct attention to a visual aid can do so simply by turning to that aid himself.

In the hands of a careless or thoughtless speaker, however, negative suggestion operates as a powerful distraction to listeners. To the injunction, "Pay no attention to this globe; it has nothing to do with my speech," a listener may react by noting the globe for the first time and finding that it distracts him. To the apology, "I'm sorry that it was necessary to meet in this room, for it is not very satisfactory for such a gathering," listeners may note for the first time, and be disturbed by the knowledge, that the room is unsatisfactory. Similarly, the speaker who apologizes for his lack of opportunity to prepare a speech is suggesting to listeners that they search for unsatisfactory elements in the speech, elements that they may never have noticed had he not forewarned them.

Faked Attention

Whether a speaker regards his prospective speech as interesting is of lesser importance than whether his audience will regard it as interesting. However, even the most skilled speaker stands in danger of misjudging his audience. The delightful new anecdote may have been related at last week's meeting. The intricate background to the issue may have been covered in a special television program the night before last. Thus, in matters of attention as in all others, the speaker must remember that the audience is the speech's end and object; he must seek verification of his estimate that the speech is interesting. Unfortunately, however, a speaker can be more readily mislead on audience reaction here than in perhaps any other area.

Every teacher and every student knows, as Ringness and his coauthors state, that "one can daydream in class to such an extent that the instructor and his words, rather than being the focus or figure, become background— not highly differentiated. This we call 'lack of attention.' "[22] Every teacher also knows that it is nearly always impossible to tell when a student is daydreaming and when he is attending. Students have learned that it pays to give attention or to give the appearance of giving attention. That is, they have learned to fake attention. They develop this ability partly because of consequences suffered when they revealed inattentiveness to teachers; but the skill also is probably developed partly so that they can conform to our society's insistence that one should give the appearance of courtesy except in unusual circumstances.[23]

[22] Thomas A. Ringness, Herbert J. Klausmeier, and Arthur J. Singer, Jr., *Psychology in Theory and Practice* (Boston: Houghton Mifflin Co., 1959), p. 188.

[23] You can illustrate for yourself your skill in faking attention. Notice how often during a lecture you think of something other than what your instructor is saying; and notice that you do not reveal this mental wandering to him. But, carried on deliberately, the experiment will be distorted by the influence of suggestion. It will be of an order with this one: "Count to 10 without thinking of a rabbit." Try it.

Audiences will usually hesitate to reveal when attention is lost. Most listeners are quite capable of assuming a rapt appearance, which better reflects the delights of tomorrow's occupation than today's speaker. Even though he may be jarred back to the immediate situation by laughter or applause in which he joins, a listener may still have missed most that went before and all that comes after, until the next burst of laughter or applause.

The speaker's common tendency toward seeing what he wishes to see complements the audience's skill in assuming the appearance of attention. A speaker wants to see an enraptured audience. To admit while on the platform that all is not well is at least a courageous thing to do, and at times it may actually be disastrous. Indeed, good sense may compel the uncertain speaker to whistle a happy tune occasionally, but he should not be beguiled into believing that the tune eliminates any dangers, even though it eases the fears. Seek confirmation that all goes well when you need that confirmation. And yet understand that the most propitious signs of attentiveness may come from the man reviewing yesterday's brilliant strategy on the golf course.

Physical Setting and Attention

Attention is given to selected stimuli out of the multitude of stimuli impinging on one at any instant. We have talked of what the speaker should do to facilitate the giving of attention to him. In addition to his own actions and speech, the prudent speaker considers the setting in which he is to speak. He takes what steps are possible to ensure that he will have the physical setting for his speech which will assist, rather than make difficult, his enterprise.

1. *As many of the competing stimuli as possible should be eliminated.* The walls of Navy classrooms used to be amply supplied with various posters, doubtless to make maximal use of a recruit's time. Experience showed, however, that recruits spent too little time attending to the immediate lecture, and Navy classrooms became fiercely bare. Bunting, flags waving in a current of air, or impressive centerpieces may all add to the mood of an occasion, and may be essential to obtaining the proper mood; but all will contribute to the competition for the listener's attention. A large platform party, particularly if it includes an uninhibited scratcher, sleeper, or conversationalist, can set up almost insuperable obstacles for the speaker. One speaker, faced with the prospect of giving a long, difficult address before a convention of educators, minimized the impact of the head table's ornate centerpieces, lovely women, and uninhibited men by arranging for a speaker's rostrum some distance in front of the head table. When the lights were dimmed, those over the head table were turned off completely.

While speakers may think of aural and visual stimuli as competitors, they often forget that all sources of stimuli may serve as a distraction. The uncomfortable chairs and the too-hot room compete as effectively as do the waving flags.

2. *Just as competing stimuli should be eliminated, arrangements should enable the listeners to receive the desired stimuli as easily as possible.* The after-dinner speaker whose auditors are seated with their backs to him or are turned awkwardly around in their chairs to hear has an extra burden in holding attention. No less than the track star gets set to hear the starter's gun, the audience must get in a position (set) to hear and view the speaker.

Visual aids must be large enough and clear enough to be seen easily. Voice must be loud enough to be heard without undue effort. Remember that giving attention is work, and hence fatiguing. The less work required of a listener, the greater the probability of his giving the needed attention.

PERCEPTION

Communication requires more than an awareness of stimuli or sensations of sound or light, even though the stimuli succeeded in holding interest. The stimuli must be interpreted. "The process of discriminating among stimuli and of interpreting their meanings" is what Morgan calls *perception*.[24] Sensation shades off into perception when one is concerned with isolated and simple stimuli. The difficulties in distinguishing between the processes need not trouble us, however; the level of interpretation demanded of a process as complex as speaking is far beyond sensation.

The speaker must be concerned with perception because what listeners perceive—the interpretation given to what they see and hear—is often markedly incongruous with what the speaker intended, even though the listeners attended closely to his speech. James A. Winans, the most influential speech teacher of this century, illustrated the problem.

> Mrs. Phillip Snowdon, the eloquent English advocate of women's suffrage, told in a speech of reading in the same Scottish paper of a man who for stealing two overcoats in order to get food for his children was given a sentence of six months, and of another man who for criminally assaulting a little girl was fined five shillings. Before proceeding to her criticisms on man-made and man-administered law, she spoke very deliberately to this effect: "Now, mind you, it is wrong to steal overcoats. Every public speaker present will sympathize with me when I say I do not wish to be represented as saying anything to the contrary. It is wrong to steal overcoats."[25]

[24] *Introduction to Psychology*, p. 299. Unfortunately, perception is not consistently used by psychologists. James Drever defines perception as "the process of becoming immediately aware of something; usually employed of sense perception, when the thing of which we become immediately aware is the object affecting a sense organ; when the object is recognized or identified in any way perception passes into *apperception*." (*A Dictionary of Psychology*, Baltimore: Penguin Books, 1952, p. 201). Morgan and many other psychologists use perception to include apperception as defined by Drever.

[25] *Public Speaking: Principles and Practices* (Ithaca, N.Y.: The Sewell Publishing Co., 1915), p. 357.

That such an explicit statement should be necessary seems less improbable if we recall that perception involves interpretation. The more complex the pattern or the more ambiguous the stimuli, the more difficult the interpretation. We hear a sound, which we interpret as a footstep. Is it the muffled step of a burglar or the cautious step of a roommate entering the house, concerned that he not waken anyone? What we regard as the most likely interpretation we generally assume is also the correct interpretation. Whether the likely interpretation is correct depends in part on whether we are aware of the alternate possibilities. The footstep may actually be nothing more than the rubbing of a branch overhanging the roof and set in motion by the wind.

The infinitely more complex pattern of stimuli in a public speech is open to even greater misunderstanding, particularly because our expectations regarding what specific people will be like influence our interpretation of their subsequent behavior, at least on first impression. Mrs. Snowden, a leader in a controversial movement, met with considerable opposition and doubtless frequent expectation that she would make irresponsible statements. Her experience showed that she must clearly distinguish between what she intended to say and what irresponsible statements she wished listeners to understand she did not make.

Further, just as wishes, needs, and motives exert considerable influence on what is attended to, they exert influence on how the received stimuli are interpreted. If he is to be clearly understood, the speaker must do more than gain attention through a variety of gesture, active voice, and compelling examples. He must seek to ensure accuracy of understanding through sufficient repetition and restatement. Berelson and Steiner remind us that

> human perceptual judgments are inexorably under the control of the particular background brought to the judgment. Perceptually, as well as logically, there is no absolute correlate of any perceived magnitude. Even the distinction between black and white, which we normally take as the prototype of an absolute qualitative dichotomy, is perceptually a matter of degree. White immediately turns to black if and when the area surrounding it becomes more brilliantly illuminated—which is exactly how areas of black on a white movie screen are produced. Thus from the simplest sensory experiences . . . to the most complicated judgments of social norms and values . . . man responds relatively—by making comparisons that detect similarities and differences and little, perhaps nothing, more.[26]

LEARNING

Psychologist Carl Hovland believed that "the extent to which a communication is effective in changing opinions depends in part on the extent

[26] *Human Behavior*, p. 120.

to which the content of the communication is attended to, understood, and remembered. When none of the supporting arguments are grasped and retained, beliefs and expectations based on them will generally be unaffected."[27]

When a speaker seeks to convince an audience of the desirability of a specific action, success depends on his auditors learning both the action sought and the reasons for it. The longer the interval of time between the speech and the action, the greater the need for effective learning. Only when the action sought is immediate and irreversible can a speaker fail to be concerned with the duration of learning. When the action sought is nonspecific and is to be based on the understanding of a concept or process, action will be modified only to the extent that learning persists.

Through thousands of experiments, the learning process has managed to stay relatively obscure. There is no universally accepted theory of learning. In spite of differences, the central fact of the learning process, and the one which is of great consequence to speechmaking, is, as stated by psychologist Ernest R. Hilgard: "Learning and motivation are inseparable. Any arrangement designed to encourage learning must provide for motivation as well."[28] Just as audiences will attend to something that is vital to them, they will more likely learn if the material is important to them.

Regardless of the motivation of the listeners, learning is limited by the degree of difficulty of what is to be learned. Things that have few parts, are concrete, and in a relationship or pattern are more easily learned than are complex, disorganized, and vague series. Speakers should particularly keep in mind the difficulty listeners have in comprehending and retaining a large number of arguments.

Although learning is an essential part of successful public speaking, a speaker must not expect too much from learning. He cannot assume that because listeners have learned a specific set of facts, they will therefore inevitably arrive at the conclusion that the proposed action is desirable. According to Berelson and Steiner, "the communication of facts is typically ineffective in changing opinions in desired directions against the force of audience predispositions. . . . Communications can change the information of the audience, and on occasion even its behavior, without changing the associated attitudes."[29]

FORGETTING

With learning comes the concomitant process—forgetting. But the more effective the learning, the less rapid the forgetting. Thus, what

[27] Carl I. Hovland, Irving L. Janis, and Harold H. Kelley, *Communication and Persuasion* (New Haven, Conn.: Yale University Press, 1953), p. 114.

[28] *Introduction to Psychology* (New York: Harcourt, Brace & World, Inc., Second Ed., 1957), p. 268.

[29] *Human Behavior*, p. 543.

facilitates and makes effective learning will also diminish the impact of forgetting. Auer states:

> A general principle is that the stronger or the more potent the stimulus, the greater impress it will make upon the responding person. The best omnibus word to describe this principle in operation is *emphasis,* the special stress or weight given to particular stimuli. In the communicative situation this means the emphasis given to particular stimulus units (whole arguments, propositional sentences, important phrases, key words) by presenting them with special potency. To give emphasis of this sort implies, realistically, that in any total learning some parts are more critical to understanding than others.[30]

Intensity, duration, and repetition or restatement (particularly if spaced) give potency to stimuli. In the speech situation the specific illustration or the apt and striking phrase often will be remembered while most of the speech is forgotten. President Kennedy's "Ask not what your country can do for you—ask what you can do for your country" is already in the familiar literature of our nation and perhaps will remain there as securely as has Lincoln's "of the people, by the people, and for the people." Even now most people who listened to Kennedy's inaugural speech would find difficulty in reconstructing it, although its organization is clear and straightforward and it encompasses few points. But to the extent that the substance of the speech is embodied in the trenchant, memorable phrase the speech is not forgotten.

Retention of material is also facilitated if subsequent use of the material is anticipated, even if the material is uncongenial. Although some students may be motivated by curiosity, a freshman class of English students is less likely to retain information on the use of a slide rule than is a freshman class of engineers. Further, pleasant things are better remembered than those that are unpleasant.

We have already suggested that the process of forgetting operates at an uneven rate. The important, the useful, the pleasant information is retained longer than the unimportant, the inconsequential, the unpleasant. But even information that is recalled goes through a transformation process. As attitudes influence attention, perception, understanding and learning, they also influence recall. What a listener later recalls about a speech will be selected, organized, and interpreted according to his expectations, attitudes, opinions, and beliefs. Berelson and Steiner state that

> qualitative changes in memory tend to comply with general perceptual principles: representations of the past, as of the present but even more so, tend to become more simple, more internally consistent, and more "stable figures" than they are in actuality; they also tend to conform to retroactive expectations and, to some extent, to the wishes of the subject.[31]

[30] *The Psychology of Communication,* p. 250.
[31] *Human Behavior,* p. 186.

The speaker often finds that his generalization is remembered, while the careful qualification is forgotten. And even that generalization, as it is reshaped through imperfect recall to the language of the listener, may undergo a metamorphosis of substance as surely as it undergoes a metamorphosis of language.[32] Mrs. Snowden's critics may not have been dishonest when they later said that she thought nothing was wrong with stealing overcoats. Rather they may have reflected Aristotle's concept of the "weakness of the hearers."[33]

Perhaps an appreciation of the problems of remembering caused Quintilian to write,

> . . . and that which an orator ought to settle in his mind before everything else, even though he purpose to offer many arguments in support of his cause, is what he would wish to be most apparent to the judge. But though this is the first thing to be considered, it does not follow that it will be the first to be stated.[34]

INTEREST AND THE ANECDOTE

Most of the factors of attention and interest are embodied in the anecdote, story, joke, parable, example, or illustration.

We recall reading an apocryphal anecdote about a legislator in ancient Greece who sought to warn his fellow legislators about the dangers from Sparta. While he talked he noticed that few people attended to what he had to say. He stopped and said that he wished to tell the story of two travelers who found themselves in Athens with no means of getting their luggage to the Piraeus, the port some miles from the city. One of the men suggested a solution. "I will buy a donkey to carry our luggage. When we are through with him I will sell him. However, since I'm taking a financial risk in doing this, you should pay me for his use." The other man agreed to the arrangement.

A donkey was purchased and loaded, and the trip began. Midway during the journey, they decided to rest. Other travelers already occupied the shade cast by the few trees in the narrow, walled corridor joining Athens to the Piraeus. Finally, the owner of the donkey thought of a solution. He lay down in the shade cast by the donkey. His companion

---

[32] Actually language can perhaps not be changed without changing thought. Hence, it is misleading to speak of style as the language in which one's thoughts are clothed. The substantial thought may be retained in spite of language change, but emphases and nuances inevitably change as the words are changed.

[33] An interesting example of this metamorphosis at work is the Churchillian statement often remembered as "I have nothing to offer but blood, sweat, and tears," but which is accurately cited as "I have nothing to offer but blood, toil, tears, and sweat." Apparently this quotation has fallen victim to our tendency, revealed in folk literature and jokes, to think in terms of three.

[34] *Quintilian's Institutes of Oratory*, John Selby Watson, Tr. (London: Henry G. Bohn, 1856), Vol. 2, Sec. 6, p. 12.

protested that while there was not sufficient shade to accommodate both men, what little there was should be shared, for he had rented half the services of the donkey. The owner refused. "I rented half the carrying capacity of the donkey to you, that is all," he argued. "You will have to find what shade you can someplace else." The men became angry, the argument became spirited, and a crowd gathered to watch its outcome.

At that point in the narrative, the ancient legislator stopped. "Oh men of Athens," he said, "I seek to warn you of the dangers to yourselves, your family, and your city from Sparta, and none of you listens. I tell you a silly little story about two men and a donkey and you listen very closely. Is this a measure of the judgment you use in fulfilling your responsibilities as leaders?"

As the legislator knew, judgment had little to do with the problem. Although no psychologist existed to tell him about the psychology of interest, some pre-Aristotelian had noted that people attend to an anecdote. Throughout this chapter we have sought to explain the psychology of interest. Yet we would guess that you read the silly little story of the donkey with far more attention than any other segment of the chapter, except perhaps for the experiences of the poker-playing physician.

Anecdotes incorporate suspense, conflict, often humor, a full portion of concreteness, and a change in pace. As nearly as any categorical statement can be made about speechmaking, one may say that the anecdote or anecdote-like material cannot fail to hold attention. Chapter 11 has a good deal more to say about anecdotes. Here we will only point out that they must be used carefully. The speaker who begins his speech with "this reminds me of a story" may realize that many speakers use that device to gain attention but not realize that those same speakers often ignore the fact that the beginning of a speech is the place where listeners are most likely to be attentive. Although initial interest may need to be heightened, the difficulties in maintaining interest increase geometrically as the speech goes on. In use of anecdotes and all other attention-getting factors, speakers will do well to recall Aristotle's opinion: "Calls for attention, when required, may come equally well in any part of a speech; in fact, the beginning of it is just where there is least slackness of interest."[35]

SUMMARY

Even though the speaker remembers well that he must be ever mindful of the difficulty in gaining attention and making a speech interesting, he must also remember that even those stimuli attended to are not always correctly interpreted, that the interpretations are not always well learned, and that things learned are often soon forgotten. In other words, as

---

[35] *Rhetoric*, W. Rhys Roberts, Tr. (New York: The Modern Library, Inc., 1954), p. 1415b.

Aristotle suggested, the speaker must remember that listeners are humans with a multitude of imperfections rather than machines with a limited repertoire of predictable responses. Though the problems are greater because listeners are humans, so are the rewards. No machine appreciates a work of art.

3   Explaining

This chapter concerns speech practices that are useful when explaining ideas in a public address. As the student speaker reads the next pages, he should not conclude mistakenly that these thoughts are meant exclusively for informative occasions or that the necessity for explaining is peculiar only to expository speaking. For, in fact, the ensuing suggestions, although important to informative speaking, are applicable in varying degrees to persuasive and entertaining addresses as well.

OBJECTIVES

Speakers intent on explaining ideas to listeners are concerned with three basic objectives: *clarity, interest,* and *retention.*[1]

Clarity

A speaker gains clarity in an address by stating his ideas with precision and concreteness, and by comparing his lesser known thoughts to better known ones in specific and illustrative ways. To be concrete, to be comparative, to be specific, however, all make one common assumption: that every speaker knows what *is* concrete, comparable, and specific to any given group of listeners. By following further the ramifications of this

---

[1] These three objectives were arrived at through an analysis of four factors interfering with communication: (1) *frustration* because the information presented exceeds the comprehension capabilities of hearers; (2) *fatigue* because the amount of information exceeds the attention span of listeners; (3) *low motivation* because the information is uninteresting or because the information is presented without constant reinforcement of attention; and (4) *resistance* because the information is revealed in a way that makes hearers avoid, attack, or compete mentally with the information. For a review of these communication problems, see Frank R. Hartman, "A Behavioristic Approach to Communication: A Selective Review of Learning Theory and a Derivation of Postulates," *AV Communication Review,* Vol. 11 (September–October 1963), pp. 155–190.

thinking, explanation is often reducible to apothegm. For if a speaker can know what an audience considers concrete, comparative, and specific, and if he is especially at home with language, he can then concentrate a whole topic development into one brilliantly clear and terse statement. Some speakers, in short, may reduce their addresses to an introduction, three or four pithy apothegms, and a conclusion—and all delivered in the space of a minute or two.

Spoken and written capsule thoughts, however, represent the conclusion of thinking and not the clarifying reasons that led to or support an apothegmatic statement. Essentially, main divisional ideas or topic sentences almost always express thoughts that need amplification for proper understanding by listeners. A speaker must decide, therefore, at what point his explanation is sufficiently concrete to his particular listeners and at what point further reinforcement by him will only bore hearers.

Ideally, a speaker might reinterpret a point over and over again until he is thoroughly satisfied he can do no more, in his explanation. Speakers, however, know that listeners have less than cast-iron constitutions and recognize that the age has passed when a person orated "briefly" for two or three hours. In a kind of natural evolution or perhaps revolution, many public speakers, trying to prevent audience boredom, reason that one explanation of a point *is* and *must be* sufficient for clarity. This conclusion leads many speech teachers to distraction—not because they like long addresses, but because a student speaker assumes one square foot of concrete is sufficient foundation to support an assertion 10 stories high.

In essence a speaker should not think that his amplification through a particular form of support is always adequate to clarify an idea. Instead, he might follow Woodrow Wilson's example in September 1919 when the champion of the League of Nations addressed a Des Moines, Iowa, audience. Wilson's point in his speech was simple: American soldiers entered World War I with a visionary outlook for the world. One illustration explained this assertion sufficiently had Wilson thought or assumed the one form of support he chose was understood immediately by his audience. Instead, he included not only comparison and short illustration, but a touch of parallelism and specificity for clarity—all in the brief span of about 350 words:

> I was saying to another audience to-day that one of the most beautiful stories I know is the story that we heard in France about the first effect of the American soldiers when they got over there. The French did not believe at first, the British did not believe, that we could finally get 2,000,000 men over there. The most that they hoped at first was that a few American soldiers would restore their morale, for let me say that their morale was gone. The beautiful story to which I referred is this, the testimony that all of them rendered that they got their morale back the minute they saw the eyes of those boys. Here were not only soldiers. There was no curtain in front of the

retina of those eyes. They were American eyes. They were eyes that had seen visions. They were eyes the possessors of which had brought with them a great ardor for a supreme cause, and the reason those boys never stopped was that their eyes were lifted to the horizon. They saw a city not built with hands. They saw a citadel towards which their steps were bent where dwelt the oracles of God himself. And on the battlefield were found German orders to commanders here and there to see to it that the Americans did not get lodgment in particular places, because if they ever did you never could get them out. They had gone to Europe to go the whole way towards the realization of the teaching which their fathers had handed down to them. There never were crusaders that went to the Holy Land in the old ages that we read about that were more truly devoted to a holy cause than these gallant, incomparable sons of America.[2]

In summary a speaker need not develop necessarily each point of an address in multitudinous ways for clarity, nor need he always deliver long speeches to insure understanding. But neither is the one-legged development always sufficient to support a table full of assertions.[3] If a speaker interprets the comments in this section as a mandate to cover fewer points in an address, then something was accomplished after all; for how much better the adequately developed, five-point speech than the undeveloped 10-point one. Perhaps an old Hawaiian proverb best climaxes the sentiments of this section: "Truth is steadfast, only so long as it is understood."

Interest

In Chapter 2 you read about stimuli, attitudes, and ways of holding attention during a speech—ideas all applicable to *interest*. Now you should consider two other aspects of this important topic.

Imaged Versus Imageless Thought

As a speaker explains a subject to listeners, they respond to his words (among several ways) in either *imaged* or *imageless* thought.[4] Perhaps you assumed previously that imaged thinking is always easier to remember, and that it is, consequently, a most effective way of keeping audience interest in an address. There is, however, no evidence at this time from behavioral scientists that unequivocally supports the merits of imaged over symbolic, or

2 *The Public Papers of Woodrow Wilson*, Vol. 2: *War and Peace: Presidential Messages, Addresses, and Public Papers (1917–1924)*, Ray Stannard Baker and William E. Dodd, Eds. (New York: Harper & Row, Publishers, 1927), pp. 20–21.

3 Of course one-legged development to increase audience comprehension is better than no development at all. See Hadley Cantril and Gordon W. Allport, *The Psychology of Radio* (New York: Harper & Row, Publishers, 1935), p. 187.

4 Whether listeners interpolate the speaker's words into their own words before coming up with imaged or imageless thought is immaterial to the point expressed in this section. In short, language as either a prerequisite or unnecessary adjunct for thought is outside the province of this discussion.

imaged over imageless thinking in terms of understanding and memory.[5] Rather the evidence indicates that *organizational coherency* within ideas as well as *degree of motivation* for learning—and not some hocus-pocus quality inherent in an idea—determine whether or not an individual better comprehends imaged than imageless thought.[6]

In their haste to generalize about implied values of imaged thinking, many speakers assume that the converse—*imageless thinking*—is less than desirable. People can comprehend ideas, however, without ever reducing their thoughts beyond the arbitrary, imageless level of language. (We are not here talking about language or thoughts that confuse listeners: we are speaking of involved ideas explained in cogent though abstract language.) A speaker concerned with explanation, therefore, can help formulate images for his hearers if he chooses and if he thinks concrete imagery best serves his particular subject and need; or he can discuss a point without attempting consciously to create images, because the treated idea seems patently clear to him or seems too complex and too intricate for reduction.

Should a speaker choose the road to imagery, he must next decide between developing either rapid- or slow-forming word-pictures for maximum audience response. If he thinks his idea requires only a burst of imagery in terms of the subject, he can follow Robert Ingersoll's example when the latter delivered a graveside tribute to his brother in June 1879:

> This brave and tender man in every storm of life was oak and rock, but in the sunshine he was love and flower. He was the friend of all heroic souls that climbed the heights and left all superstitions far below, while on his forehead fell the golden dawning of a grander day. He loved the beautiful, and was with color, form and music touched to tears. He sided with the weak, and with a willing hand gave alms; with loyal heart and with the purest hand he faithfully discharged all public trusts.[7]

In contrast if a speaker thinks his idea foreign or new to hearers, or if he wishes to give listeners time to contemplate his images, he might develop his word-pictures at the more leisurely, eighteenth- and nineteenth-century

[5] One recent study showed that listeners who heard an explanation of a syllogism in concrete terms (such as "All horses are quadrupeds.") scored only slightly higher comprehension scores than those who heard the same syllogism explained in abstract terms (such as "All A is B.") See Don Richardson, "A Study of Illustrative Material," *Speech Monographs*, Vol. 31 (June 1964), pp. 179–180. The controversy over imaged vs. imageless thought, however, is still unresolved. Generally, psychologists agree that images are sometimes present when an individual responds to language. But the degree of one kind of thought over another is still a debated question.

[6] There are numerous studies on perception by psychologists. A good single reader on the subject is David C. Beardslee and Michael Wertheimer, eds., *Readings in Perception* (Princeton, N.J.: D. Van Nostrand Co., Inc., 1958). For an elaboration on the subject of imaged vs. imageless thinking, see Joseph Church, *Language and the Discovery of Reality: A Developmental Psychology of Cognition* (New York: Random House, Inc., 1961), pp. 147–162.

[7] As printed in William N. Brigance, *Classified Speech Models of Eighteen Forms of Public Address* (New York: Appleton-Century-Crofts, 1928), p. 401.

pace of speakers. For instance when abolitionist William Wilberforce spoke before the House of Commons against the slave trade on May 12, 1789, he explained:

> Let anyone imagine to himself six or seven hundred of these wretches chained two and two, surrounded with every object that is nauseous and disgusting, diseased, and struggling under every kind of wretchedness! How can we bear to think of such a scene as this? One would think it had been determined to heap on them all the varieties of bodily pain, for the purpose of blunting the feelings of the mind; and yet, in this very point (to show the power of human prejudice), the situation of the slaves has been described by Mr. Norris, one of the Liverpool delegates, in a manner which I am sure will convince the House how interest can draw a film over the eyes so thick that total blindness could do no more. . . . "Their apartments," says Mr. Norris, "are fitted up as much for their advantage as circumstances will admit. The right ankle of one, indeed, is connected with the left ankle of another by a small iron fetter, and if they are turbulent, by another on their wrists. They have several meals a day; some of their own country provisions, with the best sauces of African cookery; and by way of variety, another meal of pulse [porridge of beans], etc., according to European taste. After breakfast they have water to wash themselves, while apartments are perfumed with frankincense and lime juice. Before dinner they are amused after the manner of their country. The song and the dance are promoted," and, as if the whole were really a scene of pleasure and dissipation, it is added that games of chance are furnished. . . .

Continuing his description Wilberforce said:

> Mr. Norris talks of frankincense and lime juices; when the surgeons tell you the slaves are stowed so close [on board ship] that there is not room to tread among them; and when you have it in evidence from Sir George Younge that even in a ship which wanted two hundred of her complement, the stench was intolerable. The song and the dance are promoted, says Mr. Norris. It had been more fair, perhaps, if he had explained that word "promoted." The truth is that for the sake of exercise these miserable wretches, loaded with chains, oppressed with disease and wretchedness, are forced to dance by the terror of the lash, and sometimes by the actual use of it. . . . Such, then, is the meaning of the word "promoted"; and it may be observed too, with respect to food, that an instrument [speculum oris] is sometimes carried out, in order to force them to eat, which is the same sort of proof how much they enjoy themselves in that instance also. As to their singing, what shall we say when we are told that their songs are songs of lamentation upon their departure which, while they sing, are always in tears, insomuch that one captain (more humane as I should conceive him, therefore, than the rest) threatened one of the women with a flogging, because the mournfulness of her song was too painful for his feelings.[8]

[8] As printed in *A Treasury of the World's Great Speeches*, Houston Peterson, Ed. (New York: Simon and Schuster, Inc., 1954), pp. 214–215. The accuracy of the statement by Wilberforce before the House of Commons is in some doubt. See Thomas Clarkson, *The History of the Rise, Progress, and Accomplishment of the Abolition of the African*

Making Explanations Impelling

Now you should consider three important ways of making information impelling: *motivation, mental set,* and *reward.* (See Chapter 5 and Chapter 9 for fuller thoughts on the subject.)

1. *Motivated hearers accept information as impelling.*—People listen best to those ideas they feel are important to them or have a satisfying effect on them. Audiences are, however, becoming more sophisticated as each year goes by, because technical advances and availability of mass media communication bring more and more speakers into the hearers' homes through television, radio, newspapers, and magazines. For speakers this means hearers quickly recognize worn-out, over-reaching, insincere motivational reasons for listening to addresses. Almost every hearer in our country, whether a speaker admits it or not, is a far more knowledgeable lay speech critic than his counterpart of a hundred or more years ago. And as the hearer listens to more speeches, unusual means of gaining attention soon pass into the realm of usual, and finally into the ranks of tired. Therefore, while our modern society requires more talk by citizens on old as well as new subjects, listeners also demand better reasons for listening.

If you look at this situation through a side window, as a speaker you may conclude that it is increasingly more difficult to stimulate genuine, motivated listening from audiences, and that mass communication brings with it some negative, undesirable effects for public speakers. But why not approach the problem positively? Speech principles culled from Aristotelian rhetoric and added to over the centuries are not moss-covered, stagnant dogmas, incapable of keeping up with advances in mass communications. And sophisticated audiences, cultivated by more and more exposure to speechmakers and their addresses, do work to a speaker's advantage: for if he has something worth saying and if he is sincere in feeling his topic is important to them, then he will satisfy more nearly the requirement of earning the right to speak. Use and value of his subject to his audience will not necessarily present itself; but neither need he sell[9] his coming explanation to them. Instead, he must only reveal it clearly to them.

2. *Mentally set hearers accept information as impelling.*—The mental set of hearers will often so influence an occasion that a speaker, through no fault of his own, finds it difficult if not impossible to communicate with listeners. Instructed by a chairman to talk on marketing trends in the automobile industry, an expert on the Lotus-Ford may find himself unable to

---

Slave-Trade by the British Parliament (London: Longman, Hurst, Rees, and Orme, 1808), Vol. 2, pp. 41–67; and Oliver Warner, *William Wilberforce and his Times* (London: B. T. Batsford Ltd., 1962), pp. 56–58.

[9] A word of warning. There is some evidence that people who are motivated too highly tend to misinterpret what they see. If this is true for hearing as well, then a speaker should probably avoid overstating his reasons-for-listening. See Bernard Berelson and Gary A. Steiner, *Human Behavior: An Inventory of Scientific Findings* (New York: Harcourt, Brace & World, Inc., 1964), pp. 114–115.

overcome his listeners' expectations of hearing a speech about this racing car. Unless a speaker is skilled enough to detect audience disappointment in his announced subject, he will proceed with the topic assigned while hearers fret continually over the question, "Why is he talking about that subject?"

Happily, the possibility of mismatching subject with audience mental set is not a common occurrence. What is common is a speaker who gets himself in trouble with listeners because he says one thing in the introduction and proceeds to talk about his subject in an entirely different way during the development of the topic. Again the successful explanation of a subject is subverted because his hearers now exclaim, "We thought he said he was going to talk about advantages, not disadvantages."

If hearers, therefore, know not only why they should listen but know also what it is they will hear, a speaker will greatly increase his chances of successfully explaining a subject to them.[10]

3. *Rewarded hearers accept information as impelling.*—Programmed learning is based on a system of small rewards wherein the student responds to questions at his own speed, checks his own progress, and receives a built-in, token reward for accomplishment. Of course no fire-bells clang in the night, no lights flash on and off, and no fountain of salutes explode whenever he answers correctly a question as "The higher the temperature of the filament, the _____ the light emitted by it." Instead, there is only a miniscule reward for correct response to a question.

In public speaking a speaker may offer his hearers similar small rewards whenever they understand a complex idea, follow his development of a subject, or grasp the subtle implications of his remarks. Thus he may assume, for instance, that his hearers understood a definition step or grasped the logical or illogical steps in an argument, or followed an involved explanation by *openly* indicating his pleasure at their ability to comprehend his meaning. At other times he might reward his listeners by proceeding further into a complex subject, thereby indicating *silently* his appraisal of their intelligence and ability to listen. And at still other times, a speaker might reward his hearers by using in-group words and expressions, and by using allusions to literature, politics, economics, and so on, that he feels most listeners will understand. He is in essence showing approval silently or overtly to his hearers, thereby giving them a means of confirming their ability to comprehend his ideas—in short, allowing the audience to reward itself for careful listening.[11]

---

10 Mental set may at times override sound judgment to such an extent that an average speech turns into a great one for those who came prepared inwardly for a masterful exhibition of oratory. For a related study, see Richard S. Crutchfield, D. G. Woodworth, and R. A. Albrecht, *Perceptual Performance and the Effective Person* (San Antonio: U.S. Air Force Personnel and Training Research, 1955).

11 The reward idea in a speech is an outgrowth of findings by such psychologists as D. Porter, D. J. Klaus, A. A. Lummsdaine, and others, and is specifically a projection of Charles O. Tucker's, "An Application of Programmed Learning to Informative Speech," *Speech Monographs,* Vol. 31 (June 1964), pp. 142–152. Tucker's recommendation is for

A section from John Pastore's keynote address before the Democratic National Convention, August 24, 1964, illustrates how a speaker might reward his hearers as they listen to him:

> Just as no Democrat has to apologize for our performance of the past [*first* opportunity for reward: the speaker assumes his hearers know the record], no Democrat will have to explain away the promises of our platform [*second* reward: assumption that hearers know the platform].
>
> We will move forward in decency and in dignity [*third* reward: in-group dig at Republicans].
>
> And we invite every American to contrast this record and our conduct here with the spectacle in the Cow Palace only six weeks ago [*fourth* reward: every American "knows" the "right" conclusion].
>
> The Cow Palace is only a continent away, but we Democrats are a world apart from all of the confusion, all of the dissension and all of the defections [*fifth* reward: every listener can congratulate himself for knowing who defected] that took place at the Cow Palace six weeks ago.
>
> And will the American viewing public ever forget how the Governor of New York was rebuffed and was jeered even when he tried to speak [*sixth* reward: in-group condemnation of Goldwater supporters]![12]

In the previous illustration, the speaker offered only silent rewards to his listeners. A speaker may, of course, *openly* reward his hearers. When Peter G. Peterson, President of Bell & Howell Company, addressed The Advertising Research Foundation in New York City, he said:

> A second reason we are not often truly creative is that we cling to *marketing folklore* that no longer is true, if it ever was. Along with our exaggerated faith in science, we retain (ashamedly, perhaps, but tenaciously) old superstitions that have little basis in reality.
>
> For example, we yearn to discover "the" marketing generalization, "the" selling trend, "the" market. It is more comfortable and easier to think in such simple terms. But we know they are not realistic terms [*reward:* verbal acknowledgement for those listeners who thought Peterson had overstated the modern practice of businessmen] . . . for people are different and therefore markets are different. And even if they weren't, people's responses change and therefore markets change.[13]

Finally in the last example, Louise Bushnell, Director of the Women's Department, National Association of Manufacturers, rewarded members of the Shenandoah Valley Manufacturers Association, Winchester, Virginia, through both silent and open affirmations:

"precisely pre-planned overt response" and not for "unguided, general reaction." The application to actual, speaker-audience situation is hinted at by Tucker only in broad terms. Gardner Murphy, "Toward a Field Theory of Communication," *The Journal of Communication,* Vol. 11 (December 1961), pp. 196–201, also suggests applications of the feedforward idea in communication. Murphy does not, however, make applications of feedforward-feedback theories in terms of reward.

12 *Vital Speeches of the Day,* Vol. 30 (September 15, 1964), p. 707.

13 *Vital Speeches of the Day,* Vol. 31 (November 1, 1964), p. 44.

Part of my material tonight comes from the Arabian Nights translations by M. Galland. I am sure you will recall from your childhood days how Aladdin came into possession of a wonderful lamp. [*Reward:* acknowledgement that listeners know this childhood story.] He could rub it, and command the power of a jinni to serve him. Through the lamp's power he grew wealthy, until one day a wicked magician appealed to his wife with a great bargain —he would trade new lamps for old. Aladdin's wife, who didn't know the secret of the wonderful lamp, was only too eager to trade a tarnished old lamp for a shiny new one. But alas, the new lamp held no jinni. And, as you know, the jinni is the Arabic for a potent spirit, which we translate into English as Genius. [*Reward:* although not too many listeners knew, probably, that jinni means Genius, the speaker nonetheless rewarded her hearers as knowledgeable persons.]

But I didn't come to Virginia to tell you fairy tales. [*Reward:* acknowledgement to those listeners who were beginning to feel the speaker was wasting time recalling a story all knew.] There is a moral in the story of Aladdin for our times. It is a lesson that we need to learn in America immediately.[14]

Retention

The last objective of explaining is *retention*. Except in speeches used as vehicles for joke sessions, a speaker almost always hopes that his listeners will go away with at least a portion of his ideas and information firmly in mind. Yet psychologists (J. G. Jenkins, J. J. Gibson, I. Lorge, F. C. Bartlett, H. Ebbinhaus, K. M. Dallenbach, B. J. Underwood, among others) tell us some interesting things about human learning and retention: we recall information best when our learning is accompanied with intermittent rest periods; our memory distorts perception; our retention drops off drastically right after learning takes place; and new learning continually interferes with old learning.[15] When these findings are applied broadly to public speaking, a speaker may think his situation hopeless: he cannot usually stand before the same audience time and again to repeat and reinforce his ideas; nor can he provide his audience with long rest periods so that his information is given at periodic intervals; nor can he control tendencies of listeners to distort his facts; nor can he be present, usually, to counter new facts presented by another speaker at some future occasion. What can a speaker do? Is the public speaking situation a hopelessly self-defeating means of imparting information to listeners?

To overcome these problems of human behavior, a speaker should consider his single speech as his own, self-contained, whirling galaxy in an awesomely large universe. In this way the speaker treats his address as an on-going experience for listeners through time and space; and, by so thinking,

14 *Vital Speeches of the Day*, Vol. 31 (December 1, 1964), p. 112.

15 Students interested in exploring more deeply the literature on retention may begin with two basic works: Ernest R. Hilgard, *Theories of Learning*, Second ed. (New York: Appleton-Century-Crofts, 1956); and John A. McGeoch, *The Psychology of Human Learning*, rev. by Arthur L. Irion, Second ed. (New York: David McKay Co., Inc., 1958).

he can make use of behavioral findings to aid his speechmaking. Through a series of rising and falling climaxes, for instance, he gives his hearers rest periods before returning to his point. Through periodic restatement of key ideas, he gives his speech a repetitious effect and spreads out learning.

Because memory distorts perception and because new learning interferes continually with old learning, a speaker set on explaining should practice two other observations learned from psychologists: *survey* and *review*. Thus a speaker who carefully reveals a planned *survey* of his subject to listeners—especially in longer addresses—will help his hearers recognize peaks of information as he unfolds ideas to them. To paraphrase a comparison from the general semanticists, by knowing the map of a speech the audience will recognize more easily the speaker's territory of development.

Jeremiah S. Black, in his well-known *ex parte Milligan* address before the U.S. Supreme Court in 1866, began his remarks with such a preview when he pleaded against the right of military commissions to try civilians:

> MAY IT PLEASE YOUR HONORS:
> I am not afraid that you will underrate the importance of this case. It concerns the rights of the whole people. Such questions have generally been settled by arms; but since the beginning of the world no battle has ever been lost or won upon which the liberties of a nation were so distinctly staked as they are on the result of this argument. The pen that writes the judgment of the court will be mightier for good or for evil than any sword that ever was wielded by mortal arm. As might be expected from the nature of the subject, it has been a good deal discussed elsewhere, in legislative bodies, in public assemblies, and in the newspaper press of the country; but there it has been mingled with interests and feelings not very friendly to a correct conclusion. Here we are in a higher atmosphere, where no passion can disturb the judgment or shake the even balance in which the scales of reason are held. Here it is purely a judicial question. . . . In performing the duty assigned to me in the case, I shall necessarily refer to the mere rudiments of constitutional law, to the most commonplace topics of history, and to those plain rules of justice and right which pervade all our institutions. I beg your honors to believe that this is not done because I think that the court, or any member of it, is less familiar with these things than I am, or less sensible to their value, but simply and only because, according to my view of the subject, there is absolutely no other way of dealing with it. If the fundamental principles of American liberty are attacked, and we are driven behind the inner walls of the constitution to defend them, we can repel the assault only with those same old weapons which our ancestors used a hundred years ago. You must not think the worse of our armor because it happens to be old-fashioned, and looks a little rusty from long disuse.[16]

Finally, a speaker should not think of *review* as coming only in the Conclusion to his address. For if retention is an objective when informing,

16 Brigance, *Classified Speech Models*, pp. 101–102.

and if repetition is a way to reinforce ideas, then timely reviews scattered strategically throughout a speech will not only help listeners know where a speaker has been at any given moment, but will help them know what he thinks they should remember. A noteworthy idea for a speaker, therefore, is for him to make his reviews progressively more comprehensive as his speech moves closer to its Conclusion, since the longer an address lasts, the greater are the demands for retention placed on the listener's memory.

ELEMENTS OF A BASIC EXPLANATORY UNIT

Now you should turn your attention to the basic unit of explanation— the topic sentence or main head, if you prefer, and its development. You should keep in mind that the *concern in this section is only with a single, basic structural unit,* and not the framework of a total speech. For the moment you should assume you decided on the central purpose and wish now to commence work on the major speech divisions.

Divisional Topic Sentence

Whereas a beginning speaker thinks of main heads in speech as contrived though convenient and as awkward though necessary thought divisions for his address, a good speaker does not accept arbitrary divisioning as an adequate foundation for effective speech composition. Instead, he first considers his divisional topic sentence as a distinct aid to listeners' comprehension, and only second as a helpmate to his own composition and memory. (Happily, our suggestion for a superior divisional sentence goes full circle and helps the speaker remember his own ideas as well.) A superior main head, therefore, is more than a haphazard compass bearing used by a speaker before he launches into an amplification of the divisional unit and is more than a transitional phrase indicating change in direction. A superior main head is a definite, carefully phrased sentence that helps hearers *organize,* and thereby retain more easily, the essential parts in his forthcoming development.

The following examples illustrate the differences between sentences speakers often use as topic ideas and sentences used for the listeners' sake:

Poor.   And, now for my third point.

Poor.   And, now for my third point about the Marquesas Islands.

Poor.   And, now for my third point, let me tell you how the natives make a living in the Marquesas.

Good.   And, now for my third point, let me tell you about the three ways natives in the Marquesas make a living.

Best.   And, now for my third point, let me describe how natives in the Marquesas make a living through fishing, trading, and the Polynesian art of weaving.

Of course a speaker often arranges his ideas from particulars-to-statement, thereby revealing his divisional topic sentence only after he develops a major portion of his sub-divisional point. Again, however, a concise statement is still an aid to listeners. In fact, since the summary sentence comes last in particulars-to-statement, a speaker needs an exceedingly accurate main head because hearers—whether intentionally or not—match wits with him in this arrangement pattern. Essentially, they test their own final generalization against the speaker's announced one. If these two generalizations are mismatched in major ways, hearers may well remain troubled and inattentive to his divisional point, and may well go away confused over his information and explanation.

Development of the Divisional Topic Sentence

In a speech to entertain, good or rollicking humor will probably mask a speaker's less than serious attention to organization. On the other hand in a speech to persuade, listeners' attention is perforce centered on organizational aspects of the address, since the development of almost any line of reasoning demands patterned (organized) arrangement if the speaker expects his hearers to follow his logic. Similarly, in a speech to explain, listeners' attention is focused on the speaker's organization of his subject, since information presented effectively consists usually of meaningful facts structured in a way to delineate important from less important ideas for the sake of aiding hearer retention and comprehension.[17]

A speaker, therefore, in a speech to persuade or inform, and even in a speech to entertain, should *first* decide carefully on his main head sentences, *second* on the method of development (definition, details, comparison, etc.) for each sub-divisional point, and *third* on what information he will include under each for balanced thought. In other words, just as it is physically impossible for a diner to consume a complete Chinese nine-course dinner in one gulp, hearers will find it equally impossible to down an entire speech in one swallow. Information must be broken up into units of convenient size for listeners; a speaker can check this phase of his speech composition by asking himself: "Does my topic sentence and its development represent easily mastered units of thought or am I overestimating the listening capacity of my hearers?"

To help listeners better follow his divisional point, a speaker often reveals a brief, oral, informal analysis before proceeding to his development. Do not here confuse *informal* with *formal* analysis. The student, scholar,

[17] The importance of structured information is emphasized *experimentally* in such diverse studies as H. B. Reed, "Meaning as a Factor in Learning," *Journal of Educational Psychology*, Vol. 29 (September 1938), pp. 419–430; H. B. English, E. L. Welborn, and C. D. Killian, "Studies in Substance Memorization," *Journal of Genetic Psychology*, Vol. 11 (1934), pp. 233–260; and Robert S. Goyer, "A Study of Individual Differences in Ability and Achievement of College Students in the Organization of Ideas," *Speech Monographs*, Vol. 22 (June 1956), pp. 89–90.

and researcher who deals in formal analysis follows the analytical process to its ultimate end. A public speaker, although concerned with formal analysis during his speech preparation, will usually reveal only glimpses of this analysis during delivery because he knows he may lose his hearers along the way if he orally segments an idea into smaller and smaller units in an ever-downward spiral towards bedrock. In short, a minutely partitioned subject is often self-defeating in public speaking, since listeners may lose sight completely of a major idea as they follow the speaker through the labyrinths of his mind.

In an address before The Economic Club of Detroit in 1963, Walter Reuther used an informal analysis that surveyed quickly the major concepts in his coming first-divisional development when he exclaimed:

> I believe that labor-management relations in America rest upon a sound philosophical and principal basis. First of all, we are all committed to a set of common values. We all believe in the essential worth and the dignity of each human individual, and that's the core of the values around which we have built our free system. Within the framework of those basic values (it doesn't matter whether you're a labor leader or a worker or a corporation executive) we have a great deal more in common than we have in conflict.
>
> Secondly, I believe that labor-management relations have to be based upon the recognition that freedom is an indivisible value.
>
> You can't have a free labor movement without free management. You can't have free management without free labor. What we need to keep in mind is the fact that neither will remain free unless we learn to work together to preserve our free society in a free world.
>
> A free society is a very complex kind of thing. I tried to explain it to Mr. Khrushchev.[18]

Conclusion of the Basic Unit

Finally, after a speaker formulates and develops his particular *divisional* topic sentence, he is ready to work on the last part of this organizational unit—the conclusion. If he is in the habit of closing each major division within the speech body with transitional phrases that summarize, connect, and forecast (sentence-link transitions), he may think this is all the conclusion necessary for any divisional point within an address. A speaker should consider, however, the merits of a more elaborate closing; for there are times when the complexity of a topic under discussion is summarized *inadequately* by a work a day transition, and he must, therefore, deliver a fuller closing for hearers.

Since most speakers are familiar already with ordinary transitions, an extended transition is presented here instead for study. When Sir Alec Douglas-Home addressed the United Nations on September 27, 1961, the British statesman closed his first point by saying:

18 *Vital Speeches of the Day,* Vol. 29 (April 1, 1963), p. 377.

And so we must face the fact that inspection and control is the crux of this matter, not for its own sake, but because, when distrust has run so deep as it has between the Communist world and the free world, confidence is the essence of the matter and, unless there is confidence, there will not be disarmament. And so I hope that the President's [Kennedy] plan will be given the most careful consideration by the Soviet Union and they will understand that when we talk about inspection there is no element of espionage which is either thought about or threatened. On the contrary, the purpose is to give confidence so that physical disarmament may proceed.

Now we turn to my second illustration on the sanctity of treaties and agreements freely signed. . . .[19]

DEVELOPMENT METHODS FOR EXPLANATORY UNITS

This section discusses how a speaker develops an explanatory unit through definition, details, specific example, analysis, comparison, cause-effect, and visual aids.

Definition

A common and sometimes unimaginative way of defining is to establish quickly the *genus* and *differentia* of key words before turning to the more important explanations at hand. The ordinary dictionary definition, heard often in speeches, includes the term defined (*definiendum*), followed by classification of the subject (*genus*), followed by distinction between objects (*differentia*). To determine the validity of a definition, a speaker should apply four tests that cover most faults.

1) Be sure the genus is not so narrow that it excludes portions of the subject defined. "A vehicle (definiendum) is an automobile (genus) used to transport people and goods (differentia)." "A Conservative (definiendum) is a Republican (genus) who believes in segregation (differentia)."

2) Be sure the genus is not so large that it includes too much. "A vehicle (definiendum) is something (genus) used to transport people and goods (differentia)." "A Conservative (definiendum) is anyone (genus) who believes in segregation (differentia)."

3) Be sure the genus is not replaced by "when," "where," or "why," and, worse, by an omitted genus. "A university (definiendum) is where (genus?) you gain an education (differentia)." "Capitalism (definiendum) is when (genus?) the rich get richer and the poor get poorer (differentia)."

4) Be sure the differentia does not include characteristics that lean towards the exception rather than the rule. "A categorical syllogism (definiendum) is a form of deductive reasoning (genus) in which conclusions are drawn from unobservable facts (differentia)."

In applying the four tests listed above, a public speaker will find that definition through *enlargement, comparison,* or *restriction* are particularly good for speechmaking, since these three methods usually generate listener interest, and probably aid retention and comprehension of an idea.[20]

Theodore Roosevelt in an address on April 14, 1906, for instance, made his now classic definition of *Muck-rake* memorable through a historical allusion that *enlarged* the traditional meaning of the word to include political and social implications as well:

> In "Pilgrim's Progress" the Man with the Muck-rake is set forth as the example of him whose vision is fixed on carnal instead of on spiritual things. Yet he also typifies the man who in this life consistently refuses to see aught that is lofty, and fixes his eyes with solemn intentness only on that which is vile and debasing. Now, it is very necessary that we should not flinch from seeing what is vile and debasing. There is filth on the floor, and it must be scraped up with the muck-rake; and there are times and places where this service is the most needed of all the services that can be performed. But the man who never does anything else, who never thinks or speaks or writes, save of his feats with the muck-rake, speedily becomes, not a help to society, not an incitement to good, but one of the most potent forces for evil.[21]

In the next illustration, Massachusetts Representative Josiah Quincy, during a Congressional debate in 1811, used a *comparative* and *restrictive* definition that propelled skillfully rather than impeded the forward motion of his address:

> Mr. Speaker, what is this liberty of which so much is said? Is it to walk about this earth, to breathe this air, and to partake the common blessings of God's providence? The beasts of the field and the birds of the air unite with us in such privileges as these. But man boasts a purer and more ethereal temperature. His mind grasps in its view the past and the future as well as the present. We live not for ourselves alone. That which we call liberty is that principle on which the essential security of our political condition depends. It results from the limitations of our political system prescribed in the Constitution. These limitations, so long as they are faithfully observed, maintain order, peace, and safety. When they are violated in essential particulars, all the concurrent spheres of authority rush against each other; and disorder, derangement, and convulsions are sooner or later the necessary consequences.[22]

[20] Although there are no direct experimental studies substantiating this view, our inference is based on studies in memory that clearly relate the importance of *resemblance* and *the known* to retention. See A. B. Blankenship and P. L. Whitely, "Proactive Inhibition and the Recall of Advertising Material," *Journal of Social Psychology*, Vol. 13 (1941), pp. 311–322; and B. J. Underwood, "Associative Inhibition in the Learning of Successive Paired-Associate Lists," *Journal of Experimental Psychology*, Vol. 34 (1944), pp. 127–135.

[21] *The Works of Theodore Roosevelt*, Vol. 16: *American Problems* (New York: Charles Scribner's Sons, 1926), pp. 415–416.

[22] Edmund Quincy, *Life of Josiah Quincy* (Boston: Little, Brown, & Company, 1874), pp. 211–212.

Before proceeding to the next section, one final reminder: since definition can be interesting and even moving, a speaker should think of defining as a lively way to forward the progress of his speech, rather than as an impeditive and dull intrusion on his theme.

Details

The commonest way of explaining an idea is to reveal related details. In a broad sense, all public speaking is simply a revelation of points that support the purpose sentence or central theme. Here, however, the reference is specifically to details that amplify an idea made *during* a main head development and that come most frequently in addresses to explain rather than persuade.

In the speech to convince, a speaker usually employs details to develop an assertion, and his aim generally is to draw a persuasive conclusion. In other words he manages his details as proof in a persuasive address so that he might in effect exclaim to listeners, "See, *there* is the evidence." Consequently, details in persuasive speaking will often take the form of substantial, explicit *reasons,* rather than unobtrusive, uncontroversial development of a generalization.

When *explaining,* in contrast, a speaker adds details not as proof of his generalization, but as a means of reinforcing or amplifying his point. And when details take the form of reasons in an informative speech, listeners are sometimes confused over the speaker's exact intent. There are, however, distinct times when a speaker states reasons in an explanatory fashion and harbors no hidden persuasion in his remarks. He is instead only using *details*—not persuasive *reasons*—to develop his divisional topic sentence, and his goal is innocent explanation. For instance when U Thant, then Acting Secretary General of the United Nations, addressed the world body on October 24, 1962, his opening words were not meant as persuasive comments. Rather, because of personal concern, he explained through details his thoughts on the Cuban crisis, so that all might know his motives for action. If hearers disagreed with him, he probably could not have cared less; he was only detailing why he addressed them:

> Today the United Nations faces a moment of grave responsibility. What is at stake is not just the interests of the parties directly involved, nor just the interests of all member states, but the very fate of mankind. If today the United Nations should prove itself ineffective, it may have proved itself so for all time.
>
> In the circumstances, not only as Acting Secretary General of the United Nations but as a human being, I would be failing in my duty if I did not express my profound hope and conviction that moderation, self-restraint and good sense will prevail over all other considerations.
>
> In this situation, where the very existence of mankind is in the balance, I derive some consolation from the fact that there is some common ground

Paine, and Benjamin Franklin. But the profession that seemed to best join prestige, power and opportunity was the law.[27]

Another procedure when offering specific examples is to arrange illustrations in a climactic order. When Edmund Burke addressed a group of constituents in September 1780, he put a series of instances together that ascended in both importance and quality, and that illustrated how religious qualifications for State positions had become less important in Europe:

> . . . the spirit of toleration began to gain ground in Europe. In Holland the third part of the people are Catholics; they live at ease, and are a sound part of the state. In many parts of Germany, Protestants and Papists partake the same cities, the same councils, and even the same churches. The unbounded liberality of the King of Prussia's conduct on this occasion is known to all the world, and it is of a piece with the other grand maxims of his reign. The magnanimity of the imperial court, breaking through the narrow principles of its predecessors, has indulged its Protestant subjects not only with property, with worship, with liberal education, but with honors and trusts, both civil and military. A worthy Protestant gentleman of this country now fills, and fills with credit, a high office in the Austrian Netherlands. Even the Lutheran obstinacy of Sweden has thawed at length, and opened a toleration to all religions. I know, myself, that in France the Protestants begin to be at rest. The army, which in that country is every thing, is open to them; and some of the military rewards and decorations which the laws deny, are supplied by others, to make the service acceptable and honorable. The first minister of finance in that country . . . is a Protestant.[28]

Finally, at other times, a speaker may decide that a balance between quality and quantity is not only apropos to his generalization but to his particular audience as well; he consequently commences his detailed development with one or two choice illustrations before following them with several undeveloped ones. When Sir Abubakar Tafawa Balewa, Prime Minister of the Federation of Nigeria, addressed the African summit conference at Addis Ababa in May 1963, he followed this pattern in describing his government's efforts toward improving communications media:[29]

> I am glad to say that the stand we have taken right from the beginning is the stand of nearly almost all the countries in this conference. . . . For our part, in Nigeria, we are already co-operating with some of our neighbours. For example, the other day, my friend, the President of Malagasy said he

[27] *Vital Speeches of the Day,* Vol. 27 (October 1, 1961), p. 760.

[28] Chauncey A. Goodrich, *Select British Eloquence* (New York: Harper & Row, Publishers, 1853), p. 305.

[29] Throughout this book we deliberately introduced speakers from countries of non-western cultures. For two articles emphasizing the near-universal practice of public speaking in today's world, see Huber W. Ellingsworth, "Anthropology and Rhetoric: Toward A Culture-Related Methodology of Speech Criticism," *The Southern Speech Journal,* Vol. 28 (Summer 1963), pp. 307–312; and Robert T. Oliver, "Culture and Communication: A Major Challenge in International Relations," *Vital Speeches of the Day,* Vol. 29 (September 15, 1963), pp. 721–724.

could not contact Lagos by telephone from Cotonou. This is no longer the case. Now he can speak direct. What we are trying to do is to link up with all our neighbours by means of telecommunications and by exchanging more postal facilities; and we are already entering into bilateral agreements with many of our neighbours. We are discussing this matter with the Republic of the Cameroun, discussing our common problems with Tchad, Congo Leopoldville, with Dahomey, and also we have a direct link with Togo.[30]

Comparison

Distinctly different from definition, detail, and example is explaining by comparison (analogy). As a common method of thinking, comparison draws its main strength and effectiveness from two sources: a hearer's tendency to match unknowns with knowns for better understanding; and a listener's interest in real or fancied resemblances between objects or ideas.[31]

A speaker who uses a comparison must decide on what two or more items will seem analogous to his audience. If he possesses a logical and imaginative mind, he will match objects that not only complement each other but stimulate his hearers' esthetic senses of harmony and beauty as well. Of course should he deliver a persuasive address, his items for analogy are usually more logical than poetic. The very nature of a speech situation, however, generally prevents cold, item-for-item revelation of long and complex lists and tables, even in a persuasive address. Hearers usually permit a speaker to indicate points of comparison from the periphery of an inclusive, fully drawn analogy because of time restrictions and because of the speaker's known integrity.

Under most circumstances of speechmaking, a speaker who uses comparison is free from a thorough, white-glove inspection of his logic by hearers, especially if his purpose is to inform or stimulate, rather than to convince. This does not imply that a speaker is at liberty to compare the improbable or to make false analogies. Rather, this means that a speaker may use safely the less objective, figurative comparison to add color, interest, imagery, and vividness to his address, without fear of hearers mentally mauling his logic.

Too often a beginning speaker thinks of comparison as a form of logical proof, unsuited to the neutral speech of explanation. Nothing is further from truth. The humorous after-dinner speaker who compares two incongruent items seeks no persuasive response; he only wants the laughs generated by exaggeration. Similarly, a speaker who compares offensive formations in college and professional football may seek no other response than under-

[30] *Vital Speeches of the Day*, Vol. 29 (August 1, 1963), pp. 620–621.

[31] The value of a comparison to improve understanding is not mythical. In fact, virtually meaningless material becomes meaningful through comparison. See Frank R. Hartman, "A Behavioristic Approach to Communication: A Selective Review of Learning Theory and a Derivation of Postulates," *AV Communication Review*, Vol. 11 (September–October, 1963), p. 184.

standing. But before a student speaker sends off a trial balloon, he should consider the following advice: (1) figurative analogies are poetic and vivid, but they have a way of becoming offensive when fancied flights outstrip common sense; and (2) literal comparisons are relatively conclusive but they have a way of becoming dull and pedantic if developed to an extreme. (See Chapter 7 for more thoughts on comparison and contrast.)

The next two examples illustrate some qualities of good comparison. Henry Grady in his "The New South" speech of 1886 employed a literal analogy that is at once inspiring as well as vivid. In comparing a victorious army with a defeated one, the newspaper editor from Atlanta owed much of his effect on listeners to an undeveloped image of the Northern Army. Instead of detailing a picture of a Union soldier, Grady allowed listeners to fill in their own elements of comparison. Depending on listener ability to depict real or fictitious details for the glorious Union Army, the Southerner concentrated his full effort on Johnny Reb. By doing so he avoided stretching his analogy beyond realism and common sense, since he forced the Northern listener to supply one half of his comparison. Grady, consequently, avoided criticism skillfully; for after all, each hearer determined, in a sense, truthful imagery for himself, and Grady let each listener supply a missing half of the picture. With this brief interpretation in mind, read what the Southerner said:

> Dr. Talmage has drawn for you, with a master's hand, the picture of your returning armies. He has told you how, in the pomp and circumstance of war, they came back to you, marching with proud and victorious tread, reading their glory in a nation's eyes! Will you bear with me while I tell you of another army that sought its home at the close of the late war—an army that marched home in defeat and not in victory—in pathos and not in splendor, but in glory that equaled yours, and to hearts as loving as ever welcomed heroes home. Let me picture to you the footsore Confederate soldier, as buttoning up his faded gray jacket the parole which was to bear testimony to his children of his fidelity and faith, he turned his face southward from Appomattox in April, 1865. Think of him as ragged, half-starved, heavy-hearted, enfeebled by want and wounds; having fought to exhaustion, he surrenders his gun, wrings the hands of his comrades in silence, and lifting his tear-stained and pallid face for the last time to the graves that dot the old Virginia hills, pulls his gray cap over his brow and begins the slow and painful journey. What does he find—let me ask you, who went to your homes eager to find in the welcome you had justly earned, full payment for four years' sacrifice—what does he find when, having followed the battle-stained cross against overwhelming odds, dreading death not half so much as surrender, he reaches the home he left so prosperous and beautiful? He finds his house in ruins, his farm devastated, his slaves free, his stock killed, his barns empty, his trade destroyed, his money worthless; his social system, feudal in its magnificence, swept away; his people without law or legal status, his comrades slain, and the burdens of others heavy on his shoulders. Crushed

by defeat, his very traditions gone; without money, credit, employment, material or training; and, besides all this, confronted with the gravest problem that ever met human intelligence—the establishing of a status for the vast body of his liberated slaves.

What does he do—this hero in gray with a heart of gold? Does he sit down in sullenness and despair? Not for a day. Surely God, who had stripped him of his prosperity, inspired him in his adversity.[32]

In the Sermon on the Mount, Jesus used *figurative* analogy to make his point clear. As you read the following selection, you should observe that Christ's figurative comparisons have a timeless quality about them; yet Grady's usage of comparison was no less effective in bringing to mind vivid images:

Beware of false prophets, which come to you in sheep's clothing, but inwardly they are ravening wolves. Ye shall know them by their fruits. Do men gather grapes of thorns, or figs of thistles? Even so every good tree bringeth forth good fruit; but a corrupt tree bringeth forth evil fruit. A good tree cannot bring forth evil fruit, neither *can* a corrupt tree bring forth good fruit. Every tree that bringeth not forth good fruit is hewn down, and cast into the fire. Wherefore by their fruits ye shall know them.

Not every one that saith unto me, Lord, Lord, shall enter into the kingdom of heaven; but he that doeth the will of my Father which is in heaven. Many will say to me that day, Lord, Lord, have we not prophesied in thy name? and in thy name have cast out devils? and in thy name done many wonderful works? And then will I profess unto them, I never knew you: depart from me, ye that work iniquity.

Therefore whosoever heareth these sayings of mine, and doeth them, I will liken him unto a wise man, which built his house upon a rock; and the rain descended, and the floods came and the winds blew, and beat upon that house; and it fell not: for it was founded upon a rock. And every one that heareth these sayings of mine, and doeth them not, shall be likened unto a foolish man, which built his house upon the sand: and the rain descended, and the floods came, and the winds blew, and beat upon that house; and it fell: and great was the fall of it.[33]

Cause and Effect

Another way of developing an explanatory unit is through cause-effect, or effect-cause arrangement. (See Chapter 5 for a full treatment of this subject.) Since this method of explaining involves a reasoning process, many students associate cause-effect development or its antithesis with argumentation for or against a contention. Let us pause here, therefore, to examine why this developmental method is as much a part of explaining as of persuading.

To help your understanding of the difference between cause-effect development in persuasion and explanation, you should consider two an-

[32] As printed in Brigance, *Classified Speech Models*, pp. 291–292.
[33] Matthew 7:15–27.

alogies. *Explanatory* causal relationships are like blasts from shotguns at a target: the order in which individual pellets hit the bulls-eye is immaterial to the final result; but collectively, regardless of sequence, the shot produce a singular, simultaneous effect. *Persuasive* causal relationships, in contrast, are like shots fired from an automatic weapon: the bullets strike the target at distinctly different intervals, and the total effect is a series of hits. In a sequential image, events occur in a definite order that lead to a particular effect. If you ever chuckled at Rube Goldberg's contraptions and his tongue-in-cheek explanations, you know that the cartoonist's imaginative devices are good examples of causal development, since the final step in a Goldberg brainstorm depends always on successful, interval accomplishments of previous steps. In speechmaking the *sequential* rather than the *simultaneous* arrangement is the concern of speakers with persuasive intent, and, as you know, one misstep in sequential arrangement results in a total collapse of cause-effect logic.

Thus where cause-effect and effect-cause arrangement are used more frequently in persuasive speaking, this fact does not deny a speaker use of the simultaneous, causal form when his purpose is explanation. The next passage, employing effect-cause arrangement, illustrates how a speaker, Mark Twain, used *simultaneous* rather than *sequential* arrangement to develop his speech on "The Babies."

> You soldiers all know that when that little fellow arrived at family headquarters you had to hand in your resignation. He took entire command. You became his lackey, his mere body-servant, and you had to stand around too. He was not a commander who made allowances for time, distance, weather, or anything else. You had to execute his order whether it was possible or not. And there was only one form of marching in his manual of tactics, and that was the double-quick. He treated you with every sort of insolence and disrespect, and the bravest of you didn't dare to say a word. You could face the death-storm at Donelson and Vicksburg, and give back blow for blow; but when he clawed your whiskers, and pulled your hair, and twisted your nose, you had to take it. When the thunders of war were sounding in your ears you set your faces toward the batteries, and advanced with steady tread; but when he turned on the terrors of his war-whoop, you advanced in the other direction, and mighty glad of the chance, too. When he called for soothing-syrup, did you venture to throw out any side-remarks about certain services being unbecoming to an officer and a gentleman? No. You got up and got it![34]

Twain, of course, poked fun in his loose effect-cause relationship and suffered from that classical disease still common today, *post hoc, ergo propter hoc* (after a fact, therefore because of it). But granting Twain's problem with flaccid reasoning, he nevertheless chose a developmental form suited to the expression of his jestful idea.

Now read the next example from a speech by J. Wayne Fredericks,

[34] *Mark Twain's Speeches* (New York: Harper & Row, Publishers, 1910), pp. 64-65.

Deputy Assistant Secretary of State for African Affairs, who in an address at St. Paul, Minnesota, in 1963, used explanatory causal reasoning in a serious effort to describe an informative point. Fredericks cannot be accused of trying to convince listeners through argumentative reasoning, since most Americans are grossly uninformed on African affairs and only a few citizens, even educated ones, can name 15 of the over 30 newly independent African nations since World War II. Thus Fredericks is merely giving the causes— without persuasive intent—that led to an effect in Africa:

> The problem of maintaining political stability in a newly independent nation is an extremely complicated and delicate task. The people demand much, and often there is relatively little to give. And the task of providing what little there is satisfactorily calls for a high degree of statesmanship.
>
> In most African colonies, only a limited number of indigenous civil servants were trained. Therefore, the new governments have had to choose between continuing all or part of the trained European civil service or employing untrained or partially trained indigenous people. This choice has been and remains a hard one between governmental efficiency and the political pressure of rapid Africanization. There is no question but that Africans can be trained to do the job, but this cannot be done overnight. Schools of public administration, therefore, become a tremendously important part of any African program.
>
> In the larger countries with well-developed tribal loyalties there is the added problem of making the power of the central government effective in the remoter regions.
>
> It is challenges such as these that tend to encourage the development of vigorous, often one-party system to provide order and direction during the transition from strong centralized colonial rule to the yet-to-be-developed African national norms.[35]

Visual Aids

Finally the last developmental method considered in this chapter is visual aids. Admittedly, this section adds no new theories to oft-repeated ideas on the subject. Yet, we would be negligent if we bypassed the topic, since basic speech textbooks vary widely on the best guidelines of usage.[36]

1. *VISUAL AIDS ARE FOR LISTENERS' BENEFIT*. Often a speaker's self-centeredness blinds his better judgment in his selection and handling of visual aids. When he thinks only of himself, he may show aids

[35] *Vital Speeches of the Day*, Vol. 29 (September 1, 1963), p. 701.

[36] Essentially, modern writers treat visual aids in four ways: there is the "Well, they're there, you figure out some principles, and then abide by them" approach; or the "There are so many rules, it's hopeless to begin" approach; or the "Here are some 50 rules out of 5000" approach; and the "Use common sense, that's all you need remember" approach. We reject immediately the first three avenues because they seem either to avoid the issue or to drown the subject eventually in an examination of minutiae. Instead, we come close to embracing the common sense idea, and herewith offer what we consider are the five most encompassing, commonsensical guidelines on the subject of visual aids in speechmaking.

barely visible to hearers or he may use the blackboard in a hit-or-miss fashion, or he may examine his own aid as though it were Gina Lollobrigida in the flesh, or he may fondle nervously the aid with his hands in Captain Queeg-like fashion. Still another self-centered speaker is satisfied easily with *any* aid, so long as *he* understands it. Thus the audience is forced to comprehend a complex chart meant for prolonged study and analysis by readers, or to witness a parade of meaningless objects introduced by a speaker as a clever mnemonic device meant for his own use. Fortunately, with a little forethought on the subject and consideration for an audience, most speakers can avoid the numerous pitfalls stemming from self-centeredness.

2. *VISUAL AIDS SHOULD MOVE THE SPEECH FORWARD.* Visual aids are meant to *aid* and not to distract from a speech. Here, of course, the line between attraction and distraction is indeed fine. A speaker who brings a 15-foot-long slide rule to an occasion is no doubt thinking about the limitations of human eyesight when he staggers onto the platform with his burden. On the other hand, his aid may prompt listeners to occupy themselves with such mental gymnastics as where the speaker got such an aid or how he managed to bring it in his car or how he got it upstairs by himself. Another speaker who delivers an address on cancer research is no doubt thinking about the value of live objects on audience attention when he brings several caged white mice with him to illustrate his lecture. On the other hand, his aid may distract hearers when he breaks a mouse's neck and proceeds to a dissection of the furry animal. Another speaker who brings his gun collection to an occasion is no doubt thinking about the ease of following a subject when listeners can see the actual objects discussed. On the other hand, his aid may result in hearers worrying for their lives as he handles an unloaded rifle. And, finally, another speaker who compares the spinal myelinization of certain chordates is no doubt thinking of his audience when he uses colored chalk to illustrate his speech. On the other hand, his aid may distract hearers because he is such a good artist that listeners are enraptured over his artistic ability, instead of his subject matter. Happily, if a speaker thinks about visual aids in terms of his *total* address, he can avoid many problems of distraction.

3. *VISUAL AIDS SHOULD BE INTEGRATED INTO THE SPEECH.* Visual aids are effective when used as integral parts rather than as vestigial appendages to a speech. A speaker who pulls a dollar bill out of his pocket and announces to hearers that money is the subject of his address is actually no worse or better than a speaker who illustrates his talk on French political attitudes toward the United States with his collection of souvenirs from Europe. Not long ago the speaker's practice of introducing aids into addresses solely for dramatic effect was common. If you attended a temperance lecture during the nineteenth century, for instance, you would not have thought it odd when a member of the Blue Ribbon Temperance Society held a bottle of whiskey high in one hand, pointed a dagger at his

heart with the other hand, and warned you that drink produced death as surely as a dagger aimed at the heart.

Unhappily, the melodramatic visual aid that turns speeches into theatricals, and that transforms a speaker into an actor, still remain in subdued forms. Today, a public speaker occasionally introduces an address with a dramatic display of a hidden object, or scrawls on the blackboard, in letters 3 feet high, words as s-e-x, c-a-n-c-e-r, or c-o-m-m-u-n-i-s-m and listeners almost expect to hear hounds baying in the distance as a pianist tinkles a high-pitched tremolo off in the wing. In essence a speaker is wiser to omit visual aids rather than to include them in an address if his only rationalization for them is a vague, phantasmal relation between his aids and his speech topic.

4. *VISUAL AIDS ARE NOT THE SPEECH ITSELF.* A speaker who comes smugly to an occasion with 1600 feet of movie film he took the previous summer in Yugoslavia may be a mediocre photographer, a better editor, and an excellent projectionist, but he is no public speaker unless he does more than introduce and conclude his film. The saying that one picture is worth a thousand words may be true enough on occasion; but it is no reason for a speaker to decide that he relinquishes subsequently his role and function as a speaker whenever he uses a visual aid.[37] He must remember: listeners can as easily go to a local theater and see a better photographed movie than to sit through underexposed, jumpy, out-of-focus pictures taken by an average speaker. And if this assertion is true, then it follows that a speaker cannot simply show his pictures and hope that they will talk for themselves.

Similarly a speaker who displays to listeners 400 coins from his collection may well be a serious numismatologist; but this is no reason for him to give up his role and function as a speaker in favor of his inanimate collection. He is, in short, a public speaker and not an exhibitor, only so long as he organizes his material, integrates his aids into his address, and develops his subject in a way that makes listener attendance worthwhile and meaningful. For him to overwhelm hearers with visual aids is impressive and may satisfy his ego; but it is not good public speaking, if it is public speaking at all.

5. *VISUAL AIDS SHOULD HEIGHTEN INTEREST.* Finally, visual aids are meant to heighten audience interest, not to kill it. Generally, listeners look forward with some eagerness to a speaker who comes before them with visual aids. Rightly or wrongly they expect an exciting address, a lively presentation, and even some entertainment value out of "seeing the speech" as well. If he shows them first one table of statistics, another, and

---

[37] For two interesting essays on the subject of whether or not a picture is worth a thousand words, see David K. Berlo, "You Are in the People Business," *Audiovisual Instruction*, Vol. 8 (June 1963), pp. 373–381; and C. M. Markvart, "Don't Overlook the Larynx," *Audiovisual Instruction*, Vol. 9 (February 1964), p. 125.

then another, he may bore them as surely with his aids as though he had droned on monotonously about irrelevancies. A speaker who uses visual aids is not likened, therefore, to a juggler adding more and more plates to his act for interest and suspense. A speaker does not have the same control over his accompanying visual aids as a juggler has over his plates.

On rare occasions a speaker's visual aids allow him to structure his address in a progressively more exciting manner. More often, however, he must use aids that he collected originally without thought of including them in a speech. When confronted later with delivering an address where he can use his collection of miscellany, he will usually find it possible to fit only some of his assorted aids into his speech with any meaning for listeners. Therefore, unless visual aids heighten instead of kill audience interest, a speaker is better off to concentrate on developing an address filled with good verbal material, rather than to accompany his speech with poor visual aids.[38]

[38] For the student interested in improving the physical make-up of his aids, Edward Minor's softbound work, *Simplified Techniques for Preparing Visual Instructional Materials* (New York: McGraw-Hill, Inc., 1962) is a highly readable, clear, and illustrative book on the subject.

4 Persuasion: Paradigm of an Argument

William Norwood Brigance, who enjoyed remarkable success both as a speaker and teacher of public speaking, often said that persuasion is 90 percent exposition. While the statement may be hyperbolic, a careful reading of speeches—the mediocre and forgotten as well as the excellent and remembered—will demonstrate that speakers believe that exposition is both a prior and concomitant process to persuasion.

For example, before listeners will agree that a certain concept should be a guide-line for action, they must understand the concept and its importance. Vera Micheles Dean, specialist in non-Western civilizations, stated in a speech that a revision of policy in dealing with the non-Western nations must be based on a realization that "anti-Westernism can exist and flourish without the help of Communism."[1] Her first task was to make clear why the statement is true. After its truth, or factual basis, had been established, it could serve as a guide-line to a proposal for action.

Before listeners will accept a specific proposal for action, they must understand it. Edward D. Eddy, Jr., President of Chatham College, urged specific action for improvement of colleges. One of his proposals, framed as a question, was: "Are we willing to encourage the judgment and selection of colleges on criteria which are in keeping with sound academic aims?"[2] What he meant became clear as he listed 15 specific criteria.

Mrs. Dean sought to establish something as fact. Eddy sought to make something clear. Both used the methods of exposition that were prerequisite to, and not the equivalent of, the methods used to secure agreement that their proposal for action was desirable. As the examples suggest, a listener may understand quite well the background to a problem, the criteria by which any solution is to be judged, and the specific recommendations for a

[1] Printed in *Representative American Speeches: 1959–1960*, Lester Thonsson, Ed.; Vol. 32, No. 4 of "The Reference Shelf" (New York: The H. W. Wilson Co., 1960).
[2] Printed in *Representative American Speeches*, 1960–1961, Vol. 33, No. 3.

solution proposed by a speaker and still remain unconvinced that the solution is desirable. *Demonstrating desirability is the province of persuasion.* Its methods are significantly different from those used in exposition.

We use the word *desirability* to suggest two salient aspects of persuasive speaking. First, public speaking in a democracy assumes that individuals are free to make a choice; hence, the speaker must constantly remember that he has to convince an audience of the desirability of something. It is not sufficient for him to believe that the proposal is desirable. As long as listeners have the privilege of saying "no," their decision will determine whether the proposition will be accepted. Second, when listeners have a choice, demonstration of fact, or "truth," or probability is not sufficient to ensure acceptance of the proposition. Speakers and writers have used millions of words to demonstrate the relation of smoking to lung cancer, yet the tobacco companies have continued to increase their sales. Why? Smokers will offer many reasons. But fundamentally individuals continue to smoke because they find it more desirable to continue than to stop. They, as well as all nonsmokers, have a hierarchy of values, some at the conscious, others at the subconscious, level, which determine how they will act. Some values are more important to the person who smokes than that of lessening the probability that he will contract lung cancer. To characterize smokers as being unreasonable may help a speaker to explain away his failure in persuasion; it will probably not, however, make a smoker a more reasonable man. Hence, we use the word *desirability* to emphasize the task a speaker has of showing the advantage of his proposition to the listener, that the listener's values will be better served by accepting rather than rejecting it.

LISTENERS' VALUES

Kenneth Burke wrote, "you persuade a man only insofar as you talk his language by speech, gesture, tonality, order, image, attitude, idea, *identifying* your ways with his."[3] What Burke means by identification is suggested by this explanation: "*A* is not identical with his colleague, *B*. But insofar as their interests are joined, *A* is *identified* with *B*. Or he may *identify himself* with *B* even when their interests are not joined, if he assumes that they are, or is persuaded to believe so."[4]

As Burke suggests, far more than ideas contribute to persuasion. The emphasis in this section, however, is on the necessity of showing that the values held by the speaker and incorporated in his proposal have an identity with the listeners' values.

Value is used here as a generic term to cover several concepts related to an individual's needs. A *need* is a condition marked by the feeling of lack or want of something. A *motive* is an inner state that moves and directs

[3] *A Rhetoric of Motives* (New York: George Braziller, Inc., 1955), p. 55.
[4] *A Rhetoric of Motives*, p. 20.

behavior toward the satisfaction of a need. The terms *needs* and *motives* are often used synonymously. A *goal* is an object, condition, or activity that will satisfy a need. An *attitude* is a predisposition to react positively or negatively toward some object, condition, or idea.

Needs, Motives, and Goals as Values

The most direct way to show the identity of values is to demonstrate that the proposal will meet some goal or satisfy some need held by the listeners.

To list the potential goals of people would be to catalog the objects conditions, and activities—real and imaginary—of heaven and earth. Potential goals are the infinite number of specifics that would satisfy every human want.

While goals are too multitudinous to consider in detail, needs or motives are more manageable—although they, too, are numerous and although there is little agreement on their number.

Most psychologists differentiate between physiological, or basic, and learned, or social, motives. The physiological motives are those related to preservation of self and species. They include hunger, thirst, sex, maternalism, avoidance of pain, and avoidance of physical danger. However, the physiological motives are rarely directly observable in humans, and seldom do they operate without being greatly influenced by learned motives —motives taught an individual by his society. The prospect of starvation brings a powerful basic motive to bear. Yet one study estimated that fewer than one third of one percent of the people in noncannibalistic societies would resort to cannibalism when faced with starvation.

While the learned social or secondary needs and motives have been classified many ways, one of the well-known classifications is the following list of "psychogenic needs":[5]

A. Needs associated chiefly with inanimate objects
    1. Acquisition: the need to gain possessions and property
    2. Conservation: the need to collect, repair, clean, and preserve things
    3. Orderliness: the need to arrange, organize, put away objects, to be tidy and clean; to be precise
    4. Retention: the need to retain possession of things; to hoard; to be frugal, economical, and miserly
    5. Construction: the need to organize and build
B. Needs expressing ambition, will power, desire for accomplishment, and prestige
    6. Superiority: the need to excel, a composite of achievement and recognition

[5] This list is based on a list originally developed by H. A. Murray in *Explorations in Personality* (New York: Oxford University Press, 1938).

7. Achievement: the need to overcome obstacles, to exercise power, to strive to do something difficult and as quickly as possible
8. Recognition: the need to excite praise and commendation; to demand respect
9. Exhibition: the need for self-dramatization; to excite, amuse, stir, shock, thrill others
10. Inviolacy: the need to remain inviolate, to prevent a depreciation of self-respect, to preserve one's "good name"
11. Avoidance of inferiority: the need to avoid failure, shame, humiliation, ridicule
12. Defensiveness: the need to defend oneself against blame or belittlement; to justify one's actions
13. Counteraction: the need to overcome defeat by restriving and retaliating

C. Needs having to do with human power exerted, resisted, or yielded to
14. Dominance: the need to influence or control others
15. Deference: the need to admire and willingly follow a superior; to serve gladly
16. Similance: the need to imitate or emulate others; to agree and believe
17. Autonomy: the need to resist influence, to strive for independence
18. Contrariness: the need to act differently from others, to be unique, to take the opposite side

D. Needs having to do with injuring others or oneself
19. Aggression: the need to assault or injure another; to belittle, harm, or maliciously ridicule a person
20. Abasement: the need to comply and accept punishment; self-depreciation
21. Avoidance of blame: the need to avoid blame, ostracism, or punishment by inhibiting unconventional impulses; to be well-behaved and obey the law

E. Needs having to do with affection between people
22. Affiliation: the need to form friendships and associations
23. Rejection: the need to be discriminating, to snub, ignore, or exclude another
24. Nurturance: the need to nourish, aid or protect another
25. Succorance: the need to seek aid, protection, or sympathy; to be dependent

F. Additional socially relevant needs
26. Play: the need to relax, amuse oneself, seek diversion and entertainment

27. Cognizance: the need to explore, to ask questions, to satisfy curiosity
28. Exposition: the need to point and demonstrate; to give information, explain, interpret, lecture[6]

Those social needs are the wellsprings of action. Anyone who would influence action must show that one or more of those needs will be satisfied if the action is taken.

Attitudes as Values

An individual's attitudes bear an exceedingly complex relation to his needs, motives, and goals. To understand that relation, it is necessary first to understand the relation between the terms *attitude, opinion,* and *belief.*

ATTITUDES VERSUS OPINIONS AND BELIEFS

Although in popular usage the three terms are almost interchangeable, many psychologists and social psychologists distinguish between them. Clifford T. Morgan, for example, defines an attitude as "a tendency to respond either positively or negatively to certain persons, objects, or situations." A belief "is *the acceptance of a statement of proposition* . . . I believe that the sun will rise tomorrow morning. Some people believe in men wearing hats in church. Such beliefs can be held without the emotional tinge of an attitude." An opinion is a combination of a belief and an attitude: "acceptance of a statement accompanied by an attitude of pro or con." He points out, however, that an opinion is difficult to distinguish from an attitude or belief.[7]

Bernard Berelson and Gary A. Steiner, on the other hand, distinguish between the concepts by the intensity with which they are held and how extensively they apply. "Thus," they write, "people have opinions on the latest economic proposal, attitudes regarding the welfare state, and beliefs about freedom."[8]

Although technical distinctions can be made, Morgan believes that "in actual practice the distinction among these terms is not of much value." And Berelson and Steiner seek to avoid misunderstanding by using all three terms in stating conclusions and by resorting to the space-saving rubric OAB to ensure that readers will recall that all three are meant.

Whether an auditor's predispositions are called opinions, attitudes, or beliefs, they concern a speaker—not only because they predispose the audi-

[6] Ernest R. Hilgard, *Introduction to Psychology* (New York: Harcourt, Brace & World, Inc., Second ed., 1957), p. 130.

[7] *Introduction to Psychology* (New York: McGraw-Hill, Inc., Second ed., 1961), pp. 529, 665, and 681.

[8] *Human Behavior: An Inventory of Scientific Findings* (New York: Harcourt, Brace & World, Inc., 1964), p. 558.

tor to decide in a predetermined direction but also because they predispose him with a strength or intensity, which varies from predisposition to predisposition. Whether one's predisposition to withhold support from public education is called an opinion or a lightly held attitude is of little consequence. That his opposition could be overcome more easily than that of another individual who fundamentally distrusts public education (has a strongly held attitude or a belief) is of consequence. Further, if a speaker is concerned with changing attitudes, his task is easier if the attitudes he must overcome are newly formed, specific, and lightly held rather than of long duration and wide applicability. Thus, while this section most often speaks of attitudes in the sense that Morgan uses the term, a reader should remember that opinions and beliefs are usually meant as well, for a speaker must be concerned with the strength, direction, and durability of attitudes related to his speech.

DEVELOPMENT OF ATTITUDES

Attitudes develop through a lifetime of learning. Some of them originate out of one's selection of goals. As an object, condition, or situation is seen as a goal or a way to satisfy a need or motive, a positive attitude toward it develops. Hence, if you aspire to become wealthy, you have a positive attitude toward those things that represent wealth.

Attitudes also develop toward those things that are seen as facilitating or hindering the acquisition of a goal object. A positive attitude toward education, for example, is extended to those things that facilitate education; those things that hinder education become objects of negative attitudes.

Concepts and ideas may be objects of attitudes. If you seek wealth, you have a positive attitude toward the concept of wealth as well as toward those objects, conditions, and situations that represent wealth.

Since humans are verbal, they can be taught attitudes toward things never experienced in any way except as verbalisms. Some of the concepts or ideas that are objects of attitudes are so far removed from personal goals that a connection is impossible to find. But people react to those attitude objects in the same way that they react to those known to be clear and specific goals.

IMPACT OF ATTITUDES AS VALUES

For the purposes of communication, it does not matter whether the object of the attitude is a goal, something associated with a goal, or a vague residual from learning in the remote past. However it was formed, an attitude will be brought to bear whenever the attitude object is associated in some way with the speaker's proposal. A speaker who characterizes something as being socialistic is likely to have leveled a cogent argument against it, even though many people who would be influenced by the argument cannot tell why they oppose socialism.

In short, *if an attitude has been attached to an object, idea, condition, or activity, a value or disvalue has also been assigned.*

The value represented in attitudes is important to a speaker for two reasons. First, an attitude may be attached to his proposal, and his task is made either more difficult or easier according to the direction and magnitude of the attitude. Second, attitudes must be used to overcome the attitude, opinion, or belief associated with the proposition. Thus, his argument must incorporate attitudes having greater value than those attached to rejection of his proposition. If such attitudes cannot be brought to bear, he will not be persuasive.

Values Used in Persuasive Speaking

The persuasive speaker deals with values in three important respects. His fundamental problem is to convince listeners that they should make a specific choice between competing values. In the process of proving that the priority he recommends is desirable, he assumes that certain values are already accepted by his audience, and he uses those values as the bedrock on which the speech is built. As his argument unfolds, the reasons offered to support his proposal are based on other values.

SELECTING BETWEEN COMPETING VALUES

An individual's values (as represented in needs, motives, goals, and attitudes) change, although at any moment they may be in a relatively stable order. A man who has been thirsty for 24 hours will have different goals shortly after his thirst is sated. Social needs, too, vary in strength according to the circumstances. If one has recently missed an opportunity by being overcautious, he may be prepared another time to give higher priority to the need to achieve and somewhat less to the need to avoid failure. Conversely, if impetuosity has brought failure, he may decide to avoid further feelings of failure by being cautious. So at times we react positively toward the platitude "Opportunity knocks but once"; a little later we will accept as true the contrary platitude "A bird in the hand is worth two in the bush."

Values may also conflict. The need to gain recognition may conflict with the need to be self-deprecating. The need to form friendships conflicts with the need to reject others; and the need to acquire things conflicts with the need to be praised by being generous. The Freudian concepts *id, ego,* and *superego* are based on a notion of fundamental conflict in human motivations.

The central problem in persuasion is to convince a listener to make a specific choice between competing or conflicting values. Whether we openly subscribe individually to the concept of the golden mean, many of our public decisions involve the selection of a compromise between competing or incompatible values. For example, one of the perpetual problems in our government is to determine the proper relation between the federal government and smaller units of government. Harry F. Byrd was one of the staunchest advocates of a diminished role for the federal government. In an address at the University of Virginia in 1963, the Senator announced that "it is in the interest of vigilance against excessive centralization of power in the Federal Government that I am speaking this evening." But he admitted that some of the federal activities "such as some aspects of the veterans' program, Federal payrolls, and retirements, and so forth, are legitimately within the Federal province."[9]

A similar problem of convincing listeners to make a specific choice between conflicting values confronted J. William Fulbright, Senator from Arkansas, in an address at the School of Law and Diplomacy, Tufts University: "The question is not . . . whether we should or should not have a space program but what priority it should have in relation to pressing and long-neglected national needs."[10]

The problem for the speaker is to demonstrate to his audience that his proposition represents values that should be given high priority.

VALUES AS BASIC SUPPORT

Every speech is based on an assumption of values that are an integral part of the speech and yet are usually not stated. These are the bedrock support for a speech. Lincoln's first inaugural, for example, carefully justifies the President's actions in meeting the crisis of disunion.[11] However, Lincoln assumed that his listeners would agree that he should uphold the Constitution. As he saw it, the issue concerned interpretation and possible amendment of the Constitution. Except perhaps for the argument on perpetuity of the government, the speech assumes rather than establishes that it is desirable to live in conformity with the Constitution. Other assumptions were that civil war is undesirable, but that if the Union can be preserved only through war, then war must come.

Although the success of Lincoln's address depended upon many things, nothing could have made it successful with a listener who rejected the assumed values. That is, any listener who refused to believe that the Constitution should be upheld or that civil war was undesirable would be unmoved by whatever the President said.

[9] Printed in *Vital Speeches of the Day*, Vol. 29 (June 15, 1963).

[10] Printed in *Vital Speeches of the Day*, Vol. 29 (June 1, 1963).

[11] Lincoln's first inaugural, although less popular than the second inaugural, is available in many anthologies. We happen to use A. Craig Baird's *American Public Address, 1740–1952* (New York: McGraw-Hill, Inc., 1956). This fine anthology has the added advantage of being a paperback.

Lincoln realized that he was making assumptions. In one point of the speech he explicitly dismissed part of his potential audience because he realized that some people would not grant his assumption:

> That there are persons in one section or another who seek to destroy the Union at all events, and are glad of any pretext to do it, I will neither affirm or deny; but if there be such, I need address no word to them. To those, however, who really love the Union, may I not speak?

Even if he thought only that there *might* be such people, why did he not address himself to them? Perhaps he thought that if there were any they were few in number, perhaps he thought that they held their opinions so firmly that they could not be persuaded, or perhaps he felt that in the time available he could not include arguments that would be effective with them.

Suppose he had concluded that he would make fewer assumptions, that he would prove, for example, that war is undesirable. He could have dwelt on the horrors of war, on the suffering, on the loss of life and property. Such an argument would still rest on an assumption—that his listeners attached value to life and property.

Could he have avoided making assumptions? If he had expanded his argument until it reached back to primary or physiological motives, he still would have assumed the value assigned to them. Even in the life-and-death business of war, social and derived motives are often more impelling than primary motives. Most of our Medals of Honor are awarded posthumously to men who acted with great bravery rather than with concern for themselves, and thus showed that they valued their nation's goals more highly than they valued their lives. And in every war men who have never considered themselves heroic have gone willingly to battle with a more or less vivid realization of the great personal risk.

Even a speech less obviously persuasive than Lincoln's inaugural must be based on assumptions. Thomas Huxley's famous lecture On a Piece of Chalk, which through all but the last segment appears to have no other purpose than to show what can be learned from chalk, seems to avoid making any assumptions when the speaker suggested the importance of knowing about chalk:

> What is this wide-spread component of the surface of the earth? and when did it come? You may think this no very hopeful inquiry. You may not unnaturally suppose that the attempt to solve such problems as these can lead to no result, save that of entangling the inquirer in vague speculations, incapable of refutation and verification. . . . I weigh my words well when I assert, that the man who should know the true history of the bit of chalk which every carpenter carries about in his breeches-pocket, though ignorant of all other history, is likely, if he will think his knowledge out to its ultimate results, to have a truer, and therefore a better, conception of this wonderful

universe, and of man's relation to it, than the most learned student who is deep-read in the records of humanity and ignorant of those of nature.[12]

What Huxley achieved, of course, was the avoidance of one assumption by making another. And doubtless he correctly believed that more of his listeners would question the assumption that knowledge of chalk was useful than would question the assumption that there is value in "having a truer, and therefore a better, conception of this wonderful universe."

It is impossible, then, to avoid making assumptions. A speech must begin somewhere. Wherever it begins, the speech rests on assumptions of values. Guided by considerations such as the time allowed, a speaker determines what he will prove and what he will assume. The success of his speech may well depend on whether he wisely chooses his assumptions.

VALUES AS SUPPORT FOR AN ARGUMENT

Not only does the speaker make basic assumptions of value when he determines where to start his speech, he also assumes acceptance of values when he develops his argument. And regardless of the pattern of development, he will have to relate his development to values held by his audience. Suppose the pattern is problem-solution. After an introduction, the speaker begins to prove that a problem exists. A problem exists for a listener, however, only if some value of his is not being met at all or only in part. To argue that a tariff problem exists because American manufacturers are forced to compete with foreign manufacturers and thereby earn less profit, would not constitute proof of a problem for most Americans. Many listeners would regard the argument rather as proof that no problem exists. Or if the pattern of organization relies heavily on the offering of reasons why something should be done, the reasons will be effective only if they are based on values listeners accept. If your friend urges you to see a particular movie because it is entertaining, he is assuming that you attach value to entertainment.

Again to illustrate from Lincoln's inaugural: While arguing that the secession movement would lead to additional secession from any newly formed confederacy, the President stated that "plainly, the central idea of secession is the essence of anarchy. A majority, held in restraint by constitutional checks and limitations, and always changing easily with deliberate changes of popular opinions and sentiments is the only true sovereign of a free people. Whoever rejects it, does, of necessity, fly to anarchy or despotism." There the argument stops. He did not seek to prove the undesirability of anarchy and despotism. He assumed that his listeners would grant it.

[12] This excellent speech, perhaps because of its length and because it was not delivered in the United States, is harder to locate than are speeches by famous Americans. It is printed in *Modern Eloquence*, Thomas B. Reed, Ed. (Philadelphia: John D. Morris and Co., 1901), Vol. 5.

Huxley, too, made assumptions in addition to those underlying his whole speech. While establishing how recent is the ancestry of man in comparison with other life forms, he stated: "The longest line of human ancestry must hide its diminished head before the pedigree of this insignificant shell fish. We Englishmen are proud to have an ancestor who was present at the Battle of Hastings. The ancestors of *Terebratulina caputserpentis* may have been present at a battle of *Ichthyosauria* in that part of the sea which, when the chalk was forming, flowed over the site of Hastings." Note that he *assumed* his listeners looked with pride to a traceable ancestry. The force of the point depended on the validity of the assumption.

To urge that a speaker should consider whether the values he utilizes in his speech are acceptable to his audience may seem like a belaboring of the obvious. Though the principle may be obvious, the frequency with which it is ignored is equally obvious—and not only by inexperienced speakers. Experienced political speakers, accustomed to addressing friendly or enthusiastic rallies, frequently have difficulty in making the transition to television speaking. While they may safely assume that most of the people who took the trouble to attend a rally believed that all the policies of the Democratic party are socialistic or that the Republican party still dwells in the nineteenth century, they forget that the nonbeliever or the indifferent will often take the trouble to turn on, and watch, a television set. The viewer at home may not consider all Democrats socialists or Republicans reactionary.[13]

First Principle of Persuasion

The discussion of values brings us to the first principle of persuasion:

The values that underlie a speech or support an argument must appear sound and important to a listener.

The values are those motives, goals, and attitudes related to the speaker's proposal.

The values serve both as the bedrock on which a speech is built and as the moving force behind reasons offered in support of the proposal.

Since different people have different values, those values used as bedrock support or as the moving force behind reasons must be regarded as sound by the listeners. Not only do people value different things, they attach varying weight to values they do hold. Thus, the values served (or the extent to which they are served) by the speaker's proposal must seem more important than the values that would be served (or the extent to which they would be served) by rejection of the proposal.

[13] It is this very problem that presents a dilemma to the keynote speaker at a national political convention. To whom does he speak: the faithful at the convention or the less faithful and varied group listening and viewing over television?

REASONING

If listeners accept the identity of interest between themselves and the speaker, there is no occasion for persuasion. There is no necessity, for example, to demonstrate to people who already will give their fair share to a united fund campaign that such giving accords with their values. On the other hand, potential donors who believe that the fair-share concept is sound but who will not actually give to a campaign, are suitable subjects for persuasion.

When identity is incomplete, the speaker offers arguments or reasons to complete the identity, to prove to listeners that their values will be served by accepting the proposition.

Logic in Speechmaking

Considerations of reasoning and adequacy of proof are the province of logic, which may be defined as "the study of the methods and principles used to distinguish sound from unsound reasoning." While the principles of formal logic are useful in understanding proof in public speaking, they do not provide an adequate theory of applied logic.

LOGICAL VERSUS PSYCHOLOGICAL VALIDITY

The logician is concerned with *logical* validity, the speaker with *psychological* validity. Formal validity is determined by whether the reasoning conforms to certain patterns, irrespective of the truth of the premises it uses and the credibility that seems to attach to the argument. Psychological validity, on the other hand, is determined by whether the premises are considered to be true and the reasoning sound, irrespective of the technical adequacy of that reasoning. Philip Wheelwright, a logician, effectively illustrated the separation of logic and truth:

> The validity or invalidity of a syllogism is to be judged independently of the truth of its premises. "Cows are intellectual; all intellectual beings are sinful; therefore cows are sinful." The syllogism looks foolish because all three of its propositions are probably false, or at any rate would usually be taken so. Nevertheless, the syllogism is logically valid. For *if* the two premises are true, *then* the conclusion must necessarily be true also.[14]

This orientation of formal logic led psychologist W. Edgar Vinacke to state: "Merely to conform to the rules of logic does not guarantee that truth will result."[15]

[14] *Valid Thinking: An Introduction to Logic* (New York: The Odyssey Press, 1962), p. 14.
[15] *The Psychology of Thinking* (New York: McGraw-Hill, Inc., 1952), p. 25.

The problems of applying logic to what Wheelwright calls "the flux of experience" (in which one cannot ignore whether the premises in his arguments are true or false) and using that logic to influence others (in which it is important that they accept the truth of the conclusion), require a number of modifications from the tests and methods of formal logic.

COMPLETE VERSUS INCOMPLETE PROOF

Of the many procedural differences between formal and applied logic, the most pervasive is the difference required to have a complete proof. This point will be illustrated by reference to but one segment of logic, although it is also true for other segments.

First, the logician may start his proof with any argument he wishes, whereas a speaker must begin his proof with an argument having psychological validity. If a logician wants to use as a premise in a syllogism the statement "men are more intelligent than women," he may do so without having to prove it. The validity of his syllogism can be tested irrespective of assumptions made in the premises. If a speaker wishes to use that statement as a part of his argument, he must consider whether it will be accepted as true by his audience.

A speaker cannot, of course, prove every statement he uses in his speech. Nor will he prove more than he has to. As pointed out above, at some point he begins to assume that his listeners will grant the truth and value in his statements. If a statement is regarded by his listeners as axiomatic, a speaker may show implicitly or explicitly its axiomatic aspect and move on. In the speech referred to above, Senator Fulbright stated: "It is axiomatic that prejudices and injustices relating to race are the products of ignorance. Only through the processes of education can men of different races learn to live together in harmony and in full respect for each other's rights." The risk the Senator took was in assuming that his audience would regard the statement as axiomatic. The point is, though, that he did not devote time to proving what he believed his audience already granted.

Second, wherever a logician begins his proof the steps leading to the conclusion must be clearly indicated if validity of the argument is to be determined, whereas a speaker may omit steps in the reasoning process and still achieve psychological validity. The argument by Senator Fulbright is an example of syllogistic-like reasoning used in speaking. The Senator's conclusion, that only through education can people overcome prejudice, is supported by only one premise: that racial prejudice is the product of ignorance. From the logician's point of view, the inference (conclusion) cannot be drawn from the premise. Both the premise and the conclusion have to do with racial prejudice, but only the conclusion says anything about education, and only the premise mentions ignorance. If the conclusion is to be drawn, the terms *education* and *ignorance* must in some way be related. In the Senator's thinking, and in the thinking of his listeners, the relationship is so obvious that it need not be stated. In syllogistic-like form (but still without formal validity) the argument would be:

> Racial prejudice is the product of ignorance.
> Education eliminates ignorance.
> Therefore, education eliminates prejudice.

What Senator Fulbright did in this argument is what most public speakers do—state only as much of any argument as they believe necessary to secure understanding and belief. The omitted portion of the argument may be one of the premises or the conclusion. In other instances the omitted portions may be links in a chain of reasoning leading from a starting point to a conclusion. This chain, called a *sorites* in logic, may appear incomplete to a critic; but completeness and adequacy of applied logic depend on whether listeners regard it as complete, not whether a critic does.

Aristotle, inventor of the syllogism, recognized that the syllogism of rhetoric differs from the syllogism of logic. The most significant differences are, first (as discussed here), that the syllogism of rhetoric often appears with one of the premises or the conclusion omitted and which the audience must supply; and, second (as will be discussed in the next chapter), that the syllogism of rhetoric deals with probabilities whereas the syllogism of logic deals with certainties. To distinguish between the two, Aristotle called the rhetorical syllogism an *enthymeme*. The term will be used in the next chapter.

Second Principle of Persuasion

The discussion of reasoning in public speaking brings us to the second principle of persuasion:

The proof that relates the proposition to the values held by the audience must appear sound.

It matters less in persuasion whether a speaker personally regards the proof of his proposition as adequate than whether the audience regards it as adequate. Cogency of an argument depends on the impact the argument has on those who receive it rather than on those who invent it.

Nor does it matter, as shown above, if formal logic pronounces an argument sound. Though formal logic may prove that "cows are intellectual," that "the Giants will win the pennant," that "John Peterson is the best candidate," or that "what's good for big business is good for everyone" a listener will be convinced only if he regards the reasoning as sound. Nor does it matter if formal logic pronounces an argument inadequate or unsound for reasons such as incompleteness of the proof.

Because the adequacy of proof is determined by the audience, the second principle of persuasion states that the proof must "appear sound" rather than "be sound." Understand, however, that an argument might achieve both psychological and logical validity. Chapter 5 will make clear that logical validity in an argument contributes significantly to, even though it may not be tantamount to, psychological validity.

PARADIGM OF AN ARGUMENT

To prove the desirability of a proposition a speaker must develop an argument according to the fundamental principles of persuasion. First, he must ensure that the values that underlie his speech or are appealed to in it will be regarded as sound and important to a listener. Second, the proof used to relate the proposition to the values must appear sound. In short, he must present cogent reasons, which show the relation between the proposition and his listeners' values.

Common sense suggests that even though the rules of formal logic may not provide an adequate theory of proof in public speaking, some standards must apply. Those standards can best be developed by first discovering the crucial points at which an argument might be rejected by listeners.

First, an argument may fail because listeners fail to see a logical relation between the proposition and the reason offered in its support. Senator Fulbright sought to convince his listeners that education needed more support in comparison with the support given military needs. Suppose he had argued, "Support education because today is Tuesday." A listener might have responded: "So today is Tuesday. What has that to do with education?" In other words, he would have agreed that the statement of fact given in the reason is true, but he would have questioned its relation to the proposition.

Second, a listener may agree that there is a logical relation between the proposition and the reason, but reject the statement of fact in the reason. That might well be your response, for instance, if a friend were to urge: "Carry an umbrella today because it will probably rain." You might agree that *if* it will probably rain you should carry an umbrella, but you are unconvinced that it will probably rain.

Third, a listener may concede the logical relation between the proposition and the supporting reason, and grant the fact contained in the reason, but still remain unmoved because the reason is based on a value he rejects, toward which he is indifferent, or to which he attaches little importance. A listener may respond to the argument "support education because it will develop more skillful business leaders," by granting the relation of education to business leadership, by agreeing that the relationship would probably result in more skillful leaders, and by rejecting the argument because he attaches no importance to the training of better business leaders. Similarly, if you enjoy walking in the rain, you may refuse to carry an umbrella even though you know it will rain. Or, if you are like many young people who regard an umbrella as appropriate only to old people and eccentric college professors, you will reject the admonition to carry one even though the clouds are about to burst.

In summary, then, in offering reasons for the acceptance of his proposition, a speaker must consider whether his listeners will grant that a relation exists between the proposition and the reason, whether the statement of fact in the reason will be accepted as true, and whether the value underlying the reason will be considered important.

The process of persuasion and its three crucial areas might be diagramed as follows:

PROPOSITION (not accepted)	RELATIONSHIP ["because"] (not accepted)	REASON (accepted as true; based on a sound value)
PROPOSITION (not accepted)	RELATIONSHIP ["because"] (accepted)	REASON (not accepted as true; based on a sound value if it were true)
PROPOSITION (not accepted)	RELATIONSHIP ["because"] (accepted)	REASON (accepted as true; based on an unsound value)

The paradigm operates only when the proposition is not accepted. As pointed out above, when identity is complete, no persuasive situation exists. The paradigm as drawn assumes only one weakness in an argument, when in fact any given argument may have more than one. A reason may not be regarded as true and may at the same time be based on an unsound value.

The proposition of the paradigm is the *specific* proposition a speaker wishes his audience to accept, regardless of what the title or announced purpose of his speech may be. Chapter 15 sets forth reasons why it may be desirable at times to leave a proposition implicit rather than make it explicit. Leaving a proposition implicit while delivering a speech is not to be confused, however, with leaving it unformed while a speech is prepared. If a speaker is unclear about his purpose, his audience can hardly expect to have a clear understanding of his intent. Had Huxley not had clearly in mind the proposition that the lessons of science argue against the Genesis theory of creation, his listeners could not have been so inexorably led to that conclusion, which is nowhere explicitly stated in the speech.

Although our paradigm assumes but one proposition, some speeches—

even some of those regarded as great—will have two or three propositions. Lincoln's "Cooper Union Address," for example, has at least two purposes —to justify the Republican position on extension of slavery and to encourage the Republicans to stand fast in their determination to stop the spread of slavery. Such a speech is in essence two speeches delivered as one and is therefore governed by two paradigms rather than one.

Speeches organized as problem solution or following Alan Monroe's motivated sequence also require more than a single paradigm for analysis. They begin with the establishment of a need and then proceed to satisfaction of the need. Whether the statement of need is implicit or explicit, it involves a proposition similar to this one: "We must change our policy of. . . ." That statement of need is the proposition to a paradigm. The next step involves another paradigm, and so on.

Frequently a proposal for action has a number of separate parts, each of which contributes to a solution of some problem. In a foreign policy speech, Richard Nixon offered a number of specific proposals for change in policy. Each of the proposals is a proposition to which the paradigm might be applied.[16]

We intend, then, that the paradigm be regarded as the fundamental unit of argument in persuasive speaking. We will see later that the elements of the paradigm can be supplied in a variety of ways and that the paradigm permits great variety in organizing a speech.

CHANGING AN AUDIENCE'S ATTITUDES

So far the analysis of an argument has assumed that the speaker would make use of existing attitudes in giving force to his argument. Often, however, his purpose will be to change attitudes or to change attitudes as a prerequisite to some other purpose.

To change attitudes is exceedingly difficult. An understanding of their development and persistence will make clearer why.

Persistence of Attitudes

An individual's complex of attitudes, opinions, and beliefs is the product of a lifetime of learning from his family, peers, acquaintances— nearly everything with which he has come in contact. As Rodgers and Hammerstein remind us in *South Pacific,* we have to be taught to hate. We also have to be taught that certain ways of gaining property (as by shoplifting) are both illegal and wrong, while others (as by bringing more duty-free items into a country than the law allows, if you are unaware that the law designating the amount has been changed) are only illegal, and still

[16] Speech delivered before the American Society of Newspaper Editors, Washington, D.C., April 20, 1963. Printed in *Vital Speeches of the Day,* Vol. 29 (June 1, 1963).

others (as accepting expensive gifts from a new admirer) are only wrong.

The lessons are learned well. Some of the opinion current at any particular moment is based on issues and events of a much earlier time. Voters who came of age during the Great Depression of the 1930s, for example, continue to be strongly influenced in their voting by economic issues.[17]

An attitude's durability results in part from attempts to protect it from change. The quest for inviolability of attitudes is so successful that Berelson and Steiner conclude that "for a population as a whole, there appears to be little lasting development of the OAB's [opinions, attitudes, and beliefs] that is independent of parental, group, or strata predispositions and is based mainly on 'objective' or 'rational' analysis of information and ideas." And "the more a person is emotionally involved in his beliefs, the harder it is to change him by argument or propaganda—that is, through an appeal to intelligence—to the point of virtual impossibility (as in cases of deeply felt matters based on strata and reinforced by primary group support)."[18]

Facts and Attitudes

Faced with the difficulties, one might ask whether there is any point in trying to change attitudes. From history, we know that attitudes of a whole population do change, although tortuously slow, perhaps, to the crusader. Between World War I and World War II Americans revised their attitudes toward involvement in foreign affairs. Experimental evidence also shows that attitudes can be altered.

As attitudes develop initially through learning, they change through learning. Although a person learns from many sources (the organizations to which he belongs and the friends he has, for example), one of the principal methods by which a speaker must seek to change attitudes is through the giving of factual information. Any newly learned fact (or what the individual listener regards as factual, whether or not it is verifiable) may have some impact on a listener's attitude.

To communicate factual information related to hearers' deeply held attitudes is made difficult by the way people receive information that endangers their attitudes.

First, people tend to seek out communications that confirm their existing attitudes and beliefs. Social psychologists Herbert H. Hyman and Paul B. Sheatsley state that "people tend to expose themselves to information which is congenial with their prior attitudes, and to avoid exposure to in-

[17] There is even some evidence that attitudes are related to personality. One study showed that female college students judged radical in attitudes are more introverted, self-sufficient, and dominant than other women students. We trust that nothing said in this book will be construed as advice on how to reorganize personality.

[18] *Human Behavior*, pp. 574–575.

formation which is not congenial."[19] A person who believes in the efficacy of fluoridating drinking water is far more likely to attend a speech in support of that position than he is one opposed to it. As Morgan states the point, "for one reason or another, people often are so reluctant to change their attitudes and beliefs that they try to avoid information that is inconsistent with these attitudes and beliefs."[20]

Second, even when exposed to information, listeners tend to misperceive and distort what they hear so as to make it more nearly conform to their existing beliefs and attitudes. This phenomenon was discussed in Chapter 2. Hyman and Sheatsley state that "it has been consistently demonstrated that a person's perception and memory of materials shown to him are often distorted by his wishes, motives, and attitudes."[21] Thus, the speaker who arranges a captive audience so that it might at least understand his position may find that the message received varies considerably from the message intended.

Third, neutrals avoid exposure to any information. Instead of being judicious individuals, independent voters tend to be uninformed and uninterested. The neutral will expose himself to information only when it is relatively easy to obtain. The interested person rarely remains neutral; he seeks out information, but (as pointed out above) information corroborating rather than challenging his existing attitudes.

Fourth, the better educated and more intelligent people tend to resort to written rather than verbal sources of information, for they have learned that fuller coverage is usually given in written sources.

The factual information a speaker attempts to communicate concerns the relation between an attitude and goals or motives.

An attitude was earlier defined as a predisposition to react favorably or unfavorably toward an idea, object, or process. If an idea, thing, or process is perceived as facilitating the realization of a goal, a favorable attitude toward it evolves; conversely, something perceived as impeding realization of a goal becomes the object of an unfavorable attitude. Therefore, to develop or alter an attitude, an object or idea must be associated in a new way with an individual's goals or values. For example, a speaker may discover that a group of property owners has a negative attitude toward a housing project because the group believes that its economic security would be threatened through loss of rent and increased taxes. If a speaker could show that more housing would accommodate population growth and that the continued economic security of the community depended on over-

19 "Some Reasons Why Information Campaigns Fail," *Readings In Social Psychology*, Eleanor E. Maccoby, Theodore M. Newcomb, and Eugene L. Hartley, Eds. (New York: Holt, Rinehart and Winston, Inc., Third ed., 1958), p. 168.
20 *Introduction to Psychology*, p. 540.
21 "Some Reasons Why Information Campaigns Fail," p. 169.

coming a labor shortage, he might succeed in establishing a previously un-perceived relation between the project and the value of economic security. With the perception of such a relation, the attitude toward the housing project would become less unfavorable. Whereas the audience previously categorized the project as a thing endangering a goal, it would now place the project in the category of things facilitating a realization of the goal.

The process just described is but another way of applying the paradigm of an argument. To recast it in terms of the paradigm, the proposition is: We should support this housing project. The reason: It will enhance eco-nomic security. The speaker's task: Show the truth or factual basis of the reason. This could be shown only by refuting the conflicting idea—eco-nomic security will be lessened by such a project. There would be little difficulty in showing that a relation between the housing project and economic security exists, for the audience (as hypothesized) already sees such a relation, although not in the desired way.

The slow development of attitudes, their resistance to modification, and the difficulties encountered in supplying the information to a hearer so that he will change suggest that a speaker be modest in his expectations of success. The persuasive process, of course, is rarely as simple as in our hypothetical example. For illustrative purposes we selected the relatively new and lightly held attitude directed toward the housing project. That attitude could be influenced far more easily than could the attitude related to the concept of economic security.

When strongly held attitudes must be dealt with, a speaker should place first priority on getting reasonably accurate and full information to his audience.

It may be important that listeners hear the full case for a proposal even though the speaker knows that they are not ready to accept it. If he recognizes his obstacles, he will develop realistic standards of achievement. He might not realize the end of his efforts, but if he has done his work well and has enjoyed good fortune, he may be at the end of the beginning.

Often it is better to ask for something less than full agreement. A speaker may conclude that the problem of getting information to un-sympathetic hearers is sufficiently great to require use of all the time he has available. Before an audience will accept the value of the housing project they perhaps need accurate information about it. Explicit attempts at proving its desirability might be left for another speech or another medium of communication.

Action and Attitudes

In Molière's *Misanthrope*, Alceste advises,

> Let men behave like men; let them display
> Their inmost hearts in everything they say;

Let the heart speak, and let our sentiments
Not mask themselves in silly compliments.

Philinte replies,

In certain cases it would be uncouth
And most absurd to speak the naked truth;
With all respect for your exalted notions,
It's often best to veil one's true emotions.
Wouldn't the social fabric come undone
If we were wholly frank with everyone?[22]

Philinte knew that often it is both easier and preferable to act contrary to belief. With Philinte, most of us would rather conceal our displeasure at meeting someone than be thought uncouth or rude; and we would rather contribute when the collection plate is passed than reveal that we do not believe in the purpose for which it is passed.

Because it can be observed, behavior is far more amenable to pressures, subtle or extreme, than are attitudes and beliefs. Thus, it is often easier to bring about changes in behavior than to alter attitudes. That fact has great importance to anyone seeking to change attitudes.

Attitudes, opinions, and beliefs are based on incomplete and often inaccurate information. As Walter Lippmann states, "inevitably our opinions cover a bigger space, a longer reach of time, a greater number of things, than we can directly observe. They have, therefore, to be pieced together out of what others have reported and what we can imagine."[23] Such a method of opinion and attitude formation leads inevitably to the widespread, oversimplified, and erroneous categories called stereotypes.

First contacts with the objects of a stereotype tend to confirm the stereotype, for we see what we expect to see. Prolonged contact eventually forces us to see the exceptions to the stereotype. A native-born American may reluctantly associate with immigrants, but if he does, he will find that they have the same strengths and weaknesses found in the native. Generalizations about the qualities of immigrants are as difficult to make as are generalizations about the qualities of any other group—Catholics, teenagers, Frenchmen, politicians, farmers, or women.

Oftentimes the best way to change an attitude, then, is to bring people into contact with the object of that attitude. A speaker who has as his ultimate purpose the dislodgment of an erroneous stereotype about Baptists knows that his audience will not likely openly reveal its distrust of Baptists and that it will not refuse to associate with them. Hence, his immediate objective may be to persuade them to *act* in a certain way (associate with

22 Act One, Scene One, Richard Wilbur, Tr., in Randolph Goodman's *Drama On Stage* (New York: Holt, Rinehart and Winston, Inc., 1961).
23 *Public Opinion* (New York: Crowell Collier and Macmillan, Inc., Paperback ed., 1961), p. 79.

Baptists), and to trust to the Baptists themselves to dislodge the stereotype once the contact has been made.

In addition to a change of attitude brought about by the information obtained from increased exposure to something, attitudes tend to be brought into conformity with actions quite apart from the information obtained. People tend to develop favorable attitudes toward what they do. Thus, the chairman of a membership drive may appreciate that each recruit, even though a reluctant recruit, has placed himself in the position of becoming a full and enthusiastic convert. Political workers constantly seek to involve individuals in campaigns. The lady who agrees to answer the telephone at headquarters or allows herself to be persuaded to address campaign literature might not even have bothered to vote had she not become directly involved in the campaign. But now she will probably vote, and for the "right" candidate; and she will probably also encourage her friends to vote, and for the "right" candidate.

SUMMARY

This chapter has been concerned with the process a speaker uses to show an audience that his proposal is desirable. Listeners will regard a proposal as desirable if the speaker can show that its acceptance will serve some value held by them. That is the function of the arguments in a speech: to show the relation between the proposition and those things valued by an audience.

Not only must the total line of argument lead toward those things valued by listeners, but each individual argument will have force only if it is associated with sound values. Further, the entire line of argument will have force only if it starts from a point of common agreement on what is true and what is desirable (what is to be valued).

The first principle of persuasion, then, is that the values associated with a speech must appear sound from the listeners' viewpoint.

Listeners will be convinced that the proposal is desirable only if the reasoning process itself meets certain minimum standards. Whatever the values on which a reason may depend for its force, the reason must be thought by the audience to bear a logical relation to the speaker's proposal, and the statement of purported fact in the reason must be regarded as true.

The second principle of persuasion, then, is that the reasoning must appear sound.

How the two principles are incorporated in a particular argument so that it achieves psychological validity was shown in the paradigm of an argument.

The paradigm assumes, however, that a speaker will use existing attitudes to prove that his proposal is desirable. Often the purpose of the speech will be to change attitudes or instill new attitudes. The section on "Changing Attitudes" shows how difficult it is to change long-standing attitudes, and suggests how a speaker may proceed in that task.

The next chapter treats of ways to apply the paradigm so that the listeners will be convinced that the reasons do bear a logical relation to the proposal, that the statement of purported facts contained in the reasons are true, and that the values associated with the reasons are sound.

5 Persuasion: Applying the Paradigm

An argument must meet three requirements if it is to have psychological validity: the reasons offered in support of the proposition must be regarded as related to the proposition, the reasons must be accepted as true, and the values toward which the reasons point and on which they are based must be accepted as sound. This chapter will be concerned with ways in which those three requirements may be met.

PROVING THE RELATION BETWEEN THE REASON AND THE PROPOSITION

Examination of arguments used to support propositions urging that we do a particular thing or accept a certain concept shows that they are usually based quite directly on the effect either acceptance or rejection of the proposition will have. Senator Fulbright, in the argument referred to in Chapter 4 and here simplified for illustrative purposes, urged greater support for education because of the effect it would have in eliminating prejudice. The injunction to take an umbrella was similarly based on an implicit argument that it would have the effect of keeping you dry. In terms of our discussion of values, speakers assume that the desirability of a proposition has been demonstrated when listeners believe its acceptance will serve their values.

In addition to arguments resting directly on cause and effect reasoning are those that are one step removed from the direct relation, but that depend ultimately on cause and effect reasoning for their cogency. One may argue that we should support education because it is our duty to do so. The argument would be effective with individuals who have a positive attitude toward duty. If a listener were to ask, however, "Why should I be concerned with public duty?" a speaker would probably be able to supply a satisfactory answer only by showing the desirable effect of performing one's duty. Sociologists tell us that most, if not all, public values, such as that one should do his duty, developed because the society believed that they had desirable effects.

Another type of argument holds that we should support a proposal on the basis of an authoritative recommendation. For example, Senator Fulbright might have argued that increased support for education is merited because the National Education Association recommends it. Although a positive attitude toward the NEA might give force to the argument, a listener could still ask, "Why should we be impressed with what the NEA recommends?" or "Why does the NEA recommend increased support?" A full answer would doubtless explain the effect of increased support.

Arguments are also leveled against or for a proposition by labeling it. The attaching of labels is a method of definition: to show the class to which a thing belongs. If listeners hold an attitude, either negative or positive, toward the class, the speaker brings that attitude to bear on the individual member of the class. Thus, an opponent to federal aid for education may class such aid as socialistic and hope that a negative attitude toward socialism will be brought to bear. Since attitudes are developed because the object of the attitude is thought to impede or assist in the realization of an individual's goals, even this line of argument ultimately goes back to cause-and-effect relations.

So far we have been examining the relation between reasons and the proposition they support in arguments that urge listeners to perform a specific action. A similar relation prevails for arguments that urge acceptance of an idea. As stated in Chapter 1, most ideas are imparted because the speaker assumes they will be the basis for action. When a speaker demonstrates why an idea should be accepted, he generally bases his arguments on its ultimate effect.

Arguments based on causal relation may be developed in several ways. First, as in the examples already given, an action may be urged because it will lead to a desirable effect. If you are urged to support education because it will decrease delinquency, the speaker is saying that a cause (education) will have a specific effect (decreased delinquency). Second, the process may be reversed, so that a cause is sought for an observed effect. By examining the effect (delinquency) a speaker may seek to show its cause (inadequate education). Third, an argument may go from effect to effect, particularly when two things are known to occur together and appear to have a common, but unknown, cause. Without knowing the proximate cause of escaping gas, a prudent man, on smelling the gas, will act to protect his family and property, because he knows that there is a possibility of a related effect of paramount consequence. Or a physician may recognize the symptoms of a well-known disease and know that other effects are or will be present even though he does not know the cause of the disease.

In examining arguments to discover whether they are causal, the unwary will be misled by the varied use of the words *because* and *for*. Psychologist Norman L. Munn wrote that "reasoning is differentiated from mere *thinking of* something, because it involves a sequence of symbolic acts."[1] He does not mean that reasoning is *caused* by symbolic activities. Rather he uses the term to explain how the processes are differentiated. When you were urged to carry an umbrella because it would probably rain, the person urging you did not mean to suggest that the rain *caused* the umbrella or vice versa. He intends *because* to mean "for the reason that" it will probably rain. Often *because* or *for,* used explicitly or implicitly, suggests only explanation or restatement rather than direct cause-and-effect relations.

Relations Based on Cause and Effect

Because (for the reason that) it is the most important type of connection between proposition and reason, causal relations will be considered in detail. Logician Philip Wheelwright says,

> We may roughly define the cause of a phenomenon as *that earlier physical condition in whose presence a certain later phenomenon occurs and in whose absence it does not occur.* In such a situation the antecedent physical condition is called the *cause* and the phenomenon which follows, or which both follows and accompanies, is called the *effect.*[2]

When analyzing cause-and-effect relations, it is important to distinguish between *sufficient* and *necessary* causes. Deprivation of liquids will lead to death and may therefore be called a *sufficient* cause of death. However, because death can be caused by other things, deprivation of liquids is not a *necessary* cause of death. Although oxygen is a *necessary* cause if wood is to burn in the usual sense, it is not a *sufficient* cause.

The two types of cause are important in solving problems. As logician Irving M. Copi states, the word *cause* is "most often used in the sense of necessary condition when the problem at hand is the elimination of some undesirable phenomenon." It "is used in the sense of sufficient condition when we are interested not in the elimination of something undesirable but rather in the production of something desirable."[3] Thus, one may argue that increased funds are a sufficient cause for improving education, that education inexorably improves as more funds are furnished to improve facilities and to pay higher salaries so that the most competent people are attracted to teaching. An argument on eliminating traffic deaths involving young drivers could be based on eliminating the necessary cause

[1] *Psychology: The Fundamentals of Human Adjustment* (Boston: Houghton Mifflin Co., Second ed., 1951), p. 228.

[2] *Valid Thinking: An Introduction to Logic* (New York: The Odyssey Press, 1962), p. 226.

[3] *Introduction to Logic* (New York: Crowell Collier and Macmillan, Inc. Second ed., 1961), p. 356.

of permitting them to drive. While there are doubtless a multitude of causes for the recklessness of young people, their effect in traffic fatalities could be eliminated by eliminating one necessary cause.

As Copi points out, "we can legitimately infer cause from effect only in the sense of necessary condition. And we can legitimately infer effect from cause only in the sense of sufficient condition."[4] The distinction is less important in rhetoric than in logic. Most people, for example, will infer from experience that there is an effect on quality of education that roughly correlates with the magnitude of financial support, even though they would also agree that generous financial support is not sufficient to ensure excellent education.

DEMONSTRATING CAUSAL RELATIONS

How are causal relations demonstrated? One way is to use the method by which they were discovered: observe the relations in a number of instances and draw a generalization from the observations. A speaker may remind listeners of their own experiences or cite examples for them. To an audience of parents who have had unfortunate experiences with an inadequate law enforcement agency, a speaker may by several illustrations adequately establish that the delinquency rate is caused by lax law enforcement. Often, however, audiences will not so willingly concede the relation. The speaker must then turn to some other method or methods to prove it.

The traditional methods of testing generalizations about cause and effect were developed by John Stuart Mill, and hence have come to be called Mill's Methods. They can readily be adapted by the speaker who wishes to show a probability of cause and effect.

1. *Method of agreement.* This method states that if all the phenomena under investigation have a single circumstance in common, that common circumstance is the cause or effect of the phenomena. Thus if an examination of six instances of juvenile delinquency shows that the only probable cause that they appear to have in common is a law enforcement agency which does not enforce a curfew law, then a probability exists that the lax enforcement is a cause.

2. *Method of difference.* This method is the obverse of the method of agreement. If all other possible causes remain constant, but it is observed that when one possible cause is present a phenomenon occurs and when it is absent the phenomenon does not occur, that possible cause is a probable cause. Thus if a number of youths come from substantially the same type homes, have in their general environment all the factors that may cause delinquency, but several are delinquent and the others are not, and it is found that the delinquents reside in an area where the curfew law is not enforced while the others reside in an area where the curfew is respected,

[4] *Introduction to Logic,* pp. 357–358.

then the failure to enforce a curfew probably contributes to delinquency.

3. *Joint method of agreement and difference.* As its name implies, this method combines the methods of agreement and difference. The probability of a phenomenon being a cause is significantly enhanced if both methods point to it. Thus the probability that failure to enforce a curfew law contributes to delinquency would be greatly enhanced if the method of difference confirmed the indication of the method of agreement.

4. *Method of residues.* Mill stated this method as follows: "Subduct from any phenomenon such part as is known by previous induction to be the effect of certain antecedents, and the residue of the phenomenon is the effect of the remaining antecedents." Thus, if in a question of juvenile delinquency a pattern of behavior is noted, and portions of that behavior may be explained by certain already predetermined causes, then that which remains unexplained in the pattern might be said to be an effect of the other possible causes.

5. *Method of concomitant variation.* Whereas the first four methods are used to discover causes through a process of elimination, this method is used to discover causes by comparing variations in the magnitude of an effect with variations in strength of a probable cause. If, for example, the extent of delinquency varies directly with the level of education attained, there is probably a relation between education and delinquency.

Many books on logic will illustrate Mill's Methods through examples of reasoning that yield high probability of discovering actual causes or effects. The method of residues, for example, is often illustrated by referring to the method used to discover a planet. By analyzing the path of a known astronomical body, and with the knowledge that its path is determined by gravitational force of other bodies, astronomers eliminate the aspects of its path caused by known bodies. The remainder is assumed to be caused by an unknown body. With careful calculation the position of the unknown body can be approximately determined, and a search for it begun. This method led to the discovery of Pluto and Neptune. Never in human activities that are the concern of public address can causes and effects be so clearly isolated. The best that can be expected is demonstration of sufficient probability for an audience to accept a statement as not only possibly but probably true. Certainly as used in our analysis of causes of juvenile delinquency, none of the methods would yield greater than modest probability that lax law enforcement had been demonstrated as a cause.

COMMON ERRORS IN CAUSE-AND-EFFECT REASONING

1. *Confusion of cause and coincidence.* Many superstitions are based on an assumption of cause and effect relations when in fact two events occur together coincidentally. Because the rise in delinquency has accompanied increased television viewing does not prove a causal relation. The growth

may be coincidental, as assuredly are the phenomena of longer life expectancy and increased viewing of television.

2. *Assuming that because one thing follows another the first must be a cause of the second.* Night invariably follows day, but is not the cause or effect of day. The argument that college education causes a man to earn greater wealth is not proven by showing that the one almost invariably follows the other. As in the sequence of night and day, things that invariably accompany or follow one another are related causally in some way, but not necessarily as cause and effect. Day and night are effects of the same causes; wealth and college education may both be effects of the same cause: ambition, or desire to excel.

3. *Overlooking intervening causes.* Economists of the New Deal argued that increased governmental spending would serve as a stimulus to increased economic activity. But economic recovery came slower than was expected. Some economists and historians now argue that the uneasiness people felt after going through the depression of 1929 led them to spend or invest more cautiously than they did before the depression, even though they had money for such purposes. The unanticipated cause disrupted the anticipated influence.

4. *Simplifying a complex of causes into one or two causes.* Although economists and historians still seek to understand the complex causes that led to economic recovery from the depression, politicians showed less caution. They had little difficulty in doing away with the complexity. The Democrats gave credit to New Deal domestic policy; Republicans argued that the expenditures made necessary by World War II brought recovery and that the New Deal domestic policy had little effect.

5. *Assuming that a necessary cause is a sufficient cause.* Much advertising is based on the premise that a particular object will lead inevitably to happiness, health, or prosperity. While an adequate and balanced vitamin intake may be necessary for health, an extremely ill person may have no vitamin deficiency. And while it may be necessary for a young man to have neatly combed hair to win the affections of the young lady of his choice, rarely will that be sufficient.

Relations Based on Indirect or Noncausal Reasons

As pointed out above, not all reasons offered by a speaker bear a direct causal relation to the proposition they support.

CLASSIFICATION

A reason can support a proposition by showing that the proposition belongs to a certain class of things. Often we can know the effect something will have, or more easily prove its probable effect, if we are able to classify it. And, of course, since listeners often hold attitudes toward classes of things, the process of classification may have probative value.

Things can be classified in almost unlimited ways: their physical properties, esthetic qualities, moral qualities, the way they react to other things, and so on.

The most obvious way to prove that something is properly classified is to show the essential attributes of the class and establish that the thing being classified has those attributes. A variation sometimes used, as in the speech by Mrs. Dean which was referred to in the previous chapter, is to show what causes things to move into a certain classification, and that those causes are operative on the thing being discussed. To show that our present handling of foreign aid would lead to making permanent pensioners of foreign nations, Mrs. Dean showed the causes that make them pensioners.

Often a speaker will be able to compress greatly the demonstration of class and the proof that the class has certain effects. Listeners may know the empirical significance of the class of things "highly inflammable." A simple statement that a particular brand of cleaning fluid belongs in the class will be sufficient for them to use it with caution.

When classification is based on other than physical properties, the process becomes more difficult, although not necessarily less effective rhetorically. Some things are classified as communistic, socialistic, or democratic. But what are the essential characteristics of each class? How does one show that a particular thing belongs to the class? And how are we to react to the class? Many of the problems in classification derive from the way we use language, which is the subject for a later chapter.

EXPLANATION

When the *because* between proposition and reason means "for the reason that," the connection is not one of direct cause and effect. If it is an indirect causal relation, as in the reason given why you should carry an umbrella, the ultimate causal relation may have to be clarified. If the relation is one of making clear, the methods used are those of exposition, and the reason's probative value will be that which comes with understanding.

PROVING THE FACT CONTAINED IN THE REASON

A reason will lend psychological validity to a proposition only when the reason is believed to be true, or—to use Bertrand Russell's phrase—when listeners have a "yes-feeling" on hearing it stated.[5] The yes-feeling is toward the purported fact contained in the reason.

[5] *Human Knowledge: Its Scope and Limits* (New York: Simon and Schuster, Inc., 1948), p. 148.

As the following examples show, reasons offered in support of a proposition contain purported facts. The point can be better shown if the propositions the reasons support are omitted.

1. "Because the square root of 256 is 16"
2. "Because education leads to a diminishing of prejudice"
3. "Because the United Nations has censured a similar action"
4. "Because Jones is incompetent"
5. "Because the symphony is majestic"

Each of the reasons has a statement of purported fact in it. A listener may ask: Is it true that the square root of 256 is 16? Does education diminish prejudice? Has the United Nations censured a similar action? Is Jones incompetent? Is the symphony majestic?

If a listener has a "yes-feeling" in response to each question, the speaker need not prove the truth of the statement. If, on the other hand, the listener responds with a "no-feeling," the speaker must prove the fact contained in the reason.

Explanation

At times an audience will reject the reason only because they do not understand it or do not recognize that it is but a restatement of a belief they already hold or included in an idea they already accept.

Thus, the statement that "the qualifications for a line appointment in a corporation differ materially from those for a staff appointment" may be rejected until the listener learns what *line* and *staff* mean in that context. Or the statement that characterizes Beethoven's third symphony as being majestic may be rejected until a listener learns that the speaker used slightly different terminology to state what the listener already accepts. Or until a listener understands that a speaker intends Dada to be early surrealism, he may object when an artist he classes as a surrealist is called Dadaist.

In all three instances, the fact contained in the reason can be proved or made acceptable through the methods of explanation discussed in Chapter 3.

If more than explanation is required to make a statement acceptable to an audience, the methods of proof available to a speaker are the methods of logic adapted to public address.

Immediate Inference

The simplest of the logical processes is *immediate inference*. Often it is possible to infer immediately from one proposition a second that must be true if the first is true. For example, if it is true that some politicians are not ambitious, it can be inferred that some are unambitious, or that some unambitious persons are politicians.

As with all logical processes, immediate inference can be used fallaciously. The statement "Some politicians are not ambitious" may seem to lead logically to the inference that "some politicians are ambitious." The original statement does not indicate, however, whether any politicians are excluded from the statement. Perhaps the term *some* was used only because the person knew few politicians and wished not to assert anything about the rest of them, even though all politicians may be unambitious. Only if the original statement said that "Some, but not all, politicians are not ambitious" could it immediately be inferred that "Some politicians are ambitious." And even that inference assumes that individuals must be either ambitious or unambitious rather than something in between.

Enthymematic Reasoning

The two major logical processes are *deduction* and *induction*. As did Robert T. Oliver, authors of speech texts customarily distinguish between the two processes by the direction in which the reasoning moves: "Induction means to reason from a specific example, or from a cluster of examples, to a generalized conclusion. Deduction means to start with an accepted generalization (such as, that all men are created equal) and to judge of a specific instance in terms of that conclusion."[6]

Logicians, on the other hand, distinguish between the processes on the basis of the purported certainty of the arrived-at conclusion. As pointed out in the previous chapter, a logician assumes the truth of premises used in deduction (syllogistic reasoning) or disregards the question of truth. This enables him to test an instance of deduction. If the process was carried out correctly, the conclusion will for a certainty be valid. Induction, on the other hand, except when every specific instance covered by the generalization has been checked, yields conclusions that have only a probability of truth.

As applied in speechmaking, however, neither process often yields conclusions that can be regarded as invariably true. Premises of syllogistic-like reasoning rarely are true beyond question. Induction is seldom based on complete enumeration. The logician's basis of distinguishing between the processes, then, is inadequate for the applied logic of public speaking. The direction the reasoning moves provides a more viable differentiation for our purposes.

Although logic serves as the basis for applied reasoning, modifications of formal logic are necessary, and particularly in deductive-like reasoning in speechmaking. To emphasize the difference between theoretical and applied deduction, we will refer to applied deduction as *enthymematic reasoning*. The term is derived from *enthymeme,* discussed in Chapter 4.

6 *The Psychology of Persuasive Speech* (New York: David McKay Company, Inc., Second ed., 1957), p. 236.

USING ENTHYMEMES

How an enthymeme is used in speechmaking can be illustrated by examining the example given in the previous chapter from a speech by Senator Fulbright. The Senator said, "it is axiomatic that prejudices and injustices relating to race are the products of ignorance. Only through the processes of education can men of different races learn to live together in harmony and in full respect for each other's rights."[7] Although the Senator was not then making the point that education should be supported so that prejudice might be eliminated, let us assume that he was.

In brief form the argument would have been: support education because prejudice will then be eliminated. This is an argument based directly on cause and effect. Two ways are open for him to prove that education eliminates prejudice. He could cite statistics and examples or draw analogies to prove inductively the truth of the cause and effect relation. However, he could seek to establish the proof through enthymematic reasoning. If that is to be his approach, the argument may take this form:

We should give additional support for education because through education racial prejudice will be eliminated. We know that this is true because all prejudice is a result of ignorance, and ignorance can be eliminated only through education.

In other words, he would have used two premises to arrive at the soundness of the statement, which is both the conclusion to the enthymeme and the reason given to support the proposition.

The proof may still not be complete, however. Listeners would grant the truth of the conclusion only if they also granted the truth of the premises. The next step would then be to prove the truth of either or both of the premises.

Bertrand Russell believes that there are three chief methods to arrive at general premises: "Sometimes they are tautologies, such as 'All widows are female': sometimes they result from induction; sometimes they are proved by complete enumeration, that is, 'Everybody in this room is male.' "[8] The premises used in enthymemes are proven more often by induction than by restatement of an accepted idea or by enumeration of every object included in the premise. Whatever the method used to prove the premise, the process must reach back to the point where listeners will respond with a "yes-feeling."

One may well ask at this point why a speaker would ever bother using an enthymeme if he had to prove by induction that one of the premises is

[7] Printed in *Vital Speeches of the Day,* Vol. 29 (June 1, 1963).
[8] *Human Knowledge,* p. 131.

true. Would it not be easier to prove the conclusion of the enthymeme, which is also the reason supporting the proposition?

The answer would depend in part on the types of evidence available to support the two approaches. It may be that the available material serves better to prove a premise of an enthymeme than its conclusion. That is, the evidence available may more readily prove that prejudice is a result of ignorance than that formal education will reduce prejudice. If the second premise were already granted (that formal education reduces ignorance) the conclusion could most easily be arrived at through enthymematic reasoning.

Even when a conclusion can be supported directly by induction, at times it is preferable, particularly if the conclusion is startling, to approach the conclusion gradually through deduction. The psychological phenomenon of the "yes response" operates powerfully in favor of enthymematic rather than inductive reasoning. Briefly the phenomenon is this: people who say yes to two things are more likely to say yes to the third. Hence, if they can be led to agree to the truth of the premises of an enthymeme, they are more likely to be led to accept its conclusion.

TESTING ENTHYMEMES

The ways of constructing and testing enthymemes can best be understood by showing how they are similar to the syllogism of logic. The importance of using some of the methods of logic stems from the two crucial basic criteria that reasoning by premises must meet if it is to yield sound conclusions. First, the soundness of the conclusion depends on the soundness of the premises on which it is based. Second, even if the premises are sound, whether they lead to a particular conclusion will depend on the form of the argument. Of course, even though they do not lead to a particular conclusion, that conclusion is not necessarily thereby disproven. For example, one may argue:

> All citizens can vote;
> John is an immigrant;
> Therefore, John did not vote.

The premises and the conclusions might all be true, yet it is obvious that the conclusion could not reasonably be based on the premises.

The way to ensure that an enthymeme is of sound form is to supply the missing premises and then subject the completed argument to tests similar to those used in testing a syllogism.[9]

[9] There are several ways to test syllogisms. One is the traditional series of rules as adapted in this work. Another popular mode is the use of Venn diagrams. Another, and particularly in the last 20 years, is the use of symbolic logic. Neither the Venn diagram nor symbolic logic has been extensively adapted to public address. William S. Howell and Donald K. Smith, in two excellent chapters in their *Discussion* (New York: Crowell

Categorical Syllogisms

Logicians customarily distinguish between three types of syllogisms: categorical, hypothetical, and disjunctive. Of the three, the categorical is most frequently adapted to public speaking. The examples so far have been enthymemes resembling categorical syllogisms.

Syllogistic reasoning is concerned with classes and properties of classes, not with causes. In its standard form, with two premises and a conclusion, it can be concerned with only three classes. In giving information about the three classes, the propositions used in a syllogism can assert that one class is or is not included in another. This determines the *quality* of a proposition. They can also say that some or all of a class is included or excluded from a class. This is its *quantity*. There are, then, four types of premises: All A is B; No A is B; Some A is B; Some A is not B.

The rules for ensuring a valid categorical syllogism are as follows:

1. *It must contain only three terms.* For example, if we have the premises "All A is B," and "All C is D," we are unable to draw conclusions about the relation of the classes other than those already stated. However, had one term appeared in both premises, a relation would be established. In popular usage synonyms are regarded as equivalent to one term. For example, the following line of argument is not invalidated by a shift from *proposal* to *measure:*

> All taxes are evil.
> The proposal is a tax.
> Therefore, the measure is evil.

A common error is to have a term shift meaning in the argument.

> All great things are desirable.
> A hurricane is a great thing.
> Therefore, a hurricane is desirable.

Great in the first premise suggests excellence, but in the next it suggests size. Thus, there are four terms.

2. *The middle term must be distributed in at least one of the premises.* The middle term is that which appears in both premises, but not in the conclusion. A distributed term includes *all* of a class. In the syllogism cited

---

Collier and Macmillan, Inc., 1956) use some elements of both techniques. We think that while the Venn diagram and symbolic logic do provide useful methods for testing syllogisms, they are less useful in testing or constructing enthymemes. The latter are rarely so simple as the standard logic-book examples. Hence, to resort to arbitrary symbols in place of language removes the testing process even further from the product being tested than does the process of converting an enthymeme to a syllogism. Further, not all logicians agree that symbolic logic has great merit in testing the thinking that people must do about real problems. For an argument against symbolic logic, see the Appendix to Wheelwright's *Valid Thinking*. Students who wish to explore the applicability of symbolic logic are urged to read Chapter 9 of Howell and Smith's *Discussion*.

earlier, the class *taxes* is the middle term. In the first premise the term is distributed; that is, it includes all taxes. If it were not distributed (if it were *some taxes*) then it would be impossible to conclude whether the proposal is evil. If there are taxes not thought to be evil (the *some* premise does not indicate whether there are), the particular tax may be one of them.

3. *A term cannot be distributed in the conclusion unless it is also distributed in the premises.* When the major term (the term that is in a premise and is also the predicate in the conclusion) is undistributed in the premises but is distributed in the conclusion the result is a fallacious argument similar to this:

> Some Republicans are wealthy.
> No Democrats are Republicans.
> Therefore, no Democrats are wealthy.

The conclusion can be valid only if the major premise said that the whole class *wealthy people* consisted of Republicans. If it is possible that there are some wealthy people who are not Republicans, it is possible that they are Democrats.

When the minor term (the subject of the conclusion) is undistributed in the premise but distributed in the conclusion the following type of fallacious argument may result:[10]

> All Communists are subversive elements.
> All Communists are critics of the present administration.
> Therefore, all critics of the present administration are subversive elements.

The conclusion would follow only if all critics of the present administration are Communists. If there are critics other than Communists, they may or may not be subversive.

4. *A categorical syllogism cannot have two negative premises.* Premises that assert that he is not a Republican and that he is not a Democrat justify no conclusion about political affiliation beyond what is already asserted in the premises.

5. *If a categorical syllogism has one negative premise, the conclusion must be negative.* The following syllogism is valid:

> All judges are lawyers.
> He is not a lawyer.
> Therefore, he is not a judge.

We could not conclude that because he is not a lawyer, he is therefore a judge. Incidentally, this syllogism, though valid, appears to violate the rule that the middle term must be distributed. However, when *he* is excluded

---

10 Taken from *Introduction to Logic*, p. 191.

from the class *lawyers* it means that *all* lawyers have been considered and that he is no part of the group *all lawyers.*

6. *A categorical syllogism having a particular conclusion must have at least one particular premise. Or, if it has two universal premises it cannot have a particular conclusion.* In the syllogism immediately above, it is apparent that no universal conclusion could be drawn. In the syllogisms given as illustrations of Rule 3, both of which have universal premises, it can be seen that since nothing is said about whether any particular individual is in one of the classes, no conclusion about a particular person can be inferred.

Disjunctive Syllogisms

One of the premises of a disjunctive syllogism states alternatives and the other denies one of the alternatives.

> Either he is a Democrat or a Republican.
> He is not a Democrat.
> Therefore, he is a Republican.

A logician will insist that a valid disjunctive syllogism can be designed only if the second premise denies, rather than affirms, one of the alternatives. The following example is therefore invalid:

> Either he is a Democrat or a Republican.
> He is a Republican.
> Therefore, he is not a Democrat.

Since the conclusion is intended to deal with one of the alternatives of the first premise, the logician will hold that if you wish to affirm that a man is not one thing the premise should be reworded to state "Either he is not a Democrat or he is not a Republican." An audience would probably be unimpressed by such a technical weakness.

The danger in assuming validity of a disjunctive argument if the second premise affirms rather than denies one of the alternatives derives from the possibility that the alternatives may not be exclusive. We assume that when someone says, "He is a Republican or a Democrat" that the person believes that it is impossible to be both. Suppose, however, that someone says, "Either the sun is shining or it is raining." To affirm that the sun is shining does not preclude the possibility that it is also raining. We have all had the experience of seeing both phenomena at the same time.

Hypothetical Syllogisms

In pure hypothetical syllogisms both premises are hypothetical. More common in public address is the argument resembling a mixed hypothetical syllogism, in which one premise is hypothetical and the other categorical. In one type of mixed hypothetical syllogism (*modus ponens*) the categorical premise affirms the antecedent and the conclusion affirms the consequent:

If he is a Republican, he voted for the Republican candidate.
He is a Republican.
Therefore, he voted for the Republican candidate.

In the other valid form (*modus tollens*) the categorical premise denies the consequent, and the conclusion denies the antecedent:

If he is a Republican, he voted for the Republican candidate.
He did not vote for the Republican candidate.
Therefore, he is not a Republican.

These two valid forms are easily confused with invalid forms. The categorical premise of the *modus ponens* cannot affirm the consequent. Suppose the premise in the example given above stated: He voted for the Republican candidate. One could not conclude that he therefore is a Republican. Other than Republicans may have voted for that party's candidate, and the hypothetical premise makes no assertion about non-Republicans. No valid conclusion can be arrived at in the *modus tollens* if the categorical premise in the example had said, He is not a Republican. Again we could not conclude that he did not vote for the Republican candidate, for the hypothetical premise does not say that only Republicans voted for the Republican candidate.

COMMON ERRORS IN ENTHYMEMATIC REASONING

Errors occur whenever an enthymeme violates the rules of the syllogistic reasoning on which it is based. To expose an error in enthymematic reasoning, one should supply any missing premises, insofar as possible place the argument in syllogistic form, and then subject it to the tests of syllogistic reasoning. The commonest errors in enthymemes are perhaps errors in distribution (rules 2 and 3 above). Let us now examine the enthymeme used by Senator Fulbright.

As reconstructed on page 73 above, and with the implied premise stated, we had the following argument:

Racial prejudice is the product of ignorance.
Education eliminates ignorance.
Therefore, education eliminates prejudice.

In checking for the number of terms we find *racial prejudice, product of ignorance, ignorance,* and *education.* That is our first clue that something is wrong. Closer examination of the enthymeme shows that the first premise speaks of causes of prejudice, whereas the next premise and the conclusion speak of eliminating ignorance and prejudice. How do we move from causes to elimination of something? We do so only by assuming another premise: that whatever will eliminate a cause will also eliminate the effects of that cause, and we assume its applicability in this particular case. To show the impact of that assumption, the first premise should be reworded so that our syllogism becomes:

> Whatever will eliminate ignorance will eliminate racial prejudice.
> Education will eliminate ignorance.
> Therefore, education will eliminate racial prejudice.[11]

The syllogism is valid only if we intend to assert that whatever eliminates all ignorance will also eliminate *all* prejudice. Suppose we intend to say that if you eliminate *all* ignorance, you eliminate *some* racial prejudice. Then the conclusion must be qualified. And if we also intend to mean that education only eliminates *some* ignorance, we cannot validly arrive at any conclusion about education and prejudice. The ignorance education eliminates may be no part of the ignorance that is related to racial prejudice.

Often, however, it is difficult to convert an enthymeme into precise logical form without moving it so far away from the original argument that the point is nearly lost. Sometimes, therefore, the most fruitful method of analysis is to supply the missing premise and check particularly for errors in distribution. Without converting the above enthymeme to a syllogism, it can be seen that only if the first premise means that *all* racial prejudice is caused by ignorance can the conclusion mean that education eliminates *all* prejudice. And the term *ignorance* must be distributed in the second premise if we are to have an unqualified conclusion.

MODALITY

The problem of ensuring that conclusions to enthymemes reflect accurately the distribution indicated in the premises brings us to the logicians' concept of *modality*. The usual conclusions in public address must be stated as probabilities. Hence, speakers use such terms as *it is likely*, or *probably*, or *almost certainly* to suggest the degree of probability. Wheelwright has devised a "modal spectrum" to suggest the various degrees of certainty represented in a conclusion:[12]

> It is necessarily so (absolutely certain)
> It is virtually certain (beyond reasonable doubt)
> It is likely (probable)
> It is a toss-up
> It is unlikely (improbable)

---

[11] A reader may recall that earlier we said deduction concerned classes, not cause and effect. Rewording will make clear that this syllogism deals with classes: All things that are things that will eliminate ignorance are also things that will eliminate racial prejudice (the classes are "things that eliminate ignorance," and "things that will eliminate racial prejudice"). The minor premise puts education in one of the classes, and, in keeping with the major premise, therefore it also goes into the other class.

[12] *Valid Thinking*, p. 34.

It is virtually impossible ("out of the question")
It is absolutely impossible

"In a modal argument," Wheelwright states, "it is never legitimate to ascribe a higher modality to the conclusion than is found in the premises. Indeed, where both premises fall short of certainty, it is sometimes questionable whether any conclusion at all can legitimately be drawn." While the logician as logician may hesitate to draw conclusions from modal arguments, as an individual he and everyone else must constantly do so. You will probably survive the night; your instructor in speech will probably attend class the next time it is scheduled; he may ask you something about the assignment, and so you conclude that you should read it. And when the logician starts for his class and makes the decision whether to cross the busy intersection at any particular moment, he is weighing probabilities.

In constructing and analyzing arguments in public speaking, the task is to discover the modality and ensure that the conclusion reflects the modality of the premises. This is not to say, however, that we should reject a conclusion having low probability. Whether we will act on low probability depends on the cost should the probabality not materialize (hence, we will spend $.50 on the church bazaar even though our chances of winning are small), the cost should the probability materialize (young men spend considerable sums on life insurance even though the probability that they will soon die is very small), or the reward should it materialize (many men will invest $1000 on a remote chance of fabulous riches).

TOULMIN'S LAYOUT OF AN ARGUMENT

Anyone who tries to apply the tests of syllogisms to practical arguments soon encounters difficulty. To restate all arguments in terms of classes oftentimes—as in the example from Senator Fulbright's speech—leads to distortion of the original argument. A valid or invalid argument may finally be evolved, but often with little assurance that the argument tested is the argument originally advanced.

Among the many attempts to improve on the syllogism, one that is relatively new and seems to have potential for public speaking is the system evolved by Stephen Toulmin, an English philosopher who has no hesitancy in showing his small regard for traditional logic.[13] Increasingly, textbooks on argumentation and debate are adapting Toulmin's system. Clearly, it is easier to diagram an argument using Toulmin's scheme than it is to form a syllogism; and, quite apart from the other advantages Toulmin claims for his system, that is a substantial one for the speaker. However, that very advantage of the system is also its weakness. Syllogisms are not difficult to

---

[13] His system is developed in *The Uses of Argument,* first published in 1958, but now made available in a paperback edition (1964) by the Cambridge University Press.

develop if one is unconcerned with testing their soundness. But the purpose in casting applied reason into quasi-syllogisms or enthymemes is to test it. Toulmin's layout lacks the devices whereby arguments can adequately be tested. However, there is insightful analysis of arguments. Oftentimes if an argument is stated in full, with the points put in their proper relation, we are able nearly intuitively to see weakness.[14]

Toulmin sought to discover how a reasoner, after making an assertion, could best answer two questions: "What have you got to go on?" and "How did you get there?" The first question is answered by a citation of what the reasoner hopes his questioner will regard as facts, and what Toulmin calls *data*. If the questioner is satisfied with the facts, the question of how the reasoner arrived at his conclusion has yet to be answered. As Toulmin states,

> Our task is no longer to strengthen the ground on which our argument is constructed, but is rather to show that, taking these data as a starting point, the step to the original claim or conclusion is an appropriate and legitimate one. At this point, therefore, what are needed are general, hypothetical statements, which can act as bridges, and authorize the sort of step to which our particular argument commits us.[15]

For example, we hear Vivian Smith addressed as "Mr. Smith." From the datum ("Mr.") we arrive at the conclusion that Vivian Smith is a male. But how did we get there? By using as a bridge the belief that "All individuals addressed as Mr. are male." This bridge, Toulmin calls a *warrant*. His diagram for an argument in its simplest form is this:

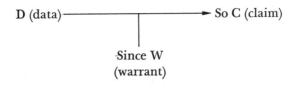

In popular argument, the appeal to the warrant is usually implicit. We would not, for example, in stating our conclusion about Mr. Smith, state the warrant. Rather, we would say: "Vivian Smith was addressed as Mr., so Vivian is a male."

Three refinements to this basic layout are what Toulmin calls the "backing for the warrant" (designated B), "modal qualifiers" (Q), and "conditions of exception or rebuttal" (R). The backing of a warrant is the proof of the warrant. Suppose an argument was stated as follows:

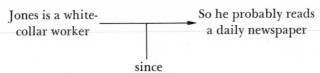

Jones is a white-
collar worker

since

So he probably reads
a daily newspaper

Nearly all white-collar workers
read a daily newspaper

The backing for the warrant may be the results of a survey that showed that 87 percent of all white-collar workers read a daily newspaper. Our example also illustrates the use of a "modal qualifier." As in enthymematic or syllogistic reasoning, a conclusion in Toulmin's layout can be stated no more positively than the least positive premise. Thus, there cannot be certainty that Jones reads a newspaper. A condition of exception might be added if we state: "Unless Jones happens to be blind, he probably reads a daily newspaper."

Illustrating the several conditions of the layout, Toulmin gives these examples:[16]

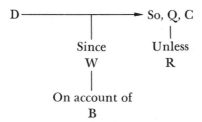

D ———— So, Q, C

Since   Unless
W   R

On account of
B

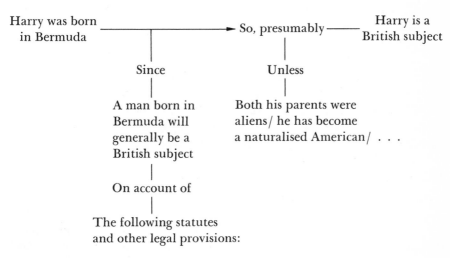

Harry was born
in Bermuda

So, presumably

Harry is a
British subject

Since   Unless

A man born in
Bermuda will
generally be a
British subject

Both his parents were
aliens/ he has become
a naturalised American/ . . .

On account of

The following statutes
and other legal provisions:

16 *The Uses of Argument*, pp. 104–105.

Reasoning by Generalization

Reasoning by *generalization* (similar to *induction* in logic) is the process of using examples to arrive at a conclusion about the class of things the examples represent. Generalization provides most of the premises used in enthymemes. If it is known that "All men are mortal," or that "Most college textbooks are expensive," the premises have been proved by generalization.

As the two above premises indicate, a generalization can vary in the extent to which it covers a class. If a check is made of the system of government used in eight cities with populations between 50,000 and 100,000 and all are found to have a mayor-council government, a conclusion concerning the mode of government for such cities could be formulated.

The generality of the conclusion could be limited to just those cities sampled: "Eight cities with populations between 50,000 and 100,000 have a mayor-council type of government." Or it could be extended beyond the sample, as this series of conclusions illustrates: "Many cities of that size have a mayor-council government," "Most cities of that size have a mayor-council form of government," "All cities of that size have a mayor-council government."

The probability that the conclusions are true range from a certainty with the first to low probability with the last. The first conclusion includes only those cities included in the sample. Hence, unless the accuracy of the sample is questioned, the conclusion is certainly true. Similarly, had the conclusion been "Some cities have a mayor-council government" the eight examples would give certainty to the conclusion. On the other hand, the sample of eight would lend little probability that all such cities have a mayor-council government. Should a continued examination of cities reveal an example of manager-council form (a negative instance), the generalization would be proved untrue.

Even though a generalization may have logical validity, it may lack psychological validity, or the reverse. Suppose an examination of 200 cities with 50,000 to 100,000 population revealed but one type of government. Most people would still be skeptical of an all-inclusive generalization. Generalizations that extend beyond the sample must seem possible and probable if they are to be accepted by an audience.

Whether a generalization has high or low probability of extending to a large number of cases has no necessary correlation to whether the generalization should serve as a basis for action. Botulism found in only three cans of tuna among thousands packed by a particular company would yield low probability that any other particular can would be affected. Yet most of us would regard as illogical the housewife who used tuna from one of the cans to make a casserole.

USING GENERALIZATIONS

Use of examples to prove a general statement is common in speech-making. As described in Chapter 3, examples are also used in exposition. Our interest here is with examples as proof of a statement, although to the extent that the examples are elaborated, the meaning of the general statement is made clearer. Note particularly in these excerpts from speeches how the generality of the conclusion varies.

1. *To Prove an Attribute of a Whole Class:*

> No revolutionary movement, no internal conflict of any magnitude can fail to affect the peace of the world. The French Revolution, which was wholly internal at the beginning, affected the peace of the world to such an extent that it brought on a world war which lasted some 25 years. Can anyone say that our Civil War did not affect the peace of the world? At this very moment, who would deny that the condition of Russia, with internal conflicts raging in all parts of that great Empire, does not affect the peace of the world . . . ?[17]

The class of things is "revolutionary movements." The attribute, "affect peace." The generalization about the whole class is based on three examples. Note that while the attribute being considered involves cause and effect, the method of proving the relation is by enumeration rather than by any of Mill's Methods.

2. *To Prove an Attribute of Most of a Class*

> . . . Most of the major problems of our day present themselves in moral terms. . . . Let me give you three instances. In the wealthiest nation in the world, at least five million families still live in squalid but remediable poverty. They are a minority. They do not have the votes to force the issue of their misfortune into the front rank of public issues. They depend, for remedies, upon the alert conscience of the majority. . . .
>
> Or take the issue of the rights and status of our colored citizens. . . . "The unfinished work" which Lincoln left us . . . can never be accomplished unless there are enough white men and women who resist to the core of their being the moral evil of treating any of God's children as essentially inferior.
>
> Nor is this simply a question of our own national community. . . .
>
> Here we are in the Atlantic world, 16 percent of the world's peoples consuming 70 percent of the world's wealth. We cannot be indifferent to the moral implications of this gigantic gap.[18]

The class of things is "major problems of our day." The attribute, "present themselves in moral terms." The generalization, based on three examples, is extended to "most" of the class.

[17] From a speech by Henry Cabot Lodge, printed in *Contemporary Forum: American Speeches on Twentieth-Century Issues,* Ernest J. Wrage and Barnet Baskerville, Eds. (New York: Harper & Row, Publishers, 1962).

[18] From a speech by Adlai Stevenson, printed in *Contemporary Forum.*

3. *To Prove an Attribute of a Portion of a Class*

In Cuba, one of our Latin American neighbors, Fidel Castro denounces the United States. In Iraq, until 1958 an active member of the Baghdad pact, crowds jeer at an American diplomat, and a Communist-dominated regime comes to power. The mayor of Manila, speaking on Edward R. Murrow's *Small World* TV program, tells us why we are losing friends in Asia in terms so bitter as to befit a foe rather than a friend of the United States.

As these and other incidents are reported from around the globe, Americans ask themselves: Why are these non-Western peoples against the West— and particularly why are they against the United States?[19]

The class of things is "non-Western nations." The characteristic, "against the west." The extent of the generalization is not precisely indicated. However, the reference to "other incidents from around the globe" indicates that the speaker intended the generalization to be extended beyond the three nations specifically mentioned.

4. *To Prove an Attribute of a Limited Portion of a Class*

Even in less turbulent areas, U.S. interests are suffering. Pakistan, formerly one of our staunchest allies, has been disillusioned by U.S. shipments of arms to India, while the U.S. refuses to consider the possibility that India may commit aggression against Pakistan as it did a short time ago against Goa. . . . Greece, where the Cold War first turned hot, has now at U.S. urging signed a twelve-point treaty with communist Bulgaria; and Turkey, our staunch ally and an enemy of communism, has with U.S. approval, signed a trade pact with the Soviet Union.[20]

The class of things is "U.S. interests in various areas." The attribute, "are suffering." The generalization applies to "areas," meaning at least two. Three examples are given. Thus, this generalization does not go beyond the examples given.

Note that the examples used clarify what the speaker meant by "interests are suffering." Any trade or military pact between a Western and Communist country is a setback for American interests.

TESTING GENERALIZATIONS

The crucial tests of generalization concern the nature of the sample used as a basis for the conclusion: Were there enough samples? Were they representative of the class? Were they relevant to the conclusion?

1. *Have a sufficient number of samples been taken to support the gen-*

[19] From a speech by Vera Micheles Dean, printed in *Representative American Speeches: 1959–1960*, Lester Thonssen, Ed.; Vol. 32, No. 4 of "The Reference Shelf" (New York: The H. W. Wilson Co., 1960).

[20] From a speech by Strom Thurmond, printed in *Vital Speeches of the Day*, Vol. 21 (February 15, 1965).

eralization? Whether there are sufficient samples depends on the generality of the conclusion. When a generalization is carefully qualified, there is no minimum number of instances that must be used in support. A "some" conclusion needs but two or three examples. Thus, there were sufficient examples to prove that United States interests are suffering in certain areas and that some non-Western nations are anti-American.

When a generalization is, or approaches being, all-inclusive, the size of the sample must be increased greatly. How many typewriters would have to be checked before one could say with reasonable probability of being correct that every machine of a certain make is better than every machine of another make: three of each, 20, 500? One could not know with full certainty that all machines of one brand are superior to the other unless he actually compared each and every typewriter made by the two companies. So that his conclusion would continue to be certain, he would need to continue his check, or manufacture of the machines would have to stop. Though each machine coming off the assembly line until this moment has fit the generalization, how could he know that the next examples would also fit? He could not know unless he presumed to predict the future.

Statistics provide a useful way of indicating the generality of a conclusion. The following generalization concerning cause and effect is based on enumeration rather than on Mill's Methods. The extent of the probability that there is a causal relation between education and unemployment is suggested by the figures cited.

> While we continue to neglect public education, the correlation between unemployment and education continues to mount. Of the 4.1 million Americans who were unemployed in March, 1959, one million, or about one-fourth of the total, had less than an elementary school education and 2.8 million, or about two-thirds, had less than a high school education.[21]

The enumeration does not, of course, eliminate the possibility that another cause leads to both unemployment and lack of education.

2. *Are the samples representative of their class?* The more nearly a conclusion approaches all-inclusiveness, the more important it becomes that listeners learn whether negative instances have been considered. If a generalization includes only some of a class, all that needs be shown is that some have the attribute, irrespective of whether the rest do. If a generalization is all inclusive, such as "All men are mortal," a single negative instance will disprove the generalization.

Lord Snow said that "scientists are not much different from other men," a generalization that appears to include all scientists. The support for the generalization came from a study of how scientists behaved. The study was directed toward discovery of negative instances, toward disproving that

21 From a speech by J. William Fulbright, printed in *Vital Speeches of the Day*, Vol. 29 (June 1, 1963).

scientists are "normal." The study showed that "the really great scientists seemed to vary from a few neutral characters to a large number who were depressingly 'normal.' The only gleam of comfort was to be found in the life of Jerome Cardan; and Cardan wasn't anything like enough to outweigh all the others."[22] The reporting and assigning of weight to the negative instance both supports and more precisely qualifies the generalization.

3. *Are the examples relevant to the conclusion?* The examples must illustrate the attributes considered in the generalization. Presumably Lord Snow's friend actually considered scientists rather than non-scientists. The generalization about United States' interests abroad would be challenged by some people on the basis that the examples do not illustrate the attribute mentioned in the generalization. The attribute is that American interests are suffering. However, two examples state that the particular condition taken as evidence of suffering was brought about by encouragement of the United States. Hence, at least those individuals responsible for the condition would question that it illustrates damage to United States' interests.

COMMON ERRORS IN REASONING BY GENERALIZATION

The general areas of errors have been suggested. Two types of errors in generalization should perhaps be emphasized here, although they are as much the fault of listeners as of speakers. The errors have less to do with technical adequacy of a generalization than with whether a listener is able to evaluate the merit of the generalization.

1. *Failure to express clearly the modality that adheres to the generalization.* Even if the speaker is clear in his own mind about the extent to which a generalization is qualified, listeners—as illustration after illustration is given—can easily be misled to assume that the generality of the conclusion is greater than is justified or intended. The generalization about the attitude of non-Western nations could easily be extended by a listener to include most or all such nations.

2. *Failure to distinguish between illustrative and probative use of examples.* As pointed out in Chapter 3, examples and comparisons are useful in exposition. Through them a concept is made clear. The tests of argument are not applied to examples used to illustrate, for the tests assume that a speaker intends his instances to be used as proof.

It is sometimes difficult to determine whether a speaker intends to use examples to form a generalization or to illustrate one already formed. The distinction is unimportant if listeners are sufficiently critical. The careful listener, on finding too few illustrations cited, will reject the conclusion, whatever the speaker intends. If he already accepts the conclusion, it will not matter that a speaker inadequately proved the point.

22 The speech is reprinted in Chapter 16.

Reasoning by Analogy

Reasoning by analogy is the process of showing through comparison that attributes of an object or event already known are present in a related object or event. Whereas generalization yields conclusions about all, or portions, of a class, analogy yields conclusions about a single member of a class. You may, for example, discover that New York and Philadelphia are alike in a great number of ways, and then conclude by analogy that, as New York has a subway system, so has Philadelphia.

When used to prove a point, a fully developed analogy first shows the number of ways in which things are alike. This comparison leads to a generalized conclusion, "because the cases are alike in those respects, there is a probability that they are alike in all, or nearly all, other respects." A specific application of the generalization is then made to prove the probability that a particular attribute known to be present in one case is also present in the other case.

USING ANALOGIES

Analogies frequently occur in speechmaking—as often, however, to illustrate a point (see Chapter 3) as to prove a point. The greatly truncated form that is typical of an analogy used in public address usually makes it difficult to determine which use is intended. Rarely is the basis established for assuming similarity in all, or nearly all, attributes. The usual practice is to show the attributes in one case and to assume that the audience knows the equivalent attribute in the other case.

1. *To prove by comparing sequences of events*

> A frightening historical parallel has occurred to me with increasing frequency in recent weeks. Fifteen or sixteen centuries ago, the Roman empire was all-powerful, rich, successful—and also complacent. Neither the Roman emperors nor the Roman Senate could bring themselves to be overly concerned with the crude and boorish people to the north. Emperors were judged by the public entertainment they arranged, and the wealth and substance of the empire were dissipated in lavish consumption. When anyone was so inconsiderate as to call attention to the gathering clouds on the horizon, he was denounced as a prophet of gloom and purged for un-Roman activity. In 1958, the critic is charged with "selling America short!"[23]

This analogy assumes that the factors that led to the downfall of the Roman Empire have their equivalents in the United States. The conclusion: just as these factors led to the downfall of the Empire, there is a probability

[23] From a speech by J. William Fulbright, printed in *Representative American Speeches: 1958–1959*, A. Craig Baird, Ed., Vol. 31, No. 3 of "The Reference Shelf."

that they will lead to the downfall of the United States. Note, however, that the speaker did not state explicitly his startling conclusion.

2. *To prove by comparing processes*

And we who search for truth or for wisdom ultimately must come to the conclusion that wisdom consists of the capacity to confront disturbing ideas, even intolerable ideas with equanimity.

Isn't it astonishing to you—it certainly is to me—that not until the fifteenth century did man invent perspective in painting, so that we could look into, and not just at, a picture? Isn't it astonishing to you that it wasn't until the nineteenth century, and the latter part of it, that professional painters had the courage to do what every child has always done in color—to paint in metaphor, to paint a face that is red with rage or green with envy? To put color into shadows? Isn't it astonishing to you that it wasn't until the impressionists that men discovered that cool colors seem to recede and warm colors seem to move forward, and that you can use color to give the illusion of depth?

Why do I mention these examples from painting? Because there is nothing there until you have been shown what to expect is going to be there. It is impossible for you or for me to see literally, simply—to see as we would have seen before the impressionists came along. You cannot look at the beauty of a cathedral, you cannot look at a bowl of fruit, and see it the way it was seen before Monet or Cezanne. And if this is true about something so simple as seeing, how much more true is it in the arena of ideas?

We seem to think that scientists are people who think very clearly, very systematically, and accumulatively, but the history of any science will give you, I think, an example of the most astounding nonsense that was long held and that man overcame only through great intellectual effort.[24]

The comparison is between seeing and thinking. It is based on the assumption that the activities are parallel and that therefore the difficulties in seeing clearly and objectively have their equivalent in thinking. Note that the speaker suggested in the last paragraph that his point could also be proved by generalization.

3. *To prove or illustrate by comparing unlike objects*

Are the universities to be stripped of students [by the draft for the Korean conflict] in order to defend our cultural heritage? The young of college age are the seed corn of a society and a nation. To survive must we eat our seed corn? And if we do, can we survive?[25]

This analogy assumes that there is sufficient parallel between seed corn and youth to support the conclusion: what will happen when seed corn is destroyed will also happen to the nation should youth be destroyed. Booker T. Washington's analogy between the search for a solution to Negroes' prob-

[24] From a speech by Leo Rosten, printed in *Vital Speeches of the Day,* Vol. 31 (April 15, 1965).
[25] From a speech by Adlai Stevenson, printed in *Contemporary Forum.*

lems and a ship in search of water (see Chapter 3) is similarly based on comparison of unlike things. Comparisons between unlike things are called *figurative analogies.*

TESTING ANALOGIES

Proof by analogy involves the assumption that because things are alike in certain respects, they will also be alike in another respect. Hence, analogy, like generalization, uses instances to draw a conclusion. Part of the test of an analogy, therefore, concerns the nature of the sample. Is it large enough in number and sufficiently representative to justify the conclusion?

Further, whether analogies can legitimately be drawn at all depends on how alike the things are that are being compared.

1. *Are there sufficient similarities to justify an assumption of additional similarities?* If one shows that several things are alike in a large number of characteristics, he will then have grounds for assuming that they will be alike in some additional characteristic. Conversely, the fewer the similarities, the less chance that the objects being compared will be alike in another and unknown characteristic. This test would lead many listeners to reject the analogy between the Roman Empire and the United States. The similarities are so remote that there is little reason to assume that the conclusion (that the United States, too, will fall) had validity.

2. *Are there sufficient dissimilarities in the cases compared to cast doubt on the conclusion?* Because proof by analogy involves an intermediate general conclusion, an analogy must be checked by a search for dissimilarities between the objects being compared. One can generally succeed if he searches for similarities between two objects. To avoid being beguiled by similarities, one should also search for dissimilarities. Imagine the similarities that can be found between Imperial and Falcon automobiles; yet imagine the magnitude of the error if one argued that because of the similarities cited, prices also must be similar. The analogy drawn between the United States and the Roman Empire could easily have been rejected on this test.

3. *Are the similarities relevant to the unknown factor of interest?* Suppose the question is whether a certain city should seek to organize a professional football team. Like three other cities that already have a team, it has two high schools, at least a half dozen major manufacturing plants, a city manager, and an airport. One could well question whether such similarities have any relevance to the point under consideration. What are the factors that were important in the other cities? Are those conditions present in the city in question?

4. *Are the things compared in the same class or are they sufficiently related to justify an attempt at comparison?* When the intermediate general

conclusion is proved, the audience has a basis for judging whether any comparisons are justified. Usually, however, the justifiability of the comparison is assumed and the speaker moves quickly to state his point. Can one compare youth and seed corn or the process of seeing with the process of thinking or the Roman Empire with the United States?

COMMON ERRORS IN REASONING BY ANALOGY

The errors considered here are those that lead an audience to assign higher probative value to an analogy than it deserves.

1. *Failure to establish the legitimacy of the comparison.* The uses of analogy illustrated above all assume that there are grounds for making a comparison. Of course, if an audience already grants the similarity between the things being compared, the legitimacy need not be proved. Often, however, a glossing-over of the question of whether a comparison is legitimate leads an audience to attach more weight to the comparison than is warranted.

2. *Failure to distinguish between illustrative and probative use of analogy.* This is often a fault of the hearers as well as the speaker. Did the speaker really intend to prove anything by his comparison between youth and seed corn? Or was he simply illustrating a point? If the analogy was intended as illustration rather than proof, the tests applied to it should be those of exposition. Whatever a speaker intended, if an analogy is inadequately developed for probative uses, it should only be assigned value as an illustration.

Proving Bedrock Statements

The discussion of reasoning in the previous pages has emphasized the importance of factual statements and described how statements may be used in proof. In contrast to attention given to how statements of fact are used to prove a higher level statement, such as a premise to an enthymeme or a generalization, attention should be given to the ways fundamental factual statements are proved. For example, statements about the impact of Urban Renewal in New York, Washington, Baltimore, and Philadelphia can be used to support a generalization about Urban Renewal. The discussion has so far been based on the assumption that each of the specific statements would be accepted as true. Suppose, however, that they are not accepted. How does a speaker establish the truth of such bedrock statements as "Urban renewal in West Philadelphia provided 623 housing units of greater convenience and safety and at less cost to the residents than housing that had been there before," or "This piece of metal weighs 6 pounds, 3 ounces?"

Our discussion will include consideration of *facts, evidence, belief, truth,* and *proof.* The terms are related as follows: selected facts are used as evidence to instill belief in the truth of a statement. The statement has been proved if the evidence led a listener to believe it is true.

The basic unit of proof, then, is one of more facts that serve as evidence. Bertrand Russell states:

> Everything that there is in the world I call a "fact." The sun is a fact; Caesar's crossing of the Rubicon was a fact. . . . If I make a statement, my making it is a fact, and if it is true there is a further fact in virtue of which it is true, but not if it is false.[26]

From this definition it follows, as Lord Russell explains, that a fact is "something which is there, whether anybody thinks so or not." The speaker is, of course, interested both in what is there and how he can convince others of its existence, for only if they agree that a statement he makes has approximate correspondence to reality will they be convinced by his argument.

That is the function of the proof of a bedrock proposition: to show the correspondence between the proposition and the reality it purports to represent. At best, however, the correspondence can be only approximate, for language, though adequate for most communicative purposes (including communication of simple facts), is an imprecise instrument.

Fortunately for speakers most audiences already know a great many things related to a particular subject, even though they may not have experienced them directly. Lord Russell says that,

> When we ask . . . "How do we come by our knowledge of the world?," subjectivity is in order. What each man knows is, in an important sense, dependent upon his own individual experience: he knows what he has seen and heard, what he has read and what he has been told, and also what, from these data, he has been able to infer.[27]

Thus audiences believe that there is a Mississippi River, that rockets have landed on the moon, that penicillin will cure many ailments, and that Caesar crossed the Rubicon. Further, they will accept without challenge many statements of fact from a speaker.

Not every bedrock statement, then, will have to be proved. For those crucial bits of evidence that need proof, a speaker can rely on demonstration of the fact itself or authoritative opinion about the fact.

On occasion the facts that purport to be represented in a statement can be observed. With a piece of dry ice a speaker can demonstrate that certain solids pass to a gaseous state without going through a liquid state. Statements about the dilapidation of a school building can be verified by a tour of the building. And in the process the meaning as well as validity of statements about the dilapidation are established.

[26] *Human Knowledge*, p. 143.
[27] *Human Knowledge*, pp. xi–xii.

At other times the facts in a statement are not immediately verifiable, but are susceptible of relatively easy verification. An audience can check the authenticity of a speaker's statement that a particular brand of coffee costs $.07 cents a pound less at the chain store than it does at the corner grocery.

Usually, however, a speaker cannot rely on immediate or relatively direct verification of the facts contained in his statement. No one can now observe Caesar crossing the Rubicon. The rate of unemployment, the impact of the federal reserve bank discount rate, the effect of a vitamin B deficiency are not facts that can be dragged to the platform and made to perform for skeptical listeners. Most of the facts that concern a speaker must be verified through the use of statements about the facts.

When something cannot be directly observed or experienced and is not already known, it can be verified only by using statements of opinion attesting to its truth or factual content. The only way, for example, that the population of a particular city can be established is by citing census figures. Regardless of the way census figures are presented, they represent someone's belief or opinion that they are approximately correct. To circulate the census reports may help an audience to understand that there is a more authoritative opinion than the speaker's to support the figure given; but it is still opinion that is being presented, not "what is there." If "something that is there" can be characterized as a rate of unemployment or the impact of the discount rate, its nature can be known only through someone's opinion.

In addition to facts concerning objects or phenomena, there are facts or pseudo-facts concerning judgment or taste. "The movie is the best of the past 10 years," "The Queen is a beautiful woman," and "Jazz is to be preferred over rock-and-roll" are all statements based largely on individual opinion. Propositions of that type frequently enter into speechmaking.

Much evidence used in speaking, then, depends on opinion and will be effective only if the opinion is acceptable to an audience. Chapter 15, on writing a persuasive speech, describes in detail how opinion should be tested before it is used in a speech.

BASING THE REASONS ON SOUND VALUES

Psychological validity depends on the values represented in an argument being acceptable, as well as on the reasoning appearing sound to an audience.

Selecting the Reasons

The easiest way to ensure that the reasons offered in support of a proposition are based on values accepted by an audience is to select the reasons carefully. There are usually many reasons that can be offered to show the proposal's desirability. For different audiences, different reasons will be effective. The man who is unable to find employment and wishes to keep his children from the same fate may be deeply impressed by an argument showing that a high school education lessens the probability of unemployment. On the other hand, the man who is secure in his job may be more impressed by an argument showing that dropouts are more likely to become delinquent than are youngsters who stay in school.

Characterizing the Reasons

As Aristotle pointed out, a specific event, condition, or object can be interpreted in more than one way. The man who jumps into a rushing river to save a dog may be called either heroic or foolhardy. Which characterization seems appropriate will depend on the values of the individual who makes the judgment. Similarly, a speaker may call a specific proposal costly when speaking to one audience, and inexpensive when speaking to another. A proposal to expend a million dollars to raise teachers' salaries may seem far less expensive to an audience of teachers than it does to an audience having large holdings in real estate.

Interpreting things in different ways and selecting varying arguments to support a proposal—particularly if the selection leads a speaker in one instance to use arguments based on a certain value and in another instance to use arguments based on a conflicting value—raise practical and ethical questions.

Chapter 4 points out that persuasion is based on an identity of interest between the speaker and his audience. Listeners assume that the speaker believes in the desirability of his proposal and that he regards as cogent the reasons used to support it. Ordinarily the speaker is anxious to make clear that he does believe in the desirability of his proposal and for the reasons he uses in the speech. Perhaps a speaker could, if he wanted, explain that he is detached from the proposal or some of the reasons he advances. However, as any teacher knows who has tried to explain a concept with which he disagrees, the separation of idea and communicator is exceedingly difficult.

The ethical problem is whether a speaker has the right to shift ground unless his beliefs shift, or to use arguments he himself does not accept. Chapter 10 deals more extensively with the ethics of speaking. Here we will only point out that separation between advocacy and belief makes a substantive alteration to the accepted procedures of speechmaking, and therefore, unless the audience is told of the change, is unethical. Part of the effectiveness of an argument comes from the assumption that the speaker believes in it. If that aspect of effectiveness is actually absent, an audience has the right to know it. To fail to tell them allows them to give more weight to the argument than it deserves.

The practical problem is that a speaker who shifts position between speeches or within a speech may be considered a sophist, liar, or fool. A charge of inconsistency is one of the most devastating arguments that can be leveled against a man. So powerful a speaker as Daniel Webster was accused of inconsistency in his famous "Seventh of March" speech, even though he carefully sought to show that he was not inconsistent with earlier positions. The most that can be said against Webster is that he changed his mind. It is a paradox of our society, however, that a politician rarely is allowed to change his mind; and in "Ichabod," Whittier mourned "the lost leader"; and Theodore Parker preached a funeral oration on the same theme.[28]

Changing the Values

Persuasive speaking characteristically attempts to convince listeners to adjust the priority assigned to particular goals or to realize that needs can be met in unanticipated ways. Such persuasion does not, however, involve a change in values as much as it does a utilization of existing values. To convince an individual that this brand of automobile is more suited to him than the one he had expected to buy involves using existing values to set a new specific goal.

As pointed out in the previous chapter, a speaker may seek to change attitudes if he wishes. If the attitude is of long standing and permeating, the task will be difficult, although in other respects not materially different from any other persuasive situation.

SUMMARY

This chapter has treated ways a speaker demonstrates to an audience that the reasons offered in support of his proposal bear a sound relation to the proposal and that the statements of fact contained in the reason are true. The methods a speaker uses are principally adaptations of formal reasoning.

While this chapter has emphasized applied argument's dependence on logic, the final test of an argument is whether the reasoning seems sound to an audience. Both because they are at times less demanding than the logician and because they are capable of understanding a truncated line of reasoning, audiences may regard an argument as sound even though it fails to meet the tests appropriate to the formal reasoning on which it is based. At other times listeners will remain unconvinced by an argument even though it meets all the tests of reasoning.

[28] An exception gave us one of the most moving speeches in our history. Senator Arthur Vandenberg, on January 10, 1945, told the Senate why he changed his position on international involvement for the United States. The speech is available in *Representative American Speeches*, Vol. 18, No. 3 of "The Reference Shelf."

Additionally, the chapter has suggested methods a speaker may use to ensure that the values associated with his reasoning are acceptable to an audience and thus give force to the argument.

Chapter 15 will deal with the problems of preparing a specific persuasive speech.

6   Language

Each year thousands of speeches are heard in our country, and most of them pass unnoticed on the national scene because of their local or microcosmic themes. The few addresses carried by wire services are spoken usually at important occasions, such as the inauguration of a president of the United States, the visit of the Soviet premier to United Nations headquarters, the announcement of a space-age accomplishment, and the statement by a succeeding president after his predecessor's assassination. Yet of these four particular events occurring in the early 1960s, only one, John F. Kennedy's inauguration, will probably fire memories and emotions in the years to come because of a speech delivered at the occasion. There is every likelihood that Nikita Khrushchev's shoe-pounding at the General Assembly session will be remembered before his address; that Astronaut Scott Carpenter's momentous space flight will be recalled before the President's congratulatory speech; and that the confusion following Kennedy's assassination will be thought of before Lyndon Johnson's first official address to the nation as President at Andrews Airport.

Why in all probability will the spoken words from only one of these four events be recalled? Because only one speech stirred the imagination of listeners and rose above the occasion itself. And, fittingly, the now widely known address of 1355 words, delivered on January 20, 1961, was, in a sense, no chance comer to fame. Kennedy deliberately studied 33 inaugural addresses before his own and set out as deliberately to rise above the occasion by matching the classic examples of Thomas Jefferson, Abraham Lincoln, Woodrow Wilson, and Franklin D. Roosevelt.[1]

Unfortunately, an attempt consciously to write a superior speech and to use words effectively, or an ability to identify an allegory, to distinguish

[1] Edmond Le Breton, "Kennedy Busy Penning Speech," Associated Press release, January 13, 1961. Kennedy considered Lincoln's second, Wilson's first, and "some" of Roosevelt's inaugurals as inspirational examples for emulation. For a scholarly study of the Kennedy address, see Donald L. Wolfarth, "John Kennedy in the Tradition of Inaugural Speeches," *Quarterly Journal of Speech*, Vol. 47 (April 1961), pp. 124–132.

aporia from zeugma, and to understand differences between oral and written style does not end necessarily in expressions that rise above the ordinary. Instead, this deliberate attention to word-choice, this understanding of stylistic devices, and this conscious interest in speech composition proves only that a student speaker studied his lesson well—it does not imply that he will speak like Lincoln, Roosevelt, or Kennedy. Nor is an imitative use of language and style even desirable.

The aim of this chapter, therefore, is modest—to make students aware of language and, hopefully, to make them slightly more imaginative in their choice of words when composing and delivering public addresses.

THE USE OF WORDS

When handing down his famous *McCulloch v. Maryland* decision, John Marshall, fourth Chief Justice of the Supreme Court, said, "Such is the character of human language, that no word conveys to the mind, in all situations, one single definite idea." "Almost all compositions contain words," reminded Marshall, "which, taken in their rigorous sense, would convey a meaning different from that which is obviously intended."[2] Because a public speaker conveys his message principally through the linguistic media, his problem is at once manifold and challenging. He becomes something akin to a symphony conductor who is trying to get each of his musicians to react with correct tonal proportion, exact volume requirement, and precise rhythm pattern demanded at any one of countless moments during a symphonic score. Or a speaker is like a football coach who hopes for the perfectly executed double reverse, when every player meets his blocking assignment, and when every man is in proper position at any given second of play.

Precision Possible in Use of Words

The problem of controlling an orchestra, guiding a football play, or conveying the exact thought from speaker to listener may seem hopeless from the beginning. Yet precision is not totally impossible since symphonic music has its Leonard Bernstein, football its George Halas, and public speaking its Winston Churchill as reminders that accuracy is a reasonable goal in a public performance. A speaker, therefore, cannot camouflage his personal obligation to communicate accurately with his listeners by shrugging his shoulders and exclaiming, "Why worry about accuracy; it's impossible to achieve whenever the human element is involved!" As the conductor strives continually for near-perfect renditions of musical scores or a coach runs through plays repeatedly in hopes of their proper execution, so a speaker should work towards narrowing the chances of failure in oral communication through proper use of words.

[2] Henry Wheaton, *Reports of Cases argued and adjudged in the Supreme Court of the United States, 1816–1827* (Philadelphia, New York, 1818–1827), Vol. 4, p. 414.

As our civilization increases in complexity, as science advances, and as most fields of learning undertake more and more research, new words are coined to express meaning with greater accuracy so that the catalogue of over a half-million so-called English words increases each year. Not too many years ago, for example, psychology students contented themselves with knowing a few terms as *claustrophobia, acrophobia,* and *olophobia* when speaking of intense fears. Today, in contrast, not even the psychology teacher, much less his students, can name the 217 different phobias classified by psychiatrists. Faced with limited memory power, students satisfy themselves with knowing that Blakiston's *New Gould Medical Dictionary* describes all 217 phobias, and if they need this information they may trudge to the nearest library. Not too many years ago, a child stood wide-eyed before an ice cream counter confronted with three choices: vanilla, strawberry, or chocolate, and, if lucky, that marvel of flavors, tutti-frutti. Today, a child needs a well-read parent to translate the meaning of over one hundred different flavors—from ambrosia to guava and from passion fruit to youngberry. Students toss off in their conversations new terms as *laser light, DNA helix,* and *existentialism* with the same confidence and alacrity their parents as students once used the words *Gamma rays, X-chromosome,* and *Nietzscheism.*[3]

Problem of Abstract Words

Yet in making more progress towards *exact* classification of knowledge, words that are vague and highly *abstract* to most people still sneak into our language. Thus a self-styled expert in government may use descriptive nomenclatures as *Afro-Asian bloc, neutralist nations,* and *conservatives* in a way that would appall the serious student of politics.

Many speakers as well as listeners, in their efforts to appear up-to-date and well-read, knowingly sacrifice language clarity on the altar of conformity. Rather than appear outside the mainstream of the times, for example, they adopt a me-too-ism attitude when vague about meaning: that is, they absorb reviews, editorials, critical writings, and news summaries in a way that allows them as speakers to talk knowledgeably or as listeners to nod knowingly when the speaker comments on the Ionesco quality in the latest shockmovie in town, or talks critically of *Who's Afraid of Virginia Woolf?,* or expounds the virtues of architect Stone over Yamasaki.

Meaning Found in Way Speaker Uses Words

Since a speaker concerns himself with audience directness, there is the temptation on his part to let one or two words signify a whole range of

[3] For two interesting essays on the subject of language change in today's fast-paced world, see James L. Jackson, "Air Force Language in the Making," *Quarterly Journal of Speech,* Vol. 42 (February 1956), pp. 14–18; and W. Norwood Brigance, "On Talking a New Language," *Quarterly Journal of Speech,* Vol. 44 (October 1958), pp. 299–302.

explanation. Worse, many a poor speaker will retreat at times to a you-know-what-I-mean position when his ideas are not clear even to himself. This self-centeredness allows him on occasion to infer that if he uses a word or speaks of an idea, then the audience understands at once what he means. He implies by this kind of thinking that each word masks its own definition and simply waits for the critical moment to reveal its meaning for the unsuspecting hearer. Or the speaker, by this one-and-one relation of words to definitions, suggests either that he always uses language in the first dictionary sense, or that his good friend Mr. Webster somehow fixed all meaning.

For the speaker employing words in this sanctimonious manner, language is always concrete and complete in itself and never abstract or in need of referents. For him words are qualitatively and quantitatively complete paint globules of primary colors on a palette, ready for instant brushing. Consequently when this speaker uses language, *he* knows what *he* means, *he* says what *he* means, and *he* means exactly what *he* says because *he* says it. By simply spouting words, he implies not only acquaintanceship, but mastery over them. Thus instead of forcing listeners to look to him for meaning, he turns hearers to the words themselves because words to him are complete entities. Words do not function as parts of sentences or paragraphs for this speaker, nor do they represent verbalization *reflecting* his total experience. Rather they are neat labels to starchy dictionary definitions. Naturally, befuddlement and bewilderment shall greet this speaker for the rest of his days, since listeners, looking for meaning from their own experiences, are confused by statements of the label-speaker who is not even talking from his own accumulated experiences.[4]

Meaning, in short, is not found in words nor in dictionaries; but in the way a speaker uses language within a sentence or paragraph, or in the way a speaker and his listeners previously encountered words in specific, environmental situations. If a speaker, therefore, chooses to use words as isolated labels, then he not only risks but blatantly invites hearers to confuse his ideas and to misunderstand his meanings. On the other hand, if he uses words within the contextual realm of occasion, audience, and his own experience, then he may not be a superior speaker; but he is at least understood.

CHOICE OF WORDS

Although language consists of nouns, verbs, adjectives, adverbs, pronouns, prepositions, and conjunctions, a speaker's primary concern over the parts of speech is with *nouns,* since they name objects; *verbs,* since they give

[4] For a related discourse on the problems of objective and ordinary language, see John B. Newman, "The Semantic Analysis of Ordinary Language," *Quarterly Journal of Speech,* Vol. 49 (December 1963), pp. 410–416.

movement; and *adjectives* and *adverbs,* since they add dimension and refinement to his basic expression. In selecting words, however, many speakers settle on the first noun or verb that occurs to them because they think fluency is more important and impressive to hearers than cogent word choice, or they are too lazy to find the most expressive words for their ideas. These speakers are like thoughtless pianists who, striving to play selections with metronomic precision, completely ignore musical mood.

Noun Selection

Plain nouns are frequently better than ornate, poetic, and ostentatious ones. There was a time, not over 100 years ago, when American speakers "orated" in a manner that would probably sicken a modern audience. For instance this next passage from a Fourth of July oration delivered in 1880 illustrates an affected choice of nouns by a speaker:

> Then spread out, O, English speaking America! Be one in mutual interest with the great Dominion that stretches from the pole to the great lakes! Go anglicize in peace and good will the Halls of Montezumas! Carry not only railroads and common schools to the lands of the Incas; and stretch forth O, American spirit of enlightenment and freedom over the Pacific Ocean, and invade Asia with conquests of commerce and manufactures.[5]

Obviously the preceding speaker gave some attention to language; but he seemed preoccupied with being different. In contrast Lucy Stone, woman suffragist, sounded sincere, despite her dramatics, because she chose apt nouns to express her idea:

> I can never look on this [American] flag without thinking that nowhere under its shadow can a woman claim her child as her own; and so I never hang it up as an object of veneration, I never bow down to it, and I never sing
>
>   "My country, 'tis of thee."

When speaking on the same theme at another occasion, she said:

> I have no country, and no hope of a country. On this wide continent there is no mountain so high and no valley so deep that there I can take my child by the hand and be protected in my God-given rights as a mother under the American flag.[6]

Verb Selection

The two previous examples from speeches also illustrate that *verb*-choice adds or detracts from the quality of a sentence or basic idea. A speaker's reliance on weak verbs, however, is not entirely his fault. In spontaneous, verbalized thought, spoken English usually passes quickly over the

---

[5] *Pacific Commercial Advertiser* [Weekly], July 10, 1880.
[6] Alice Stone Blackwell, *Lucy Stone: Pioneer Woman Suffragist* (Norwood, Massachusetts: The Plimpton Press, 1930), p. 254.

skeletal thought—expressed in *subject* and *verb*—to an emphasis upon *direct objects, subordinate clauses, adjectives,* and *adverb modifiers.* Put another way speakers are prone to open sentences with stock *subject-noun* phrases:

> *I think* that . . .
> Now here *I want* to say . . .
> *It is* my feeling that . . .
> *Man is* a . . .
> The *integration crisis is* . . .
> *This is* important to you because . . .
> While visiting Omaha, *I noticed* . . .
> Whenever possible *we should* . . .

Notice what a speaker does: he states the subject-noun or subject-pronoun, quickly adds the verb, and finally leaves himself free to leisurely develop the direct object as it occurs to him. The result is that direct objects, as compared to subject and verb development, are drawn out and decorated with adjective and adverb modifiers. During the developmental process, initial nouns and verbs are passed over quickly, as though they were poor cousins who needed little attention. English syntax, of course, is not like a normal German sentence that frequently emphasizes the verb. Thus where Englishmen say "*We spent* a month at the beach last summer," Germans say, "*Wir haben* letzten Somer einen Monat am Strant *verbracht.*" Notice the difference: the speaker in English states quickly the subject and verb, thereby freeing himself to choose words for the direct object. In contrast, German syntax, after stating initially the subject (*Wir*) and auxiliary verb (*haben*), gives the speaker time to choose a precise final verb (*verbracht*) for an exact shade of meaning. Listen to some speeches delivered by your classmates and notice how soon they state—usually within the first five words—their subject and verb in a sentence.

Adjective and Adverb Selection

Much good speaking is a matter also of proper *adjective* and *adverb* selection. A beginning speaker is likely to overwork adjectives and adverbs, since his inattention to selection of nouns and verbs forces him to depend on qualifiers for meaning. If a speaker would take more care in choosing nouns and descriptive verbs, he could rely less on compound-modifiers for meaning. However, there is no denying the importance of modifiers in good speaking, since they add life to nondescript nouns and languid verbs, and since they often generate tension in otherwise tranquil nouns and verbs. On the other hand, modifiers will not always lackey a poor noun and verb home, and emblematic adjectives and adverbs are not infallible signs of great speaking.

To more fully understand the importance of adjective and adverb selection, you should study the following passage from an 1860 address by secessionist Robert Toombs, who, torn over the slave issue, had good cause to emblazon his remarks before Congress with vituperative language. Instead, he used modifiers sparingly and relied on nouns and verbs to carry the bulk of his meaning and feeling:

> What a huge imposition is this same Black Republican party! They proclaim every day their detestation and horror of slavery. . . . But if anyone even suggests the possibility of cutting them loose from this body of death, what a patriotic rage do they manifest! Oh, no! They will die first. They hug the putrid carcass to their bosoms, and threaten us with "eighteen million" Black Republicans, carrying death and slaughter into the peaceful abodes of their deliverers. If they believed half they say, they ought to be for disunion. They should struggle continually to be relieved of this "covenant with death, this league with hell." They seem to have precisely enough of this "sum of all villanies," and [yet] they will perish ere they part with one sixteenth part of a hair of it. There is no harmony between their professions and their conduct; this argues hypocrisy, not sincerity. If you honestly want to relieve your souls from the guilt of complicity with slaveholding, say so with manly firmness. We will give you a discharge whenever you want it.[7]

CHOICE OF PHRASES

Because a certain amount of less-than-desirable language remains inevitably the stock tools of oral English, a speech professor, in contrast to an English professor, allows his students some liberties with clichés, colloquialisms, and idiomatic and slang expressions. A speech teacher knows, for instance, that even a recognized master of public address as Sir Winston Churchill used stock expressions in his speechmaking as: "At any rate . . .", "This brings me . . .", "It seems to me that . . .", "I am so glad to be able to . . .", "As a matter of fact . . .", and "I should like to say . . .".

What does in fact probably trouble a professor of speech is a student's tendency to overwork favorite words and expressions.[8] On rare occasions a student will come up with a pet word that is colorful and that adds an identifiable quality and characteristic to his speaking style. After two or three speeches, however, a word or phrase of too ordinary origin loses its attractiveness; and by the end of a semester in public speaking, these expressions may even become points for ridicule and humor to listeners. You doubtlessly recognize some of these favorites: "you see," "you know," "to get back to the point," "boy," "oh, man," to name a few. Because awareness is a partial key to improved language control, you may find the best solution for eliminating pet phrases is to get a friend to point out these idiosyncrasies as you practice.

---

7 *Congressional Globe Appendix*, 36th Cong., 1 sess., pp. 156–157.

8 We do not here imply that speech should be divorced from the characteristic traits (loosely, personality) of the speaker. For a further view, see Eliot Freidson, "The Varieties of Individual Speech," *Quarterly Journal of Speech*, Vol. 42 (December 1956), pp. 355–362.

LANGUAGE AND ITS RESPONSE

The general semanticists,[9] following what the linguistic scholar calls the triadic conception of language meaning, remind us through their mentor, Alfred Korzybski, that words (signs, maps) stand for things and are not the things themselves. That is the word *deceased* is not the actual event, but a convenient linguistic designation for a state of being; the word *dismembered* stands for the end result from cutting; or the word *pall* is a label for an act of covering, not the actual event itself. In essence the general semanticists imply that words, objectively speaking, are unemotional labels that rarely describe with accuracy an object, concept, or act, simply because words are only convenient and commonly agreed on sound combinations used by individuals for communication. For this reason a more accurate way a speaker may describe an automobile accident is for him to take his listeners to the scene, say nothing, and point, since the word *accident* is a vague, man-made verbal classification for a whole range of events.

People React to Language

Yet people do react in different ways to language. One person may unemotionally scan a newspaper item that read: "Yesterday afternoon at 2:35, a two-car accident on the Carrollton overpass caused the death of three passengers in a car driven by Albert LeBlanc of 622 Ogden Avenue." Another individual might read with some interest the following report of the same event: "Dismembered bodies of the deceased were taken away in an ambulance, and one witness said afterwards that 'a pall of death' hung about the scene." And in a more journalese description, most readers would doubtlessly react with some horror at the next accident report:

> Yesterday afternoon at 2:35 on the Carrollton overpass, a car driven at 70 miles per hour by seventeen-year-old Washington Holbrook crashed head-on with a station wagon driven by Albert LeBlanc of 622 Ogden Avenue. In the back seat of the LeBlanc car were 10-year-old Shirley LeBlanc, her 7-year-old brother, Albert, Jr., and 8-year-old Tommy Wilson, son of a LeBlanc neighbor. Police described the accident as one of the goriest in years. Severed pieces of flesh were hurled across the highway, and one witness at the accident was overcome by the sight and suffered from mild shock. Later under police questioning, the witness said that he heard distinctly the victims' screams moments before the collision, and that he immediately stopped his own car to help. Although Shirley and Albert Jr. were killed instantly, 8-year-old Tommy, his body pierced and bleeding from jagged cuts, and his legs ragged stubs below the knees, died moments after the ambulance arrived. The witness said that he was overcome by the sight of the dead and dying, and that "a sickly smell of blood" hung about the scene for several moments.

[9] For other classifications of the word "semantics," see John B. Newman, "The Area of Semantics," *Quarterly Journal of Speech,* Vol. 43 (April 1957), pp. 155–164.

Obviously, the scene can be detailed to a point where actual revulsion occurred in most readers, provided, of course, they had had a well of previous experiences to draw from for their imagery. Some readers may actually turn sick from a too vivid description. Yet the general semanticists remind us that words in isolation are not the things; they are cold, unemotional, lifeless, linguistic labels invented by man for his convenience. Then why do some people blanch at the sound of rough and crude four-letter words in our language? Why do others shrink from words as *black nigger, Chink, Jap, Wop*? And, finally, why do some of us squirm when we hear words treating personal body functions or sex?

The answer probably is that humans respond to the imagery or associative connotations created in their minds by words, whether in the context provided by a speaker, or in the context they furnish themselves based on past experience. In short, their previous encounters with words, within a given community of experiences, teach them to react in specific ways. It is useless, therefore, to argue that human responses to word stimuli are incorrect, that listeners are semantically disoriented when they react to a word that only stands for a thing, or that the popular concept of *magic* words was exploded long ago by linguistic scholars. The point and the concern of a public speaker is that listeners, regardless of the psychological, physiological, sociological, or any other applicable -ological category, *do* react and *do* emote when they hear words.

Rightly or wrongly language for one listener is magical, and he confirms his impressions of word-magic by pointing to the Auca Indians of Ecuador who think there is something mystical about language. Or he will observe his children at play and notice that magic for them includes the words *allakazam* or *hocus-pocus, dominocus*. Or he will point to Shakespeare and remind you that the witches do not simply brew potions and spells, but they incant:

> 2. *Witch.* Fillet of fenny snake,
> In the caldron boil and bake.
> Eye of newt and toe of frog,
> Wool of bat and tongue of dog,
> Adder's fork and blindworm's sting,
> Lizard's leg and howlet's wing,
> For a charm of powerful trouble,
> Like a Hell broth boil and bubble.
> *All.* Double, double toil and trouble,
> Fire burn and caldron bubble.

(Macbeth, IV, i, 12–21.)

For another listener language is the gateway to man's inner reactions based on the sum of previous experiences. This listener, perhaps more aware of language than the previous hearer, realizes that scientifically minded man is no longer plagued by witch incantations, or magical, *Arabian-Nights* words.

He will, nevertheless, add that man is forced to recognize words as more than mere signs or symbols.

Speakers Concerned with Listeners as They Are

To return to the speaker, there is no denying that ideally it would be wonderful to greet an audience, pack them into a bus, drive them to a corner, and then wait patiently for an accident to illustrate some hazard of driving. For after all, words in every instance may not adequately describe an event. Or it would be ideal to have an audience always look past words to the speaker for meaning. Or it would be even more ideal to have a language measured along a continuum of from strict-to-loose meaning so that speakers may communicate with greater precision. Public speakers are concerned, however, with hearers as they are. This is not 2966 A.D., when all humans and all languages will perhaps reach a plateau of sophistication and computer accuracy comparable to the language of mathematics. Nor is it likely that in the immediate centuries to come, mankind will one day awaken to a new generation of semantically oriented humans. Until man invents a better means of communication, speakers are chained to the rock called *language*. They are, consequently, subject to the vagaries of an unprecise and often inadequate symbolic system of expressing their ideas and of describing objects and events . . . so the general semanticists seem to infer. Does this mean a speaker should give his attention to other speech matters because he can never recreate for listeners his precise thoughts?

Shortcomings of Language not Inherently Bad

Granted that a speaker deals with immediacy; that he cannot take up the torch and crusade for semantically oriented listener-reaction to words as he delivers his address about foreign policy, demonstrates how to make a soufflé, or talks about the split between Moscow and Peking. Realistically, however, he cannot ignore the loose and flexible reaction patterns by listeners to language. He should decide, therefore, to follow a reasonable path by choosing words that more nearly express his precise meaning. And, contrary to the lamentations of fear-mongers who warn of language inadequacies, the speaker will, hopefully, keep in mind that lingual shortcomings—whether in the language itself or in the people who use it—are not evils in and of themselves. The language of mathematics, for instance, is at once precise in its symbolization and meaning. Yet it is frigid and unemotional.

Perhaps our positive attitude towards language, despite its inadequacies, has all been a horrible rationalization—an avoidance of the issues. Yet the very vagueness of language allows a speaker to create quick, sweeping images and permits him to say in a few words what may take a precise language more words to describe in certain instances. The human mind, unlike the fixed circuitry of an electronic brain, is not programmed to give one-and-one or even logical responses to words. Instead, patch-chorded in seemingly infinite patterns, man's central nervous system responds in a vast number of ways to any given word, phrase, or sentence. And although this multireaction often results in hearers misunderstanding the spoken word, this same conglomerate response allows a speaker to exclaim: "Let both sides seek to invoke the wonders of science instead of its terrors. Together let us explore the stars, conquer the deserts, eradicate disease, tap the ocean depths, and encourage the arts and commerce."[10] The speaker, John Kennedy, might be criticized for such vague generalizations as "wonders of science," "terrors," "conquer the deserts," "tap the ocean depths," and "encourage the arts and commerce." He might have, for instance, defined *wonders,* since this is a vague noun at best. Certainly the word *science* means all things to all people; and Kennedy may have enumerated, therefore, some specific classifications.

On the other hand, the necessity for such rigid encoding is not always necessary, nor particularly desirable. Kennedy was not a debater arguing against an opponent on the proposition of world peace. Instead, his message was meant to inspire hope in the future and to express the goals of all men. "Wonders of science" was vague, yet it was at once appropriate for his hearers because each listener could project into the phrase whatever seemed wondrous to him in science. For one teen-age hot rodder, *science* is a four-barrel carburetor; for one new housewife, *science* is an electric can opener; for one 70-year-old patient, *science* is an electronic heart pacer. A speaker such as Kennedy, therefore, may have intentionally placed a long, rambling, helter-skelter fence around some of his words, because whatever listeners implied would serve best his ends.

Of course another speaker, in contrast to Kennedy's positive use of language vagueness, may employ language to generate sweeping, negative images. Propaganda analysts label these latter usages of words *name calling, glittering generality,* and *transfer.* For instance when Judge Leander H. Perez, Sr., addressed the Plaquemines (Louisiana) Parish Commission Council on the evening of April 6, 1965, he used language vagueness to advantage when he exclaimed:

> Now, where will this Lyndon Johnson–Hubert Humphrey administration Voting Rights bill leave this state and the other Southern states?
> We know that during the years of the first Reconstruction when the federal government forced "manhood suffrage" and total Negro voting on the Southern Black Belt, what crude and brutal methods were used to attempt to destroy our white civilization. A noted historian wrote how the Negroes who knew nothing of the affairs of government were put into power over their old masters—assisted by two classes of whites—the northern predator—the carpet bagger—who stalked the stricken South like a jackal to filch for him-

10 *Vital Speeches of the Day,* Vol. 47 (February 1, 1961), p. 227.

self something of the wreckage—and his partner the renegade and apostate southerner—the renegade without honor, pride or patriotism,—a political unnamed, who deserted his own people in their hour of peril to became [*sic*] a scavenger, hovering like a vulture above the ruins of Negro rule. Today that scavenger is with us again—elevated to high office in Washington by our people whom he now would betray for political favors from the national administration whose sole purpose is to be the highest bidder, for the Communist dominated minority bloc votes in the largest northern and eastern states.[11]

In sum a speaker is not, in every instance, troubled by individual differences and by less-than-accurate reactions to his words. Instead, he may actually welcome human tendencies and use human traits to his advantage; for he may want his hearers to create their own images on occasion, since listeners can often personalize a subject in a more concrete and meaningful fashion than he could ever do for them.[12]

LANGUAGE EFFECTS ON SPEAKER AND LISTENER

By now it may be apparent that audiences respond to language stimuli at several levels of comprehension. Listeners, for example, may understand at once what a speaker meant if he said Freedom 7, since this word denotes a specific object used in a dated event, an object unknown to man just a few short years ago. To speak of *rocketship,* however, demands conscious discrimination by listeners, since the word designates a whole object-classification from Jules Verne's fantasy ships to the Flash Gordon and Buck Rogers rockets of a generation ago, and from the Hollywood science fiction versions to *birds* posed on *pads* at Cape Kennedy.

Confusion definitely arises and conscious understanding must take over for hearers when a speaker says *space vehicle.* These last two words confront listeners with a range of choices. Is the speaker, for example, distinguishing an interplanetary ship from a fringe-of-space craft such as the X-15? Does he mean manned or unmanned? Is he referring to a solid fuel, LOX, hydrogen, or plasma-jet craft? Does he mean a vehicle as the Russian *sputnik,* or an American, man-carrying nose cone? Or is the speaker simply using a vague term to designate any man-made object capable of orbiting around the earth? And finally does he really intend to create a specific image when he says *space vehicle,* or is he merely referring to a concept of transportation as vague as *car, boat,* and *airplane?*

Obviously, a speaker has only limited control over the listener's response to his language. A NASA engineer sitting in the audience will "hear" a

[11] Reprinted from The *Times-Picayune,* April 7, 1965.

[12] For a summary analysis of the objective-subjective approach to communication theory, see James L. Bemis and Gerald M. Phillips, "A Phenomenological Approach to Communication Theory," *The Speech Teacher,* Vol. 13 (November 1964), pp. 262–269.

speech differently from an auto mechanic or Spanish teacher. The engineer may think a speaker uses space terminology with the usual oversimplification common to laymen. The auto mechanic may marvel at the same speaker's apparent understanding of a complex mechanical device known as a *space vehicle*. The unscientifically minded Spanish teacher may accept gladly the speaker's oversimplification as a lucid explanation of a difficult subject.

Only a foolish speaker, however, would now conclude that "speechmaking is at best only purple-patched expressions of vapor-thin 'nothings,' since exact information is impossible to transmit between individuals through verbal channels." Although there is the temptation to agree with this generalization, a speaker should note how disadvantages of language are turned into advantages; and finally, how a speaker may overcome peculiar listener reaction to language. (Chapter 9 presents a fuller treatment of listeners and their reactions.)

General Imagery and the Speaker and the Listener

Because listeners identify their own experiences with words, this identification is helpful for the speaker when he uses imagery in an address. When Franklin Roosevelt asked Congress to declare war against Japan on December 8, 1941, he said, "Yesterday, December 7, 1941—a date which will live in infamy—the United States of America was suddenly and deliberately attacked by naval and air forces of the Empire of Japan."[13] The President might have been more precise in his language, for after all, "Yesterday" really meant 7:50 A.M., Hawaiian Standard Time, and actually December 8 in the Philippines. Instead of the "United States of America" he meant Pearl Harbor,[14] Ford Island, navy ships in East and South-East Loch at Pearl Harbor, Hickam Field on Oahu, Clark Field in the Philippines, and several other Pacific military installations, all representing only a part of the United States. Instead of "naval and air forces of the Empire of Japan," Roosevelt meant 351 Japanese planes and several midget submarines that passed over anti-submarine nets strung across West Loch at Pearl Harbor. Instead of "suddenly" he meant our military intelligence knew an attack was imminent but had guessed wrong on where the major blow would come.

Granting that Roosevelt had had all these facts at hand, few listeners would have thought more of him had he said:

[13] *The Public Papers and Addresses of Franklin D. Roosevelt*, Vol. 10: *The Call to Battle Stations*, Samuel I. Rosenman, comp. (New York: Harper & Row, Publishers, 1950), p. 514.

[14] Actually the Japanese launched their military attack in several places within a matter of 48 hours after Pearl Harbor. Pearl Harbor, however, became the immediate symbol of the attack because more lives were lost and more damage was inflicted there in a short morning than in the ensuing raids on Guam, the Philippines, or Midway and Wake Islands. FDR himself in the Declaration of War address centered his attention on Pearl Harbor as well.

At 7:50 AM, Hawaiian Standard Time, December 7, 1941—a date which will live in infamy—four battleships and three destroyers at anchor in Pearl Harbor and adjacent areas such as East and South-East Loch, and our planes at Hickam Field and four lesser Hawaiian fields, were caught off guard by miscalculations of our military intelligence, and this deliberate attack was carried out against our military in Hawaii by 351 aircraft and several midget submarines which represent naval elements of the Empire of Japan.

As indicated in a previous paragraph, individuals identify their experiences with words, and listeners frequently jump to first-impression meanings. These two particular traits of man worked to Roosevelt's advantage. For most Americans "yesterday" was better than a precise time, because it was 7:50 A.M. *only* at Pearl Harbor. Furthermore, "United States of America" personalized and animated the name for a political hegemony, and although the name applied usually to the continental limits of our country in 1941, Roosevelt swept our boundaries thousands of miles into the Pacific to include territories and possessions unheard of by many Americans until the war. "Suddenly" was suited more to the occasion because audiences would not become confused or sidetracked into thoughts of military blunder. Instead, the word implied "quick," "sneak," and "without warning." And finally "naval and air forces of the Empire of Japan" created images of gigantic numbers of ships and planes, and an overwhelming military force of an imperialistic nation.

The probable net result of Roosevelt's opening comments was to pit "fair-play" Americans against "foul-play" Japanese. In contrast to Woodrow Wilson, who carefully distinguished between the "Imperial German Government" and the "German people" in 1917, Roosevelt conjured immediate, sweeping images of whites against yellows, without the finer differentiation between government and people.

Listener Behavior and Reaction as They Affect the Speaker

A listener sometimes responds to language without bothering with facts because his inner, subliminal wants or fears reject all undesirable stimuli causing anxiety. He may, for instance, love praise to a point where he hears only those comments resembling acclaim, such as a friend's compliment of his appearance, a teacher's praise of his term paper, or a colleague's glowing description of his intelligence.

Sometimes this screening behavior, that allows a listener to look past facts, ends humorously; at other times his desire to suppress anxiety ends tragically. During the 1930s, for instance, many Americans, Britons, and Frenchmen wanted so much to avoid the thoughts of war that ominous events were ignored, and these people embraced Hitler's declaration before the Reichstag, "Germany needs peace and desires peace!", as the absolute truth. Men as Winston Churchill who distrusted Herr Hitler found themselves at odds with the general public and unable to overcome mass repression of war signs. Thus, thoughtful people who wanted peace even rationalized away the fall of Austria in early 1938 as a logical assimilation of German peoples. So much did some listeners wish to suppress war thoughts that they hailed Neville Chamberlain's statement, "I believe it is peace in our time,"[15] as *prima facie* evidence of Hitler's good intentions. Further, these people, shunning the unpleasant, abbreviated Chamberlain's declaration to "Peace in our time." The fact that he *qualified* his statement did not suit those who would avoid facts, and they heard, subsequently, only what they wanted to hear!

If a whole people in the 1930s deluded themselves by avoiding reality, how can a speaker hope to tear down, through language, the protective walls surrounding listeners on unpleasant subjects, and how can he hope to make audiences look at facts? The suggested procedure is that he go directly, even bluntly, to his point. Unless a speaker has enough time to lull hearers into unsuspecting response through conciliation plus impelling argument, his best approach towards an openly hostile audience may be to engage them in argument-for-argument mental clash. This does not mean that the speaker abandons his good sense and resorts to hostile language or open insults. Rather, this means only that his use of language is at once pointed and precise as he states his case.

Robert Emmet's introduction to his speech before an English court in 1803 is a good example of language usage by a speaker who knew his audience would block out facts as he saw them. Realizing that minds were made up and that facts were fixed from the court's standpoint, Emmet spoke directly and in unmistakable language; and he sought no time-consuming common ground, but began his speech directly:

> My Lords, What have I to say why sentence of death [for treason] should not be pronounced on me, according to law? I have nothing to say, that can alter your predetermination, nor that it will become me to say with any view to the mitigation of that sentence which you are here to pronounce, and I must abide by. But I have that to say, which interests me more than life, and which you have laboured . . . to destroy. I have much to say why my reputation should be rescued from the load of false accusation and calumny which has been heaped upon it. I do not imagine that, seated where you are, your minds can be so free from impurity, as to receive the least impression from what I am going to utter. I have no hopes that I can anchor my character in the breast of a court constituted and trammeled as this is. I only wish, and it is the utmost I expect, that your lordships may suffer it to float down your memories untainted by the foul breath of prejudice, until it finds some more hospitable harbour to shelter it from the storm by which it is at present buffeted. Was I only to suffer death, after being adjudged guilty by *your* tribunal . . . I should bow in silence, and meet the fate that awaits me without a murmur [;] but the silence of the law which delivers my body

to the executioner, will, thro' the ministry of that law, labour in its own vindication, to consign my character to obloquy [;] for there must be guilt somewhere: whether in the sentence of the court or in the catastrophe, posterity must determine.

Then concluding his introduction, Emmet exclaimed:

A man in my situation, my lords, has not only to encounter the difficulties of fortune, and the force of power over minds which it has corrupted or subjugated, but the difficulties of established prejudice: . . . the man dies, but his memory lives: that mine may not perish, that it may live in the respect of my countrymen, I seize upon this opportunity to vindicate myself from some of the charges alleged against me.[16]

A listener tends also to evaluate and compare each new stimulus in terms of old experiences. Without this trait life would soon grow impossible, since every stimulus would require new, unique, inductive, and deductive thoughts before reaction. Driving a car, for instance, might become too complex and disturbing an activity, since conscious effort and thinking would be required each time a person sits behind the steering wheel and turns on the ignition. Fortunately, the human mind permits an individual to compare quickly, even automatically, one experience with another and to recall specifics from a storehouse of related stimulus-response reactions essential to operating a car. Driving becomes, therefore, an almost subconscious activity in which learned reaction patterns respond automatically to normal driving stimuli.

Unfortunately, the very ability to learn has undesirable effects on occasion: a person may become disoriented when confronted with a startling stimulus, then panic and react irrationally; or worse he may become used to a pattern of learned behavior and ignore or disbelieve new experiences. Thus hearers, for instance, may grow so immune to the stimuli of oft-repeated words, phrases, and repetitive speech themes that their reaction in other than learned ways is a near impossibility.[17]

Much habitual hearer response to language, therefore, is in part the end product of nonthinking word and idea choice by speakers. For instance the callous and liberal sprinkling of sentences with worn-out qualifying adjectives—*great, super, tremendous, good, very good, best, pretty, swell, beautiful, unique,* to name only a few—result in somnambulant hearer reaction to superlatives. Some speakers, distraught by listener tendency to remain unmoved by overworked adjectives, resort foolishly to compound words for effect: *really big, brand new, terribly beautiful, very, very wonderful, super colossal,* and many more. Partly because of this avalanche of

16 Francis Plowden, *An Historical Review of the State of Ireland from the Invasion of that Country under Henry II, to its Union with Great Britain on the First of January 1801* (Philadelphia: William F. M'Laughlin, publisher, 1806), Vol. 5, Appendix, pp. 1-2.
17 Sermons and commencement addresses frequently produce a numbing effect on listeners because of oft-repeated themes and stereotyped word usage.

empty adjectives and adverbs, audiences grow even more insensitive and unfeeling to much language. Should the speaker, therefore, mean sincerely *the very best,* his audience may think his words synonymous with *okay* or *adequate.*

Some of a speaker's problems with language and hearers result from a steady diet of bagatelle ideas expressed by other speakers, with businessmen perhaps the worst offenders. Listeners, stuffed from pap, respond sluggishly as world-beater after world-beater talks of "greater sales efforts," "a go-go year," and "more team work." Civic leaders are not much better. They speak of "our growing needs," "glorious future of Homeville," and "keeping pace with the space age." Educators are no prizes. They talk of "growing opportunities," "responsibility to our children," and "personality adjustment for modern living." The result: listener resistance to tired ideas decorated with cliché-ridden language.

The good speaker, concerned with effect and audience response, realizes that he cannot ignore this shoulder-shrugging attitude of hearers. Fortunately, a listener's reaction is in part overcome when words are selected judiciously. For instance Churchill's address to Congress on December 26, 1941, is weakened by the inserted, bracketed qualifiers:

> They will [*very likely*] stop [*probably*] at nothing. They have a [*very*] vast accumulation of [*great*] war weapons of all kinds. They have [*lots of*] highly trained and [*really*] disciplined armies, [*great*] navies and [*tremendous*] air services. They have [*big*] plans and [*many*] designs which have long been contrived and [*really*] matured. They will stop at nothing that [*real*] violence or [*sheer*] treachery can suggest. It is [*certainly*] quite true that on our [*glorious*] side our [*huge*] resources in [*brave*] man power and [*gigantic*] materials are far greater than theirs. But only a [*small*] portion of your [*vast*] resources are as yet [*fully*] mobilized and [*fully*] developed, and we both of us have much to learn in the [*horrible*] cruel art of [*total*] war.[18]

Obviously Churchill did use qualifiers: *vast, highly trained, far, cruel,* to name a few. In each case, however, his qualifying words added force and meaning to his ideas because of adjective and adverb paucity in the passage. If you were composing the same paragraph, could you suggest better qualifying words?

By now you may conclude that the businessman, civic leader, or educator who purges meaningless adjectives and puffy redundancies from his addresses, may well gain more enthusiastic hearings from audiences. (We concur with this conclusion although we lack proof to back our opinion.) This is not, however, the point. Rather, the point is that public speakers should learn to develop their ideas with well-chosen language, if they would overcome listener tendency to react in an undesired, habitual manner to their speechmaking.

18 *Vital Speeches of the Day,* Vol. 8 (January 15, 1942), p. 197.

Abstraction-Conception Listener Behavior and the Speaker

Listeners also respond to language by going through an abstraction-conception process. To illustrate our meaning, we go back to an evening in Rome. It is October 1961 and several reporters and photographers follow Anita Ekberg to her villa. Annoyed by these intrusions on her privacy, she dashes into the villa and emerges moments later with bow and arrows in hand. The response is immediate: reporters and photographers scramble behind cars for protection like so many scurrying crabs.[19] In their response to the situation, these men reasoned probably as follows: (1) (abstraction process) the weapon held by Miss Ekberg—slender feathered-sticks and one longer, bent piece joined at each end by a continuous string—is like objects called bow and arrows; and (2) (conception process) the arrows she holds can kill when shot from bows.

Now let us look again at the same scene, only this time from the eyes of an expert archer. His initial evaluation of the scene (abstraction process) is similar to that of the newsmen. But the expert differs in his interpretation (conception process): the bow's size indicates a difficult 50-pound pull for even some men; Miss Ekberg is holding the arrow on the wrong side of the bow, which will impair her accuracy; she will have control problems since she is holding the extra arrows in the same hand used to pull the bow; and finally her pearl bracelet on the hand clutching the bow indicates she will be groveling on the ground after loose pearls once the bow-string snaps the first arrow away.[20]

Listeners respond initially to words in much the same way as the newsmen and the expert archer. All, for instance, go through a process of *abstraction* when a speaker exclaims "Westward the Star of Empire takes its way." The words *Westward, Star, Empire, takes,* and *way* would stimulate in each listener evaluations based on an abstraction process. Given next a large enough audience, some extreme bipolar *conceptions* (interpretations) are likely. Thus where most hearers, for instance, will abstract *star* as "a bright shining object," the range of conception may be from the "Star of David" to the "Star of Bethlehem" to "Hollywood star."

In most situations the conception process of hearers will probably lead them close enough to a speaker's intended meaning for fairly accurate understanding of a speech. Where a speaker faces a severe bipolar conceptual variation on the part of his listeners is when he uses unusual, complex, or seldomly used words. Frederick C. Schwartz, founder-director of the

[19] "Swings and Arrows of Outraged Ekberg." *Life,* Vol. 49 (October 31, 1960), pp. 28–30.

[20] Admittedly in the illustration, there is the real possibility that even an expert archer would react impulsively by scrambling for protection as well. The assumption in the illustration, however, is that once reasoning overcomes initial response, the individual will act accordingly.

Christian Anti-Communism Crusade, challenged the abstraction-conception abilities of his hearers when he exclaimed:

> Dialectical Materialism is the philosophy of Karl Marx that he formulated by taking the dialectic of Hegel, marrying it to the materialism of Feuerbach, abstracting from it the concept of progress in terms of the conflict of contradictory, interacting forces called the Thesis and the Antithesis, culminating at a critical nodal point where one overthrows the other, giving rise to the Synthesis, applying it to the history of social development, and deriving therefrom an essentially revolutionary concept of social change.[21]

Immediately many listeners would probably encounter several problems of abstraction in the Schwarz passage, and some hearers might never reach the conception stage on certain words. To understand Schwarz's definition, a hearer must abstract terms as "Dialectic," "Materialism," "Thesis," "Antithesis," "nodal point," and "Synthesis" to a level where a conceptual interpretation is possible. The danger with any involved abstracting process should be evident: the more steps needed in reducing words to meaningful comprehension, the better are chances of hearers arriving at multitudinous conceptions over a speaker's words. The speaker must, therefore, gear his language level down to a point where the abstraction process is minimized before listeners formulate conceptions.

Of course if the above suggestion is carried to an extreme, a speaker will find himself confronted with a new problem—how to say *vermilion* when he means *vermilion* and not *red*. With a little thought, a speaker should realize that if *red* matches the audience comprehension level, and if the word will not alter drastically his desired response, then *red* is necessarily the only choice left to him. Depending, however, on the experience or education of his listeners, he may decide that *vermilion* creates no abstracting hardships for them, and he will subsequently, use the word in his address.[22]

---

[21] Frederick C. Schwarz, *You Can Trust The Communists* (. . . *to do exactly as they say!*) (Englewood Cliffs, New Jersey: Prentice-Hall, Inc., 1961), p. 147.

[22] For those interested in pursuing a deeper inquiry into language, see Wallace L. Anderson and Norman C. Stageberg, *Introductory Readings on Language* (New York: Holt, Rinehart, and Winston, Inc., 1962). This one-volume paperback contains essays by such recognized authorities as Edward Sapir, Irving M. Copi, I. A. Richards, Charles C. Fries, S. I. Hayakawa, and Stuart Chase.

7   Style

Apparently the style pendulum in the United States during the last few years, so far as concerns public speaking, has swung away from nakedness of plain English towards a certain amount of controlled embellishment. Part of this swing may be the result of more and more reliance on manuscripts, which in turn permits better control over language for even an average speaker. Another reason for the swing may be the influence of such stylists as Sir Winston Churchill, Adlai Stevenson, and John F. Kennedy. Speech practice seems presently at a point where some of the stodgy, belletristic ramblings of the eighteenth-century rhetorician Hugh Blair are worth dusting off for a cursory examination by students of public speaking. In our approach to style, therefore, some old bones are exhumed for fondling. But as much as possible, the emphasis is on functional stylistic elements that may be of some practical value to a speaker and that can be illustrated with examples from speeches.[1]

APPROACHES TO STYLE

Certain considerations in the previous chapter touched the subject of this one, since language from the psychological and grammatical viewpoint helps determine a speaker's manner of expression. This chapter, however, treats specifically the constituent associated most frequently with style—combinations in language choice as exemplified through figures of speech. The assumption is that students of public speaking are interested in improving their ability at vitalizing ideas through greater control over language *clarity, accuracy, economy,* and *suitability,* without sacrifice of *sincerity.*

There are presently no magic formulas on ways of ordering and moving thoughts for maximum liveliness. Some serious scholars in linguistics, es-

[1] For those skeptical that style is teachable, see Jane Blankenship, "On Teaching of Style," *The Speech Teacher,* Vol. 13 (March 1964), pp. 88–102.

pecially Noam Chomsky (*Syntactic Structures*),[2] are nearing looking-glass land through their formula-approach to syntactical transformations of language structure. Although studies in transformational grammars open the way to a complex, *descriptive* analysis of all languages, the new age is only now on the horizon. There is still much ground for scholars to examine before critics and students will find new grammars universally useful to them when analyzing style. Of necessity, therefore, this chapter is written in terms of old-fashioned stylistics; admittedly, the analysis of style is only a step removed from popular notions held by laymen on the subject. But *any* analysis of style—other than the one hoped for through transformational theory—suffers from a lack of scientifically objective insights.[3]

Another day, in short, is not today. The discussion of figures in this chapter, therefore, is from a quasi-descriptive standpoint. The illustrations of *some* stylistic forms ignore the more than real probability that quoted speakers employed unconsciously a stylistic device. Vague *impressionistic* terms (flowing, terse, rhythmic) are used—and ashamedly—because no better ones are available at the moment. And worst of all, *imagery* is spoken of as though it might be plucked from a sentence without killing sentence-style in turn.

But all is not lost. This chapter, whatever else its inadequacies, does not resort to *statistical*, Fleschian[4] methodology as counting nouns, adjectives, and adverbs; nor does it fall back to comparing *national* styles; nor does it retreat to *synchronic* stylistics such as contrasting Asiatic with Grand style; nor does it revert to *techniques* of language usage by advising on verb tense choice and placement of modifiers (see Chapter 8 on Composing for a discussion of techniques). Rather, the aim here is to focus a student speaker's mind sharply on and make him conscious of what is termed loosely, good speaking style. Hopefully, he will see some avenues for personal improvement and will make some conscious, initial efforts at elevating his speaking style.[5]

SOME METHODS OF STYLISTIC AMPLIFICATION

This section will look closer at *some* stylistic elements that lift oral expression out of the ordinary—elements that result in the label, eloquent.

2 ('s-Gravenhage, Mouton, 1962). The curious student should see Emmon Bach, *An Introduction to Transformational Grammars* (New York: Holt, Rinehart and Winston, Inc. 1964) for an important, although involved, systematic treatment of transformational theory.

3 For those interested in an over-view of linguistics, see Charles V. Hartung, "The Scope of Linguistic Study," *Quarterly Journal of Speech*, Vol. 50 (February 1964), pp. 1–12.

4 Rudolf Flesch, *The Art of Plain Talk* (New York: Harper & Row Publishers, 1946).

5 See Donald C. Bryant, "Of Style," *Western Speech*, Vol. 21 (Spring 1957), pp. 103–110, for a thought-provoking essay on the problem of determining what *is* style.

A speaker should bear in mind, however, that an ability to identify and use figures of speech will not necessarily result in eloquence. Just as a person cannot become an Andrew Wyeth simply by knowing the terminology associated with art, so he cannot become a Churchill simply by knowing names identified with style. Nevertheless, this fact does not mean a speaker should shove his hands into his pockets, kick up the dirt with his heels, and shuffle off to that happy hunting ground where Chief Dull-Speaker presides at the council campfire. The ancient Hawaiians had a saying, "The tongue is the rudder of the words from the mouth." Since a speaker, in essence, controls the words that flow from his mouth, he is not only responsible for *what* he says, but for *how* he says it as well. It follows, necessarily, that if a speaker controls the verbalized expression of his ideas, then he can also at any moment alter his style by manipulating his language.

Comparison (Simile, Analogy, and Metaphor)

To begin a study of style, a speaker should consider the well-known *simile,* and its first cousin, *analogy.* Both, of course, are comparisons: the former employs clue words such as *like, as,* and *resembles;* the latter employs compound comparisons between attributes and propositions. Let us first analyze *simile.*

A *simile* is either a *literal* comparison of like objects ("The Germans of 1939 resembled those of 1914."), or a *figurative* comparison of unlike objects ("Like an armed warrior, like a plumed knight, James G. Blaine marched down the halls of the American Congress. . . ."). When a speaker wishes to stimulate emotional responses from hearers, he will probably find a figurative comparison more effective than a literal one, since a figurative simile simultaneously and dramatically mixes two distinct images for imaginative effect. In the next example, you should note the imagery created in a 1937 radio address by John L. Lewis:

> Those who chant their praises of democracy, but who lose no chance to drive their knives into labor's defenseless back, must feel the weight of labor's woe, even as its open adversaries must ever feel the thrust of labor's power.
>
> Labor, like Israel, has many sorrows. Its women weep for their fallen and they lament for the future of the children of the race. It ill behooves one who has supped at labor's table and who has been sheltered in labor's house to curse with equal fervor and fine impartiality both labor and its adversaries when they become locked in deadly embrace.[6]

Do not, however, underrate the literal simile, since a literal comparison is also a highly effective stylistic device when used by an able speaker. Douglas MacArthur, for example, employed a literal comparison to emotional advantage when he concluded his speech before Congress in 1951:

[6] *The New York Times,* September 4, 1937. Copyright 1937 by The New York Times Company. Reprinted by permission.

I am closing my fifty-two years of military service. When I joined the Army, even before the turn of the century, it was the fulfillment of all my boyish hopes and dreams.

The world has turned over many times since I took the oath on the plain at West Point, and the hopes and dreams have long since vanished, but I still remember the refrain of one of the most popular barrack ballads of that day which proclaimed most proudly that old soldiers never die; they just fade away.

And like the old soldier of that ballad, I now close my military career and just fade away, an old soldier who tried to do his duty as God gave him the light to see that duty. Good-by.[7]

An *analogy*, in contrast to the shorter simile, gives a speaker fuller opportunity to develop comparative relationships. He would, of course, do well to make highly *plausible* comparisons whenever possible, because the more far-fetched and unlikely his compared items, the more he stands in jeopardy of overdrawing his analogy. Items that seem more closely related permit him to cultivate his analogy for fuller effect. To illustrate the point, a speaker should study the following two examples, one by David Lloyd George, and the other by Charles Sumner. Lloyd George, in comparing two items of some relation, could extend his analogy for full effect without fear of hyperbole:

It is the interest of Prussia to break the treaty [between England, Russia, France, Austria, and Prussia to defend the integrity of Belgium], and she has done it. ("Shame.") She avowed it with cynical contempt for every principle of justice. She says treaties only bind you when it is to your interest to keep them. What is a treaty? says the German Chancellor: "A Scrap of paper." Have you any £5 notes about you? I am not calling for them. (Laughter.) Have you any of those neat little Treasury £1 notes? (Laughter.) If you have, burn them; they are only scraps of paper. (Cheers.) What are they made of? Rags. (Laughter.) What are they worth? The whole credit of the British Empire. (Cheers.) "Scraps of Paper." I have been dealing with scraps of paper within the last month. We suddenly found the commerce of the world coming to a standstill. The machine had stopped. I will tell you why. We discovered, many of us for the first time, that the machinery of commerce was moved by bills of exchange. I have seen some of them (laughter)—wretched, crinkled, scrawled over, blotched, frowsy—and yet wretched little scraps of paper move great ships, laden with thousands of tons of precious cargo from one end of the world to the other. (Cheers.) What is the motive power behind them? The honor of commercial men. (Cheers.) Treaties are the currency of international statesmanship. (Applause.)[8]

In the next example, Charles Sumner, the famous abolitionist, created a livelier and more dramatic image than Lloyd George. Yet Sumner developed only briefly his comparison of slavery to a harlot, since to overdraw this particular figurative analogy might have landed him in the ridiculous:

7 *Vital Speeches of the Day,* Vol. 17 (May 1, 1951), p. 433.
8 *The* [London] *Times,* September 21, 1914.

The Senator [Butler] from South Carolina has read many books of chivalry, and believes himself a chivalrous knight, with sentiments of honor and courage. Of course he has chosen a mistress to whom he has made his vows, and who, though ugly to others, is always lovely to him; though polluted in the sight of the world, is chaste in his sight—I mean the harlot, Slavery. For her, his tongue is always profuse in words. Let her be impeached in character, or any proposition made to shut her out from the extension of her wantonness, and no extravagance of manner or hardihood of assertion is then too great for this Senator. The frenzy of Don Quixote, in behalf of his wench, Dulcinea del Toboso, is all surpassed.[9]

Finally, a speaker reaches the comparative stylistic peak when he joins a vigorous thoughtful *analogy* with the story elements of a *narrative*. Who can forget, for instance, Booker T. Washington's famous narrative-analogy told at the Atlanta Exposition in 1895:

A ship lost at sea for many days suddenly sighted a friendly vessel. From the mast of the unfortunate vessel was seen a signal, "Water, water; we die of thirst!" The answer from the friendly vessel at once came back, "Cast down your bucket where you are." A second time the signal, "Water, water; send us water!" ran up from the distressed vessel, and was answered, "Cast down your bucket where you are." And a third and fourth signal for water was answered, "Cast down your bucket where you are." The captain of the distressed vessel, at last heeding the injunction, cast down his bucket, and it came up full of fresh, sparkling water from the mouth of the Amazon River. To those of my race who depend on bettering their condition in a foreign land or who under-estimate the importance of cultivating friendly relations with the Southern white man, who is their next-door neighbour, I would say: "Cast down your bucket where you are"—cast it down in making friends in every manly way of the people of all races by whom we are surrounded.[10]

The last form of comparison considered here is the daring *metaphor*. Instead of a cautious *simile* as "He [President Cleveland] is like an old bag of beef," a speaker removes all doubt about his personal feelings and asserts, "He is an old bag of beef and I am going to Washington with a pitchfork and prod him in his old fat ribs."[11] Note the stark difference between the two forms: a *simile* is an *inference* that allows a speaker to retreat gracefully from his statement—if he so chooses; a *metaphor,* in contrast, commits him completely to his comparison. In the first instance, Senator "Pitchfork" Ben Tillman only implied through simile that President Cleveland was *like* a "bag of beef"; in the second instance, however, Tillman's metaphoric state-ment asserted that Cleveland *was* a "bag of beef." Obviously a speaker who

[9] *Speech of Hon. Charles Sumner in the Senate of the United States, 19th and 20th May, 1856* (Washington, D.C.: Buell & Blanchard, Printers, 1856), p. 5.

[10] As quoted in Booker T. Washington, *Up From Slavery* (Garden City, New York: Doubleday & Company, Inc., 1900), p. 219.

[11] As quoted in Francis B. Simkins, *Pitchfork Ben Tillman: South Carolinian* (Louisiana State University Press, 1944), p. 315.

understands the qualifying difference between a simile and a metaphor may choose either to add blunt, brute force[12] to his ideas, or to veil them in guarded comparisons.

Contrast

Contrast, or antithesis, is a reflective process wherein a speaker balances ideas or objects against each other to heighten their differences for listeners. Kennedy often employed either the brief, undeveloped, turn-of-the-word contrast, or the rapidly reciprocating series of contrasts in his speechmaking for stylistic effect. His address before the United Nations General Assembly in 1961 illustrates vividly his use of contrast in a speech:

> We meet in an hour of grief and challenge. Dag Hammarskjold is dead. But the United Nations lives. His tragedy is deep in our hearts, but the tasks for which he died are at the top of our agenda. A noble servant of peace is gone. But the quest for peace lies before us.
>
> The problem is not the death of one man—the problem is the life of this Organization. It will either grow to meet the challenges of our age, or it will be gone with the wind, without influence, without force, without respect.[13]

But Kennedy pales next to a real master at stringing a whole series of brief contrasts together. Thomas Macaulay, when pleading the case for Jewish rights in 1833, exclaimed in the House of Commons:

> The Jew must not sit in Parliament: but he may be the proprietor of all the ten pound houses in a borough. He may have more fifty pound tenants than any peer in the kingdom. He may give the voters treats to please their palates, and hire bands of gipsies [*sic*] to break their heads, as if he were a Christian and a Marquess. All the rest of this system is of a piece. The Jew may be a juryman, but not a judge. He may decide issues of fact, but not issues of law. He may give a hundred thousand pounds damages; but he may not in the most trivial case grant a new trial. He may rule the money market: he may influence the exchanges: he may be summoned to congresses of Emperors and Kings. Great potentates, instead of negotiating a loan with him by tying him in a chair and pulling out his grinders, may treat with him as with a great potentate, and may postpone the declaring of war or the signing of a treaty till they have conferred with him. All this is as it should be: but he must not be a Privy Councillor. He must not be called Right Honorable, for that is political power.[14]

12 Our statement on the forcefulness of metaphors is based on the preliminary findings of John W. Bowers, "Some Correlates of Language Intensity," *Quarterly Journal of Speech,* Vol. 50 (December 1964), pp. 415–420. For an interesting article on the absence of scientific findings on metaphors, see Franklin L. Fearing. "The Problem of Metaphor," *The Southern Speech Journal,* Vol. 29 (Fall 1963), pp. 47–55; and for an analysis of metaphors as applied to public speaking, see Michael M. Osborn and Douglas Ehninger, "The Metaphor in Public Address," *Speech Monographs,* Vol. 29 (August 1962), pp. 223–234.

13 *Vital Speeches of the Day,* Vol. 28 (October 15, 1961), p. 2.

14. *The Works of Lord Macaulay,* Lady Trevelyan, Ed. (London: Longmans, Green, and Co., 1875), Vol. 8, pp. 103–104.

The rapid-series contrast is not the only way speakers use antithesis to develop ideas. A beginning speaker, however, may find the slow-turning contrast easier to use, because he is free to express his antithetical thought in more words and with less attention to staccato, contrasting bursts. In the next example, "Single-Tax" economist Henry George, addressing an audience in Scotland, worked out one basic idea of contrast in various ways:

> You people in Glasgow not merely erect church after church, you have the cheek to subscribe money to send missionaries to the heathen. I wish the heathen were a little richer, that they might subscribe money and send missionaries to such so-called Christian communities as this—to point to the luxury, the very ostentation of wealth, on the one hand, and to the barefooted, ill-clad women on the other; to your men and women with bodies stunted and minds distorted; to your little children growing up in such conditions that only a miracle can keep them pure![15]

Finally, before the student speaker accuses us of spending unnecessary time on this particular stylistic device, he should pause for a moment and reread a section of a *speech* that found its way into anthologies of American *literature:*

> We are met on a great battle-field of that war. We have come to dedicate a portion of that field, as a final resting place for those who here gave their lives that that nation might live. It is altogether fitting and proper that we should do this.
>
> But, in a larger sense, we can not dedicate—we can not consecrate—we can not hallow—this ground. The brave men, living and dead, who struggled here, have consecrated it, far above our poor power to add or detract. The world will little note, nor long remember what we say here, but it can never forget what they did here. It is for us the living, rather, to be dedicated here to the unfinished work which they who fought here have thus far so nobly advanced.[16]

Personification and Apostrophe

Personification, an important poetic ingredient, is also a useful figurative device for a speaker. In personification inanimate objects assume an almost miraculous, ongoing quality and a speaker talks as though inorganic matter possessed human intelligence. In the hands of an unskilled and sometimes even skilled speaker, personification is belabored often to a point where this well-meant, stylistic figure suffers from exhaustion. To give a deck of cards life, as Lewis Carroll did in *Alice in Wonderland,* may easily seem ridiculous to an audience. A speaker, therefore, will want certainly to guard against well-worn, dramatic, and trite personifications that begin: "If

[15] As quoted in Anna George de Mille, *Henry George: Citizen of the World* (The University of North Carolina Press, 1950), p. 129.
[16] Abraham Lincoln, "Gettysburg Address," from *Famous Speeches in American History* by Glenn R. Capp, copyright ©, 1963 by The Bobbs-Merrill Company, Inc., 1963, p. 89, reprinted by permission of the publishers.

Washington were here today, he would tell us . . ."; or "If these hallowed walls could speak, they would say . . ."; or "If those who fell in battle here could talk, they would tell us . . .".

To avoid the ignominy of negative criticism, a speaker often *suggests* personification rather than resurrect dramatically voices from the past. Federalist Fisher Ames, for instance, used suggestive personification when calling on faceless and nameless humanity to support the Jay Treaty:

> There is no mistake in this case; there can be none. Experience has already been the prophet of events, and the cries of our future victims have already reached us. The Western inhabitants are not a silent and uncomplaining sacrifice. The voice of humanity issues from the shade of the wilderness. It exclaims that while one hand is held up to reject this Treaty, the other grasps a tomahawk. It summons our imagination to the scenes that will open. It is no great effort of the imagination to conceive, that events so near are already begun. I can fancy that I listen to the yells of savage vengeance, and the shrieks of torture. Already they seem to sigh in the Western wind; already they mingle with every echo from the mountains.[17]

Related to personification is *apostrophe*. In apostrophe a speaker gives the impression to listeners that he is addressing the gods, deceased personages, bygone generations, and even inanimate objects. Although a short step from affected style, a modest apostrophe, as Theodore Parker declaimed to his congregation in 1852, can be effective in a speech:

> I mourned for [Daniel] Webster when we prayed our prayer and sang our psalm on Long Wharf in the morning's gray. I mourned then: I shall not cease to mourn. The flags will be removed from the streets, the cannon will sound their other notes of joy; but, for me, I shall go mourning all my days; I shall refuse to be comforted; and at last I shall lay down my gray hairs with weeping and with sorrow in the grave. O Webster! Webster! would God that I had died for thee![18]

Finally, confident in his ability to handle personification and apostrophe, a speaker may dare not only to give inanimate objects voice but to answer these imagined voices as well. Cicero followed such a technique in his first speech against Lucius Catiline:

> In truth, if my country, which is far dearer to me than my life—if all Italy—if the whole Republic were to address me, "Marcus Tullius, what are you doing? will you permit that man to depart whom you have ascertained to be an enemy? whom you see ready to become the general of the war? whom you know to be expected in the camp of the enemy as their chief, the author of all this wickedness, the head of the conspiracy, the instigator of the slaves, and abandoned citizens, so that he shall seem not driven out of the city by you, but let loose by you against the city? Will you not order him to be thrown into prison,

17 *The Annals of the Congress of the United States* 4 Cong., 1 sess., pp. 1259–1260.
18 *A Treasury of the World's Great Speeches*, Houston Peterson, Ed. (New York: Simon and Schuster, Inc., 1954), pp. 413–414.

to be hurried off to execution, to be put to death with the most prompt severity? What hinders you? is it the customs of our ancestors?"

In answer to his own intonement, Cicero exclaimed:

> To this holy address of the Republic, and to the feelings of those men who entertain the same opinion, I will make this short answer: if, O conscript fathers, I thought it best that Catiline should be punished with death, I would not have given the space of one hour to this gladiator to live in.[19]

And here a word of caution before closing: a speaker should not lose his head over personification and apostrophe, lest his audience think him an Ichabod Crane who has lost touch with sanity.

Synecdoche, Metonymy, and Antonomasia

Speakers almost intuitively substitute one word for another to embellish their utterances. Many substitutions are imaginative conjurings by teen-agers who never heard of synecdoche, metonymy, and antonomasia. Public speakers, of course, use and originate stylistic substitutions of their own. Adolf Hitler, for example, employed *synecdoche*—a description of the *whole* by its *part*—when he said, "In a few weeks' time the Brown Shirt will once more dominate the streets of Germany. . . ." Hitler used Brown Shirt, a color and *part* of a total uniform, to mean the *whole* Sturmabteilung, as contrasted with the disciplined Schutzstaffe, S.S., or Blackshirts. Speakers will, on occasion, reverse the usual pattern of synecdoche and describe a *part* by its *whole*: "There has never been any constitutional difference between me . . . and Parliament." Edward VIII in his abdication address of 1936 used the *whole* Parliament (the body of Commons and Lords) to mean a *part* (401 of the 408 House of Commons members and none of the Lords) when referring to the specific men who voted in support of his wishes.

Because a synecdoche weighs heavy on listeners when overused, speakers often resort instead to *metonymy*. In metonymy an item associated with the *whole* is substituted for the *whole*. For instance, Franklin Roosevelt in his first inaugural said, "The money changers have fled from their high seats . . ." to mean "speculators" who dealt freely in margins had left the "stock exchange."

Sometimes a speaker will use *antonomasia,* a stylistic figure wherein a substitute name of a person or place is used because the substitute is more descriptive to hearers. Thus when Churchill talked of faceless traitors, he said, "And still more fiercely burn the fires of hatred and contempt for the filthy Quislings . . .", and Kennedy in his last address before his assassination said, "I'm glad to be here in Jim Wright's city" to indicate his pleasure at being in Forth Worth.

[19] *Select Orations of Marcus Tullius Cicero* (Chicago: Regan Publishing Corporation, n.d.), pp. 15–16.

Implied Comparisons

In a broad sense, metaphor, synecdoche, metonymy, and antonomasia are all *tropes,* since a trope is any word or sentence that has undergone advantageous change from its proper signification to another meaning.[20] For our purposes, trope is narrowed to include only those changes of a word or sentence that imply rather than state another meaning. Where a metaphor bluntly and categorically compares ("Roosevelt was a fox in his personal dealings"), the narrowed use of trope, in contrast, only suggests similarity ("Roosevelt was foxy in his personal dealings"). The advantage of one comparative form over the other should be clear: a speaker who says: "Roosevelt was foxy" is less prone to criticism from hearers than a speaker who says "Roosevelt was a fox."

There are times and occasions, naturally, when a speaker wishes to emphasize his thoughts by pointing up purposefully his comparison for effect. Through direct identification and superimposition of two distinct images, a speaker may reason that his audience will arrive more precisely at his meaning. If precision is his goal, then a metaphor, "Roosevelt was a fox," suits his purpose. On the other hand, some ideas do not call for fixed imagery, but only for a hazy, inconspicuous, and suggestive reflection of reality. If generalization is a speaker's goal, then the subtler "Roosevelt was foxy" best suits his purpose. By adding *ly, ish, like,* and *en* to a verb or noun and on rare occasions to an adjective, the speaker still reinforces his thought; only he does not call listener attention to his comparison, and he does not force hearers to dwell on his imagery.

Keeping differences between comparative methods in mind, a speaker may choose the form that best meets his particular need in an address. To help him better decide on the stylistic merits of the two, a student speaker should read the following examples and observe the subtle but important difference between them.

COMPARISON	IMPLIED COMPARISON
Helen is like a man.	Helen is a manly girl.
He is an octopus when it comes to girls—all hands.	He is octopuslike when it comes to girls—all hands.
His tongue is as smooth as silk when it comes to words.	He is a silken-tongued orator.

Proverbs, Maxims, Epigrams, and Aphorisms

Stylistic figures known as proverbs, maxims, epigrams, and aphorisms are often thought of as being synonymous terms. There is, of course, a fine distinction between the four terms. Strictly speaking a *proverb* is a cogent,

[20] Thomas Gibbons, *Rhetoric* (London, 1767), p. 1.

clear, and widely accepted expression of near-universal wisdom or wit. Because of a popular association with Biblical sayings, *proverbs* are frequently thought of as moral pronouncements. Although this moralistic notion is true in some instances, speakers should understand that not all proverbs—or even the majority—are moral in their origin, intent, or teaching. Often maxims are confused with proverbs, since the application of a maxim—like a proverb—must be near-universal for all men. A *maxim*, however, usually states less profound truth than a proverb. For purposes of public address, speakers may think of proverbs and maxims as being cut essentially from the same block, with the difference between them a matter of intellectual depth rather than subject matter.

Few students ever originate a proverb or maxim of their own, because by definition both forms imply wisdom proven and reproven over the ages, or at least accepted without question by previous generations of people. Generally all a student speaker can hope for is to include the age-tested truths of others in his addresses. To illustrate what is meant by the universality of proverbs and maxims, six sayings are presented here from literally hundreds of thousands.

> Day by day anxieties and a hundred fears influence a fool: they do not affect a wise man. (*Burmese*)
> Every girl would rather be beautiful than good. (*German*)
> If a house is crammed with treasures of gold and jade, it will be impossible to guard them all. (*Chinese*)
> When the wine goes in, the wit goes out. (*Dutch*)
> Not all the people who weep over your corpse are your friends. (*Jabo tribesmen, East Liberia*)
> When force pushes on, reason draws back. (*Japanese*)

As proverb is to maxim so *epigram* is to *aphorism*. The *epigram* is a short, lively, sometimes witty statement that depends for its effect on an unexpected turn of words. On hearing an epigram, a listener's first impression is that the speaker mixed his ideas and that his words backlashed against each other in meaningless fashion. Among recent speakers, John Kennedy used epigrams with some success. A few of his better known ones were: "If a free society cannot help the many who are poor, it cannot save the few who are rich"; "for only when our arms are sufficient beyond doubt can we be certain beyond doubt that they will never be employed"; "ask not what your country can do for you: Ask what you can do for your country"; and "Let us never negotiate out of fear. But let us never fear to negotiate." Notice that in each instance from Kennedy's inaugural, there is not only contrast (such as *poor* versus *rich*), but meshing of ideas together through similar words ("help the many who are poor," "save the few who are rich"). For most speakers, the invention of epigrammatic sayings is difficult because this stylistic device depends on an ability to make language eddy back and forth over itself in meaningful ways.

A speaker may find his talents more suited to creating *aphorisms*. An aphorism, like an epigram, is brief and pithy. The differences between these two figures are:

1. an aphorism expresses a generalization, where an epigram is more speculative; and
2. an aphorism reaches the edge of overstatement, where an epigram is conservative in allegation.

Edmund Burke, famous British statesman and essayist, was a master of aphorism: "The ocean remains; you cannot pump it dry"; "When a man is robbed of a trifle on the highway, it is not the twopence lost that constitutes the capital outrage"; and "None will barter away the immediate jewel of his soul."

Let us look a little closer at Burke's aphorisms; he generalized in one sweeping sentence—most speakers do this often. He treated a part for the whole—most speakers do this, too. Finally, he began his statements innocently; just when we thought we knew what must follow logically, Burke turned off the main road down an unexpected byway. He put his imagination to work at the surprising but delightful turn in an idea. With a little practice, speakers will find that creating an aphorism is relatively easy in comparison to framing a meaningful epigram. In the following aphorisms from Stanislaw Lec's *Unkempt Thoughts*,[21] speakers may want to experiment by substituting their own words:

You have to [*decide*] even to [*hesitate*].
If the art of [*conversation*] stood a little higher we would have a lower [*birth rate*].
At the beginning there was the [*Word*]: at the end just the [*cliché*].

Like all stylistic forms, however, a speaker can overwork and overuse proverbs, maxims, epigrams, and aphorisms in a speech. Unless he creates stylistic devices artfully, exhibits his skill modestly, and suits his usage carefully to his audience, he will stand accused of an affected, artificial, and unnatural style.

Irony and Allegory

The Greeks defined *irony* as saying one thing while implying another meaning. Centuries later Jonathan Swift added a new dimension to irony by dramatically understating and underplaying ideas for effect. Today writers and speakers interchange freely the two meanings of irony, and they often employ this stylistic device to amplify ideas.

[21] Jacek Galazka, Tr. (New York: St. Martins Press, Inc., 1962).

Besides irony, speakers frequently use *allegory*—a decoy method wherein a speaker withholds a somewhat apparent point, and wherein he disguises his real meaning in a variegated, prolonged metaphorical narration. In contrast to irony, allegory is basically a nonsarcastic structural form used by speakers for its literary beauty and for its kaleidoscopic, comparative effect. Irony, on the other hand, is sometimes derisive and defamatory, or tragic in its circumstance.[22] If there is subtle beauty in irony, it perforce comes through the hearer's intellectual awareness and appreciation of the speaker's intent; whereas the beauty of an allegory is in the magnitude, imaginativeness, and aptness of compared images.

Churchill's "Finest Hour" address of June 1940 illustrates how a speaker may use *irony* in his speech. Sir Winston's method of irony follows the classic Greek form:

> Here is where we come to the Navy—after all, we have a Navy. Some people seem to forget that we have a navy . . . We are also told that the Italian Navy is to come out and gain sea superiority in these waters. If they seriously intend it, I shall only say we shall be delighted to offer Signor Mussolini a free and safe-guarded passage through the Straits of Gibraltar in order that he may play the part to which he aspires. There is general curiosity in the British Fleet to find out whether the Italians are up to the level they were in the last war or whether they have fallen off at all.[23]

In contrast "Billy" Pitt used Swiftian irony in 1792 when he attacked the English slave trade. A speaker should observe that blunt, ironic understatement, although lacking the subtlety found in classic irony, kills its intended victim as surely through slashing blows:

> But that country [Africa], it is said, has been in some degree civilized, and civilized by us. It is said they have gained some knowledge of the principles of justice. What, sir, have they gained the principles of justice from *us?* Is their civilization brought about by us! Yes, we give them enough of our intercourse to convey to them the means, and to initiate them in the study of mutual destruction. We give them just enough of the forms of justice to enable them to add the pretext of legal trials to their other modes of perpetrating the most atrocious iniquity. We give them just enough of European improvements, to enable them the more effectually to turn Africa into a ravaged wilderness.[24]

Turning next to allegory, Jesus used this method—called *parable* when a moral or religious message is implied—to impress his ideas on a multitude

---

[22] Our classification of irony is admittedly simple. The interested student should see Allan B. Karstetter, "Towards a Theory of Rhetorical Irony," *Speech Monographs*, Vol. 31 (June 1964), pp. 162–178, for a complete classification as well as analysis of irony. Karstetter concluded: *"The introduction of irony is not only possible in all argumentative circumstances, but may actually be one of the most effective rhetorical tools in almost any circumstance."*

[23] *Blood, Sweat, and Tears* (New York: G. P. Putnam's Sons, 1941), pp. 307–308.

[24] Chauncey A. Goodrich, *Select British Eloquence* (New York: Harper & Row, Publishers, 1853), p. 587.

of hearers by the sea. Notice that he did not climax his imagery with an explanation of intent. Instead the allegorical implications were left to listeners' imagination:

> Harken; Behold, there went out a sower to sow: And it came to pass, as he sowed, some fell by the way side, and the fowls of the air came and devoured it up. And some fell on stony ground, where it had not much earth; and immediately it sprang up, because it had no depth of earth: But when the sun was up, it was scorched; and because it had no root, it withered away.
> And some fell among thorns, and the thorns grew up, and choked it, and it yielded no fruit. And others fell on good ground, and did yield fruit that sprang up and increased; and brought forth, some thirty, and some sixty, and some a hundred. [St. Mark 4: 3–8]

As you probably noticed, the exact interpretation of an allegory is at once specific to an individual, yet universal in its application. In other words each hearer listening to Christ probably went away from the seashore inspired in his own way and confident in the particular meaning for himself—however right or wrong from the speaker's standpoint. There is, therefore, an inherent danger in allegory, since a too clever and too poetic comparison may escape hearers. Did you, for instance, get the full meaning of Jesus' allegory? In a later explanation of his parable to the twelve disciples, he said:

> The sower soweth the word. And these are they by the way side, where the word is sown; but when they have heard, Satan cometh immediately, and taketh away the word that was sown in their hearts.
> And these are they likewise which are sown on stony ground; Who, when they have heard the word, immediately received it with gladness; And have no root in themselves, and so endure but for a time: afterward, when affliction or persecution ariseth for the word's sake, immediately they are offended.
> And these are they which are sown among thorns; such as hear the word, And the cares of this world, and the deceitfulness of riches, and the lists of other things entering in, choke the work, and it becometh unfruitful.
> And these are they which are sown on good ground; such as hear the word, and receive *it,* and bring forth fruit, some thirtyfold, some sixty, and some a hundred. [St. Mark 4: 15–20]

RHYTHM

The stylistic beauty of a speech is sometimes imbedded in a rhythm pattern that alternates between accented and unaccented syllables, and between stressed and unstressed ideas. Unlike written prose rhythm, where a writer is dependent on sensitive readers to notice his stylistic touch, rhythm in a speech is more obvious to listeners because the speaker has full control over rate, pitch, intensity, and quality at the moment of delivery. Both writer and speaker, on the other hand, have the same basic rhythmic unit—the sentence.

Rhythm through Sentence and Word Stress

Unconscious of rhythmic possibilities in the written or spoken word, most speakers—intent on clarity—simply knit their ideas together, regardless of rhythm. Occasionally speakers such as Franklin Roosevelt, Winston Churchill, Charles de Gaulle, and John Kennedy remind us as listeners that speechmaking can be more than good delivery, clear organization, apt plans of development, and adequate support of ideas. If you listened carefully to a Kennedy speech, for instance, you often heard pleasing sentences and phrases combined with rhythmic stress:

> Let the word go forth
>   from this time and place,
>   to friend and foe alike,
> that the torch has been passed
> to a generation of Americans—
>   born in this century,
>   tempered by war
>   disciplined by a hard and bitter peace,
>   proud of our ancient heritage—
> and unwilling to witness or permit
> the slow undoing of those human rights
>   to which this nation has always been committed,
>   and to which we are committed today
>   at home and around the world.
> Let every nation know,
> whether it wishes us well or ill, that
>   we will pay any price,
>   bear any burden,
>   meet any hardship,
>   support any friend,
>   oppose any foe
> to assure the survival
>   and the success
>   of liberty.[25]

Rhythm through Periphrasis

On rare occasions a speaker gains his rhythmic effect through long sentences that seem to subordinate meaning and emphasize rhythm.[26] A

[25] *Vital Speeches of the Day*, Vol. 27 (February 1, 1961), p. 226.

[26] If *comprehension* is your goal, short sentences seem preferable to longer ones. See John W. Black, "Aural Reception of Sentences of Different Lengths," *Quarterly Journal of Speech*, Vol. 47 (February 1961), pp. 51–53. On the other hand, if *interest* is your goal, longer sentences seem superior in terms of listeners. See Hadley Cantril and Gordon W. Allport, *The Psychology of Radio* (New York: Harper & Row, Publishers, 1935), p. 189.

hearer's impression on listening to this kind of speechmaking is that the speaker is multiplying words purposefully, not for effect gained through word-meaning itself, but for effect gained through rhythmic sounds that pulsate with regularity. Richard Sheridan, for instance, used this stylistic device, called *periphrasis* by the Ancients, when he accused Warren Hastings of being a self-seeking adventurer:

> Oh Faith! Oh Justice! I conjure you by your sacred names to depart for a moment from this place, though it be your peculiar residence; nor hear your names profaned by such a sacrilegious combination as that which I am now compelled to report—where all the fair forms of nature and art, truth and peace, policy and honor, shrink back aghast from the deleterious shade— where all existences, nefarious and vile, have sway—where, amid the black agents on one side and Middleton with Impey on the other, the great figure of the piece—characteristic in his place, aloof and independent from the puny profligacy in his train, but far from idle and inactive, turning a malignant eye on all mischief that awaits him; the multiplied apparatus of temporizing expedients and intimidating instruments, now cringing on his prey, and fawning on his vengeance—now quickening the limping pace of craft, and forcing every stand that retiring nature can make to the heart; the attachments and the decorums of life; each emotion of tenderness and honor; and all the distinctions of national pride; with a long catalogue of crimes and aggravations beyond the reach of thought for human malignity to perpetrate or human vengeance to punish; *lower* than *perdition—blacker* than *despair!*[27]

Rhythm through Parallel and Balanced Phrasing

Most speakers will never deliver lines like Sheridan, since sentences of such length and involvement are difficult to reconcile with present-day thinking about pointed and clear-cut speechmaking. And probably most speakers will never merit the accolade by Edmund Burke to Sheridan of a style "something between poetry and prose, and better than either." In contrast to Sheridan, however, most speakers can add a small amount of rhythm to their speeches by linking together parallel and balanced phrases. Albert Beveridge's famous "Star of Empire" address of 1900 illustrates how one speaker used effectively rhythmic balance to make his point memorable:

> And, now, obeying the same voice
>   that Jefferson heard and obeyed,
>   that Jackson heard and obeyed,
>   that Monroe heard and obeyed,
>   that Seward heard and obeyed,
>   that Grant heard and obeyed,
>   that Harrison heard and obeyed,
> our President to-day plants that flag over the
>   islands of the seas,

[27] Goodrich, *Select British Eloquence*, p. 434.

||| outposts of commerce,
citadels of national security,
and the march of the flag goes on![28]

Rhythm through Repetition

Most speakers will probably find it easiest to instill a rhythmic, periodic beat into their speeches through *repetition*. Sometimes this rhythmic effect is gained by repetitious phrases spoken in relative slow succession, as demonstrated in this next passage from a Churchill address:

> I see the 10,000 villages of Russia, where the means of existence was wrung so hardly from the soil, but where there are still primordial human joys, where maidens laugh and children play. I see advancing upon all this, in hideous onslaught, the Nazi war machine, with its clanking, heel-clicking, dandified Prussian officers, its crafty expert agents, fresh from the cowing and tying down of a dozen countries. I see also the dull, drilled, docile, brutish masses of the Hun soldiery, plodding on like a swarm of crawling locusts. I see the German bombers and fighters in the sky, still smarting from many a British whipping, so delightful to find what they believe is an easier and a safer prey. And behind all this glare, behind all this storm, I see that small group of villainous men who planned, organized and launched this cataract of horrors upon mankind.[29]

At other times rhythmic effect depends on a swift, repetitious sequence. For instance young Pitt, when urging the House of Commons to reject Napoleon's peace offer in 1800, exclaimed:

> We have been asked in the course of this debate: Do you think you can impose monarchy upon France, against the will of the nation? I never thought it, I never hoped it, I never wished it. I have thought, I have hoped, I have wished, that the time might come when the effect of the arms of the allies might so far overpower the military force, which keeps France in bondage, as to give vent and scope to the thoughts and actions of its inhabitants.[30]

SINCERITY AND SUITABILITY

Perhaps it is unnecessary to consider some hazards arising from a too ambitious use of stylistic devices. Yet there exists the real possibility that some speakers will go away from these last two chapters impressed with the notion, "It's *how* you say something that counts; not *what* you say!" This section introduces, therefore, some crucial thoughts on the subject of sincerity and suitability in speechmaking.

Moderation the Touchstone of Good Style

A beginning speaker will often strive so hard for effect that he heavy-hands his address with figures of speech. Hearers will soon suspect this

[28] Ernest J. Wrage and Barnet Baskerville, *American Forum: Speeches on Historic Issues, 1788–1900* (New York: Harper & Row, Publishers, 1960), p. 355.
[29] *Vital Speeches of the Day*, Vol. 7 (July 1, 1941), p. 552.
[30] Goodrich, *Select British Eloquence*, p. 625.

speaker's motives, because his exhibitionism through language in fact says to them, "Look! Ain't I a wonderful critter when it comes to bee-utiful language?" Put another way will this speaker, because of his attention to stylistic devices, become another Danton who exclaimed to his executioner on the guillotine, "Thou wilt show my head to the people; it is worth seeing."

If a speaker gives undue attention to style, he is in danger of magnifying stylistic devices into the very *substance* of speech itself. Unless the style becomes the man, listeners may think that the man *is* style in its worse sense—and, nothing else. John Kennedy, for instance, is a controversial case in point. The late President's speeches, filled with stylistic turns, caused some critics to suspect the man. Was Kennedy an empty windbag, full of empty rhetoric? Was he a grandstander playing to win a niche in history? Was he thinking that he was and could be another Lincoln? One day in the future, Kennedy will have his adverse critics—as Franklin Roosevelt had his debunking, historian-biographers—who may contend that the late President's accomplishments were only a step removed from his high-sounding empty rhetoric. Will *the* man at that time stand up under examination?

But most speakers are not Presidents or persons of worldwide reputation; so these precautionary comments may seem meaningless. Then those speakers of more ordinary credentials might ask themselves these two questions: "Can I as a speaker hold up under even casual examination by my less critical listeners?"; and "Is my speaking style already my Albatross?"

Of course the coin is two-sided and speakers might reason thusly: a plain-talker, sans stylistic embellishment, is no William Jennings Bryan, no Woodrow Wilson, no Franklin Roosevelt, no Winston Churchill . . . but, he is at least free from criticism because of his style. This is a short-sighted and irrational view, and one that cannot be taken seriously. Admittedly, some speakers must content themselves with plain talk because they lack the imaginative capacity necessary for elevated stylistic touches. Even those in this category, however, have a *style* of speaking—a plain style—that can be strengthened for greater accuracy, clarity, economy, and propriety through improved control over grammatical construction and language usage.

There is no escape, therefore, from style; because the way a person expresses his thoughts *is* style—his peculiar style, however good or bad.

Fortunately, most student speakers are malleable insofar as their ways of speaking are concerned. Most use stylistic figures in their speeches and in their everyday conversations. Their usages may lack lustre; and if so, they need to polish their styles, thereby heightening the best qualities in their present manners of expression. So long as they use moderation and good sense when consciously trying to make improvements, their newly reinforced styles will help them, hopefully, to gain their ends, not lose them.

Some Specific Hazards of Style

So far this section treated the hazards and virtues of style in general terms. What of the specifics?

Ludicrous Imagery

Avoid stylistic figures that cause visualization problems. There is little excuse for a speaker who says, "He smiled like a dead Indian in the land beyond the Styx," or who proclaims, "Our ship of state sails forth like the Rock of Gibraltar," or who exclaims, "As I stand before you, I feel like a four-barrelled carburetor, all choked up from carbon deposits and gummy sludge." The three similes are vague, confused, mixed, and ludicrous. If the speaker tried to imagine the pictures formed by his words, he would see that his images were tangled hopelessly. He may conceivably through their use get some laughs from hearers; but his comparisons are far-fetched and will probably grate instead of ingratiate hearers before too many minutes pass.

Clichés

Avoid clichés whenever possible. Expressions as "He was like a bull in a china shop," "He moved like molasses in January," "We sank to the depths of despair," and thousands of other ready-made sayings, have all "seen their better days" "beyond a shadow of a doubt," and a speaker should "look with jaundiced eye" at this kind of language that goes "in one ear and out the other." At one time, of course, all clichés were "fresh as daisies." But when the expressions caught people's attention, they came more and more into common usage, so that now, all a speaker need do is say "apple of my . . .", or "hit the nail on . . .", or "heave a sigh of . . .", and a listener fills in mentally the final words. Of course avoiding clichés "is easier said than done." During the 1948 presidential campaign between Harry Truman and Thomas Dewey, for instance, both candidates mouthed their share of time-worn expressions. Here is a brief sampler: *Truman*— "We're gonna give 'em hell", "The Democratic party believes in the people. It believes in freedom and progress", "It [the Republican party] is the party of 'powerful selfish interests' "; *Dewey*—"As never before we need a rudder to our Ship of State . . . and a firm hand on the tiller", and "Our country is at the crossroads of its history."[31]

Florid Style

Avoid generally what may be referred to as florid style. Here a problem arises because the exact meaning of florid changes from time to time. As used here florid means any touches of style that attract unusual and un-

---

[31] James Reston, "Truman and Dewey Are Fast Men With the Clichés," *The New York Times,* October 19, 1948.

necessary attention to themselves, thereby causing listeners to forget meaning and to concentrate on how the speaker expressed his ideas. For example, hearers may be startled by a speaker's heavy dependence on literary allusions in his speech; or they might sicken at his overuse of repetition in his address. Remember, however, that every style—even florid—is acceptable when viewed in terms of time, occasion, and audience. This explains why a speaker as Richard Sheridan could move pompadoured ladies and powdered gentlemen to tears as he delivered his charge against Warren Hastings. Yet if Sheridan were heard by a modern audience, they might accuse him of hyperbolized language usage. In contrast, if Sheridan's audience could have heard Winston Churchill, they might have walked out on the Man of the Century because they considered his style too plain and too ordinary for their tastes.

Mismatched Style

Avoid style that is unsuited to the speaker's character and demeanor. If a speaker, therefore, is introduced as a dock worker from New Orleans, his hearers would not normally expect him to express himself in the language of a professor in international law; nor would they conversely expect a professor in international law to use the colloquialisms of a New Orleans dock worker. In a sense each person determines his own pattern of speech and sets his own speaking style. Yet audience expectations of a speaker press heavily on him. Thus to hear a would-be United States senator exclaim, "Public pap is so sweet it is hard to resist the appeals of friends for another gimlet-hole to be bored in the treasury and another teat stitched in for these pets to suck"[32] may seem incorrect stylistically for a person in the speaker's position. On the other hand, to hear a senator say, "In my understanding of the Constitution the intent written into it by our Founding Fathers, was the prohibition against the gathering of power in any one branch of our tripartite system of government or any segment of our society"[33] may sound like the natural ruminations of a person in the speaker's position.[34]

Insincere Style

Avoid style that leaves hearers with an impression of insincerity. Even when a speaker's expression is appropriate to his own character, he is still in danger of sounding insincere because his listeners, not knowing him well,

[32] As quoted in Simkins, *Pitchfork Ben Tillman*, p. 109.

[33] Barry Goldwater, "Labor-Management Relations: Unlimited Power of Labor Unions Should be Reviewed," *Vital Speeches of the Day*, Vol. 28 (September 15, 1962), p. 712.

[34] Public reaction, of course, varies from speaker to speaker. Booker T. Washington, for instance, was praised because he spoke without a stereotyped accent. On the other hand, Harry Truman was on occasion criticized for talking in language that some listeners thought unbecoming a President of the United States.

may think or detect that he is either painfully lowering his language standards to match theirs, or that he is purposefully elevating his choice of words to impress them. The line between insincerity and sincerity is admittedly narrow. A government economist addressing a state convention of Future Farmers of America, for instance, may receive compliments from one young audience for avoiding high-flown language, only to suffer chastisement by similar listeners at another state convention for his low-brow word choice. Perhaps the best rule of thumb to follow, consequently, is this: *say what you mean only in a style that expresses your ideas best.* There is, however, some frustration in the advice, because even good speakers will occasionally make stylistic mistakes. For instance the following introduction from an address by Adlai Stevenson gives the distinct impression that the Illinoian, in seeking common ground with his hearers, used language too elevated for a simple expression of pleasure:

> In less strenuous times it has been my good fortune to follow the sun to Florida a couple of times on less urgent business. And, as always, I find myself wondering today if you who live in this well-blessed land fully appreciate your fortunate estate. Or is that a minor compensation reserved for us to whom blue sky, bright sea, and white sand are a benediction after a gray Northern winter?
>
> To me, as to most outlanders, Florida has always seemed a very special place. As I have come to know this incredible peninsula of yours since I first came here as a boy more than forty years ago, I have understood why every visitor looks upon Florida with a proprietary interest—feeling a personal sense of discovery as though he alone found a green land rising from the sea. . . .
>
> Here where we stand you have brought forth a world-famous flowering park from a mangrove swamp. Behind it you have erected your shining city of the sun. Seaward you have raised from the waters that fabulous island, Miami Beach. These things you have added to God's bounty in little more than half a century. . . .[35]

ORAL AND WRITTEN STYLE

As you may know, both writers and speakers depend on language as their communication media. Some *writers* tend towards formal, compact, and grammatically correct use of English for understanding, while some *speakers* lean towards informal, sometimes redundant, and even incorrect usage of English for oral intelligibility. In practice both writers and speakers concern themselves with messages, topic sentences, suspense, climax, emphasis, clarity, and rhythm. Furthermore, both develop ideas in much the same way—by means of definition, analysis, cause and effect, detail, reason, example, comparison and analogy, narrative, and so on. Where speaking

[35] *Miami Herald*, October 12, 1952. As quoted in Eugene E. White and Clair R. Henderlider, *Practical Public Speaking: A Guide to Effective Communication* (New York: Crowell Collier and Macmillan, Inc., 1954), pp. 176–177.

differs from writing style is in the use of *repetition* and *restatement, personalization,* and *channels of communication.*[36] Let us examine briefly the three major differences between the two media.

Because the public address situation is usually a one-way communication channel from speaker to hearer, speakers reinforce comprehension through *repetition* and *restatement* with more frequency than writers. Where a reader, for instance, may re-scan for clarity, and where a reader may sink into his favorite chair to enjoy a book, a listener is no unseen button-pusher who stops and starts speakers at his pleasure, nor is he generally free from distractions—hard chairs, tight collars, cigar-smoking gentlemen, over-perfumed ladies—that divide his undivided attention. Aware of shortcomings in communication media, speakers resort to repetition and restatement as a good way of reinforcing and amplifying their central ideas.

The speaker also is given more to *personalization* than the writer. That is, because a speaker faces his audience directly, he makes use of visible and audible feedback from listeners as he addresses them. Of course writers do not sneak off to hay lofts by themselves while readers remain behind in the parlor. Writers are, however, never sure if they transport a reader successfully to the barn with them because of the feedback impossibility in the writers' communication media. A speaker's very presence before his listeners, in contrast, is an almost nagging reminder that *he* is telling *them,* and that *he* is talking to *them.* A writer, on the other hand, is lost to most readers after the first few pages, and he uses his media, therefore, to let readers take themselves on adventures. This is why you rarely read a piece of prose with author-centered phrases as "Let me tell you," "This brings to mind," "Let me say here," "As far as I'm concerned," "It occurred to me," and so on. On the other hand, a speaker takes listeners into his confidence through these same phrases, thereby personalizing his thoughts as he addresses them. Thus where a *speaker* acts as a seen guide for hearers, a *writer* acts as an unseen and usually impersonal *deus ex machina* for readers.

Finally, a speaker transforms his thoughts generally into more *channels of communication* than a writer. The writer must rely on his skill with words to communicate his message. The extemporaneous speaker, by his bearing and by his control over visible and auditory elements of sincerity, earnestness, and integrity, translates his total feelings and reactions into several stimuli for hearers.[37] Readers cannot see the writer's pleading face, or honest demeanor, or urging gesture—all they see are printed words. The

[36] Syntactical structure was omitted from our key list of differences. Those who disagree with our omission may find it convenient to skip ahead to the section on *syntactics* and *stylistics* in the next chapter for completion of the list.

[37] For a still interesting comparison of audience-communicator reactions through such media as books, television, telephone, congregate assemblies, and conversation, see Table XLV in Hadley Cantril and Gordon W. Allport, *The Psychology of Radio* (New York: Harper & Row, Publishers, 1935), pp. 264–265.

speaker, on the other hand, can allow hearers to *touch* objects through dimensional aids; he can transform part of his emotions into *visible* manifestations for listeners; he can translate the bulk of his reactions into *auditory* cues for audiences; he can on rare occasion permit hearers to experience even *olfactory* stimuli through appropriate aids; and finally he can code part of his ideas into *visible* printed words by using a blackboard or other suitable visual aid.[38]

In closing, a student speaker should study the next two passages: the *first* is from an article by Thomas M. Garrett, S.J., entitled, "TV: Who's to Blame?"; and the *second* is from a 1963 speech by Newton Minow, then chairman of the Federal Communications Commission. The student should observe that both men are discussing the same idea—only one is in written and the other in oral style.

> In short, these critics say, if the networks have full control of programs, things are bound to improve. This is somewhat naive. The American networks already control content of 85 per cent of their shows. Giving them control of the other 15 per cent is not likely to cause much improvement. The reason is simple: if the broadcaster wants big profits, he must have popular shows.
>
> A more practical approach is actually being used by the FCC. Although this body cannot censor or dictate programs, it has the right to demand that stations fulfill promises made in applying for a license. Wholesome fear about renewal of licenses has led some broadcasters to increase offerings of blue-ribbon programs. This is a step in the right direction, but it is hardly going to eliminate the westerns, action shows and quiz shows that so many find annoying.[39]

The excerpt following is from Minow's address:

Note that *as you were promised* and *I remind you* are more direct than *as indicated previously* or *be reminded.*	Third, as you were promised, renewals of broadcast licenses have not been automatic. I remind you that before the New Frontier arrived, former Attorney General Rogers recommended to President Eisenhower in 1959 that the Commission undertake "regular spot checks in depth each year (just as the Internal Revenue Service spot checks individual tax returns) of the renewal applications
A comparison for clarity. This makes for easy listening.	

38 Our list of differences is an attempt to consolidate the numerous nuances that distinguish oral from written style. Students interested in detailed differences should see Gladys Borchers, "An Approach to the Problem of Oral Style," *Quarterly Journal of Speech,* Vol. 22 (February 1936), pp. 114–117; Rudolf Flesch, "A New Readability Yardstick," *Journal of Applied Psychology,* Vol. 32 (June 1948), pp. 221–223; Orville G. Manion. "An Application of Readability Formulas to Oral Communication," (unpubl. diss., University of Michigan, 1953); Roger E. Nebergall, "An Experimental Investigation of Rhetorical Clarity," *Speech Monographs,* Vol. 25 (November 1958), pp. 243–254; Gordon L. Thomas, "Effect of Oral Style on Intelligibility of Speech," *Speech Monographs,* Vol. 23 (March 1956), pp. 46–54; and Jane Blankenship, "A Linguistic Analysis of Oral and Written Style," *Quarterly Journal of Speech,* Vol. 48 (December 1962), pp. 264–265.

39 *America* (January 27, 1962), pp. 556–557. Reprinted with permission from *America,* The National Catholic Weekly Review, 920 Broadway, New York, New York 10010.

Illustrative figures for understanding. Also there is a definite rhythm to the phrases introducing these figures.

of a number of licensees or of the licenses in a particular community."

In the last 2 years, 14 licenses were revoked or denied a renewal; 15 more are now in the hearing process on the question of revocation or renewal; 26 licenses were granted on a short-term basis. Notices of apparent liability for fines have been issued in 21 cases. In 14 hearing cases involving license renewal or revocation, the hearing was ordered held in the station's own community.

The phrase *have also been held* is fluid. In written style the same phrase is wordy.

Some hearings have also been held in the field to give the public a chance to express views on local service. These hearings have been conducted without regard to renewals of licenses. The pub-

Directness through *your* application.

lic—your real ownership—has had an opportunity to give its views—some good, some bad—and to participate to a fuller extent in your decisions on broadcast service. I believe that with

Personalization

broadcasting stations as with income tax returns, the practice of making an occasional audit in depth is an effective though sometimes painful way of finding out whether the public interest is

Personalization

being served. I cannot understand how local expression about broadcasting service can be interpreted as governmental interference with freedom. The

Personalization

public's right to insist on having a voice in your decisions will be honored and maintained.

Comparison for clarity

Some people in this industry, whom you so colorfully call "Shylock" operators and whom we call violators, have been finding out that when they promise public service to obtain a valuable license, they will be held to their prom-

Personalization

ise. And the large majority of you, who do regard the public interest as a way of long broadcasting life instead of a quick

Repetition

commercial break, silently, I repeat, silently endorse our efforts.[40]

---

[40] *Vital Speeches of the Day,* Vol. 29 (May 1, 1963), p. 426.

8   Composing

The subject of this chapter is the proper development of topic and divisional topic sentences, and the importance of unity, coherence, and emphasis for effective speech composition. The assumption of this chapter is that a student speaker knows basic principles of organization; that he is aware of the purpose and types of introductions and conclusions available to a speaker; and that he is knowledgeable of principles and practices of outlining.[1]

TOPIC AND DIVISIONAL TOPIC SENTENCES

Elements

The root of clear organization, both written and spoken, is the often abused *topic* and *divisional topic* sentence. These sentences, known also as *central themes, purpose* or *key sentences, thesis,* and *main heads,* are thought of frequently by students as singular entities pinnacled somewhere in the Himalayas of an address, or as statements representative of the best thoughts in a speaker's message. Sometimes a student thinks of a topic sentence as a forecast announced in the introduction of an address; at other times, he imagines the key sentence as a pronouncement ushered in at the conclusion to sum up his speech; and at still other times, he thinks of a topic statement as any lead-idea for body development. All these notions regarding topic sentences are substantially correct in some instances, yet entirely incorrect in others.

Then what is a topic sentence? A topic sentence is a central thought

[1] The assumption is made also that students know basically how to compose a manuscript speech. For those students who wish to review the subject, they should see Loren Reid, *First Principles of Public Speaking* (Columbia, Missouri: Artcraft Press, 1962), Second ed., Chap. 19, and Giles W. Gray and Waldo W. Braden, *Public Speaking: Principles and Practice* (New York: Harper & Row, Publishers, 1963), Second ed., Chap. 24 for especially good, instructional details.

requiring development for clarity and understanding, either (1) throughout the entire speech, in which case it is called a *topic sentence* (or purpose sentence or central theme), or (2) development within a particular section of the address, in which case it is termed a *divisional topic sentence* (or main head). There are usually *many* key statements throughout an address, and whether one sentence hems in the total speech or only part of the entire address *does not alter* the intent or fundamental requisites of development for such a sentence. The two kinds of topic sentences, in short, differ only in *location* and *magnitude*.

Every topic or divisional topic sentence consists of two parts: (1) the *subject* or *subordinate clause;* and (2) the *predicate* or *main clause*. Of the two parts, the least troublesome to students is the *subject* or *subordinate clause,* because both usually contain innocuous, neutral, and at times self-evident statements of fact or supposition. In contrast, the *predicate* or *main clause* almost always demands amplification for understanding and acceptance by hearers.

The next two topic (*or* divisional topic, as the case may be) sentences will help a speaker understand more fully his developmental obligations towards the thesis statement.

SUBORDINATE CLAUSE	MAIN CLAUSE
"United States foreign policy in Africa . . .	has been a miserable failure."

SUBORDINATE CLAUSE	MAIN CLAUSE
"Before the Congo can manage effectively her own affairs . . .	she will have to conduct a mass education program in civics for her citizens."

In the first example of subject-predicate divisioning, a speaker need only define clearly the terms of his *subject* for hearers; in other words since "foreign policy" and "Africa" may or may not be self-evident to listeners, he must decide whether or not to *define* and *classify* these terms for them. In the second example of subordinate-main clause divisioning, a speaker need only clarify the terms of his *subordinate-clause,* in other words which "Congo" is he talking about? what does he mean by "effective management"? what does he classify as the Congo's "own affairs"?—again, all matters essentially of definition and classification.

Where a speaker meets his real test is in his development of the *predicate* in the first, and the *main clause* in the second instance. Depending on predicate or main clause phrasing, he must prove (convince), arouse (stimulate), detail (inform), or narrate (entertain) this second portion of a topic or divisional topic sentence if he would fulfill his purpose and make audience attendance meaningful. How often, however, have you heard speakers concentrate their attention on the *subject* of a topic sentence to the neglect of a *predicate?* And the reason for this developmental oversight is usually because a speaker misunderstands this aspect of speech composition, or because he fails in adequate preparation for an address. If a speaker gathers minimum materials on his subject, then there is no blinking at truth—his predicate development will probably lack substance. In essence almost any speaker can mouth necessary facts explaining the subject of a topic or divisional topic sentence; but only a good speaker can develop the predicate of a topic or divisional topic sentence in an entertaining, informative, or persuasive manner.

A student speaker may take only small comfort in the fact that even skilled speakers, as in the next illustration, neglect occasionally the predicate and concentrate their attention on inane asides. For instance during a November 1938 debate in the House of Commons over the Ministry of Supply, Winston Churchill announced a predicate (italicized for convenience) that he talked around for fully 2 or 3 minutes:

> I do not think there *was ever any comprehensive plan on a scale appropriate to foreign programs.* We have had many half-measures and many afterthoughts as different courses have emerged from successive shocks to our efforts. I have always had sympathy for my right hon. Friend, the Minister for the Co-ordination of Defense. On public grounds, at considerable personal sacrifice, he accepted nearly three years ago an office for which his high gifts and lifelong specialist training had in no way fitted him. And as the House seemed to realize at the time, although it could not shake off its inertia, the office itself was framed in a manner so curious that he really never had a chance of discharging it successfully. It was a compromise which bore in every paragraph the imprint of inter-departmental interests and rivalries.
>
> I know how hard my right hon. Friend has tried within the limits to which he unwisely submitted himself, and I have no doubt that his tale of praiseworthy activities is a very long one and a very creditable one. He has told us tonight of some of the things he has been doing, and I have no doubt there is very much more to tell, and that he has played a very solid part in pushing this great process of production forward. But I continue to ask, Why was it that an office so irrationally conceived was devised by the Government, and why was it tolerated by the House? It could not have resulted in a smooth or abundant or rapid supply; it could not have resulted in clear definitions of our strategic needs. The mixture of these two opposite spheres and functions was sufficient to vitiate this administration appointment from the very outset.
>
> Such a system as I have described, with its strangely appointed, strangely shaped departmental functions, was on the face of it bound to give results which are less than satisfactory. Prima facie you would have expected a breakdown.[2]

[2] Winston Churchill, *Blood, Sweat, and Tears* (New York: G. P. Putnam's Sons, 1941), pp. 80–81.

The Churchill example is not meant as a convenient excuse for a speaker, but as an illustration of how easy it is to talk beside rather than to a point. In a debate situation, there is at least an excuse that a speaker often wool-gathers out loud as he formulates his thoughts. (The purposeful time-to-think aside appears the case in this Churchill example, since the remainder of his speech applied to the predicate.) In a prepared public address, however, the ready-made excuse is absent. Rightfully, hearers interpret a speaker's failure to develop his predicate as (1) a wish by him to side-step issues, or (2) a failure by him to analyze his speech-subject properly, or (3) a sign of sophomoric thinking on his part.

Development

Occasionally a speaker phrases a purpose sentence that is (1) based on an over-estimation of favorable or unfavorable response from listeners, or (2) premised on an incorrect assumption about hearer attitudes. The solution to the two problems, admittedly easier said than done, is in better audience analysis. Often a speaker's problem, however, is not with audience misanalysis, but with *lack of substantive supporting details* for a topic sentence. In other words a speaker, rushing to fulfill a commitment or a classroom assignment, is apt to commence his composition with only a vague purpose in mind, and to decide on his topic sentence only after completely writing out his speech. However, the resuscitation of a collapsed topic sentence, unlike the esoteric audience analysis problem, is within the realm of practical solution. The speaker's failure is either in laziness or in willingness to settle for the expedient, or worse, a combination of the two. Rather than regard topic sentences as mealy mouthed pronouncements meant to satisfy the requirements of good outlining or of finicky teachers, student speakers would do well to consider their topic statements as honest reflections of their exact attitudes, opinions, or beliefs, tempered by adequate preparation.

A speaker is not obliged to repeat his topic or divisional topic sentences to hearers, just because these sentences cogently summarize his thinking. A topic or divisional topic sentence, in other words, may appear only in his outline as a guide for himself, and he may decide, purposefully, to withhold it from listeners during the speech. Yet some speakers, confused by the predictive quality of most introductions, will invariably open their addresses with a direct statement of central theme and even divisional topic sentences to satisfy the idea of forecast.[3] When a speaker initially reveals his topic sentence to listeners in an address of entertainment or information, he is or is not hurt—depending on his subject and audience—by such

[3] There is a world of difference between a forecast ("I will try to draw some conclusions about a unified Europe") and a revelation of central theme and divisional topic sentences ("I will show you that for the benefit of the entire world, France must be unified to save Europe, and France must be unified to save Germany").

urbane announcement of intention. But in a speech to stimulate and especially in a speech to convince, his revelation of purpose is often ridiculous. Unless he decides on the direct approach in an address, he may only make his task more difficult, if not impossible, by announcing in his introduction, "My purpose today is to convince you that Old Siwash should abandon intercollegiate football."

When developing a *predicate* or *main clause* in an address, a speaker is guided by the methodical steps of such speech "plans" as chronological, cause and effect, problem-solution, motivated sequence, and progression. These plans, however, determine only the *over-all* main head requirements of speech development, and they do not dictate the speaker's internal arrangement of his subject matter. He may, therefore, follow any of three basic *sub-plans* for internal development:

1) He may arrange his ideas logically (classification, comparison, cause and effect, definition, and topical).
2) He may arrange his ideas in chronological sequence.
3) He may arrange his ideas as they occur to him, without attention to logical or to time order arrangement.

There is, of course, no *best* procedure to follow, since the sub-plan arrangement a speaker selects depends on the subject of his speech and on his purpose and personal preference. When Dwight Eisenhower radioed the peoples of Western Europe on D-Day, June 6, 1944, his purpose was to *instruct* and to *stimulate* listeners within the framework of an *over-all* topical plan for his address. In developing the predicate (italicized for you) of his *first* main head, he chose also the sub-plan of *topical* arrangement:

> All patriots, men and women, young and old, *have a part to play in the achievement of final victory.* To members of resistance movements, whether led by national or outside leaders, I say: "Follow the instructions you have received." To patriots who are not members of organized resistance groups I say, "continue your passive resistance, but do not needlessly endanger your lives until I give you the signal to rise and strike the enemy. The day will come when I shall need your united strength. Until that day, I call on you for the hard task of discipline and restraint."
>
> Citizens of France! I am proud to have again under my command the gallant forces of France. Fighting beside their Allies, they will play a worthy part in the liberation of their homeland. Because the intial [*sic*] landing has been made on the soil of your country, I repeat to you with even greater emphasis my message to the peoples of other occupied countries in western Europe. Follow the instructions of your leaders. A premature uprising of all Frenchmen may prevent you from being of maximum help to your country in the critical hour. Be patient. Prepare.[4]

4 *The New York Times,* June 6, 1944. Copyright 1944 by The New York Times Company. Reprinted by permission.

On the other hand, when Anastas Mikoyan visited Cuba in February 1960, the Russian used an *over-all* topical plan for a television address; but he developed *chronologically* the predicate of one of his divisional sentences ("The members of our Soviet Government *have many such bonds with the people*"):

> When one speaks of private matters it is better to speak of oneself than of others. Therefore I shall tell you about my bonds with the people through my family, bonds which are also important. My father, a carpenter by trade, was an illiterate but very devout man. He died 40 years ago. My mother died just a month ago. She could not read or write either. I have a 70-year-old sister who lives on a collective farm. My other sister is the manager of a small handicrafts cooperative. One of my brothers was a factory worker; now he is on pension. The youngest brother in our family designs jet fighters. The members of our Soviet Government have many such bonds with the people.[5]

Finally, when Emperor Hirohito called on his subjects to surrender during a radio address in August 1945, his *over-all* plan of arrangement was cause-effect; but he developed *topically* and *chronologically* an unstated divisional topic sentence ("I have decided to surrender *because the war has gone progressively against us*"):

> Indeed, we declared war on America and Britain out of our sincere desire to insure Japan's self-preservation and the stabilization of East Asia, it being far from our thought either to infringe upon the sovereignty of other nations or to embark upon territorial aggrandizement.
>
> But now the war has lasted for nearly four years. Despite the best that has been done by everyone—the gallant fighting of the military and naval forces, the diligence and assiduity of our servants of the State and the devoted service of our 100,000,000 people—the war situation has developed not necessarily to Japan's advantage, while the general trends of the world have all turned against her interest.
>
> Moreover, the enemy has begun to employ a new and most cruel bomb, the power of which to damage is, indeed, incalculable, taking the toll of many innocent lives. Should we continue to fight, it would not only result in an ultimate collapse and obliteration of the Japanese nation, but also it would lead to the total extinction of human civilization.
>
> Such being the case, how are we to save the millions of our subjects, nor [sic] to atone ourselves before the hallowed spirits of our imperial ancestors? This is the reason why we have ordered the acceptance of the provisions of the joint declaration of the powers.[6]

[5] *Mikoyan in Cuba: Full Texts of the speeches made by Anastas I. Mikoyan First Vice Chairman of the USSR on his tour of Cuba February 4–13, 1960* (New York: Cross-currents Press, Inc. 1960), p. 59.

[6] *The New York Times*, August 15, 1945. Copyright 1945 by The New York Times Company. Reprinted by permission.

UNITY, COHERENCE, EMPHASIS

The next section considers three demigods of written and spoken language—*unity, coherence,* and *emphasis.*

Unity

During the first four formative years of the Democratic Republic of the Congo (Léopoldville), the threat of anarchy and economic collapse so troubled this new African nation that one all-pervading question haunted Congolese citizens and officials. That question was how to maintain the country's sovereignty when pro-Communist rebels and unruly tribesmen thwarted Kasa-Vubu's moderate government at every turn. Over a period of months, public speakers in the Congo used almost every occasion for oratory as a chance to urge citizens to obey authorities and to put their trust in the Central Government. By late 1963 a predictable theme in Congolese public address appeared: almost all speakers, whether dedicating a new dormitory at Lovanium University or opening a trade fair in Léopoldville, concluded their speeches by talking about national survival. A basic theme, *unity,* had emerged in Congolese speaking.

As a student of public address, ask yourself the following two questions: "Do my speeches move surely down a grooved path like a Congolese speaker's address? Or is my speech aimless and liable to haphazard wanderings through a subject?" We suspect that most of you found yourselves faultless; for it is only a rare student speaker who has an ability to study his own masterpieces critically and objectively. On the other hand, almost all students can listen to another speaker and note when he talks around a subject or avoids the main issue, or ends mysteriously on a topic foreign to one announced initially by him. To help control unity in your speechmaking, here are *four* suggestions.

1. As a speaker composes his speech he should keep his topic sentence constantly before him. A good practice is for a learner to write out his proposed topic sentence on a card and place this reminder in a conspicuous place in front of him as he does the paper work necessary for his speech. As he composes his address, he should ask himself repeatedly, "Does this idea *directly* support my topic sentence, or is it, while interesting and close to my subject, a first cousin to my topic?" The temptation is always great and sometimes overpowering for a speaker to include fascinating materials he discovered in reading; or worse, to seek desperately for relations between materials at hand and the topic sentence; or still worse to conjure imagined or false relations. Obviously, if he invents vapor-thin connections between a topic sentence and materials gathered, he needs to re-examine his thinking on his subject and to do more research before beginning speech composition.

2. A speaker should test relations between the topic sentence and

divisional topic sentences with scrupulous care. Should a speaker have a complete working outline before him, his task of scrutinizing the bridges between ideas is much easier, since the relation of parts-to-parts is more apparent. Even a simple listing is better than none, and a skilled speaker, used to stringent thinking, will often find a rough itemization adequate for testing unity. A beginning speaker, however, may find this latter procedure best left to the "pros" than to the "comers."

3. Once a speaker completes his initial composition work, he should if possible record his speech for playback. Since his objective at this stage is solely to test the unity of his address, he should forget about word choice, sentence structure, rhythm, voice quality, and so on as he listens to his speech. A speaker, however, is sometimes his own worst enemy because he may rationalize away lapses in unity and find himself faultless. He may discover, therefore, that a better procedure is to collar an unfortunate roommate or friend into giving him a reaction at this stage, provided his friend is willing to make known negative opinions.

4. After he familiarizes himself thoroughly with his material, a speaker should find that unrelated ideas will often trouble his memory as he runs mentally or verbally through his speech. Although forgetfulness at times indicates no more than a tired or distracted mind, memory problems on other occasions point to a basic failure in speech unity, since a misplaced idea in an address offers the human memory few if any handholds. In contrast points related directly to the subject are like pitons driven into mountain faces by climbers: just as these steel spikes offer the Alpinist sure holds for his hands and climbing rope, a speaker's ideas when related to each other offer firm holds for his memory.

Coherence

Whereas unity refers to congruity of an entire speech or of a major divisional point within an address, *coherence* refers to congruity within any given section of a speech. Student problems with coherence in speech-making arise from the notion that so long as a speaker remains on his subject, he fulfills the requirement of *coherence* as well as *unity*. Thus, when a speaker delivers a speech on ways Shifty-eye Alice, Duplicate-Blue-Book Harry, and Substitute-Brother Henry cheat on exams, he may believe that by remaining on his subject and by maintaining a basic unity, his address is automatically coherent. This is, however, only a half-truth.

To attain coherence in a speech, a speaker must do more than just stay on the subject. There is a vast difference, in other words, between coherence through *kind* and *subject,* and coherence through *knit development;* and the following section from an address by Lyndon Johnson before the Associated Press, New York City, in April 1964 illustrates the point (bracketed numbers inserted for convenience):

[1] The situation in Vietnam is difficult. [2] But there is an old American saying that "when the going gets tough, the tough get going."

[3] So let no one doubt that we are in this battle as long as South Vietnam wants our support and needs our assistance to protect its freedom.

[4] I have already ordered measures to step up the fighting capacity of the South Vietnamese forces, to help improve the welfare and the morale of their civilian population, to keep our forces at whatever level continued independence and freedom require.

[5] No negotiated settlement in Vietnam is possible as long as the Communists hope to achieve victory by force. [6] Once war seems hopeless, then peace may be possible.

[7] The door is always open to any settlement which assures the independence of South Vietnam, and its freedom to seek help for its protection.[7]

This entire passage by Johnson has a coherence of *kind* and *subject:* he speaks of Vietnam, and the word "Vietnam" appears repeatedly in each paragraph or minor thought-division. The quoted section, however, is faulty insofar as coherent, *knit development* is concerned. Did you notice the following positive, questionable, and negative points regarding coherence in the passage?

POSITIVE

1) There is a clear coherence between [1] through [4] on "difficult," "gets tough," "battle," and "fighting."
2) There is a coherence through initial transitional words ("But" and "So") between [2] and [3].
3) There is a clear coherence between [4], [5], and [6] insofar as "fighting," "no possible negotiated settlement," and "hopeless" are concerned.
4) There is a coherence between [6] and [7] in "peace possible" and "door open."
5) There is an extended coherence between [5] and [7] on the idea of "settlement."

QUESTIONABLE

1) There is a coherence breakdown between [4] through [7] that is brought on partially by an absence of transitional words. This is only a questionable problem, since coherence is forged in several ways, only one of which is through transitions.

NEGATIVE

1) There is an absence of coherence in [6] between "war seems hopeless" and "then peace possible." Does Johnson mean when "war seems hopeless" for Communists, then possible peace? Or does he mean when "war seems hopeless" for South Vietnam, then possible peace?

[7] *Vital Speeches of the Day*, Vol. 30 (May 1, 1964), p. 421.

2) There is a lack of coherence in sentence [5]. If there is no possible settlement so long as "victory" is by "force," then does Johnson mean that there is possible settlement if "victory" is by "negotiation"? If he means "negotiation," then this is incoherent, since the relationship of "negotiated settlement" through "negotiation" is redundant.

3) Johnson's coherence between sentences [5] and [7] is vague. If sentence [5] means there is possible negotiation as long as Communists are willing to "compromise" at a settlement table, then the coherence between sentences [5] and [7] is obscure. What is South Vietnam willing to "compromise" in exchange for settlement? Apparently the South Vietnamese will concede nothing because sentence [7] says clearly that any settlement must *assure* independence and not just "partial" or "virtual" independence.

4) If as Johnson indicates in sentence [6] that peace is possible *only* when war is hopeless, then the coherence between sentence [6] and [7] is not clear. Sentence [6] admits the impossibility of peace until such time as war seems hopeless; yet sentence [7] says that the door to settlement is "always" open. The coherence between impossible and possible, consequently, is unclear, since this given situation cannot be *both* qualities at the same time.

The illustration from the Johnson speech was meant only to show you that what sounds good is sometimes incoherent palaver when analyzed carefully. Naturally you need not make schematic presentations of all addresses you compose. Still . . . what of your own speeches? Will they pass inspection?

Now that you reached the halfway house on the subject of *coherence,* you may proceed to an analysis of three practical ways speakers can improve coherence in their addresses.

Arrangement

Perhaps the simplest and most obvious way of gaining coherence in a speech is by means of a logical or natural developmental pattern.[8] There are, of course, numerous forms of over-all or subdivisional arrangement: from the simple *chronological* to the more sophisticated and complex pattern of *problem-solution;* from elementary *topical* arrangement to the intricate, jigsaw puzzle form called *explication.* Such patterns as *chronological, space,* and *topical* order have the advantage of universal under-

---

8 The importance of an easily grasped organizational pattern for increased comprehension by listeners has been verified to some degree in the following studies: Charles E. Irvin, "An Analysis of Certain Aspects of a Listening Training Program Conducted among College Freshmen at Michigan State College," *Speech Monographs,* Vol. 20 (June 1953), pp. 122–123; Ralph G. Nichols, "Factors Accounting for Differences in Comprehension of Materials Presented Orally in the Classroom," *Speech Monographs,* Vol. 16 (September 1949), pp. 350–351; and Donald K. Darnell, "The Relation Between Sentence Order and Comprehension," *Speech Monographs,* Vol. 30 (June 1963), pp. 97–100.

standing by listeners of all races, regardless of cultural or educational levels.

In the next example, Nikita Khrushchev used time-order to provide the coherence for his Washington, D.C. address at a Soviet Embassy dinner party in 1960. The Russian relied on the built-in coherence furnished by obvious, chronological arrangement when shifting back and forth between statement and personal, reflective comments:

> My friends and I have had a fine day today. You are real exploiters, I must say, and have made a good job of exploiting us. (*Animation.*) Mr. [Henry Cabot] Lodge has been empowered to do so, and he has worn us out completely. (*Laughter.*) I don't know whether the exploiters are satisfied with us, but on this particular occasion the exploited are satisfied with their exploiters. (*Laughter.*)
>
> We had an interesting time at your agricultural research center. You can be proud of it. We saw livestock and poultry there—they are excellent. And I did not feel in the least that they had any objection to our representing a socialist country in a capitalist one. They realized the necessity of coexistence. (*Laughter.*)
>
> My next visit today was to the National Press Club. Journalists are impetuous, quick-witted people. You and I, Mr. President [Eisenhower], are able to appreciate each other's plight when meeting journalists. (*Laughter.*) In any case, I am hale and hearty, as you can see, and I think that speaks well for the meeting. As for what they will report, we will know tomorrow. It is something I cannot guess. There were different people there, and they will probably report differently. (*Animation.*)
>
> Then we toured the city of Washington. I bear Mr. Lodge no grudge on this point. We saw little because time was short. But we did see the best section of the city. It is a wonderful city. We saw the Lincoln Memorial and paid homage to that great, most human of humans in U.S. history, whose memory as a champion of freedom will live through the ages.
>
> Then there was the talk with the members of the Senate Foreign Relations Committee. I don't know whether the Senators were pleased with me. I cannot speak for them. But I am pleased, and think that makes a half success. (*Animation.*) If the Senators are also pleased with me, I would take that to be a complete success, but I don't know if they are.
>
> I believe I speak for all my companions when I say that we are very pleased with this evening and with your presence, Mr. President, the presence of your wife and your colleagues, at so distinguished a dinner.[9]

A speaker may, of course, employ a more sophisticated plan than chronological, space, or topical order to provide the development of a particular point with necessary coherence. For instance Jenkin L. Jones, editor of *The Tulsa Tribune,* used obvious problem-solution arrangement when talking about moral decay before a television audience in Johnson City, Tennessee, on the evening of October 31, 1964:

[9] N. S. Khrushchev, *Khrushchev in America* (New York: Crosscurrents Press, Inc., 1960), pp. 43–45.

Finally, there is the status of our entertainment and our literature.

Can anyone deny that movies are dirtier than ever? But they don't call it dirt. They call it "realism." Why do we let them fool us? Why do we nod owlishly when they tell us that filth is merely a daring art form, that licentiousness is really social comment? Isn't it time we recognize Hollywood's quest for the fast buck for what it is? Isn't it plain that the financially-harassed movie industry is putting gobs of sex in darkened drive-ins in an effort to lure curious teen-agers away from their TV sets? Recently the screen industry solemnly announced that henceforth perversion and homosexuality would no longer be barred from the screen provided the subjects were handled with "delicacy and taste." Good Lord!

And we of the press are a party to the crime. Last year the movie ads in our newspaper got so salacious and suggestive that the advertising manager and I decided to throw out the worst and set up some standards. We thought that due to our ukase there might be some interruption in advertising some shows. But no. Within a couple of hours the exhibitors were down with much milder ads. How was this miracle accomplished?

Well, it seems that the exhibitors are supplied with several different ads for each movie. If the publishers are dumb enough to accept the most suggestive ones those are what they get. But if publishers squawk the cleaner ads are sent down. Isn't it time we all squawked?[10]

One more thought before proceeding to the next point: if a speaker is to benefit from matters of coherent arrangement, he should make certain that the pattern he uses is at once natural or logical to hearers. He will no doubt want to avoid the habit of Congolese public speakers who announce to listeners their division titles, their subdivision headings, and even their outline headings as "A," "1," and "a." On the other hand, he will also want to avoid going to the opposite extreme by so secreting away his general arrangement that hearers find it impossible to follow his address.

Repetition and Restatement

Like stylistic repetition, *repetition* for coherence is dependent on the periodic appearance of a key word or phrase throughout a section of an address. Unlike stylistic repetition, word repetition for coherence concentrates on *connective*-value rather than literary or emotional impact. In essence a speaker using repetition for coherence repeats a word or key phrase as an anchor-referent for listeners. As you study the next passage from Douglas MacArthur's Thayer Award speech at West Point in May 1962, see if you can identify the coherent blip that appears regularly to aid listeners:

Yours is the profession of arms, the will to win, the sure knowledge that in war there is no substitute for victory, that if you lose, the Nation will be

10 Jenkin L. Jones, "Who is Tampering with The Soul of America?" as reprinted by Giant Wholesale Grocery Corp., Johnson City, Tennessee. An earlier version of this speech was delivered before the American Society of Newspaper Editors on April 18, 1962, under the title, "The Stomach-Turning Point."

destroyed, that the very obsession of your public service must be duty, honor, country.

Others will debate the controversial issues, national and international, which divide men's minds. But serene, calm, aloof, you stand as the Nation's war guardians, as its lifeguards from the raging tides of international conflict, as its gladiators in the arena of battle. For a century and a half you have defended, guarded, and protected its hallowed traditions of liberty and freedom, of right and justice.

Let civilian voices argue the merits or demerits of our processes of government: Whether our strength is being sapped by deficit financing indulged in too long, by Federal paternalism grown too mighty, by power groups grown too arrogant, by politics grown too corrupt, by crime grown too rampant, by morals grown too low, by taxes grown too high, by extremists grown too violent; whether our personal liberties are as firm and complete as they should be.

These great national problems are not for your professional participation or military solution. Your guidepost stands out like a tenfold beacon in the night: Duty, honor, country.

You are the lever which binds together the entire fabric of our national system of defense. From your ranks come the great captains who hold the Nation's destiny in their hands the moment the war tocsin sounds.[11]

If you identified the word as *you* and its variation, *your,* then you realize how an innocent pronoun provides this passage with its basic coherence. If you did not notice the word, then go back and reread the passage to observe how this single pronoun serves as a roving referent for proper understanding of MacArthur's theme.

Repetition in its more elevated sense satisfies the function of coherence as well as stylistic embellishment. In ordinary uses of repetition, there is a balance between two results: the stylistic touch does not overwhelm the basic thought, nor does the use of repetition for coherence overpower the passage. The following selection from a radio speech by Churchill in November 1942 illustrates ordinary repetition. The repeated phrase is far from striking or vivid; yet the repetition embellishes the passage without endangering or sublimating the function of repetition for coherence:

Remember that Hitler with his armies and his secret police holds nearly all Europe in his grip. Remember that he has millions of slaves to toil for him, a vast mass of munitions, many mighty arsenals, many fertile fields. Remember that Goering has brazenly declared that whoever starves in Europe it will not be the Germans. Remember that these millions know that their lives are at stake. Remember how small a portion of the German Army the British have yet been able to engage and to destroy. Remember that the U-boat warfare is not diminishing but growing and that it may well be worse before it is better.

Then facing the facts—the ugly facts, as well as the encouraging facts—undaunted, then we shall learn to use victory as a spur to further efforts and make good fortune the means of gaining more.

[11] *Vital Speeches of the Day,* Vol. 28 (June 15, 1962), p. 520.

> This much only will I say about the future, and I say it with acute consciousness of the fallibility of my own judgment.[12]

Less spectacular and less apparent, though equally effective and perhaps suited more to most public speakers, is the use of *restatement* for coherence. Instead of a bleating word or phrase, a speaker reverts to the rhetorical device of saying essentially the same thing over and over again, only in different words. Thus where *repetition* has the advantage of unmistakable referents for listeners, *restatement* has its own advantage of variety should a speaker lack creative imagination necessary to invent a striking repetition. When used by a skilled speaker, *restatement* has an undercurrent strength that is as effective in adding coherence to a developed idea, as any elevated use of repetition can probably impart to a passage.

There is, however, an inherent danger in restatement for coherence that is absent in repetition—and that danger is the very real possibility of using misleading synonyms. Unless a speaker has a good vocabulary, he may find himself coloring his ideas with more overtones or undertones than desired. Instead of weaving a neat and subtle coherence into his address, he may patch in a whole spindle full of unwanted thoughts. Consequently, the unobtrusive repetition as MacArthur employed in his Thayer Award speech at West Point has a decided virtue—clarity. Despite the problem arising from selecting false synonyms, restatement is still, in all probability, the all-around-champion, since it adds variety to an address and since it allows a less-skilled speaker to use language without self-consciousness while maintaining coherence.

The following section from a speech by James H. Robinson, Director, Operation Crossroads Africa, delivered at Dartmouth College during the 1963 commencement exercises, illustrates the strength of restatement in terms of amplification and internal coherence.

> The first emancipation was an act of conscience, morality and decency, made law. The second emancipation must be an achievement of the respect and the support of the law, the moral code of religion and democracy and the achievement of the ultimate worth and equality of opportunity and treatment of Negroes as persons of dignity, by the will, desire and action of the majority of the citizens of this land. We can legislate laws to guarantee rights and establish grievance machinery whenever rights are violated. But the law is not and never has been enough by itself alone, important as it is. The second emancipation must be an act of conscience, voluntarily on the part of individual citizens, groups, churches, labor unions, educators, politicians and business concerns to make the race problem their problem and the nation's problem, not just the Negroes' problem.
>
> The almost hysterical reactions of a distinguished white judge, college president, business executive, society leader or ordinary citizen who finds that

---

12 *The New York Times*, November 30, 1942. Copyright 1942 by The New York Times Company. Reprinted by permission.

a Negro desires to move into the neighborhood, eat in a restaurant, join a club, get a job or position, attend a school or church, or ask for the right to equally sacrifice his life for the country in every branch of the armed services is just as disconcerting to Negroes and as damaging to America's honor, integrity and prestige as Little Rock or Greenwood, Oxford or Jackson. There can be no release from the collective discriminations until individuals attain a release for the tyrant from his fears. And what Negro has not witnessed, with anger mixed with pity, the panic in even intelligent white people when they find that the last seat on the plane is beside him.

The next emancipation will of necessity be an emancipation with a dual aspect, but its ends must be freedom of Negroes from separation by whites and freedom of whites from their fears of granting the freedom they demand for themselves to American Negroes.

It must break the bonds of economic, social, political and cultural discrimination as effectively as the first one broke the bonds of involuntary servitude of Negroes, and make it possible for Negroes to develop their full capacities and pour them into this Commonwealth as an everlasting blessing to all its people.[13]

Transition

Finally, a simple *one word* or *phrase* transition and the more complex *sentence-link* (summary, link, and forecast) transition are the devices used most frequently for adding coherence to an address. Of the two basic transitional forms, beginning speakers favor one-word or phrase connectors rather than the fuller, sentence-link transitions. There is, of course, nothing wrong in employing one-word bridges for coherence.[14] A beginner, however, is likely to overuse the simpler variety, and his transitions—especially if the same ones appear over and over again—may prove a major distraction to listeners. To help a speaker become more aware of some common transitional words, here is a list for study. Italicized words are characteristic of oral style; unitalicized ones are common to both oral and written style.[15]

also	These expressions indicate that
and	what follows is *supplementary* to
moreover	what precedes. They link matters of
furthermore	like kind and grammatical form.
likewise	
again	
in addition	

[13] *Vital Speeches of the Day*, Vol. 29 (August 1, 1963), p. 611.

[14] For the significance of one-word transitions, see Joseph Trenaman, "Understanding Radio Talks," *Quarterly Journal of Speech*, Vol. 37 (April 1951), pp. 173–178; and D. L. Thistlewaite, H. J. Haan, and J. M. Kamenetzky, "The Effects of 'Directive' and 'Nondirective' Communication Procedures on Attitudes," *Journal of Abnormal and Social Psychology*, Vol. 51 (July 1955), pp. 107–113.

[15] After Harold C. Martin and Richard M. Ohmann, *The Logic and Rhetoric of Exposition*, Revised ed. (New York: Holt, Rinehart and Winston, Inc., 1963), pp. 226–227.

therefore *and so* *so* consequently subsequently as a result	These expressions indicate that what follows is the *result* of what precedes.
but *however* *yet* on the other hand still nevertheless notwithstanding nonetheless	These indicate a change in direction. These words suggest conflict and sometimes imply concession.
although though while	These words suggest concession.
because for	These two words indicate *reason* for a subsequent statement.
then since as	These conjunctions show cause or relationship in time.
so that in order that for this reason	These show purpose.
of course *in other words* *in fact* *for example* provided that in case that that is to say more specifically naturally to be sure indeed	These words restrict or enlarge.

The following excerpt from a speech by Barry Goldwater delivered before the Economic Club of New York in January 1964 illustrates how a speaker may use one-word or phrase transitions. Connectors are italicized for your convenience.

Also, it has become apparent that just as we cannot defend the world alone, we cannot support the world alone. Multi-national efforts are needed on both counts.

We must, *at the same time,* accept the necessity of helping some of the less-developed nations. Proper ways to accomplish this are available, as through the International Development Association. *But* this way requires constant sharing of the burden, lest any of the well-developed economies, our own in particular, be crippled by an excessive lead. Other nations are able to and should contribute substantially to this course of action.

But this leaves the liberal little new choice for the spending urge. He has to express it again in the domestic poverty issue. *And so,* we have come full circle. The first question, *of course,* is how many Americans are poor? Franklin Roosevelt said that a third of the nation was impoverished and you can still hear the same figure cited, although the certified, pasteurized, homogenized, officialized figure is now one-fifth.

Also, a few years ago, some called a family poor if its income was below $1,500. *Now* it is $3,000. Others say that any family is poor if it can't afford what the Department of Labor computes to be the standard of living of the average urban worker. In a country as wealthy as ours, it is implied, everyone should be *above the average!* [Italics Mr. Goldwater's] An interesting statistical exercise!

The fact is, *of course,* that these income levels are regarded as true wealth in the rest of the world.[16]

A good speaker will often balance simple, one-word connectors with those means of coherence discussed earlier—*arrangement, repetition,* and *restatement.* He will also use the familiar, transitional *sentence-link* described in most basic textbooks on public speaking. Rather than repeat suggestions about sentence-links, here is instead an illustration of several transitional forms as used by David Ormsby Gore during his speech before the Denver Mile High Club in January 1964.

Repetitious introductory phrases for coherence.

Looking back over the last ten years the record of East-West negotiations has been disappointing but it has not been entirely negative. There was the reversal of Soviet policy in the acceptance of the Trieste Settlement. There was the withdrawal of the Soviet occupation forces from Austria some eight years ago, after the signing of the Austrian Treaty which resulted from years of negotiations. After the Geneva Summit Conference of 1955 there were a number of successful agreements made for exchanges of technical missions, artists and

16 *Vital Speeches of the Day,* Vol. 30 (February 1, 1964), p. 235.

Simple chronological arrangement for transitional coherence. This paragraph contains some simple, one-word transitions as well.

educationalists. In 1963 agreement upon a "hotline" improving communications between Washington and Moscow in time of emergency provided a safeguard against war by miscalculation. And last summer again after years of protracted negotiations with the Soviet Union by the British Government and successive United States administrations, we succeeded in reaching an agreement to limit the testing of nuclear weapons. I do not wish to exaggerate the importance of this last agreement in terms of ending the physical pollution of the atmosphere and slowing down the arms race, quite apart from improving the psychological atmosphere for new initiatives and possible new advances. Now that the agreement has been endorsed by almost all nations I think that the whole world must recognize it as an outstanding example of what a joint Anglo-American initiative can achieve.

Sentence-link transition.

Finally I should add to the inventory for 1963 another limited but useful agreement banning the placing of weapons of mass destruction in orbit in outer space,

Extended transitional sentence-link ending in a forecast.

What now are the prospects for 1964 and beyond. Can we keep up the momentum that has been accumulated and use the present slightly easier relations to remove other causes of dispute and friction between East and West. Have any new factors emerged which can encourage us to hope for further progress towards balanced and enforceable disarmament. I suggest three of particular importance in the disarmament field.

First it seems clear to me that. . . .[17]

Emphasis

We turn now to the last demigod of speech composition—*emphasis.* The discussion of this important subject is divided into seven emphatic methods useful to a speaker: *proportion, position, assertion, question, demonstration, syntactics,* and *stylistics.*

[17] *Vital Speeches of the Day,* Vol. 30 (February 15, 1964), p. 287.

Proportion

Just as a sideshow fat lady at the carnival attracts passing crowds by her unusual bulk, so a speaker draws audience attention to an idea by his bulk development of any given point in his address. In other words if a public speaker wishes to emphasize a notion, he may do so by giving unusual, though meaningful, amounts of his total speech time to this key idea.

When a speaker emphasizes through proportion, however, he runs the risk of confusing listeners if they cannot understand immediately why he spends so much time on what they consider a trivial idea, or why he gives so much attention to one point at the expense of another. Furthermore, disproportionate attention to particular ideas may cause hearers to either forget undeveloped ones or to go away with a distorted opinion of the speech. For instance when Achmed Sukarno addressed the Belgrade Conference in September 1961, the vinegary leader from Indonesia threw away his first of two steps in solving world problems:

> What, then, is the way to solve burning present-day issues? Where the conflict of the old interest and the emerging forces has become very acute and expiosive [*sic*], we must as a first step accept the status quo. As a second step we must accept the principle of peaceful co-existence, not only in words but also in deeds. Concrete action must be taken to reduce feelings of hostility by urging the contending parties to initiate talks with the aim of beginning to understand each other. Do not befog the issues by standing stubbornly by previously adopted positions in order to "save face." The aim must be to find an aceptable [*sic*] solution around the negotiating table so as to save the world from extinction.
>
> Let me issue a warning. Miscalculation of the facts as they stand— bluffing in order to see how far the other side will go, may bring us to the verge of disaster. The alternative to peaceful co-existence between the two blocs is war of unimaginable magnitude.
>
> True, peaceful co-existence does not immediately restore the position to normalcy, it does not remove conflicts. But it does remove acute feelings of hostility, and that alone is a gain. . . .
>
> That is why, Mr. Chairman, we in Indonesia firmly believe that the ideological conflict is *not,* I repeat, *not* the main problem of our time. It is not a problem which affects the majority of mankind, such as poverty, disease, illiteracy and colonial bondage.[18]

Proportional development, however, is not reducible to a matter of sums and averages. The human mind, in short, does not decide on the relative importance of given ideas by simply comparing them to previous norms on the subject. Instead, a point developed briefly by a speaker may well impress hearers as crucial because of significant changes in the perceptual

[18] A. Sukarno, "Independence, Peace and Freedom," *Belgrade Conference,* Vol. 3 (Belgrade: Review of International Affairs, September, 1961), pp. 8–9.

situation.[19] For instance when George Wallace, Governor-elect of Alabama, on January 14, 1963, exclaimed in his inaugural address, "I draw the line in the dust and toss the gauntlet before the feet of tyranny . . . ," his challenge was important and memorable, since the contemporary, social conflict over segregation altered the usual perceptual situation and turned his brief statement into an ample, proportional development of his point for hearers.

Remember, therefore, that sheer bulk for emphasis does not end necessarily in a potpourri full of positive virtues. A speaker should learn that there are several *other* means of emphasis—some, infinitely better for his purpose than deceptive *proportion*.

Position

In your development as a speaker, you are well aware of the suggestion that most important ideas are placed either first or last in a speech. You are also aware that climactic development is often used by a speaker because this arrangement situates a crucial idea in its "natural" position of emphasis for listeners. What is not understood as well by many speakers is that *position* refers also to development within any subdivisional point as well.

Students and even accomplished speakers will frequently ignore emphasis through position as they arrange their ideas *within* a main head. Thus where listeners learn to expect *ascending* or *ascending-descending-ascending* order of importance in speech arrangement, they are not expected apparently to project this pattern into subdivisional development. Logically, this oversight on a speaker's part is playing at blindman's buff. Still, there is no avoiding the fact that *ascending-climax-descending* arrangement for a development-unit is common in public speaking.

One illustration should emphasize the point. As you read the passage from John F. Kennedy's inaugural address, ask yourself the following questions: Which global problem is the most crucial one to mankind's survival? Is it national defense, the arms race, failure to negotiate, control of atomic weapons, lack of scientific cooperation, help for the oppressed, inability to proclaim a world law where the strong are just and the weak secure?

> So let us begin anew—remembering on both sides that civility is not a sign of weakness, and sincerity is always subject to proof. Let us never negotiate out of fear. But let us never fear to negotiate.
> Let both sides explore what problems unite us instead of laboring those problems which divide us.
> Let both sides, for the first time, formulate serious and precise proposals for the inspection and control of arms—and bring the absolute power to destroy other nations under the absolute control of all nations.
> Let both sides seek to invoke the wonders of science instead of its

[19] See H. Helson, "Adaptation-level as a Frame of Reference for Prediction of Psychophysical Data," *American Journal of Psychology*, Vol. 60 (1947), pp. 1–29 for details.

terrors. Together let us explore the stars, conquer the deserts, eradicate disease, tap the ocean depths, and encourage the arts and commerce.

Let both sides unite to heed in all corners of the earth the command of Isaiah—to "undo the heavy burdens . . . [and] to let the oppressed go free."

And if a beach-head of co-operation may push back the jungles of suspicion, let both sides join in creating a new endeavor not a new balance of power, but a new world of law, where the strong are just and the weak secure and the peace preserved.[20]

Obviously, until the atomic powers and would-be atomic powers agree on control of the bomb, scientific cooperation, help for the oppressed, and establishment of a just world will mock man's good intentions. As Kennedy himself said in his inaugural address:

But neither can two great and powerful groups of nations take comfort from our present course—both sides overburdened by the cost of modern weapons, both rightly alarmed by the steady spread of the deadly atom, yet both racing to alter that uncertain balance of terror that stays the hand of mankind's final war.

In short until the government solves the bomb problem, solution of secondary questions as national defense, arms race, and negotiation of differences will be defeated ultimately if there is an atomic war. Yet Kennedy placed the idea of atomic control in the *middle* of his subdivisional point.

In terms of speech practice, consequently, a speaker has precedence as his ally, and his positional arrangement of ideas *within* a subdivisional point is immaterial to speech composition. On the other hand, there is still the matter of emphasis and of a hearer's logical expectation that should not be ignored in every instance. Therefore, depending on the topic, occasion, and audience, a speaker should choose between the patterns of positional arrangement he will follow to amplify a point.

Assertion

One obvious way for a speaker to emphasize an idea is for him to announce forthrightly that his coming statement is important. Because speakers overuse such pronouncements as "Now this is important . . .", "Listen to this . . .", and "Here is my point . . .", bland emphatic assertion has probably lost much of the urgency it once held for hearers. Now if a speaker says "Get this" more than three or four times in his address, his listeners may interpret his assertive phrase as a pet expression rather than an apodictic device. Still, blatant assertion has the advantage of unmistakable intention and of predictive clarity when used sparingly by a speaker.[21]

[20] *Vital Speeches of the Day*, Vol. 27 (February 1, 1961), p. 227.

[21] See Ray Ehrensberger, "An Experimental Study of the Relative Effectiveness of Certain Forms of Emphasis in Public Speaking," *Speech Monographs*, Vol. 12 (1945), pp. 94–111; T. W. Harrell, D. E. Brown, and Wilbur Schramm, "Memory in Radio News Listening," *Journal of Applied Psychology*, Vol. 32 (June 1949), pp. 265–274; and Charles T. Brown, "Studies in Listening Comprehension," *Speech Monographs*, Vol. 26 (November 1959), pp. 288–294.

(And we are probably not too far from wrong when we guess that your speech professor prefers unimaginative clarity to imaginative cuteness.)

To make a speaker feel more at ease, here is a sampling of ordinary emphatic assertions from speeches delivered by persons of more than ordinary reputations.

> "Listen while I speak of the night before. You shall see that I watch far more actively for the safety than you do for the destruction of the republic. (Cicero, First Oration against Lucius Catiline, 63 B.C.)

> "I must emphasize this, that when sailors are fighting they busy themselves so much upon that, and take so much interest in that, that they quite forget for a long time to tell us what they are doing, which sometimes causes some embarrassment to the Admiralty and even more to the Minister of Information." (Winston Churchill, Address to House of Commons on Norway, April 11, 1940)

> "In the few words that I am speaking to my fellow countrymen tonight, I desire above all else to emphasize the thought that in just such measure as we support our Government will our Government be strong and effective and safe." (Franklin Roosevelt, Radio Address on Occasion of Sale of First Defense Savings Bonds, April 30, 1941)

> "We [the Government] emphasize that the experience of war in the Congo has borne its fruits against the day when, in spite of the numerous political parties, we understand that our safety rests in unity." (Cyrille Adoula, Address on the 3rd Anniversary of Congo Independence, June 30, 1963)

> "My brothers and children, listen." (His Holiness Pope Paul VI, Speech on Religion as a Goal in Life, March 29, 1964)

A speaker occasionally reverses the usual assertive order by stating his point first and by following his statement with a declarative remark to listeners. There is a certain risk in this procedure, since hearers may receive their cue too late to awake from their doldrums. Nevertheless, speakers—perhaps in search of unusual oral style—do reverse the assertive order, as illustrated:

> We have a right to expect that the Negro community will be responsible, will uphold the law. But they have a right to expect the law will be fair, that the Constitution will be color blind, as Justice Harlan said at the turn of the century.
> This is what we're talking about. (John Kennedy, Speech on Moral Imperative, June 11, 1963)

A speaker frequently emphasizes ideas through *lists* of important points. The very process of providing hearers with an itemized series acts probably as a magnet for attention. To stimulate further interest, a speaker will often preface his remarks with an announcement that he is about to deliver such a list.

Most itemizations in speeches, as the one Richard Nixon used in an address before the American Society of Newspaper Editors in April 1963, are mechanical, get-the-job-done revelations:

> Three elements are essential for a victory of strategy, all based on maintaining the military superiority of the West: (1) Reestablishment of unity among the Western Allies; (2) more effective assistance for the struggling free nations of Asia, Africa, and Latin America who are threatened by Communist subversion; (3) developing a new program to extend freedom to match the Communist efforts to extend slavery.[22]

There are, however, several other ways speakers introduce lists, and all of these additional ways are more imaginative and often more emphatic than the plain "first . . . second . . . third," or "one . . . two . . . three." Speakers may, for instance, omit number designations entirely and, instead, depend on the apparentness of their lists to draw listener attention. When Lyndon Johnson addressed a joint Congressional session in his state of the union message in January 1964, he declared simply:

> That tax bill has been thoroughly discussed for a year. Now we need action.
> The new budget clearly allows it.
> Our taxpayers surely deserve it.
> Our economy strongly demands it.
> And every month of delay dilutes its benefits in 1964 for consumption, for investment and for employment.[23]

Because of the lingering possibility that hearers may miss a list delivered too subtly, speakers sometimes preface each item in a series with an emphatic, attention-getting word or phrase. Arch N. Booth, Executive Vice-President, Chamber of Commerce of the United States, used the attention-getting word when addressing the National Confectioners Association, Washington, D.C., in May 1963:

> Guided by these four principles—limited government, individual freedom, free competitive markets, and steady economic progress—the next step is to take charge of the situation.
> This means: Set out to win.
> It means: Do not do the job by halves.
> Take charge of the situation.
> Work with other businessmen in your industry and in your community to bring America back to the rule of reason. . . .[24]

[22] *Vital Speeches of the Day*, Vol. 29 (June 1, 1963), p. 487.
[23] *Vital Speeches of the Day*, Vol. 30 (January 15, 1964), p. 195.
[24] *Vital Speeches of the Day*, Vol. 29 (July 15, 1963), p. 608.

In contrast to the one-word emphatic form, some speakers create metaphorical images when introducing an important series. The advantage and disadvantage of this emphatic device is, on the one hand, that a speaker may make his ideas memorable, and on the other hand, that he may reduce otherwise good points to overly dramatic notions for listeners. Consequently, should a speaker decide on creating a metaphorical listing, he must remember that the best emphatic itemizations are usually plain in their conception. Woodrow Wilson's Fourteen Points, for instance, are obviously Ten-Commandment-like in reference and draw their strength from worthwhile content. John D. Paulus, Director of Public Relations for Allegheny Ludlum Steel Corporation, used essentially the same technique as Wilson in the next example. Before a Columbus, Ohio, audience in June 1962, Paulus created a simple allusion to accompany his list:

> The myths that still prevail throughout the American public, and which we will have to overcome if the nation is to progress, are these:
>
> MYTH #1—Employment cost increases are tolerable, and consistent with price stability, as long as they are no greater than annual increases in productivity.
>
> MYTH #2—Steel is a monopoly—able to dictate its prices.
>
> MYTH #3—Automation in steel, and other industries, is the cause of unemployment.
>
> MYTH #4—As steel goes, so goes the economy.
>
> MYTH #5—Steel is extraordinarily profitable and can continue to absorb rising costs and rising taxes.
>
> MYTH #6—Productivity increases are the result of higher input per worker per hour.
>
> MYTH #7—Steel's owners—and owners of all business—are the rich people.[25]

Regardless of the emphatic method used to present lists, speakers should make certain that there is internal congruity between their introduction of items and their revelation of series-points. The following example should clarify the suggestion:

> Any settlement of the Berlin issue must provide two nonnegotiable inalienable conditions: (1) the right of the people of West Berlin to live in a system of society and under a system of government of their own free choosing; (2) guarantees of access to West Berlin from the West going beyond mere paper promises, together with all other measures necessary to insure the viability of West Berlin; (3) we regard it as essential that for the foreseeable future Western forces remain in Berlin, as of right, and as custodians of the new agreement; (4) to secure such an agreement we should be prepared to show some degree of flexibility in relation to recognizing the existence of the authorities in East Germany and working out practical measures with them;

[25] *Vital Speeches of the Day*, Vol. 28 (August 15, 1962), p. 658.

and (5) we should show a willingness to recognize on a factual basis Germany's Eastern frontier.[26]

Question

One of the most commonly used emphatic forms in speechmaking is the *direct question-answer* series. As illustrated in the following example from an address by Representative Fisher Ames during the 1796 House fight over the Jay Treaty, the speaker not only asks questions, but answers them as well:

> Will you pay the sufferers out of the Treasury? No. The answer was given two years ago, and appears on our Journals. Will you give them letters of marque and reprisal to pay themselves by force? No, that is war. Besides, it would be an opportunity for those who had already lost much to lose more. Will you go to war to avenge their injury? If you do, the war will leave you no money to indemnify them. If it should be unsuccessful, you will aggravate existing evils; if successful, your enemy will have no treasure left to give to our merchants. . . .[27]

In contrast to direct question, *rhetorical* question requires no answer because the reply is obvious and because the query is introduced primarily for its emotional impact. Charles James Fox, when supporting peace with France before the House of Commons on February 3, 1800, added vehemence to his address through the familiar rhetorical question:

> Gracious God, sir! is war a state of probation? Is peace a rash system? Is it dangerous for nations to live in amity with each other? Are your vigilance, your policy, your common powers of observation, to be extinguished by putting an end to the horrors of war? Can not this state of probation be as well undergone without adding to the catalogue of human sufferings? "But we must *pause!*" What! must the bowels of Great Britain be torn out—her best blood be spilled—her treasure wasted—that you may make an experiment? Put yourselves, oh! that you would put yourselves in the field of battle, and learn to judge of the sort of horrors that you excite![28]

Both forms of question, direct and rhetorical, emphasize ideas through the queries posed. But equal or even greater stress is gained, as in the previous examples, through the imaginative answers given by Ames to his own direct questions, and through the spurious and obvious answers implied by Fox to his rhetorical inquiries.

Vocal and Visual Demonstrations

Whereas both writers and speakers depend primarily on language for emphasis, *writers* have a singular, emphatic advantage through contrasting

---

[26] Harold Wilson, "Relationship of Britain and United States: Labor Party Politics," *Vital Speeches of the Day*, Vol. 29 (May 1, 1963), p. 420.

[27] *The Annals of Congress of the United States*, 4 Cong., 1 sess., p. 1257.

[28] Chauncey A. Goodrich, *Select British Eloquence* (New York: Harper & Row, Publishers, 1853), pp. 549–550.

letter faces and type sizes, and through unusual makeup of words or paragraphs on the printed page. *Speakers* have a singular, emphatic advantage through visual, personal demonstrations not available to writers, and through vocal clues peculiar to the spoken media.

Vocal emphasis in speech is often gained by increasing *volume*, raising *pitch*, slowing *rate*, and varying *vocal quality*. A speaker who drones at a set volume throughout a speech, hammers away at the same pitch level, or rattles on at 250 words a minute will probably emphasize only one thing to listeners—his need for a course in public speaking. If a speaker wishes to emphasize a word, phrase, or sentence, he must contrast volume-to-volume, or pitch-to-pitch, or rate-to-rate, or quality-to-quality, or any combination of these four, such as volume-to-pitch and pitch-to-rate.

Vocal stress is another means of emphasis used by speakers. Through variations in the amount of audible stress given a particular word, a speaker can shorten or stretch out a word in proportion to its normal stress, thereby calling audience attention to the emphasized word. In a manuscript speech he might take full advantage of emphatic stress variations by marking his manuscript with coded reminders. In the extemporaneous speech, however, he cannot control stress to the same pre-planned degree possible for a manuscript speaker. Still, an extemporaneous speaker who gives some attention to vocalized stress during his practice sessions may realize enough carry-over value upon delivery to emphasize—consciously or not—important words in his address.

Another means of emphatic, vocal demonstration is through expressive grunts, groans, or exclamatory words. In 1860, for instance, Giuseppe Garibaldi, the celebrated Italian patriot, exclaimed in an address to a band of heroic soldiers:

> Let timid doctrinaires depart from among us to carry their servility and their miserable fears elsewhere. This people is its own master. It wishes to be the brother of other peoples, but to look on the insolent with a proud glance, not to grovel before them imploring its own freedom. It will no longer follow in the trail of men whose hearts are foul. No! No! No![29]

Garibaldi's declarative noes surely emphasized his point. Try yourself, however, to deliver a series of noes with convincing emotional impact, and you will find it a difficult if not impossible task. In essence, therefore, passionate interjections do point vividly to ideas; but at the same time, unless exclamations are motivated sincerely and uttered spontaneously, and unless interjections are delivered skillfully, this means of emphasis may sour a listener's favorable attitude towards a speaker.

A safer emphatic course for a speaker is to use the *visual* clues of *posture* variations and of *bodily movement*. A demagogue as Fidel Castro,

[29] From *The World's Great Speeches*, Lewis Copeland and Lawrence Lamm, Eds. Second Revised ed. (New York: Dover Publications Inc., 1958), pp. 103–104.

for example, has made the overhead, pumping right hand gesture with pointed index finger an emphatic trademark for himself. A paunchy Mussolini, standing on the balcony of Chigi Palace, made the jutting jaw, tossed-back head, folded arms, and pompous bearing his emphatic trademark. Naturally, emphatic visual demonstration is not the property, nor is it the stamp, of demagogues and dictators . . . unless you classify Theodore Roosevelt and Robert La Follette in the same category as Castro and Mussolini. Except for the pumping right hand, Roosevelt speared home his points visually with a finger thrust jauntily at his listeners. Except for the balcony, La Follette occasionally aped (he was a student actor at the University of Wisconsin) his opposition in voice and action and often tossed his head back to emphasize points.

So where does this leave a student speaker? Should he embrace purposefully emphatic demonstrations of words and ideas that result ultimately in a stereotyped speaker-image—an image akin to a wringing-wet, shirt-sleeved, celluloid-collared oratorical giant from another era, as William Jennings Bryan or Huey Long? Naturally not! Yet the wish to avoid the undesirable does not mean a student speaker should abandon emphatic demonstrations in every instance. The point is many a speaker, more experienced perhaps than most students in the art of public speaking, has learned that one can gain emphasis not only through language manipulation, but through appropriately tempered visual and auditory demonstrations as well.[30]

Syntactics

A speaker frequently emphasizes an idea through unusual word or phrase placement within the syntax of a sentence. Of several syntactical means for emphasis, *four* come within the realm of practical usage by public speakers.

1. An idea is emphasized syntactically through construction. A speaker can express his thoughts in either *periodic* or *loose* sentences. In a periodic sentence, he places his crucial ideas last in a sentence; in the *loose* form, he begins with his important points and ends with subordinate, sometimes anticlimactical thoughts. Generally, a speaker will find periodic sentences are more emphatic than loose ones.

[30] We hesitate to suggest a set way of emphasis through demonstration. Apparently, a pause before an important statement, accompanied by a gesture such as banging a table, adds some emphasis for listeners. See A. T. Jersild, "Modes of Emphasis in Public Speaking," *Journal of Applied Psychology,* Vol. 12 (1928), pp. 611–620; and Ray Ehrensberger, "An Experimental Study of the Relative Effectiveness of Certain Forms of Emphasis in Public Speaking," *Speech Monographs,* Vol. 12 (1945), pp. 94–111. In fact, one study indicates that learning was increased when a speaker, hidden from his audience, used gestures while delivering his speech, as opposed to a hidden gestureless speaker. See P. W. Gauger, "The Effect of Gesture and Presence or Absence of the Speaker on the Listening Comprehension of Eleventh and Twelfth Grade High School Pupils," *Speech Monographs,* Vol. 19 (June 1952), pp. 116–117.

Loose	I never would lay down my arms—never—never—never, if I were an American, as I am an Englishman, while a foreign troop was landed in my country.	*Periodic*	"If I were an American, as I am an Englishman, while a foreign troop was landed in my country, I never would lay down my arms—never—never—never." (Lord Chatham, Speech on a Motion for an Address to the Throne, November 18, 1777)
Loose	I would say to this House, "I have nothing to offer but blood, toil, tears, and sweat," as I said to those who have joined this Government.	*Periodic*	"I would say to the House, as I said to those who joined this Government: 'I have nothing to offer but blood, toil, tears, and sweat.'" (Winston Churchill, Prime Minister Speech, May 13, 1940)
Loose	War cannot be waged without hating the enemy from morning to night, in all the hours of the day and night, without spreading hatred and without making it an intrinsic part of one's self.	*Periodic*	"Without hating the enemy from morning to night, in all the hours of the day and night, without spreading hatred and without making it an intrinsic part of one's self, war cannot be waged." (Benito Mussolini, Speech to the Chamber of Fasci and Corporation, December 2, 1942)

A speaker should keep in mind, however, that overuse of either sentence form tends to equalize all ideas. Although a speaker may agree that periodic sentences are more emphatic, he must remember that not all ideas need emphasis and the loose sentence is a valuable and necessary means of expression for a public speaker.

2. An idea is emphasized syntactically by abruptly placing important words at either the beginning or the end of a sentence. By using unusual syntactics, a speaker calls attention to key words or phrases through his purposeful violation of audience mental set towards sentence order. The following examples illustrate how some speakers used this device for emphasis:

"Finely are the Eretrian commons rewarded for having driven away your ambassadors and yielded to Clitarchus!" (Demosthenes, Speech Denouncing Philip of Macedon, 341 B.C.)

"Symbolical court of the Fugitive Slave Bill—it does not respect life, why should it death? and, scorning liberty, on it way to God, decorum?" (Theodore Parker, Philippic on Daniel Webster, October 21, 1851)

"Soldiers of France, wherever you may be, arise!" (De Gaulle, Radio Speech to Free France, June 19, 1940)

"Always will we remember the character of the onslaught against us." (Franklin Roosevelt, Declaration of War Address, December 8, 1941)

"Army and paramilitary desertion rates increased, and the morale of the hamlet militia—the 'minutemen'—fell." (Robert McNamara, Address on United States Policy Towards South Vietnam, March 26, 1964)

3. An idea is emphasized syntactically through effective placement of key *adverbs*. In contrast to written English where adverbs such as *moreover, furthermore, however,* and *therefore* appear within the body of a sentence, *oral* English positions the adverb initially for maximum effect. Thus where a *writer* might say, "I pray and exhort you, therefore, not to reject this measure," the *speaker* says, "Therefore, I pray and exhort you not to reject this measure." The reason for adverbial shift in spoken English is that speakers accent generally the first word in a sentence, thereby drawing immediate listener attention to the contrasting, corresponding, or sequential idea that follows.

4. An idea is emphasized syntactically through proper positioning of *conjunctions*. Whereas *writers* infrequently use conjunctions as *and, but,* and *or* to introduce sentences, *public speakers* often begin sentences with a conjunction because of the emphasis gained for a coming thought. Naturally, a speaker should not overuse initial conjunctions for syntactical emphasis in a speech, since he will then not only lessen its effect as an emphatic device, but he may also make his oral style seem awkward to listeners. Instances are numerous in famous American speeches when speakers employed this emphatic means. Here are some of them:

"But when shall we be stronger? Will it be the next week, or the next year? Will it be when we are totally disarmed, and when a British guard shall be stationed in every house?" (Patrick Henry, Liberty or Death Speech, March 23, 1775)

"But, in a larger sense, we can not dedicate—we can not consecrate—we can not hallow—this ground." (Lincoln, Gettysburg Address, November 19, 1863)

"For all these things I am grateful to you. But I feel no exultation, no sense of triumph. Our troubles are all ahead of us." (Adlai Stevenson, Acceptance Address, July 26, 1952)

"Nor will it be finished in the first thousand days, nor in the life of this Administration, nor even perhaps in our lifetime on this planet. But let us begin." (Kennedy, Inaugural Address, January 20, 1961)

Stylistics

This last section on emphasis covers seven distinct stylistic forms that broadly speaking belong in the previous chapter. The stylistic devices are included here, however, because they are emphatic *mechanically* rather than *artistically*.

1. A series of short sentences or phrases climaxed by a longer one, or the converse, will often emphasize an idea effectively. There is no necessity to pause long on the point, since this subject was covered indirectly under the heading *Rhythm* in Chapter 7. As illustrated in that chapter as well as in the previous section on "Coherence," balanced development when combined with *repetition* adds even more emphasis to ideas.

2. Omitted conjunctions between words and phrases emphasize key ideas in a sentence. Julius Caesar provided a memorable illustration of this device when he declared before the Roman Senate, "Veni, vidi, vici." Do not confuse the omitted conjunctional series with an ordinary series where a speaker includes a connective between the final two items in sequence, and where he harnesses together all words to make up a total idea. *Each* item in the former series is a *complete thought* in itself, regardless of other items in tandem. Thus where "Fleeing, freezing, and perishing" is normal word grouping, a speaker instead exclaims:

> They fled—they froze—they perished! And now the mighty Napoleon, who had resolved on universal dominion—he, too, is summoned to answer for the violation of that ancient law, "Thou shalt not covet anything which is thy neighbor's."[31]

In another example Lord Brougham, during the Reform Bill debates in 1831, used this stylistic means to stress his appeal before the House of Lords:

> Therefore, I pray and I exhort you not to reject this measure. By all you hold most dear—by all the ties that bind every one of us to our common order and our common country, I solemnly adjure you—I warn you—I implore you—yea, on *my bended knees,* I supplicate you—reject not this bill![32]

3. Conjunction inclusion between all items in a series emphasizes an idea by giving key words or phrases a lingering effect. The following lines delivered by Federalist speaker Josiah Quincy during the House of Representatives debates over admission of Louisiana statehood illustrate this stylistic means of emphasis:

[31] Thomas Corwin, "Against War in Mexico," in *Modern Eloquence: Political Oratory*, Thomas B. Reed *et al.* Eds. (Philadelphia: John D. Morris Company, 1900), Vol. 12, 733.
[32] Goodrich, *Select British Eloquence*, p. 936.

I hold my life, liberty, and property, and the people of the State from which I have the honor to be a representative hold theirs, by a better tenure than any this national government can give. . . . And I thank the Great Giver of every good gift, that neither the gentleman from Tennessee [Mr. Rhea], nor his comrades, nor any, nor all the members of this House, nor of the other branch of the Legislature, nor the good gentleman who lives in the palace yonder [President Madison], nor all combined, can touch these my essential rights, and those of my friends and constituents, except in a limited and prescribed form.[33]

4. Well-chosen words and phrases, matched in an ordinary series, emphasize ideas for hearers as effectively as any emphatic method described previously in this section. As fashioned by one master of language, the common series inspired courage and duty among Englishmen in 1940 when that speaker exclaimed, "I have nothing to offer but blood, toil, tears, and sweat." As fashioned in the hands of another, the common series inspired passionate hate among Cubans in 1961 when the bearded speaker said:

A worker would not have even dreamed of taking a room at the Hotel Nacional or the Hotel Habana Libre or the Hotel Habana Riviera. In those rooms and suites, left empty for a good part of the year, the executives of American companies were put up, the landowners, big latifundistas, international gangsters, smugglers, racketeers in gambling and vice, big politicians, embezzlers, and to sum up, all the top-ranking thieves that existed in this world, those were the ones who used to put up there.[34]

5. Incomplete sentences and ideas, foreign generally to written style, will emphasize occasionally an idea in oral communication. Although the manuscript speech is void usually of incomplete sentences, impromptu and extemporaneous addresses often contain sentences with missing subjects, objects and even verbs. In the next instance from an address by Adolf Hitler delivered in Munich on November 8, 1942, the German dictator emphasized ideas through disjointed sentences that throw listener attention to a subsequent phrase or word:

As for those enemies inside—well, my dear party comrades—the, of course—you understand it was easy to indulge in prophecies. It was easy to forecast that my entire work simply had to fail. On the one hand this tremendous power of the press, this terrific power of capital, this conspiracy of influential circles. These well-tested parliamentarians and these politicians. And so on and so forth. The labor unions. And on the other side the organization of the employers and then the different countries (subdivisions of Germany, such as Bavaria and Thuringia) and the parliaments and the

---

[33] As quoted in Edmund Quincy, *Life of Josiah Quincy* (Boston: Little, Brown, & Company, 1874), p. 208.

[34] Fidel Castro, *Castro Speaks on Unemployment* (New York: Young Socialist Forum, *c.* 1961), p. 2.

Reichstag—all that and against it but one single man with a little group of followers.[35]

Another means of emphasis through incomplete sentence is to break off an idea in mid-thought because of personal, overwhelming emotion. This stylistic device requires no explanation; it needs only the reminder that emotional displays should be genuine and must be appropriate to the theme of an address.

6. By feigning denial of inner thoughts that are in fact declared out loud, a speaker draws listener attention effectively to his denied statement. When used too often in an address, however, this device turns into a meaningless and empty emphatic method. The following instance illustrates how a speaker might use this device in his speechmaking:

> "I will not call him villain, because it would be unparliamentary, and he is a Privy Councilor. I will not call him fool, because he happens to be Chancellor of the Exchequer. But I say he is one who has abused the privilege of Parliament and freedom of debate to the uttering language which, if spoken out of the House, I should answer only with a blow." (Henry Grattan, Speech Ridiculing Isaac Corry, February 14, 1800)

7. Quoted material is introduced emphatically into a speech in any of five ways. Commonest and perhaps the least emphatic form is to follow the lead of high school speakers who simply—though not offensively—say, *quote;* and who frequently—and in an amateurish manner—add at the end, *unquote.* There is this to say in behalf of the word, *quote:* even experienced speakers use this sometimes painfully unimpressive means of introducing quotations. For instance when Clare Boothe Luce spoke of the crisis in Soviet-Chinese relations in 1964 before a commencement audience at St. John's University, she exclaimed:

> The official spokesman of Mao fired the first salvo at the man whom, until that moment all Communists have accepted as their Pope [Khrushchev]: (I quote) "In recklessly introducing the rockets into Cuba and then humiliatingly withdrawing them," said the Chinese, "the Soviets moved from adventurism to capitulationism, and brought disgrace to the Soviet people, the Cuban people, the peoples of the countries in the Socialist camp. . . ."[36]

If a speaker opens and closes quotations in this offhand manner, the effect on listeners may well be *de-emphasis* rather than *emphasis* of quoted materials. In a skilled speaker's hands, however, the two words add an uncommon, almost dramatic impact to an idea. John Kennedy used these two words in the best emphatic sense when he told Americans in October 1962 of Cuban arms build-up during a radio-television address:

[35] *The New York Times,* November 9, 1942. Copyright 1942 by The New York Times Company. Reprinted by permission.

[36] *Vital Speeches of the Day,* Vol. 30 (July 15, 1964), p. 592.

Yet only last month after I had made clear the distinction between any introduction of ground-to-ground missiles and the existence of defensive antiaircraft missiles, the Soviet Government, publicly stated on Sept. 11 that, and I quote, the armaments and military equipment sent to Cuba are designed exclusively for defensive purposes, unquote, that there is—and I quote the Soviet Government—there is no need for the Soviet Government to shift its weapons for a retaliatory blow to any other country, for instance, Cuba, unquote, and that—and I quote the Government—the Soviet Union has so powerful rockets to carry these nuclear warheads that there is no need to search for sites for them beyond the boundaries of the Soviet Union, unquote.[37]

Another way of introducing a quotation—although still lacking maximum emphatic value—is to follow the example of Tingfu Tsiang, Nationalist Chinese Ambassador to the United States, who before a San Francisco audience in June 1963, used the simple, work-a-day declaration:

Mao says to Khrushchev:

"You either make war or help me to make war, to promote the world revolution. You do neither. You are a traitor to Marxism-Leninism. You have abandoned the exploited classes in the capitalist countries and the oppressed peoples in the colonial and 'neo-colonial' countries. Your idea of peaceful co-existence contradicts the teachings of Marx and Lenin. You have capitulated to the United States."[38]

A speaker can also emphasize effectively quoted material by turning his introductory sentence into a qualitative forecast for his quotation. In the next example, August W. Brussat, Pastor of the Trinity Lutheran Church in Scarsdale, New York, used such an introductory sentence to tell his hearers of the relevance and importance of his coming quotation:

Daniel Webster said an important word on the subject of education:
"If we work upon *marble,* it will perish;
If we work upon *brass,* time will efface it;
If we *rear temples,* they will crumble into dust—
But if we work upon immortal minds,
If we imbue them with principles, with the just Fear of God and love of our fellow-men,
We engrave on those tablets something that will Brighten to all eternity."[39]

Finally, a speaker can introduce a quotation emphatically by setting off a key word or phrase with an interrupting, explanatory comment. When following this procedure, a speaker gives his audience a *mental,* demonstrative pause that instantly and emphatically throws their attention in two directions—toward the material *before* the qualifying insertion, and toward the material *after* the insertion. Adlai Stevenson used this means of

[37] *Vital Speeches of the Day,* Vol. 29 (November 15, 1962), p. 66.
[38] *Vital Speeches of the Day,* Vol. 29 (October 1, 1963), p. 762.
[39] *Vital Speeches of the Day,* Vol. 29 (July 1, 1963), p. 557.

introducing a quotation when speaking of human rights before a Brown University audience in January 1964:

> "Justice," President Johnson has said, "is not a partial thing which can be measured in terms of percentages. Any degree of injustice is complete injustice. And until we achieve complete justice we can regard progress only as a series of steps towards the goal. Each step should not lull us into self-satisfaction that the job has been done."[40]

[40] *Vital Speeches of the Day*, Vol. 29 (March 15, 1964), p. 326.

9   The Audience

"Of the three elements in speechmaking—speaker, subject, and person addressed—it is the last one, the hearer, that determines the speech's end and object."[1] As the reader has discovered, Aristotle's dictum is respected in every chapter preceding this one; it is respected in this chapter and every one that follows as well.

Earlier chapters emphasized the importance of the listener as an individual. This chapter, on the other hand, emphasizes the listener as part of an audience. Several steps in the speechmaking process require that listeners be considered as an audience: discovering the knowledge, attitudes, opinions and beliefs that characterize the audience; deciding toward which segment of the audience an address should be pointed; and understanding what impact the existence of the audience has on its members.

A reader should be reminded as he begins to focus on the audience that although the person addressed is the speech's end and object, concern for hearers needs balance of the sort provided by Quintilian: "But the most important of all qualities [a speaker must have] is steady presence of mind, which fear cannot shake or clamour intimidate, nor authority of an audience restrain beyond the just portion of respect that is due to them."[2]

AUDIENCE ANALYSIS

"Literary critics are all, in various way, interpreters of the permanent and universal values they find in the works of which they treat," wrote Herbert A. Wichelns. But rhetorical criticism differs from literary criticism. "Its point of view is patently single. It is not concerned with permanence,

---

[1] *The Rhetoric*, W. Rhys Roberts, Tr. (New York: Modern Library, Inc. 1954), p. 1358b.

[2] *Quintilian's Institutes of Oratory*, John Selby Watson, Tr. (London, Henry G. Bohn, 1856), Vol. 12, Sect. 5, p. 2.

193

nor yet with beauty. It is concerned with effect. It regards a speech as a communication to a specific audience, and holds its business to be the analysis and appreciation of the orator's method of imparting his ideas to his hearers."[3]

Wichelns's advice to critics should also be remembered by speakers, for most speeches are delivered to a specific audience.[4] From the time of ancient Greece when Isocrates wrote speeches for distribution as pamphlets, speeches often have reached audiences greater than that group of people physically present. Radio and television enable some speakers, as a President delivering his inaugural address, to command an immediate, world-wide audience. John F. Kennedy's inaugural contained sections specifically addressed to segments of his worldwide audience. And certainly the audience away was more important than the few thousands who stood in the cold and listened to the President. Nevertheless, though the audience reached by a speech may be extensive, that audience exists at a moment in history; it will be influenced by the set of attitudes and goals it has at that moment.

A speaker may, of course, in reaching his audience deliver a speech of literary, as well as rhetorical, worth. Thus, although Lincoln most assuredly spoke for specific purposes to particular audiences, many of his addresses are still read because of their felicity.

A speaker may deal with recurring great issues or use arguments that have been used time and time again, but they, too, must be adjusted to the specific context in which the speech is given. When Kennedy asked Americans to assume personal burdens to further the national interest, he used an argument as old as the history of nations, but it was adapted to a point in time. Few types of argument will ever be new. The ancient Greek and Roman notion of *topics,* or places to look for arguments, suggests a universality of approaches. The *specific nature* of the argument depends on the subject, occasion, speaker, and—most important of all—the audience.

The problem for the speaker, then, is to know as much about an audience as he reasonably can. He focuses, however, on common denominators, not the extremes. Although more will be said below about which segment of an audience should be addressed, not all segments should be. Range of attitudes and opinions increases geometrically with increase in the number of listeners. To tarry with the few who fail to understand a point may force the majority to boredom and exasperation and the one avenue of revenge open to them in polite society—rejection of the speaker's proposal.

[3] "Some Differences between Literary Criticism and Rhetorical Criticism," in *Historical Studies of Rhetoric and Rhetoricians,* Raymond F. Howes, Ed. (Ithaca, New York: Cornell University Press, 1961), p. 217.

[4] On rare occasions a speech is delivered with an awareness that the future joins the present audience of the important speaker delivering an important speech. A President delivering his inaugural address perhaps feels the weight of future audiences (or critics, at least) as well as of immediate hearers.

Regardless of the speaker's specific purpose, audience analysis has two aspects: discovering how much the audience knows about the subject and learning their opinions, beliefs, and attitudes toward the speaker's proposal.

Whether one is to explain the construction of a cyclotron or convince a listener that a bond issue for new schools is desirable, he must be concerned with how much his listeners already know about his topic so that he can estimate how much additional information must be given to them if he is to succeed in his purpose. Time is precious for a speaker; each moment must contribute to his prospect of effectiveness. To fail to provide essential background material is to ensure lack of understanding; to provide too much is to militate against attention.

Social Strata in Audience Analysis

Clues to an audience's knowledge of, and attitudes toward, a subject are to be found in an analysis of its social strata. Bernard Berelson and Gary A. Steiner believe that "at present, at least in the United States, differences in OAB's [opinions, attitudes, and beliefs] stem from three major factors and two minor ones. The major factors are residence, ethnic status, and class; the minor ones are age and sex."[5]

Residence

The geographical region in which a person lives (North, West, Northeast) and whether he resides in an urban or rural community significantly influences his attitudes. Certain attitudes tend to be more prevalent in the Midwest than in the far East. Isolationism, for instance, for many years has been assumed to be a Midwestern more than an Eastern belief.

While a speaker can be tragically misled in assuming a uniformity of belief for a region, when he has little specific information to go on he may have no alternative but to assume than an audience shares the prevailing regional attitude. A particular danger arises in the speaker basing his estimate on stereotypes, especially overdrawn stereotypes. While Midwestern voters are more likely to vote Republican than are Southern voters (at least until 1964), the easy generalization that any Northern audience should be regarded as Republican and any Southern audience as Democratic would be a mistake.

Residents in rural areas tend to have significantly different values from those in urban areas. Perhaps with the automobile and mass media communication such distinctions are being diminished; yet there is sufficient conflict of interest and variation in experiences for the urban and rural areas to have important differences in attitudes. The problem again is to find what those differences are in a particular setting. For the urban speaker

[5] *Human Behavior: An Inventory of Scientific Findings* (New York: Harcourt, Brace & World, Inc., 1964), p. 570.

to assume that all rural people are poorly traveled is to forget such groups as the "flying farmers."

Ethnic Status

Important and enduring opinions, attitudes, and beliefs characterize different nationality, racial, and religious groups. The influence of religious membership or identification may be stronger than the class or socioeconomic difference. The problem is to discover the predominant position of a group. Before 1954 it would have been safe to assume that Negroes believed in civil rights, but that few were inclined to do anything about what they regarded as their unequal treatment. Now, perhaps among young Negroes especially, that assumption is less valid. For some years the Catholic Church opposed federal aid to private education; by 1960 the position had changed.

Class

Whether measured by income, occupation, education, inherited status, or some combination thereof, the class to which an individual belongs influences his attitudes. Berelson and Steiner write:

> In all modern industrial countries, the upper class is in general not only more interested and more informed about public affairs but also more likely to support what is usually regarded as the conservative or "rightist" position on political affairs than are the lower classes, which tend to side with the liberal or "leftist" position.[6]

It is the lower class that tends to be more authoritarian.

Intellectual ability bears a complex relationship to persuadability. Experiments to discover whether intellectual ability (intelligence and education combined) tends to make a listener more or less persuadable have led to contradictory findings. Carl Hovland, and his associates, explain the discrepancies:

> From the evidence presented . . . , two general hypotheses can be inferred concerning the conditions under which general intelligence is predictive of responsiveness to persuasive communications:
> 1. Persons with high intelligence will tend—mainly because of their ability to draw valid inferences—to be *more* influenced than those with low intellectual ability when exposed to persuasive communications which rely primarily on impressive logical arguments.
> 2. Persons with high intelligence will tend—mainly because of their superior critical ability—to be *less* influenced than those with low intelligence when exposed to persuasive communications which rely primarily on unsupported generalities or false, illogical, irrelevant argumentation.[7]

[6] *Human Behavior*, p. 572.

[7] Carl I. Hovland, Irving L. Janis, and Harold H. Kelley, *Communication and Persuasion* (New Haven: Yale University Press, 1953), p. 183.

Age

According to experimental evidence, age bears a relationship to conservatism. *Conservatism* is not here used in the political sense; rather it is
used to generalize about an individual's willingness to change or seek to
bring about change in his society. Although it has demonstrable weaknesses
and allows for no exceptions, Aristotle's discussion of the impact of age is
as incisive and thought provoking as any. If read with Cicero's opinion in
mind, it has great value: The authority of antiquity "has great weight with
me," Cicero wrote. "I do not demand from antiquity what it has not; rather
I praise what it has, particularly because I judge their excellence of greater
concern than their deficiency."

To begin with the Youthful type of character. Young men have strong
passions, and tend to gratify them indiscriminately. . . . They look at the
good side rather than the bad, not having yet witnessed many instances of
wickedness. They trust others readily, because they have not yet often been
cheated. They are sanguine; nature warms their blood as though with excess
of wine; and besides that, they have as yet met with few disappointments.
Their lives are mainly spent not in memory but in expectation; for expectation refers to the future, memory to the past, and youth has a long future
before it and a short past behind it: on the first day of one's life one has
nothing at all to remember, and can only look forward. They are easily
cheated, owing to the sanguine disposition just mentioned. Their hot tempers
and hopeful dispositions make them more courageous than older men are;
the hot temper prevents fear, and the hopeful disposition creates confidence;
we cannot feel fear so long as we are feeling angry, and any expectation of
good makes us confident. They are shy, accepting the rules of society in which
they have been trained, and not yet believing in any other standard of
honour. They have exalted notions, because they have not yet been humbled
by life or learnt its necessary limitations; moreover, their hopeful disposition
makes them think themselves equal to great things—and that means having
exalted notions. They would always rather do noble deeds than useful ones:
their lives are regulated more by moral feeling than by reasoning; and whereas
reasoning leads us to choose what is useful, moral goodness leads us to choose
what is noble. . . . All their mistakes are in the direction of doing things
excessively and vehemently. They disobey Chilon's precept by overdoing
everything; they love too much and hate too much, and the same with everything else. They think they know everything, and are always quite sure about
it; this, in fact, is why they overdo everything. . . .

. . . The character of Elderly Men—men who are past their prime—may
be said to be formed for the most part of elements that are the contrary of
all these. They have lived many years; they have often been taken in, and
often made mistakes; and life on the whole is a bad business. The result is
that they are sure about nothing and *under-do* everything. They 'think', but
they never 'know'; and because of their hesitation they always add a 'possibly'
or a 'perhaps', putting everything this way and nothing positively. They are
cynical; that is, they tend to put the worse construction on everything. Further,

their experience makes them distrustful and therefore suspicious of evil. Consequently they neither love warmly nor hate bitterly, but following the hint of Bias they love as though they will some day hate and hate as though they will some day love. . . . They guide their lives too much by considerations of what is useful and too little by what is noble—for the useful is what is good for oneself, and the noble what is good absolutely. They are not shy, but shameless rather; caring less for what is noble than for what is useful, they feel contempt for what people may think of them. They lack confidence in the future; partly through experience—for most things go wrong, or anyway turn out worse than one expects; and partly because of their cowardice. They live by memory rather than by hope; for what is left to them of life is but little as compared with the long past; and hope is of the future, memory of the past. This, again, is the cause of their loquacity; they are continually talking of the past, because they enjoy remembering it. Their fits of anger are sudden but feeble. Their sensual passions have either altogether gone or have lost their vigor: consequently they do not feel their passions much, and their actions are inspired less by what they do feel than by the love of gain. Hence men at this time of life are often supposed to have a self-controlled character; the fact is that their passions have slackened, and they are slaves to the love of gain. They guide their lives by reasoning more than by moral feeling; reasoning being directed to utility and moral feeling to moral goodness. . . .

As for Men in their Prime, clearly we shall find that they have a character between that of the young and that of the old, free from the extremes of either. . . . To put it generally, all the valuable qualities that youth and age divide between them are united in the prime of life, while all their excesses or defects are replaced by moderation and fitness. The body is in its prime from thirty to five-and-thirty; the mind about forty-nine.[8]

Sex

According to William F. Dukes, social and cultural factors lead men to score higher than women on a test of "theoretical, economic, and political values but lower on the aesthetic, religious, and social."[9]

The test scores confirm what most people assume: that men are better informed and more active than women in political and economic affairs, while women are better informed and more active than men in religious, cultural, and social activities. The differences, of course, have nothing to do with intelligence. They result principally from expectations of what roles men and women will assume in society.

As with most generalizations about human behavior, this one can be grossly misleading when a specific audience is considered. Any political candidate who has stood before a chapter of the League of Women Voters has learned, if he did not know beforehand, that some of the most active and knowledgeable voters are women.

[8] *The Rhetoric,* pp. 1389a–1390b.
[9] "Psychological Studies of Values," *Psychological Bulletin,* Vol. 52 (1955), p. 26.

Group Membership in Audience Analysis

Analysis of social strata yields important clues to the attitudes that characterize a socially homogeneous audience. Oftentimes, however, a particular audience will include members from a variety of strata. While the Sharon Hill Ladies Bridge Club may be limited to females of wealth who have difficulty in occupying themselves, the Sharon Hill Improvement Association may include some of those same ladies as well as the physician who recently moved to the community, the plumber who lives in the house his father was born in, and the young mother of four children. Understanding of social strata may provide a speaker with all the knowledge of attitudes and beliefs he needs to address the bridge club. Knowledge of social strata would be of little help to him in preparing to address the Improvement Society.

When the audience is socially heterogeneous, the speaker must turn to an analysis of the group to which they belong if he is to obtain the necessary background information. The more stable the group (such as a continuing organization like the improvement society in contrast to a temporary group gathered only to hear a speech and then disbanding), the more useful the analysis will be except for point 2 below, which applies equally to groups requiring only temporary allegiance.

1. *Opinions, attitudes, and beliefs held by members of a group and people who identify with the group tend to be in harmony.* People join groups that are congenial to their attitudes; the groups then reinforce members' existing attitudes and develop their latent attitudes. Thus the Oak Street Businessmen's Association is likely to include only individuals who are interested in the problems of small business. One should not assume, however, that all organizations require agreement on an extensive pattern of attitudes. Perhaps all members of the businessmen's association are in substantial agreement about whether to raise property taxes, but there may be vast disagreement about whether television is a bane or blessing.

Because a speaker often wishes to know about a pattern of attitudes, he is tempted to infer that because members of a group are known to hold a certain attitude, they will also hold a particular related attitude (that is, a group that has a favorable attitude toward modern symphonic music will also have a favorable attitude toward modern art). While any particular inference may be unsound, at times valid assumptions can be made. People and groups seek consistency in their attitudes. And although there may be no inconsistency in liking the music of Copland and disliking the art of Chagall, there is inconsistency in supporting two candidates for the same office, or in supporting a public project and withholding financial support for it. Thus, even though a particular organization may not compel or even actively encourage uniformity in a wide range of attitudes or beliefs, uniformity may exist on issues of extensive public concern.

If the group members characterize themselves, for example, as "conservative," there may be marked uniformity in attitudes toward issues not necessarily closely related. As the position of "conservative" or "liberal" leaders becomes known, individuals who recognize the leadership are likely to follow the lead. Thus, there is a pattern of "conservative" positions on public issues at any particular time. In the early 1960s members of an organization formed to oppose the United Nations probably shared a distrust of federal aid to education and any increase of federal intervention in state or private affairs.

2. *The more important the issue is to a group the more uniform will be the position members take concerning it.* A group formed to encourage United States withdrawal from the United Nations will be closer in agreement on that issue than on whether there should be federal aid to education. Franklin Roosevelt speaking to a Democratic nominating convention in 1940, Charles Lindbergh addressing an America First Committee rally in 1941, and Martin Luther King addressing a civil rights group in Washington in 1964 assumed that the particular occasion assured near uniformity of attitude and made sweeping statements based on the assumption. Audience response suggested that all three made valid assumptions.

3. *The more the group encourages or requires contact between members, the more nearly uniform the members will be in their opinions.* As contacts between members of a group increase, the members become increasingly aware of any discrepancy between their view and the majority view. Those who find themselves in a minority tend either to adopt the view of the majority or to withdraw from membership. Thus, members of an audience attending a mass meeting called to "protest corruption in local government" will have less uniformity in attitudes than will the members of a small, continuing "civic improvement" society, which is sponsoring a meeting on fiscal responsibility in municipal government.

4. *The more complex a particular issue and the more difficult it becomes to estimate the impact of a certain line of action, the more individuals are likely to seek the comfort of knowing they hold views consistent with the majority.* Most of us dislike the loneliness of the small minority; few of us have courage enough to resist the pressures of the majority. Experimental evidence shows that even when an individual feels that his judgment on a relatively obvious matter is correct ("Which of these three lines is equal in length to this fourth line?"), he will tend to adjust his view to the majority position and to offer an excuse for the change ("Maybe I'm having trouble with my eyes").

The desire for corroboration of our position, the wish to know that others agree with us, is even greater when it is impossible to know whether we are right or wrong. At the time a voter must decide between two candidates for the presidency, no ruler can be placed against their future records. Further, however good or bad the performance of the one elected, no one can know how much better or worse the record of the other candidate would have been. Thus, in a presidential election people are especially influenced by group ties when they attempt to sort out the complex issues and make judgments affecting the future of their country.

GROUP OPINION LEADERS

Analysis of any audience will show that its members vary in their knowledge about a topic and have different attitudes toward it. Thus the speaker must decide how much of the disparity he should try to encompass in his speech. Does he try to cover all the members of his audience? Some authorities, such as social psychologists Richard T. LaPiere and Paul R. Farnsworth, believe that he does:

> In any audience situation the leader—actor or lecturer—addresses a hypothetical listener. This member of the audience is not the average member; *i.e.,* his personality is not the average of the personality attributes of all the audience members. The average responsiveness of an audience may remain constant as the number of members increases. . . . But what the leader endeavors to provide is an appeal that will be effective for all the members, not for a nonexistent average member. As audience members increase, the words, gestures, themes, ideas, etc., that will be effective with all, or nearly all of them, become fewer and simpler. Thus, the hypothetical listener toward whom the audience leader directs his efforts becomes, in effect, duller, more stupid, more prejudiced, and less reasonable as the audience increases in size.[10]

This "hypothetical listener" is an unlikable character, indeed: the embodiment of non-virtue, the epitome of man as animal. But he should not concern the speaker. To address such a listener is to forget about the boredom and resentment toward being patronized, which will be experienced by those of us who are better than the worst of us. Actually, the "hypothetical listener"—ignorant, prejudiced, and unreasonable—will not be persuaded. Efforts directed to him are wasted.

If the dullest listeners should not set the level of a speech, should the average man be the focus of attention? Assuming that intelligence, reasonableness, and direction of attitudes and opinions tend to group around some point, would it not be wise to direct the speech at those common points, and therefore encompass the greatest numbers of listeners? Such an approach would minimize the loss of attention by those for whom the argument is either too sophisticated or puerile. Balanced against those considerations, however, is the concept of the *opinion leader.*

[10] *Social Psychology* (New York: McGraw-Hill Inc., Third ed., 1949), pp. 427–428.

Summarizing experimental findings, Berelson and Steiner write that opinions and beliefs

> within a group are particularly subject to influence by the most respected and prestigious member(s) of the group, the opinion leader(s). . . . Virtually every group has its opinion leaders on various topics.[11]

Although the factors of leadership have been investigated almost endlessly, many of them still elude researchers. Nevertheless, some qualities of the opinion leader are known. Particularly important to a speaker is the fact that opinion leaders are better educated than the other members of the group, although not too much better. Americans still view "too much" education with suspicion. *Too much,* however, is a relative term. It means a lot more education than the individual passing judgment received. In addition to being better educated in general, the opinion leader is better educated on the particular issue. He has read more, talked more, listened more, and thought more about it.

When a speaker addresses a continuing organization, the influence of opinion leaders can be anticipated, even though the individuals who operate as opinion leaders may be difficult to identify. But what is the role of opinion leaders in a group gathered for one meeting only, in which a number of "organizations" are represented by virtue of the heterogeneity of the audience? Even here the speaker must remember that most of his auditors will check their conclusions with someone they respect. Clifford T. Morgan reminds us that "since we have relatively few firsthand facts upon which to base our beliefs, we find ourselves trusting authorities instead of facts."[12] The speaker may be regarded as such an authority; on the other hand, someone better known and better respected by the listeners may have more influence than the speaker. Thus, even in the non-periodic meeting, potential opinion leaders should be ever in the forefront of the speaker's thinking.

Rather than search for the hypothetical listener or the average man in an audience, the speaker should search for opinion leaders. Berelson and Steiner state that "the more communications are directed to the group's opinion leaders rather than to rank-and-file members, the more effective they are likely to be."

IMPACT OF BEING PART OF A CROWD

Social psychologist Kimball Young defines a crowd as "a collectivity involving essentially a considerable number of individuals responding within a limited space to some common object of attention."[13] Although

11 *Human Behavior,* p. 569.
12 *Introduction to Psychology* (New York: McGraw-Hill, Inc., Second ed. 1961), p. 537.
13 *Social Psychology* (New York: Appleton-Century-Crofts, Third ed., 1956), p. 286.

there are gradients of crowds ranging from the rioting mob to the most docile audience, writers often distinguish between three types: the action crowd or mob, the passive crowd or casual audience, and the intentional or formal audience. Young characterizes the mob by "shoulder-to-shoulder contact" of "a mass of individuals who, with the common focus of attention, unleash certain deep-lying attitudes, emotions, and action." The passive or casual audience is likely to be characterized by shoulder-to-shoulder contact, but (as with a crowd gathered to watch a building under construction) it does not turn to violent action. It often gathers out of curiosity and limits its action to relatively restrained expressions of pleasure or displeasure at what it views. The intentional audience, such as the audience for a publicized speech event, is less likely to be characterized by shoulder-to-shoulder contact and, like the casual audience, takes no action of such magnitude that it can be called a mob.

Young states that "the chief features of the formal audience are: (1) It has a specific purpose. (2) It meets at a predetermined time and place. (3) It has a standard form of polarization and interaction."

The formal audience or the passive crowd can turn into a mob. Indeed, most mobs probably start out as one or the other. And speechmaking is likely to be a part of any mob. The behavior of all crowds is determined in part by *polarization, social facilitation,* and *circular response.*

Polarization

As Jon Eisenson and his co-authors point out, polarization "is what makes a group of persons into an audience; it introduces structure into an unorganized group."[14] The members of a polarized group direct attention to one person—the speaker—rather than to each other. Without polarization there is but a group lacking the characteristics of a crowd. The people in a busy air terminal, hurrying to various ramps or idling around waiting for flights, lack polarization; hence they are not a crowd in the psychological sense.

Social Facilitation

Young defines social facilitation as "the increase in one's responses due to the presence or activity of other persons."[15] Social facilitation operates powerfully to bring individuals to act in ways they would not consider if they and the speaker were alone. James A. Winans described the differences between man-alone and man-in-a-crowd:

> Men think less keenly in a psychological crowd, their minds being more or less overcome by mass suggestion. They are, therefore, less critical and discriminating, more emotional and responsive. They will respond to senti-

[14] *The Psychology of Communication* (New York: Appleton-Century-Crofts, 1963), p. 274.
[15] *Social Psychology*, p. 294.

ments more noble and more base than those which ordinarily control them. They are credulous and accept exaggeration as wisdom. With the decrease in the sense of personal responsibility, there is a releasing of habitual restraints, reserve and caution. A crowd of men, usually polite, will hoot at strangers, women, or authorities. Men usually reserved will slap each other on the back, shake hands with strangers, parade in lock-step, laugh, shout, sing with abandon. Jokes are funnier, sorrows more grievous, sentiments more uplifting. They have more courage, but also more fear.[16]

Suggestion and imitation account for social facilitation. We have learned to imitate others and to follow implicit suggestions on how to act; hence we applaud when others applaud even though we dislike the performance; we laugh when others laugh even though we miss the point of the story; and we shout for action when others shout for action even though we may be horrified in a quieter moment to contemplate that we endorsed violence.

Circular Response

Whereas social facilitation concerns the impact members of a crowd have on each other, circular response concerns the impact the crowd and speaker have on each other. As David K. Berlo points out, "the audience exerts control" over a crowd leader's "future messages by the response it makes."[17] The interaction process is not limited to a crowd situation. LaPiere and Farnsworth believe that "in the presence of other persons, a man not only reacts to them as stimuli sources, but with rare exceptions is reacted to by them. His reactions are, therefore, at once the effect of their behavior on him and the cause of (the stimuli for) reactions on their part."[18]

This circular response is nearly inevitable. It also often seems capricious. Speakers tend to forget that, as Young states, "all behavior is a combination of present stimulation and the play of pre-existing attitudes, habits, and values."[19] A speaker who considers only himself as a source of stimuli runs the risk of finding the response less than reassuring, or at least of an unanticipated nature.

Wendell Phillips, one of the most effective of the Abolitionist speakers, developed proficiency in dealing with hostile audiences. In one of his early speeches, however, he nearly lost control of the situation. Following the shooting of Elijah Lovejoy, abolitionist newspaper editor in Alton, Illinois, in 1837, the abolitionists of Boston arranged a meeting in famed Faneuil Hall to protest the breakdown of civil authority. To the astonishment of

[16] *Public Speaking: Principles and Practice* (Ithaca, N. Y.: The Sewell Publishing Co., 1915), p. 287.

[17] *The Process of Communication: An Introduction to Theory and Practice* (New York: Holt, Rinehart and Winston, Inc., 1960), p. 113.

[18] *Social Psychology*, p. 381.

[19] *Social Psychology*, p. 291.

the abolitionists, the attorney general of Massachusetts gained the floor and seemed about to turn the meeting to the reverse of its intended purpose. Phillips, prepared to speak but unprepared to answer the attorney general, next took the floor. Aware of the audience's mood, he began: "Mr. Chairman—We have met for the freest discussion of these resolutions, and the events which gave rise to them." Cries of encouragement and discouragement rose from the floor. Phillips continued amid noisy response; when he referred to the Attorney General as a "recreant American" the tumult compelled him to stop. Only with the intervention of another person could Phillips continue.[20]

Rarely are audiences as unruly as those gathered at Faneuil Hall in 1837. Just as surely as did the Bostonians, however, listeners will give the speaker an impression of how his message is being received. The problem is to read the response correctly and, as the situation permits, make necessary adaptations.

Just as an audience can find itself moved by a speaker to unexpected and disastrous responses, a speaker can find himself feeding upon the responses of an audience and reacting in unexpected and later-regretted ways. The consummate orator, like Phillips, carefully controls his response to audience reaction. Oscar Sherwin wrote that Phillips

> never lost his head. Addressing as he did audiences bitterly hostile to him through the great part of his career, his serene self possession won him a hearing. The most prolonged applause could not disturb a muscle in his face and a storm of hisses had as little effect on him.[21]

The Setting and Crowd Reaction

Polarization, social facilitation, and circular response are functions of all aspects of the speech situation. Particular attention should be given to the physical setting in which the speech is given.

1. *Polarization is facilitated when the physical setting encourages listeners to face the speaker and when conflicting points of attention are minimized.* While a circular seating arrangement is ideal when discussion is to take place, such an arrangement encourages people to break down the effectiveness of what Elias Canetti calls the "crowd crystal."[22] Thus, most lecture halls have seating arranged so that a listener tends to face the speaker with unobstructed vision.

2. *Social facilitation is heightened with increased density of the audience.* Even in an audience situation most people are caught between a desire to stand out and a desire to be inconspicuous. Canetti argues that a

20 Oscar Sherwin, *Prophet of Liberty: The Life and Times of Wendell Phillips* (New York: Bookman Associates, 1958), pp. 58ff.

21 *Prophet of Liberty: The Life and Times of Wendell Phillips*, p. 298.

22 *Crowds and Power*, Carol Stewart, Tr. (London: Victor Gollancz, Ltd., 1962), pp. 73ff.

peculiar aspect of the mob is the willingness of its members to be in close contact with individuals, whereas those same individuals, off by themselves, would insist on separateness.

The compactness of the audience contributes in two ways to the magnitude of social facilitation. First, the more compact the audience, the less inhibited individuals will feel in making overt responses to a speaker. The individual in a scattered audience can be singled out readily by both the speaker and other audience members should he applaud, laugh, or give any other indication of his reaction. Second, the more compact the audience, the more readily the response of one member can be communicated to another. As LaPiere and Farnsworth point out, "the slight gasp, the chuckle, or the nod of approval that might stimulate a person in the next seat and thence another, and so on through the audience, cannot be effective if no one is sitting in that seat."[23]

Perhaps Faneuil Hall owes a part of its fame as a place for moving and exciting speeches to its designer, who omitted seats for the audience. It was built so that it could accommodate larger audiences through the expedient of having them stand.

3. *Circular response is intensified when setting encourages the audience to respond and minimizes distractions.* Some settings discourage audience response. Mark Twain wrote to James C. Redpath, his lecture-tour manager: "I never made a success of a speech delivered in a church yet. People are afraid to laugh in a church. They can't be made to do it in any possible way."[24]

Just as the setting determines what an audience regards as its own appropriate response, settings determine what an audience regards as appropriate to a speaker. Familiarity with the ritual (the standard form of interaction) leads audiences to expect certain types of speeches. As Mark Twain discovered, humor in a church shocks many people; and so would a political speech delivered at commencement. The skilled speaker knows the boundaries and deliberately decides when to pass beyond the usual, the expected. If he decides to go beyond the expected, he must be prepared for unusual response from the audience.

Further, setting controls circular response to the extent that an audience is encouraged to attend to the speaker rather than to distracting stimuli. All aspects of a meeting place play a part as background to audience behavior—seating arrangement and kinds of seats, temperature and humidity, wall decorations, acoustics and competing noises, and so on. As was mentioned in the chapter on interest, the speaker must remember that he is but one source of stimulation for the audience. Responses he notices

---

23 *Social Psychology*, p. 431.

24 Printed in Charles F. Horner's *The Life of James Redpath* (New York: Barse & Hopkins, 1926), p. 167.

in his listeners may more reflect dissatisfaction with the heating system than with him.

TELEVISION AND RADIO AUDIENCES

Irvin S. Cobb, lecturer and comedian, described the essential differences between speaking before a microphone and a live audience:

> To step forth before a houseful of paying customers upon an otherwise empty stage and stand there all alone except for the Lord and a pitcher of ice-water—and not be sure of the Lord, either; to consider that this essentially is a one-man show, and if the star flops, they can't rush on some educated sea lions or open a fresh crate of Albertina Rasch dancers—that, I tell you, is a job.
>
> But to walk up to a coldly unresponsive microphone in a cluttered studio, shackled by the restrictions of time and program requirements; to splash your pet joke against the frozen face of that chill disk, without ever being able to tell whether the poor little thing earned an appreciative ripple of laughter across the continent, or just naturally curled up and died—well, that isn't so easy, either. Believe me, my countrymen, it is a strain to be comical in a cuspidor.[25]

Anyone who first experiences the lift of an appreciative audience or the dead hand of unmoved listeners and then speaks to the baleful red eye or a television camera or a "coldly unresponsive microphone" knows that to be uncertain of audience reaction is worse than to know that the joke "just naturally curled up and died." If he knows it died, he may be able to send in a replacement; or he may decide that the next one should be held in abeyance lest that poor little thing, too, be frozen to death. The inability to know what every platform speaker has learned he *must* know (audience reaction) is the difficult part of radio and television speaking.

The best one can do is make the most of some generalizations about radio and television audiences.

1. *Television and radio audiences tend to be more heterogeneous than are face-to-face audiences.* The person who may feel out of place at a public meeting or who has insufficient interest to attend a public gathering may well turn on his television set to see and hear and become a part of the audience along with those who would attend a public meeting.

2. *Television and radio audiences are probably more demanding than are face-to-face audiences if they are to stay with a speech.* The viewers may have less interest in a topic to start with, hence they will be more demanding if they are to continue to view a program. Furthermore, a television set can be easily turned off or switched to another channel, whereas it is a good deal more difficult for an audience member to leave a meeting place. How-

[25] Quoted in Lew Sarett's and William Trufant Foster's *Basic Principles of Speech* (Boston: Houghton Mifflin Company, 1936), pp. 546–547.

ever, in either instance a viewer or an audience member can seem to attend and actually ignore substantially what a speaker is saying.

Part of the difficulty may derive from the public's attitude toward television. In spite of the vast educational potential of the medium, potential only realized in fragmentary amounts, people still regard television as a device for entertainment. Educational television stations struggle for existence; entertainment flourishes almost hide from view the educational aspects of successful educational television shows. Perhaps, as many textbooks advise, the speaker on television must make even more concerted use of attention factors than does the ordinary public speaker.

3. *There is little opportunity for polarization and social facilitation in television speaking.* Even if a television speech is delivered with a visible audience as well as the television audience, the viewers, in the quiet of their homes with few people in the listening group, will be far less influenced by the attitudes of other viewers and listeners. In Chapter 4 we point out that speakers at political gatherings face an almost insoluble problem when they determine whether they are to address the quiet audience at home or the enthusiastic audience before them. Just as it may be impossible to adjust one speech so that it covers the range of the faithful present to the indifferent or hostile at home, it may be impossible to adjust to the group situation of those present and to the informal group away. One rarely finds the same approach precisely suitable for a few people in their living room or den and for a few hundred people in a meeting hall or television studio.

10

The Speaker

Public speaking is the communication of ideas. As earlier chapters have shown, the communication must be considered in terms of a particular audience. It must also be considered in terms of the particular speaker. Whether he would have it otherwise or not, the speaker becomes an integral part of the communication process in a much more fundamental fashion than simply as the medium by which ideas are conveyed.

The fundamental involvement of the speaker means that you as a speaker have certain responsibilities to yourself and your ideas if you are to be effective. It also means that you as speaker have certain responsibilities to your audience. And, finally, it means that you, as an individual who will more often listen to others than deliver speeches yourself, have a responsibility to yourself and society to ensure that other speakers adequately assume their responsibilities.

This chapter is concerned with those responsibilities.

CREDIBILITY OF THE SPEAKER

Observers of public speaking have long noted that effectiveness in speaking depends on an audience's estimate of the speaker as a person as well as on its estimate of what he says. In the fourth century b.c., Aristotle wrote that a speaker's "character may almost be called the most effective means of persuasion he possesses."[1] And in the twentieth century, social psychologist Carl Hovland and his coauthors wrote, "an important factor influencing the effectiveness of a communication is the person or group perceived as originating the communication. . . ."[2] After surveying the many

[1] *The Rhetoric,* W. Rhys Roberts, Tr. (New York: Modern Library, Inc. 1954), p. 1356a.

[2] Carl I. Hovland, Irving L. Janis, and Harold H. Kelley, *Communication and Persuasion* (New Haven: Yale University Press, 1953), p. 13.

experiments on *ethos* (what we refer to as *speaker credibility* and what is often also called *ethical proof*), the rhetoricians Kenneth Anderson and Theodore Clevenger, Jr., concluded:

> The finding is almost universal that the *ethos* of the source is related in some way to the impact of the message. This generalization applies not only to political, social, religious, and economic issues but also to matters of aesthetic judgment and personal taste.[3]

Aristotle thought three things "inspire confidence in the orator's own character—the three, namely, that induce us to believe a thing apart from any proof of it; good sense, good moral character, and good will."[4] Although much has been added to Aristotle's discussion of credibility, his description of its essential components is still useful.

Competence

There has been considerable disagreement whether in what has been translated as *good sense* Aristotle meant high native intelligence or common sense. He meant at least the ability to discover the correct or best (or what at a particular time appears to be correct or best) solution. However, neither intelligence nor common sense alone ensure that a man knows what he is talking about. He needs the information about a topic necessary to make rational decisions. In other words, he needs a degree of expertness, or competence.

Anderson and Clevenger found that sincerity is no substitute for competence: "there is no evidence that the audience can perceive lack of sincerity; rather audiences appear to react to their evaluations of the competence of the speaker."

Competence as a factor in credibility is not determined by measuring a speaker's intelligence and knowledge of a topic against an ideal standard. To be a factor in credibility, a speaker's competence must be measured by his hearers and found adequate. A general audience of voters may grant the competence of the chairman of the Senate Committee on Foreign Relations to speak about complex issues in foreign policy, while a convention of political scientists may not.

Do not assume, however, that good sense is made manifest only by experts who have been fully informed and had an opportunity to evaluate carefully all the evidence. Conditions do not always permit leisurely reflection. There are times when good sense is made manifest by a hurried decision based on little evidence and arrived at by inexpert people. In periods of crisis to wait until all the evidence is in may be to wait too

---

[3] "A Summary of Experimental Research in Ethos," *Speech Monographs*, Vol. 30 (June 1963), p. 77.

[4] Lane Cooper translates the Greek as follows: "apart from the arguments [in a speech] there are three things that gain our belief, namely, intelligence, character, and good will." (*The Rhetoric of Aristotle*, New York: Appleton-Century-Crofts, 1932.)

long. We would guess that when the first arrow hit the stockade, some hasty pioneer assumed there was evidence enough of an Indian attack and sounded the alarm. And the settlement survived because of it.[5]

John Dewey stated the position well in his discussion of how we think:

> The disciplined, or logically trained, mind . . . is the mind able to judge how far each of these steps in an act of thinking needs to be carried in any particular situation. No cast-iron rules can be laid down. Each case has to be dealt with as it arises, on the basis of its importance and of the context in which it occurs. To take too much pains in one case is as foolish—as illogical —as to take too little in another. At one extreme, almost any unified action may be better than any long delayed conclusion; while at the other, decision may need to be postponed for a long period. . . .[6]

To be effective in establishing credibility, competence must be coupled with trustworthiness. Listeners have heard about or known too many corrupt experts to assume that competence is always a surety of honesty. The most successful frauds—as in medicine, for example—have been experts in their area. Hovland, therefore, distinguished between expertness and the degree of confidence the audience has in the "communicator's intent to communicate the assertions he considers most valid."

Good Will

The trustworthy and competent speaker may also be relatively self-centered or concerned with the welfare of some competing group rather than the benefit of his audience. Teddy J. McLaughlin believed that the findings in social psychology show:

> If the would-be persuader is wholly ego-centric in aims and attitudes, there can be no stirring up of feelings or meanings in his audience. The efficacy of the orator depends partially upon the degree and "quality of the social feelings" which he manifests and which are perceived by his listeners.[7]

Good will is most easily demonstrated by speakers who share values, goals, and background with their listeners. Perhaps only those Louisianians who heard Huey Long speak can understand how much a belief in a

---

[5] While we recognize the principle that at times to hesitate is to ensure loss, we also recognize that its misapplication has often led to folly and worse. Patrick Henry's whole argument in his Liberty or Death speech is based on the principle. Since most Americans prefer independence to colonial status and assume that it would have been obtained only by revolution, we now applaud the speech (even though the speech we applaud is William Wirt's) and applaud Henry for his foresight and courage. But are we quite sure that he did not misapply the principle? And how about the northern meetings when John Brown was captured? Or the southern meetings when Lincoln was elected and before he had an opportunity to show whether he would respect the rights of the South?

[6] *How We Think* (Boston: D. C. Heath & Co., 1933), p. 78.

[7] "Modern Social Psychology and the Aristotelian Concept of Ethical Proof," unpublished doctoral dissertation, University of Wisconsin, 1952, p. 80.

speaker's good will could enhance the persuasiveness of a man generally thought to be a scoundrel. Listen to Hamilton Basso.

> I had heard Long speak to the country people many times. I remember one meeting in a little town in the Teche country. It was late fall, but the long bayou summer had lingered and the evening was hot and still. There were patches of perspiration on the blue shirts of the fishermen and the women stirred the air with slow palmetto fans. Huey, his shirt plastered to his back with sweat, was speaking from the rear seat of a Ford; pouring, as they say in that part of the world, acid in their eyes. He attacked the utilities and corporations and the New Orleans ring. He promised us paved roads, free ferries and bridges, lower gas and electric rates, free schoolbooks —and most important of all—a government divorced from crookedness and graft. It was possible to believe what he said, to think that he was earnest and sincere, because as Public Service Commissioner, an office to which he was elected at the age of twenty-five, he had actually opposed the forces he now was baiting—winning, in several cases, important victories for the people. He was young too and spoke American instead of bombast, and I liked his similes and metaphors derived from the barnyard and the cornfield. I liked the stories he told and I joined the others in laughing. They understood and liked him. I liked him too. I had just become awakened politically, beginning to take an interest in such things, and I thought that here was a young and forceful radical it would be well to support.[8]

The advantage of humble beginnings has been enjoyed by many speakers less controversial than Huey Long. Abraham Lincoln and Clarence Darrow, for example, remained common people in important ways. Yet those commoners (if one may take the vast privilege of calling such extraordinary people "common") shared with the aristocrats Franklin Roosevelt and John Kennedy a reputation for understanding the problems and aspirations of the common people, for showing an interest in their welfare, and for enjoying being with them. Significantly, neither Roosevelt nor Kennedy ever pretended to be of modest beginnings, to be a commoner. Perhaps the advantage to being of the common people is limited to an initial presumption that one must therefore share much with the common people. Commoner or aristocrat, however, a speaker talks to people perceptive enough to separate affection from affectation.

CANDOR

Good will requires that the speaker candidly state what he believes necessary and desirable, even though his message may be unpleasant to his audience. The speaker who is concerned about enhancing his credibility, therefore, does not resort to misrepresentation or secretiveness when he decides how to deal with unpleasantness in his message.

[8] "Huey Long and His Background," *Harper's Magazine,* Vol. 170 (May 1935), pp. 663–664.

John F. Kennedy's inaugural address, for example, expressed a mood of confidence, but at the same time made very clear that the years ahead would be difficult.

> In your hands, my fellow citizens, more than mine, will rest the final success or failure of our course. Since this country was founded, each generation of Americans has been summoned to give testimony to its national loyalty. The graves of young Americans who answered the call to service surround the globe.
>
> Now the trumpet summons us again—not as a call to bear arms, though arms we need—not as a call to battle, though embattled we are—but a call to bear the burden of a long twilight struggle, year in and year out, "rejoicing in hope, patient in tribulation"—a struggle against the common enemies of man: tyranny, poverty, disease and war itself.[9]

COURAGE

A man of good will advocates his conception of public welfare even when his position is unpopular and efforts are made to stifle discussion. Times of greatest stress are when fullest discussion of public issues is most required. Ironically, attempts to limit discussion are most strenuous at those very times. To speak against McCarthyism in the 1950s or, in certain parts of the country, segregation in the 1960s required great courage. Not surprisingly, the period of greatest stress in our history—the Civil War period —yielded many examples of courage in speaking. Oscar Sherwin wrote of Wendell Phillips:

> And he had superb physical courage. He faced an infuriated mob in New York. He stood on the platform, rousing his listeners to a rage. Once some of the leaders rushed forward, cut a curtain rope and cried out, "We're going to hang you." "Oh, wait a minute," said Phillips quietly, "till I tell you this story."[10]

They waited, he told the story, and by that time they were sufficiently quieted for him to proceed.

HUMILITY

Implicit in a concept of good will is respect for others as well as concern for their welfare. A speaker inevitably believes that he better understands the topic of his speech than do most of his listeners. However, the speaker who is concerned with credibility is not arrogant in his views. First, he knows that public issues would not be issues were the proper manner of their resolution clear and obvious. Second, he recognizes the fallibility of humans, himself included. When the Constitutional Convention finished

[9] Printed in *Representative American Speeches: 1960–1961*, Lester Thonssen, Ed., Vol. 33, No. 3 of "The Reference Shelf" (New York: The H. W. Wilson Co., 1961).

[10] *Prophet of Liberty: The Life and Times of Wendell Phillips* (New York: Bookman Associates, 1958), p. 298.

its deliberations, Benjamin Franklin commented: "On the whole, sir, I can not help expressing a wish that every member of the convention who may still have objections to it [the Constitution], would, with me, on this occasion, doubt a little of his own infallibility. . . ."[11] Third, he knows that humility becomes the man who presumes to lecture others or prove that they are in error.

Arthur Vandenberg, in a speech renouncing isolationism, well illustrated the good will shown by respect for differing views and uncertainty that the speaker alone has right on his side.

> No man in his right senses will be dogmatic in his viewpoint at such an hour. A global conflict which uproots the earth is not calculated to submit itself to the dominion of any finite mind. The clashes of rival foreign interests, which have motivated wars for countless centuries, are not likely suddenly to surrender to some simple man-made formula, no matter how nobly meditated. Each of us can only speak according to his little light—and pray for a composite wisdom that shall lead us to high, safe ground. It is only in this spirit of anxious humility that I speak today. Politics, in any such connection, would be as obnoxious at home as they are in manipulations abroad.[12]

Moral Character

The term *character* has little standing in psychology or social psychology. The English rendering of Aristotle's writing is intended to suggest that the speaker should seem to be a man of commendable moral qualities, whether those qualities be considered traits or something else.

The previous section considered some traits and moral qualities that relate directly to the speaking situation. The point here is that when audiences pass judgment on a speaker's moral qualities and traits, they do not necessarily confine themselves to those traits and qualities that bear directly on the speaking situation.

Thus, if listeners believe that a man is shy, ambitious, or vain, that belief may lessen his effectiveness, even though the traits bear little or no relation to the adequacy of the ideas presented in the speech. Or if a man does not attend church or admits that divorce may not be sinful or believes in evolution his effectiveness with certain audiences may be diminished.

Knowing the value of seeming to accept his audience's concepts of morality even in essentially private matters, the cynic pretends to be something he is not. The man with self-respect will not give way on matters of morality and character that are his private concern. As Adlai Stevenson told the Democrats when they nominated him for President, he was no different a man after the nomination than he had been before.

---

[11] Printed in *The World's Great Speeches*, Lewis Copeland and Lawrence Lamm, Eds. (New York: Dover Publications, Inc., Second ed., 1958).

[12] Printed in *Representative American Speeches: 1944–1945*, A. Craig Baird, Ed., Vol. 18, No. 3 of "The Reference Shelf."

Credibility Compared to Other Proof

Although audiences are influenced by their estimate of the speaker and such reliance on credibility is both inevitable and necessary, credibility is no substitute for clear thinking and sound argument in a speech. In fact, part of the way in which a speaker demonstrates competence is by making a sound argument.

Even when the speaker is of highest credibility, people will at times reject his message. The evidence on this point is not conclusive, but it suggests that when the message is sufficiently repugnant, listeners will tend to disassociate the source from the message by such devices as suggesting that he really did not say that, or that the message is reported out of context. Thus, when totally unacceptable statements were attributed to President Roosevelt, people favoring him reacted by insisting that he could not have said what was attributed to him. When the speaker is held in somewhat less prestige, a listener may actually revise his estimate of the speaker's credibility rather than accept the repugnant ideas.[13]

Regardless of the extent to which credibility of a speaker enhanced or diminished his persuasiveness, time diminishes the effect. As time passes the effect of the communication depends more on what was said and less on who said it.[14]

Demonstrating Credibility

Only to a certain extent and in limited ways can credibility be improved during a particular speech. If one has a reputation with an audience, a single speech may be quite ineffectual in altering the audience's evaluation of him. Further, some of the devices that speakers might think would be helpful in enhancing credibility actually have no usefulness. After surveying the experiments on credibility, Anderson and Clevenger contend that there is no evidence to support the views "that including conciliatory remarks, statements of self-praise, and other conscious, obvious attempts at ethical appeal [that is, demonstrating credibility] enhances the speaker's status." They also question the value of giving special attention to such incidentals as dress, voice, and general manner on the platform. While these factors "apparently affect the attitude of the audience toward the speaker, [they] may not be related to persuasiveness on a given occasion."[15] Hovland suggests that those incidentals, by distracting listeners from the essential message, can interfere with effectiveness.

There are two areas in which a speaker can establish his credibility during a speech. First, he can show his good will and moral character by

13 *Communication and Persuasion,* pp. 25ff.
14 "A Summary of Experimental Research," p. 76.
15 "A Summary of Experimental Research," p. 78.

using ethical methods of persuasion. This is of such central importance that it is considered in a separate section.

Second, he can demonstrate his competence by handling his subject matter with the thoroughness and good judgment that are characteristic of the expert, and by showing in the speech how the competence was earned.

Following are two examples of how speakers revealed the manner in which competence was acquired.

Harry Truman established his right to talk to members of the American Legion about the purposes of the Legion by reminding them that "I was pretty active in Legion affairs, back in those days [right after World War I]. I helped to establish four different Legion posts in Missouri." Additionally, of course, the opening established common ground between Mr. Truman and his audience.

Winston Churchill carefully documented his right to speak about Franklin Roosevelt in a tribute delivered a few days after the President's death.

> My friendship with the great man to whose work and fame we pay our tribute today began and ripened during this war. I had met him, but only for a few minutes, after the close of the last war and as soon as I went to the admiralty in September, 1939, he telegraphed, inviting me to correspond with him direct on naval or other matters if at any time I felt inclined. Having obtained permission of the Prime Minister, I did so. Knowing President Roosevelt's keen interest in sea warfare, I furnished him with a stream of information about our naval affairs and about various actions, including especially the action of the Plate River which lighted the first gloomy window of the war.
>
> When I became Prime Minister and war broke out in all its hideous fury and when our own life and survival hung in the balance, I was already in position to telegraph to the President on terms of association which had become most intimate and to me most agreeable. This continued through all the years of the world struggle until Thursday last, when I received my last message from him. These messages showed no falling off in his accustomed clear vision and vigor on perplexing and complicated matters. This correspondence, which greatly increased after the United States entry into the war, comprises to and fro between us over 1,700 messages. Many of these were lengthy messages. To this correspondence there must be added our nine meetings, comprising in all about 120 days of close, personal contact.

By describing his acquaintanceship with Roosevelt, Churchill established his right to praise Roosevelt and to conclude by saying: "For us it remains only to say that in Franklin Roosevelt there died the greatest American friend we have ever known and the greatest champion of freedom who has ever brought help and comfort from the New World to the Old."[16]

Although a speaker is limited by modesty and good taste in what he

16 Printed in *Representative American Speeches: 1944–1945.*

can say about himself, a chairman is less limited. Hence, an astute chairman can do much to establish the speaker's competence, good will, and general character. Here is the introduction given to a speaker during World War II.

> Ladies and Gentlemen, back from the field of combat where he faced the enemy fire as an observer and participant in the opening of the Western Front has come one of America's best-known and best-liked writers. We shall hear tonight what the boys over there think about, not from hearsay but as seen, and felt at first hand by one who went side by side with our soldiers in battle. Ladies and Gentlemen, I take great pleasure in introducing to you Quentin Reynolds.[17]

Out of the context of a wartime situation, the introduction seems overdrawn, overly sentimental. But note that the introduction says things that could not have been said by Reynolds, and they were calculated to make clear that Reynolds was competent to speak on his subject. Additionally, the introduction stresses Reynold's moral character, for in war time the most applauded virtue is courage in confronting physical danger.

Television and Speaker Credibility

Television may present unique problems in credibility. An evaluation of the misnomered Great Debates of 1960 between John Kennedy and Richard Nixon led Samuel Lubell to worry that television had, and may continue to have, more impact on the speakers than on viewers. He wrote:

> We must expect that future TV debates will continue to put the prime emphasis on the personality of the candidates rather than on party and issues. Given the nature of TV, the contest between personality and issues is bound to remain an uneven one—as uneven perhaps as matching the crowd appeal of a chorus girl against a she-intellectual with horn-rimmed glasses.[18]

Other responsible observers, such as Charles Siepmann, agree that television places high premium on facets of personality that have little relevancy to the issues.

Surveys following the debate make quite clear that in the 1960 presidential campaign the kind of man voters thought the candidates to be loomed large indeed in making whatever impact the debates had. The candidates themselves anticipated the possibility of the importance of their "image." Douglass Cater, a reporter who covered the debates at the point of origin, wrote, "One thing was quite clear: as they approached this

---

[17] Delivered by Samuel D. Jackson as he introduced Mr. Reynolds to the Democratic National Convention in Chicago, July 20, 1944. Printed in *Representative American Speeches: 1944–1945*.

[18] "Personalities vs. Issues," *The Great Debates*, Sidney Kraus, Ed. (Bloomington: Indiana University Press, 1962), p. 154.

brave new frontier of television, the two candidates were far more concerned about their images than their arguments."[19]

As the candidates reasoned, and as common sense would lead one to expect, the great impersonal, probing eye of the television camera brings people into a position where they feel qualified to judge a man's character. When we want to evaluate a man, we prefer to do it by talking to him, by watching him react. When we are unable to get close to him ourselves, we rely on the TV cameraman with his zoom lens to show us the bead of perspiration (even though it may be brought about by the heat from scoop lights rather than nervousness), and the darting of the eyes (even though the speaker may be trying to find someone to tell him how much time remains rather than revealing "shiftiness" of character).

That we prefer to look a man in the eye when we pass judgment is a recognition of the fact that covert actions often are more revealing of a man's character than are overt actions or what he says. He can tell you he is brave, his actions will confirm or deny his statement.

The quarrel cannot be that viewers seek to evaluate a speaker's character. Rather it is that viewers conclude that the oftentimes adventitious clues revealed by television are clues to character. Removed from the total context, a viewer attributes the reaction to the wrong cause.[20]

The best a speaker can do is to recognize the uniqueness of the television situation and to remember that viewers do not see the lights, the buzzing confusion of the studio. He should also remember that he wishes to keep his audience attending to the subject matter of the speech, not to any mannerism or discomfort he may be feeling.

ETHICAL SPEAKING

The previous section was concerned with the ways a speaker could enhance his credibility so that his ideas would be presented most effectively. To present speech materials in an ethical fashion contributes significantly to credibility, for it demonstrates good will and commendable moral character. As this section shows, however, the necessity for ethical speaking extends beyond the advantage accruing to the speaker. To abide by a moral code in speaking is the way a speaker fulfills his obligation to an audience.

---

[19] "Notes from Backstage," *The Great Debates,* p. 129.

[20] Those who disparage voters because they seem concerned about the speaker's character as well as the issues he discusses misconceive the role of a leader in our society. Often it is more important that we know what kind of a man he is who wishes to have trust and leadership invested in him than it is for us to know his stand on a specific issue. A Presidential candidate, for instance, is seeking the right to represent us on national issues for the following 4 years. No one can know what those issues will be or what the appropriate stand would be in future years, even if the issues could be identified. The best we can do is estimate how he will deal with new issues. Whether he will be timid or forceful, open or secretive, compassionate or harsh are entirely relevant areas for voter concern.

Lists of explicit standards have often been developed in the hopes that speakers could be provided with a relatively complete guide to ethical speaking. Any statements as to whether a specific practice is ethical or un-ethical must, however, be qualified by such terms as *usually* or *ordinarily*. There are probably no practices that are generally regarded as ethical that would not also be regarded as inappropriate (if not unethical) under certain circumstances.

For example, one of the most common and seemingly inviolate tenets in codes for ethical speaking is: a speaker should not misrepresent the facts to an audience. Apart from the problem of finding the point separating the respected figure of hyperbole from the abhorred figure of prevarication, our society *does* permit, and even encourage, certain speakers under certain conditions to misrepresent. President Franklin Roosevelt did not accurately describe the extensive damage to our military installations at Pearl Harbor by the Japanese attack of December 7, 1941. And, as pointed out in another chapter, not until long after the war had been won did the British people learn that Winston Churchill doubted that his promise to repulse any German invasion could be fulfilled. If such misrepresentation was necessary to avoid panic or to keep the enemy from obtaining useful information, most of us would sanction the misrepresentation. Further, in some matters we expect dishonesty. If a chairman thanked a speaker and then said that he thought the speech was a very bad one, most listeners would be horrified.

A speaker must, then, use judgment in ethics as in all other phases of public speaking. Ethical judgments in speaking should not be settled arbitrarily or independently, however. They should be based on an understanding of the place of the persuader in our society.

The discussion that follows rests on two assumptions: that a public speaker should attempt to fulfill his role in a democratic society, and that the society has a right to define that role. The questions considered here, then, have to do with the nature of the role, and how a speaker fulfills its requirements.

Popular government requires that, insofar as possible, citizens be accurately and fully informed so that they might make rational choices on public matters. Citizens in every democracy have depended on individuals better informed on a particular problem than they are to aid in the decision process by supplying information and making an analysis of issues. In his investigations, Hovland noted that the more difficult the issue, the more people rely on advisers:

> The motivation to seek and accept advice from credible sources seems to be increased considerably when the person is in a situation which requires finer discriminations than he is capable of or which demands specialized information not at his disposal.[21]

21 *Communication and Persuasion,* p. 39.

The public speaker's role in this function has often been recognized in the United States, and those individuals who fulfilled it best have been often praised. The United States Senate formed a committee to select five outstanding senators so that their portraits might be placed in the Senate Reception Room. Henry Clay, Daniel Webster, John C. Calhoun, Robert M. La Follette and Robert Taft were selected. At least four of those men would be on any list of outstanding American speakers. Reporting on why the men were selected, John F. Kennedy said of Clay, Webster, and Calhoun: "For over thirty years they dominated the Congress and the country, providing leadership and articulation on all the great issues of the growing nation."[22]

The basic role of the speaker, then, is to assist citizens in making intelligent decisions.[23]

For sound reasons, society has insisted that speakers abide by certain standards as they fulfill the role. Public address may be thought of as competition between a speaker and his audience. The speaker wishes to get his audience to accept his proposition; even the most ethical speaker gives his best efforts to making a convincing argument. Knowing this, listeners tend to be critical of a speech, to examine the arguments for weaknesses, and to resist the proposal until they are convinced of its desirability. Experience with charlatans has shown often enough how important it is that the parties to the competition know and respect the ground rules governing the competition. As the philosopher B. J. Diggs stated, "if men are to live together there must be norms, rules, or conventions known to all and practiced by all—or almost all."[24]

Failure to respect the norms for speechmaking enables a speaker to use persuasive devices that make an issue appear to have more merit than it actually has. Therefore, to avoid giving arguments undue weight, a speaker must respect the limits beyond which society says he should not go in a particular circumstance. Conversely, one may insist that a speaker, particularly if he has been entrusted with the responsibilities as spokesman for an idea, is obligated to carry on his argument as vigorously as he can within the limits. Whether or not the criticism was justified, many Democrats thought Adlai Stevenson carried on a less vigorous campaign for the presidency than his obligations as spokesman for the Democratic party required.

[22] Printed in *Representative American Speeches: 1957–1958*, A Craig Baird, Ed., Vol. 30, No. 4 of "The Reference Shelf."

[23] For a fuller statement on the speaker's function in aiding citizens to make rational choices, see Franklyn S. Haiman's article, "Democratic Ethics and the Hidden Persuaders," *The Quartely Journal of Speech*, Vol. 44 (December 1958), pp. 385–392.

[24] "Persuasion and Ethics," *The Quarterly Journal of Speech*, Vol. 50 (December 1964), p. 367.

Even when a speaker wishes to respect the norms established by his society, he has difficulty in learning what they are. Many of them are extensions of general norms—tell the truth, keep your promises, and so on. Others pertain specifically to speechmaking. For example, the degree to which a speaker is permitted to exaggerate varies with the type of speech. If the following statement were given by a professor of political science to a freshman class, the professor would be severely condemned.

> Its [freedom's] destruction is threatened today by spending and taxation and excessive power of big government in Washington. . . . We can only preserve our liberty by putting into office men and women imbued with a hatred of that totalitarian philosophy of spending and power.

The statement was actually made by Robert Taft in the middle of a vigorous presidential campaign.[25] Probably very few people, not even the Democratic leaders, were shocked by it. In other words, the accepted standards require more objectivity and less exaggeration in a lecture before a college class than in a speech before a political gathering.

To catalog all the accepted practices and their nuances would probably fill a book as large as this one. The speaker must search out the standards that govern speechmaking in a specific situation. And he must respect those standards if he is to fulfill his function in helping citizens to make intelligent choices.

We turn now to four recurring questions about ethical speaking.

Preempting the Right of Decision and Ethical Speaking

The essence of democracy is that decisions concerning the public welfare are to be made by the public. At times, however, public welfare is best served if decisions are made for, rather than by, the public. When does a speaker have the right to misrepresent or conceal information, or in other ways deliberately manipulate persuasion so that the citizenry can no longer make intelligent choices?

As pointed out above, such situations do occur, although under very precise conditions. First, the speaker must have already been entrusted with great responsibilities, including the right at times to make substantial decisions for the public. Second, the speaker must be convinced that the dangers to the public are so great that the necessity for prompt or unique action precludes any other alternative. He cannot, of course, in such situations check with the public to see if it agrees with his decision. He alone must make the decision, and if later the citizens decide that he made the wrong decision, they will think the less of him as a leader.

Understandably, the citizenry zealously guards and defends the right to full and accurate information. The White House, for example, is under

25 Printed in *Vital Speeches of the Day*, Vol. 15 (July 1, 1952).

constant scrutiny to ensure that news is not manipulated and that the information withheld from the public is kept to the absolute minimum required for national security.

Language Use and Ethical Speaking

Careless or deliberate misuse of language is one of the commonest ways by which audiences are led to decide issues on inadequate grounds.

At least at present, the most dangerous abuse of language is in misclassification, the attaching of labels. As pointed out in Chapter 5, oftentimes an argument can be made effective simply by showing what class of things an object belongs to. The attitude bearing toward the class will then be brought to bear on the individual member.

Proof by classification is not unethical per se. It may be important for an audience to know that a certain individual is a male, or a physician, or a college graduate, or a Democrat, or a Pennsylvanian. The abuse of classification results from erroneous classification, or use of classification when it has no relevancy to the point under consideration.

Each period in our history, and particularly periods of stress, has its scare words, its way of classifying people who are regarded as dangerous. The Revolutionary war had its royalists, the Civil War its abolitionists, and the cold war has its Communists, pinks, and fellow-travelers. The charlatan knows that these scare words, many of which are so vague as to be meaningless, have great force; hence he classifies people as Communists when he does not know that they are, and he uses the classification to discredit an idea when the classification has no bearing on whether the idea is sound.

Through carelessness or design substantial errors also result from exaggeration. As William Norwood Brigance wrote: "We say 'many' when we really mean 'a few.' We say 'absolutely,' when it is only 'probably.' We insist that 'everybody knows,' when the truth is only that 'some people believe.' "[26]

Not all mislabeling or exaggeration is unethical. Although some people may insist that the excerpt from the speech by Taft cited above is an example of unethical persuasion, most people probably would not be disturbed by it. Whether it is unethical depends on two things. First, did the listeners recognize the passage for what it is—a rhetorical device? Second, were they able to place it in perspective? An audience knows that a speaker is exaggerating when he characterizes modern music as a regression to the jungle. And they know that the exaggeration emphasized a point. But can they recognize the mislabeling when someone is carelessly or maliciously called a Communist? And can they compensate for the error even if it is known? The seed of doubt is often so tiny as not to be perceptible.

[26] *Speech: Its Techniques and Disciplines in a Free Society* (New York: Appleton-Century-Crofts, Inc., 1952), p. 302.

Our society does permit exaggeration and a certain amount of careless-ness in word choice—but only when those devices serve to give emphasis, and not when they are the substance on which decision is based.

Objectivity and Ethical Speaking

Speakers are often admonished that they must be objective, that they must present with equal thoroughness and passion both sides of an argu-ment if they are to be ethical. As is shown in Chapter 15, effectiveness often depends on presenting both sides. However, failure to achieve or even at-tempt objectivity, in the sense that the term is used here, is not contrary to ethical speaking. In the first place, objectivity is impossible to achieve in matters that must be decided on so private a matter as an individual's values. Objectivity from one person's point of view may require that some aspect of a problem be classed as minor, while from another point of view the aspect may seem crucial. Further, if a speaker is expert enough to have a right to speak about an issue, he is also expert enough to have his opinion count for something. Finally, to expect a speaker to act as though he did not believe one side has more cogent arguments than the other is to require him to misrepresent his own position.

The greatest danger to society comes from the speaker who gives an *appearance* of objectivity. Listeners can better judge a man's proposals if they know where he stands. With the purpose of public discussion clearly in mind, George Bernard Shaw said, "the way to get at the merits of a case is not listen to the fool who imagines himself impartial, but to get it argued with reckless bias for and against."

As Shaw suggests, the responsibility for presenting the opposing case rests with those who believe in it.

Emotionalism and Ethical Speaking

Chapter 15 considers emotionalism from the standpoint of effectiveness. The concern here is with the ethics of emotionalism in argument.

Excessive emotional response causes listeners to decide an issue on un-reasonable grounds. That is, they are led to an emotional reaction of suffi-cient magnitude to becloud or conceal essential issues, to elevate minor points to undue importance, or to give weight to irrelevancies. To recognize the results of excessive emotional reaction does not, however, answer the crucial question of what is excessive.

The difficulty in answering the question can be illustrated by this frag-ment from a speech delivered by a lawyer pleading with a judge to sentence two men, confessed murderers, to life imprisonment rather than execution:

> I do not know but what your Honor would be merciful if you tied a rope around their necks and let them die. . . . To spend the balance of their days in prison is mighty little to look forward to, if anything.

The argument of the fragment suggests that execution may be more merciful than life imprisonment. The most striking part of the excerpt is not the argument; it is the image conveyed—that of the judge himself tying a rope around the necks of the men and standing by until they died. Unless the judge were a particularly callous individual, he would find the image highly repugnant and would probably react emotionally to it.

A critic may contend that the fragment illustrates an attempt to gain all three advantages of excessive emotionalism. He may argue that the entire fragment was designed to divert the judge from awarding just punishment (execution). It was to accomplish that objective by raising a minor consideration (whether imprisonment would be more merciful than execution) to major importance, and by bringing in a totally irrelevant point (the mode of execution). Further, that irrelevant point was advanced in an unethical manner, for the judge did not actually execute those he condemned.

A reverse interpretation is possible, however. An argument that it was unethical to picture the judge as executioner must be based on a belief that a person making decisions should be released from the responsibility for them simply because he does not carry them out. A contention that the mode of execution (hanging) should be regarded as irrelevant must rest on the belief that the way an act is accomplished has nothing to do with deciding whether it should be carried out. If hanging is thought to be inhumane for the criminal or brutalizing for society, those are relevant considerations in deciding whether to sentence a man to execution. The attempt to bring mercy into the consideration can be disparaged only if one holds that confessed criminals are unworthy of even consideration for mercy. Finally, whether one holds that the only just punishment was execution depends on whether he is willing to grant that it was the judge's responsibility to determine what was the most just of the alternatives open to him—execution or life imprisonment.

In other words, one could contend that the fragment from Clarence Darrow's summation for the defense in the Loeb-Leopold case used emotionalism to give the emphasis Darrow thought the several points merited.[27]

For reasons that are made clear in Chapter 15, limitations in the use of emotionalism may more clearly depend on effectiveness than on ethics.

ENSURING THAT OTHERS ARE ETHICAL

The earliest records of rhetorical theory are accompanied by evidence of rhetoric's misuse. Corax, who lived in the fifth century B.C. and who is credited with developing the earliest system of speechmaking, took his student Tisias to court for nonpayment of fees. After listening to the arguments, which were derived from virtuosity rather than the facts in the case,

27 A more extensive excerpt from Darrow's summation is printed in *The World's Great Speeches*.

the court dourly observed, "a bad egg from a bad crow," and turned them both out. Plato believed that an ideal rhetoric existed, although no one—not even the revered Pericles—practiced it. Hence, he banned rhetoricians from his ideal republic.

The history of speechmaking contains many examples of rhetoric's misuse. Diggs believes that "the unethical use of persuasion is one of man's most typical and most glaring faults. Misuse of 'the persuasive arts' has been so common and at times so notorious, that some have regarded persuasion as inherently evil, something which by its nature 'ought to be avoided,' like a lie."[28]

This history of misuse has led to criticism of rhetoric as well as of the malefactors who misuse it. Rhetoric has been assailed for a variety of reasons. It has been applied without regard for evidence and thus made the worst side appear better. It has served unscrupulous practitioners who concerned themselves with personal advantage rather than truth, and, therefore, as Plato charged, told audiences what they wanted to hear rather than what they should hear. Much of the suspicion of rhetoric probably results from the fear we have of the skilled speaker or writer who may lead us to do things we later regret or act for reasons we do not understand. Oscar Sherwin said of Wendell Phillips:

> Most orators coax, excite, or argue with the audience. Phillips simply stood before it and took it up quietly in his hands, turned it around as if it were a plaything, and made it behave as he wanted it to.[29]

Any speaker with that kind of power is to be feared. And as long as the potential for such effectiveness exists, a democracy must be ever watchful of rhetoric and its practitioners.

Whether to Banish Rhetoric

The history of abuse has caused an unrelenting search for ways to ensure ethical use of rhetoric's power. There are three basic approaches to guarding against abuses. First, rhetoric may be banished, as in Plato's republic.[30] Even if banishment were possible, however, reflection will show that a world with an imperfect rhetoric is preferable to one with no rhetoric. As Kenneth Burke wrote:

> Persuasion involves choice, will; it is directed to a man only insofar as he is *free*. This is good to remember in these days of dictatorship and near-dictatorship. Only insofar as men are potentially free, must the spellbinder seek to persuade them. Insofar as they *must* do something, rhetoric is unnecessary.[31]

28 "Persuasion and Ethics," p. 359.

29 *Prophet of Liberty*, p. 299.

30 Incidentally, your authors confess to some delight in the irony that those who argue most effectively against rhetoric use effectively the very process they would proscribe—Plato included.

31 *A Rhetoric of Motives* (New York: George Braziller, Inc., 1955), p. 50.

When persuasion vanishes, as it did in ancient Rome, Hitler's Germany, or in all other totalitarian societies, it vanishes because man is no longer potentially free. Our concern can never be with the abolition of rhetoric in a democratic society if that society is to remain democratic; rather our concern must be directed toward better understanding of rhetorical principles so that citizens can make intelligent choices between alternatives.

Plato's pupil Aristotle opposed attempts to abolish rhetoric, for he believed rhetoric to be useful. Further, he believed that rhetoric is self-correcting: ". . . things that are true and things that are just have a natural tendency to prevail over their opposites, so that if the decisions of judges are not what they ought to be, the defeat must be due to the speakers themselves, and they must be blamed accordingly."[32]

Most of us probably agree that in the long run at least "truth" does prevail. That seems inevitable, however. The victors, not the losers, in the world's struggles pass judgment on the past; the books they write and the speeches they make emphasize that "truth" did prevail.

Whether to Rely on Speakers

Second, abuses of rhetoric might be eliminated if speakers are trained to be ethical. Yet our history is peopled with too many malefactors, many of whom were highly trained in rhetorical skills, for us to overlook the fatuity in trusting all speakers to meet Quintilian's definition of an orator: "a good man speaking well." All of us can perhaps agree on Aaron Burr as an example of a malefactor. We add Senators Theodore Bilbo, Huey Long, and Joseph McCarthy.

Perhaps the day will come when the demagogue will find no audience. We doubt it, however. The Bilbos will, we fear, continue to gather at least a temporary following.

Hope that speakers will become increasingly ethical can be found in the expectation that as more becomes known about the methods of achieving lasting influence through persuasion, the more apparent it will become that effectiveness depends on the use of ethical techniques. In other places in this work it is pointed out:

1. That an over-use of such appeals as fear militate against the success of the speaker.

2. That the man who would have his arguments hold up under counter argument must consider both those arguments for and those against his proposition.

3. That because of the influence of opinion leaders, a speaker must be more reasonable and present a more reasoned speech than any average of listeners' intelligence or education would suggest.

[32] *The Rhetoric*, p. 1355a.

4. That the speaker whose character diverges from the public estimate of what moral character should be will have limited effectiveness as a speaker.

Whether to Rely on Listeners

The third method of controlling abuses of rhetoric is to rely on listeners to insist on ethical speaking and to expose the demagogue who fails them.

If listeners are to expose the scoundrel, they must be able to recognize him—and in time to stop him. As in the past, the method will in the future prove inadequate in the short run and for parochial speakers. Slow and cumbersome though it is, however, that method is finally what we must rely on. "Mr. W." of Silone's *School for Dictators* will be stopped only when listeners finally realize that he and others like him are dangerous.

Perhaps our society is fortunate that people move slowly against the charlatan speaker, for to call a man a scoundrel is a serious charge, indeed. However, too often slowness is brought about by indifference rather than judiciousness. Vigilance *is* the price of freedom. The significant lesson to be learned from Hitler's Germany is not what evil humans in power can achieve, but what national lethargy can achieve in permitting the enthronement of evil.

Though we must be vigilant, we have not the time or capability always to avoid assuming rather than knowing that the stranger will act in relatively predictable ways. We assume, for instance, when we stop to ask directions from a stranger that he will give us the best directions he can, and that he will not rob or falsely accuse us. If the directions sought are crucial, we may shrug off unjust comments made about a public figure while the instructions are being given. Similarly, when listening to a speaker say what we want to hear, we often excuse him of what we would at other times regard as excesses; thus we may feel that this fragment from a speech states the case not too strongly against Hitler and his Germany:

> Once again [in July of 1940] I seized the opportunity of urging the world to make peace. And what I foresaw and prophesied at that time happened. My offer of peace was misconstrued as a symptom of fear and cowardice.
>
> The . . . warmongers succeeded once again in befogging the sound common sense of the masses, who can never hope to profit from this war, by conjuring up false pictures of new hope. . . .
>
> The appeal to forsake me, made to the . . . nation by this fool and his satellites on May Day, of all days, is only to be explained either as symptomatic of a paralytic disease or of a drunkard's ravings. His abnormal state of mind also gave birth to a decision to transform the Balkans into a theatre of war.
>
> For over five years this man has been chasing around Europe like a madman in search of something that he could set on fire. Unfortunately he

again and again finds hirelings who open the gates of their country to this international incendiary. . . .

God knows that I wanted peace. But I can do nothing but protect the interests of the . . . [nation] with those means which, thank God, are at our disposal.[33]

Although we might applaud the characterization of Hitler as a madman whose actions could be explained only as symptoms of a paralytic disease or a drunkard's ravings, will we still applaud when told that the excerpts are actually from a speech by Hitler? And that he is speaking of England, the United States, and Churchill? We will probably say, "Wait a minute, now. He was wrong. He had no right to talk that way." But would it have been *right* if used to characterize Hitler? Did he suffer from a paralytic disease? Was he a drunkard? If we fail to consider the source of purported factual statements and excuse unrestrained invective, unsupported assertion, or illogical argument so long as they uphold our side, we are as dangerous to our society as the man who makes the statements. More, for without us and others like us the demagogue would find no profit in his methods.

There is probably no satisfactory alternative to assuming a speaker's good faith; but some questions can be asked. What support does he offer? What right has he to speak on this subject? And the important question, born of cynicism and nurtured by concern for one's self and his society, what does he really want?

To search for answers to such questions requires little effort beyond that already required in just listening. Listeners who expend that effort pay a part of the price for freedom. Another part is to denounce the speaker who betrays you with the same vigor that you use to denounce the treachery of one who violates any other form of public trust.

[33] Printed in *The World's Great Speeches.*

PART TWO

11

The Speech of Entertainment

Speeches of entertainment, where a speaker assumes his hearers are neutral to favorable in their attitudes towards him and his subject, may be classified in two ways: *humorous* and *serious*. *Humorous* addresses of entertainment are in turn divided into two kinds: one form has a central *theme,* while the other is *themeless.* The *serious* entertaining speech, on the other hand, is always developed around a theme.

TYPES

Let us begin the discussion by considering the humorous address, since this form is associated most commonly with the speech of entertainment.

Humorous

1. *HUMOROUS SPEECH WITH A THEME.* In the *humorous speech with a theme,* a speaker has a central thesis in mind, and he develops his address in a manner that impresses ultimately one or more key ideas on listeners. He employs, in other words, a loose framework as his rationale for telling hearers delightful details, illustrations, and narratives. He might, for example, illustrate through a series of incidents that buying a home can be a humorous experience or that living in a fraternity house can be a rollicksome adventure in human behavior. He is, in short, more than a mere jokester recounting one unrelated quip after another. Today, many successful comedians have themselves resorted to humor around a theme, because the theme not only provides them with a place to anchor their thoughts, but it also inspires them with meaningful, impromptu recollections that often prove more delightful to hearers than carefully prepared stories.[1]

[1] For more details see Leonard Hole, "Can You Make People Laugh?" *The American Magazine,* Vol. 161 (March 1956), p. 99; Steve Allen. "The Vanishing Comedian," *The Atlantic,* Vol. 200 (December 1957), p. 117; and "Comedians: The Third Campaign," *Time,* Vol. 76 (August 15, 1960), p. 43.

Part of the confusion over the speech to entertain arises from a popular notion that this speaking form treats non-controversial topics. This thinking is incorrect. For just as a speaker talking about women drivers may wish either to persuade or to inform his listeners, so may a speaker talking on the same subject wish to entertain his hearers. In essence, the speaker bent on humorous entertainment with a theme does not take himself or his subject seriously. He means only to poke good-natured fun, to relate some humorous jokes, and to narrate several amusing incidents on his subject. He realizes his logic is fallacious; he knows his instances are exaggerated; he is aware of loading his topic for its humorous effect. However, he intends no harm; he says nothing maliciously; he picks on no particular person. And, most important of all, his hearers know of or strongly suspect his humorous and good intentions.

2. *HUMOROUS SPEECH WITHOUT A THEME.* In contrast a speaker may decide to develop a *themeless humorous speech*—to deliver, in other words, a series of unrelated jokes without a thesis in mind. A speaker following this form comes close to being an entertainer or a nightclub performer. The themeless humorous speaker is in fact a raconteur who relies on his ability to tell a story for laughs or his vast storehouse of jokes to carry him through a speaking engagement. The danger in the themeless after-dinner address is that a speaker, unless extremely skilled and a near professional humorist, may bore his listeners with stories they might have heard before. Worse, he may present a false image of himself to listeners, and they might soon think of him as Lightweight Charley, or Funny Punster Harry—not as a public speaker.

There is, of course, something to say in behalf of themeless, entertaining addresses: they are easy to prepare; they allow the speaker to concentrate his complete attention on gathering "sure-fire" material; and they free him from worrying about organization.

Serious

The second major type of speech to entertain is *serious* and is dependent on mystery, suspense, and adventure for its entertainment value. If a speaker, for instance, decides to relate his experience among the Baluba tribesmen in the Congo, he may choose to describe a time when he argued heatedly with a tribal chief and almost lost his head in the process. True, there is some information gained in listening to such a speech, and there may be even some humorous value as well. Still, the address is primarily one of *serious* entertainment because mystery, suspense, and the personal thrill-of-adventure dominate the address. The speaker is delighted, of course, if listeners receive some information from his speech or laugh occasionally during the address. But his main concern—and what pleases him most— is that hearers feel swept along on a serious narrative; and whether they thought he said Kaluba or Shla-meel or what-have-you tribesmen is of minor consequence to him.

There is an instance, however, when listeners' interpretations of a *serious* speech of entertainment are important to a speaker. Although he may assume a rather blasé attitude toward information-transfer when his address borders between entertainment and exposition, he cannot usually allow hearers to confuse his intention when his speech edges between entertainment and persuasion. A speaker in this latter case may be indifferent foolishly, since there is the distinct possibility that his hearers may react negatively to comments meant only in jest. To remove any possibilities for misunderstanding, a speaker may want, therefore, to make known his exact intention at some point in the address. In this way there is no mistaking whether he is entertaining, informing, or persuading.

ORGANIZATION

In organizing the *themeless* speech of entertainment, the introduction and conclusion are relatively unimportant, since the speaker intends only to recount a series of unrelated stories. In the *serious* address of entertainment and humorous speech with a *theme,* however, the speaker divides his address into the traditional introduction, body, and conclusion to help hearers follow his development.

Introduction

Like introductions for informative and persuasive addresses, introductions for speeches of entertainment should capture attention, create good will, and if necessary forecast the speech, provide hearers with reasons for listening, and relate the subject to the occasion. Unlike informative or persuasive speaking, words opening addresses of entertainment should generate or foretell a definite *mood,* because once hearers set themselves mentally for a certain response, they often find it difficult if not impossible to suppress this expectation. If a speaker, therefore, is thought of traditionally as a serious individual, his best initial course may be to establish mood immediately in his address. For instance when James G. Blaine, unheralded as a humorist, delivered an impromptu, entertaining address in 1879 at the 11th annual banquet of the New York State Chamber of Commerce, he began: "Mr. Chairman:—I rise only to get out of the way, in order that this procession [of speakers] may go forward. [Laughter.] I am a mere chance comer—a disturber of the programme—but I do not intend to be made the butt of either the flattery or the wit of the last speaker. [Laughter.]"[2]

On the other hand, if a speaker is known as a humorist, he can

2 *Modern Eloquence: After-Dinner Speeches,* Thomas B. Reed *et al.* Eds. (Philadelphia: John D. Morris and Company, 1900), I, p. 73.

momentarily delay introducing his amusing narratives without fear of confusing listeners through a sudden shift in mood. For instance, when Mark Twain addressed the 77th anniversary banquet of the New England Society, he began simply, "The toast includes the sex, universally; it is to Woman comprehensively, wheresoever she may be found. Let us consider her ways."[3]

The humorist occasionally faces an unusual problem in mood. After a few initial entertaining comments, he may wish to be serious for a moment. How does he counter audience mental set? Sam Levenson, addressing the 99th annual meeting of the National Education Association of the United States in 1961, solved the problem by announcing candidly, "I am not going to try to be too funny in five minutes—it's really not fair!"[4]

In short an introduction to a speech of entertainment should establish a humorous mood, especially when hearers are set mentally for discourse rather than entertainment. Unless a speaker is known widely for his humor, he would do well, probably, to follow the example of Blaine by giving some attention to the business of creating unmistakable mood in the introduction.

Body

We turn now to the body. Again, the concern is with the *serious* and *thematic,* rather than the themeless entertaining speech.

Having decided on a theme for his address, a speaker is ready to divide his subject into convenient thought-units for hearers. Unlike the informative speech, however, where easily grasped divisions are an almost mandatory prerequisite to good organization, arrangement in an address to entertain is often looser, since the speaker's primary goal is entertainment rather than specific recall. And where *unity* and *coherence* share equal importance when informing, *coherence* is the more crucial of the two when entertaining. Let us examine what is meant.

Narrative climaxes, whether humorous or serious, are vital to the speech of entertainment. In fact, one could almost say that the success or failure of an entertaining address is related directly to the effectiveness of the narrative peaks within the speech. And if climax is a near-king, then the body organization of a speech to entertain may well lack balanced and proportioned development. Normally, where an informative or persuasive speaker gives each major unit within the address an equal amount of development time, a humorous speaker finds frequently that proportioned arrangement is not always possible in an entertaining speech. The humor-

---

3 *Modern Eloquence: After-Dinner Speeches,* p. 225.

4 *Addresses and Proceedings of the Ninety-ninth Annual Meeting Held at Atlantic City, New Jersey, June 25–June 30: 1961* (Washington, D.C.: National Education Association of the United States, 1961), Vol. 99, p. 67. Hereafter cited as *Addresses and Proceedings.*

ous address may therefore look odd on paper, since a speaker, for the sake of entertainment, might spend considerably more time on one point than on another. His main head divisions will, in short, seem almost arbitrary and even whimsical in some instances. Consequently, the speech of entertainment, when committed to paper, may occasionally appear as a one-point speech, or an address with several thinly developed divisions, or even a speech with a disproportionate number of main heads for a short talk.

A good humorous or serious entertaining speaker, however, remembers that he is a public speaker and not a raconteur or comedian, and he organizes the subject matter, albeit loosely, into logical units of thought.

Turning now to the subject of coherence, a speaker delivering a serious speech to entertain or a humorous one with a theme should provide continual relations between points in his address for hearers, and not simply at major divisional breaks. To understand the significance of coherence, a speaker should recall that a good entertaining speech pulsates in gradually higher peaks of humor or suspense as the address progresses, until an emotional pinnacle is reached either at the end of each main head or at the end of the entire speech. Faced with this continuous regeneration pattern between relief and humor (or relief and suspense), listeners give less and less thought to the coherent framework of the address, and more and more thought to anticipating climaxes.[5] A speaker must provide his hearers, consequently, with numerous transitions throughout his speech, since listeners probably make little attempt to ferret out coherent lines of development for themselves while in an emotional state of laughter or caught up with gripping suspense.[6] The entertaining speech could disintegrate easily into a themeless joke session or a meaningless adventure so far as hearers are concerned, *unless* the speaker provides the necessary coherence between climaxes.

A good humorous speaker, therefore, does the careful thinking for his audience by picking up threads of continuity after each humorous or serious climax. In essence he realizes listeners will not ask after each amusing or suspenseful point, "Now, let's see, where were we?" Instead, they expect him to ask the question for them and to guide them back to his theme.

The speaker aids coherent reorientation in two ways. (1) He follows audience laughter with a declarative and pointed statement that serves as

[5] Mark Twain practiced the anticipatory device with some success as a humorous lecturer. See Mark Twain, "Mark Twain Speaks Out," *Harper's Magazine,* Vol. 200 (December 1958), pp. 36–41.

[6] This statement is based on the psychological theory that humor or suspense, as a growing emotional state within an individual, climaxes in a sudden release of tension and in a state of emotional fatigue and even disruptive behavior. See David Krech and Richard S. Crutchfield, *Elements of Psychology* (New York: Alfred A. Knopf, Inc., 1959), pp. 153–159 and 258–263.

a topic sentence for the next emotional climax. Levenson used this procedure in his National Education Association address referred to in the previous section. For example he said: "(Laughter and applause) That was a great eulogy"; "(Laughter) Only a school teacher can look into the eyes of a child and see tomorrow"; and "(Laughter and applause) Other people have to be told, if they don't know, what the depression was; we never forget". (2) A speaker uses transitional phrases for coherence following audience laughter. Twain used this procedure in his 77th anniversary New England Society address referred to in the previous section. For example he said: "(Laughter.) Then, again . . ."; "(Laughter.) Such is . . ."; and "(Laughter.) Thus the . . .".

Conclusion

Regardless of the type of entertaining speech delivered, a speaker should remember always to prepare in advance a conclusion for his address, since a restatement of his theme in a rambling manner may add anticlimax to an otherwise successful humorous effort; if he relies on impromptu inspiration for an appropriate or amusing narrative, he may find his mind not up to the challenge. Frequently, the type of conclusion appropriate to an informative or persuasive address is unsuited for the speech of entertainment. For example, if a speaker summarizes, he may mislead his hearers into thinking his intention was informative rather than entertaining; and if he closes with an appeal, he may leave the impression he meant to persuade listeners rather than entertain them. Wisely, a good speaker leaves nothing to inspiration or to a hastily prepared, slipshod conclusion. Instead, he composes carefully his concluding remarks for humor, or he restates his theme cogently for thoughtful effect.

Probably nothing concludes a *humorous* speech to entertain better than humor, since hearers frequently anticipate it in such an address. Where audiences expect an informative speaker to close with his most important point, and where listeners reason a persuasive speaker saves his best argument to last, so audiences conclude—rightfully or wrongfully— that a humorous speaker reserves his peak of humor for his conclusion. Therefore, when arranging his humorous speech material, a speaker should keep his hearers' expectations in mind. The conclusion to a humorous address, consequently, is often nothing more than the speaker's last story. For instance when author-humorist Irvin S. Cobb concluded his speech before the American Irish Historical Society, New York City, in 1917, he said:

> . . . Irish blood is the strain that cannot be extinguished and it lives to-day, thank God, in the attributes and the habits and the customs and the traditions of the Southern people. Most of all it lives in one of their common characteristics, which, I think, in conclusion, may possibly be suggested by

the telling of a story that I heard some time ago, of an Irishman in Mobile. As the story goes, this Irishman on Sunday heard a clergyman preach on the Judgment Day. The priest told of the hour when the trumpet shall blow and all the peoples of all climes and all ages shall be gathered before the Seat of God to be judged according to their deeds done in the flesh. After the sermon he sought out the pastor and he said, "Father, I want to ask you a few questions touching on what you preached about to-day. Do you really think that on the Judgment Day everybody will be there?"

The priest said: "That is my understanding."

"Will Cain and Abel be there?"

"Undoubtedly."

"And David and Goliath—will they both be there?"

"That is my information and belief."

"And Brian Boru and Oliver Cromwell?"

"Assuredly they will be present."

"And the A.O.H.'s [Ancient Order of Hiberians] and the A.P.A.'s [American Protective Association]?"

"I am quite positive they will all be there together."

"Father," said the parishioner, "there'll be damn little judgin' done the first day."

[Applause and laughter.][7]

On the other hand, a speaker may decide that a formal, standard conclusion of some type is important to his success, and certainly this is a commendable practice. Generally, however, a speaker is wise to avoid mechanical *summaries,* whether delivering a *humorous* or *serious* entertaining speech, lest his hearers think they mistook his purpose and listened humorously instead of seriously to his remarks.

If a speaker delivers a *serious* speech of entertainment consisting of an extended narrative, he may close his address at the natural climax. Edward R. Murrow, in a broadcast from London on December 3, 1943, used such a conclusion to his narrative remarks when he said:

Berlin was a kind of orchestrated hell, a terrible symphony of light and flame. It isn't a pleasant kind of warfare—the men doing it speak of it as a job. Yesterday afternoon, when the tapes were stretched out on the big map all the way to Berlin and back again, a young pilot with old eyes said to me, "I see we're working again tonight." That's the frame of mind in which the job is being done. The job isn't pleasant; it's terribly tiring. Men die in the sky while others are toasted alive in their cellars. Berlin last night wasn't a pretty sight. In about thirty-five minutes, it was hit with about three times the amount of stuff that ever came down on London in a night-long blitz. This is a calculated remorseless campaign of destruction. Right now, the mechanics are probably working on "D-Dog" getting him ready to fly again. I return you now to CBS, New York.[8]

[7] From *The World's Great Speeches,* Lewis Copeland and Lawrence Lamm, Eds., Second Revised ed. (New York: Dover Publications Inc., 1958), pp. 728–729.
[8] Printed by permission of Columbia Broadcasting System, Inc.

If a speaker, in contrast, delivers a *serious* entertaining speech consisting of narratives, quips, personal reflections, and commentary, he may choose to end his address with a story that best summarizes his point. Columnist John Crosby, in his address at the New York *Herald Tribune*'s Twentieth Annual Forum on October 23, 1951, followed this procedure when he closed his speech to entertain by saying:

> One last thing, though. There are some perils to being a conformist. Back about a hundred years ago, Philipp Semmelweiss, a Hungarian physician, tried to introduce a little antisepsis into the maternity wards of Viennese hospitals. Actually, he was just trying to get the doctors to wash their hands. For this heresy, Semmelweiss was hounded out of Vienna as an iconoclast, a fool, and, I expect, also a subversive. The medical societies did most of the hounding. But—and this is important—they were greatly abetted by the mothers, who were dying like flies of childbed fever, the mothers whose lives he was trying to save. These women, good conformists all, preferred to die in the most orthodox way than to be preserved by methods that had not yet been kissed by popular fashion. They were the victims of their own conformity. The conformists always are.[9]

DEVELOPMENT OF THE NARRATIVE

Because most entertaining speeches include stories, a speaker will find it helpful if he understands the importance of five basic narrative elements (*theme, action, character, setting,* and *mood*) and four minor elements (*dialogue, dialect, illusion of originality,* and *suspense*).

Theme

If a speaker delivers a serious or thematic address to entertain, he has an all-pervading, central theme that guides the total development of his speech.[10] Besides the overriding theme, however, he has *sub*-themes that act as unifying, coalescing agents around which all narrative elements are attracted.

Should a speaker use long narratives, he faces a problem characteristic of much poor speechmaking—hazy, confused, indefinite themes. To avoid this problem, he should not deliver a story until he can sum up its point in a cogent and clear sentence. If he finds it impossible to state the theme of his narrative without deliberation and reflection, he needs to reanalyze his story; for somewhere in his narrative, there is confusion caused probably by long, interrupting details or asides.

If a speaker uses brief narratives, he is less likely to confuse hearers of

---

[9] New York *Herald Tribune,* October 28, 1951.

[10] See Jackie Gleason, "How to tell a Story," *Good Housekeeping,* Vol. 142 (March 1956), p. 69 for emphasis on the idea of organization.

the exact, central message intended through his stories. Brevity, in other words, is a virtue because it prevents a speaker from digressing to a point of distraction or confusion for listeners. Confronted with selecting 10 or 20 narratives for development of a single entertaining address, a speaker frequently includes some stories that vaguely support his major, central theme. He would, of course, do best to omit those narratives whose themes illustrate loosely the entire point or some particular sub-point of his address. Admittedly, these omissions are not feasible in every instance. Forced into choosing between humor and no humor at all, a speaker sometimes delivers anecdotes related vaguely to the point of his address.

Action

Once settled on a narrative theme, the speaker is ready to develop the important action or movement of his story.

Decide Where To Begin Narrative Action

The first problem is selecting where, in terms of time-sequence, to begin narrative movement. Often this self-evident statement is brushed aside quickly by students of public speaking and is considered by some as the proverbial mountain-out-of-a-mole-hill generalization. (Our experience as teachers, however, has taught us that students do not really understand the meaning and the problems associated with deciding where to begin a narrative. The notion, "Well, just start in at the beginning," is rarely applicable in good storytelling.)

In terms of time, each narrative has a natural starting point corresponding to the moment when a given thought, incident, or circumstance snowballs into a series of reactions culminating in a climactic event. More often than not, however, the inception point for an experience is different from the inception point for a narrative told later to an audience. A good speaker realizes, for instance, that the moment his inspiration moved him to take a motor-trip from Chicago to Mexico City is not necessarily a good starting point for a narrative. Concerned with action or movement in a story, a speaker cannot afford to conclude casually, "Well, I'll just start here!"

Should a speaker commence his story at its natural beginning, he may discover to his chagrin that he lost the attention-value inherent in the narrative form itself. What inspired him, in short, to go to Mexico City may be an exciting story in itself; but as far as listeners are concerned, these details may seem unnecessary to his narrative. Why he happened to take the route he did or how he planned his trip may be valuable information in an expository speech. These details, on the other hand, may seem like superfluous details to listeners, if they thought the narrator's purpose was to entertain them.

Decide What Details Are Vital to Narrative Action

Not all details, however interesting to the narrator, are always essential for a story told to an audience. A skilled speaker, consequently, selects and includes only those facts that (1) directly aid listener comprehension and appreciation of the narrative, and (2) necessarily seem appropriate for the particular audience or occasion. In other words narrative details that confuse listeners, appear as asides, and hold up the action should be culled from the story before it is told. Naturally what one audience calls unnecessary may seem necessary to another.[11]

The following story by Max Rafferty, California Superintendent of Public Instruction, will give you some practice in deciding what details are vital to narrative action. The story as printed here was delivered before the Pepperdine College Forum in Los Angeles on February 28, 1963. What editorial changes would you make under the following circumstances:

1) Before an audience of newspaper photographers?
2) Before an audience of college students?
3) Before an audience of the Golden Age Club, Pasadena, California?

I'm reminded of the time I was in a motorcade in San Francisco at the mid-point of the campaign [for State Superintendent of Public Instruction]. I don't know whether any of you have ever been in a motorcade or not, but it's sort of the closest thing politics have to a football serpentine, homecoming night. Everybody gets in cars, decorates them with banners, sends balloons out of windows; boys proceed down the street trying to attract votes. And on this particular motorcade, they stuck me in the lead car and I felt pretty foolish, as you can imagine.

There we were tooting horns down through the middle of San Francisco. And to make things worse, on the side of the car, they had a larger than life-size picture of me—I take the world's worst picture—look like Dracula coming out of the swamp somewhere! This particular one was the one used throughout my campaign, and it had to be posed for 22 times before they could finally get one that even looked faintly human. Finally, they caught me absentmindedly looking at the progress of a fly across the lens of the camera and they shot it quickly as my eyes were raised rather soulfully toward heaven with a sort of pious look, you know, and that's the one they used for lack of anything better.

Well, anyway, this was on the side of the car and the motorcade stopped at a San Francisco intersection, and there on the corner was a little old lady waiting for the red light to turn green so she could cross. Well, I'd always thought that all little old ladies lived in Pasadena, you know, but this one lived in San Francisco and she was a typical one. She had her hair in a bun behind her ears, and she had steel-rimmed glasses. She carried this little beaded string bag, and she was standing there waiting for the light to change. She saw the motorcade draw up. She looked at the picture on the side of the car;

11 Gleason, "How to tell a Story," *Good Housekeeping*, p. 69.

she took a step down from the curb, and she rapped with her handbag upon the glass window where I was sitting.

I carefully put down the window as quickly as possible (hoping to corral the elusive vote) and the lady said very primly and precisely, "I do not know your candidate, but my, he is goodlooking!" Well, I reacted just like Jack Benny. I said, "Well! thank you, madam." She took a step back up the curb, looked at me very severely over her steel-rimmed spectacles and she said, "Are *you* the candidate?" I said very proudly, "Yes m'am." She said, "Oh, no!"[12]

Decide Where to Place Actionless Narrative Details

Once settled on the starting point and the details necessary to a narrative, a speaker's next problem is to decide where to include narrative details that contribute to an understanding, rather than development of the action-line itself. In a short story, placement of background details essential for appreciation presents no problem, since the speaker simply groups these details at the beginning. For instance Donald I. Rogers, financial editor of the New York *Herald Tribune,* included all background materials in the first five sentences of a brief narrative he told before a Washington Roundtable audience on May 23, 1962:

> There's a story going around Israel these days about two Israeli spies who got caught in an Arab country. They were given a quick trial and, quite naturally, were sentenced to death.
>
> They were hustled to the courtyard of the prison and stood up against a wall to be shot. The Arab officer approached the first spy and offered to blindfold him. The spy glared and spit straight into the Arab officer's eye.
>
> The second spy was horrified and shouted angrily: "Meyer, why do you always want to make trouble?"[13]

In an entertaining speech consisting of several long stories, a speaker confronts a different problem. He may go on at such length in describing the setting and characters that he not only confuses listeners but he turns their attention away from the entertaining to the informative values of his address. A speaker delivering a long narrative, therefore, should support his story-theme with only necessary details and he should spread out rather than block together descriptive elements in his story. By following this procedure, he avoids strangling the theme of his narrative with prolonged pauses at points outside the main plot-line.[14]

To illustrate the problem of distributing actionless details in a long narrative, study the following selection from a speech by Samuel B. Gould, then president of the Educational Broadcasting Corporation of New York, delivered before an audience at Hunter College of the City University of

---

[12] *Vital Speeches of the Day,* Vol. 29 (May 15, 1963), pp. 450–451.
[13] *Vital Speeches of the Day,* Vol. 28 (August 15, 1962), p. 653.
[14] For details see Bennett Cerf, "How Not to Tell a Story," *The Saturday Evening Post,* Vol. 220 (March 6, 1948), p. 17.

New York on November 7, 1962. As you read the narrative, ask yourself the following questions:

1. Did Gould spread out his actionless details effectively?
2. Could Gould have improved his narrative by recasting all the details at the beginning of the story?
3. Did Gould include too many details in his narrative? Or do you think the mood was enhanced by the speaker's ability to include actionless details that aided rather than detracted from the narrative action?

A few summers ago I had occasion to spend some time in Colorado and one day chanced to stop at an Indian trading post. The post was operated by a descendant of the Blackfoot tribe, a man with the magnificent name of Charles Eagle Plume. His background, I discovered, was as magnificent as his name, for he was very well educated with an advanced degree in anthropology and a considerable amount of work behind him in the study of the history and habits of his people. His loyalty and devotion to the cause of the American Indian were quickly apparent as was his sense of bitterness over how they have been treated.

After some little conversation, Charles Eagle Plume took me upstairs in the post headquarters to show me some rare objects he had collected as part of his researches. One of these in particular he took out of its repository only after telling me the story behind it. It is this episode that I should like to share with you.

In 1851 a group of Indians lived at the mouth of the Sacramento River, a completely primitive tribe. Their homes were miserable huts built on marshy land, and the tribe was known as the Diggers. They had none of the arts we associate with other tribes, arts such as the gaily decorated baskets of the Cherokees or beautifully designed rugs of the Navajos. They merely existed.

One day during that year in 1851 a contingent of gold prospectors came to where these Indians lived and within the space of a few hours mercilessly wiped out the entire tribe, men, women and children alike. Practically every vestige of their existence was destroyed, but a few reminders of them survived and were eventually found.

At this point in his story, Charles Eagle Plume paused, his eyes still blazing with anger as he recalled the brutality of the gold miners. He took from a case behind him a tiny, closely woven basket no more than four inches in diameter and cradled it carefully in his hands.

"Imagine if you will [he said] a native woman of this primitive tribe, a woman who had never had a single object of beauty in her whole life either to see or to possess. What she had been taught of basket weaving was only for utility, for the day-to-day needs of her household. Yet somewhere within her stirred an indefinable yearning, the awakening of a sense of awareness of beauty and loveliness, a craving to create something which would bring joy to her heart as she looked at it. And so, in an almost miraculous way, she wove this basket. When she had moments to herself she trapped quail and pulled out the tufts of black on their heads. Or she sat patiently, hour after hour, completely motionless, holding a flower in her hands and waiting for a hummingbird to come and feed. When it did, she closed her hands over it and plucked from its throat the tiny downy red feathers. Or again, she searched along the marshy shore for the tiniest and most perfect of shells. All these things she fashioned into her basket with no knowledge of design or craftsmanship, with nothing but this overwhelming urge to create."

And then Charles Eagle Plume uncupped his hands, and I saw the little basket. Around its rim was carefully placed a row of perfectly matched shells, the smallest I have ever seen. The black quail tufts were interspersed with these. And all through the tightly woven reeds of the basket were the throat feathers of the hummingbirds, forming a simple pattern of reddish cast, with a texture reminding one of the softness of thistledown. It was simple and primitive, but it was almost heart-rending, for one could not look at its artless grace without thinking of the poor girl whose yearnings had culminated in the creation of this single object, her only treasure.[15]

Decide Where Turning Point Comes in Narrative

After deciding on placement of actionless narrative details, a speaker's next task is to determine where the turning point of his story comes. The turning point is that pivotal moment in a narrative when listeners sense the speaker is through revealing background details and is ready to move rapidly towards the climax.

If a speaker burdens his narrative with details after the audience senses the turning point, his listeners may not only grow impatient with him, but his climax may become an anti-climax should they predict accurately the upshot of his story. For instance, Reverend James H. Robinson, Church of the Master, New York City, told the following story to an audience at the National Education Association Convention in Atlantic City, New Jersey, on June 25, 1961. As you read the narrative, note how the first part of the story leads one to expect a climax on the point about Air Force expressions of gratitude. Instead, the incident passes, and the true turning point comes later in the story.

I was once asked to come and speak to the staff and command college down at Maxwell Field in Montgomery, Alabama. When they wrote me, they said, "Mr. Robinson, if you will come and do this three days for us, we will fly you anywhere in the world after that you want to go." Unfortunately, I was only going to Texas. I wish that I had been going to New Delhi or some-place. And then they said, "Mr. Robinson, we will be eternally grateful to you for opening up this new vista for men in the command and staff college as to how we ought to begin to think and relate toward the African continent." I wrote back and said, "I will be delighted to come but please don't send one of those boys who is still practicing." They assured me they would send a colonel. I suppose that was befitting my status as a preacher. At any rate, they picked me up in a jet and I sat piggyback, and as we got up over Knoxville, Tennessee (where I was born), at about 25,000 feet, the pilot

[15] Printed by permission of Samuel B. Gould, President, State University of New York, Albany, New York.

244 - PART TWO

said to me, "We are passing over Knoxville. Would you like to see it?" And I said, "Yes." And then I was sorry. He flipped it right up on edge. Finally we passed over Atlanta, Georgia, and he said, "We have now got to begin our descent." "But," I said, "this is only Atlanta. Why do you begin your descent here? Montgomery is a long way away." He said, "If we don't begin coming down now, we might overshoot the field." As I stood taking off the earphones, he said, "Stick around, Reverend, for fifteen minutes and you can still hear yourself coming."[16]

If a speaker, in contrast, emphasizes all background details in his story equally, his listeners may find his narrative climax no climax at all, but simply a final point that beggars an upshot. For instance when Willy Ley, popular writer on scientific subjects, addressed an audience at the summer Lecture Series, University of Colorado, on August 3, 1960, he related a narrative that might well have caused some hearers to anticipate still more story, since the turning point, if there was one, was not apparent:

> Let me tell you a little personal story of how this date [October 4, 1957] shaped up for me. On that evening I attended a small private dinner at the Harvard Club in New York, and around 10:30 the waiter came in and said, "Which one of you gentlemen is Professor Ley?" I got up, and he said, "You are wanted on the telephone." I went to the telephone, which he pointed out to me, picked up the receiver and said, "Yes, dear?" (I could do this with impunity because only Mrs. Ley knew where I could be found that evening.) "You'd better brace yourself," my wife said. "The first Russian satellite is in orbit." After a moment of speechlessness on my part, I said, "But they are late." "Yes, I know," my wife answered, "but they are in orbit now."[17]

In short, a good speaker, trying to avoid listener confusion, capitalizes on the audience pattern of narrative interest, and he moves rapidly, therefore, towards the climax of his story once he passes the turning point. The diagram on page 245 illustrates the progression of audience interest in a narrative. The schematic should help beginning speakers improve their own stories through an understanding of time-lapse and interest relations in narrative movement.

Decide Whether Unfolding (Denouement) and Conclusion Are Necessary

Frequently, when a narrative is humorous, further development beyond the climax is unnecessary and a speaker returns immediately to the main theme of his speech. On the other hand, an adventure story, and especially one with elements of mystery, often requires an unfolding or explanation following the climax. This denouement consists of any information withheld previously from listeners. However, because listener interest drops off rapidly once a speaker reveals the high point to his story,

---

[16] *Addresses and Proceedings,* pp. 19–20.
[17] "The Conquest of Space," *The Colorado Quarterly,* Vol. 9, No. 3 (Winter 1961), p. 197.

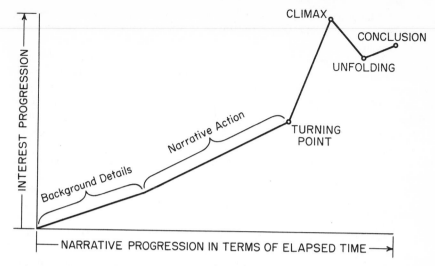

a wise narrator does not linger for more than a few moments before moving on with his speech.

Charles H. Clark's *Out of the Hurly-Burly* illustrates the typical action pattern for a narrative: background details early in the story, followed by narrative action, and then rapid movement toward the climax once past the turning point. Clark's theme, uncluttered by subplots, is exceptionally clear because of his singular goal; he used, subsequently, no unfolding and only a brief conclusion to his narrative. The American literary humorist also began his story at an eminently logical point.

> The chairman began with a short speech in which he went over almost precisely the ground covered by my introduction; and as that portion of my oration was already reduced to a fragment . . . , I quickly resolved to begin, when my turn came, with point number two.
>
> The chairman introduced to the crowd Mr. Keyser, who was received with cheers. He was a ready speaker, and he began, to my deep regret, by telling in capital style my story number three, after which he used up some of my number six arguments, and concluded with the remark that it was not his purpose to occupy the attention of the meeting for any length of time, because the executive committee in Wilmington had sent an eloquent orator who was now upon the platform and would present the cause of the party in a manner which he could not hope to approach.
>
> Mr. Keyser then sat down, and Mr. Schwartz was introduced. Mr. Schwartz observed that it was hardly worth while for him to attempt to make anything like a speech, because the gentleman from New Castle had come down on purpose to discuss the issues of the campaign, and the audience, of course, was anxious to hear him. Mr. Schwartz would only tell a little story which seemed to illustrate a point he wished to make, and he thereupon related my anecdote number seven. . . . The point illustrated I was shocked to find was almost precisely that which I had attached to my story number

seven. The situation began to have a serious appearance. Here, at one fell swoop, two of my best stories and three of my sets of arguments were swept off into utter uselessness.

When Schwartz withdrew, a man named Krumbauer was brought forward. Krumbauer was a German, and the chairman announced that he would speak in that language for the benefit of those persons in the audience to whom the tongue was pleasantly familiar. Krumbauer went ahead, and the crowd received his remarks with roars of laughter. After one particularly exuberant outburst of merriment, I asked the man who sat next to me, and who seemed deeply interested in the story,

"What was that little joke of Krumbauer's? It must have been first rate."

"So it was," he said. "It was about a Dutchman up in Berks county, Penna., who got mixed up in his dates."

"What dates?" I gasped, in awful apprehension.

"Why, his Fourths of July, you know. Got seven or eight years in arrears and tried to make them all up at once. Good, wasn't it?"

"Good? I should think so; ha! ha! My very best story, as I'm a sinner!"

It was awfully bad. I could have strangled Krumbauer and then chopped him into bits. The ground seemed slipping away beneath me; there was the merest skeleton of a speech left. But I determined to take that and do my best, trusting to luck for a happy result.

But my turn had not yet come. Mr. Wilson was dragged out next, and I thought I perceived a demoniac smile steal over the countenance of the cymbal player as Wilson said he was too hoarse to say much; he would leave the heavy work for the brilliant young orator who was here from New Castle. He would skim rapidly over the ground and then retire. He did. Wilson rapidly skimmed all the cream off of my arguments numbers two, five and six, and wound up by offering the whole of my number four argument. My hair fairly stood on end when Wilson bowed and left the stand. What on earth was I to do now? Not an argument left to stand upon; all my anecdotes gone but two, and my mind in such a condition of frenzied bewilderment that it seemed as if there was not another available argument or suggestion or hint or anecdote remaining in the entire universe. In an agony of despair, I turned to the man next to me and asked him if I would have to follow Wilson.

He said it was his turn now.

"And what are you going to say?" I demanded, suspiciously.

"Oh, nothing," he replied—"nothing at all. I want to leave room for you. I'll just tell a little story or so, to amuse them, and then sit down."

"What story, for instance?" I asked.

"Oh, nothing, nothing; only a little yarn I happened to remember about a farmer who married a woman who said she could cut four cords of wood, when she couldn't."

My worst fears were realized. I turned to the man next to me, and said, with suppressed emotion,

"May I ask your name, my friend?"

He said his name was Gumbs.

"May I inquire what your Christian name is?"

He said it was William Henry.

"Well, William Henry Gumbs," I exclaimed, "gaze at me! Do I look like a man who would slay a human being in cold blood?"

"Hm-m-m, n-no; you don't," he replied, with an air of critical consideration.

"But I AM!" said I, fiercely—"I AM; and I tell you now that if you undertake to relate that anecdote about the farmer's wife I will blow you into eternity without a moment's warning; I will, by George!"

Mr. Gumbs instantly jumped up, placed his hand on the railing of the porch, and got over suddenly into the crowd. He stood there pointing me out to the bystanders, and doubtless advancing the theory that I was an original kind of a lunatic, who might be expected to have at any moment a fit which would be interesting when studied from a distance.

The chairman looked around, intending to call upon my friend Mr. Gumbs; but not perceiving him, he came to me and said:

"Now is your chance, sir; splendid opportunity; crowd worked up to just the proper pitch. We have paved the way for you; go in and do your best."

"Oh yes; but hold on for a few minutes, will you? I can't speak now; the fact is I am not quite ready. Run out some other man."

"Haven't got another man. Kept you for the last purposely, and the crowd is waiting. Come ahead and pitch in, and give it to 'em hot and heavy."

It was very easy for him to say "give it to them," but I had nothing to give. Beautifully they paved the way for me! Nicely they had worked up the crowd to the proper pitch! Here I was in a condition of frantic despair, with a crowd of one thousand people expecting a brilliant oration from me who had not a thing in my mind but a beggarly story about a fire-extinguisher and a worse one about a farmer's wife. I groaned in spirit and wished I had been born away in some distant clime among savages who knew not of mass meetings, and whose language contained such a small number of words that speech-making was impossible.

But the chairman was determined. He seized me by the arm and fairly dragged me to the front. He introduced me to the crowd in flattering, and I may say outrageously ridiculous, terms, and then whispering in my ear, "Hit 'em hard, old fellow, hit 'em hard," he sat down.

The crowd received me with three hearty cheers. As I heard them I began to feel dizzy. The audience seemed to swim around and to increase tenfold in size. By a resolute effort I recovered my self-possession partially, and determined to begin. I could not think of anything but the two stories, and I resolved to tell them as well as I could. I said,

"Fellow-citizens: It is so late now that I will not attempt to make a speech to you." (Cries of "Yes!" "Go ahead!" "Never mind the time!" etc., etc.) Elevating my voice, I repeated: "I say it is so late now that I can't make a speech as I intended on account of its being so late that the speech which I intended to make would keep you here too late if I made it as I intended to. So I will tell you a story about a man who bought a patent fire-extinguisher which was warranted to split four cords of wood a day; so he set fire to his house to try her, and—No, it was his wife who was warranted to split four cords of wood—I got it wrong; and when the flames obtained full headway, he found she could only split two cords and a half, and it made him— What I mean is that the farmer, when he bought the exting—courted her, that is, she said she could set fire to the house, and when he tried her, she collapsed the first time—the extinguisher did, and he wanted a divorce because his house—Oh, hang it, fellow-citizens, you understand that this man, or farmer, rather, bought a—I should say courted a—that is, a fire-ex—" (Desperately.) "Fellow-citizens! IF ANY MAN SHOOTS THE AMERICAN FLAG, PULL HIM DOWN UPON THE SPOT: BUT AS FOR ME, GIVE ME LIBERTY OR GIVE ME DEATH!"

As I shouted this out at the top of my voice, in an ecstasy of confusion, a wild, tumultuous yell of laughter came up from the crowd. I paused for a second beneath the spell of that cold eye in the band, and then, dashing through the throng at the back of the porch, I rushed down the street to the depot, with the shouts of the crowd and the uproarious music of the band ringing in my ears. I got upon a freight train, gave the engineer five dollars to take me along on the locomotive, and spent the night riding to New Castle.[18]

Character

Often narrative success or failure relates directly to listener understanding and appreciation of the individuals involved in a story. In an abbreviated narrative, character development is lumped usually in a brief sentence or two, sometimes in scattered words or phrases, and at still other times in only implied statements by the narrator. Because beginning speakers find it easier to concentrate on one task at a time, they often separate action from character development; and because they lack experience in storytelling, they sometimes reveal individual motivations and traits in careless, slipshod, and verbose statements. Admittedly, a speaker delivering a brief anecdote can often take a moment out for character development without impeding seriously the narrative action.[19]

A skilled speaker, however, does not follow the aside practice when developing his dramatis personae. He will instead keep his narrative moving swiftly, and he literally makes personality development an integral part of his story. The following anecdote told by Bennett Cerf illustrates how a skilled storyteller crams crucial character details into a space of less than fifty words:

> In a remote corner of the state [of Texas], the first motorcycle Sam'l ever had seen chugged by. Sam'l seized his rifle and fired. "Git the varmint?"

18 Charles H. Clark, *Out of the Hurly-Burly* (Philadelphia: "To-day" Publishing Company, 1874), pp. 381–386.

19 A teacher of public speaking, in all probability, would much rather have a student do something, than nothing at all about personality revelations critical to understanding. And certainly if a student can do no better, his teacher will commend him for his lump-sum approach to character development.

asked his wife. "Nope," said Sam'l. "I still hear the critter but I shore made it turn that man loose."

To demonstrate the subtlety of Cerf's characterization, read the same anecdote as an inexperienced storyteller might relate it:

> In a remote corner of the state [of Texas], the first motorcycle Samuel ever saw went by. Samuel grabbed his rifle and fired. "Get the animal?" asked his wife. "No," he said. "I still hear the thing but I did make it turn the man loose."

By comparing the two versions of the same story, it should be apparent that Cerf's word choice, *Sam'l, ever had seen, chugged, seized, Git, varmint, Nope, critter,* and *shore,* conjured up his character imagery—two "seedy," slow moving, "countryfolk," one perhaps smoking a corncob pipe, and the other sitting on a rocker, and both awakened from their doldrums by the blare of a passing motorcycle. Cerf, as a skilled narrator, did not allow character development to interrupt his story. In fact, character description blends so smoothly with the action that most readers will probably guess Cerf paid no attention to this narrative ingredient.

There are times in brief narratives when characterization is unnecessary because the storyteller relies on ready-made imagery. For instance, in another anecdote by Cerf, the humorist wrote:

> A Texas rancher shot a man dead and telegraphed a slick lawyer in Forth Worth, three hundred miles away, offering a $5000 fee. The attorney wired back, "Leaving for your town on next train, bringing three eye-witnesses."[20]

Depending solely on character projections by readers of a "slick" city lawyer, Cerf brought off his humor without offering any further personal details.

Of course when a speaker delivers a *long* narrative, he may find himself giving more moments to distinct character development. Freed somewhat from the necessity of extreme brevity, a narrator may pause along the way to paint his individuals in vivid, bold strokes and colors. Such a storyteller, however, is in danger of going to an extreme by relating meaningless character details and of confusing listeners by his prolonged Unforgetable Character description.

Whenever a speaker relates a narrative involving himself, he confronts a special problem in characterization. Because he stands before his listeners, he may forget that his presence is no substitute for tacit personality revelations about himself. When a narrator omits important personal motivations or character traits in such a story, he is in danger of listeners remaining unresponsive to what he thought was a perfectly hi-

[20] Bennett Cerf, "A Texas Sampler," in *An Encyclopedia of Modern American Humor,* Bennett Cerf, Ed. (New York: Doubleday & Company, Inc., 1954), pp. 384–385.

larious or moving incident. Unless his hearers have the necessary in-common elements with him, they cannot possibly understand why his experience should be humorous or serious to them, however incongruous, exaggerated, or self-apparent it appears to him. This is the very reason why certain jokes are funny to people belonging to an in-group, but utterly incomprehensible to those eavesdroppers without identical experiences, personal traits, and cultural backgrounds. A narrator must decide, therefore, what minimum character revelations are important to his narrative theme, and how to introduce these elements to his listeners for their in-group appreciation and understanding of his story.

For instance when Negro correspondent Simon Booker of the Washington Bureau, Johnson Publishing Company, spoke to the Khayyams Club in Cleveland, Ohio, on September 26, 1964, he related the following narrative to his Negro listeners:

> Several years ago, I spent many weeks in Little Rock when they integrated the schools and came home a pretty banged-up guy—just in time to take my youngest son on his first day of school. My kids go to a parochial school in Maryland and they have to walk several blocks through a white neighborhood to board the bus. That morning, I was angry, giving the whites hell. As I stood beside my boy with a growing number of white kids, getting angrier all the time, a little white girl came up to me and said, "Mr. Booker, you don't have to stand there. I'll take Jimmy to school and I'll look after him." I went home an embarrassed man, a bigot.[21]

Unless a listener is a member of a minority group who had firsthand encounters with racial prejudice, he may miss the theme of the narrative. The significance of getting "banged-up" for what you believe is your right, walking self-consciously as a member of an out-group through the in-group's neighborhood, noticing the stare of eyes on you and your little boy because you look different, and growing angrier by the moment towards those who would consider you different—all these experiences, at once real to some and remote to others, either will make Booker's statement, "I went home an embarrassed man, a bigot," deeply meaningful, or will make his statement only an interesting, superficial observation.

Setting

On occasion a narrative fails because the speaker forgets to tell his hearers the setting of his story. In a *brief* narrative, simple statements as "Two men were one day standing on a corner . . .", "When I visited California . . .", or "Three Irishmen were talking when . . ." serve adequately to locate a story in place and time. In a *longer* narrative, however, setting development is more crucial to understanding. Fortunately, a locale described poorly tends only to bother and to confuse an audience for a moment, rather than to undermine an entire narrative theme. Still, a speaker cannot afford to brush over the setting.

There are basically two ways of introducing narrative locale. At times a speaker mentions only one or two scattered key words, and he counts on his listeners to project these words into fuller images for the setting. Dean Rusk, in the following narrative told before the Economic Club of New York on April 23, 1963, used the projection method:

> I was on my way to deliver a speech in a southern state some months ago and when I was about 30 minutes out of the airport, the tower sent a message saying, "There are a thousand people here to welcome the Secretary of State." Well, I wasn't born yesterday, so I sent a message back saying, "If there are a thousand people to meet the Secretary of State, they are obviously carrying signs. What do the signs say?"
>
> And then they came back saying, "We had a recount. There are 50 people here. Come on in, the natives are friendly."[22]

At other times a speaker uses a carefully described locale for narrative effect, and he will go on at some length to set the stage for his story. For instance Reverend William J. Kenealy, S.J., Professor of Law, Loyola University, Chicago, gave over three-fourths of his narrative time to a description of setting. Although this is an unusual practice, the Kenealy story, delivered before the Conference of Mayors and City Managers at Springfield, Illinois, on July 10, 1963, illustrates how important setting can be to proper narrative understanding.

> Once upon a time there was a tiny Negro girl who lived in the Deep South. Every time she left her home she had to sit in the back of the bus, the back of the streetcar, the back of the movie theater, the back of the church, the back of this and the back of that. While she was still a little girl her family moved to the far North. One day her mother took her to the most wonderful fairyland her eyes had ever seen. It was a beautiful amusement park, with swings and slides and tunnels and boats and roller coasters and, best of all, a fantastic merry-go-round. The child was entranced by the merry-go-round. She ran up close to listen to the gay music, and to watch the laughing children riding round and round in the lovely chariots, and galloping up and down on the charging horses. She clapped her hands and jumped with joy. Then she wanted, so much, to climb right on, to join the fun, to ride around with the other little children. But she was afraid. And puzzled, too. Finally, as the merry-go-round slowed down and the music grew softer, the tiny Negro girl turned to her mother and cried: "Oh, mother dear, tell me please, where is the back of the merry-go-round?"[23]

Mood

Failure of an otherwise good story is traced often to audience confusion over the speaker's narrative mood. This problem may turn an otherwise

22 *Vital Speeches of the Day,* Vol. 29 (June 1, 1963), p. 493.
23 *Vital Speeches of the Day,* Vol. 29 (September 1, 1963), p. 686.

normal speaking experience into an embarrassing nightmare for a narrator. The amateur, taking no chances, may fail because he smacks listeners in their faces with statements as "Now get this one; this is real-ly *funny!*", or "That reminds me of the *funny* story about two Eskimos," or "This is one of the most *exciting* stories you will ever hear." All three introductions, of course, have one important virtue—unquestionably clear forecast of narrative mood. On the other hand, a narrator cannot expect to surprise listeners when he in effect says, "Look, I'm about to tell a funny story, so watch for the trick ending."[24] There are, fortunately, several ways of introducing narrative mood, other than the climax-robbing, point-blank announcement.

Establish Favorable Mood Through Physical Bearing

If a speaker thinks it best, he may appear serious when relating a humorous narrative, but not to a point where hearers mistake his soberness when they laugh for annoyance on his part. If he thinks, in contrast, it is best for him to appear entertained as he tells his narrative, he may show signs of obvious, personal enjoyment; but not to a point where listeners begin laughing at him rather than his humor.[25]

Establish Favorable Mood Through Material Appropriate to Listeners

A speaker also establishes proper narrative mood through material appropriate for his audience. The old saw about adapting a speech to listeners is also true when selecting stories for an address. This is not to say that narratives must be always within the real or near-real experiences of listeners, although this is desirable whenever possible. Nor is this to say that anecdotes must be always humorous or exciting, although this is desirable whenever possible, too. Rather, this is to say that listeners cannot grasp mood until they are familiar sufficiently with what the narrator is talking about, either through personal experience or through details furnished by him. Students, for instance, can appreciate the humorous mood of the following story, since the narrative is appropriate for them:

> During an apparently boring lecture, the lecturer, a professor of long-standing, noticed that the [student] doctor was dozing. The miscreant was sharply awakened and asked to repeat what the lecturer was saying.
> The "student" doctor astounded the lecturer and the class by obliging with a lucid precis of all that had been said, and, as an after-thought, gave the name of the medical text-book from which the lecturer had been quoting.

24 For fuller advice on this point, see Jack Benny, "How to tell a joke," *This Week Magazine* (March 26, 1961), pp. 14–15.

25 Bennett Cerf suggests: "A hearty laugh at the end of your story, constituting yourself a sort of cheer leader, is not only permissible but, if not carried to excess, sound strategy." He cautions, however, that during the progress of the narrative, you should let the audience do the laughing. See Bennett Cerf, "How Not to Tell a Story," *The Saturday Evening Post,* Vol. 220 (March 6, 1948), p. 126.

When the professor voiced his astonishment, the erring student said, "as a matter of fact, I wrote it."

Teachers, however, may puzzle over the mood of this same story. While the upshot is humorous, some professors would decry the probability of such a situation, since their own experiences as teachers tell them such a situation is unlikely. The mood for them, consequently, may be one of incredulity rather than humor. Yet by supplying information appropriate for teachers, they, too, can understand the mood:

> OTAGO, New Zealand (UP)—Red-tape restrictions on foreign doctors who want to practice in New Zealand have had some embarrassing sequels, of which the following is perhaps the best—or worst.
>
> In order to win the right to practice, an immigrant doctor had to attend the New Zealand university for three years.
>
> During an apparently boring lecture. . . .[26]

Establish Favorable Mood Through Harmless Narrative Material

A narrator should not give listeners the impression he is picking on a person, profession, or a national group. To laugh at an individual who laughs at himself is proper grounds for humor; but to laugh at a person in pain, or one who cannot help or defend himself, shows callous disregard for others.

The following anecdote by Cerf is an illustration of a borderline narrative:

> A famous producer we will call Darryl Selznick hadn't found a story that suited him for six years and had reached a point where he was ready to listen to all comers. An unknown aspirant was ushered into his august presence one day. "They tell me you have a play," said the producer, with a reassuring wave of his hand. "Go ahead and read it to me."
>
> This was more than the author had expected. Furthermore, he had been a victim of severe stuttering since he first learned to talk. The chance was too good to miss, however, so he sat down and read his whole play, scene by scene. When he had finished, Darryl Selznick shouted for his secretary.
>
> "Sign this guy up at once," he cried. "He's got a new twist that'll have them rolling in the aisles. Every character in this play stutters."

Listener reaction to the story depends on whether an individual feels Cerf is poking fun purposefully at stutterers, or whether a hearer thinks stutterers themselves would laugh at this anecdote.

The next narrative by Cerf is also a fence-straddling story:

> Another agent story concerns a flourishing coast agency named Feitlebaum & Garfinkel. One morning Feitlebaum came to Garfinkel and explained that

[26] "Dozing Student Gives Instructor Surprising Reply," United Press International release, December 14, 1955.

he was sick and tired of his cumbersome and harsh-sounding name. "With your permission," he explained, "I have changed my name this morning to O'Brien." Garfinkel said nothing, but a few mornings later he came to his partner with the declaration that he too was tired of the name he had been bearing all his life. "With your permission," he said, "I have also changed my name to O'Brien." Thereupon, the old sign was taken down and a resplendent new one, reading "O'Brien and O'Brien" was put up in its place. A few mornings later the telephone rang and a voice demanded to be connected with Mr. O'Brien. "Very good, sir," said the cheery-voiced operator, "but which Mr. O'Brien do you want: Feitlebaum or Garfinkel?"[27]

Much of the mood in this story depends on what impression the narrator gives his listeners as he delivers the lines. Is the storyteller, for instance, capitalizing on the bigoted notion that "*All* Jews are showy, brash, and loud"? Obviously, the audience's response will depend on the mood a speaker imparts to them as he delivers the narrative. If the narrator is Jewish, then his mood is clear; his audience may laugh freely because they either conclude their storyteller is also laughing at himself, or reason he means his humor in innocent fun.

Establish Favorable Mood Through Material Appropriate for The Occasion

A speaker establishes narrative mood through the appropriateness of his stories to an occasion. Sometimes mood is so much a part of a specific occasion that no amount of explanation will make a narrative seem as humorous or as serious again to another audience.

During World War II and shortly thereafter, for instance, the atrocities at Auschwitz, Buchenwald, Dachau, Mauthausen, Sachsenhausen, and Treblinka were too real for humor. No amount of coaxing would have convinced a narrator to joke about German concentration camps and mass extermination of Russians, Jews, and Gypsies. Today, listeners born after the war can laugh at a situation that once might have resulted in a broken nose for the narrator. Time changes attitudes and moods. For some, the following anecdote will seem funny; for others, the memory is still too real for laughter:

> One day in 1944, the Führer, worried over death, called his favorite astrologer to his chamber.
> "Mein Sterndeuter," asked the little moustached man, "when will I die?"
> "Mein Führer, according to the stars, you will die on a Jewish holiday," came the reply.
> "Ja, and what day is that?"
> "Mein Führer," answered the astrologer, "any day you die will be a Jewish holiday."

27 Bennett Cerf, "Show Cases," in *An Encyclopedia of Modern American Humor*, pp. 543–545.

Further Narrative Elements

Besides theme, action, character, setting, and mood, a narrative often benefits from *dialogue, dialect, illusion of originality,* and *suspense.*

Dialogue

Dialogue between characters in a narrative contributes to the success of a story in three ways:

1. It helps create and maintain audience interest.
2. It helps hearers visualize themselves as third persons at the actual narrative event.
3. It helps humor or suspense when used as an integral part of a story.

But before a speaker plunges headlong into his use of dialogue, he should consider the following two points.

1. There is a skill in dialogue usage that depends not only on wise selection of purposeful conversation, but on the selection of oral prose appropriate to mood, characters, setting, and theme of a story. A narrator will want, therefore, to keep the principles of oral vs. written style in mind as he composes his dialogue. (See Chapter 7 on oral versus written style.)

2. The narrator must concern himself with what constitutes necessary and appropriate dialogue, as opposed to purposeless and meaningless conversation. A speaker would do well to follow the practice of Joel Chandler Harris' old Brer Fox: lay low. In other words, a narrator should not make the mistake of dialogue over-indulgence that could ruin easily an otherwise good story through bloated conversation. Rather, like the Parsee in Kipling's *Jungle Book,* who in his more than Oriental splendor waited patiently for the appropriate moment to sprinkle cake crumbs in the rhinoceros' skin, a speaker should wait to include his dialogue at crucial moments of his narrative, especially if he is not adept at storytelling.

The following narrative by General Maxwell D. Taylor, delivered at the annual meeting, Fellows of the American Bar Foundation, Chicago, on February 15, 1964, illustrates an instance of how dialogue is used sparingly but effectively by a speaker not given to storytelling:

> I am reminded of a wartime situation which confronted a chaplain in my 101st Airborne Division at the time of the parachute invasion of Normandy. Within a few hours of the invasion one of the parachute chaplains of an Infantry regiment became ill and it was clear that he could not participate in the jump on D-day. Feeling that we were going on a mission where we would have need of all of our sky pilots, we cast about to find a replacement. We found a chaplain in one of our non-jumping outfits who volunteered to replace his ailing brother and did, in fact, jump successfully and safely into action on D-Day.

Several days later I met him in Normandy and asked him how he felt when he found himself in the door of that airplane about to jump into the flaring battle below. He said, "General, I could only say, 'Good Lord, how in your wisdom did you allow me to get here?' "[28]

Dialect

A narrative technique delightful to many listeners is dialect (regional pronunciations) used in conjunction with dialogue. However, before a speaker attempts to duplicate exact language mannerisms in his own narratives, he should weigh four *important* considerations.

1. Dialect must be at once intelligible to hearers. Occasionally, a narrator with a good ear for sound can imitate precisely a foreign or local language mannerism. Since phonographic duplication of language, however, is not always understood by listeners, a narrator should examine his dialectal usages beforehand to ensure that he substitutes words and sounds whenever clarity is impaired by authenticity.

2. Good dialect, for purposes of public speaking, is not always phonetic reproduction of actual oral language. Some dialectal pronunciations, especially those associated with cultural groups, are so stereotyped and corrupted that the mass image frequently bears only passing resemblance to "real" usage. In the last 20 years, for instance, many popular dialectal distinctions between Japanese or Chinese speaking English have become confused, mixed, and restyled into a new conglomerate Oriental dialect. The "No tick-ee, no wash-ee" pronunciation once associated with slant-eyed, pigtailed Chinese laundrymen, is now confused with the "Rots of ruck" sounds of buck-toothed, four-eyed Japanese in the post-war era. Today, comedians and B-movie villains sometimes substitute one sound for another, irrespective of the two national groups; and much of the once subtle, distinctively different inflection patterns of Japanese or Chinese speaking English are mixed into the same stew. Thus it does not seem incongruous to hearers when they see a Chinese baby on television, looking very Japanese, crying out for his favorite "Amelican" dessert in a dialect concocted by an adman with the probable name of Arzanoff. Unless a speaker, therefore, takes into consideration existing language stereotypes held by most hearers, he may find his listeners giving more attention to his "poor imitation" than to his narrative.[29]

3. Dialect delivery takes practice. Nothing, perhaps, can ruin a dialect faster than an unsure speaker who bungles an imitation and who uses local pronunciations inconsistently throughout his narrative. Many listeners

---

[28] *Vital Speeches of the Day,* Vol. 30 (March 15, 1964), p. 336.

[29] For more commentary on the effects of mass media on American humor, see Kenneth Rexroth, "The Decline of American Humor," *The Nation,* Vol. 184 (April 27, 1957), p. 376; and Steve Allen, "The Vanishing Comedian," *The Atlantic,* Vol. 200 (December 1957), p. 117.

pride themselves on their fine, discerning sense of dialect, even though many of these same hearers could never illustrate exactly what they consider authentic. Should a narrator stumble, therefore, when delivering a dialect line, he is in danger of sidetracking the "expert" dialecticians in his audience away from the theme of his story into a consideration of his pronunciation.

4. Unless a speaker can *confidently* and *effectively* execute the previous three suggestions, then there is a final word of advice to him—avoid narratives with dialect.

Illusion of Originality

Most anecdotes heard today as original humor are versions of originals told many times before and are the destined forerunners of original tales for future generations of hearers and readers. Moreover, even when a humorous idea seems new to a storyteller and his listeners, a knowledgeable critic could demonstrate probably that a particular story was told in other ways in the past. A wise speaker, understanding that narrative uniqueness is more in *characters* and *setting* than in *theme,* will not waste his time worrying over originality.[30] Instead, he takes an old but good piece of humor and gives to it the illusion of originality by adding a new location, perhaps a new set of circumstances, or even a new character or two.

Essentially, a narrator should realize that stories with sound themes immortalize themselves, and that is why they are told and retold by countless after-dinner speakers, sidewalk humorists, and cigar store raconteurs. For instance read the next narrative related by Carl T. Rowan, Director of the U.S. Information Agency, to an audience of the National Student Association Congress at the University of Minnesota on August 24, 1964, and see if you can recognize the well-worn theme used in countless other narratives set in different locations and with different characters:

> There is a story told of a wealthy American tourist who was travelling through the back country of Afghanistan in his American car. The car broke down, and no one in the local villages could figure out how to get it started.
> The tourist was ready to leave the car behind and return to the capital when someone remembered that an old blacksmith who lived beyond the mountains some 50 miles away had, in his youth, tinkered with engines.
> In his despair the tourist sent for him. Three days later the old man appeared on a mule. He took one quick look at the engine and then asked for a hammer. He gently tapped one spot on the engine twice, then turned

[30] For more thoughts on the illusion of originality, see Parke Cummings, "The Art of the Off-Color Story," *The American Mercury,* Vol. 48 (September 1939), pp. 27–29; S. J. Woolf, "How To Hatch a Joke," *New York Times Magazine,* July 5, 1942; Edward (Senator) Ford, "Jokes: New Variations on an Old Theme," *New York Times Magazine,* February 20, 1944; and Burges Johnson, "The Jokes That Last," *The Atlantic,* Vol. 190 (July 1952), p. 72.

to the American and said: "Start her up." Unbelievably, the engine did start and purred as smoothly as the day it had left the factory.

"Well, that's wonderful!" said the tourist. "Now how much do I owe you?"

"A hundred dollars," replied the old man.

"What?" shouted the tourist, "A hundred dollars for just two taps with a hammer?"

"Well," said the old man, slowly, "I can itemize it for you if you like. For two taps with the hammer—ten cents. For knowing exactly *where* to tap —99 dollars and 90 cents!"[31]

A speaker faces a more difficult task, of course, than a raconteur who relates his story directly to a single listener. An individual narrating in private is not worried about the illusion of originality, since his purpose is only to reiterate a story as he heard it, and he can always stop as soon as his listener exclaims, "I heard that one before." Standing before an audience, however, that same storyteller uses poor judgment if he begins his narrative with the remark, "Stop me if you've heard the one about . . .". Instead, a skilled narrator commences by assuming that some, if not many listeners, know versions of his story. He is wise, therefore, if he takes a narrative with a good theme as his basic framework. And he is wiser still if he changes the setting from Lafayette, Louisiana, to Lafayette, Indiana, and his characters from Cajun farmers to Tippecanoe County farmers, when his hearers are Hoosiers.

Alteration of a universal, fictional narrative is ethically possible for a speaker because he is not plagiarizing nor is he really distorting facts. More often than not, a narrator telling such a story omits credits, since he considers the tale within public domain. Of course it goes without saying that he should not claim an incident happened to him when he knows full well the story is fictional or is an experience of another individual. Similarly, he should not pass off a well-known anecdote or any joke, for that matter, as a personal experience, since some hearers will know that his humor came straight from *Tested Stories for Half-witted Speakers.*

Suspense

You probably once heard a story that made you exclaim, "If that had happened to me, I could have held audience attention, too; but (sigh) nothing that suspenseful ever happens to me." There are indeed some narratives that transform hearers from bystanders into participants, and that stimulate audience interest to a point where they are mentally coaxing and even helping the action along. But is a speaker who gets this kind of response successful because he has an inherently good story, or is he successful because he has good narrative technique? In answer to both questions:

[31] *Vital Speeches of the Day,* Vol. 30 (September 15, 1964), pp. 722–723.

not every story has an element of suspense within it, but most narratives can have increased suspense-value through skillful narrative manipulation. Let us examine what is meant.

The prolongation of narrative upshot, when done to the proper degree, tickles listeners' imaginations by involving them pleasantly in the action. A good storyteller, therefore, does not plunge pell-mell toward his narrative climax until he methodically injects details that heighten suspense. Unfortunately, an ability to turn a story into a gripping or anxious experience for listeners is a matter of speaker sensitivity and judgment, and not reduced easily to a formula. All, however, is not lost. An analysis of narrative suspense technique will help a speaker understand what the storyteller does, and will subsequently help a beginning speaker in his own experiments with this technique.

To study how a narrator adds suspense to his story, you should first read an abbreviated incident from Samuel Clemens' *The Innocents Abroad,* titled, "European Guides":

> The doctor asks the questions [of guides], generally, because he can keep his countenance, and look more like an inspired idiot, and throw more imbecility into the tone of his voice than any man that lives. It comes natural to him.
>
> The guides in Genoa are delighted to secure an American party, because Americans so much wonder, and deal so much in sentiment and emotion before any relic of Columbus. Our guide there fidgeted about as if he had swallowed a spring mattress. He was full of animation—full of impatience.
>
> "Ah, genteelmen, you come wis me! I show you beautiful, O, magnificent bust Christopher Colombo!—splendid, grand, magnificent!"
>
> He brought us before the beautiful bust—for it *was* beautiful—and sprang back and struck an attitude:
>
> "Ah, look, genteelmen!—beautiful, grand,—bust Christopher Colombo! —beautiful bust, beautiful pedestal!"

Then concluding his story, the humorist wrote:

> "Ah, I see [said the doctor], I see—happy combination—very happy combination, indeed. Is—is this the first time this gentleman was ever on a bust?"
>
> That joke was lost on the foreigner—guides cannot master the subtleties of the American joke.

Now analyze carefully the dialogue omitted earlier between the opening and closing of Clemens' narrative. In the completed version below, Clemens played out his lines of dialogue like a fisherman, who, instead of landing his catch immediately, toyed with his prize to relish the supreme moment of achievement.

"Ah, look, genteelmen!—beautiful, grand,—bust Christopher Colombo!—beautiful bust, beautiful pedestal!"

The doctor put up his eyeglass—procured for such occasions:

"Ah—what did you say this gentleman's name was?"

"Christopher Colombo!—ze great Christopher Colombo!"

"Christopher Colombo! ze great Christopher Colombo! Well, what did *he* do?"

"Discover America!—discover America, oh, ze devil!"

"Discover America. No—that statement will hardly wash. We are just from America ourselves. We heard nothing about it. Christopher Colombo—pleasant name—is he dead?"

"Oh, corpo di Baccho!—three hundred year!"

"What did he die of?"

"I do not know!—I cannot tell."

"Smallpox, think?"

"I do not know, genteelmen!—I do not know *what* he die of!"

"Measles, likely?"

"May be—may be—I do *not* know—I think he die of somethings."

"Parents living?"

"Im-posseeble!"

"Ah—which is the bust and which is the pedestal?"

"Santa Maria!—*zis* ze bust!—*zis ze* pedestal!"

"Ah, I see, I see—happy combination—very happy combination, indeed. Is—is this the first time this gentleman was ever on a bust?"[32]

Perhaps you observed that there was a limit to the suspense generated in Clemens' narrative. There comes a moment, in other words, when suspense ends and climax becomes anticlimax. You may have observed, too, that suspense is by no means inherent in the narrative. The story as edited for purposes of illustration was brief and to the point. In the completed version, however, Clemens controlled[33] the pace of suspense by slowing down the narrative action four distinct times. (Can you identify these interruptions?)

There is, of course, no effective formula for creating suspense, such as "Degree of suspense is equal to the sum of interruptive actions." Only a particular audience can determine when narrative movement passes from suspense to dull repetition. A wise and skilled speaker, alert to listeners' reactions, can and does alter his story during delivery to match their responses. Actually, this impromptu technique is not as difficult or far-fetched as it seems.

[32] *The Innocents Abroad, or the New Pilgrims' Progress* (Hartford, Conn.: American Publishing Company, 1873), pp. 290, 292–293.

[33] Lest you think Clemens' narrative technique was artless, here is an earlier, complete version of the same incident as written by him for the *Alta California:* "I began to suspect that this fellow's English was shaky, and I thought I would test the matter. He showed us a fine bust of Columbus on a pedestal, and I said, Is this the first time this person, this Columbus, was ever on a bust? and he innocently answered, Oh, no."

A speaker who wishes to experiment with impromptu editing for suspense will find "shaggy dog" stories ideal for this exercise in controlling suspense, since they are delivered easily in 1 minute or 1 half-hour by merely subtracting or adding details. As the narrator experiments with such a story, he should watch hearers for telltale signs of interest and disinterest.[34] He should then experiment in excluding sections because of listener disinterest and in expanding other sections because of renewed attention. Through this exercise a speaker will gain some understanding of the relation between suspense and interest, and between suspense and length in narrative development.

CONSTITUENTS OF HUMOR

Certain characteristics distinguish American humor from other national groups. Perhaps the best, lay description of American humor was written several generations ago by Henry W. Shaw, better known as Josh Billings:

> Amerikans love caustick things; they would prefer turpentine tew colone-water, if they had tew drink either.
> So with their relish of humor; they must hav it on the half-shell with cayanne.
> An Englishman wants his fun smothered deep in mint sauce, and he iz willin tew wait till next day before he tastes it.
> If you tickle or convince an Amerikan yu hav got tew do it quick.
> An Amerikan luvs tew laff, but he don't luv tew make a bizzness ov it; he works, eats, and haw-haws on a canter.
> I guess the English hav more wit, and the Amerikans more humor.
> We have't had time, yet, tew bile down our humor and git the wit out ov it.
> The English are better punsters, but i konsider punning a sort ov literary prostitushun in which futur happynesz is swopped oph for the plezzure ov the moment.[35]

As Billings observed, American humor is not particularly subtle; in fact, it depends on exaggeration for laughs. As indicated also by Billings, Americans "luvs tew laff," and they tend to "works, eats, and haws-haws on a canter." A visiting Englishman to the United States once noted that "All over the land, men are eternally 'swopping stories' at bars, and in the long endless journeys by railway and steamer." And he added with some sadness, "How little, comparatively, the English 'swop stories'!"[36] Perhaps

---

[34] Jackie Gleason especially commends this practice to the beginner. See Jackie Gleason, "How to tell a Story," *Good Housekeeping*, Vol. 142 (March 1956), p. 69.

[35] Henry W. Shaw, *Josh Billings on Ice, and Other Things* (New York: G. W. Carleton & Co., Publishers, 1868), pp. 183–184.

[36] Andrew Lang, *Lost Leaders* (New York: Longmans, Green, and Co., 1889), p. 187.

one basic trait of American culture is its distinctive humor, described by one professor of English[37] as "native American humor."

The spawning ground for our particular brand of humor has, in a sense, been Everywhere U.S.A.; yet our humor is highly localized. Much Yankee-type imagery, for example, came from early American writers as Seba Smith, Thomas Haliburton, James Russell Lowell, Frances Whitcher, and Benjamin Shillaber, all of whom contributed to the rustic, impudent, roguish, shrewd, satirical and dialectal American character epitomized by Sam Slick, a scampish New Englander, and his philosophy that it was good to be a little shifty in a new country. From the old Southwest (Georgia, Alabama, Louisiana, Mississippi, Arkansas, Tennessee, and Missouri), American humor got its racy, oral, tall tale, frank, and incongruent qualities reflected so well in writings by James Baldwin, George Harris, Johnson Hooper, Augustus Longstreet, Thomas Thorpe, and William Thompson. From the literary comedians of less than a century ago, American humor inherited its laugh-a-line tendency, word-play inclinations, openly professional quality, and anticlimactic characteristics penned so well by writers such as Charles Browne, David Locke, Henry Shaw, and Finley Dunne. And of course as Americans we cannot forget the local colorists who touched their stories with authenticity, tenderness, nostalgia, humility, and humaneness, and who are represented by narrators such as Mark Twain, Joel Chandler Harris, Bret Harte, Edward Eggleston, and Harriet Beecher Stowe. Today our professional humorists are beneficiaries of over 150 years of maturation, which has culminated in an archetypal humor, called *American*. As for the non-professionals, they benefit also from humorous ancestors (no pun intended), and they preserve their amateur standing by "swopin' stories" at work, poker parties, dinner outings, and conventions.[38]

With this brief vignette of American humor in mind, let us now take a moment to consider the specific, basic constituents[39] of humor in some detail. Naturally, an understanding of humor does not result in an ability to create it. But for some readers, what constitutes humor is a mystery; so a

[37] Walter Blair. For good analyses of American humor, see Blair's *Native American Humor (1800–1900)* (New York: American Book Company, 1937), and Max Eastman, *Enjoyment of Laughter* (New York: Simon and Schuster, Inc., 1936).

[38] For three interesting commentaries on the status of contemporary American humor, see Max Shulman, "American Humor: Its Cause and Cure," *The Yale Review*, Vol. 51 (October 1961), 119–124; and Norris W. Yates, *The American Humorist: Conscience of the Twentieth Century* (Iowa State University Press, 1964), pp. 19–47; and "Comedians: The Third Campaign," *Time*, Vol. 76 (August 15, 1960), pp. 42–48.

[39] The basic constituents of humor vary widely from authority to authority. For some interesting classifications by scientists, see Richard M. Stephenson, "Conflict and Control Functions of Humor," *The American Journal of Sociology*, Vol. 56 (May 1951), pp. 569–574; and Jacob Levine, "Responses to Humor," *Scientific American*, Vol. 194 (February 1956), pp. 31–35. The classification used in this chapter is covered in more detail by Walter Blair, *Native American Humor (1800–1900)* (New York: American Book Company, 1937), pp. 3–16.

brief analysis here of the ingredients is in order. Hopefully, with understanding comes discrimination, and with discrimination comes an ability to select humor best suited for a particular audience.

Exaggeration

Much American humor is based on *simple* exaggeration. This type of humor, although ballooning a statement, situation, or description out of proportion to reality, is still probable as far as listeners are concerned. The following brief narrative, told by George Champion, Chairman of the Board, The Chase Manhattan Bank, at the annual Chamber of Commerce Dinner, Houston, Texas, on December 8, 1964, illustrates simple exaggeration. Champion's narrative situation, although ludicrous, does not call attention to itself and is, therefore, well within the realm of probability:

> I just hope that when you have heard me out, you won't feel a certain kinship with the professional football coach who was interviewing a college star he was about to sign to a contract.
>
> "Yes," said the player, "I run the hundred in less than ten seconds with full uniform. I block so well that last season four of our opponents had to be carried off the field with broken legs. In forward passing, I average about 60 yards a throw—against the wind. As for my grades, I've been on the dean's list since freshman year."
>
> The pro coach was understandably impressed.
>
> "But son," he said, "every one of us has some weakness or deficiency. What's yours?"
>
> "Well," replied the college lad, "I'm inclined to exaggerate a little."[40]

Another type of exaggerated humor is called *absurd*. In contrast to simple, absurd exaggeration is not only ridiculous to listeners but it is also improbable to them. Moreover, hearers tend to compare the image created in absurd humor with reality as they know it; and, in fact, the humor arises from the very improbability itself. The next narrative, told by Logan T. Johnston, President of Armco Steel Corporation, before the New York State Executives Club on November 17, 1964, illustrates how exaggerated humor can move from probable (*simple*) to improbable (*absurd*):

> A group of technicians was trying to sell a computer to a businessman and they said: "Ask it a question—any question."
>
> He thought for a moment and said, "All right, ask the machine where my father is."
>
> After the usual spinning of wheels and flashing of lights the answer was typed out:
>
> "This man's father is at this moment teeing off on the Old White course at the Greenbrier."
>
> "Well," the businessman said with some sarcasm, "there may be a golf course in heaven, but I doubt that they call it the Old White. My father is dead."

[40] *Vital Speeches of the Day,* Vol. 31 (February 15, 1965), p. 282.

This information was typed into the computer and in a few moments another answer was typed out:

"The *husband* of this man's mother is dead. But his *father* is at this moment walking down the first fairway on the Old White course at the Greenbrier."[41]

Beyond absurd exaggeration is humor known as *satire*. In contrast to absurd, satire depends for its effect on double meaning. Through overstatement or underplay, a narrator presents his hearers with a gross image meant deliberately for comparison with reality. The next story by Charles E. Shulman, Rabbi of Riverdale Temple, New York, as told to the Ad-Sell League of Omaha, Nebraska, on February 5, 1957, illustrates how a speaker may use humorous exaggeration for satirical purposes:

A fourth story concerns a new jet plane that transported a citizen in Russia from Pinsk to Minsk in four minutes thirty-two seconds. The citizen was overwhelmed. He rushed to the home of his friend in Minsk and cried: "What a nation Russia is? What a government! Not only the greatest constitution, the greatest leader, the greatest army, but now we have a wonderful plane that brought me here from Pinsk in less than five minutes!" The friend refused to be impressed. "So you got here from Pinsk in less than five minutes. What good did it do you?" "What good? It enabled me to be the first in line to buy a pack of matches!"[42]

Finally extreme exaggeration often ends in *sordid* humor—a kind of sick, irreverent, scathing look at people, ideas, attitudes, or institutions. There is still a vestigial humor of sorts in sordid exaggeration through a contrast between apparent and *real* reality. To illustrate the point, a "sick" joke comments on the futility and reality of modern life in the following manner:

Question: "Mommy, why is daddy lying so still?"
Answer: "Shut up and dig."

Many a "wayoutsville" character will find this exaggeration humorous, because the comparison is between *real* truth and ostrichlike thinking by "squares."[43]

Incongruity

The next constituent of humor is incongruity, or the unexpected juxtaposition of ideas, characters, words, or situations. A listener, in his tidy thinking, associates *Object¹* plus *Object²* with *Object³*, and he learns to expect *Incident¹* plus *Incident²* to cause *Consequence¹⁺²*. He has assumed an ordered universe where the same result always follows the same given

41 *Vital Speeches of the Day*, Vol. 31 (January 1, 1965), pp. 188–189.
42 Reprinted by permission of Rabbi Charles E. Shulman.
43 For details see Robert Ruark, "Let's nix the sickniks," *The Saturday Evening Post*, Vol. 236 (June 29–July 6, 1963), pp. 38–39.

circumstances. Whenever certain specific instances, therefore, do not produce a learned response or expected result, he is at times troubled, sometimes surprised, and often humored by the turn of events. For instance, in the next narrative told before a meeting of the Southern Gas Association, Dallas, Texas, on April 28, 1964, Alan H. Newcomb, broadcaster, counted on surprising his hearers by an incongruent turn of plausible human behavior:

> It's like the story of two little girls who had learned how to swear. One night the minister was coming to dinner, and their mother called them to her with great concern.
>
> "Now girls," she told them, "if you'll be very careful while the minister's here and not let out any of those naughty words, when he leaves, I'll give each one of you fifty cents."
>
> They promised to be very good, and they were until they sat down at the table. Grapefruit was served, and one little girl stuck her spoon down in her grapefruit and it shot up and hit her in the eye, and she said, "Oh, darn!"
>
> The other one looked over at her and said smugly, "uh-huh! There goes your fifty cents all shot to hell!"[44]

Humor that depends principally on incongruity sometimes creates a ludicrous image in the hearer's mind. For instance in the next narrative, Allen Kent, Associate Director, Center of Documentation and Communication at Western Reserve University, gained his humorous response through incongruent medical-talk in a poker-talk situation. Kent's address to the third annual Phi Delta Kappa Symposium on educational research, held at the University of Oregon in 1962, also illustrates a hazard of incongruity in humor: the speaker's resulting image, depending on the individual listener, may or may not be humorous:

> . . . I would like to tell you a story from the medical field. This is about two M.D.'s who found themselves in a hospital undergoing minor surgery. This was a hospital in which they had been residents, and they knew their way around. They had finished their minor operations and were in the intermediate situation where they were too sick to go home and too well to stay in bed. They were wandering around the halls, tired of chasing nurses, but not knowing what to do with their time. They decided to play poker, and asked the nurse for a deck of cards. The nurse informed them that no gambling was permitted and refused them the cards. So they started wandering the halls again. One of them remembered that he had a key to the medical records room, so they went in and selected fifty-two medical records. They dealt out five records apiece and looked at them. Then both men became very excited in their bidding. Finally, when the bidding stopped, one said, "I won, I have a full house—two tonsillectomies and three appendectomies." "No," said the other, "I won. I have five enemas, which is a royal flush."[45]

44 *Vital Speeches of the Day*, Vol. 30 (September 15, 1964), p. 732.
45 *Dissemination and Implementation: Third Annual Phi Delta Kappa Symposium on Educational Research*, Eds. Keith Goldhammer and Stanley Elam (Bloomington, Ind.: Phi Delta Kappa, Incorporated, 1962), p. 2.

Sometimes humor is gained by incongruently grouping objects together. Astronaut John Glenn, Jr., addressing a joint meeting of Congress on February 26, 1962, used this method when he said:

> I think all of our talk of space, this morning coming up from Florida on the plane with President Kennedy, we had the opportunity to meet Mrs. Kennedy and Caroline before we took off. I think Caroline really cut us down to size and put us back in the proper position. She looked up, upon being introduced, and said, "Where's the monkey?" [Laughter.][46]

At other times humor is generated through exhausted, unusual, or ludicrously incongruent ideas as "Phony as a $3 bill," "Slippery as a quid on a brass doorknob," or "Public meeting tonight to support Barry Goldwater for President—Place: The Lighthouse for the Blind."

Anticlimax

Anticlimax is another favorite device for humor. In contrast to normal juxtaposition where objects or ideas are thrown together for humorous effect, anticlimax groups a series of items in a crescendo of importance and dignity, only to end suddenly in the ridiculous. For instance when Winston Churchill, after Dunkirk, addressed Englishmen on June 4, 1940, he delivered the now famous line, ". . . we shall fight on the beaches, we shall fight on the landing grounds, we shall fight in the fields and in the streets" . . . and at this point he covered the microphone with his hand and said in *sotto voce,* "And we will hit them over the heads with beer bottles, which is all that we have really got."[47]

Wordplay

Wordplay, often thought of as the intellectual's humor, is associated more with wry, subtle, and witty British anecdotes, than with frank, stark, and uproarious comedy. The British, of course, have no monopoly on wordplay. Americans use language devices as *malapropisms* (boy constructor), *bad grammar* (All my brains blowed clean out), *misquotes* (I don't know what others may do, but as for me I can't go), *colloquialisms* and *localisms* (big dog in the tanyard), and double-talk (Here am I, the wickedest and blindest of sinners . . . has now come in on *narry pair* and won a *pile*).

If a narrator's humor depends on wordplay, then he should keep in mind that language devices tarnish quickly when overexposed. Malapropisms are rollicksome on occasion. As with any humorous technique, however, it may lose its effectiveness when the entire speech is based on one method of humor. Generally, therefore, a narrator is wiser to use wordplay along with exaggeration and incongruence, rather than depend only on one device throughout his speech to sustain humor. This is not to say that

[46] *Congressional Record,* 87 Cong., 2d sess. 108 (part 3), p. 2903.
[47] "Churchill's Quip of 1940 on Resisting is Revealed," Associated Press release, June 21, 1947.

listeners will always find 30 minutes of malapropisms distasteful to them; rather, that one custard pie in the face is extremely funny, but 30 face-fulls may be a bore.

Delivery

Finally, much humor derives from a narrator's delivery. Insinuation, an important ingredient of humor, is often understood by hearers through a speaker's gestures, vocal inflections, voice quality, and physical bearing. Understatement is another humorous method dependent frequently upon a narrator's delivery. Almost any speaker who ever used humor knows the importance and relation of good delivery to audience response.[48] Unfortunately, delivery as it relates to humor confuses many beginners as well as experienced speakers into imagining themselves professional comics. There is no denying that some stage, television, and nightclub comedians are, in many ways, exemplary models for the humorous speaker. The narrator who studies these professionals often benefits from them if he duplicates their polish, poise, fluency, and sensitivity to audience reaction. But here the benefits end for a public speaker.

If a narrator imitates laugh-a-line techniques, exaggerated physical antics, and anything-for-a-laugh methods of some comedians, he sacrifices his position as a speaker by transforming himself into an entertainer and comic. The more he thinks himself a comedian, the more demanding will his listeners become of his humor, and the more they will subconsciously compare him to a professional comic rather than a speaker. No longer will his audience remember that they are listening to a public address. Rather they will think of the speaker as an entertainer, and they will begin reacting like a nightclub or television audience. They will demand, and rightly so, a routine that is hilarious, clever, and smooth, rather than content themselves with the amateurish humor of a public speaker. A narrator who forgets his function and who apes Clem Kadiddlehopper, for instance, creates an unfortunate image for himself. He will be remembered as an extremely "funny guy" by listeners. One day he will find himself unable to face listeners because he exhausted his supply of new jokes. His reputation as a "funny guy" becomes an eventual millstone, and he will find himself resorting fiendishly to joke books and grinding out racy stories in a desperate effort at humor—thus further obscuring his function as a speaker.

If a public speaker wishes to become an entertainer, fine—he should get himself an agent. If he desires to be a humorous speaker, then he should remember to control his delivery and to work humor into his speech—not speech into his humor.

---

[48] The importance of timing in delivery is especially stressed by Jackie Gleason, "How to tell a Story," *Good Housekeeping*, Vol. 142 (March 1956), p. 272; and Leonard Hole, "Can You Make People Laugh?" *The American Magazine*, Vol. 161 (March 1956), p. 101.

The Speech of Exposition: *Abstract* and

12 *Instruction*

An important twentieth-century phenomenon is the increasing efficiency of global communications. Today in technically advanced nations, mass media avenues reach almost every citizen and the world communication network figuratively shrinks our globe to a fraction of its former size. Even less developed nations, such as emerging African states, find nearly instantaneous mass communications between people and between governments and people, vital if not imperative to survival in a modern world.[1]

With spectacular new advances in mass communications comes an equally startling realization: man has devised physical means of communicating information to an experimental space-probe 20,000,000 miles from earth. Yet earthlings still govern vital messages transmitted over hot-lines and telstars by a compendium of third-century B.C. to nineteenth-century A.D. generalizations about what makes information effective. The reference here is not to communication problems espoused already by general semanticists for many years; rather, the allusion is to the counterpart of available means of persuasion—*available means of informing*.

When civilized man lived in relatively isolated trade centers, and when mass dissemination of information was unknown, human progress depended in many instances on those good men who, skilled in speaking, used persuasive techniques to convince others of their share in civic, social, and moral responsibilities. Today the world is different: there are civilization centers all over the globe and even those citizens who do not live in metropolitan areas or near seats of government are aware of local, state, and world events. Persuasion is no longer the only important means of

[1] See J. Martin Klotsche, "The Importance of Communication in Today's World," *The Speech Teacher*, Vol. 11 (November 1962), pp. 322–326.

controlling men's minds; keeping the public informed has rapidly become an equally important means of control.[2]

Through the centuries, men, especially rhetoricians, theorized, philosophized, and speculated about available ways of persuasion. (We have done our share in this book, too.) Many modern scientific studies contribute to the body of findings called loosely, the psychology of persuasion. However, when the practitioner seeks methods of giving *information,* the picture is startlingly different. Thinkers and researchers have only passing words of advice—usually castoff ideas from original thoughts on persuasion—to offer students interested in the informative process. This is not to say that the body-rhetoric excludes sound advice about expository speaking or that exposition is unrelated to persuasion; rather, that emphasis is almost always on persuasion to the exclusion of information.[3]

Within recent years specialists charged with informing the masses are aware of a need for scientifically oriented information theory.[4] These men, variously called information specialists, communication specialists, information officers, and public affairs officers, are beginning to question the assumption that age-old principles of expository writing are in all instances applicable to oral, written, or visual presentation.

Even the terms used today are often outmoded and outdated: speakers talk of lecture or expository lecture; yet seldom do they mean the dictionary signification of *lecture*—reading, sermonizing, discoursing, or classroom lecturing. Even the image that goes with lecture is indicative of outdated ideas on expository speaking—it is still colored by nineteenth-century thinking and associated with formal, long, dull, dissertationese speaking by

2 For good introductory works on the control effects of mass communication on audiences, see Joseph T. Klapper, *The Effects of Mass Communication* (New York: The Free Press of Glencoe, 1960); Wilbur Schramm *et al., Communications in Modern Society* (University of Illinois Press, 1948); and Wilbur Schramm, *The Process and Effects of Mass Communication* (University of Illinois Press, 1954).

3 For a similar viewpoint, see Charles R. Petrie, Jr., "Informative Speaking: A Summary and Bibliography of Related Research," *Speech Monographs,* Vol. 30 (June 1963), p. 79.

4 In the strictest sense, *information theory* derives from *communication theory* arrived at by scientists, social scientists, and even philosophers interested in modern communication phenomenon—whether mass or personal. In the early 1930s, political scientists, along with the Social Science Research Council and the Humanities Division of the Rockefeller Foundation, became interested in the study of the communication phenomena. More recently, neurologists, engineers, physicists, sociologists, linguistic scholars, and psychologists (mainly behaviorists), among others, have contributed much assorted research data in communications. The discipline, however, is still new and only tentative theories have emerged from research. For definitions of some terms peculiar to this newly defined field, see "Communication and Information Theory," *AV Communication Review,* Vol. 11 (January–February 1963), pp. 104–108. For those interested in the historical background of this research area, see Harold D. Lasswell, "Communications as an Emerging Discipline," *AV Communication Review,* Vol. 6 (Fall 1958), pp. 245–254.

aloof, high-collared speakers. Cautiously, some writers have introduced terms as reports, instructions, and abstracts to classify a kind of straight-from-the-shoulder exposition. Even teachers themselves refer to their lectures at learned conventions as *papers*. Still, the middle ground is unoccupied. So program chairmen, sensing that *lecture* does not describe what they need for most occasions, ask would-be speakers to "Give a *little talk* about education," or "*Explain* your feelings on the administration's stand towards civil rights" or "*Say a few words* about your company" or "*Discuss* your office's policy on wage disputes" or "*Report* on research breakthroughs in your division" or "*Brief* us on the latest developments in contract negotiations," or "Give us a *run-down* on what's new at city hall."

In keeping, therefore, with current practices and needs, informative speaking is classified in four ways: *abstract, instruction, report,* and *lecture*. This chapter develops *abstract* and *instruction* and includes samples of each type for analysis. Subsequent chapters treat the *report* and *lecture*.

ABSTRACT

Probably the simplest expository form is the *abstract* or summary.[5] Based most often on a lengthier written or oral report, set of instructions, or lecture, an abstract is the end product after a speaker distills fuller materials down to minimum essentials. By its very nature the abstract is usually brief, to the point, and rather mechanical in arrangement. Concerned with precision, conciseness, and accuracy, the summarizer tends to depersonalize his oral comments because time limitations force him to use judiciously his few moments before hearers. A speaker is likely, therefore, to include only relevant material in his speech; information falling into the category of personal commentary or reaction is omitted generally to make efficient use of time.

Developmental Problems of the Abstract

In a sense, a person abstracting his own extended materials should have an easy assignment on his hands, since no one, broadly speaking, probably knows the subject matter better than he. Actually, a speaker preparing an abstract, whether working from his own or someone else's source materials, faces a most difficult task.

The reader need only think for a moment how much learning depends on an ability to draw relevant conclusions from experience, reading, and listening, and he should realize at once that the summarization process is no child's game of hopscotch. Often the very trait that distinguishes a

---

[5] Other terms used interchangeably with *abstract* are *brief* (not to be confused with legal briefs) and *run-down*. Whereas *brief* suggests formality in the oral presentation and preparation of the remarks, *run-down* suggests informal delivery and impromptu comments.

superior student from an average one, an administrator from a clerk, a judge from a lawyer, or a noted historian from an unknown one is the ability to condense page upon page of detailed information into several, brief, meaningful, and accurate statements.

When abstracting another person's work, a speaker does well to consult the originator for judgments on major points. When this is impossible, the abstractor's preparatory procedure is still essentially the same one followed when the material considered is his own.

1. *PROBLEM OF ANALYSIS.* In analyzing the raw materials for his speech, an abstractor should not delude himself into assuming that all written or oral information clearly and methodically follows a deductive or inductive arrangement pattern. If he makes the deductive assumption, he is in danger of seeking summary points only at paragraph *beginnings;* if he makes the inductive assumption, he is in danger of searching for summary points only at paragraph *endings.* In many instances these two assumptions are true enough; but in nearly as many cases the writer of the original report will not have thought as neatly as the abstractor desired. Essentials may appear within a paragraph as randomly as black pepper on breakfast eggs; occasionally summary thoughts are omitted entirely because the originator of the material concluded that his points were too obvious to mention. Moreover, the abstractor should not assume that printed *I, II, III,* and *IV* are infallible indexes of broad divisional points or that capsule headings are necessarily accurate or that comments as "And this is significant" or "This was a most interesting point" always indicate important ideas for inclusion within the oral abstract.

2. *PROBLEM OF CLARITY.* Having completed the analytical step, a speaker is ready to construct a working outline. As he draws up his more detailed plan he should give prime attention to precision and clarity of his statements; otherwise he should not bother to hamstring himself with limitations imposed by the oral abstract media. In short, he is better off to deliver a report or lecture if all he is doing in the so-called abstract is squeezing a 30-minute delivery into a 3-minute time-slot. If a speaker must rush along madly as he delivers his abstract, he probably failed to analyze his subject properly; in fact, he defeated the intention and purpose of this expository speaking form.

Since abstracts are often meant to accompany a report, a handout, or a set of instructions available to hearers for reading, a speaker may unfortunately assume a rather lackadaisical attitude toward the entire affair. Thus, instead of striving for clarity, an abstractor may conclude, "Well, if they don't understand me, they can always read the complete report." If he thinks this way, he is once again undermining the purpose of an abstract; he is, moreover, defeating his own function as a speaker. The danger of negative thinking is that an abstractor will devote little time to his task and to his problem of composition and delivery. The speaker should assume, therefore, that very few listeners will actually read the original report once he abstracts it for them.

3. *PROBLEM OF DELIVERY*. Because oral abstracts are usually brief, terse, and cogent in comparison to some other expository forms of address, speakers tend, perhaps naturally, to give little, if any, attention to the problems of effectively delivered summaries. However, the very process of abstracting begs for clarity, and a summarizer is obliged, consequently, to deliver his abstract in a manner that both reinforces and emphasizes his prepared material. This means that oral presentation should be reasonably direct, especially emphatic in gestures indicative of major points, clearly enunciated, and easily heard. In fact, if the abstractor remembers that his remarks are the essence of a lengthier idea, he should conclude that his listeners cannot afford, almost literally, to miss a single uttered word. Effective delivery, therefore, becomes nearly a *sine qua non* for the abstractor.

Sample Abstract

The following sample is a special briefing held for Lyndon Johnson and Hubert Humphrey at Headquarters, National Aeronautics and Space Administration, Washington, D.C. The subject of the abstract is the Mariner IV Mars satellite launched at Cape Kennedy on November 28, 1964.

In the audience at the briefing, beside the speakers, the President, and Vice-President, were: Glenn Reiff, Director, Lunar Planetary Division; Edgar Cortright, Deputy Associate Administrator for Space Science and Applications for NASA; Dick Sloan, Chief Scientist, Jet Propulsion Laboratory; John Pasonic, Systems Manager for Mariner IV project; several other distinguished space scientists; and invited members of the press.

The analysis included in the left-hand column with this sample brief is on two levels: major considerations are represented by **bold face** type; secondary questions are presented in regular type. Students and teachers may wish to use both sets of analytical questions, or only bold face ones, as the case may be.

MARINER IV BRIEFING FOR THE PRESIDENT
OF THE UNITED STATES[6]

by members of the *National Aeronautics and
Space Administration,* Washington, D.C.

(This abstract is prepared from a tape recording, February 25, 1965.)

**Discuss the merits of this precise intro-
duction to the coming remarks.**

Note that the briefing session abstracted
a 2-day meeting as well as 3 months of
work.

NEWELL [Dr. Homer E., Associate Administrator for Space Science and Applications for NASA]: . . . My task here
this morning, Mr. President and Mr.
Vice President, is to provide a few introductory remarks. Following those, Dan
Schneiderman [Mariner Project Manager for the Jet Propulsion Laboratory]
will discuss the mission of Mariner. And
then, following this discussion, Jim Van
Allen [Professor of Physics, State University of Iowa (and briefing the President in his capacity as Mariner scientific
investigator)] will present some of the
scientific results.

We have had a two-day meeting here
on the Mariner IV. It is a quarterly review of the project, the sort of things
we carry out on all of our projects, and
as I think you will find, some very interesting results have come from this
project.

May I have the first slide, please?

[6] This sample brief was provided by Richard T. Mittauer, Public Affairs Officer for
Space Science & Applications, National Aeronautics and Space Administration, Washington, D.C. The visual aids reprinted with the text are those used by the speakers and
are reproduced here by permission of NASA.

Evaluate the attention value of this first visual aid.

In what arrangement order would you place the pictures if you were to reorganize the four photographs as a composite aid?

Could I have the lights out, please?

In this slide we remind you very quickly that there are many elements to the Mariner project, as in all projects of this sort. There is the spacecraft, and the spacecraft is launched with a space vehicle.

During the launching operations and following the launching operations, there must be a brain center. This one is at the Jet Propulsion Laboratory, which controls the over-all operation. And, of course, we must have the "ears" that listen to the signals that come back from the spacecraft.

Discuss the skillful manner in which Newell got in facts as he transitioned to the first main speaker.

Evaluate the merits of rounding off figures for oral presentation in describing a scientific project that allows little error in its planning and execution.

Discuss the manner in which the speaker explained his point about the distance traveled in 15 minutes.

This is a dish at the Goldstone station. It is similar to other 85-foot dishes in the deep space net around the world.

Now, you will recall that after your visit to the Cape last fall, you saw the actual Mariner shortly before it was launched. You have in front of you a model of that Mariner. The actual version is about 575 pounds, carrying 60 pounds of instruments. It is about those 60 pounds of instruments and what they hope to do and actually are doing that Dan Schneiderman and Professor Van Allen will talk to you.

First, may I introduce Dan Schneiderman.

SCHNEIDERMAN: The machine that you saw at the Cape last year is at the present time approximately 23 million miles away from the Earth. It was launched on November 28 [1964] for the planet Mars, and it is traveling at the present time at a velocity of approximately 20,000 miles per hour.

Indeed, at this velocity, while we are speaking, its travel during the entire time of the presentation, the machinery would have gone over the entire country—approximately 5,000 miles every fifteen minutes.

Could I have the first slide, please?

MARINER IV TRAJECTORY TO MARS

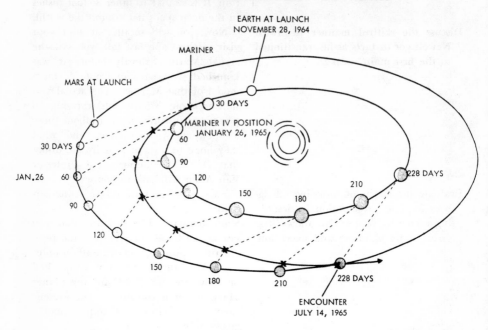

EARTH AT LAUNCH
NOVEMBER 28, 1964

MARINER

MARS AT LAUNCH

30 DAYS

MARINER IV POSITION
JANUARY 26, 1965

60

30 DAYS

90

JAN.26   60

120

90

150

180

120

210

228 DAYS

150

180   210   228 DAYS

ENCOUNTER
JULY 14, 1965

What are the merits and demerits of this diagrammatic presentation? Would the oral remarks accompanying the aid clarify any objections you may have had with the diagram? If *yes*, why? If *no*, why?

This is a graphical description of the trajectory of the Mariner IV spacecraft which was launched on November 28 from Cape Kennedy. It is traveling away from the sun in a manner so as to intercept the planet Mars approximately July the 14th, 1965, a total flight time of 228 days.

At the present time, this is our position, right here. This is some concept of the present location of the spacecraft. In order to impact or to not impact, or to pass by the planet at the proper distance and time, to take the photographs which are scheduled in the mission, we performed a mid-course maneuver.

Could I have the next slide, please?

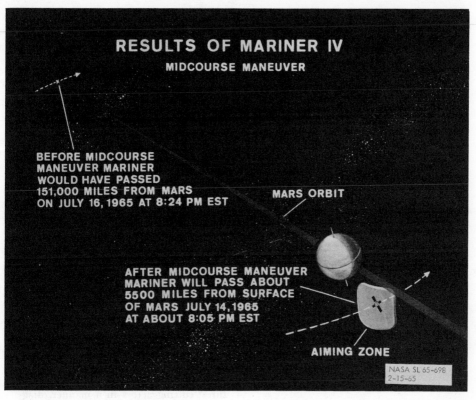

Correlate the aid with the oral commentary. What remarks of praise and criticism would you make?

If we had not performed the correction maneuver and simply gone past the planet on the initial injection, then we would have passed by it approximately so, or 102,000 miles from Mars itself.

Our aiming zone for the pictures to be taken was this area indicated here. Our present predicted encountered distance is approximately 5500 miles from the surface of the planet Mars. We have an uncertainty of approximately plus or minus 500 miles in this number.

May we have the lights on, please?

Note the manner in which Schneiderman abstracted succinctly the present status of Mariner IV.

The engineering condition of the spacecraft at the present time is excellent. All systems are operating well. The communications systems are transmitting at the present time 10 watts of power, which is the power necessary for us to transmit from the planet Mars the pictures and information.

The temperature of the spacecraft is slightly less than originally designed, but this is not a matter of concern on our part.

It is a matter of interest, if you look at the model [of Mariner IV in briefing room] and you observe those little side panels, they are at the present time working sufficiently well enough. So we now expect to have enough gas on board to last six years, which is far in excess of our requirements.

What is the meaning of the sail reference?

WEBB [James E., Administrator, NASA]: It is a sail, you see. The solar pressure on it makes it sail faster than you could—

SCHNEIDERMAN: The system is stabilized by gas. These little vanes you see support the gas system, and they are working well enough to give us enough flight time, if the machine lasts this long.

As I said, we expect to encounter the planet Mars on July 14. That is Washington time, about eight o'clock in the evening. The spacecraft will pass by the planet Mars in a manner that takes pictures, cutting across in a manner, diagonal across the poles this way, touching upon both the light and dark areas, and hopefully going into the dark areas, crossing the terminator. So that 21 pictures will be taken, stored on a tape recorder, and played back to Earth, and we will receive our first picture and will be able to reproduce our first picture, hopefully, approximately 24 hours after the first picture is taken.

Next slide, please.

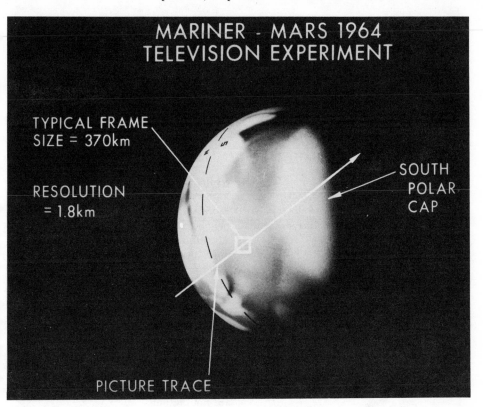

Discuss the virtues in offering a verbal explanation, followed by a visual aid, and climaxed by restatement. Would this be true in an informal and technical report as well? What of a lecture where a general impression is often more important than precise recall?

What form of support is the speaker using here?

This is a slide showing you what I described a minute ago, the pass of the planet Mars, and covering the—what did I say, the diagonal across—of the size of frame that I think—It varies actually as a function of distance as you can see from the planet. Well, this is not truly representative of the frames that we will see.

The resolution is approximately that of a mile and a half. Now, when we scale this in concept, the pictures that Mariner will take are equivalent in history to the moment which Galileo first observed the moon through a telescope several hundred years ago. I don't remember the date.

Notice Schneiderman's use of under-statement to reinforce the importance of the Mariner IV project.

Observe the way Van Allen makes every word count in his introduction by dropping in facts as he introduces his function.

What form of arrangement is Van Allen using? Discuss its clarity.

At the present time our pictures of the planet Mars are as you see here. We expect to see Mars to a resolution of about that which we can see through telescopes at the present time of the moon, which I think is considerable improvement.

Could we have the light on here, please?

The next speaker is Dr. Van Allen, who will describe to you the kind of results we have thus far.

VAN ALLEN: Mr. President, Mr. Vice President, gentlemen: Mariner IV has now been flying 89 days. This is the 89th day of its flight. It is now 23 million miles away from the Earth.

Now, during the past two days we have had about 20 hours of intensive review of the fate of the spacecraft, the state of the mission, and especially the review of scientific results which have been obtained up to this point.

My role here this morning is to try to compress these 20 hours of discussion into a five-minute summary of what we are finding out.

There are three main phases to the Mariner flight from the point of view of the scientific experimenters. The first phase is the escape from the vicinity of the Earth, which already had given some quite interesting scientific results as we swing out away from our own planet.

The second phase is the long coasting phase, which is interplanetary space, coasting in the direction of Mars. This is a period of about seven-and-a-half months.

Finally, on the special objective of this investigation is to encounter the near approach to the planet Mars, ex-pected on the 14th of July.

Now each one of these regions of space has distinctive scientific interest and properties, and I propose to give a very brief review of the sorts of things we have found so far.

What is your evaluation of Van Allen's team-effort comment?

I might say I am only a representative of a large group of experimenters, in addition to the television-photographic coverage of the planet, which is the principal objective. There are some 28 scientific investigators that stretch all the way across the United States who are engaged in quite sophisticated experiments, using this spacecraft as a base for our operations. So I am here only as a representative of this very large group of competent people working in this field.

I would like to show a series of slides, giving some impression into the kinds of things we are finding out.

This is an old slide [not available for reproduction] which shows the general nature of the Earth's magnetosphere, which has been extensively explored by NASA satellites for the last seven years, beginning with one in 1958. I will not dwell on the details, but I wish to call your attention to the fact that the Mariner IV flight was launched here, made a rather spiral path, and went out away from the vicinity of the Earth in this general direction, thus cutting through the entire magnetosphere of the Earth, this very interesting region we have been studying now for about seven years.

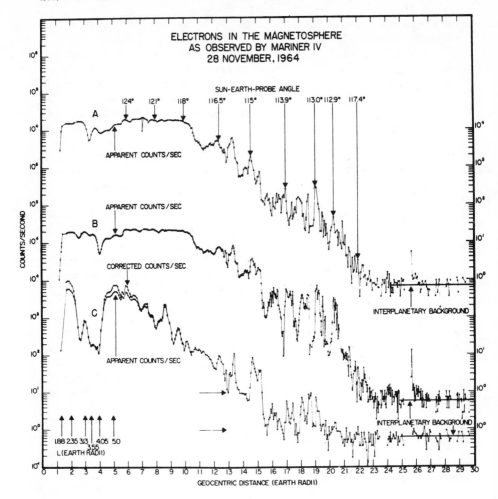

ELECTRONS IN THE MAGNETOSPHERE
AS OBSERVED BY MARINER IV
28 NOVEMBER, 1964

This visual aid is quite technical. Why is it appropriate to the occasion? What general impression does such an aid make on the hearer? Or would you say that its highly technical nature distracts rather than adds to the abstract?

This is a technical slide showing detailed results. I thought it was not inappropriate to show at least a few slides to the sort of data that we actually work with. I call your attention particularly to the following features.

As we pass out away from the area at a distance of about 23 times the radius of the Earth, we then become interplanetary space, as defined by this instrument in a functional sense.

This slide is particularly of interest in illustrating the nature of the data which we may receive in the vicinity of Mars. At the present time it is not known whether Mars has a magnetic field, and whether it has a radiation belt similar to that of the Earth. This is one of the principal objectives of the group of people which we have at the [State] University of Iowa.

Now, the next slide, please.

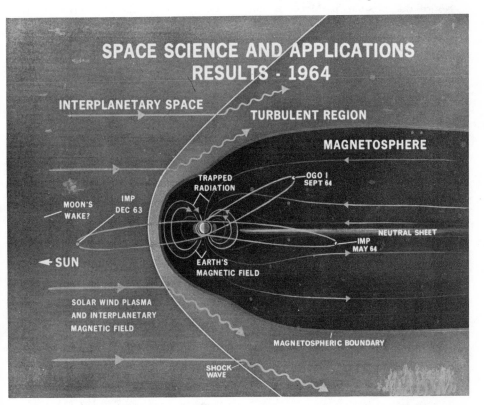

If you reacted negatively to the previous aid, study the next presentation and then answer the question: Is an aid's usefulness determined by the technical nature of the subject treated, or by the audience addressed?

Why is comparison so important to a highly technical abstract?

This gives a photographic summary of the knowledge of the Earth's magnetosphere and its immediate physical environment. The crucial causative agent for all these varieties of phenomena shown here is what is now known as solar wind, a blast of very tenuous gas, mostly hydrogen gas, which is emitted from the sun, flows through interplanetary space, and encounters the Earth's magnetic field.

There are a great variety of phenomena which result from that wind. The

Notice the peculiar problems of language posed by the space-age—the apparent necessity of earth oriented terminology to describe space oriented phenomena. Do you think that this will introduce problems of oversimplification as well as inaccurate imagery on occasion?

most well known ones, I think, here on the Earth are the appearance of the northern and southern lights in polar regions, and the occurrence of magnetic storms. This has been a region of intensive investigation by NASA satellites beginning in 1958.

One of the specific questions we have been interested in is to see how far downstream this turbulent wake of the Earth extends. We have now settled that with Mariner IV. We have cut through that tail on the 28th of January and found that 3,000 times the radius of the Earth in the downstream direction there with [was?] no influence of the Earth.

Next slide, please.

[See slide on opposite page 285.]

This shows one of the significant events we have discovered during the interplanetary cruise of Mariner IV. This was a so-called solar cosmic ray event, an occasion on which the sun emits energetic particles in a dulsatory and so far in an unpredictable manner. This type of event is of special concern with persons who are planning extended manned flights in interplanetary space.

So we are making a systematic study, monitoring this type of phenomena, throughout the 7-$\frac{1}{2}$ month period of Mariner IV's flights.

In addition to that, there are several near-earth satellites. The OGO-I satellite, the Injun-IV satellite, the IMP-II satellite, and the new OSO-II, the solar-monitoring satellite, all in orbit simultaneously. So we are able to obtain and compare different pictures between conditions remote from the Earth, and conditions near the Earth.

This event occurred on the 5th of February with the—two or three weeks ago. We have the results presented here. The event was one that would not have been dangerous for interplanetary manned spacecraft and was a small

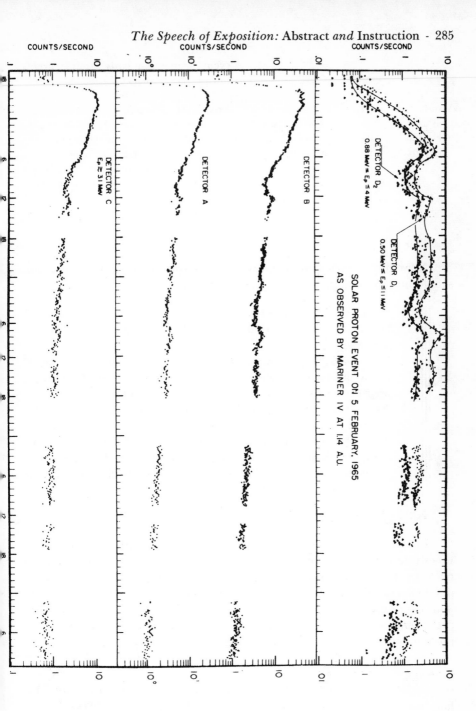

Would you classify these last comments as the conclusion? If *no*, was a conclusion necessary? If *yes*, evaluate the effectiveness of the conclusion.

event by the standards of such events during recent years.

Thank you very much.

VOICE: Mr. President, that completes our review of Mariner IV to date.

I might remind you again that the total mission will take until the summer of this year, and then as Mariner passes by Mars, we will be looking to see what pictures we can get from Mars and what we can see about any possible radiation belts and so on. So the mission is far from over.

Now that you read the remarks at the Mariner IV briefing session, you should answer the following general questions.

1. What basic methods of support did the speakers use during the briefing? Do you think that narratives and humor have a place at such occasions?
2. What evidences of personal commentary did you find in the abstract? If you found *none*, would you have included some? If you found *some*, what is your reaction to such comments in an abstract?
3. Discuss the organization plan used by each speaker. What are the virtues of clear arrangement in such a short presentation?
4. Discuss the implications of briefs as a method of apprising those charged with policy making. Are the responsibilities of the speaker to his audience greater at briefing sessions than at other occasions of speechmaking?

INSTRUCTION

Instructions, unlike abstracts, reveal a complete body of facts. Sometimes referred to as directions, instructions give hearers exact information on steps, procedures, modes of operation, plans of action, or methods of development, all important and essential to the accomplishment of a goal. This expository form, like the abstract, depends usually for effectiveness on precision, conciseness, and accuracy. Additionally, there are two other important objectives of instruction—*clarity* and *retention*.

In contrast to the oral abstract where hearers are interested usually in *general* points of information, an audience listening to instructions is concerned with *specific* recall. Aware that they are to receive directions for later use, hearers alert themselves to their speaker's coming remarks. Unlike other expository forms of address where, if anything, more responsibility rests with the speaker than listener for successful communication, the instructional situation tends to equalize the communication burden genuinely between listener and communicator. Whereas hearers at a lecture may reasonably expect the speaker to deliver a good, clear, and lively address for casual recollection, listeners receiving instructions vital for later recall are forced generally into attentiveness, regardless of the speaker's presentational ability. The necessity, therefore, of remembering particular information demands more concentrated listener attention to a speaker's remarks than is usually found in other expository situations.

Developmental Problems of Instruction

When preparing a set of oral instructions, a speaker should consider three problems peculiar to this expository form of address.

Problem of Delivery versus Content

Since clarity, accuracy, and retention are essential ends of instructional presentations, a speaker may consider himself relatively successful if hearers go away with his information and with general understanding of his remarks. And good physical action, of course, often aids this success.[7] But delivery, regardless of its polish, is never a substitute for the information itself.

Because hearers expect brevity and cogency when listening to instructions, a speaker delivering such remarks may read his prepared, step-by-step set of instructions to his audience in a matter-of-fact, offhand fashion.[8] And certainly if his instructions are not long, if the information is delivered in easily grasped sentences,[9] and if the expository material is presented in a logical and methodical manner, hearers will probably go away enlightened from such an occasion.

Problem of Checking Effect

Since clarity, accuracy, and retention are essential ends when giving instructions, a speaker frequently uses forms of support for his speech as definition, comparison, contrast, example, restatement, repetition, and in-

[7] In fact, one study showed that even when the audience could not see the speaker, comprehension was improved if the speaker used gestures during delivery. See P. W. Gauger, "The Effect of Gesture and the Presence or Absence of the Speaker on Listening Comprehension of Eleventh and Twelfth Grade High School Pupils," *Speech Monographs,* Vol. 19 (June 1952), pp. 116–117.

[8] Some experiments have shown that even poor vocal delivery does not interfere with comprehension to any great extent. See Vernon Utzinger, "An Experimental Study of the Effects of Verbal Fluency upon the Listener," *Speech Monographs,* Vol. 20 (August 1953), p. 161; K. C. Beighley, "An Experimental Study of the Effect of Four Speech Variables on Listener Comprehension," *Speech Monographs,* Vol. 21 (November 1954), pp. 248–253; C. F. Diehl and E. T. McDonald, "Effect of Voice Quality on Communication," *Journal of Speech and Hearing Disorders,* Vol. 21 (June 1956), pp. 233–237; and Charles F. Diehl, Richard C. White, and P. H. Satz, "Pitch Change and Comprehension," *Speech Monographs,* Vol. 28 (March 1961), pp. 65–68.

[9] There is some evidence indicating that short sentences definitely increase accuracy of recall when giving directions. See Hadley Cantril and Gordon W. Allport, *The Psychology of Radio* (New York: Harper & Row, Publishers, 1935), p. 189.

ternal summaries. The experienced speaker realizes, however, that the situation demanding instructions is different from some other occasions for public address where accuracy and retention are less crucial to success. In the directional circumstance, the speaker expects listeners to carry out his suggestions or edicts. If hearers are, however, to execute properly his instructions, he should whenever possible check on his own effectiveness in advance.

Because applause and apparent audience interest are often misleading, a speaker may rely on more accurate means of evaluating his success at an instructional session. He may test his effectiveness in several ways:

1. he calls for questions after the instructions
2. he invites limited interruption whenever listeners are confused
3. he asks hearers to repeat his directions orally when feasible[10]
4. he quizzes them randomly on essential points of instruction to check his accuracy[11]
5. he requires his hearers either to take notes, or to study summary sheets containing his information[12]

Here the student may ask, "If the speaker is going to distribute a complete set of instructions, why should he bother even to speak?", or "Why not just hold a session for questions and answers?" The reason for accompanying instructions with oral presentation is that a writer's set of printed directions are as liable to misinterpretation as a speaker's words. The speaker, consequently, serves a definite function; indeed, he meets a particular need—he gives instructions an oral interpretation and an emphatic direction sometimes impossible to impart through printed words.

[10] There is some evidence to indicate that a speaker, when addressing persons of low motivation or when giving complex instructions, increases comprehension by making individual listeners verbally repeat his instructions. See Carl I. Hovland, Irving L. Janis, and Harold H. Kelly, *Communication and Persuasion: Psychological Studies of Opinion Change* (New Haven: Yale University Press, 1953), p. 218.

[11] Some evidence indicates that listeners, when motivated by a coming quiz, recall information better than those who are surprised by a quiz. See Franklin H. Knower, David Phillips, and F. Koeppel, "Studies in Listening to Informative Speaking," *Journal of Abnormal and Social Psychology*, Vol. 40 (1945), pp. 82–88; and B. L. Prince, "A Study of Classroom Listening Effectiveness to Certain Other Factors," *Speech Monographs*, Vol. 16 (September 1948), p. 352; and Charles E. Irvin, "Motivation in Listening Training," *The Journal of Communication*, Vol. 4 (Summer 1954), pp. 42–44.

[12] Since listeners vary in their ability to take notes, a wise speaker can increase the recall of his instructions if he provides hearers with a set of notes. See Ralph G. Nichols, "Factors Accounting for Difference in Comprehension of Materials Presented Orally in the Classroom," *Speech Monographs*, Vol. 16 (September 1949), pp. 350–351; and Charles E. Irvin, "An Analysis of Certain Aspects of Listening Training Program Conducted among College Freshmen at Michigan State College," *Speech Monographs*, Vol. 20 (June 1953), pp. 122–123. Should the speaker, however, find it impossible to distribute a handout, listeners forced to take all or even part of the instructions down will retain more information than those hearers who merely listen to the speaker. See Frank R. Hartman, "A Behavioristic Approach to Communication: A Selective Review of Learning Theory and a Derivation of Postulates," *AV Communication Review*, Vol. 11 (May–June 1963), p. 184.

Finally, his presence allows listeners to ask questions for clarification when necessary.

Problem of Composition

Instructions are developed generally in two major ways. (1) A speaker will find that *chronological* arrangement is often easiest for hearers to follow and grasp. (2) There is often a natural, relative, or real importance to sections of his material. When the latter is the case, instructions developed *topically* may prove easiest for listeners to remember accurately, since arrangement of ideas in this manner permits a speaker to control his placement of instructional ideas within the address.

An important emphatic means for *effective* presentation of instructions is proper and frequent use of *transitions.* (See Chapter 8 for further details on transitions.) Even if a speaker arranges his set of directions chronologically, there is still need on his part at times to indicate clearly when he is taking another step forward. If his development is topical, then transitions are even more important for effective presentation of instructions. Therefore a good speaker will want to signal each new step with appropriate and unmistakable language as well as physical action. Sometimes content-movement is indicated by a simple *First, Second,* and *Third* joined with an appropriate counting gesture. Certainly a speaker delivering instructions need not feel ashamed that he took the easy way out, since there is merit in the direct though less imaginative way of bridging instructional points. Some speakers may prefer to combine an internal summary with a forecast, saying, for instance, "After your interview with the personnel manager, the *third* step in getting a job with NASA is to report to the security office for preliminary clearance." In any event, since recall is the communicator's goal—and this is almost always the case when giving instructions—he cannot afford to miss opportunities for rerunning information past his audience for second, third and even fourth hearings.

The final two points of composition concern the *introduction* and the *conclusion* to instructions. Introductions to directional speeches usually proceed along traditional lines of capturing attention, demonstrating need for the coming information and forecasting impending remarks. There are, of course, some deviations from the norm. *First,* because instructions are often presented quickly, the speaker's one opportunity for some informality and rapport with hearers is during his introduction. *Second,* because anxious and impatient listeners concern themselves with receiving and carrying out instructions, a speaker may choose to limit his preliminary remarks before proceeding to his instructions. *Third,* because instructions sometimes take only 1 or 2 minutes for delivery, a speaker may reduce his entire introduction to such pointed sentences as: "Ladies and Gentlemen, as you go to your various inspection posts, there are only two things to keep in mind. First . . ."; or "Good afternoon. Before you begin your evaluative tests for the Peace Corps, I need remind you of only two things. First . . ."; or "Good evening. I am your referee for tonight's fight, Sam Lavine. Mr. Fernandez, Mr. Jones, you know the rules of the New York Boxing Commission. I expect . . .".

Conclusions to instructions may contain an informal or formal summary whenever the speaker wishes to reemphasize his directions.[13] A speaker may even go a step further at times by including appeals for action when he feels the occasion is especially important or when he realizes that hearers lack proper motivation. Frequently, a speaker will deliver final wishes for the success of an operation whose accomplishment depends on implementing his instructions. Often, he will intone some benedictorylike pronouncement on hearers charged with executing directions. (Here, a word of caution: the standard closings, "Good luck" or "God be with you" can be sincere, or they can sound melodramatic.) Finally, a speaker will sometimes emphasize one particular instruction over all others as essential to consummating a plan. Not all instructions, naturally, lend themselves to this technique.

Sample Instructions

The first sample speech illustrates how a speaker may use *chronological* arrangement when delivering a set of instructions. As you read the remarks by Ewald Turner before the 1962 National Education Association convention in Denver, you should note particularly how the speaker, after capturing attention for his coming instructions, proceeds directly to a concise and clear explanation of procedure:

> We now proceed to the nomination of officers for the National Education Association. Each delegate will be charged with the responsibility of selecting the candidate they believe can best serve the profession. I urge you to listen carefully, weigh your decisions judiciously, and vote early on Friday.
>
> I have a bit of advice for those who are going to speak for the candidates and for the candidates themselves. I shall label my advice "SOS"—*S*, speak slowly, *O*, open your mouth, *S*, stay near the microphone.
>
> The ground rules for the speeches are as follows: Nominating speeches are in alphabetical order of the states from which the candidates come. Following all nominations, the candidates will then be presented in reverse order of their nomination. Candidates for Executive Committee will be allowed three minutes, and candidates for president-elect-vice-president, will be allowed five minutes. A timer has been provided and a green light will flash when the speaker has two minutes left to speak. A yellow light will flash when the speaker has one minute left to speak, and a red light will flash when the time has expired.

[13] Bernard Berelson and Gary A. Steiner in *Human Behavior: An Inventory of Scientific Findings* (New York: Harcourt, Brace & World, Inc., 1964), pp. 552–553, conclude that effectiveness is increased by explicitly drawing ideas to a conclusion.

The member of the Rules Committee in charge of this will stand when the red light appears, the gavel will sound, and the speaker's opportunity to orate will be terminated.

At this time, the Chair recognizes *Robert Morton* of Colorado to present a candidate.[14]

The second address illustrates how a speaker may use *topical* order when delivering a set of instructions. As you read Dwight Eisenhower's remarks delivered by radio from London on May 20, 1944, you should observe how the speaker relies upon the importance of the occasion to capture attention, how he moves rapidly to his instructions once he informs listeners in occupied Europe of his purpose, and how he emphasizes one key point in closing his speech. Like the Turner address, Eisenhower is precise and clear in his remarks to hearers:

> When the Allies come to liberate you, they will rely on your help in many ways. . . . In no more valuable way can this be given than by information about the enemy.
>
> Start, therefore, today to observe him more and more closely. Observe the numbers of men and of vehicles by type. Note when they come and how, and the direction in which they are going.
>
> Note the markings on their vehicles and try to find out the regiment, formations or groups to which they belong. Note their arms and their arrangements for supply of food and petrol. Note especially any large movement and the exact date.
>
> Observe the faces and appearances of officers, especially senior officers, and of leaders among civilians. Endeavor to find out their names; note when they come and go and where they go to; learn the badges of their rank.
>
> Try to discover the locations of petrol, ammunition and supply depot and stores. Locations of headquarters and signal stations are especially important.
>
> Note the times and routes of dispatch riders and whether they go singly or escorted.
>
> Keep a watch on all bridges and note the water and lighting key points, which, if damaged, would destroy water and lighting systems.
>
> Keep a look-out for the laying of mines or preparations for demolitions. Note especially any suspicious preparations that might be the laying of booby traps.
>
> Let nothing escape you. Pool your knowledge. Take utmost care to give information to none but known patriots.
>
> Be patient, above all, and hide your actions until the word is given.[15]

The third address illustrates how a speaker may use a combination of *topical* and *chronological* order when delivering a set of instructions. As you read a section of the hearings on President Kennedy's assassination,

[14] *Addresses and Proceedings of the One-Hundredth Annual Meeting Held at Denver, Colorado, July 1–July 6: 1962* (Washington, D.C.: National Educational Association of the United States, 1962), Vol. 100, p. 100.

[15] *The New York Times,* May 21, 1944. Copyright 1944 by The New York Times Company. Reprinted by permission.

you should note how the speaker asks for confirmation during his remarks. The chairman presiding at the President's Commission on the Assassination, February 3, 1964, was Earl Warren, Chief Justice of the Supreme Court. Attorney for Mrs. Lee Harvey Oswald was John M. Thorne, and general counsel for the commission was J. Lee Rankin.

> The CHAIRMAN. Now, Mr. Thorne and Mrs. Oswald, I want to say to you that we want to see that Mrs. Oswald's rights are protected in every manner and you are entitled to converse with her at any time that you desire. You are entitled to give her advice that you want, either openly or in private; if you feel that her rights are not being protected you are entitled to object to the Commission and have a ruling upon it, and at the conclusion of her testimony if you have any questions that you would like to ask her in verification of what she has said you may feel free to ask them.
>
> After her testimony has been completed, a copy will be furnished to you so that if there are any errors, corrections or omissions you may call it to our attention, is that satisfactory to you?
>
> Mr. THORNE. Very satisfactory, Mr. Chairman.
>
> Mr. CHAIRMAN. I might say also to her we propose to ask her questions for about 1 hour, and then take a short recess for her refreshment, and then we will convene again until about 12:30. At 12:30 we will recess until 2 o'clock, and then we may take her to her hotel where she can see her baby and have a little rest, and we will return at 2 o'clock, and we will take evidence until about 4:30. If at any time otherwise you should feel tired or feel that you need a rest, you may feel free to say so and we will take care of it.
>
> Mrs. OSWALD. Thank you.
>
> The CHAIRMAN. The questions will be asked of you by Mr. J. Lee Rankin, who is the general counsel of the Commission.
>
> Mr. RANKIN. Mrs. Oswald, you be at your ease, and the interpreter will tell you what I ask and to take your time about your answers.
>
> Will you state your name, please?[16]

[16] *Hearings Before the President's Commission on the Assassination of President Kennedy* (U.S. Government Printing Office, Washington, D.C., 1964), Vol. 1, 2.

The Speech of Exposition: *Informal* and *Technical* Reports

13

Reports, in contrast to abstracts, are fuller ʻand more detailed summaries. Based on personal study or experience, or on conclusions or observations of others, a speaker preparing a report is usually allowed more time to deliver his remarks than the speaker presenting an abstract or summary.

TYPES OF REPORTS

Depending on the content, reports are of two broad types: *informal* and *technical.*

Informal Report

Many addresses, termed lectures for want of a better term, are actually informal reports. For instance, the speaker who represents his company at a businessmen's luncheon and who talks about new production developments in his plant is often delivering nothing more than an informal report. He will probably include several abstracts within the total speech because listener fortitude, hard chairs, and clock-watching chairmen still put time restrictions on him. He may even include instructions in his address concerning directions for visiting his plant, or steps when applying for work at his company. Then what, exactly, distinguishes an informal report from an abstract, a set of instructions, or a lecture?

Beside time allotments, the significant characteristic of an informal report is the freedom permitted a speaker in choosing his developmental details. He is at once at liberty to include such lengthier forms of support in his address as illustrations and narratives. Then, too, because he feels the situation is less rigorous than a formal lecture, his physical presentation is frequently more relaxed. He may often use his notes sparingly because he sees less urgency for precision, conciseness, and accuracy when giving an informal report than when delivering an abstract or set of instructions. Furthermore, he may conclude that since his points are broad, he will give less attention to precise content for later recall and more to the general effect his remarks will have on listeners.

In essence many speakers prefer the looser form of exposition because the informal report is usually delivered in circumstances of more rapport between speaker and listener than is present in a formal lecture situation. You doubtlessly delivered one or two informal reports in your lifetime, although you called them broadly, expository speech, informative speech, or speech to inform.

Technical Report

The technical report, as contrasted to the informal, is decidedly more precise in terms of composition and delivery. Often called papers, findings, factual reports, and even, though mistakenly, abstracts, technical reports are based on serious and methodical study, research, or experience and are almost always more detailed than the true abstract. This difference between a technical report and an abstract, however, is sometimes confusing. A speaker who talks for half an hour may be in a sense only "abstracting" an original study that runs to four or five volumes in length. The difference between the abstract and the technical report is determined more accurately by *detail* than by time.

Where the abstractor has room only to indicate main developmental points, a speaker delivering a technical report may explain more fully the hypothesis, the experimental steps of a study, the implications of a project, and the observations and reactions of himself and others to the study. Often associated with detailed lists, avalanches of figures and statistics, and intricate and complex lines of reasoning, technical reports are sometimes dull to outsiders and to the uninitiated, because these hearers could not care less about a speaker's topic, or because they cannot understand his use of language, choice of idioms, and jargon, or because they cannot comprehend his basic premises. Thus a report, for instance, on the eightfold system of quantum mathematics as applied to theoretical physics is meaningless for most hearers. To the knowledgeable, however, technical reports can be exciting and informative. In contrast, an informal report is a more popular treatment of a subject, and most listeners with a modicum of inside knowledge will probably find the address meaningful to them. Admittedly, there are many occasions when an informal report is still too technical for the general public.

Because technical reports are steeped with facts, speakers presenting such addresses often concentrate their attention on content rather than methods of development and delivery. A technical report is frequently, therefore, no more than a paper meant for readers rather than listeners. The tendency toward reader oriented reports is encouraged by publication of technical papers on the heels of or even before oral presentation, as in the case of the American Statistical Association. The speaking occasion, consequently, becomes a chance genuflection to the goddess of tradition and a bothersome trifle to the reader-speaker.

Possible publication of a technical report, however, is still a poor excuse for sloppy delivery and for inattention to listener limitations. Hearers are human whether they be members of an important board of directors or fellows of a scientific academy; materials presented dully and organized in highly obtuse ways will as easily confuse a listener with five academic and 20 honorary degrees after his name as a hearer with Mr. before his.

DEVELOPMENT PROBLEMS OF THE REPORT

There are four problems associated with the development of informal and technical reports.

Problem of Feedforward-Feedback Stimuli

Audience adaptation is a rhetorical injunction accepted by most speakers. Unfortunately, the edict to adapt is issued more easily than executed and the reasons for this are generally twofold: (1) a speaker is unaware the situation calls for a change in his speech plan; (2) he discovers, even when conscious of a situational change, that it is one thing to realize the need for adaptation, and quite another to scissor prepared remarks as demanded by the circumstance.

Is there a premeditated procedure available for speakers who wish to solve the adaptation problem? There is, happily, a three-step solution.

Since the communication process is a two-way street between informer and informee, a speaker should *first* release exploratory balloons during his speech to sample audience reaction at crucial communication moments between himself and hearers.[1] Using *feedforward* stimuli (as opposed to *feedback* responses), the speaker, for instance, probes audience reaction by offering them sacrificial sentences as "Eisenhower is thought by many to be one of our best Presidents in recent times," or "Economists say we face a serious business recession next year," or "The President of a California university said that co-educational dorms will be in vogue throughout the country within ten years."

Second, the speaker then watches for negative feedbacks such as frowns, surprise or troubled fidgeting from listeners (referred to as *jamming,* in

---

[1] The procedure presented here is based on Gardner Murphy, "Toward a Field Theory of Communication," *The Journal of Communication,* Vol. 11 (December 1961), pp. 196–201.

communication lingo). To observe audience feedback, a speaker needs good eye-contact with his hearers. Most speakers are aware, probably, of the eye-contact mandate; many speakers, by practicing this commandment, have learned already to classify a whole range of audience feedbacks. If the practice of looking for jamming is new to a speaker, then a suggestion is in order: after deciding on those listeners whom he thinks are the most likely barometers of reaction to feedforward information, he should watch them carefully for telltale responses.[2]

Once a speaker decodes feedback, he is ready for the *third* step: to choose a path of reaction that overcomes audience jamming. The skilled speaker, armed beforehand with several trial sentences, proceeds through his speech as planned when his listeners respond favorably. If their reactions are negative, however, he counters with prepared, emergency illustrations reserved for such possibilities, in the same way a lawyer or college debater counters from his reserve of just-in-case information contained in his brief. There is, however, a significant difference between the information held in reserve by a lawyer presenting a legal case and a speaker delivering a report. Whereas the former will usually include a wealth of facts and arguments in his brief to substantiate a particular viewpoint, the latter includes in his outline only those reserve facts based on specific, problematic responses by hearers. Naturally, the success or failure of such a technique depends on how accurately the speaker delivering a report predicts audience response, and whether or not his substitute information satisfies listeners.[3]

The idea of simultaneously juggling more than one idea in the air may frighten some speakers and may even seem like a devilishly impossible trick. Furthermore, if a speaker has never debated formally, he may at first find the feedforward-feedback practice difficult and awkward to use in his speech. A beginner, however, may console himself, since he does not need a sense of timing and physical agility necessary to a circus juggler. All he needs is practice at interchanging support required by audience circumstances. Moreover, he need not join a debate club for practice; he need only find himself a responsive listener-critic on whom he can test his feedforward sentences during practice sessions. Hopefully, the student speaker should discover that his mind is capable of keeping several assorted ideas in the air without their falling to the ground in heaps.

2 John F. Kennedy, realizing the significance of audience feedback, used this device to tell him whether or not he was reaching the "personal audience"—"men in work shirts and sports shirts, the women in house dresses with babies in arms, the farmers observing silently, the students listening intently, the bobby-soxers yipping and squealing." See Theodore H. White, *The Making of the President: 1960* (New York: Atheneum Publishers, 1961), p. 255.

3 For an interesting account of a speaker who followed essentially this practice of speech composition and audience adaptation, see Carroll P. Lahman, "Robert M. La Follette," in *A History and Criticism of American Public Address*, William Norwood Brigance, ed. (New York: McGraw-Hill, Inc., 1943), II, pp. 942–967.

Problem of Analysis and Assumption

Even a beginning speaker in a persuasive address will take pains to analyze listeners in terms of their fundamental attitudes, opinions, or beliefs on a topic. Thus, before arguing the point that airline companies can afford to pay flight engineers on jets, a beginner knows he must first remove the fundamental objection—featherbedding is undesirable. The speaker delivering a report essentially confronts the same evaluative problem of assumption as the advocate. Yet in practice an informative as contrasted to a persuasive speaker often appraises casually his listeners' beliefs, opinions, and attitudes towards his topic. Common, therefore, are the following analytical questions asked by a speaker preparing a report: "What does the audience know about my subject?" and "Is my topic truly within the area of information?" Certainly these vital questions need answers before a speaker should prepare his informative report, but these questions represent only the first steps of audience analysis.

If a student speaker ever permitted hearers to quiz him after delivering an informative report, he may recall some of their inquiries. Usually a better part of the questions sought further information—an indication of his success or failure at stimulating curiosity or at explaining ideas; and another series of questions fell into an unrelated category—a sign of listener woolgathering. Finally, there was a group of inquiries that should have given the speaker pause and concern. These last questions, dismissed frequently by a speaker as listeners' misunderstanding of his intentions, are argumentative audience comments that disagree with his interpretation of supposedly factual, informative points. Far from harmless probes, these cuts at him illustrate a fundamental problem in much expository speaking —the assumption that a speech intended as informative rather than persuasive will seem unbiased to hearers.

The very decision to use one quotation over another, or one illustration in preference to another, or one fact instead of another is a *qualitative,* selective judgment by a speaker, and his choices are subject, therefore, to attack from hearers.[4] The problem of objective versus subjective analysis, in short, emphasizes an important point: *the analytical process cannot end until the speaker utters his final word to hearers.*

Problem of Superficiality

The *informal report* also presents a speaker with the problem of *superficiality.* Readers have probably heard (perhaps delivered themselves) expository speeches that left listeners unimpressed because the speaker's development was too common, too shallow, and too elementary. Those

---

4 We are not here engaging in a metaphysical debate over the possibility or impossibility of a truly objective judgment. We take the view that regardless of a speaker's position on a topic, he must plunge in and make evaluations.

responsible for this *genre* of superficial oral reports are generally innocent beginners who think glibness makes up for poor content, and who, after spending precious time selecting their perfect subjects for presentation, devote a pitiable amount of energy to gathering and ordering their materials. Worse, much information collected in haste is—and at times necessarily—superficial and monumentally inconsequential to hearers. A good speaker, therefore, should find worthwhile topics for presentation, thereby saving hearers from the creeping plethora of time-wasting, informal reports.

To illustrate what is meant by superficiality, a speaker might talk about his trip to West Germany and he may think he fulfilled the requirements of an informal report as long as he related his experiences in one section of his address, expounded his reactions in another, and offered personal advice in closing. Actually, this kind of an address is more nearly a narrative and entertaining speech than an expository report. A speaker's proximity to a subject, in other words, does not always license him to fulfill his speech purpose by merely relating personal reactions and experiences. On occasion a subject lends itself exclusively to introspective treatment— if the speaker commanded the Seventh Fleet in World War II, his ruminations in an informal report are truly informative; or if he headed the American Embassy in Viet Nam during the overthrow of the Diem regime, his observations in a report are indeed valuable.

Unfortunately, most speakers have had experiences of unheroic proportion: they must report instead on their travels to Europe, restate experiences as door-to-door salesmen, or explain their jobs at a summer resort. When treating conventional subjects, a speaker is in danger, consequently, of reporting more ordinary information to his hearers. Certainly the three commoner topics above can be informative . . . and they will be informative if a speaker uses his experiences as a springboard for development, rather than the development itself. The concern here, therefore, is with the speaker who reports informally on his trip to Europe and who treats his subject in tired, movie-travelogue fashion. The as-the-sun-sinks-in-the-West-we-leave-our-land-of-enchantment report only impresses hearers with the speaker's fulsome sentimentality. This kind of so-called informal report may meet the rhetorical requirement of *interest,* but it does not fulfill the necessity of *information.*

The last illustration may lead a speaker to conclude that informal reports are either researched subjects or unusual, saga experiences. Obviously, this is not so; for then only a handful of people in every 10,000 could ever feel free enough to deliver reports. What is meant is that a speaker should add *meaningful,* informative facts to his informal report, which go beyond the reflective step of elementary-level speech composition. If a speaker, therefore, is going to report on his European trip, his job as a door-to-door salesman, or his experience as a busboy at a resort, he should ask himself: "Can I add some significant data to my personal, sometimes superficial, and often frivolous impressions on a topic?"

In contrast to a person preparing an informal report, the speaker composing a *technical* one has little problem discovering enough significant information for hearers. By its very nature, the technical report, if anything, is engulfed in too many facts. A speaker, subsequently, faces the problem of *selectivity,* of deciding what information can be understood when presented verbally to hearers, and of finding ways to enliven his topic for oral presentation. When an average speaker preparing an informal report is compared to one composing a technical report, a startling paradox often emerges: a speaker who spent a month in Italy may discover that all he remembers are superficial facts about the country; in contrast, a speaker who never visited Italy, who instead spent a month researching a paper on the Italian economy since World War II, may find himself confronted with so much factual material that he has difficulty eliminating data from his oral, technical report on his subject. The dissimilarity between the two speakers is much like the difference between one student in a course on English Literature who exclaims, "I didn't learn a thing," and another student in the same class who concludes, "I learned so much in a semester." Where one speaker and student were *observers,* the other two were *participants.*

If a speaker, therefore, is merely an observer on a subject, he may well find himself with inadequate material for a good oral report. Before he inflicts himself on listeners, he should participate actively by either researching additional concrete information on his subject or by carefully recording facts as he observes them.

Problem of Composition

So far as the composition of informal and technical reports are concerned, both require careful organizational plans. Usually, *topical, chronological,* or *space* arrangement is used. Reports, however, can also follow the cause-effect pattern. For instance, a speaker delivering an informal report on new trends in marketing may decide to build his speech around a series of examples that illustrate vividly an *effect* to listeners. (As demonstrated in Chapter 3 on explaining, cause-effect development is not intentionally persuasive in every instance.)

Even a modified problem-solution plan is possible when developing certain informative topics. If a speaker wished to deliver a progress report on proposals for increasing policemen's wages, he might follow an amended problem-solution plan, *provided his basic assumptions about hearers' attitudes are valid.*[5] Once the speaker felt certain that his listeners agreed with his assumptions, he could then devote the first part of his address to

[5] In the hypothetical illustration about policemen, the speaker's assumption is that listeners agree that these men deserve a wage increase.

restating the *problem* and the second part to considering the possible *solutions* under advisement by the city council. The speaker, meanwhile, remains neutral on the subject; he implies no preferences nor does he align possible solutions into an inevitable, preferential pattern. Instead, he reports the four or five proposals under study; in place of indicating preferred ones, he reports the city council's criteria for final judgment. Here at the third step, a speaker delivering such a progress report may find it difficult to leave his own preferences out of his speech. He may decide, consequently, to omit the test-step from his address. Finally, the speaker makes no appeal; he reverts instead to neutral conclusions used by informative speakers as summary, quotation, and illustration.

SAMPLE REPORTS

A word about procedure before the student reads the next two sample reports. *First,* the analysis included with each speech is on two levels. Major considerations are in **bold face** and secondary ones are in regular type. The student should give his attention to the major analysis in the left-hand column, and then—if he or his teacher is so inclined—to the minor questions and comments. *Second,* instead of telling the reader what the speakers are doing in every case, the analysis includes questions meant purposefully to force the student into making evaluations for himself. Hopefully, he will be inspired to inquire about his own reports in an equally introspective manner, since the student speaker must often rely on his own best judgment as a prediction of effectiveness before actually delivering his address. Some of the questions and comments, consequently, verge on nit picking. Until the student develops a *highly critical approach* to his own speech-making, he may proceed blindly through life trusting in a superficial analysis and pronouncing only one verdict—*Great!*—on all his speeches. These questions of analysis, therefore, are meant to initiate students in a more critical appraisal of their addresses.

An Informal Report

THE JOB WAS TOUGH: OUR SUCCESS HAS BEEN YOUR SUCCESS[6]

by Robert Sargent Shriver, Jr.,[7] *Director, Peace Corps, Washington, D.C.*

(*This informal report was delivered at the 17th National Conference on Higher Education at the Morrison Hotel, Chicago, on March 6, 1962. There were as many as 1600 college educators listening to Shriver when he delivered this address. In preparation for the speech, Shriver wrote that he was fairly sure of a friendly audience, although he confessed that I don't think the question—whether the*

[6] As reprinted from *Vital Speeches of the Day,* Vol. 28 (April 15, 1962), pp. 407–411.
[7] For a collection of speeches by Shriver, see Robert Sargent Shriver, Jr., *Point of the Lance* (New York: Harper & Row, Publishers, 1965).

audience would be friendly or unfriendly—would have made a lot of difference in what I planned to say. . . . *Continuing, Shriver wrote:* In the case of this Chicago talk on March 6, 1962, I was making corrections on the [5 x 7 note] cards as late as ten minutes before I was introduced to the audience.

I don't think I have ever given a speech exactly as it appears on the cards. Since I don't like to read a speech, I usually glance at the cards for cues. This means that I will often alter a talk as I go along—sometimes in response to the mood of the audience, sometimes for other reasons. . . . I recall that I spoke quite freely off the cuff [to the Chicago audience] whenever something occurred to me that I thought they would be interested in hearing. The printed version of the speech contains passages which I confess to have said but which were plainly never written out in advance. *Shriver cautioned further* that printed texts are almost always not the exact words that I use at the moment of delivery. . . . *Robert Sargent Shriver, Jr.*)[8]

What is the value of this initial compliment?

A year ago tonight, the Peace Corps was just six days old. And just a year ago, at your 1961 meeting, this association had the courage, the faith and the foresight to pledge its support to our fledgling enterprise.

What effect would Shriver's informal idioms—*backed a winner* and *home free*—have on his audience of college administrators?

So, tonight I especially welcome the opportunity to participate in your Conference on Higher Education. It's a pleasure to report that you backed a winner.

Three months ago I might have hesitated to make that statement. But when Barry Goldwater endorsed the Peace Corps, I knew we were home free. Do you remember his candid comment?

Evaluate this reward to listeners.

"I think the Peace Corps is beginning to remove the doubts from the doubters' minds. I have been impressed with the quality of the young men and women that have been going into it. At first, I thought that it would be advance work for a group of beatniks, but this is not so. As a businessman, I know that the two years overseas experience will be invaluable and rewarding. I'll back it all the way."

Why did he bring in Walter Judd? Why did he use *Charlie* instead of *Charles?* Is this due to the relaxed atmosphere of an informal report?

He has since been joined by the Republican Keynoter, Walter Judd. Tomorrow I expect Charlie Halleck to announce that he has joined the major-

8 Letters to James C. Ching, July 11, 1964, and August 7, 1964.

Why was the speaker wise to call attention to this nonpartisan fact?

ity of the Republican party which voted for the Peace Corps when it was first proposed in the Congress. Most people don't remember that fact—that the majority of the Republicans in the House of Representatives voted for the Peace Corps last Fall. They did, and it's important. Their support made the Peace Corps a truly national enterprise —not a partisan political endeavor.

The President's Message to Congress establishing the Peace Corps called for a pool of trained Americans—volunteers to go overseas for the United States government, to help foreign countries meet their urgent needs for skilled manpower.

Is this the beginning of Shriver's first main point? Or is this part of the introduction? If this is the beginning of the body, what do you think of Shriver's transition?

A particular kind of person was required. That person had to have the physical and intellectual capacity to cope with the demands of swiftly evolving economies, the dedication to put that capacity to work—and to keep it working—in remote villages, in mountain areas, in towns, in factories, and in the schools of dozens of struggling nations. For them, the "age of revolutions" would mean service abroad—the new frontier for international education.

Discuss the choice of phrase, *new frontier,* at this point in the speech.

The job of the Peace Corps was tough. Some said it was impossible. Yet in the past year, the Peace Corps has recruited, selected, and trained more than 900 Volunteers. They are already at work in 12 countries.

Would you have named the 12 countries here or named them only in a technical report?

By the end of this calendar year, we expect to have almost 5,000 Peace Corps Volunteers working in 30 countries.

That record is ours. But it is also yours.

What is Shriver doing here? Why is he doing it?

It could not have been written without the full cooperation of colleges and universities.

From the beginning, the Peace Corps organizers knew that our assignment could not . . . and should not . . . be undertaken by government alone. To get the job done, to get it done quickly, and done well, we needed the help of experienced hands and minds. So we turned to higher education.

This was a decision we never once regretted. American higher education has responded promptly, and expertly, to our needs. Our success has been your success.

But the skeptics are still with us. Even though their initial doubts have not been fulfilled, they still have their nagging questions:—

"What difference," they say, "does all this success mean? What you are doing is just a drop in the bucket. In the long sweep of history no one will remember whether the Peace Corps existed or didn't exist. Its influence will be negligible. Time, energy, and money will have been expended, but the results will be unimportant."

"Go ahead with your idealistic ventures," they say. "Americans have always over-simplified foreign affairs. The Peace Corps is no exception. Waste your money and your energies, but don't expect us to attach much significance to your effort."

Fortunately, all the experts are not skeptics.

Last week Arnold Toynbee wrote these words about the Peace Corps:

"Here is a movement," Toynbee writes of the Peace Corps, "whose express purpose is to overcome the disastrous barriers that have hitherto segregated the affluent Western minority of the human race from the majority of their fellow men and women. And the initiative in this has come from the country that is now the recognized leader of the Western world. Service in the Peace Corps (he

---

Why does he admit tacitly to this audience that JFK's administration relied on "eggheads"?

What is the importance of compliment in an informal report?

The speaker uses hypothetical dialogue. Is this a good way to enliven the contrary point of view? Do you think factual dialogue is more effective?

Discuss Toynbee as a source for this part of the report. Why not Arthur M. Schlesinger, Jr., or Dean Rusk?

Why does Shriver emphasize these characteristics? Do they seem to fit Aristotle's description[9] of youthful character?

What do you think of Shriver's forecast?
Discuss the use of *guesses* in terms of informal and technical reports.
What do you think of comparing Toynbee to Goldwater?

Has Shriver shifted ground? In the previous paragraph he talks of *quality*, and here he talks of *effective education*. Should this be *Second, I think . . . ?*

goes on) is not an easy option. It calls for adventurousness, adaptability, human feeling, and, above all, self-sacrifice. There is something in human nature that responds to a challenge like this. I believe that, in the Peace Corps, the non-Western majority of mankind is going to meet a sample of Western Man at his best."

It was encouraging for us at the Peace Corps to read what Arnold Toynbee wrote. We have pondered over his words. Why does Mr. Toynbee say that the Peace Corps Volunteers will give an example of Western Man at his best?

I have no private insight into the great historian's mind, but tonight I'd like to venture a couple of guesses about his thoughts.

First, I think that he, like Barry Goldwater, must have been impressed by the quality of the Volunteers he has seen. Mr. Toynbee visited the Peace Corps overseas training center in Puerto Rico. He spent two or three days talking to the Volunteers, living with them, eating with them. In such a time it is possible for a perceptive person to evaluate the quality of our Peace Corps manpower. Mr. Toynbee was visibly impressed.

I think Mr. Toynbee has probably been impressed also by the highly concentrated, effective education which we, with your help, have given to the Volunteers. Fourteen American colleges and universities,—public and private, large and small, representing every section of the United States—have conducted training programs for the Peace Corps.

This summer we will have some 30 Peace Corps training programs being

[9] Aristotle in his *Rhetorica*, 1389a 1–37 and 1389b 1–11, described young men as impulsive, confident, courageous, and idealistic. He went on further to describe them as thinking they are equal to great things, as desiring to do noble deeds rather than useful ones, and as reacting more to moral feeling than reasoning.

conducted simultaneously on campuses throughout the United States. In every one of these training programs the universities of America have marshalled unrivaled resources for instructing young Americans, and older ones, too, in the languages of the foreign countries, in the history, customs, traditions of the foreign countries; in world affairs, in American studies, in physical education and health education, as well as in professional fields such as teaching, engineering, geology, agriculture extension and nursing. No other country in the world could have mounted such specialized courses on such short order. And, we already have dramatic evidence of the effectiveness of this effort made by American higher education on behalf of the Peace Corps.

Are the instances concrete enough? Discuss the value of going a step further, for instance, and saying *history such as that of the Congo.* Does an informal report, however, demand such specificity?

Yesterday in Washington, the visiting Foreign Minister of Thailand and his colleagues told us that the recent group of Peace Corps Volunteers who arrived in Thailand had stunned the people and the officials of that country by their facility in speaking the Thai language, and by their knowledge of Thai history and traditions. Never before, he said, had any group of Americans arrived in his country as well prepared for their work.

Discuss the validity of this assertion.

The USIA stated that the most effective, single piece of news favorable to America in the last months in Thailand had been the advent in that country of the Peace Corps contingent, speaking Thai, singing Thai songs, knowing Thai history.

Why is Thailand a good example? Does her geographical location make her an apt illustration? **Does this particular kind of illustration seem suited for an informal report?**

The University of Michigan created this special course in Thai culture and customs and language. For three months our Volunteers worked 12 hours a day, 6 days a week. That's the reason why they were enthusiastically welcomed in Thailand. That's the reason why their work in that country will be successful.

Could Shriver in this case assume his hearers knew what *USIA* stood for? Would this be true of all audiences?

Discuss the cause-effect relation in this paragraph.

In what way, if this were a technical report, would the idea of training schedules have differed?

At Ohio State, the Peace Corps trained a group destined for agricultural work in the Punjab region of India. The Dean of the School of Agriculture at that great university told me personally that the fully packed training schedule —66 hours a week long—gave to the Peace Corps Volunteers at Ohio State almost the equivalent of a full year's graduate work.

The Minister of Economic Planning for the Punjab region, a distinguished Indian Civil servant, came to this country, spent two weeks at Ohio State, and on his return to India stopped by in Washington specifically to congratulate Ohio State and the Peace Corps on the thoroughness and skill which he had observed in the training program at that institution.

What is the value of the Tanganyikan example in this report? In what way would the example have differed in an *abstract*?

I could easily go on. Our first training program, for example, at Texas Western College where we trained Volunteers for Tanganyika was the subject of much skepticism in this country, and overseas the Tanganyikan government had some doubts that we could actually train people effectively for service in that remote African nation; so they sent the Minister of Communications and Public Works to our country and he spent ten days at Texas Western College in El Paso observing the Volunteers and their study program.

Tanganyika originally asked for 25 people, but after this British Civil Servant saw the quality of the people and the kind of program of training, he came to Washington and asked us to send every one of the 35 Volunteers to his country. Today, in fact, all of those Texas Western Volunteers are in Tanganyika. They have been there seven months, and not one complaint has been lodged against them by the government or by the people of that important African nation.

Is this a summary to a whole main head development, or is this an internal summary for clarification?

Are these the important stereotypes about Americans?

What stylistic device is Shriver using?

Why is this significant?

What makes this important in March 1962?

I think Arnold Toynbee was thinking of these kinds of training programs when he said that the Peace Corps would send to the non-Western world examples of Western Man at his best.

Toynbee may also have been thinking of certain other qualities of the Peace Corps Volunteers and the program under which they're serving. I mean— some of the psychological factors involved.

A Peace Corps Volunteer arrives in a foreign country not only speaking the language of that country and knowledgeable about its customs and traditions, but he comes ready, willing, and able to live the way they live, under *their* laws.

He does *not* try to change their religion.

He does *not* seek to make a profit from conducting business in their country.

He does *not* interfere in their political or military affairs.

He works within *their* system for *them.*

He helps to fill *their* needs as *they* see them.

He arrives on schedule.

In Ghana three of the first 51 teachers sent to the high schools of that country by the Peace Corps were elected assistant principal, or principal, of the schools to which they were assigned within four months of their arrival on the scene.

How many times in recent months have you heard of black men in Africa electing white men to positions of authority?

I suggest the Ghanaians were happy to accord these positions of influence to Peace Corps Volunteers because the Volunteers came to Ghana asking nothing, demanding nothing, except an opportunity to serve. They were not hanging around the PX Commissary. In

What is the stylistic value in the choice of these particular, foreign-sounding names?

Discuss Shriver's choice of details. What of their imagery value? How would narrative development of the instance differ?

What value is this internal restatement to over-all coherence?

Discuss the merits of *unusual* and *unique* over *different*.

Has Shriver come to a new main development? If so, evaluate his transition.

What is the *language* of *teaching*? Do the two series used here end in climax or anticlimax?

fact, they are excluded from such American perquisites.

They were not concentrated in the capital of that country, Accra. They were 300 miles up country in Tamale, —250 miles to the west in Half Assini, —450 miles away in Navrongo flush against the border of Upper Volta.

In Sierra Leone, when the Volunteers disembarked in Freetown, they were not surprised to see a small group of officials waiting for them. This has become rather customary. But they were surprised when, as they walked up the streets of Freetown, the local inhabitants came out and stared at them as they went by. Only later did they discover the real reason for the unusual turnout of local inhabitants:—

The inhabitants of Sierra Leone had never seen a white man walking up the street carrying his own luggage.

Once more, I suggest that Arnold Toynbee may be thinking of small, but significant, psychological factors such as these.

These Peace Corps Volunteers are clearly *different* Americans. These facts explain more eloquently than any words I can commend why it is that every one of the 12 countries to which the Peace Corps has sent Volunteers has required more of the same.

Over and above these factors, let me speculate for just a few minutes on another aspect of Peace Corps service abroad which may have been in Mr. Toynbee's mind and which will, I hope, be of interest to you.

The Peace Corps is attempting to communicate, humbly and compassionately, in the many languages of man,— not just the spoken languages like French, Spanish, Urdu, Hindi, Swahili, or Tagalog,—but the languages of poetry, of music, of law, of science, of painting and of teaching,—the myriad methods by which man has learned to communicate his inmost thoughts and sensitivities to his fellow creatures. Let me illustrate what I mean:

Discuss the merits of this illustration.

We have sent 500 teachers overseas, most of them secondary school teachers. We brought one of them back because he refused to participate in the social and recreational life of Nigeria. He wanted to be only a teacher. But we're not sending people overseas who want to be only teachers. Formal education is one method of communicating the culture of past centuries to upcoming generations. It is essential. But a teacher

Discuss Shriver's choice of simile.

whose role is restricted to the classroom is like a fighter with one hand tied behind his back. Our Peace Corps teachers must be human beings who participate in the full life of a foreign country, who communicate the substance of our culture on the playing field, in a social gathering, yes, even at a dance.

Can you identify the traditional logic used here?

When the English said that the battle of Waterloo was won on the playing fields of Eton, they meant it. The battle of Africa may be won on the athletic fields of Ibadan University, just as much as in the classroom.

Discuss the implications of Shriver's statement to doctors at home.

We have sent doctors overseas, and nurses, and nurses aides, and we want to send many more. But we haven't sent any doctor whose idea of medical practice is restricted to large fees and comfortable office hours. A Peace Corps doctor is a man or woman who has voluntarily surrendered the high income which every doctor in our country can now command and in its place has accepted a different sort of reward. One of them expressed it to me in these words:

"The future of my children may be determined more by what happens in Africa, South of the Sahara, than by what happens in Washington or Cleveland. I want the Africans to know that we Americans are interested in them as human beings, that

Discuss the merits of the adjective, *warm*. What image does it connote? Is it more British than American?

If this were a feedforward idea, what range of response might it have gotten?

What humorous device did Shriver use? What effect do you think the humor had on this particular audience?

Discuss the contradiction here between the *ordinary* and *different* Americans mentioned several paragraphs back.

we are there to help them as human beings, and that we would be there to help them if there were not Communism in the world at all."

None of our doctors goes overseas to wait upon the expatriate community, to hang around the local country club drinking warm beer. Our doctors are all assigned to indigenous medical institutions where they can give an example of what Toynbee called Western Man at his best.

In South America we are trying a couple of ventures at which skeptics may well scoff and the sober-minded citizens may well laugh. But, among intellectual leaders such as this audience contains, I hope to find an understanding reception for these projects.

We have contacted some young American poets and have asked them to go to South America as faculty members at universities. We have asked poets to do this because many Latin Americans think of the United States as a place inhabited 100% by businessmen working for Sears-Roebuck, Socony Vacuum, Anaconda Copper and Pan American Grace, not to mention United Fruit.

In general, they have no idea that ordinary North Americans, gringoes like you and me, are interested in music, or poetry, or art. These aspects of life are often more important to many South Americans than economic matters. But they think we are "Philistines" preoccupied only with money and profits. And the Communists encourage them to think so.

There is a newspaper published in Colombia for the campesinos—the small peasant farmers of that land—most of them uneducated, untraveled and, until recently, ignored.

Page One in the last two issues of this newspaper has been devoted to a poetry contest. Why to a poetry contest? There wasn't a word on Page One about Wallace's Hybrid Corn, or Olin Mathieson's phosphate pill to increase food production. Probably there should have been, but instead there was a poetry contest. Can you imagine how successful a poetry magazine for Iowa farmers would be?

We've got to learn to communicate with people who prefer poetry to peanuts; otherwise we will never be able to reach inside of them and get them interested in food production, health, economic development, or any other of the subjects to which we attach so much importance.

Take another example: At Peace Corps headquarters we're now exploring the possibility of sending a jazz combo to a specific South American nation. Music is a language which opens many minds as well as many hearts. Jazz is popular, especially with the younger people in South America, and we have been lucky enough to find a group of brilliant young jazz musicians, all of them college graduates, three with M.A.'s, who have indicated that they are willing to give up their promising careers here in the United States to serve in the Peace Corps for two years, at $75 a month.

I think these young musicians may well be able to reach into the minds and hearts of young South Americans more effectively than politicians. These musicians would not be wandering troubadours. They would have full-time jobs on a full-time music faculty. Like all Peace Corps teaching personnel they would be an integral part of a foreign academic community.

Poetry and music and the healing arts of medicine are not the only languages we use. We are now exploring a project with American schools of journalism whereby young Americans with special gifts and training in the journalistic arts can become teachers of

---

What is the value of contrasting *peanuts* to *poetry*?

Why is a statement as *I think* more apt in an informal than technical report?

Discuss the value of sacrificing clarity for an inspiring emotional effect.

Discuss the use of *ways to skin a cat* and *That's our tough luck* (two paragraphs hence) in an informal report.

What method of development is used in this and the next paragraph? Why is it effective?

these skills in universities around the world. Once again we believe the language of journalism may be as effective as formalized instruction in English grammar or literature. We want classroom teachers of English literature. The world wants them. But we also believe there are many ways to skin a cat—and journalism may be one way in which to attract and instruct enterprising young people of foreign nations.

Science, too, has its language and we are fortunate at the Peace Corps to have with us already overseas more than 100 young teachers of science who are using that language as a means of communication between us Western men and the non-Western majority of mankind in the world today.

You will note that the word "young" Americans slipped out just then. There's no doubt that most of us in this room tonight consider someone 25 years old to be young. That's our tough luck. The 32 year old Minister of Economic Development for Tunisia, however, does not share our feelings. Nor does the 34 year old Foreign Minister of the Congo, Justin Bambalo [*sic*]; or the 31 year old Party Leader in Kenya, Tom Mboya; or the 32 year old Secretary General of the Labor Congress in Ghana, John Tettegah; or the 33 year old Prime Minister and King of Morocco, Hassan II; or the 33 year old Prime Minister of Tanganyika, Rashidi Kawawa.

Youth is not a liability for the Peace Corps or for our country. It's a great asset. The Peace Corps is fortunate to have placed instructors of approximately 25–26 years of age on the faculties of various universities around the world. We now have 10 teachers on the faculty of Chulalongkorn University in Bangkok; 30 teachers on the faculty of the University of the East in Venezuela; and soon we shall have 8 teachers at the

University of Huamanga at Ayacucho in Peru; 20 additional teachers at the University of the East in Venezuela; 25 teachers at the University of Ife in Nigeria; 25 teachers at the University of the Philippines in Quezon City and Los Banos.

What are the outstanding features of this internal summary?

All of those Volunteers, on the job, and others like them, have done more than anyone else to dispel the skepticism at home and even the skepticism expressed by some people abroad. When the Peace Corps came into being many foreign officials thought they had enough Americans in their countries. What they did not know then, but what many of them know now, is the fact that the Peace Corps provides a "new American," the sample of Western man at his best, to which Toynbee referred.

Has the speaker moved to a new main head development? Or is this a major sub-heading under the previous point?

It would be foolish for me to leave the impression with you that everything has been all sweetness and light at the Peace Corps during the first year of operations. We have had our problems. But it's extraordinary how understanding nearly everyone has been.

I'll venture the guess that no one in this room knows that a Peace Corps Volunteer driving a jeep in the Philippines a couple of months ago struck and killed a native of that country.

What has been our historical relationship with the Philippines? How does the past influence the conclusion inferred here by Shriver?

Nobody in this room knows that fact although we made no effort to conceal the information. The extraordinary reality is that in the Philippines the newspaper stories describing that accident featured the news that a Peace Corps Volunteer had been injured. They almost buried the news that a Filipino had been killed. What a change from the stoning of Embassy windows.

Nobody in this room knows that a near psychotic was discovered among the early Peace Corps trainees. We had to escort this particular young man home from a Peace Corps training center in a strait jacket.

Evaluate the merits of appendectomies and hepatitis as instances.

No one in this room knows that three girls in training for Peace Corps service smashed up a car in the middle of the night in the Pennsylvania mountains and nearly killed themselves.

No one here knows that we've had four emergency appendectomies, 5 cases of infectious hepatitis, 30 cases of dysentery, and other routine illnesses.

Fortunately, we have not lost even one person. But we will. The actuarial statistics disclose that if all these Americans who are now in the Peace Corps had stayed at home, five of them would have died over the next two years. So, we're to have our cases of Peace Corps Volunteers coming home in wooden boxes. And we're going to have other tragedies which will be harder to understand and to forgive.

Why is *wooden box* more effective than *coffin?*

Sometime, somewhere, some Peace Corps Volunteer is going to do something disgraceful to himself, to his parents, to the Peace Corps and to the United States. The President of every college or university in this audience knows that this is going to happen. Tonight I can only say that when it happens, I hope that the sober-minded, experienced, intelligent and informed people in this audience will be among the first to understand and reply to the inevitable critics who will cry havoc.

Why is the comparison of the director of the Peace Corps to a college president a good one for this audience?

And now for a few closing points.

Is this the beginning of the conclusion, or is this an instance of *abstract* in an informal report?

1) The total number of people volunteering for the Peace Corps in February was the highest of any month in our history. More than 3,000 new Volunteers responded in February alone to the President's challenge: "Ask not what America will do for you, but what together we can do for the freedom of man."

2) The head of our Selection Division, Professor Lowell Kelly, Chairman of the Department of Psychology of the University of Michigan, has reported to

me that the quality of the men and women volunteering for the Peace Corps today is as good, and in some cases, better than those who first responded to the President's call. We are in no danger of running out of qualified Americans of high character and ability to serve in the Peace Corps overseas.

3) Every state in the Union has already produced members of the Peace Corps. Every race in our country is represented,—every creed. There has been no discrimination on the basis of race, color, or creed in the recruitment, the selection, the training or the assignment of Peace Corps Volunteers.

4) Overseas, the Peace Corps Volunteers have been received everywhere by the people of foreign lands and by government officials with enthusiasm, warmth and generosity. In Nigeria, where expatriate university teachers have been present in large numbers for over a quarter of a century, the government staged an official reception at the Federal Palace Hotel in Lagos when the first small Peace Corps contingent of 35 Volunteers arrived, and more than 1,000 civic leaders and government officials showed up to welcome this small but pioneering group.

What is Nigeria's relation to the U.S., especially in terms of foreign aid? In view of your answer, what is your evaluation of Shriver's choice of illustration?

In Ghana, the Foreign Minister, the Minister of Information, the Minister of Interior, and other Cabinet members said of the Peace Corps: "That's one thing your country is doing properly."

Why was it important to climax the speech with the Camargo quotation rather than the Ghanaian statement?

In Colombia, the distinguished President of that country, Alberto Lleras Camargo, said: (The Peace Corps) "is the finest way in which the United States could prove to the humble people of this and other lands that the primary purpose of its international aid program is to build a better life in all of the free world's villages and neighborhoods."

Before you proceed to the next speech by Arjay Miller, ask yourself the following questions about Shriver's informal report:

1. Do you think the speaker successfully accomplished his purpose in reporting the progress of the Peace Corps to his particular audience? If *yes*, why? If *no*, why?
2. What indications in the speech lead you to believe that the speaker may have aimed his remarks at a larger audience—the general public.
3. In your opinion was the address organized clearly? If *yes*, why? If *no*, why? What improvements if any would you have made?
4. Did Shriver show any indications of audience awareness? If so, what were they? If he made attempts to adapt to his hearers, did they seem spontaneous or preplanned?
5. Does the address seem more persuasive than informative to you? If *yes*, why? If *no*, why? If you answered *yes*, then suppose you knew Shriver intended no persuasion in his remarks: would this dismiss the controversy over his exact purpose?
6. Do you think Shriver used his limited time effectively, thereby avoiding the impression of superficiality? If you were giving the same speech as a *technical report* and an *abstract*, what would you change and edit out? What would you add?

A Technical Report

REPORT OF OPERATIONS[10]

by Arjay Miller, *President* Ford Motor Company

(This technical report was delivered at the 1964 Annual Meeting of stockholders, Henry and Edsel Ford Auditorium, Detroit, May 21, 1964. There were approximately 1200 people at the occasion. Of this number 1163 were stockholders, invited guests, and members of the press. The occasion was not open to the public.)

Good afternoon.

Compare Miller's introduction with Shriver's. What is the major difference between the two openings? Does the fact that one is a technical report influence this difference?

I want to join Mr. [Henry] Ford [II] in welcoming you this afternoon. We are happy indeed to see so many of our stockholders interested in the Company's affairs.

Last year, as you know, sales and earnings set new records. Earnings rose to $4.42 per share—six cents above the previous high in 1962. Quarterly divi-

[10] As reprinted from a Ford Motor Company News Department release at 2 P.M. (EST), Thursday, May 21, 1964. The visual aids included with the speech text were those used by Miller during his report and are reproduced here by permission of Ford Motor Company through the courtesy of James W. Harris, Public Relations Staff, Ford Motor Company, The American Road, Dearborn, Michigan.

dend payments this year have been raised to 50 cents—an increase of 11% over last year and up 67% from the quarterly payments in 1956 when our stock first went on the market.

These gains have reflected both the growing car and truck market and our own strong competitive position. With the help of slides, I should like to discuss these factors in some detail.

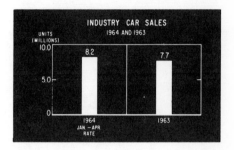

Notice that the speech settles down quickly to a factual presentation of material. Would you expect this in a technical report?

Turning first to U.S. activities, retail car sales are now breaking all previous records. During the first four months of this year, industry sales, including imports, were at an annual rate of 8.2 million cars, half a million above last year's record sales. We believe car sales this year may well pass the eight million mark for the first time.

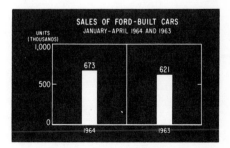

Ford has shared fully in this growing market. During the first four months, our car sales were 673,000, compared to 621,000 last year—an improvement of 8% and a record for the period. Our share of the market through May 10 this year is 24.7%, up four-tenths of a point from last year.

The Comet line—this is the Caliente hardtop—has made impressive gains. Sales during the first four months were up 58%, and Comet increased its market share by nearly one percentage point. The public has reacted very favorably to the Comet Durability Run at Daytona—where each of four specially-equipped Comets completed 100,-000 miles at an average speed of more than 105 miles per hour. We think this is a real testimonial to the durability designed and built into all our car lines.

Why will gains by the Peace Corps in Shriver's report probably seem more important to most readers than gains by the Ford Motor Company? What does this suggest as a difference between informal and technical reports?

The Lincoln Continental's outstanding quality continues to earn increasing recognition. So far this year, sales are up 24% from a year ago.

Sales of the standard Ford car in the first four months were up 10% from a year ago. Shown here is the Galaxie 500 XL in our new 4-door hardtop model.

Thunderbird sales are running 76% ahead of the 1963 pace. Since its introduction in September, the new Thunderbird has been even more popular than its predecessors.

By now you may have been impressed by the impersonal nature of this report. Would you expect a technical report to have the same personal touch as an informal report? Would you expect a technical report to have more personal commentary than an abstract?

Here is the Company's newest product, the Mustang, which went on sale April 17. Customer demand for this car is exceeding even our most optimistic forecasts. Equally encouraging, about half of the trade-ins on Mustangs have been cars made by competitors. This fact, together with the market strength of our other lines, gives us confidence in our outlook for future car sales.

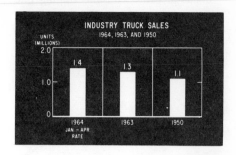

Compare the clarity of the visual aids used by Miller with the ones used by NASA (Chapter 12) during the briefing for Lyndon Johnson.

Industry truck sales also are breaking . . . records. Sales in the first four months this year were at an annual rate of 1.4 million, up from full year sales in both 1963 and 1950, the previous peaks.

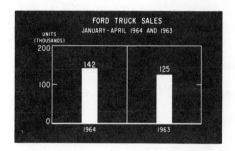

Ford truck sales in the first four months totaled 142,000, up 13% from last year—and a new record. . . .

Compare the previous developments on domestic gains with the coming one on foreign markets. Which section is developed more clearly? Why?

Outside the United States, car sales scored another impressive gain last year, rising 18% to 7.4 million. As the slide shows, U.S. consumers still buy more new cars than all the rest of the free world combined, but the gap is narrowing steadily.

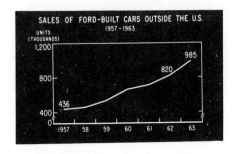

Despite intense competition in foreign markets, almost a million Ford-built cars were sold in other countries last year, an increase of 20% from 1962. In Europe, our share of industry sales was 12.8%, second only to Fiat's.

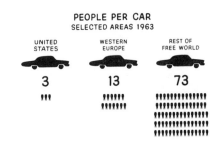

Miller speaks of growth potentials as did Shriver. How does Miller's explanation of growth differ from Shriver's?

Great as the increase in car sales overseas has been, the potential is still greater. The U.S. has three people for each car, Western Europe has 13 people per car, and the rest of the free world has 73 people per car. Ford is a world-wide enterprise, organized to compete effectively on a global basis. Our plans are geared to serve the dynamic growth in world demand that lies ahead, as other nations continue to raise their standard of living.

This plant being constructed in England will help us keep up with similar growth in the world demand for tractors. Last year, Ford world-wide tractor sales totaled 111,000 units, 9% higher than in 1962.

Compare this aid with the ones used previously by Miller. What might make this one seem out-of-step with the others?

Here you see the basic U.S. line of nine tractors. We produce a large number of variations to meet the diverse

Since the speaker has now turned away from foreign markets back to domestic ones, how might he have improved clarity?

needs of agriculture and industry. The Tractor Division recently completed a program to improve its marketing system in the U.S. by selling directly to dealers rather than through distributors. This change puts our U.S. tractor marketing in line with the method of distribution used by our automotive divisions, as well as by all other major U.S. tractor manufacturers.

Discuss the speaker's assumption that hearers knew Philco was a subsidiary of Ford and not an independent company. In what way is the assumption influenced by the fact that this is a technical rather than informal report?

Our defense and space capabilities were strengthened by the transfer of Aeronutronic Division to Philco last year. The Shillelagh missile, shown in action in this drawing, is being developed and tested by Aeronutronic under a contract amounting to nearly $40 million.

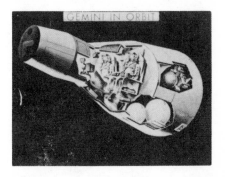

In the national space program, Philco has a contract of more than $35 million to develop and equip the mission control center near Houston, Texas. The tracking of manned Gemini rendezvous flights and the Apollo moonshots will be coordinated at this center. Installation of equipment has already begun, and mock missions are scheduled to start later this year.

Turning now to Philco's consumer products, here is one of the color TV sets in its 1965 line, to be introduced in a few days. We are continuing our intensive efforts to realize the potential we know Philco has in consumer markets. In the past two years, management has been concerned primarily with the development of fully competitive consumer products such as the one shown here.

Discuss the pros and cons of a speaker using a visual aid to indicate shifts in development.

Our finance and insurance subsidiaries have had another year of rapid growth. Ford Motor Credit Company has opened 20 new offices since the beginning of last year, bringing the total number to 123, as shown on this map.

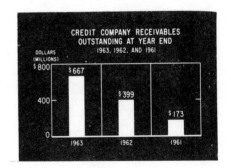

With receivables of $667 million at the end of 1963, Ford Motor Credit Company was the fifth largest sales finance company in the U.S. Its average charge to a customer who finances a new car through one of our franchised dealers is now about $115 less than other finance companies charged in 1958, the year before our own credit company was formed.

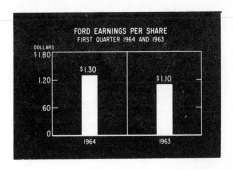

What reward is the speaker offering his hearers?

As you know, our First Quarter report showed record sales and earnings. Earnings were up 19% from the First Quarter of last year and were $1.30 per share. This improvement was mainly the result of three factors—first, higher Company sales; second, vigorous management efforts to improve efficiency; and, third, the recent changes in Federal income tax laws.

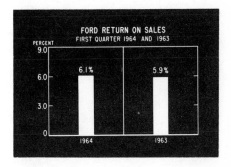

Despite these favorable factors, our First Quarter return on sales was up only slightly from the First Quarter of last year. Increased product value (which I shall discuss in a few moments) and higher wage rates and fringe benefits have not been offset by price increases.

The long-term trend in automobile use and sales is up. We are, however, in a cyclical industry. In some years, industry sales will go down, rather than up. Our goal is to increase our share of total industry sales—whatever that total may be—by strengthening our basic competitive position.

INVESTMENT IN TOMORROW

1. GREATER PRODUCT VALUE AND QUALITY
2. MODERNIZED AND EXPANDED FACILITIES
3. EMPHASIZED STYLING, ENGINEERING, AND RESEARCH
4. STRENGTHENED MARKETING AND DEALER ORGANIZATIONS
5. IMPROVED CUSTOMER SERVICE

At this point Miller introduces a theme into his address ("Investment in Tomorrow") that he develops effectively throughout the remainder of the report. As you read the speech from here on, you should notice how this theme adds interest-value to his remarks.

At last year's meeting, I outlined our long-range program for future growth. Here is the slide I showed you then. Our "Investment in Tomorrow" includes: (1) greater product value and quality; (2) modernized and expanded facilities; (3) emphasized styling, engineering and research; (4) strengthened marketing and dealer organizations; and (5) improved customer service. Today, I should like to summarize our progress in each of these programs.

Building ever-increasing value into our products is the first requirement for continued growth in sales and profits. We must continually improve the quality, appearance, performance, safety and diversity of appeal of our products. To illustrate the progress we have made, let me cite just a few of the many improvements in our 1964 models.

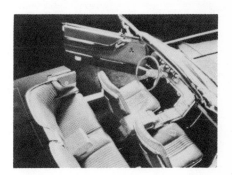

Why is this next part of the report informative rather than persuasive? Might this section of the report seem inspirational? If *yes*, why? If *no*, why?

In our Thunderbird for 1964, we have achieved a new level of luxury for the most demanding customer. We have coupled the most unusual interior design of any car with a superior ride.

A completely new and unique type
of ventilation—Silent Flo—pioneered
by Ford, is just one of many new
comfort features we have added.

Our attention to "comfort engineering" has produced major improvements
up and down the line. On our Lincoln
Continental, a three-inch increase in
wheelbase permitted a 28% increase in
knee room in the rear seat, and more
trunk space.

Evaluate Miller's assumption that his hearers knew the meaning of a *three-speed manual transmission with all forward speeds synchronized.*

Our newly-designed automatic transmission, which provides improved efficiency and performance, is still another example of our progress in improving our present products. Ford is the only U.S. company producing a three-speed manual transmission with all forward speeds synchronized.

The Mustang is an example of our aggressive program to develop new automotive concepts to meet the changing demands and tastes of the car-buying public. For those who want solid transportation with low cost of operation, the Mustang is an economical car with unique styling, comfort and convenience. Offering a broad line of optional equipment which permits

customers to tailor their cars to individual tastes and driving needs, the
Mustang may also be purchased as a
luxurious personal car, or as a sports-
type car. And all of this comes at a most
attractive price.

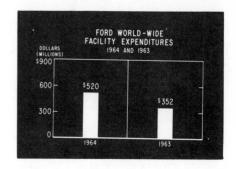

Modernized and expanded facilities
are the second element of our "Investment in Tomorrow." Last year, our
world-wide capital expenditures totaled
$352 million. This year, we expect our
spending to increase to more than half
a billion. As Mr. Ford mentioned, the
new capacity expansion plan is expected
to bring our total expenditures for
1964, 1965 and 1966 up to $1.6 billion.

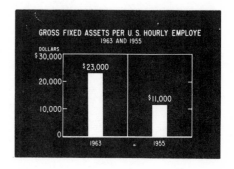

At this point in the report, Miller has used already several terms peculiar to business. Some of these words and phrases are *receivables, cyclical, competitive industry, capital expenditures,* and *fixed* assets. Discuss the probabilities of jargon appearing in an informal report. Did Shriver use any in his speech?

From 1955 through 1963, our spending for facilities in the U.S. alone totaled more than $1.6 billion. As a result, our fixed assets per hourly employe in the U.S. were $23,000 last year, more than double the 1955 level. Without this additional investment, increased efficiency would have been negligible. In the face of constant upward pressures on wages, new developments and new methods must be conceived and introduced continuously by all levels of operating management. This is the only way to keep costs in line.

As one example, the basic oxygen steelmaking facilities shown on this slide will completely replace our open hearth operations in the Detroit area. We now have just two furnaces doing the work formerly done by eight, and fuel costs alone have been reduced by more than $2 million per year.

Investments such as these provide the basis for increased future earnings. Growth in earnings, in turn, is vital to safeguarding your present investment and the market value of your stock. For these reasons, funds for new production facilities and for keeping our operations at maximum efficiency must have first call on Company profits.

Here the speaker reminds hearers pointedly that he is on the third item of his theme. Previously, he did not follow this procedure. Evaluate the place of consistency when using transitional indicators in a speech.

Emphasized styling, engineering and research is the third item in our "Investment in Tomorrow" program. We have sharply expanded our personnel and expenditures for styling. The Company has a long record of styling leadership, and we are going to maintain that leadership. Our pre-eminence in styling has just been demonstrated again by the outstanding success of the Mustang.

Evaluate the merits of visual comparison as used in this slide.

The Mustang also serves as an example of our engineering creativity. Shown at the top of this slide, the Mustang is about the same size as the 1957 two-passenger Thunderbird shown below—but that is where the similarity stops and progress begins. In roughly the same size car—

Observe the way Miller itemizes progress. What emphatic-value does it have?

This is the first time Miller has switched from the *our* or *we* to the *you* reference for Ford Motor Company. Discuss the implications of comments as *your Company* in this report. Keep in mind that Miller is delivering a technical report.

The Mustang seats four people, not two;

Has 6 inches more wheelbase for a much improved ride;

Weighs almost 550 pounds less, because of design efficiency and new material applications.

With comparable V-8 engines, the Mustang—

Out-performs the original Thunderbird; and

Gives 25% better fuel economy using regular fuel (not premium fuel, which the 1957 Thunderbird required.)

With all of these improved characteristics, the Mustang has a price about $1,000 lower and a sales potential ten to twenty times greater than the original Thunderbird. This is the kind of progress that we believe demonstrates the ability of your Company to forge ahead in response to new market challenges.

Our world-wide experience in performance competition has contributed to our all-out efforts to build cars with improved ruggedness, power, handling, comfort and safety. Participation in races, rallies and durability tests has led directly to substantial improvements in engine, drive train and suspension components. Widespread news coverage and our own "total performance" advertising have converted our victories in open competition into public awareness and sales.

A stronger marketing and dealer organization is the fourth point in our long-range program. The heart of a sound marketing program in our industry is a sound and profitable franchised dealer system. And this, in turn, requires careful planning for thorough market coverage, together with adequate sales potential for each dealer. Our Dealer Development Program helps to provide better market coverage by making it possible for outstanding dealer prospects who lack capital to start their own dealerships. Some of our best dealers have started this way.

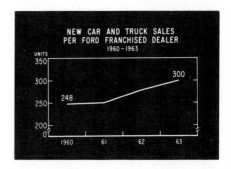

Comparatively speaking, Miller used many more figures and statistics than Shriver in his report. The NASA briefing (Chapter 12) also used many figures. Decide whether or not these statistics tend to kill interest. Keep in mind the speaker's audience and purpose in each instance.

This slide illustrates the progress of our dealer representation plans. It shows we now have a stronger dealer system than in 1960. On the average, each Ford and Lincoln-Mercury dealer sold 300 new vehicles last year, compared with 248 in 1960--an increase of 21%.

Six Ford Marketing Institutes, located throughout the U.S., are an outstanding example of the assistance we offer our dealers. Last year, more than 15,000 dealer and Company personnel took sales, service or general management courses at the Institutes. The training they received is paying off: dealers who have taken our courses have increased their sales and profits significantly more than those who have not yet participated.

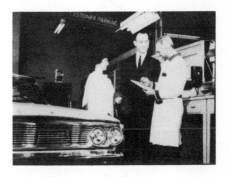

Giving our customers the kind of service that will keep them loyal to Ford-built products is our final "Investment in Tomorrow." At the time of last year's meeting, we were just launching a multi-million dollar service improvement program. More than 170 Company employees have been added to help and encourage dealers to provide better service.

As part of this program, both the Company and its dealers have conducted a series of owner panels. At each panel meeting, 15 to 25 owners are invited for dinner and a full discussion of what they like—and do not like—about their cars and the service they have received. These meetings have been helpful in identifying product and service problems, in making dealers aware of the importance of good service, and in building good-will among our customers.

Our efforts to improve service have been directed toward expanding and improving the training of the more than 60,000 service technicians who work for our dealers—and toward helping Company-franchised dealers obtain the latest, most efficient repair equipment. We now offer 40 courses for dealership service people, many of whom take several courses a year. When they return to their dealerships, they demonstrate the new techniques they have learned to additional thousands of dealership employees.

Discuss the merits of a formal or informal summary at the end of a technical report.

This, in summary, is what we are doing to assure the growth of Ford Motor Company now and in the years ahead. Although most of my examples have been drawn from our activities in the U.S., similar programs are being carried out in our foreign subsidiaries. Ford companies all over the world make full use of the best methods and techniques available—wherever they are developed or discovered.

Evaluate the manner in which Miller appended this last point on planning to his report. Does the idea fit his theme of "Investment in Tomorrow"? If *yes*, where? If *no*, discuss the possibilities of Miller adding a sixth long-range plan for future growth to his initial list.

I should mention one other aspect of our planning, which is crucial to the success of everything else we do. It engages the best thoughts and efforts of our whole management team, from top to bottom, throughout the world. I am speaking of the development of management. The immediate future of our Company depends heavily upon the abilities of the people who are now key members of our management team.

In the longer run, our future depends on what we are doing at the present time to attract and develop the people who will be making the major decisions 10 to 20 years from now. We are growing management competence in depth in order to attack the problems that will confront a company of great growth— and great growth (both in profits and sales) is exactly the goal we have established for Ford Motor Company.

We are continuing to emphasize recruiting. This spring, 180 of our management people have devoted part of their time to recruiting outstanding graduates from colleges and universities throughout the U.S. Last year, these efforts resulted in our hiring over 1,000 graduates, 220 more than the year before.

We are seeking and we are finding young men—and young women, too— with brains and backbone—people who have the ability and the desire to make room for themselves at the top. We give our trainees challenging assignments with as much responsibility as they can carry. We promote them as fast as they are ready. Those who are interested in easy security soon drop out. Those who have what we want stay with us, and move up quickly to increased responsibility and the pay that goes with it. Thanks to the quality of the people we are recruiting and developing, I am firmly convinced that our outlook is most promising.

Miller closes his report with an appeal. Discuss the pros and cons of such a closing in a technical report; in an informal report; in a briefing.

I want to close my remarks this year —as I did last year, by asking you, our stockholders, for your enthusiastic support of all our products. Your help and your confidence will be of great assistance to our plans for the Company's future.

Now answer the following questions about Miller's technical report:

1. Do you think the speaker successfully accomplished his purpose in reporting the progress of the Ford Motor Company (between 1963–1964) to his particular audience? If *yes,* why? If *no,* why?
2. What makes Miller's speech a technical rather than informal report?
3. Discuss the merits of visual aids in terms of the speaker and the listener when presenting a technical report.
4. In your opinion did Miller use clear organization for his technical report? If *yes,* why? If *no,* how might he have improved his organization?
5. What forms of support did Miller use in his report? Can you identify at least four of them?
6. What evidences did you find of abstracts in Miller's report?
7. Miller's speech is obviously pro-Ford. May you therefore classify his speech as persuasive? as inspirational?
8. Why is Miller's speech of less general interest than Shriver's? What does this suggest as a difference between the technical and informal report? Does it follow that a technical report is always less interesting to the general public than an informal one?
9. Why is the team-approach to the preparation of a technical report desirable, undesirable?

The Speech of Exposition:
14
Lecture

Lecture is an abused term used often to include all types of exposition. A lecture, to distinguish it from other expository forms, is usually academic or pseudo-academic in its content, generally personal in its observation or comment, and sometimes narrative in its development. Unlike abstracts, lectures are longer; and unlike instructions, they provide listeners information of broad application. Unlike technical reports, lectures are often less detailed and frequently more personal in approach; unlike informal reports, they are usually more stylized and decidedly more occasional.

The lecturer frequently breathes a certain human warmth and quality into his sometimes cold topic. He may often use a careful and considered organizational plan; he may explain his ideas in a concrete and clear manner; he may give hearers, along with factual information, benefit of his considered and educated judgment; he may develop subjects in a slightly popular fashion; he may approach the occasion with some formality; and he may present his ideas in a manner suited for listeners rather than readers.

SPECIAL PROBLEMS IN PREPARING A LECTURE

A lecturer, like the person preparing a technical report, faces a problem of selecting information from his usually vast reserve of facts on the subject. Should he find it necessary to seek further information, his more than lay understanding of the topic should simplify his research problems because he knows exactly where and how to locate specific information and facts. Furthermore, since he is often considered an expert or a near-expert in his lecture area, he has the additional advantage of a respectful if not friendly audience. Finally, because the lecturer is concerned with broad more than precise recall of his information by listeners, he does not have to order his materials with the same stringency necessary for the speaker delivering instructions.

Problem of Audience

Unlike the goal-centered hearers listening to instructions or technical reports, listeners addressed by lecturers are less homogeneous in their makeup. To be sure, many people who attend lectures are drawn to these occasions because their own *specific interests* match closely those of the lecturer's. Thus, for instance, if the speaker were John Russell Brown from Birmingham University, England, and his announced topic were "Shakespeare Today," he would attract several kinds of listeners. *Theater authorities* would attend the lecture because of their professional interests, and they would understand almost anything Brown said on the topic because of their academic kinship with the lecturer. *Near-authorities* may also go to the lecture in hopes of discovering new insights on the subject. Hearers with *related interest* would attend the lecture on the chance the speaker may add new dimensions in an area allied to their own. Finally, a few listeners, without special foreknowledge on the subject, may attend the lecture because of a *curious interest* in learning about or exposing themselves to a subject unknown to them. Thus whether an occasion is a paid or a free one, or whether a lecture is delivered at a convention, conference, public meeting, or forum, or whether the audience attends voluntarily or not, a speaker may frequently find hearers with more divergent interests at a lecture than found at occasions for abstracts, instructions, or technical reports.

Problem of Adaptation

The lecturer should decide, therefore, at what level of understanding to key his speech and to what group or groups of his hearers he will address his remarks. Obviously, if he receives a fee for his services, or if the occasion is by paid admission only, a lecturer should feel a strong obligation to inform and interest most of his listeners. On the other hand, if the lecture is free, he may still feel this same obligation, since those hearers who attend out of curiosity have in fact paid him a high compliment by their presence. How will he reach such a varied audience with his information? Should he simply talk to the opinion leaders and, in a sense, bypass the remainder of his listeners?

If the lecturer is using the occasion as a chance to persuade his hearers on a subject, then his problem of adaptation is eased, because he can aim his remarks at the opinion leaders. (See Chapter 9 for details.) Most speakers, however, approach a lecture in its more usual sense—as an informative occasion. What then of the lecturer, who, flattered by general public attendance, seeks to communicate with almost all of his hearers? Is there no recourse for him?

Fortunately, there is an escape tunnel if he seeks one: for the more specialized or academic the title of his lecture, the fewer curiosity seekers will probably attend the occasion. The speaker may decide, therefore, to discourage the curious by announcing as his topic, "Tagmemic Formulas and PS Rules in Transformational Grammars," or to attract as many comers as possible by announcing a more popular title, "A New Approach to Language." Should he choose the former course, he then assumes a certain minimal level of listener knowledge on his topic before he commences his address.[1] Conversely, if he decides on the latter course, his decision would seem to force him into informing the curiosity seekers as well. If a lecturer, however, has ever delivered an address before an audience of divergent backgrounds, interests, intelligence, and age levels, or, for that matter any kind of speech before such an audience, he should know how difficult it is to communicate with *all* of his hearers. Better advice to the lecturer, therefore, is for him to inform as many hearers as possible without sacrificing his integrity, subject, and general effectiveness.

Problem of Selecting Materials

Invited to deliver a lecture, a speaker is usually considered an expert on the topic of his address. May he, consequently, simply rehash his well-known or published ideas on the topic or can he assume his listeners are relatively ignorant of his opinions and printed works? And may he dust off a lecture he delivered before an audience in Alaska and redeliver it before another group in Florida?

Certainly a speaker is unwise to try what William F. Buckley, Jr. did when addressing the University of North Carolina's Forum—read one of his essays published previously by *Playboy* on "Freedom and the Welfare State." The Forum considered Buckley's fee of $450 unrealistic, since he had already received $1,000 for the same reading in Chicago and $3,500 from *Playboy* for the article.[2] In short, most listeners, with some justification, anticipate more than an oral reading of a printed work by the expert. They expect the lecturer to give them benefit of (1) his experience, (2) his candid and considered judgment on his topic, and (3) his findings—some old when necessary as well as new when appropriate—that explain his thesis.

Problem of Variety in Support

A lecture, somewhat like an informal or technical report, usually calls for a variety of supporting materials as helpmates for clarity and for main-

---

[1] In a sense by announcing a complex title, the lecturer gives the distinct impression he will deliver a technical report. In reality, however, the simplicity or complexity of a title does not determine the difference between a lecture and a technical report.

[2] "People," *Time*, Vol. 80 (December 28, 1962), p. 28.

taining audience interest. Where the report is normally a short, single address on a subject, the lecture, in contrast, is usually longer and delivered occasionally in series. This comparison between the two speech forms raises a significant practical difference between a lecture and an informal or technical report: where a speaker may rely on one or two forms of support to bolster a report, he cannot usually depend—especially as a beginner —on only one or two forms to sustain a lecture. A skilled lecturer, of course, can maintain audience attention over long time-periods with repeated use of only one or two supporting forms. However, until a speaker reaches a high level of speech competency, he is generally wiser to promote audience interest through several developmental forms in his addresses.

The beginning speaker, therefore, is cautioned against relying on only one or two forms of support for a lecture. He should strive initially for variety in speech development, until such time that he has sufficient experience at lecturing. When he knows finally what is involved in delivering a compelling lecture of an hour or so, and when he realizes how much work is required in preparing a series of lectures, then and only then should he depend on fewer forms of support to hold audience interest. And when he arrives at this point of maturation as a lecturer, he may decide to rely on his established pattern of variation, rather than shift to a newer, untried one. If this be his decision at that time, it will still be a wise one.

Sample Lecture

Again as in the previous two chapters, analytical questions in **bold face** are for primary study, and questions in regular face are for secondary use.

THE CLASSICAL FRENCH TRADITION: CONTRADICTIONS AND CONTRIBUTIONS[3]

by Michel Saint-Denis, *Director and Theater Theoretician*

(*This public lecture, given before faculty and students at Harvard University, is essentially the same as originally delivered by Saint-Denis, except for corrections of what the lecturer described as his "corrupted" English. In preparing the lecture, Marion Watson and Barbara Goodwin helped the famous European and English director compose the address. In describing his preparation for the occasion Saint-Denis said:* I gave . . . [this lecture] soon after my arrival in the United States in March 1958. It was my first visit. I had been invited to America as "consultant" to the Juilliard School of Music following upon the completion of an enquiry about

---

[3] As reprinted from Michel Saint-Denis, *Theatre: The Rediscovery of Style* (New York: Theatre Arts Books and Tadworth, Surrey, England: Heinemann Educational Books Ltd., 1960), pp. 17–34.

theatre training conducted in Europe and the United States by the Rockefeller Foundation.

The Lincoln Centre for the Performing Arts was being planned, and the Juilliard School of Music had agreed to establish a progressive institution for advanced training in theatre art.

I had met representatives of the Rockefeller Foundation very briefly in Strasbourg where I was working at the time, and preliminary conversation in New York led me to understand that I had been called upon as a result of my familiarity with the classical theatre both in England and France, combined with a contemporary approach to education and training for the state.

My former acquaintanceship with members of the American Group Theatre and the information I had gathered particularly from reading Harold Clurman's *The Fervent Years* had prepared me to appreciate in America the development of a realistic tradition more or less based upon Stanislavski's example and teachings. I found that the American theatre, not only by "method", but in basic outlook and, so to speak, by constitution, was realistic. Any evolution, whether in subject-matter or style, the need for which was being expressed by several dramatists, directors, and critics, would have to start from the deeply ploughed fields of realism in its different aspects.

During my first fortnight in New York, in the atmosphere of the Broadway and off-Broadway theatres, I remodelled my lectures. It seemed to me essential that my European attitude, formed out of a fusion between traditional "theatricality" and the ever-growing influence of European realism, should be presented within the framework of the young but already ingrained American realistic tradition. . . . The Theodore Spencer lecture, which I gave in Harvard University, is devoted to the French theatre, classical and modern, in which theatrical evolution is greatly nourished by tradition. . . . *Michel Saint-Denis*)[4]

Evaluate the manner in which honor is tied to the occasion.

LADIES AND GENTLEMEN. Knowing the names of the poets, the scholars, and of the men of the theatre who have spoken here before me, I realise the great honour you have paid me in inviting me to speak for the first time in Harvard in memory of a man whom you cherish for all that he did for letters, the arts, and the theatre of your country [Theodore Spencer].

Discuss the merits of telling listeners that a forthcoming lecture is based on personal authority.

How did the speaker create a feeling of warmth in his introduction?

I shall try to tell you simply of my experience in the theatre. Next year I shall have been in the theatre for forty years. I began in 1919, just after the First World War; I've only been interrupted once in that work, and that was by the Second World War. I mention the two wars because they have been of great importance to me: in tragic cir-

4 *Theatre: The Rediscovery of Style*, pp. 13–14.

cumstances, they have connected me with other men. It is thanks to these wars, perhaps, that I have avoided being confined to the world of the theatre, the atmosphere of which is sometimes rarefied and artificial.

Why is the confession a good one?

If I have partly escaped the theatre, I am glad also that I have partly escaped my French nationality. I know that it is a dangerous attitude to take . . . I've spent twenty years of my life, the best years of my maturity, living in England and working with the English theatre. What I probably mean is that I feel in a position to understand my own country better through having been so long away from it.

At this point in the lecture, what kind of development do you anticipate?

Now I've got to make a final preliminary confession. I've always belonged to non-conforming organisations. I began in Paris with Jacques Copeau at the Théâtre du Vieux Colombier, the beginnings of which were not easy. When I became myself the head of a company —it was the Compagnie des Quinze—I played a repertory of plays of the sort that were not fashionable in Paris at the time. I have established three different schools of the theatre and I have always encouraged my students to join me in discovering new ways of stimulating their creative imagination and an approach to their interpretative work which could give reality to style. I have never directed a play I did not like. I have never directed "boulevard" or "West-end" plays. I must say that I have not often been asked to. The theatre is divided into very definite families.

Finally, in spite of appearances—for I was a part of the Old Vic for six years —I've always been much more concerned with the modern than with the classical theatre. I could say of my work that during these forty years it has been, and still is, an experiment directed towards the discovery of all the means

Discuss the lecturer's pointed admission that he is through with his introduction.

Evaluate the lecturer's method of defining *classics*.

If this were a highly specialized report, how might the definition of *classics* differ?

by which reality can be given to fiction on the stage.

I have now finished what is called an "introduction": and you know the ghosts and shadows with which I am accompanied in my first contact with Broadway, with the American theatre, with America and Americans.

I am French: there's no doubt about it. I leave it to you to appreciate the normal consequences of being French. People have many different ideas about it. But from a theatrical point of view these consequences are precise, even if they are not always well known.

I discovered, once I was outside France, that the English, and, I believe, the American people mean by "classics" all the great dramatists of the past, including those of the recent past; so that in your terms, Ibsen and Chekhov are "classics"; and I believe it is true that you even refer to Bernard Shaw and Eugene O'Neill as classics.

With us it is not at all the same. For a Frenchman, classicism is a spirit, a philosophy, a form. In fact if you speak to a French purist, and we have a few, you will find him asserting that only one aspect of his own civilisation is worthy to be described as "classical": the period that was born from Rabelais and Montaigne in the pre-classical age, and went on to blossom with Descartes and Pascal in philosophy, Poussin in painting, Lulli in music, Corneille, Racine, and Molière in drama. Here we are at the summit of the true French classical period. The sixteenth century is excluded: the style of Louis XIII, easily remembered as that of *The Three Musketeers,* is too heavy, too fleshy. The style of Louis XV is too mannered, too frail. No, Louis XIV, "le Roi Soleil", the king who modestly chose the sun as symbol of his glory, stands in the centre of the classical age. Regnard and Marivaux, dramatists of the eighteenth century, will

Discuss the assumption by the lecturer that hearers knew who Beaumarchais was, but not who the Greek and Roman writers of the period were.

Evaluate Saint-Denis' use of restatement.

Discuss the imagery used by the speaker. What of the humorous value?

be admitted into it by extension, but the door will shut in front of Beaumarchais, already corrupted in spirit and form.

It is by a sort of considered need for affiliation that French classicism has recognised its ancestors: the classical period of Greece (Aeschylus, Sophocles, Euripides); Roman comedy (Terence and Plautus); and even the comedians of the Comedia dell' Arte. But those buffoons from the south needed Molière, to give their work shape.

Such is really the nature of the milk by which every French child is nurtured at school and in life. He is educated in the Humanities according to the classical disciplines. The same discipline survives in Universities, in Academies, in literature, in the arts, and in the theatre. To this classical tradition we revert continually; very often to oppose it. But it remains a basic measure, the standard of quality. It is embodied most tellingly in Molière: La Comédie Française is called "La Maison de Molière; The Home of Molière"; it is supposed to have transmitted up till today the traditions of Molière's company. You can see it symbolised by the very armchair in which Molière died while playing *Le Malade Imaginaire.* Very often this chair travels with the company. When they went to Moscow they took it with them; they were not playing *Le Malade Imaginaire;* just as a sign of Molière; complete Molière in wood. And the French National Conservatoire, the official school of dramatic art, is a place where some great actors "de la maison" teach; and they take seriously their function, which is to pass on to the young the traditional way of playing classical texts and consequently the meaning of the classical style.

Now it is very easy to laugh at such a conservative spirit, especially if one is

Evaluate the reward offered to listeners here.

completely foreign to it. We have suffered from this spirit enough, we French, to see the merit in laughing also. It is evident that one cannot transmit a literal tradition from generation to generation and keep it alive. Nobody with any intelligence ever thought that that was possible.

Fortunately we have the texts which should lead us to the spirit. To be classical is to be impersonal and objective. It does not mean to avoid detailed characterisation, but to create characters which instead of being detailed, with a subjective, realistic psychology, remain objective. It tends to create types which in a balanced civilisation will be generally recognised. The language, usually eloquent, is loaded with human matter. Born of an aristocratic society, this form of art is aristocratic in expression: vigorous and heroic in Corneille, tender and passionate in Racine, more popular in Molière. And in the tragedy of Racine and Corneille, or in high comedy, like Molière's *Misanthrope*,

Discuss the logic of something being at once rigid (12 feet divided in half) and still flexible.

the text is written in verses of twelve feet, usually divided in the middle, with a rhyme at the end. Nothing less. You can imagine that actors do not find this style easy to tackle, though at the same time it has flexibility. Needless to say that to discover this flexibility and to preserve the form of the verse requires considerable art. Similarly the prose, the great prose of Molière, is also calculated, numbered prose, so written that it tends towards prosody.

Now you may find such a style so exacting that it becomes boring. It is the contrary of naturalism: probably the most isolated, but at the same time the highest form of theatre in the whole of Western Europe. It is also, as I know from experience, the most remote from the Anglo-Saxon world. I have had the opportunity of reading

Evaluate the merits of climaxing these series of instances with dialogue.

some Molière to audiences in London, and they were often pleased; but when I tried Racine, even those English people most familiar with French culture and ready to appreciate a certain form of classicism, could not "take" him. And I had chosen *Phèdre,* which is rich in dramatic events and tension; but even so they could not accept it— "talk, talk, talk," they said, "it's too rhetorical, too formal, at the expense of action, of life, of reality."

One must say that it is becoming increasingly difficult for us to find actors capable of playing in the style of Corneille and Racine because the kind of classical measure and discipline it requires goes further and further away from modern life.

I have always worked, I've said, with non-conforming people, who, starting afresh from the texts, have re-created the tradition, very often against the rulings of the Comédie Française.

When a speaker says *First of all,* do hearers expect to hear later *Second of all?* Or is this simply a meaningless expression?

First of all, in 1913, I saw Charles Dullin play Molière's *L'Avare.* I saw it again in 1922. Dullin was still playing *L'Avare* when he died, a few years ago. He brought to the role, not realism, but a reality which restored the vitality that a conventional respect for tradition had destroyed.

What kind of response might the lecturer have gotten from this feed-forward sentence?

In 1922 I heard some public readings by Copeau. He was an extraordinary reader. A lot of his influence came through his readings. He read *Bérénice.* Do you know *Bérénice?* It is the most motionless of Racine's plays. Its subject comes from Tacitus and is expressed by "invitus invitam dimisit" —"in spite of himself, in spite of herself, they parted." That's all. No other matter: solely the movement of lovers quitting and lovers coming back. It concerns four people with their servants. Copeau always said that such plays, instead of being played in the open air, in big places, should be performed in

Discuss the use of contrast between Copeau and Racine.

Why is the imagery in the simile especially effective?

Would you classify this revelation about Copeau as a narrative, an illustration, or a specific instance?

a small auditorium made of wood, where the sound of the text would have the quality of chamber music; the tone of the voices, the variety of pitch, the positions of the characters, their extreme economy of movement and gesture, all must be arranged so that nothing should trouble the air but beautiful sound and rare motion. Racine requires near immobility; the whole of the action being an inner one, it has to be expressed outwardly with the utmost sensitivity. You see that it is all very refined.

In 1920 Copeau gave a production of *Les Fourberies de Scapin* by Molière. Set on a bare platform, ruthlessly lit like a boxing ring, it recaptured the spirit of the Comedia dell' Arte without any laborious imitation of the past.

In 1923 *Le Misanthrope* was directed and acted by Copeau. I was the stage-manager. It was performed in front of a tapestry, with four armchairs and a stool in the middle of the stage. A few hats, a few sticks, and a few swords: no other properties. Two letters, I think. When Copeau, who played Alceste, came on to the stage before the show, I used to be told every night that the armchairs, set on a very beautiful carpet, so that I could not mark the positions, were wrongly set. And I assure you that they were always exactly in position. Copeau was in the mood of Alceste for about two hours before the curtain rose—such was the "reality" needed to animate the great style of the play.

In 1935 there was Jouvet in *L'École des Femmes*, playing Arnolphe in the famous Bérard set.

In 1949 there was Jouvet in *Tartuffe* with scenery by Braque.

In 1952 a newcomer, Jean Vilar, was acclaimed as an innovator because of his interpretation of Corneille's *Le Cid*, a tragedy in rhetorical and lyrical style. Gérard Philipe was Rodrigue.

What insights do you get about the speaker when he exclaims, *I was standing on my feet and shouting . . . ?*

In 1954 I saw Vilar's *Don Juan* by Molière, at the Avignon Festival, a magnificent performance. At the end I was standing on my feet and shouting: the relationship between Don Juan and Sganarelle appeared in a new light, much more illuminating than at the Comédie Française. Don Juan was more of an atheist than a seducer; and Sganarelle was the common man serving the aristocratic unbeliever and watching with terror and admiration his master's challenge to God.

Discuss and identify the various forms of support used by Saint-Denis beginning with the lines, *First of all, in 1913* . . . (eight paragraphs back) to this point in the development.

All these productions have had a profound influence on the contemporary theatre in France and abroad. I've mentioned them because they are milestones: the "classics" have made an important contribution to the modern style. You yourselves have seen here Jean-Louis Barrault in *Les Fausses Confidences* by Marivaux. Not very long ago Moscow applauded La Comédie Française in *Le Bourgeois Gentilhomme* by Molière, and Jean Vilar in *Le Triomphe de L'Amour* by Marivaux and also in Molière's *Don Juan* and *Marie Stuart* by Victor Hugo. I went to Moscow in June 1957 and when I asked the Russians what they liked best from the repertories of Brecht, the Comédie Française, and Jean Vilar, they answered without any hesitation, Marivaux. I asked them why. They said, "Because of its style: it's something we cannot do ourselves. From Brecht we have nothing to learn, we have done it before him. But the kind of diction and physical elegance required by the French plays of the eighteenth century, that's what we need."

What is the thesis sentence for the development up to this point in the lecture?

Why is the Russian example a good climax to this part of the speech?

Why are the Russians so sensitive to that kind of art? Why do they want to learn from it? Why on their own stages do they regularly act Molière and Shakespeare?

Is this the transition to another main head? If *yes,* is it a good one? If *no,* what are these sentences ending in question marks?

According to French rule, custom,

By now you have been impressed or unimpressed with Saint-Denis' method of developing an assertion. If you were impressed, why is it good? Does it depend on a good theatre background? If you were unimpressed, what faults do you find?

Saint-Denis keeps adding to his definition of French classicism. Do you find the definition process interesting in a speech?

Discuss the speaker's assumption that listeners know the meaning of naturalism.

and vocabulary, Shakespeare is not a classic. Everybody knows that up to the time of Victor Hugo in the middle of the nineteenth century, the French considered Shakespeare a barbarian. His plays were excessive, without discipline, without taste; he was a man without balance, mixing comedy with tragedy, which according to the rules of the classicist you cannot do: each style must be kept separate. Then the French Romantics, Hugo and Musset, tried to imitate Shakespeare, but in most of their plays they failed; they retained only superficial likenesses: they never got to the heart of Shakespearian reality, which is something of flesh, of passion, of blood, which gives body to the spirit; and all expressed in a language which is less restricted than the French, but which is all the same perfectly measured, with its own subtle laws. Until about 1910 the French considered Shakespeare in the light of French romanticism and the literary battle between the classics and the romantics. Shakespeare was a romantic and Racine was a classic, the representative of the truly French tradition. During this intermediate period, translators and adaptors tended to simplify Shakespeare, to bring order to his plays, to "classicize" them.

Since 1910 the influence of Shakespeare has prevailed in France to an extent I doubt whether you realise. The naturalists of whom the first was André Antoine, got hold of Shakespeare and produced, for instance, *King Lear* with so much emphasis upon the storm as to drown the words. A little later Firmin Gémier gave popular shows of a spectacular kind in a circus. When the anti-naturalistic school triumphed with Copeau—that was from 1913 onwards —not only Shakespeare but many of the Elizabethan dramatists began to be performed, and on the architectural or

Who are some of the other English writers referred to here? Is this knowledge necessary to the listener?

Discuss the merits of *Don't you find these facts significant* as a feedforward sentence to test audience understanding.

Did you notice Saint-Denis' constant use of restatement? What do you think of this stylistic device for clarity, especially in terms of a lecture?

formal stages of Copeau, Dullin, and Pitoëff, there were to be seen the plays of Webster, Tourneur, Ford and Thomas Kyd, alternating with Ben Jonson, Thomas Heywood, and Beaumont and Fletcher. The Théâtre du Vieux Colombier opened in 1913 with *A Woman Killed with Kindness* by Heywood. It closed its first season in 1914 with the great success of *Twelfth Night,* and it reopened in 1920 with *The Winter's Tale.* Don't you find these facts significant? This new development in France is in line with the influence of Freud and of surrealism. New translations, together with less constrained productions, cultivate the contrasts in Shakespeare's style, give expression to his violence, mark the changes in tone and in location. But up to the war these productions remained the privilege of cultured people belonging to the "avant-garde." Shakespeare and the Elizabethan dramatists were performed because they combined "theatricality" with deep meaning.

When in 1934 I went to work in the London theatre, I found the popular Shakespeare of the English. I arrived at a moment when the reforms brought about by William Poel and Granville Barker had placed Shakespeare again in a suitable architecture, with a minimum of scenery, so that the original composition of the plays could be respected without undue pauses between the scenes.

It was also the time when interpretation and production were being influenced by modern realism, with the effect that human truth had come to be considered more important than the famous "music of words": the result was that rhetoric or lyrical delirium had to go. It was then that I understood, more clearly than I have ever done with Racine and Corneille, how poetry is better able to express reality than the so-called "realistic" language of everyday life; and how style is the only penetrating instrument of authentic "realism", whatever the period.

I went many times to sit in the gallery of the Old Vic. There were four hundred excellent seats which at that time were sold for six pence each. Every night they were filled with English working people. I went there once with some French friends. *Hamlet* was being performed in its entirety; it lasted four hours; the seats were wooden benches; it was a bit hard. But the audience sat there motionless. They were listening to the story of a national hero told by a national poet: that is always impressive. At the end my French friend asked me, "Do you think they understand?" "What?" I replied. "The meaning of the play, the philosophy." "Oh," I went on, "certainly not. They have listened to the story which has unfolded in front of them as if it were a chronicle, a royal chronicle, in keeping with their traditions. They are fascinated by poetry, by sound, by rhythm" (which, by the way, my friends could appreciate even less than I), "And that," my French friends asked with a smile, "is enough for them?" "Probably they gather some kind of meaning," I replied, "their own individual meaning, and at the same time they enjoy being soaked in the words. It's a mysterious exchange, a sort of 'osmosis', an intermingling of various elements in which sense cannot be separated from form. They are the voluntary victims of the power of incantation which belongs to poetry and which is no more and no less mysterious than the power of music."

What is the interest-value in developing a point through narrative-like dialogue?

Here, you see, are two guides, two guards, two beacons—French classicism and English dramatic poetry—which

Evaluate Saint-Denis' transition extending over the next two paragraphs. What are its virtues? Its faults?

have continually accompanied me on my journey through the contradictions of the modern theatre.

This journey is not an easy one, no more easy for the English or the French than it is, I imagine, for you Americans.

We live in the theatre as well as in life in the most indefinite, indeterminate period. And possibly the French and English suffer from this uncertainty more than you do because in the past we have been definite; in the past we have been determinate.

By now you should be impressed with Saint-Denis' control of English. What do you find appealing in his use of words?

Now we feel uprooted. Believers or unbelievers, we cling to what convictions we have and we work; but our minds are ⸱in chaos. We don't know where we are going. Those who have kept faith and balance, observe this chaos; but it is not in their power to stop or organise it. Our best minds are given to analysing this period of disintegration.

Why does Saint-Denis assume his audience will not be surprised? Or is this a polite way of stating an idea he thinks his listeners should know, but do not?

At the present time the world presents us with a spectacle which is so passionately interesting and so full of anxiety that one wonders how the theatre can keep pace with it. You won't be surprised if I tell you that in this vast waste of anxiety France is as deeply involved as any. She has been materially, morally, and spiritually struck down. In fact she has never fully recovered from the 1914–18 war and the humiliation of defeat in 1940 has accentuated all her previous dissensions. We try continually to show the world that we are better than this defeat has shown us to be. It's a dangerous state of mind. And, to the sorrow of our best friends, I am sure it will be many years before we shall recover.

To what *events* does Saint-Denis refer?

Were the previous three paragraphs necessary to an understanding of this

During the winter of 1957–8 in connection with certain events in North Africa, journalists and politicians in other countries spoke of French stupid-one? If *yes*, why? If *no*, what did the paragraphs add?

Has the lecturer suddenly moved his address down to reach *all* hearers? Or do these ideas seem clear and "simple" because he has been lucid in explaining complex ideas up to this point?

Discuss why *kitchens* and *bedrooms* are in the same category.

ity. That is something new; for we have generally been criticised for our excessive intelligence, what is called our incurable tendency towards intellectualism. Be assured, if you want to be, that intellectualism in France is not dead. We remain—and I say it with simplicity, for after all one must find one's strength where it lies—we remain intellectuals, and also artists. And the way in which we are reacting to our trials is particularly evident in our theatre.

For our theatre, like our society, goes in many different directions and it is only our traditions, which lie behind the contradictions, which tend to create any sort of unity. We are naturally exposed to the assaults of modern realism, including American realism: you know that your dramatists are played in France a great deal. We closed our doors to popular or bourgeois naturalism, a long time ago. Kitchens and bedrooms are banished from our stage. "Parisian" comedy, so dear to our grandfathers, is all but dead. We have even been so determined to avoid presenting a photograph of real life on the stage that we made the mistake of ignoring Chekhov for many years. During the last forty years of course we have played Chekhov, but I believe that it is only in the last four or five years that the French public has felt Chekhov deeply, intimately. And now we welcome Chekhov but we have no use for his imitators.

Recently you have given a kindly reception in your theatres to the work of two of our dramatists who have enjoyed longstanding reputations in France: Jean Giradoux, who died towards the end of the war, and Jean Anouilh, who is younger and in perfect health. They are two very different

The description of Giradoux's stylistic inheritance is explained clearly. Then what is the meaning of the phrase, *sometimes his style is a little precious?*

Notice that the lecturer is contrasting Giradoux with Anouilh, and then Claudel with Sartre and Camus. Would you commend Saint-Denis for this? If *yes*, why? If *no*, why?

What is *existentialism?* Does Saint-Denis suddenly talk to knowledgeable hearers only? Or would you say any college audience should know the meaning of this term?

writers who both began writing for the stage at the same time, in the thirties.

Giradoux belongs to the tradition I have defined as classical. Fed upon the mythical sources of the Greeks he seems to be the heir to both Aristophanes and Racine. He has elegance and satirical wit. He is a writer with a style. For him, writing counts: he was unable to separate thinking from style: though sometimes his style is a little precious.

Anouilh is a realist, often aggressively so, both in matter and in language. It is difficult to define Anouilh's style: while it moves from naturalism to expressionism, it is always darkly coloured by modern pessimism, the despairing sense of loss belonging to fallen angels. Anouilh's passion for absolute integrity, so difficult to achieve, has inclined him towards anarchy. This uncompromising attitude, which drives him to escape from a world of compromise, leaves in its wake a train of insults and invectives.

Here now is a pair of dramatists in striking contradiction. Paul Claudel died only a few years ago. He was a poet, one of the most powerful French poets we have known. Though anti-classical by position, he studied the Greeks and Shakespeare, he studied the Bible and the scriptures. He shaped a prosody and a syntax of his own. But because he is a Catholic poet his public tends to be specialised. Claudel always wanted in his work to remain outside actuality.

Now let us look at the other extreme: Jean-Paul Sartre, the existentialist, the promoter of "littérature engagée" (committed), living in close touch with the events and values of our time; and Albert Camus, a Nobel prize-winner, who was a disciple of Sarte and then parted from him. The writing of Camus became increasingly classical, in the French sense of the term.

As presented by Saint-Denis, the relationship of dramaturgy to other literary forms converges in this last period of development. Discuss the lecturer's assumption that listeners know these novelists and short-story writers, and understand, consequently, his comparison.

Discuss the imagery created here to explain Ionesco.

Now, to mention only the more important of the younger people, we have got Vauthier, a realist, who seems to be a kind of descendant of Strindberg, full of dreams and visions. We have G. Schehadé, the Lebanese poet, whose third play was produced by Jean-Louis Barrault in October, 1957. We have Jean Genet and H. Pichette, both poets and realists. And finally there is the trio of the "avant-garde", at present the most important group of all. Arthur Adamov, who in his most recent play *Paolo Paoli* seems to come near to Brecht; Samuel Beckett, who has been influenced by Joyce and Proust and who is related in his work to Kafka. His transcendental realism is close to the expression of modern anxiety in its most acute form, a sort of disease of the soul caught between the need for and the absence of God. Eugène Ionesco is the third representative of this "Theatre in Hell", as one critic called it. Like Beckett, Ionesco uses a realism which makes use of invented characters, transplanted from humble areas of the world into a sort of Punch and Judy show where perfectly ordinary life disintegrates into nightmare. And very often this disintegration, which affects the language itself, makes us laugh. In Paris, while a rather small public is fascinated by Beckett, a larger one enjoys Ionesco as a comic dramatist, and laughs at his new world, the logic of which is curiously related to the feelings of a modern audience. The phenomenon Beckett-Ionesco is a very French one. Here we have two writers of foreign origin—one is Irish, the other Roumanian—both writing in French, and both born into the theatre in the intellectual Parisian atmosphere where their plays have not yet enjoyed great commercial success whatever their repercussions. And they are becoming known throughout the world.

A dramatist or theatre director concerns himself with ideas, and he effectively transforms those ideas for listeners into images, partly through clear writing and partly through stage directions. Does it follow, therefore, that a good writer makes a good lecturer?

Evaluate the clarity of this summary statement.

Waiting for Godot was played for nearly a year on Piccadilly Circus, at the Criterion Theatre. I have just been to San Francisco: a group was rehearsing *Waiting for Godot.* I arrived in Los Angeles: I was taken to see a show—it was *Waiting for Godot.* You see the deep sort of realism practised by these two dramatists belongs to the world of poetry and of style. To penetrate to the heart of reality, far beyond appearances, they cannot make use of naturalistic methods.

In France those plays could not be born if behind the contradictions of our stage there was not some kind of basic unity between the intellectual movement and the development of the theatre.

Two men are leading the French theatre at present: Jean-Louis Barrault and Jean Vilar; they are both pupils of Charles Dullin, himself an actor in Copeau's company and one of his main disciples.

Here, in my view, is the main contribution of France to the theatre: men, and a tradition. We work within the framework of our classical tradition and under its constant pressure. We struggle to free ourselves: tradition has become not so much a guide as a constant provocation.

I have seen the same thing in England with the admirable tradition of Shakespeare, easier to adapt, I believe, to modern times.

For very many years in France tradition has quite logically been supported by institutions. Up to 1939 the state helped only the official theatres: Opéra, Opéra Comique, Comédie Française.

At the Comédie Française every generation can see masterpieces of the past, French and foreign, together with revivals of the most important works of the last thirty years. From time to time

Saint-Denis does not state that old people are for the Comédie Française. Do you think he meant that his listeners should imply this?

Here, Saint-Denis makes an educated judgment of uniqueness to France. Since a lecturer may in a sense rely on his own expertness, the next paragraphs may seem unnecessary. Why do you think Saint-Denis included them? What, in fact, is he doing in the next paragraphs? Has he successfully combined factual information with his own educated judgments?

there is a "creation", because it would be fatal never to give a new play. The Comédie Française informs and provokes you: when you are young you are always against it; frequently it drags behind the times, so that at intervals it has to be brought up to date.

Up to 1935 all the unofficial theatres and companies were financed and supported by private money. The advent of the "popular front" in 1936 brought more generous support from the state under the guise of popular education. But it must be said that while at the end of the nineteenth century there was a theatre building in France for every ten thousand inhabitants, most of them were transformed into cinemas between the two wars. Today, when Jean-Louis Barrault plays in Paris, he receives no grant from anybody. He is under the constant threat of bankruptcy. What I find unique in France is that people of the theatre have always been ready to die for their art: and this is no pompous nonsense.

If today, in spite of invasions, in spite of wars, of political and economic disorders, there exists a living theatre in France, it is because in 1887 André Antoine, an employee of the Gas Company, opened the "Théâtre Libre" with very little money: it was the beginning of naturalism ten years before Stanislavsky. Since 1913 men like Copeau, Dullin, Pitoëff, Jouvet, Baty, have taken upon themselves the *total responsibility*, financial and artistic, of their undertakings. This is no nationalistic outburst or uncontrollable French flourish: Pitoëff died before he was fifty, Jouvet and Dullin at sixty-four. None of the three retired. They were stopped by their heart or their kidneys while they were still acting.

Copeau and Dullin had schools attached to their theatres, not the kind

A lecture is suited for listeners rather than readers. What evidence do you find in this lecture that indicates it may *hear* better than *read?*

of schools that exist to find jobs for pretty girls, or to bring money to star actors in decline. Not at all. Schools that cost money.

Barrault today is in the same heroic situation. But the state has partially taken the place of private capital. It gives to Vilar a theatre and a grant of 125,000 dollars a year. Moreover as the theatre has disappeared from the provinces since the coming of the cinema, the state has created five dramatic centres in the main areas of France. These centres play modern and classical repertory. They have a relationship with the universities, which in France do not have theatres. They are also in touch with the amateur movement. Each of them plays, at popular prices, three to six different shows a year, in anything between forty to eighty different towns, giving single performances in the smaller, and more in the larger. Repertory and presentation are generally of high quality. The T. N. P. (Théâtre National Populaire) plays at the price of little more than a dollar a seat.

These centres, together with the better touring companies from Paris, maintain the theatre in provincial France. It has been found that only by living and working in the heart of the provinces can artists and technicians generate a creative impulse. That's why the state does not subsidise touring companies. Instead, for instance, it sends people like me to Strasbourg to build up an organisation, with the help and participation of the local people themselves. Rooted in the provinces there is a chance that the organisation will slowly grow, calling upon and training local talent. In ten to twenty years' time we may find that this artistic initiative has helped to give expression to original talent in many parts of France other than Paris. Then

Saint-Denis, by his own admission, spent *the best years of my maturity* in England. At the same time he includes himself among the *us* of such *French* directors as Barrault and Vilar. What has he assumed or admitted about himself?

Discuss the lecturer's conclusion. What are its merits? Demerits?

the real goal of the theatrical decentralisation will have been reached.

The dramatic centres, together with men like Barrault and Vilar, are all far more concerned, I assure you, with modern plays than with the classics. Don't consider us a lot of old bores, obsessed with the past. That isn't true. But we are all trained in classical disciplines, having found that our modern theatre, with all its contradictions, cannot present us with a solid enough basis for development. A complete actor cannot take shape, a dramatist cannot grow out of photographic naturalism. True representation of reality requires transposition and style.

There is only one theatre. The Greeks, the Chinese and the Japanese, Molière and Shakespeare can provide food for our realism. True realists have made a great contribution to the interpretation of the classics.

I've finished. France has been my subject. I'm not doing propaganda for my country. I do not like nationalism in any form. But I want to seize this opportunity of thanking from the bottom of my heart those few people who have seen my work in Europe [and who] were instrumental in bringing me here. It has allowed me to discover a great country very different from what I had been told it was. It's a new stage in my later development, for which I am most grateful.

Now ask yourself the following questions about the Saint-Denis lecture.

1. What assumptions would you guess Saint-Denis made about his audience, their knowledge of his subject, and their attitude towards him and his topic?
2. What is your evaluation of the title for the lecture? Would you say it was meant to attract all comers or to eliminate most curiosity seekers? The words *theatre* and *drama* are absent from the title; yet the lecture is rooted in both. Discuss the merits of such an omission, and whether

or not the inclusion of *classical, French,* and *tradition* in the title would attract a more diverse audience.

3. From a speech standpoint, what did you find objectionable in the Saint-Denis lecture? What did you find admirable?

4. Without having met Michel Saint-Denis, what is your impression of this man? Is he an *old bore* as he describes himself? If you find him exciting and warm, what gives you a favorable reaction: his candor, his authority as a theatre expert, his use of language, his knowledge of theatre and literature as demonstrated in the address?

5. Do you feel you would go away from this lecture with more specific information than with a general impression? Which is more important in a lecture situation?

6. Suppose you knew that Harvard University has no Theater Department. Would this influence your evaluation of the Saint-Denis lecture in terms of its suitability to listeners?

7. We classified this speech as a lecture. Saint-Denis classified it similarly. Do you agree that this is indeed a lecture or is it more an informal report?

15   The Persuasive Speech

The speech of persuasion, designed to demonstrate desirability, is the ubiquitous genre. Persuasion can be the dominant purpose in nearly any speech situation. Election campaigns, legislative gatherings, religious services, legal trials, keynote addresses at conventions or meetings, and debates within meetings or on public issues all call for persuasive speeches.

Speeches delivered at occasions of commemoration, such as Fourth-of-July gatherings, and at occasions of celebration, such as graduation exercises or reunions, often are persuasive speeches for which the occasion provides the platform.

Although each of these situations has uniqueness, they all share the common problem of the persuasive speech: that of relating the speaker's proposition to the listeners' values so that the listeners will decide to accept, rather than ignore or reject, the proposition. In terms of the analysis in Chapters 4 and 5, the speaker must apply the paradigm of an argument in a specific instance.

THE DECISION-MAKING PROCESS

The process by which people arrive at decisions is important to a speaker as he prepares a persuasive speech because, as will be shown in later sections of this chapter, it often influences the selection and development of a topic.

To understand the process, one must distinguish between two types of proposals that a speaker may advance. A speaker may attempt to influence his audience in areas of individual decision, such as that his listeners should read more books, be more patriotic, or donate to a charity. In other instances, he may attempt to influence his hearers on public issues, such as that they should support a particular candidate for public office or join in the drive to raise funds for a community playhouse.

In matters of private concern, the listener can arrive at a decision and action will be taken quite apart from what anyone else does. In matters of public concern, action will be taken only if enough people arrive at an agreement. One person can go to a library; whether a new library will be built depends on the opinions of a number of people. An individual determines whether a particular automobile will be purchased; public consensus determines who will serve on the city council.

Philosophers, psychologists, and sociologists have analyzed the process people go through to arrive at decisions. The analyses have shown that the process by which public consensus develops is basically an extension of the process by which private decision evolves.

The process may be described, then, either from the standpoint of an individual as he solves personal problems, or from the standpoint of a public as it arrives at a consensus. The description of the process as given here is based on sociologist Kimball Young's analysis of how public problems are solved.[1] To state the steps in terms of public, rather than private, problems emphasizes that, regardless of the nature of the proposal, the speaker is more than likely dealing with a problem that is of general concern and in which individual decisions will be influenced by the decisions of other people. That is, although the decision on whether to send a son to college is a private one, what other parents are deciding will significantly influence that decision.

Young divides the process of decision-making into four steps.[2]

1. *There must be an awareness that a problem exists.* The problem may have reached awareness through a physical catastrophe, a periodic election, or a gradual awakening of the community. According to Young, "the essence of the first stage is an attempt to state the issue in such terms as will permit its discussion by individuals and groups." For years Americans rested secure in the certainty that their educational system surpassed any other in the world. With the Russian Sputnik of 1957, a re-examination of the system began.

2. *Awareness of a problem is followed by preliminary analysis of the nature, seriousness, and causes of the problem.* The shock of finding that Russia excelled the United States in at least one area of technical development precipitated a frantic search for causes and for individuals and institutions to blame. Schools of education provided the most obvious point for criticism. Although much of the preliminary investigation of American

[1] The best known description of how an individual arrives at a decision was developed by John Dewey. In *How We Think* (Boston: D. C. Heath & Co., 1910, p. 72) Dewey analyzed an individual act of thought into its component parts. Such examination, he said, ". . . reveals, more or less clearly, five logically distinct steps: (i) a felt difficulty; (ii) its location and definition; (iii) suggestion of possible solution; (iv) development by reasoning of the bearings of the suggestion; (v) further observation and experiment leading to its acceptance or rejection; that is, the conclusion of belief or disbelief."

[2] *Social Psychology* (New York: Appleton-Century-Crofts, Third ed., 1956), pp. 334ff.

education led only to fault finding, the analysis ultimately turned to a systematic consideration of strengths and weaknesses. Comparison of American education with European systems proved fruitful.

3. *Analysis of the problem leads to suggestions for solutions and active advocacy of plans to remedy the problem.* Continued discussion about education showed that the problem was multi-faceted. A number of solutions were proposed, such as acceleration in education at all levels, increased financial support for education from governmental sources, and revision of curricula.

4. *From the advocacy of the various proposals, consensus is reached on which is the best solution.* Prolonged and vigorous discussion and debate, carried on in newspapers, television and radio broadcasts, professional journals, school meetings, and conversations between individuals, established that many of the proposed changes could contribute to an overall improvement of education. Many of them have now been put into effect. All of the suggested solutions mentioned above have been adopted in some form or other in various places throughout the country.

Many public, as well as private, problems are never solved in the sense that one solution remains viable. Although the problem of choosing between candidates for office is terminated by the calendar, the problem of ensuring that education is sound continues indefinitely. And the discussion continues at all levels of the decision-making sequence. New analyses are being made, new ideas are being suggested, and new proposals are being put into effect.

PREPARING THE PERSUASIVE SPEECH

The steps to prepare a persuasive speech are the same as the steps to prepare any speech: selecting a general subject for consideration and determining the specific purpose of the speech, analyzing the audience, gathering materials, selecting the points to be included, organizing the material, and writing the speech. There are, however, particular problems in building the persuasive speech. They will be considered here.

Although the problems are discussed below in the order in which they are most likely to occur, they will often be dealt with concurrently, just as the steps in the building process are taken more or less concurrently. A speaker will decide early on a specific approach to his topic, for example, but as the speech develops he may discover that time will not permit the development he had anticipated; hence, his purpose will be altered, probably by being narrowed. His preliminary selection of reasons to support his proposition may be changed as he discovers that there is insufficient evidence to support them or their proof would take too much time. Thus, all facets of the process undergo constant evaluation as the speech takes form.

Selecting the Specific Topic

There is no shortcut, no satisfaction-guaranteed-or-your-money-back method of selecting any speech topic. This problem, so much in the forefront of problems for student speakers, is likely to become less troublesome once you leave the speech class. Whereas you are now assigned to speak to accomplish a general purpose in the classroom, you will in the future most likely be invited to speak because of a known competence you have in an area of interest to the potential audience. An organization will often even suggest a topic, general or specific, that it would like to have considered. However, audience expectations on topics, even if made clear through a suggestion for a title, need not bind the speaker beyond what Quintilian suggested as the proper respect due them.

The selection of a topic should be based on considerations of your interests, your adequacies as a speaker, and the time you will be able to devote to preparation; the audience's expectations, its knowledge and attitudes about a potential topic, and its estimates of you; the limitations and obligations of the specific occasion; and the status of issues that interest, or should interest, your audience.

The careful speaker gives particular attention to the appropriateness and freshness of his topic.

APPROPRIATENESS

Occasionally the uniqueness of the occasion will dictate the specific topic or general theme around which a speech must be built. Only patriotic themes are appropriate at a Fourth-of-July celebration. A keynote address to a convention of educators must be related to education. At other times the uniqueness of the occasion will not dictate a specific theme or topic but will preclude consideration of some. Usually it would be inappropriate, for example, to speak in behalf of a candidate for a political office at a Parents and Teachers Association meeting, even though such a wide range of topics as the adequacy of police protection, the implications of the new tax bill, and the emotional problems of youngsters would be appropriate.

The topic must also be appropriate to the speaker and the audience. The speaker must have competence in his subject, and the audience must agree that he is sufficiently competent. The best topics enable the speaker to apply his expertness in areas of interest to the particular audience. G. Keith Funston, President of the New York Stock Exchange, adapted his particular competence to his audience when he addressed a graduating class at Maryland. He spoke on the economic problems facing young people.

FRESHNESS

A relatively fresh or new topic may better hold the interest of an audience than will an old standby. Freshness is even more to be valued, however, because persuasion is most likely to be effective when it concerns a relatively new topic.

Recall that a person who has made up his mind becomes increasingly hard to dissuade. Once his decision has been made, he seeks out information compatible with that position and even calculated to reinforce it. An existing opinion interferes with the reception of information that would alter it. Interference is especially likely if the individual has given public evidence of his opinion, such as signing a petition or encouraging others to accept his view.

The most propitious time to speak on a particular topic is *after* the audience has already become aware of the problem and *before* it has decided on a solution. Bernard Berelson and Gary A. Steiner state that "communications are most likely to convert or establish opinions for those members of the audience who are neutral on the issue, and least likely to affect those with strong feelings or those whose positions are strongly reinforced by group memberships."[3]

In other words, a single effort at persuasion will probably be most effective if the audience has advanced beyond the first stage in decision making but has not yet reached the final stage, where opinion is already fairly well solidified.

NARROWING THE TOPIC

Many speakers, particularly beginners, select too broad a topic. The more general and broad the topic, the more superficial its treatment must be. William Norwood Brigance gave sound advice: "A speech must be specific. To be specific, it must say 'more and more' about 'less and less.' Ergo, choose a subject that covers 'less and less' in order that you can say 'more and more' about it."[4]

Analyzing the Audience

A speaker is concerned with what an audience knows about his particular topic and what attitudes, opinions, and beliefs they have concerning it. Thus, when a speaker uses those methods of audience analysis discussed in Chapter 9, he limits his search to areas that are relevant to his topic.

What he learns from an examination of social strata and group membership will enable him to estimate where the audience tends to be in the decision-making sequence associated with his topic. The number of steps the audience has taken determines the development of the speech.

If the speaker concludes that there is insufficient awareness of the

---

3 *Human Behavior: An Inventory of Scientific Findings* (New York: Harcourt, Brace & World, Inc., 1964), p. 542.

4 *Speech: Its Techniques and Disciplines in a Free Society* (New York: Appleton-Century-Crofts, Inc., Second ed., 1961), p. 177.

problem, his first task must be to develop an argumentative paradigm that will create awareness; and that alone may be enough of a task for one speech. On the other hand, if he finds that his listeners are already convinced that something needs to be done, he should not waste his or their time by trying to prove the existence of a problem. To remind listeners of its existence and importance will be sufficient.

The extent of audience awareness and interest in the problem also determines how much background information must be included in a speech. The more people are aware of a problem and the more they have become interested in it, the more they will know about it.

Remember that audience analysis should be directed toward discovering what the opinion leaders, rather than what the average members, know and think about the topic.

Often it is easier to know what to look for than where to look. A speaker cannot poll his audience or telephone the opinion leaders to learn what they know and believe about his topic. A logical starting point is to ask the person who arranged for the speech. Usually he will be an officer in the organization and hence familiar with its goals and objectives. He can provide detailed information about the composition of the membership, the expected audience, and what they in turn will expect of a speaker.

When there is a lack of specific information, a speaker may assume that the audience will tend to agree with his opinions as they are known and understood by the audience. In keeping with the tendency to hear information calculated to strengthen rather than weaken existing opinions, few audiences invite speakers who are known to disagree with the audience's predominant opinion on the subject of the speech. Of the many reasons for being asked to speak, one of the commonest is a belief that the speaker will reaffirm the majority opinion in an organization.

Gathering Material

As soon as a speaker tentatively chooses a topic, he begins to consider ways in which it might be developed; he begins, from his own thoughts, his reading, and his conversations with other people, to gather material that may be useful in its development. Both the selection of a topic and the way it is developed depend on whether evidence is available to prove the statements about facts that are used in the speech.

Relatively few of the statements will need proof. An audience will already know that most of the statements have sufficient correspondence to reality. Inevitably, however, a persuasive speech will include statements about simple facts or relations between facts that will not be acceptable to an audience. The problem is to find the material that will provide the proof.

As pointed out in Chapter 5, some of the facts can be demonstrated to an audience. Others can be verified by the audience itself. Most of the statements that need verification, however, must be proved by use of other statements; in other words, through statements of opinion.

Since the material used as evidence must be acceptable to an audience, statements should be tested by asking the questions about their source that members of an audience may ask.

TESTING OPINION FROM A WITNESS

If the statement is about a particular event or happening, supposedly experienced in some way, it will have probative value if the audience can answer "yes" to the following questions, should any of them be asked:

1. Was the witness in a position to observe or otherwise experience the events?

2. Does the witness have the ability to observe that to which he testifies?

3. Is the witness reliable to report what he actually saw or experienced?

4. Is the explanation given by the witness the most plausible explanation of what took place?

5. Is the opinion of the witness reliably reported?

TESTING OPINION FROM AN AUTHORITY

In contrast to statements of witnesses to a certain event are the statements of interpretation made by authorities. Statements of authoritative opinion draw conclusions from facts, evaluate other statements, or express matters of judgment and taste. Competent testimony about the causes of a depression requires different standards from testimony about whether a depression exists. Testimony of an authority will have probative value if an audience can answer "yes" to the following questions, should any of them be asked:

1. Is the person known as an individual of integrity?

2. Is the person competent to draw conclusions or weigh the statements of others about the matter at question?

3. Has the authority carefully weighed the facts that bear on his conclusion?

4. Is the opinion reliably reported?

USING THE STATEMENTS OF OPINION

Although the reliability of a witness or authority may be clearly established, audiences may still reject the opinion if it is incompatible with what they already know or expect to be true. The plausibility of the statement can often be established if the grounds for the opinion are shown. Thus, in support of an argument that the probe of Mars is not worth the cost, a speaker may wish to use the opinion of a well-known astronomer, who believes that nothing unusual will be found on Mars. The acceptability of the astronomer's judgment could be enhanced by explaining the basis for his conclusion.

From the statements about facts available to him, the speaker develops his arguments in the manner discussed in Chapters 4 and 5. As pointed out in those chapters and again at the beginning of this one, the object is to use the materials to develop lines of argument that will relate the speaker's purpose to listeners' values so that the audience will conclude that it is more desirable to accept than to reject or ignore the proposition.

Selecting the Arguments

In the ancient Greek and Roman classes in rhetoric, the discovery of arguments received attention first both in time and importance. By the time of Quintilian, the first century A.D., elaborate suggestions for *invention* (the apt title applied to the process) had already been developed. Quintilian himself offered many specific suggestions, although he ended his discussion with a warning that too much attention to system could stifle the process it was intended to facilitate. With Quintilian, however, we believe that system can be of help to speakers.

FINDING AVAILABLE ARGUMENTS

Cicero stated the first precept in discovering available arguments: "The speaker must investigate the facts thoroughly." "For what savors so much of madness," he asked, "as the empty sound of words, even the choicest and most elegant, when there is no sense or knowledge contained in them?"[5] That should still be the first precept, not only because a thorough investigation of the facts will yield the most cogent arguments, but because no speaker has the right to offer advice about something he does not understand thoroughly.

A second ancient precept, which is still valid, held that the student should discover the main issues or "the hinge"—to use Donald Lemen Clark's term—"upon which a case turns." Even though many arguments may be offered in support of a proposition, whether the proposal will be accepted depends oftentimes on but one or two crucial points. Of the many arguments that can be developed against capital punishment, two "hinges" are these: Is the death penalty a significantly better deterrent to crime than is life imprisonment? Is the taking of a life appropriate to our society?

[5] In *De Oratore*, printed in *Cicero on Oratory and Orators*, J. S. Watson, Tr. (London: George Bell and Sons, 1891), Vol. I, p. xii.

The hinge of an issue is usually the argument that is most difficult to prove conclusively. But the persuader who ignores the hinge to an issue almost assuredly will fail.

The kinds of reasons that may be offered in support of a proposition and the ways they can be proved have been discussed in Chapters 4 and 5. An awareness of the types of arguments should be ever present in the mind of the speaker as he investigates his subject and gathers materials. Classical rhetoricians discussed this concept under *topics,* from the Greek word meaning places. They wrote of the places of arguments, or, as did Quintilian, of "the seats of arguments, where they lurk and whence they are to be sought."

Summarizing the concept of topics, Clark wrote:

> One of the most important places or topics of arguments is that of cause and effect. The teacher trains the student to ask, "What might have caused the effect we are investigating? What effects might result from this situation?" Other important places or topics of argument are similarity and dissimilarity. "What is it like? What is it different from." Two very important places are definition and division. "What is it? What are its parts?"[6]

What the classical rhetoricians recommended was, of course, critical and perceptive investigation of a topic. Speakers learned to become well-informed on a topic; to discover the crucial points in that topic; and then, with an awareness of the types of argument that could be developed, to investigate available material. Such a procedure brought forth the crucial arguments, thoroughly supported. It still will.

Limiting the Number of Arguments

When selecting arguments, speakers must remember that listeners are limited in the number of arguments they can grasp at one time. Psychologist Donald Johnson believes that

> any intellectual activity is limited to consideration of only a small number of things at any one time, in most cases about five or six. . . . When people are asked to decide a controversy on the basis of more than six separate arguments, the surplus arguments are usually ineffective.[7]

The time available for a speech also limits the number of arguments that a speaker may use. Even when no specific limit has been suggested, an audience usually has an expectation of the maximum and minimum time limits for a speech. No longer are listeners willing to listen to speeches

[6] *Rhetoric in Greco-Roman Education* (New York: Columbia University Press, 1957), p. 76.
[7] *The Psychology of Thought and Judgment* (New York: Harper & Row, Publishers, 1955), p. 82.

that last hours, except the captive audiences of jurors in trials at law or legislators in legislative assemblies. And even those captive audiences may be annoyed by speeches of unusual length.

MEETING OPPOSING ARGUMENTS

The paradigm of an argument developed in Chapters 4 and 5 stressed the affirmative reasons offered to support a proposition. In application, however, a speaker oftentimes must consider reasons why audiences will reject a proposition, as well as reasons why they should accept it. Common sense suggests that a proposal will not be accepted if the arguments against acceptance are sufficiently strong. Thus, listeners who believe that education is a local affair will remain unconvinced by even a cogent argument that shows the desirability of federal over state aid to education.

Carl Hovland and his coauthors summarized the results of two important experiments designed to discover whether it is better to present only those arguments favoring a controversial proposition or to discuss as well strong arguments opposed to it:

> 1. A two-sided presentation is *more* effective in the long run than a one-sided one *a*) when, regardless of initial opinion, the audience is *exposed* to subsequent counterpropaganda, or *b*) when, regardless of subsequent exposure to counterpropaganda, the audience initially *disagrees* with the commentator's position.
>
> 2. A two-sided presentation is *less* effective than a one-sided if the audience initially *agrees* with the commentator's position and *is not exposed* to later counterpropaganda.[8]

Note that the conclusions stipulate that, regardless of a listener's initial position (that is, whether he tends to agree or disagree with the speaker), if he is subject to counterarguments, it is more effective to state and refute the opposing arguments.

Omnipresent mass-communication media grant insulary to few people even on issues of only local concern. Opinion leaders particularly are likely to be exposed to, if not actually seek out, the "other side."

Chauncey Goodrich, perceptive speech critic of over a century ago, told how well Charles James Fox, one of the great speakers of all times, understood the importance of meeting opposing arguments:

> He struck instantly at the heart of his subject. He was eager to meet his opponent at once on the real points at issue; and the moment of his greatest power was when he stated the argument against himself, with more force

[8] Carl I. Hovland, Irving L. Janis, and Harold H. Kelley, *Communication and Persuasion* (New Haven: Yale University Press, 1953), p. 110.

than his adversary or any other man could give it, and then seized it with the hand of a giant, tore it in pieces, and trampled it under foot.[9]

One of President Franklin Roosevelt's fireside chats illustrates one way of meeting opposing arguments. The President wished to convince Americans that their country should serve as "the great arsenal of democracy." To be that arsenal required greater efforts. "But all of our present efforts are not enough," he insisted. "We must have more ships, more guns, more planes—more of everything."

Intermingled with the arguments for the proposal are arguments designed to overcome beliefs inimical to the President's purpose. Here are some of the negative attitudes and opinions he sought to counter, and the ways he tried to overcome them:

That the dangers should not be told:

During the past week many people in all parts of the nation have told me what they wanted me to say tonight. Almost all of them expressed a courageous desire to hear the plain truth about the gravity of the situation. One telegram, however, expressed the attitude of the small minority who want to see no evil and hear no evil. . . .

Frankly and definitely there is danger ahead—danger against which we must prepare. But we well know that we cannot escape danger, or the fear of danger, by crawling into bed and pulling the covers over our heads.

That the western hemisphere stands in no danger:

There are those who say that the Axis powers would never have any desire to attack the Western Hemisphere. That is the same dangerous form of wishful thinking which has destroyed the powers of resistance of so many conquered peoples.

That what is proposed would involve the United States in war:

If we are to be completely honest with ourselves, we must admit that there is risk in any course we may take. But I deeply believe that the great majority of our people agree that the course that I advocate involves the least risk now and the greatest hope for world peace in the future.

That the proposal would lead to undue economic adjustments when the war is over:

Our defense efforts must not be blocked by those who fear the future consequences of surplus plant capacity. The possible consequences of failure of our defense efforts now are much more to be feared.

And after the present needs of our defense are past, a proper handling of the country's peacetime needs will require all of the new productive capacity, if not still more.[10]

[9] *Select British Eloquence* (New York: Harper & Row, Publishers, 1854), p. 461.
[10] Speech delivered on Dec. 29, 1940, printed in *The World's Great Speeches*, Lewis Copeland and Lawrence Lamm, Eds. (New York: Dover Publications, Inc., 1958).

CHOOSING BETWEEN AVAILABLE ARGUMENTS

To the extent that a speaker can choose between arguments, preference will be given those that can be proved most adequately and easily. Adequacy and ease of proof both depend on the availability of suitable material for proof (discussed in a previous section) and the existing attitudes of an audience.

1. *Audiences will tend to believe what they want to believe.* That is, they will more readily be convinced that reality corresponds to their hope of what it is like than the reverse. Thus, it is easier to prove to a man that the incumbent party is corrupt if he hopes to find corruption.

2. *Audiences will tend to believe what they expect to be true.* Even though a man may be grieved to learn that corruption exists, if he expects corruption, he will require less proof of it than will a man who considers corruption highly improbable.

3. *When audiences have no particular hope or expectation, they will be more easily convinced of a fact if it conforms to what they already know and does not require rejection of existing beliefs.*

WHETHER TO USE EMOTION-LADEN ARGUMENTS

Jon Eisenson and his coauthors refer to emotion as

a component of a complex reaction that an individual undergoes in a given situation. The component *emotion* is characterized by: (1) a marked change in the internal state of the organization, (2) awareness of the change, and (3) behavior indicative of an attempt to adjust to the given situation.[11]

Although at times emotions themselves may become motives, emotions do not exist apart from goals and motives. We experience no emotion toward something that is unrelated to our motives or goals. As Clifford Morgan states,

Anger . . . is provoked by restraints, including any interference with goal-directed activity. This means that anger is produced by frustration—by not having or getting what one wants. Frustration may not always elicit anger, but anger is usually caused by frustration or by circumstances that have previously caused frustration.

Conversely, pleasure "is the accompaniment of satisfying a drive."[12]

Emotions also have a close relation to attitudes. Since an attitude is a tendency to respond positively or negatively toward its object as the object is seen either to facilitate or hamper the realization of a goal, an attitude

[11] Jon Eisenson, J. Jeffery Auer, and John V. Irwin, *The Psychology of Communication* (New York: Appleton-Century-Crofts, 1963), p. 69.

[12] *Introduction to Psychology* (New York: McGraw-Hill, Inc., Second ed. 1961), pp. 111 and 109.

may also be considered as a tendency to react emotionally toward something. The greater the role of the attitude object in facilitating or hampering goal realization and the more important the goal is to an individual, the greater will be his tendency toward emotional response.

Because any argument that is related to a listener's values (motives, goals, and attitudes) will elicit some degree of emotional response, it is doubtful that a distinction can be made between *logical* and *emotional* arguments. A distinction can be based on *degree* of emotional response elicited by an argument.

A speaker must decide whether he will use arguments that elicit extensive emotional response. The answer is partly based on ethics. That part was considered in Chapter 10. Another part is based on effectiveness. That is the concern here.

The impact of emotion in speechmaking can be illustrated by examining the particular emotion that has been most fully investigated—fear. Theoretically, the emotion *fear* lends force to a persuasive message by motivating the listener to seek some ease of his fear; thus, the emotion becomes a motivating force.

To implement the theory, however, is difficult. Although people can be made fearful, not all people fear the same things. Further, whether a specific and realistic danger is more frightening than a vague threat varies with the individual and the subject. Whether fear can be aroused also depends in part on the hearer's estimate of the speaker's intent. If the listener believes that the intent is to arouse great fear, he may be on his guard and dismiss the speaker as a "rabble-rouser" and the methods as "propaganda techniques."[13]

Even when successfully instilled, fear has a variable impact on the communication. Hovland and his coauthors describe in detail an experiment using the subject of dental hygiene to explore the effectiveness of fear appeals. In seeking to gain conformity to recommendations, three messages were developed. They were judged to make strong, moderate, and minimal use of fear appeals. The results were these:

> The main findings of the fear appeal experiment indicate . . . that when the goal of persuasive communication is to create sustained preferences or attitudes, a relatively low degree of fear arousal will sometimes be the optimal level—that too strong a fear appeal can evoke some form of interference which reduces the effectiveness of the communication. The results definitely contradict the assumption that as the dosage of fear-arousing stimuli in a mass communication is increased the audience will necessarily become more highly motivated to accept the reassuring recommendations contained in the communication.

[13] *Communication and Persuasion*, pp. 56ff.

Further, the subjects not only conformed more closely to the recommendation when minimal fear appeals were used, but "the minimal appeal proved to be the most effective form of the communication with respect to producing *resistance* to the counterpropaganda."[14]

The interferences are apparently of three types: First, rather than be subjected to fear-inducing messages, the listener may become inattentive. Perhaps everyone has had the experience of finding something too fearful to observe or hear and simply quit looking or listening. Second, fear appeals may actually lead to aggressive feelings toward the communicator rather than to acceptance of his proposal. Third, listeners may resort to defensive-avoidance reactions; that is, the audience may ignore or minimize the danger.

If the impact of other emotions resembles the impact of fear, the disruptive nature of an intensely emotional argument may be more of a hindrance than an aid to effectiveness.[15]

Organizing the Speech

The term *organization* is used here, as it ordinarily is, to include two different, though related, problems in speech composition: (1) selecting the materials that introduce and conclude a speech, and (2) deciding on the order in which the arguments should be presented.

The overriding objective in determining organization of the persuasive speech is to enhance the psychological validity of the arguments. Hence, although many considerations bear on organization, none is as important as the character of the audience. In *The Fundamentals of Speaking*, Wilbur E. Gilman, Bower Aly, and Loren Reid remind students that the plan of development for a speech depends on (1) a speaker's opportunities for preparation, (2) his reputation as a speaker, (3) the implications of his purpose, (4) the requirements of his subject, (5) the composition of his

---

14 *Communication and Persuasion*, pp. 81 and 83.

15 A study more recent than Hovland's bears on this point. Kenneth D. Frandsen investigated how the media of communication influences the effectiveness of "threat appeals." Using three media of communication (tape recording, television, and face-to-face), two messages having different levels of threat appeal, and students in college lecture sections as subjects, he found that "none of the three media and neither of the two messages produced a significantly greater shift of opinion or a significantly greater amount of immediate recall when compared with the other media or with the other message." While both messages were effective, "the level of threat did not affect the degree of effectiveness." ("Effects of Threat Appeals and Media of Transmission," *Speech Monographs*, Vol. 30, June 1963, pp. 101–104.)

This experiment does not, of course, contradict Hovland's findings. Had the threat appeal been large enough, there might have been a disruptive response. The finding that there was no significant difference in effectiveness between the messages of lesser and more threat suggests that, as stated above, fear often may be overrated as a persuasive factor.

audience, and (6) the nature of the occasion. "Of all the factors governing the selection of a plan," they point out, "the foremost is likely to be the audience."[16]

INTRODUCTION

Whether it is called an introduction, attention step or something else, the beginning of a speech should, according to most textbooks, attract the attention of the listeners to the subject matter of the speech and prepare them for what is to follow.

While describing the process a speaker uses to organize a speech, Cicero indicated the relation of the introduction to the arguments in the speech:

> The results of his invention he will set in order with great care. . . . The orator will certainly make fair "porches" and gorgeous approaches to his oration. And when he has gained attention by the introduction, he will establish his own case, refute and parry the opponent's argument, choosing the strongest points for the opening and closing, and inserting the weaker points in between.[17]

Here, as in other areas of speech composition, great speakers have regarded the *rules* as suggestions rather than inviolate principles. Cicero, better known to his contemporaries as a speaker than as a writer about speechmaking, exhibited no hesitancy in ignoring his own admonitions. Although there is no evidence that Lincoln read the classical rhetoricians, he did learn from his reading and from Mentor Graham some of the theory of public speaking. He must have known that this introduction seems calculated to discourage rather than encourage attention:

> Mr. President and fellow citizens of New York:—
> The facts with which I shall deal this evening are mainly old and familiar; nor is there anything new in the general use I shall make of them. If there shall be any novelty, it will be in the mode of presenting the facts, and the inferences and observations following that presentation.[18]

No "fair porch" or "gorgeous approach" there. Yet that was the opening Lincoln prepared for what he must then have regarded as his most significant speech: his Cooper Union address, delivered on February 27, 1860, before New York Republicans anxious to see if the man from Illinois, who had attracted so much attention in his debates with Douglas, possessed real substance. Lincoln was so successful that his Cooper Union appearance is often called his President-making address.

[16] New York: Crowell Collier and Macmillan, Inc., 1951, p. 73.

[17] *Orator*, 15, 50, H. M. Hubbell, Tr., in *Cicero* (Cambridge, Mass.: Harvard University Press, 1939), p. 343

[18] Printed in *American Speeches*, Wayland Maxfield Parrish and Marie Hochmuth, Eds. (New York: Longmans, Green and Co., 1954).

Why did Lincoln utilize such an introduction? He may have believed that his audience expected something sensational, something totally new and original, and thus he wished to orient them immediately to his approach: one of utilizing the closest type of reasoning to prove a proposition.[19] Whatever his reason for using that kind of an introduction, he demonstrated that a skilled speaker is not afraid to defy convention.

BODY

The *body* carries the substance, the arguments, of the speech. When determining the order in which his arguments are to be presented, the speaker must look first at the logic of the material. Occasionally the logic will determine the order. If one uses a chain of reasoning, the obvious order is to start with the first link and continue to the last. Most often the logic of the argument will permit latitude in organization. A speaker generally uses several relatively independent arguments, which also may be of varying strength.

Logic of the material is not the sole consideration in ordering arguments, however. A suggestion made by Wayland Parrish to students reading speeches of others merits the speech writer's attention: "It is helpful to separate the structure of the speech from the structure of the reasoning that supports it, and to outline both. Rarely will they coincide, for rarely do experienced speakers put their thoughts into . . . mechanical form. . . ."[20] Experienced speakers seldom place their arguments in mechanical form because they know that psychological validity is not earned mechanically. It is earned through a sensitivity to both the astonishing limitations and incredible capacities of the human mind.

One of the most successful attempts to implement the principle that concern for the listener should determine the mode of arrangement is Alan H. Monroe's *motivated sequence,* an adaptation of John Dewey's analysis of how we think, described above.

Speakers should not assume, however, that any one mode of development is the best. No single pattern of organization can be applicable at all times. Our preference is that an auditor have a feeling of movement and direction as a speech progresses. But even that should not be regarded as an admonition. C. P. Snow's "The Moral Un-Neutrality of Science," discussed

[19] The speech is worthy of close study. Using as his text Douglas' statement that "Our fathers, when they framed the Government under which we live, understood this question [of the position of the federal government towards slavery] just as well, and even better, than we do now," Lincoln ranged through history to show the various ways in which the fathers had acted on problems involving slavery. The result is an impressive document in support of the position that on slavery there was no "division of local from federal authority," and that no "part of the Constitution forbade the Federal Government to control as to slavery in the federal territories." The speech is perhaps most readily available in the source we cite. See footnote 18.

[20] *American Speeches,* p. 14.

at length in the next chapter, fits together somewhat as a jigsaw puzzle. Many of his listeners must have been curious to see how the apparently almost random development of points could fit together into a pattern.

Although the artist has full opportunity to show his art in the organization of his speech, social science offers several tentative suggestions. Findings in this area are fragmentary, partly because research has been limited, and partly because the complexities of the problems being investigated have occasionally led to inconclusive and even contradictory results.

The results of one experiment coincide with what common sense would lead us to expect. Raymond G. Smith found that complete randomization of the major points in a speech led to a negative audience reaction.[21] From either resentment at having been exposed to a poor speech or a belief that a reasonable argument cannot be constructed in support of a position, listeners may be expected to agree less with a speaker at the end of a poorly organized speech than they did at the beginning.

Carl Hovland and his associates provided partial answers to several of the questions on organization asked by a speaker. They did so, however, only after acknowledging that decisions on speech organization are as yet "much more an art than a science."

1. *Is it more effective in a speech supported by arguments of different strength to present the strongest arguments at the beginning or the end?*

Although studies have yielded contradictory results, the answer probably depends on the degree of audience interest and involvement in the topic.

> The most useful generalizations will . . . be concerned with "interaction" effects. Two tentative propositions of this type are advanced: that climax order [presenting the major arguments last] will be favored on issues with which the audience is familiar and where deep concern is felt, but that anticlimax order [presenting the major argument first] will be favored on unfamiliar topics and with uninterested audiences.[22]

Hovland pointed out, however, that other considerations may override considerations of initial interest and involvement. An argument that arouses considerable anxiety may better be left until last even though an audience initially has little interest in the topic. Utilized without a gradual buildup, the argument may be so disruptive that it would immediately cause an audience to cease listening. Some initially uninterested audiences may experience disappointment at the anticlimactic nature of arguments.

Robert E. Lana explored the relation between order of argument and information known about the topic. He found that "a communication presented first, whether pro or con, is more effective the more familiar the

21 "An Experimental Study of the Effects of Speech Organization Upon Attitudes of College Students," *Speech Monographs*, Vol. 18 (November, 1951), p. 299.

22 *Communication and Persuasion*, p. 120.

subject is with the topic." He also found "a recency effect [greater effectiveness of a climactic order] when the subjects' familiarity with the topic of communication is near zero. . . ."[23]

2. *When the speaker presents arguments both for and against his proposition, does it matter which are presented first?*

Hovland answers: "When an authoritative communicator plans to mention pro arguments and also nonsalient con arguments, the pro-first order is superior to the con-first order." Con arguments are "nonsalient" when "the audience is either initially unfamiliar with the con arguments or for some reason fails to recall them."[24] The finding is not to be interpreted to apply conversely. That is, there is not sufficient evidence to state what is the most efficacious approach for a non-authoritative communicator or salient arguments.

3. *When seeking to satisfy needs of an audience, does it matter whether the information is presented first or whether the need is pointed out first?*

The answer conforms to what we would expect from the way people approach problems: "Presentation of information relevant to the satisfaction of needs after these needs have been aroused brings about greater acceptance than an order which presents the information first and the need-arousal second."[25]

CONCLUSION

The *conclusion* to a speech can serve a variety of functions. It can bring the line of reasoning to culmination; it can summarize and restate the points of the speech; it can reinforce the speaker's thesis.

A reading of great speeches will show that the outstanding characteristics of a closing, regardless of its specific functions, are strength and vigor. Lincoln concluded his Cooper Union address in this way:

> Neither let us be slandered from our duty by false accusations against us, nor frightened from it by menaces of destruction to the Government nor of dungeons to ourselves. *Let us have faith that right makes might, and in that faith, let us, to the end, dare to do our duty as we understand it.*

The care with which great speakers plan conclusions is suggested by how often bits from the closing to a speech have become part of our popular literature: Lincoln's "government of the people, by the people, for the people"; Webster's "Liberty and Union, now and for ever, one and inseparable"; Henry's "give me liberty, or give me death"; and Kennedy's

[23] "Familiarity and the Order of Presentation of Persuasive Communications," *Journal of Abnormal and Social Psychology,* Vol. 62 (May, 1961), p. 575 and 577.
[24] Carl I. Hovland, Ed., *The Order of Presentation in Persuasion* (New Haven: Yale University Press, 1957), p. 137 and 128.
[25] *The Order of Presentation in Persuasion,* p. 135.

"ask not what your country can do for you—ask what you can do for your country."

Social science offers assistance in answering only one of the questions a speaker must ask about the closing to a speech.

Does it matter whether the point of the speech is explicitly stated or left implicit?

The major experiment in this area led Hovland to conclude that when the arguments are complicated and on impersonal topics, "it is generally more effective" to state the point explicitly.[26]

That finding, however, is based on two important assumptions. First, it assumes that the subject is so complex that listeners need assistance if they are to see the implications of the reasoning. If the implications are easily seen, there is no reason to expect that it will make much difference whether they are stated by the speaker. Whether the implications are easily seen depends on the audience as well as on the nature of the argument. An audience that is familiar with the topic or experienced in following complex arguments may quite easily carry an involved line of reasoning to its culmination.

Second, the finding assumes that the issue is not one in which the implications of the argument are so objectionable or repugnant that a listener will refuse to grant immediately that the logic of the case compels him to the disruptive conclusion. If the implications are disruptive, time and reflection may bring a listener closer to the desired conclusion than would an explicit statement from the speaker. Perhaps all of us find ourselves saying to someone: "If you need an answer now it will be *no*. But I'd rather think about it awhile." In Chapter 4 we cite Thomas Huxley's "On a Piece of Chalk" as an example of a speech in which the major point is not explicitly stated. To grant immediately that the Genesis narrative of creation is unscientific may have been too difficult for a group of workingmen in nineteenth-century England. Huxley apparently believed that more of his listeners would acknowledge the implications of his argument if they had additional time to ponder his remarks.

Cicero believed that "it is the treatment of the subject matter . . . that makes the speech admirable; the facts themselves are easy enough to acquire." Whether or not the facts are easy enough to acquire, the ordering of materials in a speech certainly contributes to whether the result is admirable. The process of selecting and ordering materials for a speech may well be considered in Francis Bacon's terms: Reason applied to imagination for the moving of the will.

The possible patterns of development are nearly limitless. Some of them are discussed in other chapters. Any listing is arbitrary, for under the touch of imagination "pure" forms become corrupted—and are often better for it.

26 *Communication and Persuasion,* pp. 100ff.

The best way to learn how to organize a speech is to read speeches. Other speakers can teach you a great deal about how to handle the complex problems of selecting and ordering speech materials.

Wording the Speech

The use of language in a persuasive speech, considered in its entirety, differs materially from the use of language in an expository speech. The persuasive speech as a unit uses language to direct behavior by proving that one action, concept, or object is to be preferred over another—in other words, to prove desirability. The expository speech, on the other hand, uses language to gain understanding.

When language of the persuasive speech is examined in smaller segments—individual words, sentences, and paragraphs—rather than the whole speech, the distinction between language for exposition and language for persuasion vanishes.

First of all the language of the persuasive speech must be clear. If audiences are to understand the reasons why they should accept the speaker's proposals, the reasons must be stated clearly. From the standpoint of effectiveness, then, Stendahl's rule for the use of language is applicable. "I see but one rule: *to be clear*. If I am not clear all *my world* crumbles."[27]

The ethical speaker is also concerned with accuracy of statement. As pointed out in Chapter 10, failure to use language accurately can cause audiences to arrive at decisions based on misinformation. The persuasive speaker uses exposition in two fundamental ways. First, he seeks to describe and explain "what is there." Second, he describes and explains his evaluation of "what is there." That is, he describes what is there so that he can explain his evaluation of it and its implications for his audience. With either use, accuracy is necessary.

Both the persuasive and expository speaker also are concerned with vivid use of language, and for the same reason—to heighten interest in what is said.

In summary, the methods of achieving accuracy, clarity, and vividness, which are described in Chapters 6 and 7, are the methods to be used both in exposition and persuasion.

RESTRAINT IN DESCRIPTION

One of the problems shared by expository and persuasive speakers should be re-emphasized here: How to achieve vividness without at the same time arousing an emotional response of such magnitude that the effectiveness of the argument or the speech is destroyed.

[27] In *Writers on Writing*, Walter Allen, Ed. (New York: E. P. Dutton & Co., Inc., 1949), p. 205.

Speakers seek to give force to arguments by associating them with powerful motives, prized goals, and dynamic attitudes. The more vital and significant the argument seems to a listener, however, the greater its potential for eliciting strong and disruptive emotional response.

The disruptive response is usually evoked when the speaker too vividly describes the consequences of failure to accept the argument. How much detail should be given to support an argument that seat belts in automobiles reduce the chances of death and injury? How completely should a speaker describe the consequences of being unprotected by a bomb shelter in case of nuclear war? Should he describe, as John Hersey did in *Hiroshima*, how skin pulls away from a man's hand when he touches something, the appearance of a man whose eyes have been burned out, or the way a child dies from radiation sickness?

The problem is not one of accuracy or clarity. Vivid description is always clear, as is Hersey's, and it can be precisely accurate. The problem concerns completeness or fullness of description. A speaker would have to decide whether what Hersey considered appropriate for his purpose in a book would be appropriate in a speech having a similar purpose.

Lord Snow's speech, printed in the next chapter, illustrates that a speaker can deal forcefully with an urgent problem (the subject is nuclear war) and at the same time minimize the probability of disruptive reactions from his listeners.

16   Persuasion in Use

One of the most fruitful ways to learn about public speaking is to read and analyze speeches of others. Printed here in full is an address worthy of your close study. Not that you will try to imitate it, but from studying it, you will better understand how the principles of persuasion can be used by a speaker to build a speech about a specific problem for the purpose of persuading an audience at a certain moment in history.

The chapter also includes an analysis of the persuasive factors in the speech. The analysis is not complete. You will find much left for study. Further, you may well disagree with points in the analysis, for, as we said in Chapter 1 and as this speech proves, public speaking is an art. No one's opinion about art is final.

THE SPEECH SITUATION

The Speaker

The speaker is Charles Percy Snow. He was born into a middle-class English family in 1905. He attended University College in Leicester, his birthplace, and in 1930 earned a Ph.D. in physics from Christ's College, Cambridge. From 1930 to 1950 he was a fellow of Christ's College, where he performed distinguished work in physics. In 1932 he published his first novel and thus began a long and distinguished literary career. His best-known fiction is his series of novels *Strangers and Brothers,* which deal with the problems of finding personal and intellectual commitment in the turmoil of the twentieth century. His best-known nonfiction is *The Two Cultures,* which analyzes the conflict and difficulty in communication be-tween the "culture" of the sciences and the "culture" of the humanities.

From 1945 until 1960 he served as Commissioner of Civil Service. He was knighted in 1957. At the time he spoke—December 1960—he was a visiting professor of English at the University of California, Berkeley. He is well known for his university lectures both in England and the United States.

In October 1964 he was made a life peer and is now known as Lord Snow of Leicester. At that time he accepted a position as Parliamentary Secretary in the Ministry of Technology, the second-ranking position in the Ministry. When he accepted the appointment he said, "I was terribly impressed by Dag Hammarskjold, who believed in the moral value of participating in a complex world."

At the time of the speech, a reporter for The New York *Times* wrote:

> Perhaps the most surprising thing to persons meeting Sir Charles for the first time, it has been said, is that his erudition, a share in the making of great decisions and continuing popularity as a novelist have never made him arrogant or mean. He is almost invariably described as just a hard-headed, warm-hearted, intelligent midlander who has come up the hard way.

The Occasion

Seven thousand members of the American Association for the Advancement of Science gathered in New York on December 26, 1960, for what The New York *Times* called "a five-day potpourri annual meeting." Subjects considered in conference sessions ranged from the problems of delinquency to the status of nuclear research and weapons development in Communist China. The sessions, announced daily in the newspapers, were open to the public.

On the morning of December 27, the *Times* announced that Sir Charles would address an evening session on the topic, "The Challenge to Science of World Conditions Today."

The topic seemed appropriate. World conditions concerned many people. Of all the world's troubles—hunger, sickness, conflict—, none seemed so threatening as those associated with atomic-weapons development. People worried about the radiation fallout from past and future weapons testing. Did radiostrontium get into milk and thence into the bones of children and ultimately lead to bone cancer? Did it cause mutations and assure deformity to thousands of unborn children?

People worried even more about what use might be made of atomic weapons. Could the United States and Russia agree on a test ban? Talks began in 1958, but there seemed to be no progress. In October 1960 the Chairman of the Atomic Energy Commission accused Russia of failing "to deal seriously with the issues." The United States grew increasingly restive under a voluntary test moratorium that extended through 1959 and 1960. By late 1960 the United States had made extensive plans to resume testing the following year. How far would the weapons race expand? There were already four atomic powers. The night before Sir Charles spoke, participants in a session of the conference predicted that China would soon explode an atomic device.

Scientists had long been concerned about their role both in the development and uses of the weapons. That concern was reflected in a conference symposium held the day before Sir Charles spoke. The topic was, "The Scientist's Role in the Community: New Responsibilities in the Nuclear Age." The participants gave particular attention to the problems of radiation and the scientist's role in educating the public about the extent and hazards of nuclear radiation.

On the evening of the 27th, Sir Charles delivered the main speech at a session held in the Grand Ballroom of the Commodore Hotel. Theodore M. Hesburgh, C.S.C., President of Notre Dame University, and Dr. William O. Baker, Vice-President for Research at Bell Telephone Laboratories, were to deliver prepared comments on the speech as soon as Sir Charles finished.

The speaker was introduced by Dr. Warren Weaver, Vice-President of the Alfred P. Sloan Foundation. After a brief review of the spectacular changes in science during recent times, Dr. Warren said:

> Sir Charles Percy Snow has become recognized as the most authoritative and most moving spokesman for the view that we must rejoin the pieces of our fractured culture, must restore the unity of the world of the mind. Himself a distinguished practitioner in science and in the creative arts, he has made a responsible and reasoned plea that our culture be a unified one.
>
> He speaks to us on a theme which deals with one of the most interesting and difficult aspects of the interrelatedness of science with all the rest of life, an interrelationship which many disregard, which most debate, and which some deny—the moral unneutrality of science.

THE SPEECH[1]

[1] Scientists are the most important occupational group in the world today. At this moment, what they do is of passionate concern to the whole of human society. At this moment, the scientists have little influence on the world effect of what they do. Yet, potentially, they can have great influence. The rest of the world is frightened both of what they do—that is, of the intellectual discoveries of science—and of its effect. The rest of the world, transferring its fears, is frightened of the scientists themselves and tends to think of them as radically different from other men.

[2] As an ex-scientist, if I may call myself so, I know that is nonsense. I have even tried to express in fiction some kinds of scientific temperament and scientific experience. I know well enough that scientists are very much like other men. After all, we are all human, even if some of us don't give that appearance. I think I would be prepared to risk a generalization. The scientists I have known (and because of my official life I have known as

[1] The speech has become well known under the title, "The Moral Un-Neutrality of Science." The text used here is that published in the magazine *Science* (January 27, 1961), a publication of the American Association for the Advancement of Science. The paragraphs are numbered for later reference.

many as anyone in the world) have been in certain respects just perceptibly more morally admirable than most other groups of intelligent men.

[3] That is a sweeping statement, and I mean it only in a statistical sense. But I think there is just a little in it. The moral qualities I admire in scientists are quite simple ones, but I am very suspicious of attempts to over-subtilize moral qualities. It is nearly always a sign, not of true sophistication, but of a specific kind of triviality. So I admire in scientists very simple virtues —like courage, truth-telling, kindness—in which, judged by the low standards which the rest of us manage to achieve, the scientists are not deficient. I think on the whole the scientists make slightly better husbands and fathers than most of us, and I admire them for it. I don't know the figures, and I should be curious to have them sorted out, but I am prepared to bet that the propor-tion of divorces among scientists is slightly but significantly less than that among other groups of similar education and income. I do not apologize for considering that a good thing.

[4] A close friend of mine is a very distinguished scientist. He is also one of the few scientists I know who has lived what we used to call a Bohemian life. When we were both younger, he thought he would undertake historical research to see how many great scientists had been as fond of women as he was. I think he would have felt mildly supported if he could have found a precedent. I remember his reporting to me that his researches hadn't had any luck. The really great scientists seemed to vary from a few neutral characters to a large number who were depressingly "normal." The only gleam of comfort was to be found in the life of Jerome Cardan; and Cardan wasn't anything like enough to outweigh all the others.

[5] So scientists are not much different from other men. They are certainly no worse than other men. But they do differ from other men in one thing. That is the point I started with. Whether they like it or not, what they do is of critical importance for the human race. Intellectually, it has trans-formed the climate of our time. Socially, it will decide whether we live or die, and how we live or die. It holds decisive powers for good and evil. *That* is the situation in which the scientists find themselves. They may not have asked for it, or may only have asked for it in part, but they cannot escape it. They think, many of the more sensitive of them, that they don't deserve to have this weight of responsibility heaved upon them. All they want to do is to get on with their work. I sympathize. But the scientists can't escape the responsibility—any more than they, or the rest of us, can escape the gravity of the moment in which we stand.

[6] There is of course one way to contract out. It has been a favorite way for intellectual persons caught in the midst of water too rough for them.

[7] It consists of the invention of categories—or, if you like, of the division of moral labor. That is, the scientists who want to contract out say, *we* produce the tools. *We* stop there. It is for *you*—the rest of the world, the politicians—to say how the tools are used. The tools may be used for purposes which most of us would regard as bad. If so, we are sorry. But as scientists, that is no concern of ours.

[8] This is the doctrine of the ethical neutrality of science. I can't accept it for an instant. I don't believe any scientist of serious feeling can accept it. It is hard, some think, to find the precise statements which will prove it wrong. Yet we nearly all feel intuitively that the invention of comfortable categories is a moral trap. It is one of the easier methods of letting the conscience rust. It is exactly what the early 19th century economists, such as Ricardo, did in the face of the facts of the first industrial revolution. We wonder now how men, intelligent men, can have been so morally blind. We realize how the exposure of that moral blindness gave Marxism its apocalyptic force. We are now, in the middle of the scientific or second industrial revolution, in something like the same position as Ricardo. Are we going to let our consciences rust? Can we ignore that intimation we nearly all have, that scientists have a unique responsibility? Can we believe it, that science is morally neutral?

[9] To me—it would be dishonest to pretend otherwise—there is only one answer to those questions. Yet I have been brought up in the presence of the same intellectual categories as most western scientists. It would also be dishonest to pretend that I find it easy to construct a rationale which expresses what I now believe. The best I can hope for is to fire a few sighting shots. Perhaps someone who sees more clearly than I can will come along and make a real job of it.

[10] Let me begin with a remark which seems some way off the point. Anyone who has ever worked in any science knows how much esthetic joy he has obtained. That is, in the actual *activity* of science, in the process of making a discovery, however humble it is, one can't help feeling an awareness of beauty. The subjective experience, the esthetic satisfaction, seems exactly the same as the satisfaction one gets from writing a poem or a novel, or composing a piece of music. I don't think anyone has succeeded in distinguishing between them. The literature of scientific discovery is full of this esthetic joy. The very best communication of it that I know comes in G. H. Hardy's book, *A Mathematician's Apology*. Graham Greene once said he thought that, along with Henry James's prefaces, this was the best account of the artistic experience ever written. But one meets the same thing throughout the history of science. Bolyai's great yell of triumph when he saw he could construct a self-consistent, non-Euclidean geometry; Rutherford's revelation to his colleagues that he knew what the atom was like; Darwin's slow, patient, timorous certainty that at last he had got there—all these are voices, different voices, of esthetic ecstasy.

[11] That is not the end of it. The *result* of the activity of science, the actual finished piece of scientific work, has an esthetic value in itself. The judgments passed on it by other scientists will more often than not be expressed in esthetic terms: "That's beautiful!" or "That really is very pretty!" (as the understating English tend to say). The esthetics of scientific constructs, like the esthetics of works of art, are variegated. We think some of the great syntheses, like Newton's, beautiful because of their classical simplicity, but we see a different kind of beauty in the relativistic extension of the wave equation or the interpretation of the structure of deoxyribonucleic acid,

perhaps because of the touch of unexpectedness. Scientists know their kinds of beauty when they see them. They are suspicious, and scientific history shows they have always been right to have been so, when a subject is in an "ugly" state. For example, most physicists feel in their bones that the present bizarre assembly of nuclear particles, as grotesque as a stamp collection, can't possibly be, in the long run, the last word.

[12] We should not restrict the esthetic values to what we call "pure" science. Applied science has its beauties, which are, in my view, identical in nature. The magnetron has been a marvelously useful device, but it was a beautiful device, not exactly apart from its utility but because it did, with such supreme economy, precisely what it was designed to do. Right down in the field of development, the esthetic experience is as real to engineers. When they forget it, when they begin to design heavy-power equipment about twice as heavy as it needs to be, engineers are the first to know that they are lacking virtue.

[13] There is no doubt, then, about the esthetic content of science, both in the activity and the result. But esthetics has no connection with morals, say the categorizers. I don't want to waste time on peripheral issues—but are you quite sure of that? Or is it possible that these categories are inventions to make us evade the human and social conditions in which we now exist? But let us move straight on to something else, which is right in the grain of the activity of science and which is at the same time quintessentially moral. I mean, the desire to find the truth.

[14] By *truth,* I don't intend anything complicated, once again. I am using the word as a scientist uses it. We all know that the philosophical examination of the concept of empirical truth gets us into some curious complexities, but most scientists really don't care. They know that the truth, as they use the word and as the rest of us use it in the language of common speech, is what makes science work. That is good enough for them. On it rests the whole great edifice of modern science. They have a sneaking sympathy for Rutherford, who, when asked to examine the philosophical bases of science, was inclined to reply, as he did to the metaphysician Samuel Alexander: "Well, what have you been talking all your life, Alexander? Just hot air! Nothing but hot air!"

[15] Anyway, truth in their own straightforward sense is what the scientists are trying to find. They want to find what is *there.* Without that desire, there is no science. It is the driving force of the whole activity. It compels the scientist to have an overriding respect for truth, every stretch of the way. That is, if you're going to find what is *there,* you mustn't deceive yourself or anyone else. You mustn't lie to yourself. At the crudest level, you mustn't fake your experiments.

[16] Curiously enough, scientists do try to behave like that. A short time ago, I wrote a novel in which the story hinged on a case of scientific fraud. But I made one of my characters, who was himself a very good scientist, say that, considering the opportunities and temptations, it is astonishing how few such cases there are. We have all heard of perhaps half a dozen open and notorious ones, which are on the record for anyone to read—ranging

from the "discovery" of the L radiation to the singular episode of the Piltdown man.

[17] We have all, if we have lived any time in the scientific world, heard private talk of something like another dozen cases which for various reasons are not yet public property. In some cases, we know the motives for the cheating—sometimes, but not always, sheer personal advantage, such as getting money or a job. But not always. A special kind of vanity has led more than one man into scientific faking. At a lower level of research, there are presumably some more cases. There must have been occasional Ph.D. students who scraped by with the help of a bit of fraud.

[18] But the total number of all these men is vanishingly small by the side of the total number of scientists. Incidentally, the effect on science of such frauds is also vanishingly small. Science is a self-correcting system. That is, no fraud (or honest mistake) is going to stay undetected for long. There is no need for an extrinsic scientific criticism, because criticism is inherent in the process itself. So that all that a fraud can do is waste the time of the scientists who have to clear it up.

[19] The remarkable thing is not the handful of scientists who deviate from the search for truth but the overwhelming numbers who keep to it. That is a demonstration, absolutely clear for anyone to see, of moral behavior on a very large scale.

[20] We take it for granted. Yet it is very important. It differentiates science in its widest sense (which includes scholarship) from all other intellectual activities. There is a built-in moral component right in the core of the scientific activity itself. The desire to find the truth is itself a moral impulse, or at least contains a moral impulse. The way in which a scientist tries to find the truth imposes on him a constant moral discipline. We say a scientific conclusion—such as the contradiction of parity by Lee and Yang— is "true" in the limited sense of scientific truth, just as we say that it is "beautiful" according to the criteria of scientific esthetics. We also know that to reach this conclusion took a set of actions which would have been useless without the moral nature. That is, all through the marvelous experiments of Wu and her colleagues, there was the constant moral exercise of seeking and telling the truth. To scientists, who are brought up in this climate, this seems as natural as breathing. Yet it is a wonderful thing. Even if the scientific activity contained only this one moral component, that alone would be enough to let us say that it was morally un-neutral.

[21] But is this the only moral component? All scientists would agree about the beauty and the truth. In the western world, they wouldn't agree on much more. Some will feel with me in what I am going to say. Some will not. That doesn't affect me much, except that I am worried by the growth of an attitude I think very dangerous, a kind of technological conformity disguised as cynicism. I shall say a little more about that later. As for disagreement, G. H. Hardy used to comment that a serious man ought not to waste his time stating a majority opinion—there are plenty of others to do that. That was the voice of classical scientific nonconformity. I wish that we heard it more often.

[22]   Let me cite some grounds for hope. Any of us who were working in science before 1933 can remember what the atmosphere was like. It is a terrible bore when aging men in their fifties speak about the charms of their youth. Yet I am going to irritate you—just as Talleyrand irritated his juniors —by saying that unless one was on the scene before 1933, one hasn't known the sweetness of the scientific life. The scientific world of the twenties was as near to being a full-fledged international community as we are likely to get. Don't think I'm saying that the men involved were superhuman or free from the ordinary frailties. That wouldn't come well from me, who have spent a fraction of my writing life pointing out that scientists are, first and foremost, men. But the atmosphere of the twenties in science was filled with an air of benevolence and magnanimity which transcended the people who lived in it.

[23]   Anyone who ever spent a week in Cambridge or Göttingen or Copenhagen felt it all round him. Rutherford had very human faults, but he was a great man with abounding human generosity. For him the world of science was a world that lived on a plane above the nation-state, and lived there with joy. That was at least as true of those two other great men, Niels Bohr and Franck, and some of that spirit rubbed off on to the pupils round them. The same was true of the Roman school of physics.

[24]   The personal links within this international world were very close. It is worth remembering that Peter Kapitza, who was a loyal Soviet citizen, honored my country by working in Rutherford's laboratory for many years. He became a fellow of the Royal Society, a fellow of Trinity College, Cambridge, and the founder and kingpin of the best physics club Cambridge has known. He never gave up his Soviet citizenship and is now director of the Institute of Physical Problems in Moscow. Through him a generation of English scientists came to have personal knowledge of their Russian colleagues. These exchanges were then, and have remained, more valuable than all the diplomatic exchanges ever invented.

[25]   The Kapitza phenomenon couldn't take place now. I hope to live to see the day when a young Kapitza can once more work for 16 years in Berkeley or Cambridge and then go back to an eminent place in his own country. When that can happen, we are all right. But after the idyllic years of world science, we passed into a tempest of history, and, by an unfortunate coincidence, we passed into a technological tempest too.

[26]   The discovery of atomic fission broke up the world of international physics. "This has killed a beautiful subject," said Mark Oliphant, the father figure of Australian physics, in 1945, after the bombs had dropped. In intellectual terms, he has not turned out to be right. In spiritual and moral terms, I sometimes think he has.

[27]   A good deal of the international community of science remains in other fields—in great areas of biology, for example. Many biologists are feeling the identical liberation, the identical joy at taking part in a magnanimous enterprise, that physicists felt in the twenties. It is more than likely that the moral and intellectual leadership of science will pass to biologists, and it is

among them that we shall find the Rutherfords, Bohrs, and Francks of the next generation.

[28] Physicists have had a bitterer task. With the discovery of fission, and with some technical breakthroughs in electronics, physicists became, almost overnight, the most important military resource a nation-state could call on. A large number of physicists became soldiers not in uniform. So they have remained, in the advanced societies, ever since.

[29] It is very difficult to see what else they could have done. All this began in the Hitler war. Most scientists thought then that Nazism was as near absolute evil as a human society can manage. I myself thought so. I still think so, without qualification. That being so, Nazism had to be fought, and since the Nazis might make fission bombs—which we thought possible until 1944, and which was a continual nightmare if one was remotely in the know— well, then, we had to make them too. Unless one was an unlimited pacifist, there was nothing else to do. And unlimited pacifism is a position which most of us cannot sustain.

[30] Therefore I respect, and to a large extent share, the moral attitudes of those scientists who devoted themselves to making the bomb. But the trouble is, when you get onto any kind of moral escalator, to know whether you're ever going to be able to get off. When scientists became soldiers they gave up something, so imperceptibly that they didn't realize it, of the full scientific life. Not intellectually. I see no evidence that scientific work on weapons of maximum destruction has been in any intellectual respect different from other scientific work. But there is a moral difference.

[31] It may be—scientists who are better men than I am often take this attitude, and I have tried to represent it faithfully in one of my books— that this is a moral price which, in certain circumstances, has to be paid. Nevertheless, it is no good pretending that there is not a moral price. Soldiers have to obey. That is the foundation of their morality. It is not the foundation of the scientific morality. Scientists have to question and if necessary to rebel. I don't want to be misunderstood. I am no anarchist. I am not suggesting that loyalty is not a prime virtue. I am not saying that all rebellion is good. But I am saying that loyalty can easily turn into conformity, and that conformity can often be a cloak for the timid and self-seeking. So can obedience, carried to the limit. When you think of the long and gloomy history of man, you will find that far more, and far more hideous, crimes have been committed in the name of obedience than have ever been committed in the name of rebellion. If you doubt that, read William Shirer's *Rise and Fall of the Third Reich*. The German officer corps were brought up in the most rigorous code of obedience. To them, no more honorable and God-fearing body of men could conceivably exist. Yet in the name of obedience, they were party to, and assisted in, the most wicked large-scale actions in the history of the world.

[32] Scientists must not go that way. Yet the duty to question is not much of a support when you are living in the middle of an organized society. I speak with feeling here. I was an official for twenty years. I went

into official life at the beginning of the war, for the reasons that prompted my scientific friends to begin to make weapons. I stayed in that life until a year ago, for the same reason that made my scientific friends turn into civilian soldiers. The official's life in England is not quite so disciplined as a soldier's, but it is very nearly so. I think I know the virtues, which are very great, of the men who live that disciplined life. I also know what for me was the moral trap. I, too, had got onto an escalator. I can put the result in a sentence: I was coming to hide behind the institution; I was losing the power to say no.

[33] Only a very bold man, when he is a member of an organized society, can keep the power to say no. I tell you that, not being a very bold man, or one who finds it congenial to stand alone, away from his colleagues. We can't expect many scientists to do it. Is there any tougher ground for them to stand on? I suggest to you that there is. I believe that there is a spring of moral action in the scientific activity which is at least as strong as the search for truth. The name of this spring is *knowledge*. Scientists *know* certain things in a fashion more immediate and more certain than those who don't comprehend what science is. Unless we are abnormally weak or abnormally wicked men, this knowledge is bound to shape our actions. Most of us are timid, but to an extent, knowledge gives us guts. Perhaps it can give us guts strong enough for the jobs in hand.

[34] I had better take the most obvious example. All physical scientists *know* that it is relatively easy to make plutonium. We know this, not as a journalistic fact at second hand, but as a fact in our own experience. We can work out the number of scientific and engineering personnel needed for a nation-state to equip itself with fission and fusion bombs. We *know* that, for a dozen or more states, it will only take perhaps six years, perhaps less. Even the best informed of us always exaggerate these periods.

[35] This we know, with the certainty of—what shall I call it?—engineering truth. We also—most of us—are familiar with statistics and the nature of odds. We know, with the certainty of statistical truth, that if enough of these weapons are made, by enough different states, some of them are going to blow up, through accident, or folly, or madness—the motives don't matter. What does matter is the nature of the statistical fact.

[36] All this we *know*. We know it in a more direct sense than any politician because it comes from our direct experience. It is part of our minds. Are we going to let it happen?

[37] All this we *know*. It throws upon scientists a direct and personal responsibility. It is not enough to say that scientists have a responsibility as citizens. They have a much greater one than that, and one different in kind. For scientists have a moral imperative to say what they know. It is going to make them unpopular in their own nation-states. It may do worse than make them unpopular. That doesn't matter. Or at least, it does matter to you and me, but it must not count in the face of the risks.

[38] For we genuinely know the risks. We are faced with an either-or, and we haven't much time. The *either* is acceptance of a restriction of nuclear

armaments. This is going to begin, just as a token, with an agreement on the stopping of nuclear tests. The United States is not going to get the 99.9-percent "security" that it has been asking for. This is unobtainable, though there are other bargains that the United States could probably secure. I am not going to conceal from you that this course involves certain risks. They are quite obvious, and no honest man is going to blink them. That is the *either.* The *or* is not a risk but a certainty. It is this. There is no agreement on tests. The nuclear arms race between the United States and the USSR not only continues but accelerates. Other countries join in. Within, at the most, six years, China and several other states have a stock of nuclear bombs. Within, at the most, ten years, some of those bombs are going off. I am saying this as responsibly as I can. *That* is the certainty. On the one side, therefore, we have a finite risk. On the other side we have a certainty of disaster. Between a risk and a certainty, a sane man does not hesitate.

[39] It is the plain duty of scientists to explain this either-or. It is a duty which seems to me to come from the moral nature of the scientific activity itself.

[40] The same duty, though in a much more pleasant form, arises with respect to the benevolent powers of science. For scientists know, and again with the certainty of scientific knowledge, that we possess every scientific fact we need to transform the physical life of half the world. And transform it within the span of people now living. I mean, we have all the resources to help half the world live as long as we do and eat enough. All that is missing is the will. We *know* that. Just as we know that you in the United States, and to a slightly lesser extent we in the United Kingdom, have been almost unimaginably lucky. We are sitting like people in a smart and cozy restaurant and we are eating comfortably, looking out of the window into the streets. Down on the pavement are people who are looking up at us, people who by chance have different colored skins from ours, and are rather hungry. Do you wonder that they don't like us all that much? Do you wonder that we sometimes feel ashamed of ourselves, as we look out through that plate glass?

[41] Well, it is within our power to get started on that problem. We are morally impelled to. We all know that, if the human species does solve that one, there will be consequences which are themselves problems. For instance, the population of the world will become embarrassingly large. But that is another challenge. There are going to be challenges to our intelligence and to our moral nature as long as man remains man. After all, a challenge is not, as the word is coming to be used, an excuse for slinking off and doing nothing. A challenge is something to be picked up.

[42] For all these reasons, I believe the world community of scientists has a final responsibility upon it—a greater responsibility than is pressing on any other body of men. I do not pretend to know how they will bear this responsibility. These may be famous last words, but I have an inextinguishable hope. For, as I have said, there is no doubt that the scientific activity is both beautiful and truthful. I cannot prove it, but I believe that, simply

because scientists cannot escape their own knowledge, they also won't be able to avoid showing themselves disposed to good.

THE SUBJECT

The speech illustrates the typical area of persuasion. Persuasion deals with the future and, because the future cannot be predicted, with probabilities. The persuasive speaker assumes that man can at least to some extent control his future; he also assumes that man understands himself and the forces around him well enough to make reasonably accurate predictions of what will happen. This is what Snow sought to establish: the high probability that certain things would happen and that man could control these events if he would but make sufficient effort.

The subject could hardly have been more appropriate to either the speaker or audience: a scientist (or ex-scientist, as Snow would have it) talking to scientists about an urgent problem in science.

While the subject was not a new one, it was timely—and particularly if Snow correctly states that scientists know with the certainty of statistical truth that bombs will explode unless the arms race is halted.

DEVELOPMENT OF ARGUMENTS

In developing his arguments—determining what elements should be included, what order they should be taken up and the form of their presentation—a speaker seeks to give force to truth as he sees it, to demonstrate the probability of that truth to his listeners so that they will be brought to agreement with him; in other words, he seeks to give psychological force to reason.

The purpose of this section is to see how Snow met that problem. The analysis will be made easier if his arguments are first summarized.

Summary of the Arguments

The first paragraph hints at Snow's point: "At this moment, the scientists have little influence on the world effect of what they do. Yet, potentially, they can have great influence." The last sentence of the speech states the full implication of his arguments: "I cannot prove it, but I believe that, simply because scientists cannot escape their own knowledge, they also won't be able to avoid showing themselves disposed to good."

The route by which Snow moved from the idea that scientists "can have great influence" to the point that they "won't be able to avoid" exerting influence seems complex, indeed. The sequence is roughly this (the numbers refer to the paragraphs of the speech in which the points are made):

[1–4] Scientists as individuals are not different from other men (they have the same virtues), except that what scientists do is of "critical importance for the human race."

[5–8] They have a responsibility that they cannot escape by the invention of moral categories. The invention of comfortable categories "is the doctrine of the ethical neutrality of science." Categorizing "is a moral trap. It is one of the easier methods of letting the conscience rust," as happened in the nineteenth century.

[9] We cannot accept the concept that science is morally neutral. To construct a rationale to prove that it is not neutral will be difficult, however. "The best I can hope for is to fire a few sighting shots."

[10–13] Science has esthetic joy (beauty) in its activity, constructs, and engineering applications. Attempts to separate esthetics from morals may be attempts to "make us evade the human and social conditions in which we now exist."

[14–19] Science also has a moral aspect in the search for truth, which has been respected except for a "vanishingly small" number of scientists. Scientists thus illustrate "moral behavior on a very large scale."

[20] "The desire to find the truth is itself a moral impulse, or at least contains a moral impulse." Science is morally un-neutral.

[21–25] The scientific world community of former times existed with an air of benevolence above the nation-state. The movement of scientists within that community was "more valuable than all the diplomatic exchanges ever invented."

[26–32] "Atomic fission broke up the world of international physics." The moral leadership in science will probably now pass to biologists, for with the discovery of atomic fission, physicists became a military resource. Although there was little else they could do, they have paid a moral price. "Soldiers have to obey," while "scientists have to question and if necessary to rebel." Loyalty and obedience can turn into conformity and "a cloak for the timid."

[33] The duty to question needs support. "There is a spring of moral action in the scientific activity which is at least as strong as the search for truth": *knowledge.* "Most of us are timid, but to an extent, knowledge gives us guts."

[34–39] For example, scientists *know* the risks involved in a continued expansion of the nuclear arms race; "we are faced with an either-or" situation. On one side, there is some risk if the race is restricted; on the other, there is a certainty of disaster if bombs continue to be made. "It is the plain duty of scientists to explain this either-or."

[40–41] As another example, scientists *know* that "we possess every scientific fact we need to transform the physical life of half the world." We also know, however, that if we solve that problem, it will lead to others, such as overpopulation. But that should be regarded as a challenge.

[42] Thus, "the world community of scientists has a final responsibility upon it." Because "the scientific activity is both beautiful and truthful," and

because scientists *know,* they "won't be able to avoid showing themselves disposed to good."

Interpretation I

The speech is clearly intended to be a reasonable argument addressed to reasonable men. The essential elements in the argumentative structure of the speech are stated in the conclusion [42]. They are: (1) the "final responsibility of scientists" (earlier referred to as the duty to speak out on uses made of scientific discoveries), (2) the "beautiful and truthful" nature of science, (3) the force of knowledge, and (4) the "showing themselves [scientists] disposed to do good" (in other places specified as the act of speaking out).

The elements are related in this fashion: You must speak out concerning the uses made of scientific discovery because it is your duty as a scientist to tell the truth. That it is your duty devolves from the morality (the beauty and truth) of science. Your knowledge will compel you to do your duty.

The relation and functions of the elements can be better understood if they are placed in the paradigm described in Chapters 4 and 5.

Proposition: You must speak out about the uses made of scientific discoveries [because]

Reason: It is your duty as a scientist to tell the truth.

How are the proposition and reason related? By classification. The proposition is one of the things a scientist does if he assumes his duty to tell the truth.

How does one know that a scientist has that duty? Or, in terms of the paradigm, what is the proof of the statement of "fact" contained in the reason? The nature of scientific activity (its beauty and the moral impulse of truth) compel a scientist to be truthful.

Why should a scientist be concerned with doing his duty? Or, in terms of the paradigm, what values underlie the reason and give it force? The word *duty* was deliberately selected, and doubtless because Snow expected his audience to have a positive attitude toward the concept. He did not rely solely on that attitude, however. The argument is extended to show the significance of a failure to assume the duty in one area. Here is where the final element of the argumentative structure is brought in. The scientist *knows* the significance of failure to speak out on atomic weapons; what he knows will force him to assume his duty.

The two illustrations of areas in which scientists should speak out perform subtle but significantly different functions in the argumentative structure of the speech. Snow introduced his discussion of atomic weapons development by saying that he was going to "take the most obvious example" of his point. Thus, one might regard that part of the speech as an application of the proposition "you must speak out." Similarly, the discussion of science's benevolent powers may be regarded as an application of the proposition.

As suggested above, however, the atomic weapons illustration serves an additional function. It gives force to the reason why one should do his duty. The argument might be paraphrased in this way: "For example, you must do your duty and speak out about the military applications of your discoveries. You must do your duty in this area, for if you do not, you will contribute to the likelihood that atomic weapons will explode."

The second illustration, on the other hand, does not add force to the reason why one should speak out. Rather, it detracts from the force adhering to a concept of duty, for, as Snow mentioned, if scientists do speak out about the benevolent applications of scientific knowledge, new problems will be created. This admission led Snow to bolster the force adhering to a concept of duty by talking of the newly created problems as a *challenge*.

The differing functions of the illustrations can be diagramed as follows:

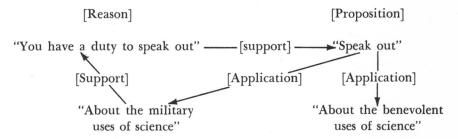

[Reason]   [Proposition]

"You have a duty to speak out" ——— [support] ———➤ "Speak out"

[Support]   [Application]   [Application]

"About the military   "About the benevolent
uses of science"   uses of science"

Because the one illustration adds support to the reason offered as justification for insisting that a scientist should speak out and the other detracts from that reason, the order in which the illustrations were presented seems nearly inevitable. The more firmly the proposition was established, the better the chance that it would be applied in the second instance.

Essentially, then, this is a one-reason speech: scientists must speak out because it is their duty to do so.

Three other arguments appear in the speech, and at first glance they seem unrelated to the main development. They perform vital functions.

The first of these is the long, initial point in the development: that scientists as individuals are moral [1–4]. This point prevents the speech from resting on an assumption that scientists are sufficiently moral to be able to meet the moral demands of science. Snow obviously feared he could not safely assume agreement on the point. He said, "the rest of the world, transferring its fears, is frightened of the scientists themselves and tends to think of them as radically different from other men." This argument may have been developed in part for the benefit of nonscientists who may be listening or who may later read the speech.

Even with that assumption removed, another one of importance still remains: "that a moral man will do what the morality of his occupation requires." In the argument against "contracting out," Snow seeks to show why scientists must do what the morality of science demands that they do [5–8]. He thus eliminated the assumption and at the same time prevented his listeners from escaping his line of reasoning.

The third point that seems to be outside the main development appears immediately after Snow had proved that science is morally un-neutral. The forward motion of the speech seems to stop while he reviews the science of the twenties and speaks of loyalty and obedience, which "can often be a cloak for the timid and self-seeking" [27–32]. The argument closed a gap that a listener might have found. Without the development of that argument, a listener could have thought, "All well and good; but we must, after all, recognize that our first responsibility is to our nation."

The speech assumes that listeners will grant many things: that atomic bombs should not explode, that the world can become overpopulated and that it should not, and that people should not go hungry. Snow made few assumptions in the reasoning, however. He sought to make his line of argument complete.

The question now becomes, why might that particular arrangement have been selected?

LOGICAL VALIDITY

The order of development serves well the logic of the argument. Two important basic premises are established: scientists are moral and scientists must fulfill whatever moral obligations are imposed on them by their activity. Then the nature and basis of the obligation imposed by the scientific activity are explained. The point that loyalty and obedience do not release one from the obligation is next developed. And, finally, the significance of the obligation is illustrated by applying it in two instances.

Certainly there is nothing illogical about the pattern. One might almost say that this leading-into development is the most reasonable of all from the standpoint of his material.

PSYCHOLOGICAL VALIDITY

The handling of the material may seem to be more open to criticism on the grounds that it was too much governed by the logic of the material and too little by concern for the audience. If Snow gave any thought to the difficulties an audience might have in following his speech, would he not have outlined his development at the beginning, and thus aided his listeners in following the line of argument? Doubtless, a clear indication of direction would have helped many listeners (and readers) of the speech to follow the progression of ideas.

Why did Snow not begin with such a concession to the "weakness of his hearers"? He might have assumed that his listeners were sufficiently familiar with a complex line of argument not to need such assistance. A more compelling reason, however, would seem to derive from the startling and highly controversial nature of one of the examples he gave: speaking out on the control of nuclear arms.

Snow must have anticipated that most attention and controversy would be directed toward his point on weapons control. If the newspaper reports of the speech (including reports of what other scientists said) are indicative, many people lost sight of the rationale and assumed that the discussion of atomic weapons was the principal point of the speech rather than just an illustration. And, indeed, that may be the correct interpretation. The speech does not make clear whether Snow actually attached more significance to the rationale or the examples of the rationale in operation. One suspects, however, that Snow would not have bothered to construct the rationale had he not believed that it needed urgent application. In other words, perhaps he saw the need for speaking out first and then developed the rationale to provide a basis for meeting the need.

Whatever the significance of the illustration, had that highly controversial aspect of the argument been introduced early in the speech, many of his listeners would have said, "that point cannot be proved," and would have dismissed Snow and his speech at the start.

Snow handled this problem by delaying the startling conclusion until late in the argument. This delay gave him two advantages in developing his speech.

First, the delay enabled him to lead listeners gradually through the line of argument until eventually they had to face his striking conclusion. Each time a listener might think he saw an avenue of escape, Snow paused to shut off the avenue. An early point in the speech, for example, was that scientists have a moral responsibility. Snow suspected some people would try to escape the responsibility by moral categorizing. He paused to show the untenability of such categorizing. He then proceeded to develop the rationale that showed the nature of the moral obligation. After the development of the point, he stopped to ensure that no one escaped by pleading loyalty and obedience.

Thus, by advancing positive arguments and by stopping to close up openings as he proceeded, Snow sought to move his listeners inexorably to his startling conclusion.

Second, to place the most controversial part of the speech near the end enabled Snow to introduce the controversial points in climactic order, thus postponing as long as possible the moment when a listener might find that he had to disagree. This invoked the "yes-response" technique discussed in Chapter 5. Additionally, it meant that even though a listener might not accept the whole argument, he might be carried along for some distance at least. Finally, the climax in controversy helped to hold audience interest.

Here is how the climax was built: The first point, that scientists are at least as moral as other people [1–4], probably invoked no controversy. An audience made up of scientists and people sympathetic to science could be expected to agree enthusiastically with that conclusion. The second point, that scientists must not contract out through a belief in the neutrality of science [5–8], is more controversial than the first. The next series of arguments deals with the moral obligations imposed by science [10–20]. Although Snow said that "all scientists would agree about the beauty and truth" [21], his earlier concern with moral categorizers indicates that he assumed there would be opposition to his argument. He next argued that the moral imperative of science compelled scientists to question and rebel [21–32]. That point is most assuredly controversial. He then moved to the most controversial point of all—that scientists must speak out because they *know* that atomic bombs will explode if the arms race is not halted [34–39]. That is the high point of the climax. The final point, that the scientist has a duty "in a more pleasant form" [40–41], provides a relief from the climactic progression.

The pattern may be diagramed as in figure 16.1:

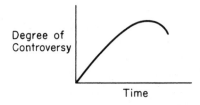

Not even Snow's best novel could better illustrate the use of climax to hold attention and interest. Here the climax served the even more important persuasive purposes.

Interpretation II

The first interpretation views the speech as an intellectual argument addressed to logical men who act, or at least think they act, for logical reasons.

The speech can, however, be viewed from a quite different position. It can be viewed as a plea for virtue addressed to each individual scientist in the audience.

RELEVANT VIRTUES

Although the speech is about morality in a broad sense, it is concerned principally with morality as revealed by manifestations of several virtues.

Snow makes very clear that he wants scientists to tell the truth. A scientist must, then, possess and manifest the virtue *truthfulness*. He must be truthful about the way discoveries of science are used in two specific areas.

First, the scientist must be truthful about atomic-weapons development. However, truth-telling about atomic weapons would, as Snow said, "make them [scientists] unpopular in their own nation-states. It may do worse than make them unpopular" [37]. Therefore, if a scientist is to speak out on weapons control, truthfulness must be combined with the virtue *courage*.

Second, the scientist must be truthful about "the benevolent powers of science," which could "transform the physical life of half the world."

> We are sitting like people in a smart and cozy restaurant and we are eating comfortably, looking out of the window into the streets. Down on the pavement are people looking up at us, people who by chance have different colored skins from ours, and are rather hungry [40].

But effective use of the benevolent potential in science would lead to new problems. Therefore, if a scientist is to speak out concerning benevolent uses of science, truthfulness must be combined with the virtue *kindness*.

THE PLEA FOR VIRTUE

Forget for the moment Snow's rationale. Forget the various reasons and the way they were organized in the speech. Look now at the speech from the standpoint of an individual scientist who is in the audience. Before he hears the speech, he has no way of knowing how the topic will be developed. The speech begins:

"Scientists are the most important occupational group in the world today." What they do is of "passionate concern" to all of society. Non-scientists, transferring their fear of science, now also fear scientists. The transfer is unwarranted, for scientists are not much different from other men.

> The moral qualities I admire in scientists are quite simple ones, but I am very suspicious of attempts to oversubtilize moral qualities. It is nearly always a sign, not of true sophistication, but of a specific kind of triviality. So I admire in scientists very simple virtues—like courage, truth-telling, kindness—in which, judged by the low standards the rest of us manage to achieve, the scientists are not deficient [3].

A scientist in the audience would have more likely noticed than would a reader the specific virtues mentioned. The scientist, after all, was being

406 - PART TWO

talked about. A scientist would perhaps have acknowledged that he possessed the three virtues mentioned, although he would have no reason to suspect that he would be called upon to demonstrate his possession of them. He probably would have noted, too, that they were mentioned in conjunction with the statement about oversubtilizing moral qualities.

You should now reread the section on "contracting out" [6–8]. Note that it seems to be a plea for virtue (that is, "are we going to let our consciences rust?") as much as it seems to be a part of an argument to construct a rationale. It gives a strong implication that the speech is to be a plea for virtue.

Note, too, that the section emphasizes the joy to be found in scientific work—including the joy in applying scientific discoveries—as much as it emphasizes the beauty in science. The section closes with a warning against moral categorizing: "Is it possible that these categories are inventions to make us evade the human and social conditions in which we now exist?" [13]. Might Snow have intended that the joy and beauty found in applying scientific discoveries to engineering problems can also be found in applying them to human and social problems?

If you now reread the section that establishes that concern for truth is an integral part of scientific activity [14–20], and if you search for its impact on a listener rather than for its logic, you will find an emphatic plea that scientists must continue, as they have in the past, to manifest the virtue *truthfulness*.

Turn next to the section of the speech that describes science in an earlier period [22–25]. Notice that when you have the several specific virtues in mind, the section takes on meaning beyond providing a description of recent changes in science and scientists. The science described there was permeated with kindness and joy. "The atmosphere of the twenties in science was filled with an air of benevolence and magnanimity" [22]. Rutherford "was a great man with abounding human generosity. For him the world of science was a world that lived there with joy. That was at least as true of those two other great men, Niels Bohr and Franck" [23]. The discussion of the Kapitza phenomenon suggests that the speaker was obviously concerned that science live above the nation-state on military matters. But the discussion of magnanimity and joy has perhaps even greater applicability to the benevolent uses of science. Implicit in the whole section is a plea for a return to the benevolence, generosity, and kindness of that great period in science.

Now reread the section on loyalty and obedience [28–32]. In the first interpretation that section was seen as an argument that loyalty and obedience cannot be used to justify an escape from responsibility. When read with a recollection that Snow is concerned with courage, the section becomes also an eloquent plea that scientists be courageous.

Which of the two interpretations made here did Snow intend? The question may be pointless. There is no reason to have to choose between them, for they are not in conflict. Snow may, however, have wished to place greater emphasis on the construction of the rationale than on the plea for virtue. The plea was kept subordinate by at least two techniques.

First, he kept the plea subordinate by using synonyms for the virtues after he named them early in the speech. The closest he came to using again the word "truth-telling" was when he spoke of "the constant moral exercise of seeking and telling the truth" [20]. He used the word "kindness" only once in the entire speech, although he talked of "benevolence" and "magnanimity." Nor does the word "courage" recur in the speech. When Snow stressed the impulse that knowledge gives to courage he said, "Most of us are timid, but to an extent, knowledge gives us guts. Perhaps it can give us guts enough for the job in hand" [33]. Thus, the plea was not emphasized through internal summaries or repetition, whereas the rationale was.

Second, the conclusion was designed to stress the development of the rationale rather than the plea for virtue. It is in a low key, more appropriate to a reasoned discussion than a plea for virtue. Further, it is a summary of the specific items developed in the rationale rather than a listing of the virtues scientists must possess and manifest.

Why might Snow have written a speech that could be interpreted in two ways? First, it should be recognized that the approach to analysis used here emphasizes the separateness of the points of view, whereas they are actually carefully integrated in the speech. A listener probably would have been carried along by both points of view as the speech progressed.

A strong justification for deliberately combining the approaches derives from the way people think and act. Logical argument may help a man to demonstrate truthfulness, courage and kindness. He may even require that his manifestations of those virtues be supported by sound reason. Fundamentally, however, people are not impelled through reason alone to be courageous, truthful, and kind.

PROOF OF THE ARGUMENTS

Snow's speech illustrates how proof of a point derives from the material, the audience, and the speaker. From the material comes those facts and statements about facts that provide the substance for reasoning; from the audience comes attitudes, values, and knowledge about the subject that serve as starting and end points of the reasoning; from the speaker comes the force of credibility.

How these three sources of proof may be combined can be seen by examining several of the points in Snow's speech.

Scientists are Moral [1-4]

In the first paragraph of the speech, Snow said:

> The rest of the world is frightened both of what they [scientists] do—that is, of the intellectual discoveries of science—and of its effects. The rest of the world, transferring its fears, is frightened of the scientists themselves and tends to think of them as radically different from other men.

The statement concerns attitudes toward scientists as a group. Those people who transfer their fears have arrived at a generalization that scientists are radically different from other men.

Snow wished to prove that the generalization is unsound. Although the generalization could be weakened by showing that some or most scientists are like other men, the error in opinion could most emphatically be demonstrated by proving that the reverse generalization is true; that is, that scientists *are* like other men. Snow used that approach. When he ended discussion of the point he stated this generalization: "so scientists are not much different from other men. They are certainly no worse than other men."

The first item in the proof is Snow's statement of his own belief: "As an ex-scientist, if I may call myself so, I know that [the statement that scientists are radically different] is nonsense." The introductory clause is important. It reminded the audience that there was reason to respect the speaker's opinion.

That item of proof is expanded a few moments later: "The scientists I have known (and because of my official life I have known as many as anyone in the world) have been in certain respects just perceptibly more morally admirable than most other groups of intelligent men." Snow there gives an additional basis for his competence to have an opinion: not only has he been a scientist himself, but he has known "as many as anyone in the world."

The second major item in the proof is based directly on an analysis of the objects covered in the generalizations—scientists. Snow tells how a friend of his sought to discover whether many great scientists had been fond of women. The investigation was specifically directed toward showing that scientists are not moral; so it was a search for negative instances to the generalization that Snow wished to prove. Together the two items establish a generalization and then check it by a search for exceptions. (Incidentally, the generalization that most scientists are truthful in their scientific activities [16-18] illustrates a much fuller use of a search for negative instances as a way to prove a generalization.)

The third type of proof depended on the knowledge and attitudes of the audience. Snow explained what evidence he thought provided proof that scientists are as moral as other men:

> I think on the whole the scientists make slightly better husbands and fathers than most of us, . . . I don't know the figures, . . . but I am prepared to bet that the proportion of divorces among scientists is slightly but significantly less than that among other groups of similar education and income.

While Snow probably intended those comments to serve as amplification of his point, to the extent that his auditors agreed already with the generalization, they would doubtless support it from their own knowledge of scientists as husbands and fathers.

Thus this relatively simple proof depended on the material, the audience, and the speaker.

Moral Categorizing is Undesirable [6–8]

To show that moral categorizing is undesirable requires proofs quite different from those used in the other parts of the speech. Most of Snow's statements could be proved through a demonstration of truth in the sense that he used the term in the speech: "what is *there*." The morality of scientists, as measured in divorce rate and so on, "is *there*." So is the honesty of scientists as determined by whether they fake evidence or perpetuate hoaxes. But one does not prove that moral categorizing is undesirable by considering whether or not it exists. This question, then, is one of judgment rather than what "is there."

Snow's first approach to the argument is simply to make clear his own judgment concerning moral categorizing. In what seemed an incidental comment in an earlier point, he said: "I am very suspicious of attempts to oversubtilize moral qualities. It is nearly always a sign, not of true sophistication, but of a specific kind of triviality" [3]. Whether or not Snow intended that comment as a forecast of his position, it served to prepare his listeners for the attack on division of moral labor that was to come.

The attack on moral categorizing and division of moral labor is made in part through associating them by metaphor with objects toward which his audience would have negative attitudes. Snow speaks of the division of moral labor as "a favorite way for intellectual persons caught in the midst of water too rough for them" [6]. He calls the invention of moral categories "a trap," and a way "of letting the conscience rust."

The negative-association approach is both followed and accompanied by an analogy to suggest the consequences of contracting out. Snow compares the first industrial revolution with "the scientific or second industrial revolution." He implies that a refusal to face facts will have consequences as serious as those that resulted from the refusal of the nineteenth century economists to face facts. "The exposure of that moral blindness gave Marxism its apocalyptic force."

The final element in the proof is really no proof at all. Rather, it is a shift of the burden of proof and an insinuation about the motives of the categorizers:

> But esthetics has no connection with morals, say the categorizers. I don't want to waste time on peripheral issues—but are you quite sure of that? Or is it possible that these categories are inventions to make us evade the human and social conditions in which we now exist?

The substantial argument against moral categorizing came in the rest of the speech, even though the categorizers were not mentioned again. If a scientist was moved to be truthful, courageous and kind, he could not still be a moral categorizer.

The handling of the attack seems ill-designed to persuade a categorizer to change his ways, unless he should feel unable to withstand Snow's scorn and contempt. The method could be expected to elicit a response from those under attack. In his comments on the speech, Hesburgh read to the audience a lesson about scientists being too quick to dismiss philosophical distinctions, particularly those included in ethics and moral philosophy. Perhaps annoyance with the method of proof caused Hesburgh to miss the emphasis Snow placed on kindness, which is an aspect of "the good"—the precise area of concern to ethics and moral philosophy.

Either We Control Atomic Weapons Or [34–39]

As the speech approached its climax, Snow moved to what he called "the most obvious example" of the scientist's moral compulsion to speak out. The illustration was the either-or alternatives concerning the development of nuclear weapons.

A non-scientist may believe that the speaker sought to prove that bombs will go off. Actually, however, Snow's point was that his audience of scientists already *knew* that bombs will explode. He used the either-or condition of atomic weapon's development as an illustration that what they *knew* would compel them to speak out.

How does one prove to a person that he already knows something? Simply to assert that he knows may give little force to the point. Further, if that which is supposedly known is complex, the person may not realize that he knows all that is encompassed within it. Thus, the proof or illustration must be expanded beyond an assertion that he knows.

There is a limit beyond which the elaboration cannot go, however, without being self-defeating. Suppose someone set out to prove that you *already know* how to find the square root of 2304. Could he lead you through the whole process, and then say, "there, didn't you know that all along?" But *did* you know if he had to take you through the whole process? And *did* he really believe that you knew if he reminded you by reviewing all the steps? It is doubtful that the answer could be "yes" to either question.

It was imperative that Snow not put his listeners in a position of themselves doubting that they knew or himself in a position of seeming to doubt that they knew.

His approach was to remind the audience of the method by which a proof that bombs will explode might be developed. To prove that bombs would explode would require a three-part proof: (1) that enough nations have the capacity in resources and technical ability to produce a substantial number of bombs, (2) that those nations actually will build the bombs, and (3) that statistical analysis establishes that some bombs will explode.

Instead of developing a full proof, Snow reminded his listeners that they knew plutonium is "relatively easy to make," that they could prove to themselves that a dozen or more nations have the needed resources in personnel to equip themselves with bombs, and that they knew from statistics that some bombs will "blow up, through accident, or folly, or madness" if enough are built.

A significant part of the convincingness of the point derives from Snow's insistence, shown through repetition and emphasis, that the scientist *knows* the either-or condition. In a section of the speech that probably took less than 4 minutes to deliver, the words *knowledge* or *know* recur 14 times [mid-33 to the beginning of 38].

Even with the repetition, however, the proof of this point is shorter and simpler than the proof of other points that were both less controversial and less essential to the line of argument. Given the nature of the point, there seems to have been no other satisfactory alternative.

The risk Snow took, of course, was in the assumption that his audience *did* already know. If they did not know that there is a certainty of an explosion, the illustration added no force to his general argument and may even have weakened it.

The proof can be tested by two questions, neither of which has to do with traditional tests of reasoning: First, did his audience already know that an either-or situation existed? Second, did he illustrate that they knew? This proof shows how imperative it is that arguments be developed by speakers (and evaluated by critics) within the total context of the speech situation.

LANGUAGE

As one reads the speech (and almost assuredly as a listener heard it), he gets an impression that here is language for talking rather than for writing or reading. It is direct, personal, uncomplicated, straightforward and informal.

Although the structure of the speech is complex, word usage is not. There is no reaching to display erudition, no striving for elegance. Clarity in word choice, sentence structure, and paragraph development seems always to have been a prime objective. When Snow wished to ensure that he not be misunderstood he paused to define his terms, as when he defined *truth* [14], or to clarify his intention by stating what he meant to say and what he meant not to say, as when he discussed *loyalty* [31].

The conversational aspect of the speech almost conceals the care with which manner of expression was made to serve the persuasive purpose. The concern for persuasive use of language can be illustrated in several ways, but perhaps, as Snow said, we had better take the most obvious example.

Although the implications of the speech are not made clear until near the very end, Snow gradually led his listeners to realize that the demands on them would be great. As the speech progresses, a listener heard his role described in these terms:

You can have great influence on the world effect of your work [1]. You have a responsibility you cannot escape [5]. You must not let your conscience rust (thereby, Snow indicated that more than passive acceptance of responsibility was needed) [8]. The nature of science compels you to tell the truth [20]. You must tell the truth even if it means that you have "to question and if necessary to rebel" [31]. To speak out and rebel if necessary is your duty [32]. You have a plain duty to speak out on the either-or of the nuclear arms race [39].

This changing characterization of the demand being made on the listener is, of course, precisely in keeping with the climactic nature of the speech. But the climax was scrupulously carried through in language as well as argument.

The word *duty* plays a significant part in the climactic development. Notice first how easily the statement "scientists have to question" [31] becomes "the duty to question" [32]. That is the first use of the word in the speech. The next time it is used it appears as "the plain duty." Having gradually worked toward the use of *duty* to characterize the listener's responsibility, Snow adds force to the notion by repeating the word three times in quick succession at the climactic point in the speech [39]:

> It is the plain duty of scientists to explain this either-or. It is a duty that seems to come from the moral nature of the scientific activity itself.
>
> The same duty, though in a much more pleasant form, arises with respect to the benevolent powers of science.

EVALUATION OF THE SPEECH

The New York *Times* gave Snow's speech front-page coverage and reprinted a substantial part of it. A reporter wrote that "Sir Charles's flinty viewpoints have struck many sparks," and that the speech was in that tradition, for it, too, "struck some sparks." Lester Thonssen, editor of *Representative American Speeches,* wrote: "Excepting President Kennedy's inaugural address, no speech of the past year has attracted as much attention and provoked as much controversy."

Most attention was directed, of course, to the contention that scientists know there is an either-or situation concerning atomic weapons development. Hesburgh, for example, doubted that the mathematics of probabilities can be assumed to prevail in the area of human affairs.

Should the speech be evaluated by whether it accurately forecast the future? That is an essential part of the evaluation, for the speech is sound only if the view of the future turns out to be reasonably accurate. No atomic bombs have been used in malice, although within four years after the speech, China did explode an atomic device. Snow's purpose, however, was not to predict a gloomy future. Rather, he sought to convince men to act so that the future would be less dismal.

Should the basis of evaluation, then, be whether the speaker accomplished his purpose? That, too, is an important part of the evaluation; but the question can be taken to imply that all good speeches should succeed in the sense that what the speaker proposed finally came about. Measured by that criterion many great speeches have failed. Lincoln's two inaugural addresses, for example, failed to achieve their objective. The First Inaugural did not convince the southern states to wait and see whether the President would respect their constitutional rights. The Second did not convince the north to finish the war and "bind up the nation's wounds" with "malice toward none" and "with charity for all." Some speeches are delivered at a time when the state of public opinion makes success seem almost impossible. In those instances it is the effort and the nature of the effort that count. We do not think less of a man because he failed against insuperable odds. Rather, we praise him if he attempted to do the right thing in the right way.

But even when a speech appears to have succeeded, it rarely is possible to know what part a single effort played in subsequent events. Persuasion on public issues occurs in a milieu of persuasion. Thus, even had the southern states remained in the Union, there would be no way of knowing how much Lincoln's speech might have contributed to that decision. And there is no way to know how much Snow's speech moved scientists—and non-scientists—to work for a test ban (a limited ban was finally agreed to in 1963) and for a cessation of the weapons spread (the spread appears to have slowed down at least).

Evaluation of a persuasive speech finally must depend on one's judgment about the speaker's objective and method—whether he tried to do the right thing and whether his views were soundly and well articulated within the persuasive context. On those grounds, we agree with Thonssen: the speech was "a significant addition to the oratorical literature of 1960."

The Speech of Praise:
Introduction, Welcome,
17   ## and *Presentation*

The speech of praise has six forms: *introduction, welcome, presentation, tribute, eulogy,* and *farewell.* This chapter considers principles applicable to the initial three ceremonial (occasional) addresses of praise.

INTRODUCTION

James Redpath, who in the last century acted as agent for some of America's famous public speakers, issued the following advice to his business managers: "Abolish the practice of introducing lecturers wherever it is practicable to do so; it is a nuisance and an excrescence, and always, to some extent, destroys the effect of the first appearance of the lecturer." "In many cases, in large cities especially," Redpath concluded, "the introducer ought to be introduced first; for often nobody knows, and always nobody cares, who he is; and everybody does know the lecturer."[1]

Notwithstanding Redpath's injunction there is a place for the speech of introduction, since preliminary evidence indicates a high correlation between introductory remarks and audience attitude towards a guest speaker's credibility.[2]

Problem of Originality

When presenting a guest speaker, an introducer should avoid three all too familiar opening formats:

[1] Charles F. Horner, *The Life of James Redpath and The Development of The Modern Lyceum* (New York: Barse and Hopkins Publishers, 1926), pp. 195–196.

[2] See Phillip K. Tompkins and Larry A. Samovar, "An Experimental Study of the Effects of Credibility on the Comprehension of Content," *Speech Monographs,* Vol. 31 (June 1964), pp. 120–123; Carl I. Hovland, "Reconciling Conflicting Results Derived from Experimental and Survey Studies of Attitude Change," *American Psychologist,* Vol. 24 (1959), pp. 12–13; and Harold H. Kelley, "The Warm-Cold Variable in First Impressions of Persons," *Journal of Personality,* Vol. 28 (1950), pp. 431–439.

> "Our speak-ah, Ladies and Gentlemen, needs no-o-o Introduction. May I present the Honorable Hen-ry M. (as in Micawber) Jackson, Sena-tah from the gr-reat State of Washington."
>
> "Orville L. Freeman [nervous cough] is known sufficiently well by anybody interested in the field of agriculture [nervous sigh] not to need any introduction. His topic today has something, I think, to do with the farm problem. Secretary Freeman?"
>
> "Ladies and Gentlemen: [hrmmph] At this momentous occasion celebrating the birthday of that great and famous Cuban hero, José Martí, I take great pleasure in introducing [audible sniffle] Carlos Todd, former Editor, *Havana Times* [visibly folding notes and putting them in pocket], who will speak to us on the topic, 'Cuban Independence.' Mr. Todd [leading the claque like a cheer leader]."

There is, obviously, some virtue in brevity; for certainly an introducer stands unaccused of stealing thunder from a guest speaker by any of the above openings. Furthermore, a pattern emerges whenever an introducer confines himself to a box-top, 25-words-or-less introduction: inevitably, the same elements appear—audience (*Ladies and Gentlemen*); speaker (*Carlos Todd*); speaker's authority (*former Editor*, Havana Times; introducer (*I*); introducer's reaction (*pleasure*); introducer's function (*introducing*); the speaker's topic (*Cuban Independence*); and finally, when appropriate, reference to the occasion (*birthday* of *José Martí*). Logically, a speaker may ask, "How can I be original when I must be brief?"

This, of course, is the very point: if an introducer is unimaginative, he should not worry about originality. Instead, he should simply fulfill his immediate function and keep to a minimum his use of tired phrases ("It gives me great pleasure . . .", "I consider it a high honor to . . ."). He may follow the basic pattern for a brief introduction suggested below:

> Our speaker at this celebration is the distinguished President of the Italian Republic. His topic is "The Atlantic Partnership; Necessity for a United Europe." I present to you His Excellency, President Antonio Segni.

Problem of Genuine Compliment

An introducer should compliment genuinely the guest speaker. An introduction of too laudatory proportions not only embarrasses the introducee, but places an extra burden of proof on him as well. Grave-digging opening remarks have caused doubtlessly many a listener to think, "How can the speaker possibly live up to *that* introduction?" or "Well, let's just see if he is as great as the introducer says he is!"

The next speech by John G. Buchanan, president of the Pennsylvania Bar Association in 1946, illustrates the effusive introduction:

When the great Oliver Wendell Holmes, Jr., sat upon the Supreme Court bench, some said that there was no Roland for that Oliver. A like remark cannot be made of another Federal tribunal which for nearly two decades has been graced by two great lawyers. Shall I say of the same name? The prophetic parents of one of them christened him "Noble" and the equally prophetic parents of the other christened him "Learned." Each of the children earned right to both of the appellations; each of them is noble and each of them is learned. The Honorable Augustus Noble Hand had a distinguished career as a student at Phillips Exeter Academy, Harvard College and the Harvard Law School, and has served as president of the Alumni Association of each of those institutions of learning, as an overseer of Harvard University and as a trustee of the Episcopal Theological School at Cambridge. He is a Doctor of Laws of Yale University, of the University of Pennsylvania (represented here by a number of other alumni), of Williams College, of Middlebury College, and of Harvard University. What can be better than that? He practiced for nineteen years in the city of New York, where he was a member of a leading firm. Thirty-two years ago he was appointed United States District Judge by President Wilson, and thirteen years later he was appointed a judge of the Circuit Court of Appeals for the Second Circuit by President Coolidge. For the past ten years he has served as a member of the Council and of the Executive Committee of the American Law Institute, and there are many of us who can testify to the laborious and invaluable services which he has rendered to the Institute. Knowing as I do his great distinction as a scholar, as a jurist, and as a churchman, I was prepared to find that he left no field of learning untouched and that he touched nothing which he did not adorn. However, I was scarcely prepared to find, as I did a little more than a month ago, that he is also an eminent vocalist. Whether he speaks or whether he sings, or whether to take an Episcopalian middle course, he chants, what he has to say to us, we will, I am sure, attend closely to his winged words.[3]

In contrast Harry Truman in 1946, when presenting Winston Churchill at Westminster College, Fulton, Missouri, omitted all references to the Prime Minister as an orator, and included only a few comments about him as a statesman. (Why reiterate what hearers already knew!) Because Truman's remarks were personal, unaffected, and almost plain, the visiting Englishman, on a vacation in this country at the time, was unencumbered by opening remarks that led anyone to expect much more than an ordinary talk by an extraordinary man on the rather ordinary subject of world peace:

> You know, this is one of the greatest pleasures and privileges I have had since I have been President of the United States. (Applause.) I appreciate most highly Governor Donnelly's welcome to Mr. Churchill and myself, and I am very thankful that Dr. McCluer suggested to me that Mr. Churchill be invited to deliver this lecture today. (Applause.)
>   I had a letter from Mr. Churchill—oh, six months ago or more—in

[3] Guy R. Lyle and Kevin Guinagh, compilers, *I am Happy to Present: A Book of Introductions* (New York: H. W. Wilson Company, 1953), pp. 145–146.

which he said he was considering a vacation in the United States or in North Africa. (Laughter.) I sent him Dr. McCluer's invitation and made a longhand note on the bottom of it telling him that if he would spend his vacation in the United States, at whatever point he chose to pick, and then would deliver this lecture, I would make it a point to come to Missouri and personally welcome him and introduce him for that lecture.

I had never met Mr. Churchill personally until the Berlin Conference between Mr. Stalin, Mr. Churchill, and myself. I became very fond of both of them. They are men, and they are leaders in this world today when we need leadership. It is a pleasure for me to introduce Mr. Churchill. He is one of the great men of the age. (Applause.) He is a great Englishman, but he is half American. (Applause.)

Mr. Churchill and I believe in freedom of speech. I understand that Mr. Churchill is going to talk on "The Sinews of Peace". I know that he will have something constructive to say to the world in that speech. I am happy that he came here to deliver it, and it is one of the great privileges of my lifetime to be able to present to you that great world citizen, Mr. Churchill. (Applause.)[4]

Not expecting eloquence of a Blood, Sweat, and Tears address, listeners must have been surprised pleasantly when Churchill rose above the occasion and fashioned the memorable image, *iron curtain.*

Of course the line between a genuine compliment that embarrasses a speaker, and one that does not, is indeed fine. Generally, praise can be given without embarrassment to the guest speaker if the introducer avoids grandiloquent adjectives and adverbs, if his praise is cast within the framework of a plausible situation, and if his accolade avoids hyperbolized comparisons or contrasts. In the next brief introduction, G. Lynn Sumner, president of the New York Advertising Club in 1939, complimented skillfully the main speaker:

It is a traditional example of the busman's holiday that when a sailor gets a day's shore leave, he goes rowing in Central Park. And if you would know what advertising men are doing these autumn nights—well, they are flocking to the Morosco Theatre, where some aspects of the advertising business have been cleverly put into a play called *Skylark.* The scintillating star of that play—Miss Gertrude Lawrence—is our special guest of honor today. That is the reason why we had no trouble whatever getting a complete set of our vice presidents at the head table.

In *Skylark,* Miss Lawrence plays a familiar part—the neglected wife of an advertising agency executive who is so busy with his clients and his speculative plans for prospective clients that he too often forgets to come home. Of course this is just a play—just a comedy—all in fun—for I am very sure that if Miss Lawrence were *really* the wife of an advertising executive, his chief problem would be to keep his mind on his work.

From observation of her theatre audiences, supplemented by observations

4 "President Truman Introducing Mr. Churchill," *Westminster College Bulletin,* April 1946.

of this audience, Miss Lawrence has some observations of her own to make about advertising and advertising men. I hope she doesn't pull her punches. It is a great pleasure to present one of the most charming and talented actresses of the English and American stage—Miss Gertrude Lawrence.[5]

Problem of Accuracy by Introducer

An introducer should rely on notes when necessary for important facts about the guest speaker. There is, in other words, no excuse for an introducer who mixes dates, distorts facts, and mispronounces names. The remedy is almost too obvious for statement: (1) he should prepare in advance as many of his remarks as possible; (2) he should note carefully any last-minute facts for inclusion after conversing with the speaker at the occasion. By following these two suggestions, the introducer may—should he consider reliance on notes a sign of mental weakness, rather than the better part of wisdom—still deliver most of his introduction without notes, confident in the knowledge that his additional notations are available on paper as needed.

Problem of Paving Way for a Speaker

An introducer should check on physical arrangements for the guest speaker. Often a program chairman, who is not necessarily the person delivering the introduction, provides speaker needs as rostrum, projector, and blackboard. A person skilled at introducing speakers, however, knows that program chairmen are occasionally unaware of all their responsibilities. A chairman, for instance, may consider his duties completed once he receives a commitment-to-speak from a guest speaker. To save the sponsoring group embarrassment, an introducer should ask his introducee, either beforehand or at the actual occasion, if all arrangements are satisfactory and if any last minute physical changes are needed.

During his introductory remarks, an introducer must still remain alert to the changing scene. This may mean delivering impromptu comments to gag private conversations among listeners; stalling long enough for waiters to pick up dishes; prolonging the introduction as last-minute arrivers play musical chairs; or requesting a small audience to group down front for the speaker's convenience.

Once the guest speaker begins, an introducer can usually sit back to enjoy the address. His duties, however, are not over. He is, for example, in a much better position than the speaker to remedy unexpected disturbances and interruptions, and to correct failures in the public address system. Naturally, an experienced speaker knows how to cope with unfortunate and unforeseen commotions; nevertheless, an equally experienced introducer remains alert for the unexpected situation that needs his attention.

[5] Lyle and Guinagh, pp. 47–48.

Problem of Congratulatory and Transitional Remarks between Speakers

An introducer is often the official congratulator as well as chairman. At the close of a speech, an introducer should make some sincere comments about the address to the guest speaker. Should he as chairman have to introduce a series of speakers, he may find it convenient to (1) make a brief, appropriate remark or two about the previous address, before (2) beginning his prepared introduction for the succeeding speaker.

WELCOME

The formal procedure for welcoming a group or a single visitor varies throughout the world: among Bantu-speaking African tribesmen, the pre-scribed method of greeting depends upon the individual's social position, age, and sex; some East African tribes exchange welcomes through third persons to avoid any unfortunate outbursts of temper or insults between greeters; the Javanese employ one of five language-styles when saluting strangers, and the exact choice depends on the rank of the person addressed; and among the Chinese, a special idiomatic spoken language is used for welcoming.

Guidelines for Welcoming Speeches

As Westerners our customs for welcoming have been fixed more or less through centuries of usage. Today, speakers charged with delivering official greetings should follow four Guidelines:

Guideline 1. Express honor and privilege when welcoming visitors.
Guideline 2. Indicate the reason for the visit and/or the significance of an occasion to hearers.
Guideline 3. Wish the visitor success, if his trip is purposeful, and a pleasant time.
Guideline 4. Extend cooperation and hospitality to the visitor.

Let us examine briefly each of the four Guidelines before studying sample speeches.

1. *EXPRESS HONOR AND PRIVILEGE. First,* when delivering welcoming addresses, a speaker should usually include a cordial greeting to the visitor or visiting organization. On occasion a speaker dwells on the honor of saluting a distinguished visitor. This attention to expressions of privilege is motivated often by a sincere desire to make a visitor feel truly welcome. Some greeters, however, think that their success or failure rests on quantity rather than quality of expression. A student speaker is reminded that a too enthusiastic welcome can produce an opposite impression—*in-*

sincerity. Furthermore, listeners, and worse, the person greeted, may be embarrassed by pronouncements of honor that ooze on at unnatural lengths.

2. *INDICATE REASON FOR AND SIGNIFICANCE OF VISIT OR OCCASION. Second,* a good welcomer indicates the significance of an occasion in one of two ways: (1) by stressing the historic proportions of the visit in terms of an organization, a person, or a group represented by the visitor; or (2) by recounting events or incidents leading to the trip. Obviously a welcomer should not distend the significance of a visit. To inflate the importance of Mr. Unknown's arrival in Mudville is not only unforgivable, but a sham on the whole welcoming process. If the visit, therefore, is unhistoric, the welcomer might shift his attention to a summary of events initiating the trip.

A welcomer should also indicate the purpose (work or pleasure) of the visit. Depending on its importance, a speaker may wish to describe in some detail the aspirations of both visitor and welcomer, as they relate to the goal of the trip.

3. *EXTEND WISHES FOR SUCCESS. Third,* a welcomer should wish his guest success in accomplishing the purpose of the trip. This wish is in terms of the welcomee's own objectives, or of the welcomer's projected goals, or of both.

Most speeches of welcome also include wishes for a pleasant time and visit. In welcoming addresses delivered to a person intent on pleasure, a speaker often includes a descriptive summary of those things he considers pleasurable for the visitor, as a well-meaning account of outstanding landmarks or tourist attractions.

4. *EXTEND COOPERATION AND HOSPITALITY. Fourth,* a welcomer should offer his cooperation to the visiting person or group, or his aid in the name of the organization he represents. This part of the address is climaxed often by presenting the visitor with some token of esteem as keys-to-the-city or a certificate of honorary membership.

Sample Speeches of Welcome

Before preparing a speech of welcome, a speaker should study the following sample addresses illustrating different approaches to this occasional form of public speaking. The first address is by Adolf Schaerf who greeted John Kennedy upon the latter's arrival in Austria for talks with Nikita Khrushchev in 1961. The speech contains only the bare skeleton and hint of the four guidelines for a welcoming address.

Guideline 1   I am very happy to be able to welcome you in Austria. You are the first [United States] President to visit Austria while in office.

Guideline 2   We know that you will have had

many and important reasons to come here.

Diplomacy today is not only carried out by diplomats, but also through personal contacts. And we Austrians are pleased that you, Mr. President, did not spare the effort to choose Austria as the stage for your talks with Premier Khrushchev.

Guideline 1

I myself, and I believe many Austrians, millions of Europeans and the peoples of our globe wish that your talks will be crowned by success. This we wish from the bottom of our heart.

Guideline 3

Your stay here will be short. That is why I cannot offer you much. For yourself and your work, I wish you much success.[6]

Guidelines 3 and 4

In the next address, Harold Macmillan conveyed more cordiality in his remarks to Kennedy than did Schaerf in his. Part of the warmth in Macmillan's speech delivered at London airport in 1961 comes from the conversational quality of the remarks; part of its cordiality stems from his choice of adjectives; and part of its friendliness arises from expressions of sympathy as well as the personal *you* and *I.* Macmillan included only three of the four guidelines. Why did he omit one?

Guideline 1

I need hardly tell you how glad all my countrymen are to welcome you on your first visit to this country as President of the United States.

Guideline 1

I am particularly happy that Mrs. Kennedy is with you. You will soon have an opportunity of seeing the welcome which will be given by the citizens of London, and I am sure that that welcome would be repeated, if it were possible, in every part of this land.

Guideline 2

You have had a long journey and seen many distinguished personalities. I won't disguise from you that I am looking forward to hearing just what happened [in the talks with Khrushchev]. Meanwhile, I would add only this:

Guideline 2

I recall with pleasure my visit to you

[6] The New York *Times,* June 4, 1961. Copyright 1961 by The New York Times Company. Reprinted by permission.

both at Key West and Washington a very short time ago. I am looking forward to renewing and, I hope, strengthening the friendship we made then.

Guideline 4

I think we are all, Mr. President, glad to have you with us. We hope you will soon come back again and next time stay a bit longer.[7]

The last welcoming speech stresses Guidelines 1 and 2 and is by Khrushchev to Antonin Novotný, President of the Czechoslovak Republic in 1958. What effect does the heavy-handed attention to naming individuals, as well as to an unusual emphasis on doctrine, party, and Communist aspirations have on impressions of sincerity and cordiality?

Dear Comrade Novotný,
Dear Comrades and Friends,

Guideline 1

Allow me on behalf of the Central Committee of the C.P.S.U. [Communist Party of the Soviet Union], the Presidium of the Supreme Soviet of the U.S.S.R. and the Soviet Government, on behalf of the entire Soviet people, to welcome you heartily in our capital —Moscow.

Guideline 1

The visit to the Soviet Union of Comrade Novotný, First Secretary of the Central Committee of the Communist Party of Czechoslovakia and President of the Czechoslovak Republic, is a big and joyous event for our Party and all the Soviet people. The Soviet people know you well and respect you deeply, dear Comrade Novotný, as an outstanding leader of the revolutionary working-class movement and tireless fighter for socialism, for peace.

Guideline 1

We also heartily welcome the prominent leaders of the Communist Party of Czechoslovakia and the Czechoslovak Government who have come with you —Comrade Václav Kopecký, member of the Political Bureau of the Central Committee of the Czechoslovak Communist Party and Deputy Chairman of

[7] *The New York Times,* June 5, 1961. Copyright 1961 by The New York Times Company. Reprinted by permission.

the Government, Comrade Rudolf Barák, member of the Political Bureau and Minister of Interior, Comrade Jiři Hendrych, member of the Political Bureau and Secretary of the C.C. [Central Committee], Comrade Rudolf Srehaj, candidate to the Political Bureau of the C.C., Chairman of the Corps of Representatives of Slovakia, and Comrade Václav David, member of the C.C. and Minister of Foreign Affairs.

Guideline 1

Dear comrades, in your persons we greet the glorious Communist Party of Czechoslovakia, which holds high the victorious banner of Marxism-Leninism, and the fraternal peoples of socialist Czechoslovakia who have enduring bonds of long-standing inviolable friendship with the Soviet people.

Guideline 2

You have come to our country at an auspicious moment in Czechoslovak history. The 11th Congress of the Communist Party of Czechoslovakia, which has drawn up a programme of completing the building of socialism in your country in the next few years, closed a few days ago. The Soviet people received the results of your congress with a sense of profound satisfaction. The completion of socialist construction in Czechoslovakia will have a tremendous international impact. Your successes in building socialism go to strengthen the might of the socialist camp and cement the forces of peace and democracy throughout the world.

Guideline 2

This is not the first time we meet as close friends and brothers brought together by the great ideas of communism, the ideas of peace and people's happiness. It is good to know that your present visit, just as our frequent meetings in the past, is not bound up with the need of settling any controversial questions and misunderstandings, because such controversial questions have never existed and do not exist now.

Guideline 2   The friendship between our countries, based on principles of proletarian internationalism and all-round mutual support, accords with the basic vital interests of our peoples, the interests of the socialist camp as a whole. At the same time, this cordial and inviolable friendship helps to strengthen the peace in Europe and the world.

Guideline 2   We do not doubt that during your stay in the Soviet Union you will again see how profound and sincere are the sentiments of love and friendship which the Soviet people have for the peoples of Czechoslovakia.

Allow me, dear friends, to express the trust that your arrival in the Soviet Union will contribute to a still greater strengthening of fraternal relations and co-operation between our Communist parties, between the peoples of the Soviet Union and Czechoslovakia.

Guideline 4   For our part, we shall do our best for you to feel at home in our country.

Welcome, dear friends!

(Stormy applause, Cheers for inviolable Soviet-Czechoslovak friendship.)[8]

PRESENTATION

Related closely to the welcoming address is the speech of presentation.

Guidelines for Presentational Speeches

A speaker making an award should follow five Guidelines:

Guideline 1. Indicate pleasure, honor, and privilege in delivering the speech and presenting an award.

Guideline 2. Relate the reason why the recipient is receiving the award.

Guideline 3. Signify the importance of the award, or the occasion, or both.

Guideline 4. Stress the recipient's inspiring qualities.

Guideline 5. Express good wishes and thanks to the recipient.

Special Problems of Guidelines 3 and 4

Although Guidelines 1, 2, and 5 are self-evident, Guidelines 3 and 4 need some explanation.

[8] Nikita S. Khrushchev, *For Victory in Peaceful Competition with Capitalism* (New York: E. P. Dutton & Co., Inc., 1960), pp. 502–504.

1. *PROBLEM OF GUIDELINE 3.* When making a presentation, a speaker should keep in mind that the award is almost always a token of esteem, and is, therefore, a poor substitute for actual feelings and true regard of a receiver's accomplishments. Unless the prize has remarkable value, either sentimentally or materially, the presenter should give only passing attention to a description of the award itself. To overinflate the importance of a commendatory letter, citation, keys to a city, trophy, watch, or cash award is to devalue the honoree's success.

On rare occasions, as in the first sample speech for study, a speaker presents an award of priceless value in terms of dollars and cents. When this is the case, a speaker should refer to the object's intrinsic or extrinsic value. More often, however, a speaker presents an award of microscopic monetary significance compared to the recipient's sacrifice or service. When this happens, the presenter should shift his attention to importance of the occasion and to impressiveness of the honoree's contribution.

2. *PROBLEM OF GUIDELINE 4.* When delivering a speech of presentation, the speaker will sometimes feel compelled to describe the recipient's life and accomplishments at length, even though many of these details are well-known to hearers and, in some cases, related vaguely to the particular award. From the presenter's standpoint, however, an enumeration of the honoree's successes and biographical milestones may seem a necessary part of the address, since the receiver will serve as a model for emulation by hearers. On the other hand, a person so honored is embarrassed usually by an overloquacious, picayune, ostentatious, and exaggerated billboarding of his accomplishments. The presenter, consequently, must *catalogue* and then *select* those facts worth recounting.

Naturally, constituents of good taste are personal judgments; for what is complimentary to one person is often offensive to another. Moreover, the speaker's modesty is at stake—perhaps more so than the honoree's at times. A speaker is wise, therefore, to include only those accomplishments related directly to the award and to consult others involved with the occasion for their lists of praiseworthy facts. By doing so, the presenter may avoid embarrassing himself and the recipient of an award as well.

Sample Presentational Speeches

In 1963 John Kennedy gave the first address for study. The occasion was unusual: Sir Winston Churchill, the recipient of a proclamation, was 3000 miles away from the scene of the speech; David Bruce, United States Ambassador to Great Britain, made the physical presentation of the award to Churchill as the President spoke. The address was usual in that it included most of the Guidelines: Kennedy outlined the reason for the award, indicated its importance, recounted some of the recipient's accomplishments, and emphasized the value of the award.

Guideline 3

Guideline 1

Guideline 3

Guideline 2

Guideline 4

Members of the Congress, members of the Cabinet, His Excellency the British Ambassador, Ambassadors of the Commonwealth, old friends of Sir Winston led by Mr. Baruch, ladies and gentlemen:

We gather today at a moment unique in the history of the United States. This is the first time that the United States Congress has solemnly resolved that the President of the United States shall proclaim an honorary citizenship for the citizen of another country, and in joining me to perform this happy duty the Congress gives Sir Winston Churchill a distinction shared only with the Marquis de Lafayette.

In proclaiming him an honorary citizen, I only propose a formal recognition of the place he has long since won in the history of freedom and in the affections of my—and now his—fellow countrymen.

Whenever and wherever tyranny threatened, he has always championed liberty. Facing firmly toward the future, he has never forgotten the past. Serving six monarchs of his native Great Britain, he has served all men's freedom and dignity.

In the dark days and darker nights when England stood alone—and most men save Englishmen despaired of England's life—he mobilized the English language and sent it into battle. The incandescent quality of his words illuminated the courage of his countrymen.

Indifferent himself to danger, he wept over the sorrows of others.

A child of the House of Commons, he became its father.

Accustomed to the hardships of battle, he had not distaste for pleasure.

Now his stately ship of life, having weathered the severest storms of a troubled century, is anchored in tranquil waters, proof that courage and f[a]ith and zest for freedom are truly indestructible. The record of his triumphant passage will inspire free hearts all over the globe.

Guideline 1

By adding his name to our rolls, we mean to honor him—but his acceptance honors us much more. For no statement or proclamation can enrich his name now. The name Sir Winston Churchill is already legend.[9]

In the next address, Watson Pierce presented a 200-year-old Indian peace pipe to Khrushchev in the latter's New York hotel suite in 1960. The emphasis in the Pierce address is almost entirely on the reason for and importance of the presentation, with only passing attention to a description of the object for exchange. Is the Pierce speech weak because the speaker omitted reference to his personal pleasure and privilege in presenting the pipe? Or are circumstances such that the American was wise in his omission?

Guideline 2

I am presenting this peace pipe to the Premier of the Union of the Soviet Socialist Republics. My colleagues at Archaeological Artifacts and Antiques and I look upon this pipe as a symbol which the Indians of the Black Foot tribe used to mark an end to tomahawks and wars on the great plains of America. Our ancestors thought they belonged to different nations. They fought, were frightened, and again fought until they found that they could expel the spirit of sorrow by quietly chatting as they sat round the campfire. The pipe was then passed from hand to hand. Smoke curled. And they became blood brothers and good neighbors in the human community.

Guidelines 3 and 4

May A- and H-bombs and other weapons no longer frighten the men, women, and children of the world. When they talk, may the leaders of our two great powers, the USSR and the USA, see in this pipe a new age for the recently recognized African nations and

[9] *The New York Times,* April 10, 1963. Copyright 1963 by The New York Times Company. Reprinted by permission.

for all other countries assuming the full responsibility for the establishment of a fair and desirable peace.

Mr. Prime Minister, now this pipe is yours. And may you and the heads of other states symbolically smoke it together.[10]

In contrast to the previous addresses, the next one by Calvin Coolidge comes close to the overloquacious presentational speech. The cyclorama for Coolidge's remarks is the immediate area surrounding Washington Monument; the object of presentation is the Distinguished Flying Cross; the date is June 11, 1927; the deserving hero is Charles A. Lindbergh. After reading the address, what suggestions for improvement—if any—do you have?

Guideline 3

My Fellow-Countrymen:

It was in America that the modern art of flying of heavier than air machines was first developed. As the experiments became successful, the airplane was devoted to practical purposes. It has been adapted to commerce in the transportation of passengers and mail and used for national defense by our land and sea forces.

Beginning with a limited flying radius, its length has been gradually extended. We have made many flying records. Our Army fliers have circumnavigated the globe. One of our Navy men started from California and flew far enough to have reached Hawaii, but being off his course, landed in the water. Another officer of the Navy has flown to the North Pole. Our own country has been traversed from shore to shore in a single flight.

It had been apparent for some time that the next great feat in the air would be a continuous flight from the mainland of America to the mainland of Europe. Two courageous Frenchmen made the reverse attempt and passed to a fate that is as yet unknown.

[10] *Khrushchev in New York: A documentary record of Nikita S. Khrushchev's trip to New York, September 19th to October 13th, 1960, including all his speeches and proposals to the United Nations and major addresses and news conferences* (New York: Crosscurrents Press, 1960), p. 95.

Guideline 4

Others were speeding their preparations to make the trial, but it remained for an unknown youth to attempt the elements and win. It is the same story of valor and victory by a son of the people that shines through every page of American history.

Twenty-five years ago there was born in Detroit, Michigan, a boy representing the best traditions of this country, of a stock known for its adventure and exploration.

His father, moved with a desire for public service, was a member of Congress for several years. His mother, who dowered her son with her own modesty and charm, is with us today. Engaged in the vital profession of schoolteaching, she has permitted neither money nor fame to interfere with her fidelity to her duties.

Too young to have enlisted in the World War, her son became a student at one of the big State universities. His interest in aviation led him to an Army aviation school, and in 1925 he was graduated as an airplane pilot. In November, 1926, he had reached the rank of Captain in the Officers' Reserve Corps.

Making his home in St. Louis, he joined the 110th Observation Squadron of the Missouri National Guard. Some of his qualities noted by the Army officers who examined him for promotion, as shown by reports in the files of the Militia Bureau of the War Department, are as follows:

Do you find this an unusual list of character traits? Do you find this parade of qualities offensive?

"Intelligent," "industrious," "energetic," "dependable," "purposeful," "alert," "quick of reaction," "serious," "deliberate," "stable," "efficient," "frank," "modest," "congenial," "a man of good moral habits and regular in all his business transactions."

One of the officers expressed his belief that the young man "would successfully

If someone had described you thus, would you be proud or embarrassed?

Guidelines 2 and 4

Guideline 2

complete everything he undertakes." This reads like a prophecy.

Later he became connected with the United States Mail Service, where he exhibited marked ability, and from which he is now on leave of absence.

On a morning just three weeks ago yesterday this wholesome, earnest, fearless, courageous product of America rose into the air from Long Island in a monoplane christened "The Spirit of St. Louis" in honor of his home and that of his supporters.

It was no haphazard adventure. After months of most careful preparation, supported by a valiant character, driven by an unconquerable will and inspired by the imagination and the spirit of his Viking ancestors, this reserve officer set wing across the dangerous stretches of the North Atlantic.

He was alone. His destination was Paris.

Thirty-three hours and thirty minutes later, in the evening of the second day, he landed at his destination on the French flying field at Le Bourget. He had traveled over 3,600 miles, and established a new and remarkable record. The execution of his project was a perfect exhibition of art.

This country will always remember the way in which he was received by the people of France, by their President and by their Government. It was the more remarkable because they were mourning the disappearance of their intrepid countrymen, who had tried to span the Atlantic on a western flight.

Our messenger of peace and goodwill had broken down another barrier of time and space and brought two great peoples into closer communion. In less than a day and a half he had crossed the ocean over which Columbus [and his men] had traveled for sixty-nine days on their way to the New World.

Guideline 3

But, above all, in showering applause and honors upon this genial, modest American youth, with the naturalness, the simplicity and the poise of true greatness, France had the opportunity to show clearly her good-will for America and our people.

With like acclaim and evidence of cordial friendship our Ambassador without portfolio was received by the rulers, the Government and the peoples of England and Belgium. From other nations came hearty messages of admiration for him and for his country. For these manifold evidences of friendship we are profoundly grateful.

The absence of self-acclaim, the refusal to become commercialized, which has marked the conduct of this sincere and genuine exemplar of fine and noble virtues, has endeared him to everyone. He has returned unspoiled.

Particularly has it been delightful to have him refer to his airplane as somehow possessing a personality and being equally entitled to credit with himself, for we are proud that in every particular this silent partner represented American genius and industry. I am told that more than 100 separate companies furnished materials, parts or service in its construction.

Guideline 1

And now, my fellow-citizens, this young man has returned. He is here. He has brought his unsullied fame home. It is our great privilege to welcome back to his native land, on behalf of his own people, who have a deep affection for him and have been thrilled by his splendid achievement, a Colonel of the United States Officers' Reserve Corps, an illustrious citizen of our Republic, a conqueror of the air and strength for the ties which bind us to our sister nations across the sea.

Guideline 5

And, as President of the United States, I bestow the Distinguished Flying

Cross, as a symbol of appreciation for what he is and what he has done, upon Colonel Charles A. Lindbergh.[11]

Thirty-five years after Coolidge pinned the DFC on Lindbergh, John Kennedy, at Hanger S, Cape Canaveral headquarters of Project Mercury, pinned the National Administration Distinguished Service Medal on another pioneering first. In contrast to the 1927 speech, the 1962 address is brief, pointed, and stripped of sentimentality.

Now Colonel Glenn, will you step forward.

Guideline 3

Seventeen years ago today, a group of marines put the American flag on Mount Surabachi, so it's very appropriate that today we decorate Colonel Glenn of the United States Marine Corps and also realize that in the not too distant future a marine or a naval man or an Air Force man will put the American flag on the moon.

Guideline 1

I present this citation:

"The President of the United States takes pleasure in awarding the National Administration Distinguished Service Medal to Lieut. Col. John H. Glenn Jr., United States Marine Corps, for services set forth in the following:

Guideline 2

For exceptionally meritorious service to the Government of the United States in a duty of great responsibility as the first American astronaut to perform orbital flight.

Lieutenant Colonel Glenn's orbital flight on Feb. 20, 1962, made an outstanding contribution to the advancement of human knowledge, of space technology and demonstration of man's capabilities in space flight.

Guideline 4

His performance was marked by his great professional skill, his skill as a test pilot, his unflinching courage and his extraordinary ability to perform most difficult tasks under conditions of great physical stress and personal danger.

His performance in fulfillment of

[11] *The New York Times*, June 12, 1927. Copyright 1927 by The New York Times Company. Reprinted by permission.

Guideline 5

this most dangerous assignment reflects the highest credit upon himself and the United States."

Colonel, we appreciate what you've done.

President Kennedy pinned the medal on Colonel Glenn's lapel.[12]

---

[12] The New York *Times,* February 24, 1962. Copyright 1962 by The New York Times Company. Reprinted by permission.

The Speech of Praise:
Tribute, Eulogy,
18   and *Farewell*

This chapter considers important Guidelines applicable to three forms of praise: *tribute, eulogy,* and *farewell.* Since the three differ in sufficient ways, each form is treated as a distinct kind of speechmaking with its own special considerations.

TRIBUTE

A tribute is a ceremonial address that memorializes a *recently*[1] deceased person, commends a still living individual, or praises such inanimate objects as political, social, or cultural institutions.

Before considering specific Guidelines, a speaker should understand an important difference between encomiums for the living as opposed to praises for the dead: tributes to the living are less emotional, sweeping, and laudatory than praises for the deceased. The reasons for this are: (1) the dead cannot confound the speaker by later actions that increase or decrease the need for praise; (2) the dead do not veil themselves behind man-made cloaks of modesty, whereas the living—even when they think they deserve praise—indicate usually some embarrassment over salutatory remarks.

---

[1] Since *recently* is a relative term, it needs clarification. A "recently deceased person" is one who has not been dead long enough for objective, critical evaluation. Thus the term varies according to the individual praised. For instance, the tragic circumstances surrounding John Kennedy's death still make it difficult to avoid subjective, emotional appraisals of the 35th President, whereas the natural death of Winston Churchill after a full life and many public honors makes critical analysis of the man easier. Consequently, a speaker would be guided by the Guidelines for a *tribute* when talking of Kennedy, and the Guidelines for a *eulogy* when speaking of Churchill.

434

Guidelines for Tribute

When composing a tribute, a speaker should follow three guidelines:

Guideline 1. Demonstrate reasonable pleasure or grief according to the circumstances of the tribute.

Guideline 2. List the recipient's accomplishments.

Guideline 3. Evaluate and praise (or blame) the tributee for his deeds.

Five Considerations when Using the Guidelines of Tribute

There are five important considerations that a speaker should follow when preparing a tribute.

1. *Temperance.* The first consideration guiding a speaker's choice of encomiums is temperance. The temptation is almost overwhelming, when moved by grief or swept by pride, for a speaker to shower praise like manna from heaven. Worse, there is an inclination on the speaker's part to predict a place of honor for the honoree in terms of contemporaries, or, even more flattering, in terms of all recorded time. A speaker is wiser to avoid grandiloquent and reckless forecasting and to list simply the tributee's accomplishments.

2. *Selectivity.* The second consideration is selectivity. When inventorying the honoree's accomplishments, the speaker will find that (1) he can cheer about man-made assets (bank balance, yachts owned, and match covers collected), (2) he can applaud mental and physical accomplishments (academic degrees, books published, and Olympic records held), and (3) he can praise human characteristics (generosity, fair play, and courage).

In deciding on the subject's laudable features, a speaker may find that the tributee accomplished a long list of things, not the least of which were material. Certainly tangible successes deserve some acclaim. A human being, however, is a paradoxical creature: he may, for instance, willingly work himself to death hoarding his first million dollars; yet faced with reckoning, he often denies materialism, embraces spiritualism, and sings hosannas about his good deeds. Consequently, a speaker delivering a tribute should pass out some encomiums on topics as the subject's love for his fellow man, his cheerful demeanor, his trustworthiness, or his high intellectual capacity.

The speaker's problem, therefore, is not so much in cataloguing man-made accomplishments—a little research will uncover these facts; rather his problem is deciding what personal traits deserve mention, because to praise another is akin to advertising one's own character, as well as urging a course of action. Naturally, to present here a list of all praiseworthy *human characteristics* is folly, since the English language, at last count, had roughly 1800 descriptive adjectives fitting this category. Fortunately, psychologists have done the pruning; so the list below is borrowed from them.[2]

BROAD TRAIT	SPECIFIC TRAITS
SOCIABILITY	Like to meet people, considerate of others, conversationalist, tactful, adaptable, polished, poised, cheerful, humorous, witty
EMOTIONALITY	Steadfast, frank, calm, free from neuroses, mature, ego suppression, dependable, realistic, confident, self-assertive, courageous
CONFORMABILITY	Conventional, cooperative, balance between serious and frivolous, trustworthy, good-natured, generous, conscientious
INTELLECTUAL ABILITY	Factual, objective, independent judgment, decisive, imaginative, broad interests, intelligent, logical mind, level-headed
SELF-EXPRESSIBILITY	Expressive, language control, frank, confident, organized, introspective

A speaker preparing a tribute may find the above list of *traits* insufficient, because man is motivated also by *goals* that affect his behavior toward his fellow man. Humans, for instance, generally despise the self-seeker who, like the *doctrinaire* in the French Revolution, is so mesmerized by a principle that he loses sight of humaneness along the way. Thus a man who sets out to lead and who steps on colleagues in the process is subject to our contempt rather than admiration. In essence, to seek greatness is one thing; to achieve greatness without self-seeking is another. A speaker may desire, therefore, to concentrate some attention on the following motive-goal characteristics of man.[3]

MOTIVE	GOALS AND EFFECTS
ACHIEVEMENT	To set difficult tasks for one's self, and to accomplish them.
AFFILIATION	To seek friendship and acceptance, and to realize those ends.
ALTRUISM	To help others and to sacrifice one's self for others.
AUTONOMY	To free one's self of restraints and obligations, and to act freely.
COUNTERACTION	To master a task and to persevere—

[2] As interpreted from Donald W. Fiske, "The Consistency of Factorial Structures of Personality Ratings from Different Sources," *Journal of Abnormal Social Psychology*, Vol. 44 (1949), pp. 329–344.

[3] Modified from *Introduction to Psychology*, Second ed. by Clifford T. Morgan. Copyright ©, 1961. McGraw-Hill, Inc.,

	within the bounds of social acceptance—toward that end.
DEFERENCE	To support others and to yield willingly or to accept blame graciously when necessary.
DOMINANCE	To control and influence others and to become a leader in the best sense of the word.
ORDER	To seek order in things and to achieve orderliness and organization.
PLAY	To give free time to joyful activity and to enjoy participation in sports, games, and entertainment.

3. *Objectivity.* The third consideration when preparing a tribute is objectivity. Occasionally, a person preparing such a speech will develop only the tributee's positive virtues. But, few men are saints . . . few institutions, perfect. Must the speaker, consequently, balance good against evil? virtue against vice?

The answer is not a simple *yes* or *no.* Rather, the answer is determined partially by audience expectation and partially by the speaker's personal preference. In many instances a speaker only praises because he feels listeners will decry his censuring remarks. In as many other instances, a speaker tempers praise with blame because he feels objectivity adds credulity to praise.

4. *Sincerity.* The fourth consideration of praise—and perhaps the most important one of all—is sincerity; for without it, a speaker is subject to criticism by hearers and to loss of his personal integrity.

5. *Composition.* The final consideration of praise is composition. Reduced to its simplest level, tributes generally follow chronological, or topical, or topical-chronological arrangement. At first glance time order seems most desirable, since the speaker need only marshal his material consecutively by dates into a ready-made formation. On second glance topical development appears superior to time arrangement, since the subject is segmented according to traits and motives. On close analysis, however, a speaker should find topical-chronological the best organizational framework. This combination plan permits a speaker to organize his material by traits and goals, before developing chronologically his selected characteristics. Regardless of the plan used, a speaker should remember that a tribute is a speech of *advocacy* in which his basic contention is a *proposition* of fact. Essentially, he is proving to listeners in his address that "Mr. Retiree was one of the Company's most loyal employees," or that "Mrs. Deceased was a loving and faithful mother and wife," or that "The AFL-CIO is a great union." Faced with supporting a proposition of fact, the

speaker should establish criteria for judgment acceptable to his hearers before matching traits or accomplishments against his norms.

Now for the final two considerations of composition: *introduction* and *conclusion*. An introduction to a tribute should refer to one of three circumstances inspiring the address: death, success, or dedication. Since the reason for a tribute is usually well known to hearers, and since the occasion is foremost in listeners' minds, clever introductions are generally out of place. This is not to imply that originality or imagination are undesirable in speeches of tribute; rather the point is that if a speaker lacks an inventive mind, there is certainly no loss of honor if he bows to a simple recognition of the occasion.

The conclusion to such an address is more than a formal expository summary. Sometimes an appropriate and stirring quotation is in order. Often the conclusion is an inspirational appeal. At other times the conclusion indicates the significance of, or illustrates the crucial points in, the tribute.

Sample Tributes

Now turn to a comparison of three tributes. All were delivered at moments of bereavement—one by a Malayan, one by a Congolese, and one by an American. There are similarities in the pronouncements; yet, at the same time, each speech differs sufficiently to suggest that a cultural background may initiate an originality of its own. (Before reading the first tribute, the reader should go back to the beginning of this chapter and review quickly the Guidelines.)

The first address, delivered in English and translated into Malayan and Mandarin, was delivered in 1961 by Toh Chin Chye, Deputy Prime Minister of the State of Singapore. This speech, given before the Singapore Legislative Assembly, honored Inche Baharuddin bin Mohammed Ariff, who, until his death, served the Assembly as a member from the district of Anson.

Guideline 1

Mr. Speaker, no one can speak of sorrow unless he has felt the anguish of sorrow. No one can write of pain unless he has suffered the pangs of pain. And if those in sorrow and pain ask for the answer to the eternal question of life and death, who can blame us if we give no answer? We can only give consolation. And if an epitaph were to be written, I can find no better phrase than this simple verse from the Rubaiyat:
"Then said another, 'Surely
not in vain

My substance from the common
earth was taken
That he who subtly wrought me
into shape
Should send me back to common
earth again.' "

Sir, if we lived in an age of despair, then little else could be said. But today we live in an age of faith and hope, faith in ourselves and hope for the future of the Malayan nation and our country. And it is with faith and hope that the late Member for Anson, Inche Baharuddin, came forward to take part in the leadership of the country.

Guideline 3

Guideline 2

He sacrificed security in his old position as a journalist in the *Utusan Melayu* to face insecurity as a leader of the people. Inche Baharuddin had served the people in the City Council and in the Legislative Assembly. He was rare as a leader. He was broadminded and tolerant in accordance with the tenets of his Islamic faith. He was loyal to the people whom he represented, and on the very evening of his death he was with them in Anson listening to their complaints and trying to find an answer to their questions.

Guidelines 1 and 3

Sir, I speak not as a partisan, not because Inche Baharuddin was a member of the P.A.P. [People's Action Party], but I speak in respect of his virtues and qualities as a leader among the people who had sat among us in this Chamber. There was so much to hope in a man so young, and can you blame us if we are bitter that that hope is knocked out without any warning?

The people today have a great need for leaders who are prepared to be self-sacrificing. If we hope to build our budding nation, if we hope to succeed in our quest for building our united Malayan nation, then it is absolutely necessary that leaders from all communities must work together to achieve

Guideline 3

this purpose. Inche Baharuddin, young as he was, had the faith that a Malayan nation could be built. He had the hope, although he did not live to see his faith and hope fulfilled, that the time will come when we will all be marching from strength to strength in our task of nation-building.

Guideline 1

Mr. Speaker, you have been in this Chamber for the last six years. You have witnessed stormy scenes. You have heard words flung across the Floor of this Chamber in anger, in bitterness, in acrimony. But Sir, all anger, all bitterness, all pain, are finally dissolved in death.[4]

The next tribute was delivered by Justin Bomboko, Minister of Foreign Affairs, Democratic Republic of the Congo, on the occasion of Dag Hammarskjold's untimely death in 1961. This address, delivered in Léopoldville over the state's radio facilities, is translated from French.

Guideline 1

In the name of the Government of the Republic, it is my very unhappy duty to inform you of a tragic event that happened today, not only for the Congo, but equally for the entire world.

Mr. Dag Hammarskjold, Secretary General of the United Nations Organization, died this evening, the plane that brought him from Ndola in Rhodesia having crashed.

Guideline 2

Mr. Hammarskjold was Secretary General of the United Nations Organization for more than eight years. It was on the seventh of April 1953 that he was elected for the first time. His first five-year commission was renewed by the General Assembly at the end of September 1957.

Guideline 3

In a very brief time, Mr. Hammarskjold, who had already given proof to the ages of his administrative and economic abilities in Sweden and in several international organizations, was not slow in demonstrating greatness as

[4] *Legislative Assembly Debates: State of Singapore: Official Report*, 1 Assembly, 2d sess. (Singapore: Lee Kim Heng, Acting Government Printer, 1961), p. 1403.

Secretary General of the United Nations.

He was the man in whom all the States of the world had placed their confidence and had placed their hope for a better world, sheltered from war.

It was in this man that the Congo attached its hopes since appealing for United Nations intervention.

Guideline 2

His clairvoyance, his wisdom, his intelligence and his courage in the conduct of international affairs, had served as our motto for the contentions before the Organization and accordingly for the harmonious development of a strong and unified Congo.

Guideline 3

This great champion of peace, in the service of all humanity, made special efforts of service for the Congo's well-being.

Mr. Hammarskjold died in the course of a mission for the Congo. He had stopped in Léopoldville for several days, on the invitation of our government, to discuss the continuation and the new programs of the United Nations in the Congo.

Mr. Hammarskjold died for the Congo.

In his mission, unfortunately his last, he showed the enterprising spirit that had guided him since July 1960: the elimination of all foreign influence and the defense of a united Congo.

Guideline 1

In your name, in the name of all Congolese, I render a heartfelt homage to him who gave his life in accomplishing his duty for the Congo, to him who, in carrying out his Congo mission, sought only to contribute to the reinforcement of peace in the world.

Also I take this occasion to address a solemn appeal to the people of the entire world, to the great powers as well as to the little nations, to the independent member States of the United Nations Organization, to the people of Asia and of Africa who aspire and strive for independence, to join in sorrow with us who are touched closely by the disappearance of the Secretary General of the United Nations.

Let the confidence, the will to safeguard world peace be the watchword of all governing officials.

So it is that the Congolese people keep faith in peace and in a better future.

Let unity prevail in all the Nations.

Long live the United Nations Organization.[5]

In 1963, upon John Kennedy's death, Earl Warren delivered the final tribute in the trilogy. The scene for this address was the Rotunda of the Capitol Building, Washington, D.C.

Guideline 1

There are few events in our national life that unite Americans and so touch the heart of all of us as the passing of a President of the United States.

Such misfortunes have befallen the nation on other occasions, but never before shockingly than two days ago.

We are saddened; we are stunned; we are perplexed.

Guidelines 2 and 3

John Fitzgerald Kennedy, a great and good President, the friend of all men of good will, a believer in the dignity and equality of all human beings, a fighter for justice and apostle of peace, has been snatched from our midst by the bullet of an assassin.

What moved some misguided wretch to do this horrible deed may never be known to us, but we do know that such acts are commonly stimulated by forces of hatred and malevolence, such as today are eating their way into the bloodstream of American life.

What a price we pay for this fanaticism!

Guideline 1

It has been said that the only thing we learn from history is that we do not learn. But surely we can learn if we have the will to do so. Surely there is a

[5] Doc. 252, Ministre de l'Information, Léopoldville, September 21, 1961.

lesson to be learned from this tragic event.

If we really love this country, if we truly love justice and mercy, if we fervently want to make this nation better for those who are to follow us, we can at least adjure the hatred that consumes people, the false accusations that divide us and the bitterness that begets violence.

Is it too much to hope that the martyrdom of our beloved President might soften the hearts of those who would themselves recoil from assassination, but who do not shrink from spreading the venom which kindles thoughts of it in others?

Guidelines 2 and 3

Our nation is bereaved. The whole world is poorer because of his loss. But we can all be better Americans because John Fitzgerald Kennedy has passed our way, because he has been our chosen leader at a time in history when his character, his vision and his quiet courage have enabled him to chart for us a safe course through the shoals of treacherous seas that encompass the world.

And now that he is relieved of the almost superhuman burden we imposed on him, may he rest in peace.[6]

Now that you read the three addresses, ask yourself the following questions:

1) Of the three speakers, which one best accomplished his purpose—praise of an individual?
2) Of the three which one did you find most pleasing from a stylistic viewpoint? Does your decision coincide with the address you considered the most sincere?
3) Did you find that one of the speeches, more so than the others, predicted the deceased's place in history? If yes, what did you think of the guardedness in the prediction?
4) Compare the introductions of the tributes. In your opinion which speaker had the best one? Why?

[6] *Vital Speeches of the Day,* Vol. 30 (December 1, 1963), p. 99.

5) All three addresses linked the deceased to the country of the speaker. Would this be a normal practice in most tributes delivered on such occasions?

6) Compare the conclusion of each tribute. In your opinion which speaker had the best one? Why?

Finally, lest the reader leave this section with an impression tributes are delivered only on sorrowful occasions, he should read the next address by George Graham Vest, Senator from Missouri between 1879 and 1903, in which the speaker wove all three Guidelines into his speech.

Gentlemen of the Jury:—The best friend a man has in this world may turn against him and become his enemy. His son or daughter that he has reared with loving care may prove ungrateful. Those who are nearest and dearest to us, those whom we trust with our happiness and our good name, may become traitors to their faith. The money that a man has he may lose. It flies away from him, perhaps when he needs it most. A man's reputation may be sacrificed in a moment of ill-considered action. The people who are prone to fall on their knees to do us honor when success is with us may be the first to throw the stone of malice when failure settles its cloud upon our heads. The one absolutely unselfish friend that man can have in this selfish world, the one that never deserts him, the one that never proves ungrateful or treacherous, is his dog.

Gentlemen of the jury, a man's dog stands by him in prosperity and poverty, in health and sickness. He will sleep on the cold ground, where the wintry winds blow and the snow drives fiercely, if only he may be near his master's side. He will kiss the hand that has no food to offer, he will lick the wounds and sores that come in encounters with the roughness of the world. He guards the sleep of his pauper master as if he were a prince. When all other friends desert he remains. When riches take wings and reputation falls to pieces he is as constant in his love as the sun in its journey through the heavens. If fortune drives the master forth an outcast in the world, friendless and homeless, the faithful dog asks no higher privilege than that of accompanying him to guard against danger, to fight against his enemies. And when the last scene of all comes, and death takes the master in its embrace and his body is laid away in the cold ground, no matter if all other friends pursue their way, there by his graveside will the noble dog be found, his head between his paws, his eyes sad but open in alert watchfulness, faithful and true even in death.[7]

EULOGY

The difference between *tributes* and *eulogies* is usually a matter of *time*. The former is given during the lifetime or shortly after an individual's death, whereas the latter is normally delivered years afterwards.

[7] [Chicago] *Herald*, September 17, 1897. As quoted in Manuel I. Kuhr, "The Speaking Career of George Graham Vest," unpublished doctoral dissertation, The University of Missouri, Columbia, Missouri, 1963.

Guidelines for a Eulogy

Like the tribute speaker, a speaker composing a eulogy should concern himself with *sincerity, temperance, selectivity, objectivity,* and *composition;* and like the tribute speaker, a speaker composing a eulogy follows the same *three* Guidelines mentioned in the previous section:

Guideline 1. Demonstrate reasonable pleasure or grief according to the circumstances of the eulogy.

Guideline 2. List the recipient's accomplishments.

Guideline 3. Evaluate and praise (or blame) the subject for his deeds.

Special Considerations of a Eulogy

Unlike the tribute, however, the eulogy has four peculiar considerations.

1. *HISTORICAL OBJECTIVITY POSSIBLE IN EULOGY.* Delivered years and sometimes centuries after the demise of an individual or institution, a speaker can present his memorial in a much more objective manner than possible for an individual preparing a tribute. If a eulogizer, for instance, chooses to praise the contribution of a man or institution, he can do so with some assurance that time has borne out his statements. Moreover, the naked edges of criticism that frequently slash a man shortly after his death have healed sufficiently for a more objective appraisal of the subject. This is not always true, of course, since man is known to move through cycles of debunking when he besmirches everything from Jesus Christ to George Washington, and from Whistler's mother to the Blarney stone. The converse is also true when everything old becomes sacred and blameless. This very movement between condemnation and laudation, however, is probably healthy; certainly this human tendency aids a eulogizer, since he can study both sides of a person's character, apply his own judgment to the matter, and decide finally on the extent of praise or blame he will heap on his victim.

2. *CANDOR POSSIBLE IN EULOGY.* A major consideration when preparing a eulogy is *candor.* Not to be confused with sincerity, selectivity, and objectivity, *candor* means frankness. Because a tribute is given shortly after a man's death, or because a tribute is delivered when the individual praised is still alive, a speaker does not talk as openly as he might on his subject for praise. Furthermore, the speaker's *objectivity* is blurred sometimes by the sorrow or magnificence of the occasion; his *selectivity* is limited because the facts are still unknown for the most part; and his *sincerity,* however heartfelt, cannot possibly make up for his lack of foresight. In contrast a eulogizer can develop his subject with an openness uncommon to a tribute. He may speak of the praised with critical detachment, and he may concern himself with delivering a frank appraisal. The

reception of his praise or blame depends, of course, on listeners' previous inclinations towards the subject. If hearers wear earmuffs as they listen, then a speaker's candor may be mistaken as blasphemy; if they are suspicious, then his frankness may be mistaken as a "white wash" of the subject eulogized.

3. *CALMNESS EXPECTED IN TREATMENT OF SUBJECT*. An audience listening to a eulogy is usually detached emotionally from the subject praised. For instance a eulogy to John Garfield, assassinated while President in 1881, would not evoke the same bewildered memories as a tribute to John Kennedy, assassinated in 1963. In other words, if there is any emotion left in an event already several decades old, that emotion is found usually in a few professional mourners who delight ghoulishly in maudlin displays. The eulogizer, therefore, who becomes oversentimental in his speech will probably seem insincere to most of his hearers.

4. *PROBLEM OF RELATING PAST TO PRESENT*. A eulogizer often takes the opportunity provided by the occasion to relate his topic to some present problem or subject. This practice of tying together the old and new is commendable, since it generates audience interest. A speaker, however, will sometimes emphasize the present to an extent that the *raison d'être* for his eulogy is lost to hearers.

5. *DIFFERENCE BETWEEN EULOGISTIC AND COMMEMORA-TIVE ADDRESSES*. Perhaps it occurred to some speakers that the hairline is often fine between *eulogy* or *tribute* and *commemoration* or *celebration*. Rightly, all four categories belong under one heading—the speech of praise. There is, however, a distinction—admittedly tissue thin—between eulogy or tribute, and commemoration or celebration; that is whether or not a *dedicatory function* is implied in the address. A speech is classified as either one of *celebration* or *commemoration* if (1) a direct dedication is involved, as unveiling a monument; or (2) a *re*dedication of listeners, spiritually or mentally, to an *ideal, institution,* or *event* is implied in the occasion.[8] Conversely, if a dedicatory function is absent from the address, a speech of praise is classed as either a tribute or a eulogy. Although both major types—tribute or eulogy, and celebration or commemoration—are developed similarly, the act of dedication poses persuasive problems, unknown to the speaker delivering a simple tribute or eulogy. (For persuasive considerations see Chapter 5 and Chapter 15.)

Sample Eulogies

Here are two speeches that should give the student speaker some idea of how others developed eulogies. The first one is by Franklin D. Roosevelt, who planned a Jefferson Day radio address for April 13, 1945, but who died

[8] Since Americans do not, in the strictest sense, worship individuals, a speech praising a person long dead is technically a *eulogy* used to "commemorate" an individual's birth or death.

the day before he could deliver it. The student should note particularly that the President was decidedly more interested in the contemporary circumstances of the speech than in the man eulogized.

Americans are gathered together this evening in communities all over the country to pay tribute to the living memory of Thomas Jefferson—one of the greatest of all democrats; and I want to make it clear that I am spelling the word "democrats" with a small *d*.

I wish I had the power, just for this evening, to be present at all of these gatherings.

In this historic year, more than ever before, we do well to consider the character of Thomas Jefferson as an American citizen of the world.

As Minister to France, then as our first Secretary of State and as our third President, Jefferson was instrumental in the establishment of the United States as a vital factor in international affairs.

It was he who first sent our Navy into far-distant waters to defend our rights. And the promulgation of the Monroe Doctrine was the logical development of Jefferson's far-seeing foreign policy.

Today this Nation which Jefferson helped so greatly to build is playing a tremendous part in the battle for the rights of man all over the world.

Today we are part of the vast Allied force—a force composed of flesh and blood and steel and spirit—which is today destroying the makers of war, the breeders of hatred, in Europe and in Asia.

In Jefferson's time our Navy consisted of only a handful of frigates headed by the gallant U.S.S. *Constitution—Old Ironsides*—but that tiny Navy taught Nations across the Atlantic that piracy in the Mediterranean—acts of aggression against peaceful commerce and the enslavement of their crews—was one of those things which, among neighbors, simply was not done.

Today we have learned in the agony of war that great power involves great responsibility. Today we can no more escape the consequences of German and Japanese aggression than could he avoid the consequences of attacks by the Barbary Corsairs a century and a half before.

We, as Americans, do not choose to deny our responsibility.

Nor do we intend to abandon our determination that, within the lives of our children and our children's children, there will not be a third world war.

We seek peace—enduring peace. More than an end to war, we want an end to the beginnings of all wars—yes, an end to this brutal, inhuman, and thoroughly impractical method of settling the differences between governments.

The once powerful, malignant Nazi state is crumbling. The Japanese war lords are receiving, in their own homeland, the retribution for which they asked when they attacked Pearl Harbor.

But the mere conquest of our enemies is not enough.

We must go on to do all in our power to conquer the doubts and the fears, the ignorance and the greed, which made this horror possible.

Thomas Jefferson, himself a distinguished scientist, once spoke of "the brotherly spirit of Science, which unites into one family all its votaries of whatever grade, and however widely dispersed throughout the different quarters of the globe."

Today, science has brought all the different quarters of the globe so close together that it is impossible to isolate them one from another.

Today we are faced with the preeminent fact that, if civilization is to survive, we must cultivate the science of human relationships—the ability of all peoples, of all kinds, to live together and work together, in the same world, at peace.

Let me assure you that my hand is the steadier for the work that is to be done, that I move more firmly into the task, knowing that you—millions and millions of you—are joined with me in the resolve to make this work endure.

The work, my friends, is peace. More than an end of this war—an end to the beginnings of all wars. Yes, an end, forever, to this impractical, unrealistic settlement of the differences between governments by the mass killing of peoples.

Today, as we move against the terrible scourge of war—as we go forward toward the greatest contribution that any generation of human beings can make in this world—the contribution of lasting peace, I ask you to keep up your faith. I measure the sound, solid achievement that can be made at this time by the straight edge of your confidence and your resolve. And to you, and to all Americans who dedicate themselves with us to the making of an abiding peace, I say:

The only limit to our realization of tomorrow will be our doubts of today. Let us move forward with strong and active faith.[9]

The next address by William W. Scranton, delivered at Soldiers National Cemetery, Gettysburg, on November 19, 1963, eulogizes the 100th Anniversary of Lincoln's famous speech. Scranton, like Roosevelt, emphasized circumstances surrounding the occasion. In contrast, however, Scranton kept his subject (Lincoln) in sight for most of his address.

To this hallowed ground one hundred years ago came the 16th President of the United States to voice the solemn hope that this nation, under God, might have a new birth of freedom.

He stood here humbly in the presence of a ghostly army of Gettysburg dead. Reflections of his heart's agony were etched in the craggy furrows of his countenance as he admonished his countrymen:

"The brave men," he said, "living and dead, who fought here, have consecrated it, far above our power to add or detract."

One hundred years later we stand in the long shadow cast by that gentle man both on this field and on the pages of history. Our purpose is to commemorate his memory—and, we are, of course, engaged in a needless task far above our poor power.

His memory to endure has no need of our faint applause.

[9] *The Public Papers and Addresses of Franklin D. Roosevelt*, Vol. 11: *Victory and the Threshold of Peace*, Samuel I. Rosenman, Comp. (New York: Harper & Row, Publishers, 1950), pp. 613–616.

His life's work—or even the few eloquent words he spoke here—need no commemoration from us to insure their honored place in the annals of mankind.

If we are but one-tenth as humble as he was, we will realize that we are not here for his sake.

Rather, we are come for our own sake, as free men, to refresh ourselves at this shrine. We are come to find increased devotion for the unfinished cause of human freedom. We are come to take comfort in the victories of the past because we know that for liberty there lies fierce battles in the future.

Long before Abraham Lincoln spoke here, the homeless visionary Thomas Paine had been able to rally an embryo nation to the cause of liberty by writing that the aspirations of a few people were little more than "Common Sense."

Lincoln rallied what was left of a nation to fight for the cause of union by appealing to that same common sense.

Abraham Lincoln was of the people . . . not because he was born in a log cabin, or because he split logs, or came from a poor, but honest, family . . . but because he had a superb appreciation of the honest common sense that came to a public official from the American people, if he will but let it. And to that, Lincoln was willing to contribute his own quite considerable talent for leadership.

In Lincoln, the two great mainstreams of American political philosophy converged, and he drew deeply from both. From the Jeffersonians, Lincoln took an appreciation of the people's ultimate wisdom. From the Hamiltonians, he took a belief in the need for strong leadership.

Thus, Lincoln, though a master politician, did what our American folklore has come to say is impossible to do . . . he was able to fulfill his own campaign slogans. He was great as a man and as a President because he had faith in the people, listened to them, but yet led them.

This same strong mixture of following and leading is what is needed in America today.

There are those who would say, of course, that there is no valid comparison between the America of today and the America of Abraham Lincoln.

They would say that we have entered the nuclear age and everything has changed.

Everything has not changed.

Grape shot fired at Manassas ripped life from a man just as surely as an atomic bomb dropped at Hiroshima.

What is more, the ultimate way in which man may die does not change the ultimate way in which he must strive to live.

That ultimate striving for us, as a nation, can be nothing less than eternal warfare on the forces of tyranny, no matter the garb in which the tyrant comes disguised.

Whether the tyranny is of power, or of money, or of unjust privilege . . . whether it's a tyranny of fear, or of hunger, or of censorship . . . whether the tyrant wields the dagger of prejudice or of demagoguery . . . whether he comes openly mounted on a high horse, or more subtly disguised on a soap box

. . . in every case the great unfinished work to which each generation of Americans must be dedicated is to strike down tyranny and destroy the tyrant.

In the 187 years that have passed since the American colonies declared their independence, we have found no sounder formula for destroying tyranny than that of Abraham Lincoln.

America will survive so long as we have leaders of the people who use as their guidelines the people's common sense.

While politicians, and even statesmen, for instance, may argue mightily about the relative danger to the republic from the far right or from the far left, the people in their common sense reject both.

While politicians and lawyers discuss the legalistic fine points of civil rights legislation, the tyranny of prejudice is doomed because the American people in their deep common sense realize it is wrong.

While men of great importance carry on erudite debates over the relative merits of Total Victory versus Total Co-Existence, the American people long ago decided that though we are not a nation of belligerents, we must never abandon the ultimate effort to free captive peoples wherever they are imprisoned in the world.

The wise and gentle Mr. Lincoln would have understood today's American people. Their common sense would have appealed to him.

"Human nature," Lincoln told an audience shortly before he died, "will not change. In any future great national trial, compared with the men of this, we shall have as weak and as strong, as silly and as wise, as bad and as good."

Today, 100 years after Abraham Lincoln on this field gave the world his few appropriate remarks, let us resolve to keep faith with the memory of the man who had such great faith in us as a nation.

If we but do that, this nation, under God, *will* have a new birth of freedom. If we do that, we shall *not* perish from the earth.[10]

FAREWELL

The farewell address gives a speaker an opportunity to express appreciation and regrets, to denounce and exhort, and to reminisce and predict. Like the eulogy, the farewell speech is controlled by elements of *candor, sincerity, selectivity, temperance, objectivity,* and *composition.*

Special Considerations

Delivered usually at a formal, climactic moment, the farewell speech is pronounced in an atmosphere of some sadness or happiness, or both. Because of this emotional overtone, a speaker should decide whether or not he will match his own feelings with those of his hearers and of the occasion. This statement is not at once self-evident. Some speakers, guided by their personal mood, ignore listeners' feelings; other speakers sublimate

[10] *Vital Speeches of the Day*, Vol. 30 (December 15, 1963), pp. 132–133.

their own inclinations in deference to those of hearers; and still other speakers disregard their own and audience feelings in favor of the emotional requirements demanded by the occasion.

Once the speaker decides whose feelings should guide the tenor of his remarks, he may next consider a special problem of *selectivity*. His choice of ideas for development should fall into one or more of five broad categories.

1. He may stress accomplishments as related to himself and hearers.
2. He may review events leading up to the speech.
3. He may emphasize apologetic, soul-baring, or even vindictive aspects of an occasion.
4. He may center his attention on predictions for the future.
5. He may offer public thanks.

A farewell speaker should learn that selectivity is knotted frequently with considerations of sincerity, temperance, objectivity, and even candor. Moved sincerely by the occasion, by hearers' emotions, and by his own personal feelings, a speaker in his remarks may find it difficult to remain objective. At other times a speaker may find that he cannot in good conscience say what is on his mind without hurting innocent bystanders; that he must, therefore, so temper his praise or blame that candor is impossible. Rather than stoop to conquer, he resorts to the moral that only "small" men demonstrate publicly their vendetta, and that "big" men swallow and temper their personal feelings for the sake of others.

Like the speaker delivering a tribute or eulogy, the farewell speaker parades his ego before hearers as he speaks his mind. But more important where a speaker bares only his vanity in a tribute, a farewell speaker may bare—unfortunately—his personal acrimony. Thus, for instance, when Richard Nixon took leave of the press in 1962, he said in a farewell statement: "Just think how much you're going to be missing. You [reporters] won't have Nixon to kick around any more, because, gentlemen, this is my last press conference." Then revealing his bitterness, he concluded: ". . . if they're [the press services] against a candidate, give him the shaft, but also recognize if they give him the shaft put one lonely reporter on the campaign who will report what the candidate says now and then."[11] (And although we have no proof, we suspect that listeners are inclined to be more tolerant of a speaker who reveals his vainness in a farewell address than one who advertises his personal bitterness.)

Having decided on matters of selectivity, a speaker may proceed with the business of composition. As he composes his speech he should consider

11 This quotation is a compilation from two sources of the same occasion: "You Won't Have Nixon to Kick Around . . .", *Newsweek,* Vol. 60 (November 19, 1962), p. 32; and "Nixon Bows Out . . . Has 'Last' News Conference," *U.S. News & World Report,* Vol. 53 (November 19, 1962), p. 19.

only one more item: a farewell address includes generally an appeal step developed either in the body or conclusion. This appeal is usually inspirational; that is the speaker urges his listeners to carry on, to look toward a brighter future, to support a successor, or to have faith in some man-made or God-given ideal.

Sample Speeches of Farewell

The next three addresses illustrate what some speakers have said at farewell occasions. Each speech is different from the others, either in its developmental approach, in its style, or in its revelation of personal character.

Napoleon's farewell to his Old Guard before his exile to St. Helena in 1814 exemplifies a well balanced, parting speech. In slightly more than ten score words, Napoleon covered three of the five subject-areas for development mentioned earlier in this section. (The areas omitted are apology and prediction.) With his Old Guard in tears and Napoleon moved visibly by the occasion, the General exclaimed:

> Soldiers, I bid you farewell. For twenty years that we have been together your conduct has left me nothing to desire. I have always found you on the road to glory. All the powers of Europe have combined in arms against *me*.
>
> A few of my generals have proved untrue to their duty and to France. France herself has desired other destinies; with you and the brave men who still are faithful, I might have carried on a civil war; but France would be unhappy. Be faithful, then, to your new king, be obedient to your new commanders, and desert not our beloved country.
>
> Do not lament my lot; I will be happy when I know that you are so. I might have died; if I consent to live, it is still to promote your glory. I will write the great things that we have achieved.
>
> I cannot embrace you all, but I embrace your general. Come, General Petit, that I may press you to my heart! Bring me the eagle [standard], that I may embrace it also! Ah! dear eagle, may this kiss which I give thee find an echo to the latest posterity! Adieu, my children; the best wishes of my heart shall be always with you: do not forget me![12]

In the next farewell radio address by Edward VIII upon his abdication in 1936, the speaker emphasizes soul-baring more than a review of events, and open rather than guarded and cryptic thanks. Like Napoleon's speech Edward omitted predictions for the future; unlike the General, the ex-king excluded any talk of his accomplishments. The reader should observe too that where Napoleon showed a certain vainness through comments as "All the powers of Europe have combined in arms against *me*," and ". . . do not forget me!" Edward leaves an impression of a sincere desire for commonness.

[12] *A Treasury of the World's Great Speeches,* Houston Peterson, Ed. (New York: Simon and Schuster, Inc. 1954), p. 325.

At long last I am able to say a few words on my own.

I have never wanted to withhold anything, but until now it has not been constitutionally possible for me to speak.

A few hours ago I discharged my last duty as King and Emperor, and now that I have been succeeded by my brother, the Duke of York, my first words must be to declare my allegiance to him. This I do with all my heart.

You all know the reasons which have impelled me to renounce the Throne, but I want you to understand that in making up my mind I did not forget the Country or the Empire, which, as Prince of Wales and lately as King, I have for 25 years tried to serve.

But you must believe me when I tell you that I have found it impossible to carry the heavy burden of responsibility and to discharge my duties as King, as I would wish to do, without the help and support of the woman I love, and I want you to know that the decision I have made has been mine, and mine alone. This was a thing I had to judge entirely for myself. The other person most nearly concerned has tried, up to the last, to persuade me to take a different course. I have made this, the most serious decision of my life, only upon the single thought of what would in the end be best for all.

This decision has been made less difficult to me by the sure knowledge that my brother, with his long training in the public affairs of this Country and with his fine qualities, will be able to take my place forthwith, without interruption or injury to the life and progress of the Empire, and he has one matchless blessing, enjoyed by so many of you, and not bestowed on me, a happy home with his wife and children.

During these hard days I have been comforted by Her Majesty, my Mother, and by her [Mrs. Wallis Simpson?], by my Family.

The Ministers of the Crown, and in particular Mr. Baldwin, the Prime Minister, have always treated me with full consideration. There has never been any constitutional difference between me and them and between me and Parliament. Bred in the constitutional tradition by my Father, I should never have allowed any such issue to arise.

Ever since I was Prince of Wales, and later on when I occupied the Throne, I have been treated with the greatest kindness by all classes of the people, wherever I have lived or journeyed throughout the Empire. For that I am very grateful.

I now quit altogether public affairs, and I lay down my burden. It may be some time before I return to my native land, but I shall always follow the fortunes of the British race and Empire with profound interest, and if, at any time in the future, I can be found of service to His Majesty in a private station, I shall not fail.

And now we all have a new King.

I wish Him, and You, His people, happiness and prosperity with all my heart.

God bless you all!

God Save the King![13]

[13] As transcribed by Robert W. Smith in "Rhetoric in Crisis: The Abdication Address of Edward VIII," *Speech Monographs,* Vol. 30 (November 1963), pp. 338–339.

The last address is Lincoln's well-known farewell to friends at Springfield, Illinois, in 1861. In evaluating this speech, the reader should notice that unlike the two previous addresses where the speakers confined themselves generally to circumstances and to their stations in life, Lincoln concentrated on his inner emotions during his farewell remarks. The reader should observe, too, that Lincoln stressed the future, that he gave considerable attention to an appeal to God, that he omitted accomplishment in preference to momentary review of events, and that style and sincerity contribute much to this speech. The ominous note, "I now leave, not knowing when or whether ever I may return" added a predictive overtone to the address.

My Friends: No one, not in my situation, can appreciate my feeling of sadness at this parting. To this place, and the kindness of these people, I owe everything. Here I have lived a quarter of a century, and have passed from a young to an old man. Here my children have been born, and one is buried. I now leave, not knowing when or whether ever I may return, with a task before me greater than that which rested upon Washington. Without the assistance of that Divine Being who ever attended him, I cannot succeed. With that assistance, I cannot fail. Trusting in Him who can go with me, and remain with you, and be everywhere for good, let us confidently hope that all will yet be well. To His care commending you, as I hope in your prayers you will commend me, I bid you an affectionate farewell.[14]

[14] *A Treasury of the World's Great Speeches*, p. 509.

SUBJECT AND AUTHOR INDEX

SPEAKERS AND SPEECHES INDEX

SPEAKERS CITED

464

SPEECHES, SPECIMEN (reprinted in full)